The Handbook
of Research
on Black Males

The Handbook of Research on Black Males

Quantitative, Qualitative, and Multidisciplinary

EDITED BY Theodore S. Ransaw, C. P. Gause, and Richard Majors

Michigan State University Press | *East Lansing*

The paper used in this publication meets the minimum requirements
of ANSI/NISO Z39.48-1992 (R 1997) (Permanence of Paper).

Michigan State University Press
East Lansing, Michigan 48823-5245

Printed and bound in the United States of America.

28 27 26 25 24 23 22 21 20 19   1 2 3 4 5 6 7 8 9 10

LIBRARY OF CONGRESS CATALOGING-IN-PUBLICATION DATA
Names: Ransaw, Theodore S., editor. | Gause, C. P., editor. | Majors, Richard, editor.
Title: The handbook of research on Black males : quantitative, qualitative, and
multidisciplinary / edited by Theodore S. Ransaw, C.P. Gause, and Richard Majors.
Description: East Lansing : Michigan State University Press, 2018. | Series: International
race and education series | Includes bibliographical references and index.
Identifiers: LCCN 2017055650| ISBN 9781611862973 (cloth : alk. paper) | ISBN
a9781609175771 (pdf) | ISBN 9781628953411 (epub) | ISBN 9781628963410 (kindle)
Subjects: LCSH: African American men—Social conditions. | African American men—
History. | African American boys—Education. | African American men—Education.
Classification: LCC E185.86 .H286 2018 | DDC 305.38/896073—dc23
LC record available at https://lccn.loc.gov/2017055650

Book design by Charlie Sharp, Sharp Des!gns, East Lansing, MI
Cover design by Shaun Allshouse, www.shaunallshouse.com
Cover art is *My Brother's Keeper* by Julian Van Dyke (www.vandykeart.com)
and is used with permission of the artist. All rights reserved.

Michigan State University Press is a member of the Green Press Initiative and is
committed to developing and encouraging ecologically responsible publishing
practices. For more information about the Green Press Initiative and the use of
recycled paper in book publishing, please visit www.greenpressinitiative.org.

Visit Michigan State University Press at *www.msupress.org*

CONTENTS

Part 5. Criminal and Social Justice

Part 6. Hip-Hop

Foreword
and Preface

FOREWORD

Jerlando F. L. Jackson

One's "Blackness" and "Maleness" are inescapable; at least they were for me, being from the Deep South. I was born in Ashburn, Georgia. I would be surprised to learn that anyone reading this foreword has been there, or even knows where it is on a map. Allow me to spare you the trip. Ashburn, also known as the Peanut Capital of the World, has an estimated population of 4,435 people. This small city is comprised of 65.2 percent African Americans, and the average income for residents in Ashburn is $18,702. Approximately 38 percent of the residents have a high school diploma or equivalent, 15.8 percent with some college or an associate's degree, 5.4 percent with a bachelor's degree, and 5.3 percent with a graduate degree. Now, let me visualize it for you, to understand what life has been, and still is, like in a place like this. Many of the houses in the Black community are so small and primitive that they could be considered shacks. Multiple generations of families live in these homes collectively. oftentimes with no father figure present.

A turning point for my family was when my father joined the army. This led to a life that presented access, opportunity, and education as viable options for my family, and especially for me. After his basic training, we relocated temporarily to Germany, then finally to the Fort Benning—Columbus area in Georgia, where I lived until I went to college. That said, I had access to quality-of-life experiences not available to me before, such as sound housing, medical and dental care, youth centers, and education. The schools on the military base had vested teachers and schools for a diverse student population that varied by race, ethnicity, cultural background, and nationality.

However, when I reached middle school (eighth grade, to be specific), it was time to choose a high school diploma track. I selected the highest track in Georgia, which was designated as college preparatory. The teacher immediately scheduled a parent-teacher conference with my mother. The teacher informed her that, not only would I not be able to receive this elite high school diploma, I would not graduate high school at all. She attested to this in spite of the fact that I had never had any academic problems throughout my educational experience, did not demonstrate behavioral problems, and actually performed quite well in school.

When my mother came home to explain it to me, I officially entered the "quandary of the Black male." I was in a state of perplexity, uncertain what to do with the difficult situation presented to me. The teacher did not say, "Oh, no, your son should not pursue this college preparatory track, he should just be on the regular track." She said, "Not only will he not be able to achieve the diploma track he selected, he will be lucky to graduate high school." I searched for answers; I wondered whether it was true. What did I do to make her believe that? Why had all the grades I earned not mattered? How could we arrive at two completely different interpretations of my abilities? She is a teacher; she should know, right?

I was at a crossroads with this information. I could acquiesce to what the teacher believed, or I could prove her wrong. Imagine what hearing this lack of confidence and support from a teacher does to the psyche of young Black boys. It can be damaging. And indeed, it does discourage the dreams of young Black boys every day. Fortunately, for me, I saw it as an opportunity and motivation to be a premier student. I used this opportunity to reshape my thoughts and views about education and its importance. I immediately became my most critical evaluator and my biggest advocate at the same time. It became clear that merit was not enough. I realized that I needed to take my educational process very seriously, because the only person in the classroom who cared about my success was me—and that included the teacher who was supposed to be a supporting mentor. I did get the elite college prep diploma, and the rest is now history.

It was not until many years and several degrees later that I had a framework to understand this turning point in my life. The experience was largely shaped by teacher expectations and views, and less so by in-classroom experiences. While I was fortunate to find a productive way to manage a misaligned assessment of my abilities based on views held by the teacher, far too many stories of Black male experiences in education do not end the same way. *The Handbook of Research on Black Males* is designed to fill the void in seminal resource for researchers, policymakers, practitioners, and concerned citizens in need of an empirically driven road map for those who seek clarity about the "quandary of the Black male." I was able to rise above the odds working against me as a Black male in the education system, and my story should be viewed not as the exception, but as the norm. Erasing those odds should be a national goal and future reality. The editors and authors of *The Handbook of Research on Black Males* have taken a very important step in the direction of making that case.

PREFACE

Theodore S. Ransaw

H ow did this Handbook come to be? My students asked for it. And not just my Black male students, but my female students as well. Incidentally, I've always had more female students in my masculinity classes than male students.

While working on my doctorate, I created and then taught an African American Music and Culture Hip-Hop class. That class covered all four elements of hip-hop: graffiti, b-boying/break dancing, d-jaying as well as rap. An interdisciplinary class, graffiti was taught from a historical and political lens, b-boying was taught from a non-verbal communication and business commercialization perspective, d-jaying was interpreted through musicology and rap was discussed using classic rhetorical analysis. Every semester, when the topic of girls and music videos came up, the women in the class had much to say. The men did not. Many of the young men were interested in particular women in the class and did not want to take any chances to offend them. Other men in the class were reluctant to talk because they did not feel their comments would be accepted. Because of their silence, I realized that the Black men in my hip-hop class needed a "safe place" to talk. So, I created a Black masculinity class.

Although every class had more women than men, one of the commonalities between the men and the women was that they all kept asking for more and more information. What is compelling is that much of the knowledge they accumulated was channeled into their scholarship and personal lives. As I observed through reading assignments, reflection papers, and a culminating term paper, the men and the women in the class became able to express themselves in ways they were unable to do before. They even had a course activity where they created a personal shield or family crest. The Black masculinity class taught both my students and myself how important such a marker of ancestry can be to identity. The class had an additional benefit. The more the students learned, the more they were eager to share with others.

The students of the first masculinity class created an hour-and-thirty-minute multimedia presentation for their final project. The next class started a mentorship program for Black males at an at-risk elementary school. That mentorship requirement continued as the class's final project until I finished my PhD program, when there were four programs operating in three elementary schools. What is more inspiring is that all of the students in the class were undergraduates. In addition to watching my students' academic growth, I was also personally rewarded when I saw my Black male students' inner growth as they worked with young Black men. Having Black boys that looked up to the them made these young men stand a little taller, move a bit more purposively, and talk with even greater alacrity. Most of the Black males in class graduated; some even went on to graduate school. One of the Black male students from the masculinity class is now a professor as well as a contributor to this Handbook.

Six months after I completed my PhD, I was hired at Michigan State University as a Black male research specialist. My job was to work with the Michigan Department of Education to help close achievement gaps for males of color. The masculinity class prepared me with both the research component and the civic engagement experience necessary for the job. In a way, my entire career thus far has focused on giving students of color, especially Black male students, information about Black masculinity.

What about the young women in my classes who asked for information? This Handbook was created with them in mind too. The women in the Black masculinity class contributed, helped, pushed, supported, and inspired all of the Black male students, and myself as well.

The Nature of the Handbook

The main purpose of this Handbook is to encourage researchers in various fields to explore the nuanced and multifaceted phenomenon known as the Black male. Simultaneously hypervisible and invisible, Black males around the globe are being investigated now more than ever before. However, much of the well-meaning media attention to Black males is not well informed by research. Additionally, Black males are not uniform in nature and have varying strengths and challenges as well as differing opportunities and struggles, making one-size-fits-all perspectives inaccurate. A comprehensive tool that can serve as a resource to articulate and argue for policy change, suggest educational improvements, and provide resources for judicial reform fills a void long overdue to be filled.

The overarching goal of the Handbook is to share multiple methods and perspectives that can help improve the lives of a population who are often the most vulnerable, Black males. To that end, the chapters in this Handbook are written by scholars and researchers from various fields, including, psychology, communication, education, sociology, and criminal justice.

Organization of the Handbook

The Handbook is divided into seven parts. Part 1, introduced by Bernard K. Duffy, describes the history of and contributions by Black males using oral traditions who advocated for critical thinking about race and exploring what it means to be an American. The major purpose of the chapters in this part is to provide an overview of the intricate complexity, influence, and impact that Black males have had on national identity throughout American history. Several significant issues that pertain to trends in research on Black males are highlighted in Part 2, introduced by Darryl Holloman and Corey Givens, including the often-ignored issues of Black males with disabilities and contemporary issues related to gender identity.

Part 3, introduced by Brent Johnson, focuses on underdiscussed topics that influence Black male health, including graduation rates and macroaggressions. Part 4, introduced by Theodore Ransaw, concentrates on education and how the lack thereof or the successful implementation thereof influences the lives of Black males. The reader will find research related to Black male learning styles, grit, persistence, and cultural competency in this part. In addition to math pedagogy and literacy teaching strategies, part 4 also includes firsthand perspectives as well as programing suggestions to help improve the education of juveniles who are sentenced like adults in the school-to-prison pipeline. Consequently, Part 5, introduced by Steven Cureton, examines how the criminal justice system is influenced by fear, the media, and lack of empathy for ethnic groups, especially Black males.

Part 6, introduced by Toby S. Jenkins details how hip-hop can be a form of artistic expression, an avenue that supports mental health and a way to unpack the complexities of Black masculinity. Part 7, introduced by Spencer Platt, summarizes program initiatives that support Black males, including approaches to culturally responsive pedagogy, college athletic program reform, and suspension and expulsion alternatives.

The cover art, *My Brother's Keeper* was drawn by Julian Van Dyke using pen and ink. The different tones reflect the premise that Black males are multifaceted and unique, while still unified by a common experience. The title *My Brother's Keeper* is a metaphor for the Handbook, that reminds us to watch out for one another despite the obstacles we face.

In keeping with the theme of working collectively, you will find an adinkra symbol (Owusu 2000) at the beginning of each part that represents the part's specific theme, drawn by Elijah K. Hamilton-Wray using charcoal on paper. *Dwennimmen*, or ram's horn, represents the overarching theme of the book, the strength of working together with humility. *Sankofa* is the symbol that implores us to remember to learn from the past and represents the history part. *Hwe Mu Dua* is a symbol for quality control and represents the research and research issues part. *Akoma*, the heart, is a symbol of patience and tolerance and represents the health part. *Nea Onnim No Sua A, Ohu* is a symbol for lifelong learners and represents the education part. *Epa* is a symbol of law and justice for criminal justice and represents the criminal justice part. *Ananse Ntontan*, also known as the spider's web, is a symbol of wisdom and creativity and represents the hip-hop part. *Woforo Dua Paa A* is a symbol of support, cooperation, and encouragement and represents the programs and initiatives part.

At the end of each part, you will find vignettes of one Black man's journey from primary school to graduate school penned by Ryan J. Henson. A vignette is a short composite, impressionistic scene, that focuses on one character to give a personalized perspective. Ryan was one of the first students in the aforementioned masculinity class. The portraits serve to ground the complexities of the Handbook by providing snapshots of the life experiences of a Black male named Ronnie. These vignettes can be used by readers to conceptualize academic research as a heuristic way to understand the individual lives of Black males.

Acknowledgments

It is imperative that others know the significant amount of time and energy that contributors other than the authors, reviewers, and part leaders have made to this Handbook. To that end, it is with pride that we publicly acknowledge the sacrifice, dedication, and hard work of the staff at Michigan State University's Press. MSU Press has been supportive, encouraging, and helpful throughout this entire process. We would also like to thank the members of the advisory editorial board for their advice and wisdom.

We are grateful to the leadership, sacrifice, and expertise of the section leaders and the authors of the Handbook. We are deeply thankful for the helpful comments and revision suggestions of the reviewers.

The editors of the Handbook are especially thankful to Michigan State University's Associate Provost and Associate Vice President for Academic Human Resources Theodore "Terry" Curry and his staff for their tireless efforts supporting the achievement and academic advancement of Black males.

■ **Reference**

Owusu, H. (2000). *Symbols of Africa*. New York: Sterling Publishing.

PART 1

History

INTRODUCTION

Bernard K. Duffy

Of the social problems in America that have engendered passionate oratory, none has been more long-standing or pervasive than racial injustice. In every era, from slavery, to Jim Crow laws, lynching, segregation, the civil rights movement of the twentieth century, to racial profiling, police brutality, and consequent cries that "black lives matter," black men and women have engaged in a struggle, most often peaceful, to achieve the American dream of equal treatment and access to the constitutional protections and economic opportunities of a nation whose riches are both philosophical and material. It has been a long and arduous struggle that can be cataloged by the speeches delivered by blacks who became famous for their ability to rally others in their communities by speaking truth to power. Each of the speakers represented here made demands that were met with recalcitrance and, at times, force and violence by those in positions of authority. Some of the speakers in this part, such as Henry McNeal Turner, Marcus Garvey, Malcolm X, and Stokely Carmichael, believed that the United States was inherently racist and in desperate need of systemic change. Others, such as Frederick Douglass, Vernon Johns, A. Philip Randolph, and Martin Luther King, wanted substantive reform. However, the passion of their oratory and the strength of their convictions were not diminished by the size of their demands. The speeches of these historic voices are testaments to the courage of black orators in the face of uncertain, and at times impossible, odds. Each of the speakers in this part took the country a step further toward racial equality, although its complete attainment has not occurred. Even after Barack Obama's idealistic two-term presidency, racial reconciliation remains a too distant hope.

This part begins with Richard Besel's and my study of two of Frederick Douglass's Fourth of July orations. My interest in African American orators began when I coedited the first volumes of an encyclopedia of American orators, which featured a number of black speakers. Professor Leeman and I edited *The Will of a People: A Critical Anthology of Great African American Speeches*. Professor Besel, my chapter coauthor, is a scholar of political, scientific, and environmental rhetoric including environmental justice, that is, how the degradation of the environment disproportionately affects racial minorities and the poor.

Although Fourth of July orations delivered by white men most often extolled the virtues of democracy and the success of the young nation, Douglass, like other abolitionists, such as his mentor, William Lloyd Garrison, used the occasion to underscore the hypocrisy of white Americans. We argue that in his Independence Day addresses of 1852 and 1857, Douglass made use of the rhetorical device of anamnesis, or recollection. In "What to the American Slave Is the Fourth of July?," delivered in 1852, Douglass effusively, but ironically, praised the "fathers" of his white audience for risking all in the revolution against the British Crown, while condemning the present generation for not adequately supporting the abolition of slavery and greater equality for free blacks in the North. "This Fourth of July," he declares poignantly, "is *yours*, not *mine*. To drag a man in fetters into the grand illuminated temple of liberty, and call upon him to join you in joyous anthems, were inhuman mockery and sacrilegious irony" (Douglass, 2012, p. 65).

Using paralipsis, the rhetorical figure in which the speaker says what he first denies he will say, Douglass denounces slavery and argues that blacks are in every respect human and deserve equal rights. While Garrison saw the Constitution as an irreparably proslavery document and called for disunion and secession, Douglass parted company with Garrison when he concluded that the Constitution could be reinterpreted radically to include blacks as well as whites. In 1875, Douglass reminded his audience that both blacks and whites had shed their blood in the Civil War and that they were also together in the Revolutionary War and the War of 1812. Compared to his better-known 1852 speech, the 1875 speech was subdued and written in a much plainer style. In 1875 Douglass feared that white paternalism would prevent blacks from taking their rightful place in society, criticizing "benevolent societies" that were ostensibly aimed at helping blacks but undercut the perception that they could manage their newly gained freedom independently.

After the Civil War, blacks were elected to the state legislatures of southern states, but many, such as Georgia legislator Henry McNeal Turner, were expelled. In the second chapter in Part 1, Andre E. Johnson examines Turner's eloquence on behalf of the equality of blacks during Reconstruction. Like Frederick Douglass, Turner demanded the extension of liberty embodied in the Declaration of Independence to blacks. As Turner saw it, during the slavery era, whites had sinned by failing to educate blacks and thereby had broken "a sacred trust." Turner, who proudly served as the first black chaplain in the armed forces and established the African Methodist Episcopal (AME) Church in Georgia, also believed that the "divine" mission of America was to promote freedom and equality internationally. He agreed with Lincoln, who in his Second Inaugural had interpreted the Civil War as the "woe" that befell America because of the sin of slavery. Yet, in his Emancipation Day speech Turner expressed optimism that the "Southern gentleman" would help unify blacks and whites. In carefully measured speech, Turner argued that the Constitution declared him a man because it fell short of sanctioning slavery, the Framers having made a conscious effort to avoid even so much as the word "servitude." Turner's optimism was deflated, however, when Georgia state legislators refused to seat black representatives. In "On the Eligibility of Colored Members to the Seats in the Georgia Legislature," delivered from the floor of the statehouse, Turner ferociously defended the right of blacks to serve in the legislature, characterizing the refusal of white politicians to allow blacks to hold office as "political slavery." He realized that to accomplish this end he must "fight the devil with fire," and his rhetoric thereafter reflected this new perspective. As a preacher, Turner took solace in the ultimate judgment of God on those who attempted to enslave blacks politically. While the US Congress reseated Turner and other blacks in state legislatures to which they were elected, intimidation and violence at the polls prevented many from winning reelection.

Richard Leeman next examines the rhetoric of four black leaders in the first half of the twentieth century. Leeman's discussion bridges the Reconstruction period with the modern civil rights movement. The first figure he considers is Marcus Garvey, who attracted hundreds of thousands of followers in a Black Nationalist movement to edify and inspire blacks. Garvey founded the Universal Negro Improvement Association and called for a return to Africa and the establishment of a pan-African nation. Like Turner he emphasized the need for education and encouraged racial and personal pride. Among his accomplishments was the establishment of various businesses including a steamship company, the Black Star Line, which would be used to transport blacks to the new African nation hoped to create. Ultimately convicted of mail fraud, related to selling stock in the Black Star Line, Garvey was imprisoned and later deported, but the effect of his uplifting Black Nationalist rhetoric continued to be felt and emulated by other black leaders.

The Reverend Vernon Johns infused the civil rights movement with the idea of "the Social Gospel," the application of Protestant Christianity to social problems. Educated at Oberlin College and the University of Chicago Divinity School, Johns was well positioned to serve as president of Virginia Theological Seminary and later to become pastor of Dexter Avenue Baptist Church in Montgomery, Alabama. His pastorate at the venerable church immediately preceded that of Martin Luther King's. In Johns's most famous sermon, "Transfigured Moments," he finds the rise from the ordinary to the extraordinary exemplified in the figure of Lincoln, a common man who removed slaves from bondage, while Moses, a noble man, had pursued the ordinary by leading the Jews into bondage. In the rich and powerful sermon, Johns also inveighed against pseudoscientific representations of blacks as inferior based upon skull size. Speaking at a time when segregation, discrimination, and lynching were the order of the day in the South, Johns expressed certainty that God would see an end to these un-Christian practices as houses that were built upon sand rather than the rock of Jesus and would be washed away.

Garvey and Johns focused on the self-efficacy and spiritual well-being of blacks, while A. Philip Randolph took the cause of racial equality to the economic world, fighting for the cause of the black workingman and soldier. Randolph was in the advance guard of black labor unions in America. He organized elevator operators and black dockworkers and later served as president of the Brotherhood of Sleeping Car Porters. In that role he helped organize opposition to the Pullman Company, on whose sleeping cars many black porters toiled for low wages. Randolph also called for the integration of the US armed forces and lobbied Franklin Roosevelt to provide jobs for blacks in the defense industry. Randolph threatened to persuade black youth to disobey orders from their draft boards. He also compared the fight for racial equality with Gandhi's nonviolent protests for an end to British colonial rule of India, comparing American blacks to Indian colonial subjects. Randolph's influence was keenly felt as the person who envisioned the March on Washington for Jobs and Freedom. He was the first of nine speakers who took the lectern before Martin Luther King spoke on the steps of the Lincoln Memorial.

Finally, Leeman discusses the contribution of Supreme Court justice Thurgood Marshall, who worked for racial justice within the legal system. As a lawyer, Marshall successfully brought a case against the University of Maryland for a prejudicial admissions policy that had prevented him from being admitted. Most famous, however, was his success in arguing a series of school desegregation cases, culminating in the *Brown v. Board of Education* case in 1954, which brought a legal end to segregation in the public schools with a nine-to-zero decision. As an attorney for the NAACP, Marshall encouraged the bringing of as many cases of discrimination before the courts as possible. "Many people," he said, "believe the time is always 'ripe' to discriminate against Negroes. All right then—the time is always 'ripe' to bring justice." He himself brought thirty-two cases, winning twenty-nine of them. Marshall's singular success as a civil rights lawyer led Lyndon Johnson to name him to the Supreme Court, the first African American to hold that post.

Although the contributions of Garvey, Johns, Randolph, and Marshall were substantial, no figure in twentieth-century African American rhetoric looms larger in the national memory than Martin Luther King. His "I Have a Dream" speech, delivered in Washington as part of the March on Washington for Jobs and Freedom, was only one of ten speeches by civil rights leaders the physical and television audience heard that day, including that of A. Philip Randolph. In the fifth chapter in this part, Richard Besel and I consider how King's speech became recognized as perhaps the most memorable address delivered in the twentieth century. Retrospectively, it is difficult to understand why the *Washington Post* failed to recognize the significance of the speech—failed in fact, even to mention it—while featuring A. Philip Randolph's instead. *New York Daily News* television critic Kay Gardella believed that the cutaways to the brooding statue of Abraham Lincoln were the most affecting part of the performance. In short, the speech was not immediately acknowledged by all as a masterpiece of oratory—few speeches are—although King presciently copyrighted it, requesting that the proceeds of sales benefit the Southern Christian Leadership Conference. Over time, however, the speech, particularly the "I Have a Dream" refrain, has come to signify King's contribution to the movement and has indeed become an emblem of the movement itself. In 1963, King was acknowledged as the religious leader of the civil rights movement, but his reputation as an organizer and a speaker were amplified when, after his assassination, the speech was replayed to memorialize his contribution to the civil rights movement.

The establishment of the Martin Luther King holiday in 1983 provided still more opportunities for Americans to watch the most moving passages of the speech. Valerie Strauss of the *Washington Post* recently noted that in 2013, Taylor Branch, King's biographer, opined that Americans might know more about the speech had the King Foundation put it in public domain, which otherwise will occur automatically in 2038 (Strauss, 2017). However, apart from the Gettysburg Address, it is difficult to imagine a more recognizable speech. While permission to reprint or to include the speech in film can be prohibitively expensive, there is little question that the speech has achieved the status of what Frederick Douglass, addressing a predominantly white audience, called "your national poetry and eloquence" (Douglass, 2012, p. 63).

Great speeches such as Lincoln's Second Inaugural, which Lincoln modestly thought would "wear well" and Frederick Douglass considered "a sacred effort," are often not immediately recognized for their singular eloquence, let alone their potential impact. Exactly what King thought of the speech on the day it was delivered is difficult to know. Surely he realized the impact of its scintillating dream section and dramatic conclusion. He had told his wife, Coretta Scott King, that he would redeploy the rhetorically potent, extemporaneously delivered "I Have a Dream" material he used recently in a speech in Detroit if it seemed the moment was right. Ms. King presented the words as inspired by a higher power, while John F. Kennedy, a student of oratory, welcomed King into the Oval Office after the speech, admiringly intoning its most famous phrase. King himself recognized the prophetic power of the dream passage and incorporated references to the dream in later speeches.

For the American public the "dream" came to represent the unexpressed context of the celebrated speaker and his cause. The Martin Luther King Memorial in Washington draws inspiration from the speech, including in its design physical representations of phrases taken from the text, such as "a mountain of despair," "a stone of hope," and "justice" rolling "down like water and righteousness like a mighty stream." While King was a brilliant organizer and a charismatic leader whose efforts on behalf of civil rights spanned his adult life, shortened by an assassin's bullet, his public memory is fixed by the words he spoke in the heat of Washington, DC, on August 28, 1963.

Dr. King's message of nonviolence might not have been as effective in drawing public support had it not been for the militancy of Malcolm X. In his contribution to Part 1, Robert Terrill weaves together the biographical and rhetorical narratives of Malcolm Little, later Malcolm X, suggesting that he underwent a number of transformations both in his life and in his rhetoric. These transformations also would affect his audiences, as Malcolm X invited them to see the world through a more refractive lens.

Little was born into relative poverty in Omaha, Nebraska, and lost his father to a streetcar accident that some thought was actually a murder committed by the white-supremacist Black Legion. His mother was consigned to a state mental hospital. A good student, Malcolm became rebellious, fell into a life of criminality, including petty larceny and burglary, which led to his incarceration. While in jail he was introduced to the tracts of Elijah Muhammad, who led the Nation of Islam (NOI).

In the NOI Malcolm found his vocation and his voice. He became the minister of the Harlem NOI Temple No. 7 and increased its congregation exponentially. When Malcolm became disenchanted with Elijah Muhammad and the NOI, he was transformed, as Terrill says, "from being the best public speaker in a little-known religious sect to being a recognized leader and thinker on the national and global stage." After the difficult and bitter split with Elijah Muhammad, Malcolm formed his own religious organization and a political outlet, the Organization of Afro-American Unity. Political comments had been forbidden by Muhammad, which was one of the reasons for Malcolm's decision to leave the NOI.

A trip to Mecca softened Malcolm's perspective on white people, who had been roundly condemned by Elijah Muhammad. Now unfettered by the NOI, Malcolm X was able to express his political sentiments. Terrill focuses on three speeches he delivered: "Black Man's History," while Malcolm was still in the NOI, "The Ballot or the Bullet," and his speech in Rochester, New York. Terrill argues that "for Malcolm X, public address *is* social change, his words *are* his deeds," in the sense that his rhetoric created a different worldview for blacks and made them conscious of actions they could take to effect change. "Black Man's History" was the complex mythical account of human genesis according to the NOI, which is Manichaean in perspective, representing blacks as entirely good and whites as entirely evil.

Among his political speeches, "The Ballot or the Bullet" is the most widely anthologized and is representative of Malcolm's politics after he broke with the NOI. In contrast to the nonviolent activism of Martin Luther King, Malcolm X sees the potential need for the synecdochical "bullet," should blacks not be allowed to exercise their rights to the ballot. "It'll be ballots, or it'll be bullets. It'll be liberty, or it will be death" (Malcolm X, 2012, p. 284). He opposes Martin Luther King's plea for nonviolence and the "turning of the other cheek." "Die for what you believe in. But don't die alone. Let your dying be reciprocal" (p. 286). In the speech, the fiery orator explains the concept of Black Nationalism from an international point of view. He also points to the successes of "dark people" in fighting guerrilla wars against white foes. He rails against the Johnson administration for allowing the Dixiecrats, the southern Democrats, to block the Civil Rights Act of 1964, but also denies that blacks can be given rights that they already have as human beings. The speech, which was delivered extemporaneously in various versions, is highly provocative, and Malcolm X's rhetoric produced a sense of anxiety among many Americans concerned about further igniting racial tensions.

FBI director Herbert Hoover feared that Malcolm X would galvanize the black community with his militant rhetoric. After Malcolm X's assassination in 1965, Hoover speculated that either Martin Luther King or Stokely Carmichael would assume his role (Leeman & Duffy, 2012, p. 297). Carmichael, briefly a Black Panther, and head of the Student Nonviolent Coordinating Committee, was a prolific and versatile speaker, but none of his speeches received the same attention as "Black Power," delivered at UC Berkeley in 1966, a speech that Richard Besel and I consider. Governor Pat Brown and his challenger in the gubernatorial race, Ronald Reagan, both expressed concern about the speech. Brown flew to Oakland to meet with police so that provisions could be made in case the speech incited violence. Carmichael, educated at Howard University and author of articles in outlets such as the *New York Review of Books*, was only twenty-five when he delivered the speech (Leeman & Duffy, 2012, pp. 298, 295). Followed by the press, Carmichael had made a reputation as a provocative speaker, often addressing his messages to black audiences at historically black colleges. In the "Black Power" speech, Carmichael mentioned many of the same ideas as Malcolm X, including the idea that violence should be reciprocated with violence in defense ("If you play like Nazis, we playing back with you this time around") and that the civil rights bill was for whites who did not recognize the innate freedom of blacks (Carmichael, 2012, pp. 309, 306). Among the themes Carmichael addressed was his insistence that blacks be able to define themselves and articulate their own identities; his plea for separate action by whites to involve other whites as allies, rather than participants, in the black power movement; his demand for access to education and economic power for blacks; and his criticism of the draft and the Vietnam War.

The concept of black power was intended for black audiences as a symbol of racial pride and self-worth. So much was this the case that the Afro-American Student Union at Berkeley asked Carmichael not to use the term with white audiences. Although Carmichael agreed nominally, a large portion of the speech explains black power and criticizes those who were antagonistic toward blacks for using the term. Martin Luther King, for example, saw it as the parallel to white supremacy and thought it equally evil (Leeman & Duffy, 2012, p. 296). Carmichael viewed the Vietnam War as an expression of American imperialism justified by the idea that the Vietnamese needed democracy at any price: "We'll just wipe them the hell out, 'cause they don't deserve to live if they won't have our way of life'" (2012, p. 312). His stance on the Vietnam War was embodied in the phrase "Hell no, we ain't going," a sentiment commonly heard as "Hell no, we won't go" in antiwar demonstrations.

When Barack Obama ran for the presidency the advent of the Great Recession eclipsed the issue of the lingering and frustrating wars in Iraq and Afghanistan. As the first black to win the Democratic nomination for the presidency, Obama was also forced to confront the issue of race. David Frank's chapter on Obama's speech on race, "A More Perfect Union," during his first campaign for the presidency suggests alternate arguments that might have set the stage for greater national unity and suppressed the political rise of Donald Trump. Obama's so-called race speech was a reaction to the criticism of the Reverend Jeremiah Wright, the pastor of a Chicago church that Obama had attended. Quotations from Wright's sermons, including "God damn America," all taken out of the context of sermons criticizing racism in America, had been broadcast both by the news media and by Republican opponents to Obama's presidential candidacy. Obama's speech was an attempt to blunt the criticism, but also to reflect on American racism. In some ways it was an apologia not unlike John F. Kennedy's "Speech to the Greater Houston Ministerial Association," which answered accusations about his fitness to run for office as a Roman Catholic. Although Frank regards the speech as President Obama's most brilliant, worthy of the "pantheon of great orations," he also wonders if the project of unifying America might have been enhanced with a rhetoric that considered race differently. He imagines arguments and appeals that Obama might have expressed that would have broadened his message.

After all, as Frank notes, "The word 'race' does not describe something essential to human biology or identity." Therefore, many in the scientific community prefer "ancestry" or "population" to "race." Had Obama taken a broader view, he might have emphasized other factors that might describe himself or his audience members, for example, the fact that he descended from an immigrant father, or that his maternal grandfather and great uncle served in the military during World War II. Many things bind Americans together other than race, class, religion, or national origin. Although Obama speaks of slavery as America's "original sin," sins were also committed against indigenous people and ultimately against impoverished European settlers such as the Scots-Irish who like blacks were classified as an underclass. White working-class Americans who believed they had been ignored and disenfranchised were successfully courted by Donald Trump. Had Obama made an effort to take them into account in his unifying rhetoric, they might have been less receptive to candidate Trump's nationalistic message. As Frank and Cornell West note, people disadvantaged by race and by class have in the past collaborated successfully, as when President Johnson's Great Society and Franklin Roosevelt's New Deal improved conditions for both poor whites and poor blacks.

The presidential elections of 2008 and 2012 both emphasized economic disabilities experienced by a large swath of Americans during the Great Recession. Frank speculates that white voters, including those in the crevices of rural and industrial America who had voted for Obama in those two elections, were "primed" to think in racial terms during the 2016 Clinton-Trump campaign. Counties that had been Democratic victories in 2008 and 2012 shifted Republican.

Racial reconciliation is, therefore, still unfinished work that will require sincere acknowledgments of responsibility and blame. If scapegoating racial minorities continues to be part of increasingly divisive political campaigns, the racial divide will expand and there will be little chance of reconciliation in the near future.

In this environment, one can only hope for a sustained and resounding clarion call of civil rights rhetoric not only from blacks but from all groups who consider themselves at risk, including blacks, Muslims, Middle Easterners, Asians, Hispanics, women, the LGBTQ community, the elderly, the disabled, immigrants, and refugees from tyranny and poverty. In the matter of civil rights, black orators historically led the way, providing the arguments and passionate appeals that over time struck at the core of Jim Crow legislation and stripped away the false front of paternalism. While the 1963 March on Washington for Jobs and Freedom was the first and last such event fully covered by television, the recent women's march of more than one million in Washington and throughout the United States and around the world was impressive in numbers and organization (Stein, Hendrix, & Hauslohner, 2017).

The history of black oratory is remarkable for its eloquent truths and courage, while the stimulus for that oratory is frightening for its inhumanity and its suppression of freedom and the voices of the oppressed. As John Lewis, congressman and civil rights activist, has urged: "You cannot be afraid to speak up and speak out for what you believe, you have to have courage, real courage" (Brinlee, 2017).

■ **References**

Brinlee, M. (2017). These John Lewis quotes about justice & civil rights are the perfect example of how words become action. January 14. Https://www.bustle.com/p/these-john-lewis-quotes-about-justice-civil-rights-are-the-perfect-example-of-how-words-become-action-30445.

Carmichael, S. (2012). Black power. In R. W. Leeman & B. K. Duffy (eds.) *The will of a people: A critical anthology of great African American speeches.* Carbondale: Southern Illinois University Press, 295–303.

Douglass, F. (2012). What to the American slave is the Fourth of July? In R. W. Leeman & B. K. Duffy (eds.) *The will of a people: A critical anthology of great African American speeches.* Carbondale: Southern Illinois University Press, 57–82.

Duffy, B. K., & R. W. Leeman (eds.). (2005). *American voices: An encyclopedia of contemporary orators.* Westport, CT: Greenwood Press.

Johnson, A. (2012). *The forgotten prophet: Bishop Henry McNeal Turner and the African American prophetic tradition.* Lanham, MD: Lexington Books.

———. (2010–17). *An African American pastor before and during the American Civil War.* The Literary Archive of Henry McNeal Turner. 6 vols. Lewiston, NY: Edwin Mellen Press.

Leeman, R. (ed.). (1996). *African-American oratory: A biocritical sourcebook.* Westport, CT: Greenwood Press.

———. (2012). *The teleological discourse of Barack Obama.* Lanham, MD: Lexington Press.

Leeman, R. W., & B. K. Duffy (eds.). (2012). *The will of a people: Great speeches by African Americans.* Carbondale: Southern Illinois University Press.

Malcolm X. (2012). The ballot or the bullet. In R. W. Leeman & B. K. Duffy (eds.) *The will of a people: A critical anthology of great African American speeches.* Carbondale: Southern Illinois University Press, 268–76.

Strauss, V. (2017). The price of using King's "Dream" speech. *San Luis Obispo Tribune,* January 16, pp. 1, 7.

Stein, P., S. Hendrix, S., & A. Hauslohner. (2017). Women's marches: More than one million protesters vow to resist Donald Trump. *Washington Post,* January 22.

Terrill, R. (2004). *Malcolm X: Inventing radical judgment.* East Lansing: Michigan State University Press.

——— (ed.). (2010). *Cambridge companion to Malcolm X.* Cambridge: Cambridge University Press.

———. (2015). *Double-consciousness and the rhetoric of Barack Obama: The price and promise of citizenship.* Columbia: University of South Carolina Press.

Recollection, Regret, and Foreboding in Frederick Douglass's Fourth of July Orations of 1852 and 1875

Bernard K. Duffy and Richard D. Besel

Nineteenth-century American Independence Day orations were as much a part of the celebration as festoons, flags, fireworks, cannonades, parades, and pealing bells (Travers, 1997, p. 54; Engels 2009, pp. 311–12). Every city sought an orator to perform a skillfully crafted reaffirmation of the principles for which Americans had risked their lives. Most prized undoubtedly were those who simultaneously were civic leaders, public philosophers, and wordsmiths—important people who possessed both moral authority and the literary and oral ability needed to impress and inspire their audiences. Silver-tongued senators Daniel Webster and Edward Everett were obvious choices. Lincoln as president delivered an Independence Day oration, as did national anthem author Francis Scott Key, humorist Mark Twain, and abolitionist William Lloyd Garrison (Heintze, 2010). In all, twenty-five hundred printed Independence Day orations survive from those delivered in nineteenth-century America, the bulk by orators less celebrated than these, but never by ordinary citizens (Martin, 1958, p. 397; Travers, 1997, p. 6). Without exception invited speakers treated their compositions seriously, laboring over them for weeks, if not months, in advance (Banninga, 1967, pp. 45–46; Martin, 1958, p. 393). Significant speeches were printed and circulated, often in pamphlet form, sometimes stimulating the publication of pamphlets written in response (Martin, 1958, p. 397; Goetsch and Hurm, 1992). The fact that most important speeches were destined for print helps to explain the atavistic grandiloquent style of nineteenth-century oral discourse, particularly of ceremonial speeches.

Abolition orators used the July Fourth oration to plead their cause. Frederick Douglass, unquestionably the greatest abolition orator, delivered several such orations, the most famous of which is "What to the Slave Is the Fourth of July?," delivered in Rochester, New York, on July

5, 1852. The speech ranks as one of the most important abolition speeches of the nineteenth century and Douglass's most celebrated oratorical achievement. Douglass's use of irony in this speech has captured the attention of many rhetorical scholars (Lucaites, 1997; Fulkerson, 1996; Terrill, 2003). Less well known, yet still important, is Douglass's 1875 speech "The Color Question." Delivered in Hillsdale, just outside of Washington, DC, also on July 5, this address provides an important comparison point for understanding the development of Douglass's rhetoric. Unlike in previous analyses, Douglass's penchant for irony is not the singular focus of this essay. Instead, we argue that the use of anamnesis, often understood to mean "recollection," or an attempt to remind people of what they have forgotten, saturates both of his speeches (Allen, 1959; Scott, 1987). Following his break with the Garrisonians, Douglass used a specific recollection of the Declaration of Independence to create a mythic vision of what America could and should become.

Rhetorical and Historical Context

William Garrison's Fourth of July oration, "Address to the Colonization Society," delivered at Park Street Church in Boston in 1829, was the first major speech of the man who would become Douglass's mentor and helped establish a subgenre of Fourth of July orations delivered by abolitionists (Rohler, 1987, pp. 184–85). Garrison exploited, although to a much lesser extent than Douglass would, the great paradox of celebrating liberty within the context of slavery in the United States. Slavery was to Garrison "a gangrene preying upon our vitals [that] . . . should make this a day of fasting and prayer, not of boisterous merriment and idle pageantry—a day of great lamentations, not of congratulatory joy." Although his speech violates the expectation that speakers praise the Constitution and the government it established, Garrison's speech embodied the revolutionary spirit also valued in speeches within this genre (Martin, 1984, p. 395). Fourth of July speeches such as Garrison's and Douglass's boldly took issue with the fulfillment of the ideals of the Founding Fathers, if not with the ideals themselves.

There was not a more famous or more eloquent African American abolitionist than Frederick Douglass. Born a slave, the unacknowledged son of an unknown white father and an African American mother in Maryland, Douglass found his voice as an abolitionist and advocate of the equal rights of African Americans in Baltimore. He listened to and participated in debates among free Blacks in the city, becoming a member of the East Baltimore Mental Improvement Society. At the age of twelve he had read Caleb Bingham's *The Columbian Orator*, a collection of patriotic works including essays and dialogues, used in schoolrooms early in the nineteenth century to develop literacy and an appreciation of eloquence and the importance of public discourse in a free republic. Bingham, whose book had a profound impact on Douglass, preached the importance of combining eloquence with content that merited such eloquence, for example, the ideas of liberty and equality (Lampe, 1998, pp. 9–13; Martin, 1984, pp. 139–40). As an abolitionist orator, Douglass initially aligned himself with the radical views of Garrison, who claimed that the US Constitution immorally supported slavery and that slaves should be immediately emancipated (McClure, 2000, pp. 428–29). Garrison ultimately came to believe that the only solution was disunion and secession (Lucaites, 1997, p. 55). The Garrisonians made significant inroads in persuading the American public of the immorality of slavery, but Douglass broke with the Garrisonians in 1847, only briefly continuing to support their view of the Constitution. By 1850 Douglass thought differently, preferring to see the Constitution as embodying tenets of equality that, if properly interpreted, would lead Americans to abandon slavery (McClure, 2000, pp. 428–29).

As an orator, Douglass quickly became a celebrity. The Massachusetts Anti-Slavery Society hired him as a paid lecturer, a position he held from 1841 to 1845. Among the African American speakers who satisfied the public interest in the life of the slave, the uncommonly literate and eloquent Douglass rose to stardom. So literate was Douglass that rumors circulated he was an imposter; such an educated speaker could not be a fugitive slave. To establish his bona fides, he published *Narrative of the Life of Frederick Douglass* in 1845. As his fame increased, so did the danger that bounty hunters would seize him and return him to slavery, however, and so Douglass sailed to Britain and, until 1847, lectured across the British Isles. He returned to the United States after reluctantly allowing British supporters to purchase his freedom so that he could continue his abolition work in America itself. A career as an editor and journalist followed in publications such as *North Star, Frederick Douglass's Paper, Douglass Monthly*, and *New National Era* (Martin, 1984, pp. 140–42; Fulkerson, 1996, pp. 82–83). Douglass availed himself of every opportunity to remind audiences of problems many of his contemporaries wanted to sublimate.

Fourth of July orations provided a great opportunity for shaping historical memory, for active "recollection," and even the creation of myth, as Douglass later realized in witnessing how white civic leaders chose to remember the Civil War. Many layers of speeches delivered at commemorative ceremonies—whether praising the Founding Fathers, the Army of the Potomac, or the Union Army—created a collective national consciousness through a process of steady inculcation. Conservative rhetorical critic Richard Weaver claims that grandiloquent speeches of the nineteenth century reminded their audiences of received truth, of a *textus receptus*, in a day when there was greater homogeneity of cultural belief (Weaver, 1953, p. 171). Therefore, audiences judged ceremonial speeches not by the originality of their claims, but by how artfully accepted truths were represented. Fourth of July orations deepened preexisting belief and provided instruction in public virtue for the young (Duffy, 1983). In such speeches, history was to be experienced with sentiment rather than remembered objectively in its factual details, as "felt" rather than "passive" history (Blight, 1998, p. 212). Weaver argues that the modern decline in the importance of rhetoric is commensurate with the decline in the importance of socially cohesive memories (1964, pp. 55–56).

From one point of view, then, nineteenth-century American orators, recalling the virtuous words and deeds of past generations, created "a meditative relationship with history" wherein audiences with shared beliefs about religion, morality, and government remembered the past in light of those beliefs (Weaver, 1953, p. 178). Recollection, "an act of gathering things together again," inspired by ceremonial discourse, is typically regarded as a force for conservatism, although, as Blight also notes, reformers such as Douglass strove to modify perceptions about the past to stimulate change (1998, p. 218).

The appraisal of nineteenth-century sentimental oratory characterized by Fourth of July orations depends upon one's stance on the value of conservatism and of reform. Liberal rhetorical critic Edwin Black believes that the common run of nineteenth-century sentimental oratory operated through "willful distraction," wherein audiences were encouraged to repress recognition of social problems, most notably slavery. Sentimental orators, Black argues, directed the emotions of their audiences, leaving no room for individual response (1992, pp. 100–104). In his historical study of Fourth of July celebrations, Len Travers suggests that "the ritualized celebrations of the Fourth of July helped to mask disturbing ambiguities and contradictions in the new republic, overlaying real social and political conflict with a conceptual veneer of shared ideology and elemental harmony." Thus, while political partisans used Independence Day as a vehicle to air their disputes, "Other Americans employed the rituals, rhetoric, and symbolism of Independence Day to minimize the conflicts and to assert the idealized (but dubious) unity of the American people" (Travers, 1997, p. 7). Blight provides an important example, addressed later in this chapter, in which the "causes and consequences of the Civil War—the role of slavery and the challenge of racial equality," were "actively suppressed," as Douglass feared they would be in his Fourth of July oration of 1875 (1998, p. 214).

Douglass's 1852 Address

Douglass delivered "What to the American Slave Is the Fourth of July?" as part of an 1852 Independence Day celebration at Corinthian Hall in Rochester, New York, the city where he had taken up residence after his return from Britain. The Rochester Ladies' Anti-Slavery Society invited Douglass to deliver the main address, and Douglass wished to speak on July 5, following a tradition in the New York State African American community. The audience comprised six hundred people who had paid the ticket price of twelve and a half cents each, the equivalent of $3.20 in current dollars (Fulkerson, 1996, pp. 90–91; Blight, 2005). Since many in Douglass's mostly white, immediate audience were abolitionists such as himself, in large measure he was "preaching to the choir." Among Garrisonian abolitionists, though, his antislavery interpretation of the Constitution would have been controversial. Before Douglass took the podium to address his audience, a clergyman first read the Declaration of Independence (Blight, 2005). Douglass's speech, subdued and circumspect at the outset, abruptly turns to mordant criticism of the nation and, apparently, of his audience: "America is false to the past, false to the present, and solemnly binds herself to be false to the future. . . . I will not equivocate; I will not excuse."

As the speech unfolds, Douglass deliberately violates the norms of the occasion, but it is difficult to believe that his inviters might not have expected as much from the fiery thirty-four-year-old abolitionist. Surely, the immediate audience would have recognized the rhetorical artifice in his acutely uncomfortable question: "Do you mean, citizens, to mock me, by asking me to speak to-day?" The women abolitionists who invited Douglass would not have been surprised by the tension he deliberately creates between himself and his audience. As the editor of the *Frederick Douglass Papers* remarks, "Sarcasm, invective, and ridicule were constants in Douglass's orations" (Blassingame, 1979, p. xxxiii). Those who knew his reputation as an abolitionist speaker would have been disappointed had his speech lacked the firebrand qualities that had made him a sought-after orator. Douglass's ironic treatment of his subject might have been a thrillingly provocative oratorical strategy, but it is difficult to believe that an audience of abolitionist sympathizers would have found it personally offensive. The implied audience to whom Douglass directs his criticism served as a foil for his charge of mockery, and a critical component of the rhetorical drama he created.

Customarily, ceremonial (or *epideictic*) speeches take noncontroversial themes, the praise or blame of what is acknowledged as praiseworthy or blameworthy. Although belonging to the epideictic genre, this speech does not fulfill the conventional purpose of a Fourth of July address—to praise America and its institutions among Americans. Its praise is reserved for the sacrifices made and the risks taken by the Founders on behalf of liberty, and even that praise serves to heighten Douglass's argument of blame—that Americans in the present are guilty of the sin of hypocrisy for accepting the institution of slavery in their midst. Douglass, though a free man, assumes the position of a representative of African Americans callously enslaved in a nation dedicated to liberty and of free, northern African Americans accorded, at best, second-class citizenship. If indeed Douglass were only speaking on behalf of abolition, the irony of the speech would be less meaningful. Although Douglass appears to criticize his immediate audience, the people he wishes to make most uncomfortable with his criticisms are the larger audience that would read his carefully burnished speech in print. He reveals as much in saying midway through the speech: "O! had I the ability and could I reach the nation's ear." A journalist, Douglass well understood both the power of the printed word and the power of committing an act of oratorical defiance that would make his speech newsworthy. Northern journalists were known to describe Douglass in provocative terms: "'saucy negro,' 'the impudent negro,' 'an impertinent black vagabond,' 'that black disgrace to human nature'" (Blassingame, 1979, xxxviii).

The main body of the speech is divided into two broad sections, the first praising the Founders, and the second criticizing the present generation for not acting in the same spirit of liberty as their forebears. Douglass begins by lowering expectations about his speech, a nineteenth-century rhetorical custom he regularly followed: "I evince no elaborate preparation nor grace my speech with a high sounding exordium. With little experience and less learning, I have been able to throw my thoughts hastily and imperfectly together" (Blassingame, 1979, p. xxxvii). In reality, Douglass had departed from his normal practice of extemporaneous and impromptu speaking and had spent fully three weeks preparing the speech (Chesebrough, 1998, p. 45). Despite Douglass's claims to the contrary, the exordium, or introduction, that follows *is* distinctly "high sounding" and replete with carefully contemplated, if not sometimes labored, metaphors. He speaks of the nation as a "great stream" that might "rise in quiet and stately majesty and inundate the land, refreshing and fertilizing the earth with their mysterious properties," but warns that it might "rise in wrath and fury" and that the "river may dry up, and leave nothing behind but a withered branch, and the unsightly rock, to howl in the abyss-sweeping wind, the sad tale of departed glory. As with rivers so with nations." Although easy to overlook as a rhetorical embellishment, this carefully constructed metaphor contains the central idea of the speech. Douglass saw that to live, the nation must continue to renew itself from the same sources that had created it—the idea of equality in the Declaration of Independence and the idea of liberty in the Constitution. Douglass's hydrological metaphor sounds the same chords as "a Nation conceived in Liberty," tested by the Civil War (the "wrath and fury in Douglass's metaphor) and destined for "a new birth of freedom," that Lincoln would memorably envision eleven years later in the Gettysburg Address (cf. Jasinski, 1997, pp. 80–82).

In narrating the nation's birth, Douglass celebrates the deeds of *the audience's* fathers, not *his*. With each successive use of "you" and "your," Douglass coils the spring of an invective that is released in the major portion of the speech focused upon the present and the future. He tendentiously describes the circumstances that led to the nation's foundation based upon the principle of liberty: "Oppression makes a wise man mad. Your fathers were wise men, and if they did not go mad, they became restive under this treatment." After many paragraphs in which Douglass distances himself from his audience by referring repeatedly to "your fathers," he breaks the tension of this deliberate alienation from the audience: "Fellow citizens, I am not wanting in respect for the fathers of this republic. . . . The point from which I am compelled to view them is not, certainly, the most favorable; and yet I cannot contemplate their great deeds with less than admiration. . . . I will unite with you to honor their memory." While Douglass cannot but admire the impulses toward liberty of the Founding Fathers, he reminds his audience that as a former slave and disenfranchised citizen, his perspective is at a great remove from theirs, and that his admiration is less filial than intellectual. The "causes of this anniversary" are a branch of knowledge in which you feel "a much deeper interest than your speaker." Douglass has only half-fulfilled the purposes of a Fourth of July speech, which was in the nineteenth century a most important ritual in American patriotism. His narrative meets out praise, but is underlain by a grim and glowering detachment from the object of praise.

Douglass's caveats and self-conscious, ironic positioning in the historical section of the speech prepare the ground for his discussion of the present problem. "My business" he says, "if I have any here to-day, is with the present." Circumspect historical narrative and personal distancing give way to imperatives, exhortations, and embarrassing questions: "You have no right to wear out and waste the hard-earned fame of your fathers to cover your indolence," thunders Douglass. "What have I, or those I represent, to do with your national independence?" He presses the irony of his being asked to speak when he is "not included within the pale of this glorious anniversary": "You may rejoice, I must mourn." Douglass invokes the image of his former bondage to press the irony of his delivering a speech celebrating independence: "To drag a man in fetters into the grand illuminated temple of liberty, and call upon him to join you in joyous anthems, were inhuman mockery and sacrilegious irony. Do you mean, citizens, to mock me, asking me to speak today?" Douglass's question and the metaphor of the manacled African American in the "temple of liberty" might seem melodramatic and unwarranted. There is a double irony here since Douglass was not then a slave, nor was he being physically forced, as a slave might be, to speak that day. Yet, like all African Americans who lived in the United States in 1852, including those, such as himself, who were nominally free, Douglass was fettered by discriminatory practices of the North reflecting the same racial prejudice that made slavery possible. Even many abolitionists, although opposed to slavery, supported such discrimination. As John Lucaites observes: "Douglass came to recognize the latent, if well-intentioned, racist paternalism that underscored the efforts of many white abolitionists like Garrison. He thus came relatively quickly to the conclusion that the social and political implications of such racism were even more significant than the problem of slavery, for they pervaded not only the plantation, but the world of the free black as well" (Lucaites, 1997, pp. 55–56). Douglass would again revisit the realities of northern discrimination and Black consciousness in his 1875 Fourth of July address.

In his 1852 address, irony is not merely a stylistic device, it is a strategic response, a refrain that thunders from deep within the speech. "At a time like this, scorching irony, not convincing argument, is needed. O! had I the ability and could I reach the Nation's ear, I would to-day, pour out a fiery stream of biting ridicule, blasting reproach, withering sarcasm, and stern rebuke." Although coyly denying his broader influence, he uses the interest of reaching a much larger audience to justify his use of "scorching irony." In this section, Douglass employs the rhetorical trope of paralipsis, arguing points that he claims are so obvious that they do not require argument—that the slave is a man, that slavery is wrong. He reasons, for example, that if slaves are not men, there would not be laws in the South forbidding their education. Seeking to prove undeniably the wrongfulness of slavery, he presents a litany of specific wrongs that slavery produced: "to make men brutes, to rob them of their liberty, to work them without wages . . . to beat them with sticks, to flay their flesh with the lash, to load their limbs with irons, to hunt them with dogs, to sell them at auction, [and] to sunder their families." Douglass's self-evident indictments against southern slave culture would today come under the heading of "crimes against humanity," although then many southerners callously questioned the very humanity of Black slaves.

Another aspect of the present is the internal slave trade, which Douglass describes in haunting detail. He contrasts the "mandrover," the "inhuman wretch who drives" the pitiable "sad procession" of shackled slaves to the Baltimore pier to sail to the New Orleans slave market and ultimately to the cotton fields and sugar mills of the Deep South. As if describing a tableau that he creates with image-laden language, Douglass moves from one detail of the tableau to the next: "There, see the old man with locks thinned and gray. Cast one glance if you please, upon the young mother, whose shoulders are bare to the scorching sun, her briny tears falling on the brow the babe in her arms." The appeals are auditory as well as visual; Douglass describes the "chain rattles" and the crack of the slave whip, the anguished scream of a young woman flayed (see also Terrill 2003, pp. 224–25).

Douglass maintains that the Fugitive Slave Law essentially nationalized slavery. The law made it possible for an African American man living in the North to be consigned to slavery in the South upon the testimony of two witnesses. He questions why the churches have not publicly criticized this law. Religion, he says, should not be simply a "form of worship" but "a vital principle requiring active benevolence, justice, love and good will towards man." It should offer support and protection to Blacks who fear deportation to the South. Most prominent ministers, north and south, he claims, cling to the idea "'that we ought to obey man's law before the law of God.'" In his Second Inaugural Address, Lincoln would echo Douglass's thoughts about the sin of silence in the face of evil. Lincoln saw the Civil War theologically as God's punishment of the South for having slavery and of the North for allowing it. In the climax of this section, Douglass warns ominously and presciently that the existence of slavery would damage the nation. He sets before the audience's eyes the image of slavery as a lurking, parasitic beast. "Oh! Be warned! Be warned! A horrible reptile is coiled up in your nation's bosom; the venomous creature is nursing at the tender breast of your youthful republic; for the love of God, tear it away." In less than ten years the reptile would spring forth in a civil war wherein 603,000 American lives were lost and the circumstances of Black Americans changed forever.

Finally, Douglass comes to the question of the Constitution. Whether the Constitution was a proslavery or an antislavery document was hotly debated by abolitionists (Chesebrough, 1998, pp. 40–41). In the early years of his abolitionist career, Douglass had taken the view of his compatriot William Lloyd Garrison that the Constitution was a proslavery document and argued the position in a formal debate in 1850. Earlier he had wavered in that belief, maintaining in 1849 that "I am satisfied that if strictly 'construed according to its reading,' it is not a pro-slavery instrument." He admitted, however, that the Framers had made it a proslavery instrument (Chesebrough, 1998, p. 39). After he broke with Garrison in May 1851, Douglass came to espouse the views of "political abolitionists" such as Gerrit Smith, who argued that the Constitution, understood outside of its historical circumstances, opposed slavery (McClure, 2000, pp. 428–29; Lucaites, 1997, p. 55). If that proposition was true, then political action could be used to bring about its abolition.

In the 1852 Independence Day oration, Douglass attempts to redeem the nation's founders from the charge that in writing the Constitution they contradictorily affirmed both liberty and slavery. Douglass's use of anamnesis first appears in the paradoxical request to remember what is *not* written in the Constitution. He asks: "If the Constitution were intended to be by its framers and adopters, a slave-holding instrument, why neither slavery, slaveholding, nor slave can anywhere be found in it?" Douglass argues a literalist interpretation of the Constitution: "Now take the constitution according to its plain reading, and I defy the presentation of a single pro-slavery clause in it." He then declares that it is a right, if not an obligation, for "every American citizen . . . to form an opinion of the constitution, and to propagate that opinion, and to use all honorable means to make his opinion the prevailing one." Douglass sees the correct understanding of the Constitution as a vehicle by which to expand the idea of liberty to include African Americans, to keep the "great stream" from drying up. Surely this is his aim, although he leaves the "full and fair discussion" of the subject for a later time.

In his conclusion, Douglass returns to the Declaration of Independence and its "great principles." He also expresses faith in the future and in the promise that technology and commerce will make known American social evils that formerly could be hidden: "Oceans no longer divide, but link nations together. . . . Space is comparatively annihilated. . . . No abuse, no outrage whether in taste, sport or avarice, can now hide itself from the all-pervading light." The conclusion offers further ironies. Although opposed to William Lloyd Garrison's views on the Constitution, Douglass concludes with Garrison's five-stanza poem "The Triumph of Freedom." Douglass had spoken earlier of slaves "whose chains . . . are . . . rendered more intolerable by the jubilee shouts that reach them." Garrison's paean anticipates "the year of jubilee," but in contrast to the celebration of American liberty that Douglass had acknowledged and then scorned as hypocritical, the heartfelt jubilee the poem prophesies would occur when the "oppress'd" "wear the yoke of tyranny like brutes no more." Unlike the American Fourth of July, this is the celebration to which Douglass could lift his voice in unqualified support.

Douglass's 1875 Address

In argument, style, and tenor, Frederick Douglass's Reconstruction rhetoric differs markedly from his antebellum addresses. Unlike his 1852 declamation, Douglass's 1875 speech made little use of irony and matched many of the changes to the genre adopted by other Fourth of July speakers in Reconstruction. For critic Cedric Lawson, the oratory of this period was "somewhat acrimonious in character and dealt with charges and countercharges arising out of the war." Speakers often adopted styles featuring "simplicity of diction and optimism over the future" (Lawson, 1940, p. 23). A careful observer of social trends, Douglass likewise adapted his Independence Day oratory to the new plain style, but continued to challenge the genre's conventions with a prophetic and foreboding tone.

Delivered in Hillsdale, just outside of Washington, DC, Douglass's 1875 oration "The Color Question" is perhaps one of the least studied of Douglass's canon. Conscious of dramatic change in the societal position of former slaves, Douglass used this opportunity to "say a few plain words of matters suggested by the facts of the present hour" and to speculate on what the future might hold for the newly freed Americans in light of the imminent Centennial celebration in the year ahead. Roughly following a chronological order, Douglass's typed speech of eight pages, less than half the length of his 1852 address, is divided into three main points: the past and present status of newly freed Americans, the great change in their condition, and the means by which they should work out their destiny. Because the Fourth of July fell on a Sunday that year, Douglass again addressed his audience on the fifth.

Mirroring the style of other Reconstruction Fourth of July orations, Douglass directly states: "I am not here to glorify the heroes of the American Revolution." Douglass's opening remarks suggest that he will reanimate the well-worn paradox of expressly refusing to praise what the occasion should impel him to praise. However, this is not the case, for Douglass concedes the nation's founders were "great men" responsible for "great events." His praise is tempered only by his desire to address the pressing problems facing former slaves.

In 1852, Douglass asked what to the slave *is* the Fourth of July. His answer then bore upon the exclusion of the slave from the blessings of liberty. The first main point of his 1875 speech references another question. If asked "what colored people have to do with the Fourth of July," he would readily answer, "almost everything of vital importance." Recollecting the role Blacks played in relation to whites allowed Douglass to illustrate to his audience how whites and Blacks were forever bound by blood shed in wars and a shared cultural history:

> We have never forsaken the white man in any great emergency, and never expect to forsake him. We have been with him in times of peace and in times of war, and at all times. We were with him in the darkest hours of the Revolution of 1776. We were with him in the war for free trade and sailors rights in 1812. We were with him in 1861. We were with him at Bunker Hill and at Red Bank. We were with him on the land and with him on the water, and with him everywhere.

In this passage the repetition of "we have and "we were," an example of the stylistic device of anaphora, adds emphasis to his point that Blacks and whites were separated by race but are now united by Nation. For Douglass, the freed slave was lucky to have been on the winning side of the recent war: "Fortune favored us with a liberal hand." But following the war, Douglass no longer wanted the free Black to rely on fortune, insisting that people are only free when they can determine their own destinies.

The Civil War sealed the great divide between the North and the South over slavery, but not over the treatment of Blacks. As Reconstruction speeches began to reflect a "healing" motif for former white combatants, Douglass well understood that the once-warring whites would soon make peace among themselves. For example, Roger A. Pryor, a brigadier general in the Confederate army, would declare in a Decoration Day speech in 1877 that the Civil War was not about slavery, but that it had only been the "occasion not the cause of secession" (Blight, 2001, pp. 89–91). For Douglass, the upcoming Centennial in 1876 would almost surely mark an inflection point in the process of reconciliation spearheaded by northern and southern politicians and orators. In the second main point of the speech Douglass turned his attention to the importance of the recent war and what it represented to Blacks—a "change in our condition." In a relatively short point, only two paragraphs long and less than one typed page, Douglass notes that people "will not quarrel and fight forever," anticipating the upcoming Centennial as a moment in history when the once-divided nation would "lift to the sky" its voices "in one grand . . . hosanna of peace and good." This imminent and lasting peace among the whites, although a welcome change, was for Douglass also a cause of grave concern.

In the longest and concluding point of his speech, Douglass shifts his primarily Black audience's attention away from the peace among whites to a consideration of what is to become of the newly freed, masterless slave: "If war among the whites brought peace and liberty to the Blacks, what will peace among the whites bring?" He even notes that the "signs of the times, are not all in our favor." Douglass argued for the development of a new Black consciousness, one in which former slaves no longer depended on white paternalism. If Ulysses S. Grant was "our shelter in the storms of the past," then determining "who will shield us in the future" was of the utmost importance. For Douglass, Blacks not only could, but must, produce their own leaders to give voice to their perspective in a new nation recovering from a Civil War, which many saw as bringing "a new birth of freedom," as Lincoln had urged in the Gettysburg Address. Douglass used this opportunity to assure his audience "that the colored race is capable of living more than a life of dependence, and can think and speak for itself."

Douglass's use of a celebratory oration that traditionally reflected on the Revolutionary War to discuss what the Civil War meant for the future of newly freed slaves follows Douglass's decision to break with the Garrisonians nearly twenty-five years earlier. If the Declaration of Independence was an antislavery document, the Civil War could be interpreted as the next step in the fulfillment of an American promise of equality made by the "great men" Douglass had briefly praised at the start of his speech. The citizenship granted to African Americans by the Fourteenth Amendment in 1868 incited a new spate of racist pronouncements during Reconstruction. Many whites who had once favored slavery contended that some free Blacks were actually safer and better served as slaves. Blight observes: "the entire racist theory that slavery protected and nurtured blacks" was the exigency that "forced Douglass to argue for an aggressive use of memory" (1998, p. 211). Douglass could not allow racist romanticism to taint what was to be a newly shaped national history.

In his attempt to call for a new Black consciousness, a new voice of Black self-determination, Douglass recollects why the Revolutionary War was fought. The issue of equality and self-determination is so important for Douglass that he chooses to offer a new declaration closely modeled after the "Great Declaration" of 1776. For nearly twenty-five years, Douglass had directed his audiences to recollect, and thereby revise in memory, the Declaration of Independence as an antislavery document. On this point he was consistent and unwavering. But the realist in Douglass also understood it would be difficult for newly freed slaves to resist the "so-called benevolent societies" that wished to "help" them. Even northern whites who truly did wish to help the freed slaves should be approached with skepticism. The rise of "freedmen's aid societies" spread like an infestation after the Civil War, some legitimate and some filled with swindlers. Eventually, northern whites had to compromise with southerners when they realized Reconstruction would require participation from all parties (Drake, 1963). Given the compromises, Douglass observes: "We have been in many instances injured more that benefitted." To play upon the emotions of wealthy benefactors, it was not unusual for these aid societies to portray freed Blacks as incompetent and in need of white assistance. Douglass knew this all too well: "They draw the most distressing picture of the black man's character and condition. They keep the public mind constantly upon the poor, wretched negro, and thus damn the whole race." In the new, free America, Douglass told his audience to resist this new form of self-imposed slavery: "We must not beg men for us what we ought to do ourselves." His final exhortation is that all Americans "now and here denounce and repudiate all such shams."

Conclusion

In many respects, Frederick Douglass's 1852 and 1875 Fourth of July speeches are opposite yet complementary. The first is prolix in argument and copious in language, is addressed primarily to whites, and relies heavily on irony. The second is concise and linguistically spare, addressed primarily to newly freed Blacks, and virtually free of irony. How might one summarize the comparison of the two speeches? Following his break with the Garrisonians, Douglass invited his audience to recollect the ideals of the Declaration detached from its historic context. By looking backward with a new lens, Douglass took his audience forward to a day when his vision of what the Declaration truly means would be fulfilled. Liberally used in both of his Fourth of July orations, anamnesis, the stylistic device embodying the idea of recollection, was the means by which Douglass could envision the future ideal. Unlike the Garrisonians, Douglass remembered a revered American text in a light that made it possible for African Americans to identify themselves with the nation. Additionally, a racial dialectic is consistently at work within Douglass's rhetoric. While urging all Americans to unite under the banner of equality, he simultaneously recognizes the need for a unique and independent Black consciousness and voice. W. E. B. DuBois would later refer to this dialectic as the "double-consciousness" of Black America. In 1897 DuBois asks: "Am I an American or am I a Negro? Can I be both?" (Bell, 1992, p. 140). As John Lucaites notes, "Many of the advocates of American racial equality have since treated this 'two-ness' as the primary problem facing the cultural assimilation of the black person into American culture" (1997, p. 64). In recent American history, the dialectic informing Douglass's speeches surfaces in the rhetoric of such diverse voices as Malcolm X and Martin Luther King Jr. (Lucaites & Condit, 1990). Tellingly, the important questions first posed by Douglass so many years ago are the same questions all Americans are still struggling to answer.

■ References

Allen, R. E. (1959). Anamnesis in Plato's *Meno* and *Phaedo*. *Review of Metaphysics 13*, 165–74.

Banninga, J. L. (1967). John Quincy Adams' address of July 4, 1821. *Quarterly Journal of Speech 53*, 44–49.

Bell, B. W. (1992). The African-American jeremiad and Frederick Douglass's Fourth of July 1852 speech. In *The Fourth of July: Political oratory and literary reactions, 1776–1876*. P. Goetsch & G. Hurm (eds.). Tübingen: Gunter Narr Verlag, 139–54.

Black, E. (1992). The sentimental style. In *Rhetorical questions: Studies in public discourse.* Chicago: University of Chicago Press.

Blassingame, J. W. (ed.). (1979). *The Frederick Douglass Papers*, series 1: *Speeches, debates, and interviews*, vol. 1: *1841–46*. New Haven: Yale University Press.

Blight, D. (1998). "What will peace among the whites bring?": Reunion and race in the struggle over the memory of the Civil War in American culture. In *When the shooting is over: The order and the memory.* L. V. Mannucci (ed.). Milan: Universita di Milana. www.library.vanderbilt.edu/Quaderno/

Auaderno4/quaderno4.html. Web.

———. (2001). *Race and reunion: The Civil War in American memory.* Cambridge: Harvard University Press.

———. (2005). What to the slave is the Fourth of July. *Time*, June 26.

Chesebrough, D. W. (1998). *Frederick Douglass: Oratory from slavery.* Westport, CT: Greenwood Press.

Douglass, F. (1852). What to the slave is the Fourth of July? Rochester Ladies Anti-Slavery Society, Rochester, New York. July 5, Address. In Leeman, R.W. & Duffy, B. (eds.). *The will of a people: A critical anthology of great African American Speeches.* Carbondale: Southern Illinois University Press, 2012.

———. (1875). The color question. Hillsdale. July 5, Address. Https://www.loc.gov/item/mfd.23001/. Drake, R. B. (1963). Freedmen's aid societies and sectional compromise. *Journal of Southern History 29*, 175–86.

Duffy, B. K. (1983). The Platonic functions of epideictic rhetoric. *Philosophy and Rhetoric 16*, 79–93.

Engels, J. (2009). Uncivil speech: Invective and the rhetorics of democracy in the early Republic. *Quarterly Journal of Speech 95*, 311–34.

Fulkerson, G. (1996). Frederick Douglass (1818–1895), abolitionist, reformer. In *African-American orators: A biocritical sourcebook.* R. W. Leeman (ed.). Westport, CT: Greenwood Press, 82–97.

Garrison, W. L. (1829). Address to the colonization society. Park Street Church, Boston. July 4. Address. Http://teachingamericanhistory.org/library/document/address-to-the-colonization-society/.

Goetsch, P., & Hurm, G. (eds.). (1992). *The Fourth of July: Political oratory and literary reactions, 1776–1876.* Tübingen: Gunter Narr Verlag.

Heintze, J. R. (2010). *A primer for the study of Independence Day orations.* Http://www1.american.edu/heintze/Primer.html.

Jasinski, J. (1997). Rearticulating history in epideictic discourse: Frederick Douglass's "The meaning of the Fourth of July to the American Negro." In *Rhetoric and Political Culture in Nineteenth-Century America.* T. W. Benson (ed.). East Lansing: Michigan State University Press, 71–89.

Lampe, G. P. (1998). *Frederick Douglass: Freedom's voice, 1818–1845.* East Lansing: Michigan State University Press.

Lawson, C. (1940). Patriotism in Carmine: 162 years of July 4th oratory. *Quarterly Journal of Speech 26*, 12–25.

Lucaites, J. (1997). The irony of "equality" in black abolitionist discourse: The case of Frederick Douglass's "what to the slave is the Fourth of July?" In *Rhetoric and Political Culture in Nineteenth-Century America.* T. W. Benson (ed.). East Lansing: Michigan State University Press, 47–69.

Lucaites, J., & Condit, C. (1990). Reconstructing <equality>: Culturetypal and counter-cultural rhetorics in the martyred Black vision. *Communication Monographs 57*, 5–24.

Martin, H. H. (1958). The Fourth of July oration. *Quarterly Journal of Speech 44*, 393–401.

Martin, W. E., Jr. (1984). *The mind of Frederick Douglass.* Chapel Hill: University of North Carolina Press.

McClure, K. (2000). Frederick Douglass's use of comparison in his Fourth of July oration: A textual analysis. *Western Communication Journal 64*, 425–44.

Rohler, L. (1987). William Lloyd Garrison. In *American orators before 1900: Critical studies and sources.* B. K. Duffy & H. Ryan (eds.). Westport, CT: Greenwood Press, 183–89.

Scott, D. (1987). Platonic anamnesis revisited. *Classical Quarterly 37*, 346–66.

Travers, L. (1997). *Celebrating the Fourth.* Amherst: University of Massachusetts Press.

Terrill, R. E. (2003). Irony, silence, and time: Frederick Douglass on the Fifth of July. *Quarterly Journal of Speech 89*, 216–34.

Weaver, R. M. (1953). The spaciousness of old oratory. In *The ethics of rhetoric.* Chicago: Henry Regnery.

———. (1964). *Visions of order: The cultural crisis of our time.* Baton Rouge: Louisiana State University Press.

Fighting the Devil with Fire

The Political Rhetoric of Henry McNeal Turner during Reconstruction

Andre E. Johnson

In November 1871, while testifying before Congress to the Joint Select Committee to Inquire into the Condition of Affairs of the Late Insurrectionary States (Turner, 2013, p. 205) the chair of the committee asked Henry McNeal Turner his present occupation. Turner replied that he was a "minister of the gospel and a kind of politician." At the time of his testimony, he was both the presiding elder of the Georgia district in the African Methodist Episcopal (AME) Church and a member elect of the state legislature. The reason for Turner's "kind of politician" reference was that on the same day that he gave his testimony, members from the state house of representative had *again* expelled Turner from his seat and replaced him with a Democrat. When asked if his career in politics had ended, Turner acknowledged that for the time being it had.

A political career could not have been what Turner would imagine for himself. Born "free" in 1834 in New Berry Courthouse, South Carolina, state laws forbade Turner from learning to read and write. His father died when he was quite young, leaving his mother, Sarah, and maternal grandmother, Hannah Greer, to raise him. Turner's childhood consisted of working alongside enslaved persons in cotton fields as a "hired hand" to help feed his family. During the winter months, he labored in a blacksmith shop, and this early exposure to the "real world" made him physically strong and painfully aware of society's inhumane treatment of blacks.

When Turner was young, dreams guided his life. One in particular had him standing in front of a large crowd of both blacks and whites looking to him for instruction. Turner interpreted those dreams as God distinguishing him for great things, along with the desire for an education. Understanding that the state laws of South Carolina forbade African Americans to receive an education, Turner nevertheless acquired a spelling book and began to teach himself. Through the help of a divine "dream angel," who Turner believed appeared to him in his dreams to help him learn, he taught himself how to read and write. Further, by the time he was fifteen, he had read the entire Bible five times and memorized lengthy passages of Scripture (Johnson, 2012, pp. 17–18).

After hearing the preaching of plantation missionary Samuel Leard in 1851, Turner accepted his call to preach two years later at the age of nineteen. One of the first places Turner preached was Macon, Georgia, where he received a warm welcome from both black and white audiences. After gaining a reputation around Georgia for his preaching acumen, Turner traveled to St. Louis, where he officially joined the AME Church.

Anticipating the frustrations and angst he would have later with society limiting African Americans from opportunities, he had become disillusioned with the Southern Methodist Church because it did not allow blacks to be ordained or to become bishops. He had learned about the AME Church during a visit to New Orleans for a preaching assignment, where he also met Willis H. Revels, pastor of the St. James AME Church. Revels shared the story of the church's beginnings, describing its founder and first bishop, Richard Allen. The AME story impressed Turner, as he had not heard of the denomination before, complete with black bishops and pastors (Johnson, 2012, p. 19).

While Turner had enjoyed some success as a Southern Methodist preacher, it was only after he joined the AME Church that his preaching career catapulted. After joining the AME Church, Turner moved to Baltimore in 1860 to serve as pastor of Waters' Chapel AME Church and the Tissue Street Mission. After leaving Baltimore in 1862, Turner served as pastor of the large and influential Israel AME Church in Washington, DC. Here Turner formed relationships and friendships that would serve him throughout his life. Turner invited his newfound friends to speak to the black citizens of the city, and he spent hours in the Capitol listening to debates and arguments on the floor of the House of Representatives and the Senate Chamber. Turner quickly learned about the Constitution, the Declaration of Independence, politics, and the art of deliberative oratory. During this time, Turner also started a lyceum at Israel Church, in which he served as president and participated in debates about these and many other issues of the day (Johnson, 2012, p. 20).

As an AME minister, not only was Turner ordained, but he also became a regular correspondent for the *Christian Recorder*, the AME's weekly newspaper. During the Civil War, President Lincoln commissioned Turner as a chaplain in the Union Army, making him the first black chaplain in any branch of the military. In this capacity, he also became a war correspondent, publishing many articles in the *Christian Recorder* about the trials and tribulations of the First Regiment of US Colored Troops. When the Civil War ended, President Johnson assigned him to the Freedmen's Bureau in Georgia as army chaplain (Johnson, 2012, p. 20).

When Turner returned to Georgia in 1865, he was preoccupied with the idea of building the AME Church. However, as time went on, Turner also discerned another call—politics and helping to establish the Republican Party in the state. Neither would be easy. In a letter to the editor in the *Christian Recorder* dated August 31, 1867, Turner chronicled some of the experiences of these dual professions. He wrote about being "depressed with so many cares, responsibilities, and anxieties," even more so than he had while serving as "chaplain in the United States Army." He mentioned that he had "been away from my family so long, roaming over hills and through the valleys of this country" that his own children no longer recognized him. He wrote that his "encounters, cares, labors, travels, night studies and such other burdens have made my head as gray at thirty-four years, as my family of people generally are at fifty-four years" (Turner, 2013, p. 42).

In this chapter, however, I focus on the rocky political career of Turner primarily by examining two speeches that helped shape his political persona. In the first of these, the Emancipation Day speech, Turner demonstrates his willingness to reconcile after the war. When Turner returned to the South after a Union victory and serving as the first African American chaplain in the armed forces, Turner was optimistic about the future of the country. It was with this optimistic tone that Turner began his work in the South. Grounded in the belief that "bygones should be bygones" and that blacks and whites could work together in the South, Turner involved himself in a host of activities. He not only established the AME Church in Georgia, but also helped in establishing Loyalty Leagues and writing pamphlets for the Republican Party. As Turner's popularity grew, he would serve as a representative of the Georgia State Constitutional Convention and one of the members of the Georgia State House of Representatives.

However, he did not stay optimistic for long. In the second speech, after white members of the house of representatives made a motion to remove all the black elected officials, Turner's conciliatory tone shifted to one of disgust and indignation. In an impassioned speech, "On the Eligibility of Colored Members to the Seats in the Georgia Legislature," delivered from the floor of the Georgia statehouse, Turner said he needed to "fight the devil with fire" and offered a prophetic rebuke of his opponents as he defended the right of blacks to serve in the legislature. I argue that this speech began Turner's shift that would grow more pessimistic as America continued to default on its promise to African Americans.

Emancipation Day Speech

Turner starts his speech by directly considering the occasion:

> Gentlemen and Ladies, or Fellow Citizens, I should have said, we have assembled to-day under circumstances, unlike those of any other day in the history of our lives. We have met for the purpose of celebrating this, the first day of the New Year, not because it is the first New Year's day we ever saw, but because it is the first one we ever enjoyed. O! how different this day from similar days of the past. The first day of January hitherto, was one of gloom and fearful suspense. The foundation of our social comforts hung upon the scales of apprehension, and fate with its decisions of weal and woe looked every one of us in the face, and dread forebodings kept in dubious agitation, every fleeting moment that passed. But to-day we stand upon no such a sandy foundation. Uncertainty is no more the basis of our existence; we have for our fulcrum the eternal principles of right and equity. (1866, p. 4)

According to Turner, the reason for the celebration this year was that blacks finally were "citizens." By correcting his salutation and adding "fellow citizens," Turner announced to his audience, both black and white, that he considers himself and his fellow blacks to be "citizens." Next, Turner appropriated the doctrine of the sacred mission of America. As he continued to celebrate this day by comparing it with other celebrations, Turner shifted his attention to the Fourth of July. Independence Day was important in Turner's narrative because not only did America declare independence from English colonialism, but also the Fourth of July was when America discovered its true mission in the world. Speaking about July 4 and the Declaration of Independence, Turner declared:

> The white people have made it a day of gratitude and general rejoicing ever since 1776 because on that day they threw off the British Yoke and trampled underfoot the scepter of despotic tyranny. They raised the standard of independence on that ever memorable day and every man rallied to its support by the Declaration of Independence. . . . As soon as every name of that august assembly convened within was appended to that mighty document, which has ever since defied the world, a little boy shouted out "ring, ring"! and with all the power of a freeman, he struck that bell one hundred blows, (the same number of days it took Abraham Lincoln to smelt out the bell of liberty from September 22nd, 1862, to January 1st, 1863) and the bell in response chimed out the iron words engraved upon its rim, "Proclaim liberty throughout the land, and to the inhabitants thereof" and thus the stone cut out of the mountain without hands, as seen by the ancient king, makes its first revolution towards filling the whole world, as was predicted, for I hold that America and her Democratic principles and institutions is the great stone which is spoken of by the prophet Daniel. (1866, p. 6)

This passage grounded Turner's rhetoric in the belief that America was divinely inspired to "proclaim liberty throughout the land." However, he also added scriptural authority from the biblical book of Daniel, and he equated "America and her Democratic principles and institutions" with the great stone spoken of by Daniel. The "divine mission" of the country requires the abolition of inequality (slavery) that the "democratic principles and institutions" promoted. This is why Turner can later proclaim, "God seemed to have held it (America) back for some important purpose" (1866, p. 7). This purpose of America, divinely inspired and proclaimed in the book of Daniel, was for America to promote equality not only at home, but also throughout the whole world.

However, by defining America through its association with biblical prophecy and assigning the nation's "divine mission" to promote equality throughout the world, Turner constructed a rhetorical problem for himself—the same problem that confronted many nineteenth-century African American orators and social thinkers—the problem of slavery. How can Turner explain slavery if America was divinely inspired by the "prayers of the Puritans" and "founded upon free principles and recognizing equality in all men" (1866, pp. 6–7)? Turner found his answer through a prophetic reinterpretation of the institution.

He began by adopting what many considered a proslavery argument.

> The African was, I have no doubt, committed to the care of the white man as a trust from God. That he should clear up the land and pioneer the march of civilization by agricultural labor and domestic pursuits is a fact about which I have no hesitancy in admitting. That the white man should have made him work and exacted so much daily toil as was commensurate with the necessities of life and the developments of the nation's resources was all in keeping with order and sense, for he was by virtue of his superior advantages thereby his superior in intellect and the guardian of the negro. (1866, p. 8)

Turner's interpretation of slavery, while sounding conciliatory, was in fact very radical. By appropriating a "proslavery argument," Turner then could prophetically critique the argument by offering a reinterpretation of this "sacred trust."

> But that the white man should bar all avenues of improvement and hold the Black man as he would a horse or cow; deface the image of God by ignorance, which the Black man was the representative of, was the crime which offended Heaven. We gave the white man our labor, yes! Every drop of sweat which oozed from our face he claimed as his own. In return, he should have educated us, taught us to read and write, at least, and to have seen that Africa was well supplied with missionaries. (1966, p. 8)

Turner rejected the argument that slave owners only purchased the labor from enslaved people. The labor came from humans who were not like a "horse or cow" because unlike horses and cows, blacks can improve their stations or status in life. Nevertheless, there was a problem with this sacred trust. Whites barred all avenues of improvement, and, in so doing, they "defaced the image of God" by causing "ignorance" to the black race. What whites should have done with the sacred trust from God was to teach the slaves how to read and write, and to send missionaries to Africa.

Framed this way, Turner placed whites in a position of sin. The sin of whites was the breaking of the sacred trust. Not only did whites not educate enslaved people, they also did not educate Africans by sending missionaries to the continent. In other words, whites were sinful because of their lack of commitment to the intellect of the enslaved person.

Through a reinterpretation of proslavery arguments, Turner has *placed* blacks as citizens and *displaced* whites from their position of moral superiority. Whites failed as caregivers of the sacred trust and "insulted God" by failing to perform their duty to educate black people. Therefore, God had to exact judgment, not on everybody, but only on the "guilty heads of the violators of this law." More specifically, Turner referred to slave owners and ministers who failed as caregivers. However, to what law did Turner refer? He referred to the trust God gave white people to care for the African. God had to exact judgment because whites failed to see Africans as created in the "image of God" and continually defaced that image by enslaving them.

Turner believed that the judgment God exacted for the sin of slavery was the Civil War itself.

With the promise of blacks fulfilled, now was the time to celebrate. Turner's audience was free to celebrate America as the "stone cut from the mountain" and to celebrate America's divine mission as one that proclaimed and promoted liberty and freedom. For Turner, there was no need to charge or challenge the people to live up to the covenant. The people were living up to the covenant because, in Turner's estimation, God acted on behalf of the oppressed and through the Union victory in the Civil War, through the ending of slavery, and through leading Congress to pass the Thirteenth Amendment, Turner as *prophet* can see God's handiwork in all that had transpired. In short, since God has acted in this way, God blessed or affirmed the covenant, and now Turner and his fellow blacks could take part.

Turner's hope sprang from the belief that America had a divine mission to promote freedom and equality throughout the world. He believed that since slavery, that "horrid monster and curse," was dead, America could live up to its promise of equality. Turner believed that whites and blacks could eventually "live in friendship," but this belief was conditional: "I must say, as I believe, that as soon as old things can be forgotten, *or* all things common, that the Southern people (whites) will take us by the hand and welcome us to their respect and regard" (1866, p. 13). The key word was "or." The possibility of blacks and whites coming together depended on either forgetting the past or making "all things common."

Here Turner did not want to forget the past. He had spent the majority of the speech recalling past events because remembering the past was of paramount importance. In fact, Turner insists on recounting the horrors of slavery not because he wanted to "incite passions" against white people, but to demonstrate why blacks should "thank God" and "hold this day in special remembrance" (1866, p. 14). In other words, Turner believed that his slavery narrative was reason to celebrate God's goodness and that God's Providence was evident in the destruction of slavery. Therefore, out of this Providence, Turner's hope was for equality between blacks and whites, and the only way for this to occur is for all things to be common.

Turner's hope also leads him to offer a challenge and charge to blacks in his audience:

> Let us love the whites, and let by-gones be by-gones, neither taunt nor insult them for past griev-
> ances, respect them; honor them; work for them; but still let us be men. Let us show them we can
> be a people, respectable, virtuous, honest, and industrious, and soon their prejudice will melt
> away, and with God for our father, we will all be brothers. (p. 14)

By all accounts, Turner's speech was a success, and despite the rainy weather and the fact that the "streets and roads were almost impassable," almost three thousand people showed up for the "first anniversary of freedom." The crowd was thoroughly impressed with Turner, and according to Robert Kent, chairman of the event, the crowd was "amused and astonished" at the "lofty language and eloquence" of Turner (1866). He further wrote; "Even the whites could not conceal their admiration, nor restrain the applause due him, as the best orator of the day."

Given, as the pamphlet noted, on "the spur of the moment," Turner attempted to place the new day of "emancipation" (January 1) within the context of other days celebrated by Americans.

This new day or new era could only come about in Turner's estimation because America was divinely inspired. For Turner, America was the "stone cut from the mountain"—fulfilling biblical prophecy as a messianic nation called by God to promote liberty and freedom for the oppressed. Although slavery (in the form that it took) was a stain on the country and a sin, Turner's belief in the American creed allowed him to offer a reinterpretation of slavery. For Turner slavery, while wrong in the sight of God (he would later call slavery a providential institution and not a divine one), did not displace America from its chosen position. God did in fact judge America for its sins, and for Turner, that judgment took the form of the Civil War. It was through the Civil War and the Union's victory that God answered the prayers of millions of blacks and finally destroyed slavery. Therefore, for Turner, with slavery abolished, America could finally live up to the covenant and be a place of liberty for both blacks and whites.

After his successful speech, Turner turned his attention to Colored Convention movement. It was at these conventions that African Americans could voice their opinions and concerns about issues and problems faced on a daily basis. Delegates also promoted ideas of equal treatment under the law, suffrage, temperance, education, and moral reforms. One historian argued that the conventions not only "mirrored progress, but influenced Negro opinion, and demonstrated to the American public that the man [person] of color was ready to assume the full responsibilities of citizenship" (Bell, 1969, p. 4).

Ten days after his Emancipation Day address, Turner joined other African Americans to hold a Freedmen's Convention in Augusta, Georgia. From this convention, delegates created the Georgia Equal Rights Association that met in April 1866. The convention's president, J. E. Bryant, named Turner as one of the editors of the Association's organ, the *Loyal Georgian*. In addition, the convention also named Turner as its delegate to Congress to represent the interest of the convention.

At the Equal Rights and Education Convention in October 1866, Turner served on the Committee on Address and Condition of the Colored People in the State. As with previous conventions, Turner was selected to serve as the Washington delegate on behalf of African Americans in Georgia, and he offered the recommendation that the leaders of the convention publish the proceedings from the meeting.

When writing weeks later in the *Recorder*, Turner praised the work of the African American delegates.

> The convention of colored men from all parts of the State, which was held here a few weeks since, did honor to our race, and exhibited a degree of progress intellectually, and highly commendable, in a people so recently freed. There was marked ability developed in their entire proceedings, the idea that colored men could not govern themselves, if permitted, is all a hoax. The addresses which they prepared and memorialized the legislature with, will stand as a monument of colored ability in Georgia for centuries. (Turner, 2013, p. 25)

While working within the Colored Convention movement during this period of his career, Turner's rhetoric continued to be both hopeful and optimistic. In a speech to the Union League Association on April 29, 1867, he said that it "behooves both colors to cooperate, to join hands, and strive to the same goal." He called for a unified South and argued that the "Southern gentleman was the best and truest friend of the Negro" (*New York Times*, May 5, 1867).

In addition, Turner popularity reached some of the leaders of the Republican Party. Hired as an official spokesperson for the party, Turner turned his attention to helping freed people understand their rights under Reconstruction. Letters written to the Union Republican Congressional Committee demonstrate strategies he incorporated to teach the formerly enslaved about the Reconstruction measures. Turner wrote that he and others would participate in "dialogues" that instructed the freed people about their rights. They would "read over the dialogues to the delegates" and comment on them at "great length, so that no mistake might be entertained" (Turner, 2013, p. 151).

With Turner acting as the freed person and his friend Tunis Campbell playing the role as the "true Republican," Turner would ask questions about the new Reconstruction measures and Campbell would answer in a "suitable voice, giving emphasis to the facts being related." Turner wrote, "You ought to have seen the effect which it produced. When Campbell would read some of those pointed replies, the whole house would ring with shouts, and shake with the spasmodic motions and peculiar gestures of the audience." Turner suggested that this way of learning had double the effect upon uneducated masses and ordered them to be read until the people knew them by heart and could "relate them from memory" (2013, p. 151).

Even with conservatives fighting against every measure proposed during Reconstruction, Turner, grounded in his optimism and belief in democracy, held out hope. In an editorial in the *Recorder* published August 31, 1867, while admitting there had been a "vast amount of ignorance here among all classes, relative to the state of the country," he "thanked God that all parties are to be elevated through the ordeal (Reconstruction) we are passing." He believed that reconstruction in the state of Georgia was inevitable. In addition, he did not believe that a majority of whites were going to "vote to keep up civil commotion and political strife, which would follow opposition to reconstruction (Turner, 2013, pp. 44–45).

Due to the hard work that Turner provided Republicans, when it was time to create the state constitutional convention, Turner served as a delegate and made an impact. According to one historian, Turner's "conduct throughout the course of the convention reflected a sincere desire to cooperate with the white community in formulating a sound and workable constitution for the state" (Herndon, 1967, p. 18). Another one noted that Turner's demeanor, while "strategic in character," was nevertheless "quite conservative, almost to a fault (Angell, 1992, p. 85). An examination of Turner's actions while a delegate to the constitutional convention would tend to support Herndon's claims that Turner demonstrated a "naive faith" in the white citizens of Georgia. For instance, Turner favored protecting property rights of the Confederate upper class while also removing suffrage restrictions against them. He favored pardoning Jefferson Davis and proposed an educational amendment for voting. He also favored what many would later call a poll tax that conservatives used to disenfranchise African Americans (Herndon, 1967, pp. 18–21; Angell, 1992, pp. 85–86).

However, according to Herndon, the biggest example of Turner's naïveté was "his failure to foresee the implications of the omission from the Georgia Constitution of an explicit provision" that guaranteed African Americans the right to hold public office (1967, p. 21). Members of his own party convinced Turner that the state constitution did not need this provision in order to protect African American rights. So Turner did not vote for the provision—a mistake that he would later regret.

This opportunity to serve in the state constitutional convention led the people of Georgia (Bibb County) to elected Turner to the Georgia House of Representatives in June 1868. However, Turner's hope and optimism took a serious blow when on August 8 of that same year, a resolution was introduced that would deny all African American members the right to serve in the legislature (Martin, 1975, p. 48). Led by conservatives in both parties, the most frequently articulated argument against African Americans holding office was, of course, the one Turner voted against when it came up at the state convention, that neither the United States or the Georgia state constitution had granted the rights of African Americans to hold elected office.

After much debate on the measure to expel African American members of the house of representatives, Turner addressed the body on September 3, 1868. The speech consisted of an introduction in which Turner established his "position," followed by a series of rhetorical questions aimed at securing this position. Second, Turner focused his attention on disputing and refuting his opponent's claims, which refutation makes up the majority of his speech, and finally, Turner offered a prophetic warning that house members would have to answer to God for the actions that they took.

On the Eligibility of Colored Members to Seats in the Georgia Legislature

Turner wastes no time establishing the tone and tenor of the speech:

> Before proceeding to argue this question upon its intrinsic merits, I wish the Members of this House to understand the position that I take. I hold that I am a member of this body. Therefore, sir, I shall neither fawn nor cringe before any party, nor stoop to beg them for my rights. Some of my colored fellow-members, in the course of their remarks, took occasion to appeal to the *sympathies* of Members on the opposite side, and to eulogize their character for magnanimity. It reminds me very much, sir, of slaves begging under the lash. I am here to demand my rights, and to hurl thunderbolts at men who would dare to cross the threshold of my manhood. There is an old aphorism which says, "Fight the Devil with fire," and if I should observe the rule in this instance, I wish gentlemen to understand that it is but fighting them with their own weapon. (Turner, 1932, p. 82)

By establishing this position, Turner frames his argument as a fight against the Devil. In this way, Turner can prophetically stand with God, stand against his opponents and stand up for the other African American members who in Turner's estimation needed someone to stand and speak for them. Turner felt that the members were returning to slavery by appealing to their opponents' sympathies and eulogizing their "character[s] for magnanimity." Turner's belief in his opponent's "sympathy" and "magnanimity" disappears when his opponents introduce the motion to expel the African American legislators.

This realization for Turner also helps to strengthen his prophetic persona—Turner does not have to worry about consensus building or being a prophet for everyone (the entire audience). Here he represents the feelings and emotions of the African American members of the house of representatives. To buttress this claim, when Turner proclaimed that he was speaking for himself, while black members of the house might not endorse his sentiments, they all cried out "we do" (p. 86), thus allowing Turner to become the leader of the African American representatives and to strengthen his prophetic persona.

Further, for Turner, the expelling of the African American members of the house of representatives grounded itself in the belief that African Americans were not human. Positioned this way, Turner can later ask, "Am I a man—If I am such, I claim the rights of a man" (p. 83). Foreshadowing the Memphis sanitation workers' struggle for just and humane treatment from the city when the worker declared, "I am a man," Turner prophetically aimed at what he believed was the most significant part of his opponent's arguments. For Turner, it was simple: if one believed that he and his fellow African American members were human, then they could serve; if they were deemed not human, then they could not serve in the house or take any part of elective office. When Turner claimed the "rights of a man," he included in those rights the right to participate in the political process. Turner believed he was "entitled" to his seat in the house and was ready to argue the question "upon its intrinsic merits."

How did Turner argue this question "upon its intrinsic merits"? I maintain that he grounded himself in prophetic discourse that allowed him not only to criticize his opponents but to establish himself as a spokesperson-prophet both for African Americans representatives that day, and also for the entire African American community.

Grounded in a representative prophetic persona, Turner pivots to ask a rhetorical question; "Am I a man?" Turner offers a twofold answer. First, he grounds his answer in the *sacred character of God*.

> God saw fit to vary everything in Nature. There are no two men alike—no two voices alike—no two trees alike. God has weaved and tissued variety and versatility throughout the boundless space of creation. Because God saw fit to make some red, and some white, and some black, and some brown, are we to sit in judgment upon what God has seen fit to do? As well might one play with the thunderbolts of heaven as with that creature that bears God's image—God's photograph. (p. 84)

By grounding his argument in the *sacred character* of God, not only did Turner highlight the diversity of God, who has "weaved and tissued variety and versatility throughout the boundless space of creation," he also attacked the position of his opponents. Since his opponents attempted to expel African American members from the house of representatives because of their racist beliefs, Turner grounded his answer in the sacred character of God. Turner placed the onus of the "color problem," framed this way, not on African Americans, but on God. "Because God saw fit" to do this, Turner then can ask, "Are we to sit in judgment upon what God has seen fit to do?"

Here Turner invited his opponents to reflect on the events taking place in the house. By expelling the African American members of the house, Turner's opponents in essence rejected a part of the *character and nature of God*. Turner was then able to extend this concept of the sacred character and nature of God when he declared, "I do not regard this movement as a thrust at me. It is a thrust at the bible—a thrust at the God of the Universe, for making a man and not finishing him; it is simply calling the Great Jehovah a fool" (p. 93).

The second way that Turner answers the question "Am I a man?" is by grounding himself in the sacredness of the US Constitution. Turner argues that since a "good deal of reference has been made to the Constitution; *I am as much a man as anybody else.*" He reasoned that the document "neither proscripted, or has it ever, in the first instance, sanctioned slavery" (p. 87). However, how did the Constitution declare that he was a man?

It made him a man because the Constitution never sanctioned slavery. Recall that in Turner's Emancipation Day speech, there was a clear line of demarcation between being a slave and being free. Turner reasoned that to be a slave meant that one was not a citizen, but to be free amounted to being a citizen and enjoying the rights and privileges thereof. Thus, Turner juxtaposes slavery and personhood. To be a slave is not to be a person, but to be free is to be a person, and free persons have rights assigned to them.

Turner started his defense of the Constitution by arguing against what he believed was a false interpretation.

> The Constitution says that any person escaping from service in one state, and going to another, shall on demand, be given up. That has been the clause under which the democratic fire-eaters have maintained that that document sanctioned slavery in man. I shall show you that it meant no such thing. It was placed there, according to Mr. Madison, altogether for a different purpose . . . Mr. Madison declared, he "thought it wrong to admit in the Constitution the idea that there could be property of man." . . . The word "SERVITUDE" was struck out, and "service" unanimously inserted—the former being thought to express the conditions of SLAVES, and the latter the obligation of free person[s]. (p. 87)

Turner's opponents argued that slavery was lawful because the Constitution "sanctioned slavery in man." Turner countered this argument by offering a reinterpretation of the Constitution. Invoking the Founding Fathers' position on slavery, Turner restructured the debate about the Constitution.

First, while the Constitution provided that any person escaping from service in one state and going to another "shall on demand be given up," it could not have referred to slavery. Turner highlighted the Founders' intent and provided the audience with a *history lesson* of sorts as he explained that the Founders took out the word "SERVITUDE" and replaced it with "service." This, he argued, was a *conscious choice* because the Founders did not want to be misinterpreted. Turner's argument was simple; if the Founders wanted slavery, they would have used that word in the Constitution. Since it was not there, he concluded that they never wanted the United States to be a slaveholding nation.

Therefore, by adopting the "neutral position" argument about the Constitution and its relation to slavery, Turner embraced the fullness of the document and held it up as *sacred text*. By engaging the text in this way, Turner grounded his speech within this covenant that leads him later to declare, "Every law, therefore, which is passed under the Constitution of the United States, is a portion of the Supreme Law of the Land, and you are bound to obey it" (p. 87). Moreover, framing the argument this way, Turner placed the Georgia house on notice. Any law or any bill must pass constitutional muster, because Georgia law was under the US Constitution and the US Constitution was the "supreme law of the land," and he and his opponents were "bound to obey it."

The second and longest part of Turner's speech comprised refutations. Turner's first refutation came when he addressed the charge that "Negroes wanted to hold office." To refute this charge, he developed a four-pronged argument that takes up the majority of his speech. First, Turner argued that the "negro never wanted office," and when candidates were needed for the constitutional convention, blacks went "door to door in the 'negro belt' and begged white men to run" (p. 85). In fact, according to Turner's refutation of the charge, white men "induced the colored man to place his name upon the ticket as a candidate for the Convention." All the black people wanted to do, according to Turner, was to be able to "walk up to the polls and deposit our ballots" (p. 85).

The reason why whites wanted blacks to run was that one of the white leaders, Benjamin Hill, told them that it was a "nigger affair" and advised whites to stay away from the polls. By recalling this bit of history, Turner proclaimed:

> If the "niggers" had "office on the brain," it was the white man that put it there—not carpet-baggers, either, nor Yankees, nor scalawags, but [the] high bred and dignified democracy of the South. And if anyone is to blame for having Negroes in these legislative halls—if blame attaches to it at all—it is the Democratic Party. Now however, a change has come over the spirit of their dream. They want to turn the "nigger" out; and, to support their argument, they say that the black man is debarred from holding office by the Reconstruction measures of Congress. (p. 85)

His critique of the Democrats was reminiscent of his critique of whites for slavery in his Emancipation Day speech; he placed the blame on his opponents. The reason why blacks went to the polls and voted for a constitutional convention that eventually led to blacks being elected was that whites not only did not participate in the voting process, but *whites encouraged blacks to run and serve*. It was the height of hypocrisy for Democrats to argue that African Americans were not entitled by the Reconstruction measures to hold the very offices that they were encouraged to seek.

The second part of his argument against the charge of "negroes holding office" was to refute the belief that *Congress never gave the right to African Americans to hold office*. Turner argued that Congress based the Reconstruction measures "on the ground that no distinction should be made on account of race, color, or previous condition" and therefore they permitted blacks to hold office. Speaking further on the Reconstruction measures, Turner stated:

Was not that the grand fulcrum on which they rested? And did not every reconstructed state have to reconstruct on the idea that no discrimination, in any sense of the term, should be made? There is not a man here who would dare say "no." If Congress has simply given me merely sufficient civil and political rights to make me a mere political slave for Democrats, or anybody else—giving then the opportunity of jumping on my back, in order to leap into political power—I do not thank Congress for it. Never, so help me God, shall I be a political slave. (p. 86)

Opponents also had argued that neither the Fourteenth Amendment nor Georgia's current state constitution provided a place for African Americans to hold office. However, here Turner did not appeal to either of these documents individually but to the "Reconstruction measures" in their entirety. When he used the term "Reconstruction measures" Turner did not want to limit the debate to any particular law or measure—he wanted to address the spirit of the measures. In Turner's mind, the Reconstruction measures provided a space for nondiscriminatory practices, and any "reconstructed" state had to accept the spirit of the measure, or in Turner words, "reconstruct on the idea that no discrimination . . . should be made." In other words, the former Confederate states had to turn from their position of discrimination to a newly constructed idea of racial equality.

Turner further argued that refusing to allow African Americans to hold office was not only to stand against the Constitution and God, but was also tantamount to placing African Americans back into a type of slavery. Turner maintained that it is "political slavery" for a group of people to have "civil and political rights" but not to allow them to hold office. Turner saw this as an attack on his personhood that would allow whites to assume political power on the backs of blacks. He declared later, with other black representatives cheering him on, that those "assisting Mr. Lincoln to take me out of servile slavery, did not intend to put me and my race into political slavery. If they did, let them take away my ballot—I do not want it and shall not have it" (p. 86).

The third part of Turner's refutation referred to the claim that African Americans could not hold office because holding elective office was not "conferred" upon blacks by "specific enactment." To answer this objection, Turner posed a rhetorical question; "Were we ever made slaves by specific enactment?" Then he added:

I hold sir, that there never was a law passed in this country, from its foundation to the Emancipation, which enacted us as slaves. . . . If, then, you have no laws enacting me a slave, how can you question my right to my freedom? . . . Why then do gentlemen clamor for proof of our being free "by virtue of specific enactment?" Show me any specific law of Georgia, or of the United States, that enacted black men to be slaves, and I will tell you that, before we can enjoy our rights as free men, such law must be repealed. (p. 89)

Turner drew upon the use of rhetorical questions to counter the argument that passage of a specific enactment was necessary before blacks could hold office. However, Turner addressed more in this passage; he equated the right to hold office with the right of *freedom*. As we recall in Turner's Emancipation Day speech, there are only two positions one can hold in America—slave or free. For Turner, the denial of his "right" to hold office infringed on his right to be free and made him, as he had said earlier, a "political slave" (p. 86).

The final refutation against the view that African Americans could not hold office related to the claim that blacks had not built any monuments. This charge, aimed at the intellectual capacity of blacks, was predicated on the belief that since they had not built any monuments, they did not have the capacity to serve in politics. Turner could have answered the charge in vindicationist terms by invoking the pyramids of Egypt, the civilizations of Africa, or even by talking about the many structures and buildings that enslaved Africans erected in the South. However, Turner chose a different approach that challenged his audience:

> I can tell the gentlemen one thing; that is, that we could have built monuments of fire while the war was in progress. We could have fired your woods, your barns and fences and call[ed] you home. Did we do it? No sir: and God grant that the Negro may never do it, or do anything else that would destroy the good reputation of his friends. No epithet is sufficiently opprobrious for us now. I say sir that we have built a monument of docility, of obedience, of respect and of self-control that will endure longer than the Pyramids of Egypt. (p. 95)

Instead of speaking about literal monuments, Turner spoke about symbolic ones. First, Turner spoke about the "monuments of fire" that could have been built during the war. As in his earlier Emancipation Day speech, Turner deployed one of the rhetorical strategies blacks used to illicit sympathy from whites, which was to invoke the response of Southern blacks during the war. Many blacks argued that slaves could have run away or destroyed their master's property while they were away fighting in the war, but because of an obedient and docile nature, blacks did not take that course of action. Why did slaves not take this action? Turner answered the question when he explained that blacks did not want to destroy the "good opinion" they had with their friends, and blacks were at work building monuments of docility, obedience, respect, and self-control.

Turner then turned his attention to a series of critiques of his audience that centered on two major opponents. The first one was the "Anglo-Saxon race," or white people in general.

> The Anglo-Saxon race, sir, is a most surprising one. No man has ever been more deceived in that race than I have been for the last three weeks. I was not aware that there was in the character of that race so much cowardice, or so much pusillanimity. The treachery which has been exhibited in it by gentlemen belonging to that race has shaken my confidence in it more than anything that has come under my observation from my birth. (p. 82)

Many blacks had internalized the views of nineteenth-century orators and writers that the Anglo-Saxons were "lovers of liberty" who had the "spirit of individual enterprise and resourcefulness" and a "capacity for practical and reasonable behavior" (Fredrickson, 1971, p. 98). In fact, many African Americans held up Anglo-Saxons and their views as ideal—the height of true civilization. As Turner noted earlier in his speech, many other black members of the house appealed to this character construction of whites.

However, Turner did not appeal to this conventional wisdom. Instead, he adopted a prophetic persona that allowed him to view his situation as different from that of other representatives. He spoke from the moral high ground, saw the error of his ways, and confessed that he too had bought into Anglo-Saxon thought, admitting that he had been "deceived" by the white race and was not aware of the "cowardice and pusillanimity" of their characters. Far from regarding whites as courageous and fair-minded, Turner had been shaken in his "confidence" in them.

The second critique came when Turner likened the Democrats to Pharaoh in the book of Exodus of the Bible.

> I say to you, *white men*, today, that the great deliverance of the recent past is not altogether dis-similar to the great deliverance of ancient times. Your *Democratic Party* may aptly said [*sic*] to represent Pharaoh; the North to represent one of the walls, and the South the other. Between these two great walls the black man passes out to freedom, while your Democratic Party—the Pharaoh of today—follows us with hasty strides and lowering visage. (p. 90, emphasis mine)

Although Turner spoke to the entire house of representatives, he specifically addressed "white men" and associated them with the Democratic Party—thus he lambasted the Democratic Party as a political party that served the interest of white men. Moreover, grounded in the sacredness of a biblical story, Turner again not only adopted the moral high ground, which was intended to encourage his audience to reflect on their actions, but also gave Turner a *safe place* from which to criticize the Democrats. In the biblical story of the Exodus, the Israelites, released from bondage, head for freedom only to find out that Pharaoh and his army had followed to enslave them again. The point Turner made was clear—the Democrats represented Pharaoh, and black people represented Israel. As black people attempt to pass to freedom, the Democrats (Pharaoh) follow behind ready to enslave them again.

However, Turner's argument did something more. First, it represented African Americans as the ones who were victims of oppression and not whites, who argued throughout the Reconstruction process that they were victims of black political domination. Second and probably even more importantly, to be *Israel* in the story is also to be a *child of God*. Though Turner did not develop this line of thinking fully here, he definitely implied as much. Even though the Israelites were oppressed and placed in slavery, they were still the *children of God*, and just as Israel received its freedom, African Americans, who were also children of God, had received their freedom and were walking toward that freedom despite resistance from the Democrats who were acting the part of Pharaoh.

At first glance, there seems not to be any hope or optimism in this speech. However, this view assumes that the only audience present was white people promoting African American exclusion. African Americans were there as well. Therefore, Turner, understanding that expulsion was a foregone conclusion, was not speaking primarily to his opponents—they had already rejected him and his arguments. He was speaking for the "ninety thousand black men—voters of Georgia," and Turner would continue to speak "until God, in His providence, shall see proper to take me hence," and he trusts that God "will give me the strength to stand, and the power to accomplish the simple justice that I see for them" (p. 89).

By adopting a prophetic persona, Turner positions himself not in his opponents' community, but in the African American community. Understanding whom Turner claims to represent gives us a different perception of *audience*. Therefore, the question is not whether Turner offers hope and optimism, but how he does it for the African American audience he claims to represent.

> You may expel *us*, gentlemen, by *your* votes, today; but, while *you* do it, remember that there is a just God in heaven, whose All-seeing Eye beholds alike the acts of the oppressor and the oppressed, and who despite the machinations of the wicked, never fails to vindicate the cause of Justice, and the sanctity of His own handiwork. (p. 96, emphasis mine)

Clearly, Turner is speaking on behalf of the African American members of the house of representatives when he uses "us" and "your." Turner knows there is nothing that he or his fellow members can do about expulsion. However, he does not leave *his* people hopeless. What Turner does is to invoke the presence of God, who is in "heaven" and who has "all seeing eyes." The hope here is not that the members of the house of representatives would repent and change their mind about expulsion. Nor is the hope that African Americans can just trust in the "covenant" that Turner had lifted up in his Emancipation Day speech. The hope here is that God is watching, and since God "never fails to vindicate the cause of Justice," God will hear their pleas and rectify the situation.

Turner invited his African American audience to take a hopeless situation and see a ray of hope to help them continue to move forward. Expulsion was the fate of the African American members, and no matter how Turner or others spoke, their opponents did not hear them; they would not change their minds. Therefore, Turner invited his audience to remember that their opponents would not get the last word. The last word comes from a God who sits high, looks low, and will "vindicate the cause of justice," and is a call for African Americans to remain "just" and continue to wait on the Lord.

Conclusion

It took Turner only two years to start questioning some of his earlier assumptions. In his Emancipation Day speech, Turner affirmed the American creed, believing that America was the "stone cut from the mountain" from the biblical book of Daniel, and that America was ready to live up to its covenant. The *sacred* in that speech was America as *chosen* to lead the cause of liberty, and Turner would have believed this even more strongly because of his participation in Georgia governmental affairs and his becoming a leader in the Republican Party. While there was still prejudice and racism throughout the South during this time, Turner would have chalked that up to individual situations. He would not have accepted a systemic view of prejudice because he believed that America was the chosen nation and had taken on messianic qualities in spreading liberty, freedom, and justice throughout the world.

Turner's actions during this time reflected these assumptions. Angell wrote that Turner "did not advocate a free distribution of lands among the freed people," and he adhered to a "strict Puritan ethic, arguing that hard work would be suitably rewarded" (1992, p. 63). Therefore, he held black business owners in high regard, making sure in his letters to the *Christian Recorder* to offer a report about their successes. The rest of his time focused on building both the Republican Party in Georgia and the AME Church.

However, by 1868 Turner's views began to change. Still embodying a prophetic persona, Turner would no longer ground himself in the American creed. No longer would he believe that America itself was sacred and was the stone cut from the mountain for messianic purposes of distributing liberty and freedom to all. Though he did draw upon the sacredness of the Constitution for political purposes in defining his manhood, what Turner did in this speech and throughout the rest of his career was to appropriate the sacredness of God.

The other noticeable change in Turner's prophetic rhetoric was in his conception of encouragement and hope. In his Emancipation Day speech, Turner saw the day where blacks and whites could come together to make the South a better place for all. He saw blacks working hard and demonstrating their worth to whites, and he saw whites respecting blacks and receiving them into the larger society. The hope promoted in the speech was one of general unity where Turner acted as prophet for both communities.

In his "Eligibility" speech, Turner's hope was that God, seeing injustice, would act on behalf of oppressed African Americans. This version of hope was not the inclusive one that Turner proclaimed in his Emancipation Day speech, but was directed at the people whom Turner represented. Turner's hope was that God would act because his opponents had already acted and acted in opposition not only to the American covenant, but also to God's will. It was a hope that African Americans could embrace.

It was indeed this hope that God would act on their behalf that prompted African Americans members, led by Turner, to go to Washington, DC, and petition members of Congress for their seats in the House. Congress did return Turner and the other African American representatives to their seats; however, many of them lost reelection efforts in 1870 through voter intimidation and outright violence at the polls. Turner actually won his reelection bid only to have it taken away again by an overwhelming majority of white conservatives in the legislature. After his time in electoral politics, Turner turned his attention back to the church. He served as the presiding elder and superintendent of missions for the state of Georgia, and under his leadership, the church grew exponentially.

After serving in both positions, Turner later became the publications manager of the church in 1876 and bishop in 1880. His career as bishop is worthy of a full-length study by itself because between 1880 and his death in 1915, apart from Frederick Douglass, who died in 1895 and Booker T. Washington, who would not come to national prominence until 1895, Turner stood alone as the leading rhetorical figure in black America. One could rightfully argue that Turner, along with Douglass, was one of the first African American public intellectuals whose influence extended beyond African Americans. Even when Turner became a wholesale emigrationist, he could still command an audience. His bitter denunciations of America, his insights on race and class, his enlightened position on women leaders in the church, and even his critiques of other black leaders' positions on the ubiquitous "Negro Problem" made Turner both one of the most admired but yet most controversial figures in the latter half of the nineteenth century. One cannot help but think that his oratory, shaped in the political crucible of Reconstruction, gave rise to what he would later become.

■ **References**

Angell, S. W. (1992). *Bishop Henry McNeal Turner and African-American religion in the south.* University of Tennessee Press.

Bell, H. (1969). *A survey of the negro convention movement: 1830–1861.* Arno Press.

Fredrickson, G. M. (1971). *The black image in the white mind: The debate of Afro-American character and destiny, 1817–1914.* Harper and Row.

Herndon, J. W. (1967). Henry McNeal Turner: Exponent of American negritude. M.A. thesis, Georgia State College.

Johnson, A. E. (2012). *The forgotten prophet: Bishop Henry McNeal Turner and the African American prophetic tradition.* Lexington Books.

Kent, R. F. (1866). Letter from Augusta. *Christian Recorder*, January 27.

Martin, Elbert T. The Life of Henry McNeal Turner: 1834–1870. MA Thesis: Florida State University, 1975.

Turner, H. M. (1866). *Celebration of the first anniversary of freedom.* Georgia Union League.

———. (1932). On the eligibility of colored members to seats in the Georgia Legislature. In Participation of Negroes in the Government of Georgia, 1867–1870, by Ethel Maude Christler. MA thesis. Atlanta University.

———. (2013). *An African American pastor before and during the American Civil War: The literary archive of Henry McNeal Turner,* vol. 3: *1866–1880.* Edited by A. E. Johnson. Edwin Mellen Press.

Fanning the Flame

African American Leaders and the Agitation for Change, 1918–1954

Richard W. Leeman

In 1918, as World War I concluded, two major sociological events had shaped the African American community. The first event was the series of "Great Migrations," when blacks moved from the rural, legally resegregated South to the northern urban population centers that promised better employment opportunities in their factories. By 1920, over three hundred thousand African Americans had emigrated from the South in the World War I era, almost exclusively to the northern cities. The second event was World War I itself. During the war, factory jobs opened up for African Americans as young white men joined the army and were shipped overseas, thus stimulating additional migrations. However, those jobs were almost universally taken away from African Americans when the white men returned from the war, thus increasing blacks' frustration over racial discrimination. Then, too, many African American men had also joined the army, and through their military service had traveled through Europe, where they did not experience the discrimination they faced in the United States. Even as an African American urban culture grew, through movements like jazz and the Harlem Renaissance, African Americans chafed under the de jure discrimination in the South and the de facto discrimination in the North. Many African American speakers sought to channel this frustration and to effect needed reforms. This chapter will examine four representative speakers of this period between World War I and the rise of the modern civil rights movement: the urban populist Marcus Garvey, the rural southern preacher Vernon Johns, the labor organizer A. Philip Randolph, and the legal advocate Thurgood Marshall. Together, these speakers represent the range of arenas in which African Americans agitated for change and the variety of strategies these leaders employed.

Marcus Garvey

Marcus Garvey was undoubtedly the most popular, though controversial, political figure of the three decades following World War I, even though his time on the national stage was relatively brief. Garvey was the first Black Nationalist to assemble a mass following, but he also attracted many powerful enemies who represented very diverse aims and ideologies. He was a flamboyant writer and orator, one whose penchant for pomp and exaggeration provided fuel for his critics. Yet the philosophy to which he gave voice was sophisticated and well developed, and many subsequent leaders such as Malcolm X, Louis Lomax, and Stokely Carmichael were his intellectual heirs. He spoke assertively of black pride and racial purpose to an audience who had heard so often that their skin color proved their lack of worth. Although Marcus Garvey was often dismissed as a "showman," there was considerable substance to the show.

Marcus Garvey was born in Jamaica in 1887, the son of a stonemason and small farmer descended from the Maroons, the escaped Jamaican slaves who had fought for and won their independence in the eighteenth century. Garvey was a bright, inquisitive learner, and at the age of fourteen was apprenticed to a printer, from whom he learned his trade and in whose company he also participated in literary and political societies. At sixteen, he moved to Kingston, Jamaica's capital, and by the age of eighteen he had already been appointed the manager of a printing house. Not only was Garvey one of the youngest printers to be thus promoted, but Jamaicans of African descent were rarely given managerial positions. In 1907, Garvey lost his position when he helped lead a printers' strike, siding with the workers rather than management. Throughout his life, Garvey would incur personal costs for political positions he took on behalf of those who were less well off than himself.

Although fired and blacklisted from private printing firms, Garvey quickly found employment with the government printing agency, and on the side he published his first political newspaper, *Garvey's Watchman*. He left Jamaica in 1910, and from there moved to Costa Rica, Panama, and then Ecuador, where he always found ready employment as a master printer. Wherever he traveled in Latin America, Garvey was struck by the poor working conditions imposed on those of African descent, and in each country he quickly became involved in local politics. From Latin America, Garvey traveled back to Jamaica and then on to England, where he delivered speeches at the famed Hyde Park Speaker's Corner, attended law lectures at Birkbeck College in London, and traveled to a variety of European countries. His political philosophy was further shaped while he worked at the *Africa Times and Orient Review*, which regularly published articles written by prominent African Americans such as Booker T. Washington and W. E. B. DuBois. In 1914 he returned to Jamaica, where he founded the Universal Negro Improvement and Conservation Association and African Communities League, later shortened to the Universal Negro Improvement Association (UNIA). The UNIA was part of the larger pan-African movement, committed to bettering the living conditions of black persons around the world and to the establishment of a central African nation that blacks could govern and in which they could grow and prosper.

In 1916, Garvey embarked on a yearlong tour of the United States that included visits to thirty-eight states. The following year, he settled in Harlem, the center of the African American intellectual "renaissance," and on June 12 of that year he delivered his famed Liberty League address, a speech that catapulted him to the attention of blacks. In that speech, Garvey called for new leadership that would advance the race through militant assertion of control over their own destinies (Stein, 1986, pp. 41–42). Building on the attention his Liberty League address drew, the UNIA rapidly expanded to a membership of hundreds of thousands. Garvey launched the successful and influential *Negro World*, and his speeches at UNIA functions drew widespread attention.

Committed to a platform of black self-help and separatism, the UNIA was part business operation, part social organization, and part political agitator. Among other enterprises, it operated "laundries, restaurants, a doll factory, tailoring and millinery establishments," but its most famous operation was its cargo and passenger steamship corporation, the Black Star Line (Martin, 1976, p. 13). The steamship line was envisioned as a highly visible business that would connect blacks around the world and demonstrate their economic acumen and purchasing power. It also would provide the means of conveying blacks from around the world back to Africa and the pan-African nation Garvey and the UNIA envisioned. The line was highly popular, drawing stock purchasers from around the world, and helped fuel interest in the UNIA.

The *Negro World*, Garvey's newspaper at the time, played a significant role in the rapid growth of the UNIA. Published in New York but distributed worldwide, the weekly *Negro World* enjoyed an audience of about a half million readers. In contrast to the cultural drumbeat from the white media that the African continent was "backward" and "uncivilized," the readers of *Negro World* were provided with articles that described Africa's storied past and great accomplishments. They were also treated to stories that condemned European colonization of Africa and attacked those of African descent who cooperated with whites or who promoted integration. Each week, a column written by Marcus Garvey appeared on the front page. Through this forum, Garvey advanced his ideas of race pride, the economic uplift of the black community, and the necessity of reclaiming the African continent for Africans and those of African descent, themes he regularly developed in his speeches as well. Marcus Garvey's speeches were opportunities for his followers and himself to come together and give physical voice to the ideas and programs they already believed in. "The Principles of the Universal Negro Improvement Association," delivered in 1922, is representative. In it, Marcus Garvey speaks to his audiences' frustration, renews their pride in self and race, and provides them with hope for a far better, more opportunity-laden future.

The speech is developed on the political principle of "self-determination," the idea that the nation-state should be constructed around a homogenous ethnic group. Articulated by many and codified in Woodrow Wilson's Fourteen Points at the close of World War I, self-determination was the idea that each race or ethnic group had a unique cultural identity and that each was entitled to its "homeland." In Wilson's language, each group of "peoples and nationality" was entitled to "autonomous development." Self-determination was grounded in the belief that the bonds of *ethnicity* or *race*—two terms that are often blurred in this discussion—are stronger than those based on national boundaries or political philosophy. Thus, Garvey asserted, "When our [blacks'] interests clash with those of the ruling faction [whichever race is in control of a nation] then we find that we have absolutely no rights" (1922, p. 96). Thus the UNIA's primary goal was to create a nation across the African continent for those of African descent: "We are not engaged in domestic politics, in church building or in social-uplift work, but we are engaged in nation building" (p. 94). In pursuing this goal of full rights in the citizenship of the world, Garvey said that his UNIA was the vanguard: "We of the Universal Negro Improvement Association demand that the white, yellow and brown races give to the black man his place in the civilization of the world. We ask for nothing more than the rights of four hundred million Negroes" (p. 95).

Appeals to black pride assured his listeners that a pan-African, self-ruled nation would provide blacks with the room to thrive and excel, and told them that the race was capable of realizing that promise. "The black man of Africa has contributed as much to the world as the white man of Europe and the brown man and yellow man of Asia," he told them (p. 95). "If it takes manpower," he said, "if it takes scientific intelligence, if it takes education of any kind, or if it takes blood, then the four hundred million Negroes of the world have it" (pp. 98-99). Moreover, the achievements of the black race assured his audience that blacks could demand their freedom and their country. He spoke with pride about "black hell fighters" in Europe's recent war, concluding that "under the leadership of the UNIA, we are marshaling the four hundred million Negroes of the world to fight for the emancipation of the race and for the redemption of the country of our fathers" (p. 93). Black pride meant that Garvey could confidently demand first-class citizenship: "Why should [the white man], because of some racial prejudice, keep me down and why should I concede to him the right to rise above me and to establish himself as my permanent master? . . . I refuse to stultify my ambition, and every true Negro refuses to stultify his ambition to suit any one" (p. 98).

Along with this positive message of pride and self-determination, however, Garvey wove a lesser, but critical theme that challenged blacks to do better. This theme echoed the work of Booker T. Washington. "We have been satisfied to allow ourselves to be led, educated, to be directed by the other fellow," Garvey declared, and "allowed ourselves for the last five hundred years to be a race of followers" (p. 97). Just as the UNIA's businesses and revenues served as the basis of its power, so too should individual blacks build their power through hard work and thrift.

Garvey reminded his audience that they were four hundred million strong, and that together they could achieve the "redemption of our own country, our motherland, Africa" (p. 100). Rights that African Americans had sought as they migrated northward and served in World War I had been denied to them even as the Europeans' colonization of Africa had been renewed with increased vigor. In his speech, Garvey spoke persuasively for the reclamation of those rights, and of the race's ability to succeed in this reclamation. His was a popular message to many who looked for renewed hope in the future. Garvey told his audience that "we should say to the millions who are in Africa to hold the fort, for we are coming, four hundred million strong" (p. 100).

In "The Principles of the Universal Negro Improvement Association" can be discerned all the common rhetorical themes that Garvey sounded in his speeches. The black race could and would reassert itself, ultimately by liberating Africa from European colonization and establishing on the continent a nation that would be governed by Africans. To that nation of Africa those in the diaspora could return, and there they would reestablish African civilization, wealth, and glory. Those of African descent were demanding nothing less than what was being granted to other races and ethnic groups around the globe, but especially in Europe.

"Cheering Negroes Hail Black Nation," wrote the *New York Times* following one of Garvey's speeches in 1920, and the reporter wrote of the crowd's "applause that shook the building." Many contemporary observers noted Garvey's energetic delivery, and one political activist from another organization thought that Garvey was "one of the most powerful personalities" he had ever seen on the public speaking platform (Martin, 1976, pp. 101–2).

Harassed by critics and opponents on many fronts, in 1923 Garvey was convicted by the US government on charges of mail fraud in connection with solicitation of stock purchases of the Black Star Line. He was imprisoned in 1925, but after many protests on his behalf, the US government freed Garvey in 1927 upon condition of his deportation from America (Stein, 1986, pp. 189–208). Although Garvey remained active in the UNIA for the remainder of his life, political infighting reduced both the popularity of the organization and his influence in it. He frequently traveled between Jamaica and England, attending international conferences, establishing new publications, and speaking to audiences on behalf of those causes he continued to support most deeply: pan-Africanism, black pride, and black self-help. Even after his death in 1940, Garvey continued to attract the allegiance of thousands of followers, typically termed "Garveyites." Biographer Edmund David Cronon writes that Garvey's major contribution was fundamentally rhetorical, that is, "More than any other single leader he helped to give [blacks] everywhere a reborn feeling of collective pride and a new awareness of individual worth" (1969, p. 202).

Vernon Johns

African American ministers similarly preached hope, pride, and self-improvement, and one of the most intriguing and highly regarded preachers of the era was the Reverend Vernon Johns. By all accounts, the Reverend Johns was a brilliant, iconoclastic preacher, one who sometimes accepted a congregational appointment but other times traveled as an itinerant minister and scholar who provided guest sermons to church and college audiences with great eloquence. Most of Johns's lectures and sermons were never recorded, and many of those that were written down were destroyed in a house fire, although a collection of undated sermons has been reprinted in Samuel Gandy's *Human Possibilities*. Vernon Johns's 1926 sermon, "Transfigured Moments," was the first homily by an African American to be included in the highly regarded *Best Sermons* collection, an annual volume that published sermons written by influential theologians such as Reinhold Niebuhr and noted ministers such Harry Emerson Fosdick. Like many African American intellectuals in the first half of the twentieth century—such as Mordecai Johnson or the Grimke brothers—Vernon Johns was well known throughout the African American community, but largely ignored and then forgotten by white Americans. His public speeches and sermons, although individually styled to reflect his particular messages, resembled those of many African American leaders of the first half of the twentieth century. Grounded in the Social Gospel, his oratorical canon was staunchly pro-civil rights, but he also demanded that African Americans work diligently to improve their circumstances in America.

Vernon Johns was born in 1892 in Farmville, Virginia, the oldest son of Willie and Sallie Price Johns. Reflecting the complicated and generally unspoken family relations of the time, Johns was the grandson of slaves and a slave master. His paternal grandfather was famous in that part of Virginia for having reputedly cut his white master in two with a scythe, an act for which he had been promptly hanged. His father, Willie, was a full-time farmer and part-time preacher. Vernon himself became a full-time preacher, but remained a part-time farmer as well.

Self-educated on the family farm, from an early age Vernon Johns displayed a prodigious intellect. He recited long biblical passages and poetry, and as a teenager talked his way into several schools in Virginia, including Virginia Seminary in Lynchburg. Due either to rebelliousness or just his contrary nature, he was either dismissed or voluntarily left them all. He applied to Oberlin College in Ohio and, when he was turned down, went to argue his case in person. As the story goes, when the associate dean pointed out that the Johns had been denied admission due to invalid educational credits, Johns replied, "I got your letter, Dean Fiske, but I want to know whether you want students with credits or students with brains" (Branch, 1988, p. 8). After he translated passages from German and Greek, the school took him on as a "provisional" student, and in 1918 Vernon Johns graduated from Oberlin Seminary first in his class (Branch, 1988, p. 9). After graduation, Vernon attended the University of Chicago graduate school of theology, the intellectual home of the Social Gospel movement. This group of theologians argued that the teachings of Christ required his followers to work vigorously for the physical and emotional care of everyone, and not just their spiritual well-being.

Following his studies at the University of Chicago, Johns accepted a series of teaching and pastoral positions, including stints at the Virginia Theological Seminary and as pastor for the Court Street Church in Lynchburg and then First Baptist Church in Charleston, West Virginia. From 1929 to 1933, he served as president of Virginia Theological Seminary, and was credited with saving the college from financial bankruptcy during the early days of the Great Depression. After his presidency, he returned to holding a series of pastorates, intermixed with itinerant lecturing and preaching as well as farming. Branch writes that Johns seemed happiest when touring, traveling from college to college, church to church, delivering guest lectures for which he received sufficient remuneration to support himself and his family (1988, pp. 9–11).

From 1948 to 1952, Johns took the position for which he is most famous today—as the pastor of the Dexter Avenue Baptist Church in Montgomery, Alabama, immediately preceding Martin Luther King Jr.'s becoming the preacher for that church. Johns's intellectual prowess was prized by the middle- and upper-middle-class Dexter congregation, but the part-time farmer's vehement espousal of manual labor—in sermons such as "Mud Is Basic" and through practices such as selling watermelons outside church after Sunday worship—created friction between the pastor and his more dignified church members. Johns was also an outspoken critic of seg-regation and the racist practices common in Montgomery, which drew the ire and negative attention of the white power structure in Birmingham. As with all Johns's formal positions, the Dexter pastorship did not last. He returned to his itinerant preaching and lecturing, and continued to do both in conjunction with his family farming until his death in 1965 (Branch, 1988, pp. 11–25).

In 1926, Johns published "Transfigured Moments" in the highly respected *Best Sermons* series. These volumes were published by liberal theologians and preachers who were contest-ing with their fundamentalist brethren for the philosophical leadership of the Christian church. Although the headnotes in *Best Sermons of 1926* suggest that it was a sermon delivered at "Court Street Baptist Church (Colored), Lynchburg, VA," it is not clear that "Transfigured Moments" was actually ever delivered as a sermon. Several times Johns had submitted to the editors copies of sermons that had been delivered by better-known African American ministers, such as Mordecai Johnson, president of Howard University, and Howard Thurman, a noted theologian. Frustrated by the rejection of those sermons by the editors, Johns penned one of his own, "Transfigured Moments," which became the first sermon by an African American to be included in the series.

Unlike most of his sermons, "Transfigured Moments" is designed for a predominantly white audience, and a theologically oriented one at that. Johns takes as his text for the sermon the Gospel story of Jesus climbing a mountain with three of his disciples and there being met by Moses and Elijah. The apostle Peter proclaims, "It is good to be present here," and Johns (1926b) expands on why it is good to be present in such transfigured moments. It is good, he argues, to rise above the everyday to the mountaintop where one can take stock of what is important. Sounding a Social Gospel theme, Johns reminds his audience that it is also good to see the ordinary transformed into something extraordinary, because it reminds one of the presence of God in the lives of the rich and poor alike. He then says that it is good to be in the presence of heroic figures such as Moses, Elijah, and Jesus who can inspire us to greater deeds and truer morals. Finally, he concludes that the mountaintop is a place where one can see the connections of one age with the other—Moses to Elijah to Jesus and beyond—that points toward the Second Coming and the end of times.

Although the sermon primarily touches on Social Gospel themes, the further Johns draws his audience into the sermon the more frequent become his allusions to civil rights issues. Moses, he says, was a man born into nobility, becoming ordinary to lead his people out of bondage, while Lincoln was an ordinary man becoming extraordinary to remove the chains of bondage. Discerning God's presence in the life of those normally considered "lowly" fights back against the tendency of the powerful to dehumanize those they will later abuse, as when "masters avow[ed] their slaves' inability to learn [yet] at the same time penalize[d] them if caught with a book" (p. 55). As Johns nears the conclusion of his sermon, he uses his metaphor of mountaintop vision to attack race prejudice, particularly the pseudoscience of measuring head skulls to claim that African Americans have less intelligence: "Up there [on the mountain-top] we can read history with our eyes instead of our prejudices. Up there we do not hear the clamor of time-servers and self-servers: and as we look down from the heights, it is too far to descry the hue of faces or the peculiarity of skulls, all we can see is the forms of men, toiling or contending in the valleys: swayed by the same hopes and fears, the same joys and sorrows. The whole creation groaning in travail and pain together and waiting for deliverance; one in need, one in destiny" pp. 58-59). Social Gospel theology, Johns is saying to this audience, requires them to reject race prejudice and to work toward the improvement of conditions for African Americans.

Like Marcus Garvey, Vernon Johns's sermons to his black congregants preach black pride and encourage self-help, as they provide reassurance that better days are coming if African Americans will keep working for them. However, while Garvey emphasizes that ultimately blacks will literally need to fight for those better days, Johns grounds his metaphorical fight in the principles of Christianity. "Rock Foundations" was a sermon delivered at Johns's Court Street Baptist Church late in 1926, around the same time as he wrote "Transfigured Moments." Recent lynchings in Wytheville, Virginia (August 25, 1926) and Aiken, South Carolina (October 23, 1926) provide an important contextual backdrop to his discussion of race and justice in the sermon.

There is hope, he tells his congregation, in Jesus's pronouncement in the Gospel of Matthew that he is a rock upon which they should build their houses. Houses built on sand, Jesus says, wash away in time, and Johns agrees. The practice of segregation, discrimination, and lynching that whites have built their houses upon will be washed away, he assures them, for those practices are not built upon the Gospel of Jesus. Johns argues that, ironically, the idealism of Jesus will outlast the apparent pragmatism of others. "Civilizations practice [apparent pragmatism]," Johns says, "and destroy themselves" (1926a, p. 61). Only God's principles are permanent: "An enduring civilization must be one that exists for the good of all" (p. 64).

Johns especially mocks the religious arguments over theology that then miss the heart of the Christian message. "If we say the world was made in six days," he asks, "will the statement guarantee to all men 'life, liberty, and the pursuit of happiness?' If we say Jesus was born of a virgin, will the dictum cause every valley to be exalted, every mountain and hill to be brought low?" (p. 63). Calling to mind the terrible carnage of World War I, Johns asks whether carefully reciting these religious orthodoxies "muzzle our deadly guns" or "kindle in humanity that redeeming spirit of brotherhood?" (p. 62). As Johns twice avers with biting irony: "The phraseology would be wonderful magic if it did" (pp. 62, 63). He thus links the racial and ethnically caused destruction of World War I to the racially motivated lynchings in the American South, and uses those two social issues to condemn the modern-day pharisees who do not understand the spirit and fundamental principles of their own Christianity. In the eyes of the white, orthodox, southern Christians, he says, a science textbook that included evolution was "a tragedy like the sacking of Troy," while lynchings ironically recurred "as regularly as Holy Communion" (p. 63). "If one opens his mind on the subject of religion," Johns observes sardonically, "he may have to keep it open on questions of justice" (p. 63).

Although the Reverend Johns was obviously a highly educated man, he was, like many others, a preacher who talked *with* his audience to help them to manage the deep irony at work in the world around them. It is a world that believes it is building upon rock, but its foundations are set in sand. It is a pragmatic world that does not understand that the ultimate pragmatism is found in the Gospel's idealism. It is a world that calcifies the orthodoxy of its dogma, but abandons the spirit of its religion. As Vernon Johns succinctly puts it, "There is a world of disparity between the idealism of Jesus and the practices of men." "But," he observes, "Jesus is not crazy. We are crazy" (p. 61).

A. Philip Randolph

While Marcus Garvey and Vernon Johns preached hope and black pride, with an emphasis on self-help, A. Philip Randolph focused on changing the institutional barriers to economic progress and political rights that prevented black upward mobility regardless of how much hope, pride, or self-improvement African Americans acquired. The leading black labor leader in America, Randolph extended the trade union model of organizing to his plan for achieving civil rights broadly. Just as he did as president of the Brotherhood of Sleeping Car Porters, Randolph blended calls for mass actions and demonstrations with demands for specific policy changes in his drive to improve political, economic, and social conditions for African Americans. He was the first to envision an African American march on Washington, the 1963 version of which provided the backdrop to Martin Luther King Jr.'s famous "I Have a Dream" speech.

Asa Philip Randolph was born in 1889 to James and Elizabeth Randolph. His father was an African Methodist Episcopal (AME) minister who deeply admired Henry McNeal Turner, the firebrand AME bishop who rejected accommodation and preached that blacks should return to Africa in a manner similar to Marcus Garvey's rhetoric several decades later. Randolph was also an avid reader of Frederick Douglass, W. E. B. Du Bois, and Shakespeare, and he briefly pursued an acting career in New York City. Randolph grew up in Jacksonville, Florida, graduated from Cookman Institute, and moved north to New York when he was twenty-two. There he became involved in the Socialist Party and cofounded *The Messenger*, "the first voice of radical, revolutionary, economic and political action among Negroes in America" (Kersten & Lang, 2015, p. 17).

Simultaneously, Randolph worked as a union organizer, beginning with elevator operators in 1917 and organizing black dockworkers in 1919 into the National Brotherhood of Workers in America. After *The Messenger* experienced financial difficulties, Randolph moved full time into labor organizing. In 1925, he became president of the Brotherhood of Sleeping Car Porters (BSCP). For twelve years, the BSCP battled the corporate giant Pullman Company for better pay and working conditions for its members, and in 1937 the company finally agreed to a deal that significantly improved the compensation it paid to the porters.

This signal victory provided Randolph with stronger leverage with which to agitate for greater inclusion of African Americans in the larger labor movement, despite continuing resistance from white workers to the integration of black workers into their unions. Randolph moved into the broader civil rights movement as well. Threatening to bring massive African

American protests to the nation's capital, Randolph successfully lobbied for the integration of the US armed forces. A campaign that began in 1941 prior to the United States being drawn into World War II, and finally concluded in July 1948 with President Truman's executive order, this was an effort marked by Randolph's dogged perseverance. Randolph's repeated calls for massive, nonviolent protests by African Americans coupled with demands for specific changes in policy provided the blueprint for the public face of the modern civil rights movement of the 1950s and 1960s (Welky, 2014, pp. xii–xxiii).

To African Americans, Randolph preached that they aggressively demand their rights. Here was the labor organizing model at work. "True liberation," Randolph said to the National Negro Conference in 1937, "can be acquired and maintained only when the Negro people possess power; and power is the product and flower of organization—organization of the masses." They could not wait for white Americans to see the sense in providing freedom, democracy and equality to all its citizens. "Securing [those rights] is the task of the Negro," Randolph declared, for "Freedom is never given; it is won. And the Negro people must win their freedom. They must achieve justice. This involves struggle, continuous struggle."

In order to organize and create the mass action he saw as necessary, Randolph's speeches and rallies were reminiscent of those of Marcus Garvey and the UNIA in the early 1920s. Calling on his training as an actor, Randolph was dramatic and emotive in his delivery. At one rally, held at Madison Square Garden, his entrance was accompanied by a line of marching Pullman car porters in their uniforms. As he entered, the band played "Hold the Fort for We Are Coming," a title that repeats the line from Garvey's famous speech discussed above. Where Garvey turned the attention of his followers inward and toward Africa, however, Randolph focused on agitating for economic and political equality in the United States.

In 1940, one year into World War II being fought in Europe, and with the United States as a tacit ally and munitions supplier to Great Britain, Randolph combined his calls for mass action with his drive for labor equality by lobbying President Franklin Roosevelt for equal job opportunities for African Americans in the defense industry. To secure concessions from Roosevelt, Randolph threatened to call on African Americans to march on Washington. Federal defense money, he argued, should not be spent to uphold discriminatory employment practices. While the argument was sound, it was the threat of controversy at a time when Roosevelt was running for reelection and fending off the "America First" isolationist movement that yielded the creation of the Fair Employment Practice Commission. Randolph's ability to gather a national audience had produced tangible gains. Recognizing the power of mass protests—in this instance, simply threatened—led him to create the March on Washington Movement. The Movement maintained and developed the organizational framework for later marches.

Randolph recognized the political opportunity afforded African Americans by US involvement in World War II, and for the remainder of the conflict he lobbied for the desegregation of the armed forces. Randolph was unequivocal in his condemnation of what he labeled the "Jim Crow" army. "So long as the Armed Services propose to enforce such universally harmful segregation not only here but also overseas," he told the Senate Armed Services Committee, "Negro youth have a moral obligation not to lend themselves as world-wide carriers of an evil and hellish doctrine" (Randolph, 1948, p. 308). Now he threatened to call on African American youth to boycott the military and disobey draft orders. Promises were made and progress was slow, but in 1948 President Harry Truman finally, and fully, desegregated the armed services.

In conjunction with his agitation for mass political action, Randolph's speeches and essays also argued for the political and moral legitimacy of his calls. Historically, African American protests have been labeled by white Americans as "unpatriotic," and Randolph sought to blunt that criticism. As have many African American speakers over the years, Randolph co-opted language that white Americans used in their own political discourse. In early 1941, for example, Franklin Roosevelt enunciated what became known as the "Four Freedoms" that justified providing supplies and shipping to the Allies in Europe: freedom of speech, freedom of worship, freedom from want, and freedom from fear. Randolph asserted that, for their part, African Americans were also demanding "Freedom from want! Freedom from fear! Freedom from Jim Crow!" (1941, p. 224).

Perhaps most significantly, in the 1940s Randolph identified the agitation for African American civil rights with Gandhi's nonviolent, mass demonstrations for Indian independence from British colonial rule. Like the Indian protesters halfway around the world, Randolph said, "the Negro masses will be disciplined in struggle. Some of us will be put in jail and court battles may ensue but this will give the Negro masses a sense of their importance and value as citizens and as fighters in the Negro liberation movement" (1942, p. 230). Gandhi's protests found a sympathetic audience in the United States. For his part, President Roosevelt was pressuring the British to guarantee Indian independence in exchange for enthusiastic Indian support for the Allied war effort against the Japanese. Americans were suspicious of European colonial rule, suspecting that it was one of the root causes of the war into which they felt they had been dragged. By identifying Gandhi's movement with that of African Americans, Randolph simultaneously asserted African American status as colonial subjects in their own country, and legitimated the use of mass, nonviolent protest as a method of enacting change. A decade later, Martin Luther King Jr. would also find inspiration for nonviolent protest in the example of Gandhi, and in that of A. Philip Randolph as well.

Throughout the civil rights movement of the 1950s and 1960s, and even until his death in 1979, Randolph continued to be an important force in support of African Americans' civil rights. Due in large part to his good work, African Americans became full partners in America's labor unions, and Randolph himself was an officer of the AFL-CIO. As noted above, his March on Washington Movement was a force behind the 1963 March on Washington at which King delivered his "I Have a Dream" speech. Randolph, too, spoke on the same occasion, and his speech that day serves as an apt summary of his long, influential career. "Let the nation and the world know the meaning of our numbers," he said. "We are not a pressure group. We are not an organization or group of organizations. We are not a mob. We are the advance guard of a massive moral revolution for jobs and freedom" (Randolph, 1963, p. 261). Although he delivered those words in 1963, Asa Philip Randolph had been working and organizing that "advance guard" since 1917.

Thurgood Marshall

While Garvey, Johns, and Randolph spoke broadly to the spirit and community of African Americans during the interwar period, other speakers such as Thurgood Marshall focused like a laser on changing the law and, perhaps more importantly, on the interpretation and application of the law. The law and social practice were intimately intertwined, and it would not do to change one but not the other. "Segregation and discrimination," Marshall declared, "are so tied up together that you can't tell one from the other." Separate but equal, the legal principle established in 1896 in the Supreme Court's decision in *Plessy v. Ferguson*, would have to be dismantled before equality could be attained in fact. Marshall spoke to judges, lawyers, and the public in support of laws and court rulings that would make real the promise of the Declaration of Independence that the United States was a nation where "all men are created equal," and that government guarantees to all the citizens the promise of "life, liberty and the pursuit of happiness."

Thurgood Marshall was born in 1908 to Norma Williams Marshall, a teacher, and Will Marshall, a railroad porter. Although born and raised in the segregated, southern-leaning city of Baltimore, Marshall enjoyed a decidedly middle-class childhood. His parents both stressed getting a good education, and his father often took Thurgood to watch courtroom trials in order to learn how to argue and support his ideas. Although Marshall did well in high school, he could not attend the segregated University of Maryland, and so went to college at Lincoln University in Pennsylvania, one of the elite, liberal arts, historically black colleges of the day. At Lincoln, he joined the debate team, where his trial-watching served him well. He was a very successful debater, winning many matches against top debate teams from whites-only colleges.

Marshall was a good, though not outstanding, student in college, but his love of debate led him to a career in law. Still denied entry to the law program at the University of Maryland, he earned his law degree at Howard University in Washington, DC. At Howard, Marshall not only studied with some of the best African American legal minds in the country, but he could hear cases being argued before the US Supreme Court and attend guest lectures given by judges and lawyers such as Justice Felix Frankfurter and famed defense attorney Clarence Darrow. Marshall thus received an excellent legal education at Howard, and he graduated at the top of his class (Tushnet, 1994, pp. 4–5). In 1933, he opened up a solid, private legal practice back in his hometown of Baltimore.

Shortly after starting his practice, Marshall became involved in civil rights litigation. He helped reorganize the Baltimore chapter of the National Association for the Advancement of Colored People (NAACP) and in collaboration with Carl Murphy, the editor of the *Baltimore Afro-American*, began working local civil rights cases. In 1934, working with the national NAACP office, Marshall prosecuted a case against the University of Maryland Law School's discriminatory admissions policy, the segregation policy that had barred Marshall himself from applying. Marshall won the case, and in 1936 he left private practice and took a position as assistant counsel with the NAACP, and in 1940 he became director-counsel of the NAACP Legal Defense

Fund. In that role, the most famous case Marshall would argue would be *Brown v. Board of Education* in 1954, the landmark case that legally desegregated public schools across the nation.

One of Marshall's primary tasks was to address the public about segregation and the law. Marshall needed to articulate the legal case against segregation and to rally African Americans in support of that cause. His 1944 speech "The Legal Attack to Secure Civil Rights," delivered to an NAACP conference, is representative. He argued that the Thirteenth, Fourteenth, and Fifteen Amendments, together with the 1875 Civil Rights Act, provided all the legal ground necessary to bring complaints of discrimination before the courts. A key Supreme Court ruling, he said, was the language of the court that held that "the plain objects of these statutes, as of the Constitution which authorized them, was to place the colored race, in respect to civil rights, upon a level with the whites. [The congressional statutes] made the rights and responsibilities, civil and criminal, of the two races exactly the same" (p. 91). Here was the legal precedent, stated in plain, straightforward language that any layperson could understand, that guaranteed that African Americans would be treated equally under the law. Unfortunately, Marshall noted, the equal rights promised by the Court "will never become a reality until the U.S. Department of Justice decides that it represents the entire United States and is not required to fear offending any section of the country which believes that it has the God-given right to be above the laws of the United States Supreme Court" (p. 93).

If the Department of Justice *could* be convinced to prosecute discrimination cases, Marshall was confident that things would change. For example, he said, "One wholehearted prosecution of a judge or other official for excluding Negroes from jury service because of their race would do more to make that particular law a reality than dozens of other cases merely reversing the conviction of individual defendants" (p. 93). Until judges and other government officials paid the price for supporting discrimination, the unequal treatment of African Americans would continue unabated.

Not only were government officials who discriminated open to criminal charges, Marshall also noted that, according to the Civil Rights Act they could be sued in civil court as well. Civil cases, which did not have to wait on the Justice Department prosecutors to bring a case, appealed greatly to Marshall's legal mind. "Officials who discriminate can be sued," he reminded his audience, and civil suits had yielded success: "This statue has been used to equalize teachers' salaries and to obtain bus transportation for Negro school children. It can be used to attack every form of discrimination against Negroes by public school systems" (p. 95).

For civil or criminal cases to succeed, however, the NAACP needed plaintiffs as well as prosecutors. Marshall's strategy was to inundate the Justice Department until justice was done. In regard to voting rights abuses, for example, "There is no reason why a hundred clear cases of this sort should not be placed before the United States Attorneys and the Attorney General ever year until the election official discover that it is both wiser and safer to follow the United States laws than to violate them" (p. 94). African Americans could not wait for the government to initiate these cases; rather, "It is up to us to see that these officials of the Department of Justice are called upon to act again and again wherever there are violations of the civil rights statutes" (p. 94). "Unfortunately," Marshall observed, "there are plenty of such cases.

It is equally unfortunate that there are not enough individuals and groups presenting these cases and demanding action" (p. 94). Several times in the speech Marshall argued that African Americans and the NAACP Legal Defense Fund had "only scratched the surface" of what could be prosecuted legally. African Americans must "continue with ever-increasing vigor to enforce those few statutes, both federal and state, which are now on the statute books," and the time for prosecuting those cases was now:

> We must not be delayed by people who say "the time is not ripe," nor should we proceed with caution for fear of destroying the "status quo." Persons who deny to us our civil rights should be brought to justice now. Many people believe the time is always "ripe" to discriminate against Negroes. All right then—the time is always "ripe" to bring them to justice. The responsibility for the enforcement of these statutes rests with every American citizen regardless of race or color. However, the real job has to be done by the Negro population with whatever friends of the other races are willing to join us. (p. 97)

It was "necessary and vital" that the NAACP keep up its unrelenting legal campaign to end voting, jury, education, and job discrimination.

Once the cases were brought before the courts, they needed to be argued, and Marshall appeared frequently before state and federal courts. In the 1940s and 1950s, Marshall argued thirty-two cases before the US Supreme Court, a remarkable number for any trial lawyer. He won twenty-nine of them. His 1953 argument before the Court in *Brown v. Board of Education* illustrates Marshall's blend of the principled and the pragmatic. In his case, Marshall provided the justices with two arguments as to why school desegregation was wrong. On the one hand was the legal rights argument. The law said that discrimination against any citizen was illegal. He analogized segregation laws as the equivalent of the post–Civil War "Black Codes," which had reestablished slavery in a de facto manner through a series of laws targeting African Americans. "We charge that [school segregation laws] are Black Codes," Marshall told the Court. He continued: "They obviously are Black Codes if you read them. [The opposing attorneys] haven't denied that they are Black Codes, so if the Court wants to very narrowly decide this case, they can decide it on that point" (1953, p. 209). The Fourteenth and Fifteenth Amendments had been passed by Congress explicitly to make the Black Codes illegal. Apply the law dispassionately, Marshall argued, and school segregation would be made illegal.

Marshall could not count on all the justices to be dispassionate, however, and the law had previously been interpreted to provide leeway to the states to provide "separate but equal" facilities and accommodations. So Marshal advanced a social effects argument as well. Pragmatically speaking, separate facilities could never be equal, he argued. African American children forced into segregated schools inherently received a different, and inferior, education. The only practical remedy to the problem was desegregation. "Segregation and inequality [are] equivalent concepts," Marshall argued. "They have equal rating, equal footing, and if segregation thus necessarily imports inequality, it makes no great difference whether we say that the Negro is wronged because he is segregated, or that he is wronged because he received unequal treatment" (p. 207). If the justices upheld school segregation, they would continue to consign African American children to a second-class education and permanent status as an underclass in the United States, the "classless" society. Marshall delivered both lines of reasoning to the justices because he wanted a decision whose legitimacy was unmistakable. In *Brown v. Board of Education* the Court decided to order the desegregation of schools on a nine-to-zero decision.

In 1961, Thurgood Marshall was appointed by President Kennedy to the US court of appeals. Four years later, President Johnson appointed him to serve as solicitor general. Just two years later, in 1967, Johnson nominated Marshall to the US Supreme Court, and most remember him as the nation's first African American to serve as a Supreme Court justice. Just as significant as his work as a judge, however, was Marshall's advocacy for African Americans' legal rights, inside and outside the courtroom.

Conclusion

Marcus Garvey, Vernon Johns, A. Philip Randolph, and Thurgood Marshall were hardly alone in their agitation for African American rights and opportunities. Many men and women advocated for African Americans between the end of World War I and the beginning of the "modern" civil rights era in Montgomery, Alabama. These four black men represent four of the major streams of advocates who spoke to and for African Americans during this period: raising black consciousness, preaching moral conviction, agitating for economic opportunities, and fighting for the just application of the law. They spoke in different styles and on different specific topics, but they reflected the determination of black men and black women to achieve their rightful place in the national community.

■ References

Branch, T. (1988). *Parting the waters.* New York: Simon and Schuster.

Bynum, C. L. (2010). *A Philip Randolph and the struggle for civil rights.* Urbana: University of Illinois Press.

Cronon, E. D. (1969). *Black Moses: The story of Marcus Garvey and the Universal Negro Improvement Association.* Madison: University of Wisconsin Press.

Garvey, M. (1969). A speech on the principles of the U.N.I.A. *Philosophy and opinions of Marcus Garvey.* Edited by A. Jacques-Garvey. New York: Arno.

Gilbert, K. R. (2016). *A pursued justice: Black preaching from the Great Migration to Civil Rights.* Waco, TX: Baylor University Press.

Grant, C. (2008). *Negro with a hat: The rise and fall of Marcus Garvey.* New York: Oxford University Press.

Hamilton, C. V. (1972). *The black preacher in America.* New York: Morrow.

Johns, V. (1977). *Human possibilities: A Vernon Johns Reader.* Edited by S. L. Gandy. Washington, DC: Hoffman Press.

Johns, V. (1926a, 1977). Rock foundations. *Human possibilities: A Vernon Johns Reader.* Edited by S. L. Gandy. Washington, DC: Hoffman Press.

Johns, V. (1926b, 1977). Transfigured moments. *Human possibilities: A Vernon Johns Reader.* Edited by S. L. Gandy. Washington, DC: Hoffman Press.

Kersten, A. E., & Lang, C. (2015). *Reframing Randolph: Labor, black freedom and the legacies of A. Philip Randolph.* New York: New York University Press.

Leeman, R. W. (1996). *African American orators: A biocritical sourcebook.* Westport, CT: Greenwood Press.

Leeman, R. W., & Duffy, B. K. (eds.). (2012). *The will of a people: A critical anthology of great speeches by African Americans.* Carbondale: Southern Illinois University Press.

Marshall, T. (1944, 2001). The legal attack to secure civil rights. *Thurgood Marshall: His speeches, writing, arguments, opinions, and reminiscences.* Edited by M.V. Tushnet. Chicago: Lawrence Hill Books.

Marshall, T. (1953, 2003). Argument before the U.S. Supreme Court in Brown v. Board of Education. *Ripples of hope: Great American civil rights speeches.* Edited by J. Gottheimer. New York: Basic Civitas Books.

Martin, T. (1976). *Race first: The ideological and organizational struggles of Marcus Garvey and the Universal Negro Improvement Association.* Westport, CT: Greenwood Press.

Randolph, A. (1941, 1977). Call to the march. *Black protest thought in twentieth century*, 2nd ed. Edited by A. Meier, E. Rudwick and F. L. Broderick. Indianapolis: Bobbs-Merrill.

Randolph, A. (1942, 1977). Keynote address to the Policy Conference of the March on Washington Movement. *Black protest thought in twentieth century*, 2nd ed. Edited by A. Meier, E. Rudwick and F. L. Broderick. Indianapolis: Bobbs-Merrill.

Randolph, A. (1948, 2014). Testimony before the Senate Armed Forces Committee. *For jobs and freedom: The selected speeches and writings of A. Philip Randolph.* Edited by A. E. Kersten and D. Lucander. Amherst: University of Massachusetts Press.

Randolph, A. (1963, 2014). Address of A. Philip Randolph at the March on Washington for Jobs and Freedom. *For jobs and freedom: The selected speeches and writings of A. Philip Randolph.* Edited by A. E. Kersten and D. Lucander. Amherst: University of Massachusetts Press.

Stein, J. (1986). *The world of Marcus Garvey: Race and class in modern society.* Baton Rouge: Louisiana State University Press.

Tushnet, M. V. (1994). *Making civil rights law: Thurgood Marshall and the Supreme Court, 1936–1961.* New York: Oxford University Press.

Welky, D. (2014). *Marching across the color line: A. Philip Randolph and civil rights in the World War II era.* New York: Oxford University Press.

Williams, J. (1998). *Thurgood Marshall: American revolutionary.* New York: Times Books.

Martin Luther King Jr.'s "I Have a Dream" and the Politics of Cultural Memory

An Apostil

Bernard K. Duffy and Richard D. Besel

In 1998, an Atlanta Federal District Court judge ruled that Martin Luther King's "I Have a Dream" speech was part of national history and that CBS did not need to seek permission to air it in n historical documentary that included a segment on the civil rights movement. The documentary, broadcast in 1994, incorporated a nine-minute excerpt of King's historic speech. The King Corporation lawyers in the case argued that CBS had unlawfully used King's "eloquent, creative, literary expressions." Arguing the decision before the Eleventh Circuit Court of Appeals, the King family succeeded in having it overturned two years later. Although the decision was the first to legally cement the King family's rights, this was not the first time the copyright had become an issue, nor would it be the last.

Presciently, King had copyrighted the speech a month after it was delivered, and his heirs clung tenaciously to the idea that it was a bequest to them (Stout, 1998, p. 16). Clarence Jones, King's lawyer and confidant, filed suit against Twentieth Century Fox Records and Mr. Maestro Records for issuing bootleg copies of the speech (Branch, 1998, p. 886). However, King granted Motown Records permission to release two recordings of his speeches ("Great March to Freedom" and "Great March to Washington"), but told Motown founder Berry Gordy that he wanted the entire proceeds to be donated to the Southern Christian Leadership Conference (SCLC). When Gordy urged King to keep half of the royalties for himself and his family, King insisted it go to the SCLC so as not to give the impression that he was benefiting from the cause of civil rights (Posner, 2002, pp. 175–76). King's family, like Gordy, has seen the speech as an important source of revenue, some of which undoubtedly has been used to promote King's legacy. Since winning their appeal against CBS, the King family has continued to exploit the copyright of the speech, agreeing to sell the French telephone company Alcatel the right to use a digitally altered version of the event for a 2001 television commercial. The commercial shows King speaking, jarringly absent the 250,000 people who had on that day lined the reflecting pool on the national mall. The commercial asks what would have happened if King's words had not been able to "connect" with his audience (Szegedy-Maszak, 2001, p. 20).

Selling permission to use the speech for a television commercial and engaging in legal wrangling about the news media's right to rebroadcast the speech are not developments that could be predicted from the iconic status the speech has achieved in national history. Although the legal dimensions of the speech's dissemination are of interest, we are primarily interested in how King's speech has become a permanent fixture in the collective memory of American citizens despite the copyright controversy. In a recent book on the speech, Drew Hansen suggests that it is "the oratorical equivalent of the Declaration of Independence" (2003a, p. 214). What Edwin Black said of the Gettysburg Address is equally true of "I Have a Dream": "The speech is fixed now in the history of a people" (Black, 1994, p. 21). Far more than an ordinary written or performed text, King's speech is now viewed as a text belonging to the nation, despite its current legal status. Coretta Scott King suggested that when King delivered the speech he was "connected to a higher power" (King, 2003). Whether or not divinely inspired, the speech has come to symbolize the civil rights movement and anchors collective public memory of the 1963 March on Washington for Jobs and Equality and of King himself.

Although King's "I Have a Dream" speech is now recognized as one of the most important speeches of the twentieth century, this has not always been the case. Reactions to the speech immediately following its delivery were mixed. Some praised the speech, while inexplicably others completely ignored it. How did King's speech achieve its iconic status given the mixed reaction immediately following its presentation? Thinking of the speech as generative of its own fame supports the legendary aura that now surrounds it, but its elevated stature resulted from a gradual process of media dissemination and cultural amplification. The touchstones in this process included eventual comparisons of King's rhetoric to Lincoln's, media portrayals of King's role in the civil rights movement following his assassination, and the appropriation of the speech as a synecdoche for that movement.

The memory of Lincoln's speech was fixed by print, while King's speech was fixed by the electronic media. In 1863 no one realized that Abraham Lincoln's humble "Remarks by the President" at the Gettysburg ceremony would become part of national iconography. Years later Carl Sandburg referred to it reverentially as the "great American poem," but part of the apocryphal lore of the speech is that Lincoln truly believed the world would not "note nor long remember" what he and others said at Gettysburg. Senator Edward Everett, one of the great ceremonial orators of his day, had satisfied every expectation of his audience with an address that took him two hours to deliver. It had taken Lincoln only three minutes to utter his 272 words (Wills, 1992, p. 68). Lincoln's speech gradually reached a secondary audience through the accounts of newspapers; King's speech was instantaneously heard and seen by radio listeners and television viewers numbering in the millions. For all its compelling metaphor and soaring imagery, "I Have a Dream" is more drama than poetry; as drama, it must be heard and seen. King's rhetorical genius was oral, Lincoln's written. Lincoln spoke transcendentally, while King spoke in the moment. Journalist Richard Carter, an eyewitness of the speech, reminds us that never before had a civil rights demonstration been aired live on national television (2004, p. 38). It was also the last such mass meeting to be broadcast (Branch, 1998, p. 876). Of the ten civil rights leaders who spoke at the rally, King did most to ignite the crowd, but the impact on television audiences derived from the interplay of King, his speech, the response of the crowd, and even the frequent cutaways to Lincoln's statue. Carter finds it "inexplicable" that television critic Kay Gardella of the *New York Daily News*, who acknowledged that the speech was the most moving of the rally, subordinated the impress of King's words to the visual images that the television camera associated with them: "Most effective and meaningful," she said, "were the cutaways to Lincoln's statue" (2004, p. 38). To those in the television medium who recorded the speech, and probably to those who watched it, the stone statue of the Great Emancipator amplified the combined effect of King's lyrical words, mellifluous voice, and determined countenance. The symbolic interplay between King and Lincoln was also not lost on E. W. Kenworthy, who filed the front-page story for the *New York Times*: "It was Dr. King—who had suffered perhaps most of all—who ignited the crowd with words that might have been written by the sad brooding man enshrined within" (1963, p. 1).

James Reston, on the same *New York Times* front page, declared that King "touched the vast audience. Until then the pilgrimage was merely a great spectacle" (1963, p. 1). The *Time* magazine article about the rally clearly understood the importance of King's speech: "King's particular magic had enslaved his audience," *Time* said of the prepared portion of King's text, while particularly praising the extemporized section with which the speech ended as "catching, dramatic, inspirational" ("Beginning," 1963). Not every major news outlet recognized the importance of King's speech. The *Washington Post*, for example, focused on the speech delivered by A. Philip Randolph, without even mentioning King's (Branch, 1988, p. 886). The historic and literary brilliance of Lincoln's address at Gettysburg had also not been universally recognized by journalists. The fact that Lincoln's speech became so famous is doubly remarkable when one considers how few people actually heard it or saw so much as a photograph of Lincoln delivering it. Illustrators would fill in the visual gaps that photographers like Matthew Brady had left out. There is only one photograph of Lincoln on the speaker's platform and it was taken from some distance away (Kunhardt, Kunhardt, & Kunhardt, 1992, p. 315). King's speech, by contrast, was forever wedded to a set of visual images—of Lincoln's statue, of the responsive throng, and of King himself, visibly moved by his own words.

It is difficult to explain precisely how King's speech went from privately copyrighted words to cherished public property, but surely the number of people who saw and heard and felt his speech live was an important ingredient. In the case of Lincoln's speech, it helped that it was apparently spare and simple, something schoolchildren could easily read, memorize, and declaim. At eighteen minutes, King's speech is roughly six times as long as Lincoln's, but the dramatic climax of the speech is short enough to replay in honoring King or in the retelling of civil rights movement history, and the imagery of the speech is often striking. Both King's and Lincoln's speeches were tied to a momentous event, and the messages of both can be appreciated, if not fully understood, by successive generations without providing detailed historical context.

The same cannot be said of Lincoln's lawyerly and highly nuanced First Inaugural Address, or for that matter King's Vietnam-era antiwar speech, "A Time to Break Silence." The addresses at Gettysburg and the Lincoln Memorial abridge tumultuous chapters in American history.

Martyrdom, Memorialization, and Mass Circulation

The martyrdom of Lincoln and King did much to propel rehearsals of their deeds and words. Pulitzer Prize–winning historian David Garrow agrees with King biographer Drew Hansen that the speech received little further mention until after King was assassinated (Garrow, 2003; Hansen, 2003a). Although King was honored by *Time* as its Man of the Year in 1964, the same year he won the Nobel Peace Prize, prior to King's assassination there was not a reason for the press to commemorate King's biography or place in history. The identification between King and his enunciated "dream" heard by millions was unavoidable and seemingly inevitable. Soon after his death, Motown Records reissued a single recording of the "Dream" speech (Waller, 1985, p. 48). Eulogizing King in 1968, *Time* spoke of the "dream" peroration of his speech as the peak of his oratorical career ("Transcendent," 1968). While Coretta King asked supporters to "join us in fulfilling his dream" (Rugaber, 1968, p. 1), the *New York Times* structured its eulogy of "the fallen martyr" by discussing aspects of his "dream" ("He had a dream," 1968, p. E12), and in another article judged that his speech at the Lincoln Memorial was "the high point of Dr. King's war for civil rights" (Mitgang, 1968, p. E1). King himself perpetuated his identification with "the dream" by introducing it into his later speeches.

Immediately after the assassination, Democratic congressmen proposed the establishment of a Martin Luther King Jr. holiday, but it did not come to fruition until 1983 (Hansen, 2003a, p. 216). The holiday itself has given impetus for annual memorializing of King and synoptic renderings of his life. Thus, the speech, particularly the prophetic "dream" section and dramatic conclusion, continued to be heard by virtually every generation of Americans. The speech was widely anthologized and was so widely taught in college public speaking classes that in 1982 Haig Bosmajian published an article in *Communication Education* to correct inaccurate versions of the speech. In 1998, *Time* listed it as one of only four of the "century's greatest speeches," putting the speech in a firmament with speeches by Churchill, Roosevelt, and Kennedy and offering an abbreviated quotation of the "dream" section and peroration ("Four," 1998). Within recent years, two books have been written about the speech, as books were also written about the Gettysburg Address (Sunnemark, 2004; Hansen, 2003a). There are few American speeches so important as to inspire book-length treatments.

The anointing of the speech by the media has been a mixed blessing. Historians and civil rights proponents caution against the condensation of a rich life into a single event. King's later speeches, which include continued references to his dream, proved less successful in the North than they had in the South. "I have felt my dreams falter," he said in Chicago in 1965, and on Christmas Eve 1967, reflecting on his own life, he added a dream reference made famous by poet Langston Hughes: "I am personally the victim of deferred dreams, of blasted hopes."

In his final years, the sweeping imagery of his famous 1963 speech gave way to a more focused advocacy on behalf of African Americans in their struggles for jobs, higher salaries, better working conditions, and integration (Hansen, 2003b, p. E11). King also adamantly opposed the Vietnam War and called for a guaranteed family income. Worried about the dissolution of the civil rights movement, he argued for a more aggressive and disruptive brand of nonviolence, threatened boycotts, and even suggested obstructing the national Democratic and Republican conventions ("Transcendent," 1968). Because King's rhetoric is defined by the celebrated dream speech, his later speeches, which do not fit this model, are relatively unremembered.

How much "I Have a Dream" has come to represent Martin Luther King is revealed by the national memorial in Washington, DC. Sited between the Lincoln and Jefferson Memorials, the Martin Luther King Memorial includes structures and elements that materially evoke King's speeches, particularly "I Have a Dream." Clayborne Carson, the director of the King Paper's Project at Stanford University, offered suggestions for the design selected from among more than nine hundred submissions. He proposed that King's public words be used as inspiration for the structures in the open-air memorial. Thus the features of the memorial include a "mountain of despair" and a "stone of hope," reflecting a phrase from the speech. There is a fountain meant to symbolize the biblical quotation King used in the speech: "Justice rolls down like water and righteousness like a mighty stream." There are naves, representing the leaders of the civil rights movement, "hewn from rock, with rough edges on the outside, and smooth stone on the inside," again a homage to a biblical passage in King's dream speech ("The rough places shall be made plane and the crooked places shall be made straight) (Konigsmark, 2000, p. 1B). The importance of King's speech in American history is also illustrated by its incorporation at the Lincoln Memorial. Visitors can watch footage of King's speech, and note the spot where King delivered the speech, which is conspicuously marked with an X.

Conclusion

Historical interest in how King came to include the "I have a dream" section is comparable to the interest in how Lincoln composed his Gettysburg Address, which has produced tales of fanciful composition on an envelope while en route to Gettysburg. King had been given seven minutes to deliver his speech, and his prepared text fit roughly into that time limit when King had departed from his text to declare: "We will not be satisfied until justice runs down like waters and righteousness like a mighty stream." The voluble affirmation from the audience made King reluctant to continue reading from his manuscript. At this crucial turn, King recast the subdued request that the attendees should "go back to our communities" with a dynamic series of imperatives: "Go back to Mississippi. Go back to South Carolina. Go back to Louisiana. Go back to the slums and ghettos of our Northern cities, knowing that somehow this situation can and will be changed. Let us not wallow in the valley of despair." Mahalia Jackson, who had earlier sung a black spiritual, shouted from behind King: "Tell 'em about the dream, Martin." Whether through the singer's prompting or by his own initiative

King launched nearly seamlessly into the now-famous sentences that embodied his dream (Branch, 1988, pp. 881–82).

There are competing accounts of why King chose to depart from his text and prepared conclusion to improvise the "I have a dream" refrain. While Coretta said that he had considered including this section beforehand, if the moment was right, in a 1963 interview King remembered that he included it on an impulse: "I just felt I wanted to use it here. I don't know why. I hadn't thought about it before the speech" (Garrow, 1986). King's version lends credence to Coretta's idea that it was inspired by a higher power (King, 2003). Inspired prophecy should not require a prepared text, and extemporaneous speech, like the "winged words" of Homer's heroes, is regarded as more authentic than written ones.

No one, not even King, could anticipate the place his scintillating speech would take in public memory. In 1963 King delivered 350 speeches and sermons. His message and rhetoric were often the same, although the size of his audience and the amplitude of his public exposure were never so great. Of course, the speech itself is powerful and memorable, but contextual forces, including the live airing of the speech, King's assassination, and the enactment of a national holiday celebrating King all contributed to making "I Have a Dream" a symbol of King's life, which in turn is a symbol of the civil rights movement. It was and continues to be a media event. It expresses in shorthand the sentiments that the public is supposed to recall. What was a performed text delivered with a political purpose has been translated by the media into a symbolic narrative that casts King as the heroic voice of those for whom the dream had not yet become a reality.

■ **References**

Beginning of a dream. (1963). September 6. Time.com.

Black, E. (1994). Gettysburg and silence. *Quarterly Journal of Speech 80*, 21–37.

Bosmajian, H. (1982). The inaccuracies in reprintings of Martin Luther King's "I Have a Dream" speech. *Communication Education 31*, 107–14.

Branch, T. (1988). *Parting the waters: America in the King years, 1954–63.* New York: Simon and Schuster.

Carter, R. G. (2004). TV captured magic and tragic moment. *Television Quarterly 34*, 38.

Four of the century's greatest speeches. (1998). April 13. Time.com.

Garrow, D. J. (2003). King, the march, the man, the dream. *American History 38*, 26–36.

———. (1986). *Bearing the cross: Martin Luther, Jr., and the southern leadership conference.* New York: William Morrow.

Hansen, D. (2003a). *The dream: Martin Luther King, Jr., and the speech that inspired a nation.* New York: Ecco.

———. (2003b). King's dreams for demise of racism, poverty continue today. *USA Today* August 27: E11.

———. (1968). He had a dream. *New York Times* April 7: E12.

Kenworthy, E. W. (1963). 200,000 march for civil rights in orderly Washington rally; President sees gains for Negro. *New York Times* August 29: 1, 16.

King, C. S. (2003). Interview with Coretta Scott King. August 28. CNN.com.

Konigsmark, A. R. (2000). Stanford historian assists design of King memorial; Man who witnessed "Dream" speech contributes to winning plan built on imagery, interpretation of leader's life. *San Jose Mercury News* Septembe4 24: 1B.

Kunhardt, P. B., Jr., Kunhardt, P. B., III, & Kunhardt, P. W. (1992). *Lincoln: An illustrated biography.* New York: Alfred A. Knopf.

Mitgang, H. (1968). The race crisis: A non-violent man is martyred. *New York Times* April 7: E1.

I have a dream: The nature of great speaking. (2004). Perf. Michael Osborne. Davidson Films.

Posner, G. (2002). *Motown: Music, money, sex, and power.* New York: Random House.

Reston, J. (1963). Peroration by Dr. King sums up a day the capital will remember. *New York Times* August 29: 1, 17.

Rugaber, W. (1968). Plea by Mrs. King: "Fulfill his dream." *New York Times* April 7: 1.

Stout, D. (1998). "Dream" speech by King is held as the public's. *New York Times* July 23: A12.

Sunnemark, F. (2004). *Ring out freedom: The voice of Martin Luther King, Jr.* Bloomington: Indiana University Press.

Szegedy-Maszak, M. (2001). The marketing of Martin. *U.S. News & World Report* April 9: 20.

Transcendent symbol. (1968). April. 12. Time.com.

Waller, D. (1985). *The Motown story.* New York: Scribner's Sons.

Wills, G. (1992). *Lincoln at Gettysburg: The words that remade America.* New York: Touchstone.

The Biographical and Rhetorical Transformations of Malcolm X

Robert E. Terrill

The story of the life of Malcolm X can be told as a series of transformations. Between his birth on May 19, 1925, in Omaha, Nebraska, and his assassination in Harlem on February 21, 1965, he evolved from an adolescent involved in petty crime, to a prison inmate, to the charismatic spokesperson for the Nation of Islam, to a human rights activist with an international reputation. A second approach, however, would be to describe his evolution as a public orator. These two approaches to the life of Malcolm X would produce two different, but complementary, narratives. Neither alone would capture the entirety of Malcolm, of course, but taken together they can illuminate more of this remarkable individual than either narrative could on its own. With that in mind, in this brief essay I sketch the basic outlines of these two narratives. The first of these is a *biographical* narrative, and it is the organizational strategy that appears most commonly in the literature: it informs Alex Haley's *Autobiography of Malcolm X* (1964); Manning Marable's *Malcolm X: A Life of Reinvention* (2011), which is the most comprehensive and detailed biography to date; and Spike Lee's 1992 Hollywood film. The second strategy for organizing Malcolm's life I will refer to as a *rhetorical* narrative, because it focuses on his identity as an orator. It is a less common and familiar approach, and for that reason I spend more time with it in this essay.

Biographical Transformations

Malcolm's parents, Earl and Louisa Little, were followers of Marcus Garvey and at the time of Malcolm's birth were attempting to establish a chapter of Garvey's Universal Negro Improvement

Association in Omaha. They faced persistent resistance from local white supremacist groups, and in the face of that, coupled with their own financial hardships and Garvey's legal troubles—he would be convicted of mail fraud in 1923, and was imprisoned until President Coolidge commuted the sentence in 1927, with the stipulation that Garvey be immediately deported—Malcolm's parents moved their family to Milwaukee, Wisconsin, and then East Chicago, Indiana, before finally settling in Lansing, Michigan. There they faced continued harassment and threats from local whites, including a firebombing of their home. When Malcolm was about six years old, his father was killed when he was run over by a streetcar. His death was ruled an accident, though the family was certain that Earl had been murdered, perhaps by the Black Legion, a local white supremacist group. His mother kept the family together, receiving public assistance and working when she could, but her health steadily deteriorated. In January 1939, she was found mentally unfit to care for her children and was admitted to the Kalamazoo State Hospital, where she would remain for the next twenty-four years. Malcolm's older siblings, Wilfred, then twenty, and Hilda, eighteen, were considered old enough to assume responsibility for the youngest children, and Malcolm became a ward of the Ingham County Juvenile Home in Mason, Michigan.

This brief summary of Malcolm's early years provides context for the first of Malcolm's transformative moments, from innocent youth to cynical outsider. Despite the many complexities and deficiencies in his home life, Malcolm was a good student in junior high in Mason, and popular with his classmates. It was during this time that he told one of this white teachers that he wanted to be a lawyer when he grew up. In the *Autobiography of Malcolm X*, Malcolm attributes this response to the teacher:

> Malcolm, one of life's first needs is for us to be realistic. Don't misunderstand me, now. We all here like you, you know that. But you've got to be realistic about being a nigger. A lawyer—that's no realistic goal for a nigger. You need to think about something you *can* be. You're good with your hands—making things. Everybody admires your carpentry shop work. Why don't you plan on carpentry? People like you as a person—you'd get all kinds of work. (1964, p. 36)

Marable portrays this conversation as precipitating a profound change in Malcolm. Soon after this encounter, the realities of being poor and black in the United States crowd into Malcolm's world, deflating whatever potential there might have been for his to have been a story of achievement within the system. In his autobiography, Malcolm reports that "the more I thought afterwards" about what his teacher had said, "the more uneasy it made me. It just kept treading around in my mind" (p. 36). Marable notes that soon after this incident, "Malcolm's grades plummeted and his truculence increased. Within several months, he found himself expelled" (2011, p. 38).

Soon afterward, he moved to Boston to live with his half sister Ella. It was early in 1941, and Malcolm was not yet sixteen years old. Ella attempted to rein in some of Malcolm's more rebellious tendencies, but the city held powerful attractions. Malcolm soon began working as a shoeshine boy at the Roseland Ballroom, where he met many celebrities and musicians, and became known as "Red" because of the copper tones in his hair. He later got a job as a cook on the train that ran from Boston to New York City, and eventually he moved on his own to Harlem. He began to supplement his income with petty crime, and then became involved in the numbers racket and in burglary. Early in 1946, Malcolm and his small-time criminal gang were arrested, and he was sentenced to three concurrent six- to eight-year sentences (Marable, 2011, p. 68).

Being sent to prison facilitated the second important transformation in Malcolm's life, because it was while he was incarcerated that his younger brother Reginald first introduced him to the teachings of Elijah Muḥammad, the leader of the Nation of Islam. It may be that the influence of Marcus Garvey on the NOI helped to make the organization especially attractive to Malcolm X and to his family. C. Eric Lincoln, for example, writes that in the NOI's "commitment to racial uplift and to the unification of black peoples . . . the echo of Garveyism is loud and distinct" (1994, p. 248). Many of the NOI's early converts were former Garveyites casting about for leadership after Garvey's deportation in 1927. Louis DeCaro suggests that Garvey was "influenced by Edward Wilmot Blyden's earlier, positive assessment of Islam" and that "Garvey provided Muslim missionaries in the United States with a friendly platform. Indeed, some members of the UNIA were themselves converts to Islam" (1996, p. 16).

Whatever the reason for the affinity that Malcolm X felt for Elijah Muhammad and his then-fledgling Nation of Islam, it was undeniably powerful. He began writing letters to Elijah Muhammad from prison, and with each reply he received his religious fervor grew stronger. Frustrated at his inability to express himself as well as he wished, Malcolm began a lifelong project of self-education, famously beginning by copying pages from the dictionary. His religious conversion, in this way, was linked to an intellectual conversion, and together they defined this moment of transformation. Where before Malcolm was a petty thief and Harlem hustler, now he had turned toward becoming a minister who reached out to those who resembled his former self; where before he was inarticulate and out of control, afterward he was eloquent and almost preternaturally restrained. His spiritual commitments became intertwined with his dedication to the value of education in all its forms, and these twin commitments would inform his life and character until his death. This interdependence of faith and fluency is suggested by Louis E. Lomax, when he compares Malcolm X to St. Paul:

> Malcolm X is the St. Paul of the Black Muslim movement. Not only was he knocked to the ground by the bright light of truth while on an evil journey, but he also rose from the dust stunned, with a new name and a burning zeal to travel in the opposite direction and carry America's twenty million Negroes with him. (1994, p. 15)

Malcolm himself writes in his autobiography, "I do not now, and I did not then, liken myself to Paul. But I do understand his experience" (1964, p. 163). DeCaro provides a particularly thoughtful commentary on Malcolm's Pauline associations (1996, pp. 33–37).

After his release from prison in 1952, Malcolm rose quickly through the ranks of the NOI until, by 1954, he was minister of the key Temple No. 7, in Harlem (the Nation of Islam referred to its places of worship as "temples" until 1961, when Elijah Muhammad ordered that they should be referred to as "mosques"). He had been given command of the Harlem post as a reward for his hard work and leadership in helping to grow the NOI from a small group of a few hundred members. Precise membership numbers are difficult to obtain. Archie Epps suggests 40,000 at about the time that Malcolm X took over Temple No. 7 (1968, p. 29); E. U. Essien-Udom estimates the membership at close to 250,000 (1962, p. 4). The actual numbers undoubtedly lie somewhere between these two estimates. In any case, the precipitous growth of the NOI, and Malcolm's responsibility for much of it, are well established. Soon he was serving as Elijah Muhammad's chief spokesperson, crisscrossing the country establishing new temples and shoring up existing ones. He was a tremendous boon for the NOI, because his reputation as an orator meant that large crowds were guaranteed wherever he appeared, and that the media often sought him out for interviews. During this time, Malcolm rarely missed an opportunity to praise Elijah Muhammad and to credit him with whatever success and wisdom he might have attained. The NOI went from being a small and somewhat cultish group to one of the most prominent black religious organizations in the United States.

Perhaps paradoxically, the astonishing growth of the NOI and the correspondingly more elevated profile of Malcolm X contributed to the next conversion in his life: his rejection of the esoteric teachings of Elijah Muhammad and his embrace of Sunni Islam. This transformation can be understood, in part, as being precipitated by his evolution from being the best public speaker in a little-known religious sect to being a recognized leader and thinker on the national and global stage. As Malcolm's fame grew, so did his sphere of experience and influence until his thoughts, and his audiences, exceeded the confines of the Nation of Islam.

The nominal event that precipitated Malcolm's split with the NOI was a comment he made in December 1963, regarding the assassination of President John F. Kennedy. Muhammad had barred all of his ministers from making any mention of the assassination, and Malcolm initially complied. But during a question-and-answer session, following a speech on another topic, Malcolm referred to the assassination as a case of the "chickens coming home to roost"—meaning that the assassination was the inevitable outcome of the culture of violence fostered by the United States. Muhammad summoned Malcolm to Chicago and "silenced" him for ninety days, forbidding him even to address his own followers in Harlem. Eventually it became clear that the silencing actually was intended to be permanent, and on March 12, 1964, Malcolm X held a press conference to announce that he was leaving the Nation of Islam.

Tensions between Malcolm X and the Nation of Islam had been long in building. Contributing factors included the mounting jealousy of some other ministers regarding Malcolm's international fame and close relationship to Elijah Muhammad, Malcolm's chafing under Elijah Muhammad's stern policy against political activity of any kind, Malcolm's discovery of Muhammad's adulterous relationships with several female members of his staff, and Malcolm's growing acknowledgment of differences between Elijah Muhammad's teachings and Sunni Islam. Still, when he was being ousted from the NOI, he "felt as though something in *nature* had failed, like the sun, or the stars" (1964, p. 304). According to Bruce Perry, Malcolm even sought medical attention for the physical symptoms brought on by his anguish over the split (1991, pp. 243–44). But the loss of one structuring ideology was quickly repaired by adherence to another.

While it would be an oversimplification to attribute this conversion to any single cause, the impact on Malcolm of the traditional hajj, or pilgrimage to Mecca, that he undertook in 1964, should not be underestimated. E. Victor Wolfenstein argues that when Malcolm visited Mecca he experienced *ihram*, the "ultimate form of Islamic group-experience" in which the "group's leader . . . is not a man but Allah himself" and "the individual is immediately identified with the abstract universal of the God-idea and the potentially concrete universal of unified humanity" (1981, p. 307). This may or may not be an accurate description of Malcolm's experience, but it does portray Malcolm as giving himself up to new structures of belief, which was evident in letters sent home, and then in his autobiography, where Malcolm described in detail his reaction to seeing people from all over the world worshipping together in massive multiethnic communion.

This conversion is as powerful and as complete as the others Malcolm experienced. Before his hajj, Malcolm X was a Black Muslim who issued a blanket condemnation of all whites and white institutions; when he returned, as El-Hajj Malik El-Shabazz, he was a Sunni Muslim who relented, somewhat, and offered whites almost a redemption. Just as his split from the NOI had placed him beyond the reach of many of his former followers, this transformation also alienated some. As Peter Goldman puts it, Malcolm returned from Mecca "with his wispy beard and an astrakhan hat, both of which immediately became fashions in Harlem, and a slightly moderated view of white people, which did not" (1973, p. 182). Freed from Muhammad's isolationist strictures and claustrophobic doomsday revelations, Malcolm X could finally begin to draw upon his own extraordinary talents to craft a new vision of race relations. He softened his views on interracial marriage, rescinded somewhat his blanket condemnation of whites, and explored the political possibilities of an international perspective on racial issues in the United States. He established two new organizations: the Muslim Mosque Inc., intended to provide Malcolm with the religious pulpit necessary to his style of leadership, and the Organization for Afro-American Unity, modeled on the Organization for African Unity.

Malcolm X was assassinated on February 21, 1965, at one of his regularly scheduled Sunday afternoon meetings at the Audubon Ballroom, in Harlem. Longtime associate Benjamin Karim, one of the few who followed Malcolm out of the NOI, had "opened up" for him that day, and Malcolm had just begun to speak. A man in the middle of the audience created a diversion, shouting that someone was picking his pocket; another man charged the stage and fired a 12-gauge shotgun into Malcolm's chest. He was dead before he could be rushed to the medical center across the street. This followed months of both public and private acrimony between Malcolm X and the Nation of Islam, including in the pages of *Muhammad Speaks*, the official NOI newspaper. The assassins were members of the Newark, New Jersey, mosque, faithful followers of Elijah Muhammad who saw Malcolm X as a dangerous apostate (Goldman, 1973, pp. 273–78; Perry, 1991, pp. 357–67; DeCaro, 1996, p. 274; Breitman, 1988; Evanzz, 1992; Friedly, 1992).

The narrative I have described fits a familiar sinner-redemption narrative structure and is partially responsible for Malcolm's continued resonance in American popular and political culture. It might stand as a sort of parable for the evolution and uplift of the race, which seems to have been at least partly Alex Haley's purpose in fashioning the *Autobiography of Malcolm X*. Or it might serve as a structuring narrative to frame any number of personal challenges, as it serves Spike Lee in his story of the trials and tribulations of making his Malcolm X movie. But attending only to this biographical narrative can deflect our attention away from another set of transformations that are at least equally important: those that are evident in Malcolm's public address. Oratory was Malcolm's medium. For Malcolm X, the actual performance of public address was the primary process through which he impacted the world. He did not sit down and write any systematic ideological tract, nor did he formulate any programmatic response to America's racial strife. He stood up and spoke. As Goldman notes, Malcolm "did his cerebrating on his feet, in the heat of battle" (1973, p. 13). And the point can be made more forcefully yet; it is not merely that Malcolm X was eloquent, nor that public eloquence was his chosen instrument. Rather, for Malcolm X, public address *is* social change; his words *are* his deeds. It is through his public discourse that members of Malcolm's audiences are made to see the limits imposed upon them by the dominant white culture and are shown attitudes and strategies that invite them to resist, and to transgress against, those limits. Most significantly, it is through his oratory that Malcolm X provides to his listeners interpretive frameworks that they are encouraged to use in their efforts to make sense of the world.

Rhetorical Transformations

I described Malcolm's biographical narrative by focusing on moments of transition between phases of his life; in describing his rhetorical narrative, I will focus instead on speeches that are representative of different stages of his public career. The first of these speeches is "Black Man's History," which Malcolm delivered in December 1962, at his home Mosque No. 7, in Harlem, and is typical of the sermons Malcolm would deliver to the NOI faithful. The second is one of Malcolm's best-known speeches, "The Ballot or the Bullet," delivered April 3, 1964, and typical of the addresses he gave after he split with the NOI and before his journey to Mecca. The third is one of the very last speeches he delivered, which he gave no title but was delivered at the Corn Hill Methodist Church in Rochester, New York, on February 16, 1965, just five days before he was assassinated.

Black Man's History

"Black Man's History" conveys "the central myth of the Black Muslim Movement" (Lincoln, 1994, p. 72), and versions of it were repeated regularly in each NOI temple in order to attract new followers and to reinforce the faith of the converted. The content is drawn, for the most part, from Elijah Muhammad's teachings, and it was the task for NOI ministers to translate those teachings into effective rhetorical prose. Malcolm describes his relationship to Elijah Muhammad this way:

> When you hear Charlie McCarthy speak, you listen and marvel at what he says. What you forget
> is that Charlie is nothing but a dummy—he is a hunk of wood sitting on Edgar Bergen's lap. . . .
> This is the way it is with the Messenger [Muhammad] and me. It is my mouth working, but the
> voice is his. (Lomax, 1964, p. 81)

"Black Man's History" primarily is a genesis story, which explains that the white race is the by-product of a plot by an evil scientist who is attempting to rule the world. This text invites Malcolm's audience to understand the world as starkly bifurcated between good and evil, with whites being entirely wicked and blacks being entirely noble.

The speech frames its genesis story as a product of biblical interpretation. "The Honorable Elijah Muhammad's mission," Malcolm tells his audience, "is to teach the so-called Negroes a knowledge of history, the history of ourselves, our own kind, showing us how we fit into prophecy, Biblical prophecy" (1971, p. 33). The Bible presented something of a dilemma, for Malcolm X and for the NOI, because at the same time that they recognized it as a foundational and authoritative text, especially for many of their potential converts, they also viewed it as a book that had been corrupted by white people so that its true meaning had become obscured. This dilemma is resolved through peculiarly literal and concrete reading strategies. The Bible is not understood as a compendium of metaphors or parables, but instead as a predictive history referring distinctly and directly to the Nation of Islam. The job of NOI ministers, then, was to unmask the Bible so that it was no longer understood as a mystical or religious tract but instead as a reference book of future and past African American history.

For example, while there is a long history in African American public address of presenting the Exodus story as analogous to the experiences of African Americans in the United States, in "Black Man's History" the story is presented as being not actually about Jews at all, but about black people in America. "Not *these* things that you *call* Jews," teaches Malcolm X. "They weren't in Egypt, *they* weren't the people that Moses led out of Egypt, and the Jews know this. But the Bible is written in such a tricky way, when you read it you think that Moses led the Jews out of bondage" (1971, p. 36). Moses is not merely an exemplar for future black leaders; he *was* a black leader, leading out of bondage in Egypt the actual tribe that later would become the black race. The book of Genesis is given similar treatment. Malcolm quotes, for example, Genesis 15:13:

> And he said unto Abram, Know of a surety that thy seed shall be a stranger in a land that is not theirs,
> and shall serve them; and they shall afflict them four hundred years; and also that nation, whom
> they shall serve, will I judge: and afterward shall they come out with great substance. (1971, p. 34)

"Now The Honorable Elijah Muhammad," Malcolm continues, "teaches that the so-called Negro is the one that the Bible is talking about" (1971, p. 34). The biblical narrative illustrates a historical event; specifically, it refers to the moment when Adam was cast out of the Garden, which itself actually is a reference to the time "the white man was run out of the East by the Muslims six thousand years ago into the caves of Europe" (1971, p. 61).

Perhaps the boldest appropriation is the direct insertion of Elijah Muhammad into biblical narrative. The "Bible is a book of history," Malcolm assures his listeners, and then quotes from Deuteronomy 18, in which "God told Moses: 'I will raise them up a Prophet.'" This Bible story, like the others, is "talking about you and me" and promising "a prophet like Moses whose mission it would be to do for you and me the same thing that Moses did back then." Malachi, further, prophesied that the name of this prophet would be Elijah, and that he would "turn the hearts of the children to the fathers and the hearts of the fathers to the children" (1971, p. 37). And this, Malcolm continues, "is something that The Honorable Elijah Muhammad is doing here in America today" (1971, p. 38). This realist attitude toward the Scriptures presents the audience with an opportunity to sense a connection with history: They, or their ancestors, were the gods who created the universe, and they can witness Elijah Muhammad continuing this divine work today.

The central narrative of NOI theology, at the time that Malcolm delivered this address, begins sixty-six trillion years ago, before the white race existed, when the world was populated exclusively by black scientists (1965, pp. 110–22). One of these scientists had a disagreement with the other black scientists about what language the people of Earth should speak, and he determined to destroy civilization when the others rebuffed him. "So this scientist drove a shaft into the center of the Earth and filled it with high explosives and set it off," Malcolm explains. The explosion did not destroy civilization—"the black man can't destroy himself" (1971, p. 45)—but instead destroyed one of the original thirteen tribes of black scientists (it also created the moon). To replace this missing tribe, a black scientist named Yacub—whom Malcolm reveals to be John, the author of the book of Revelation (1971, p. 53)—crafted a new race. Yacub/John set up "a birth control law" that involved a combination of selective breeding and infanticide, and which over the course of six hundred years created a white race that was inherently wicked: "At the outset the nurses had to kill the little black babies, but after a while it got so that the mother, having been brainwashed, hated that black one so much she killed it herself. . . . So that at the end of the six hundred years . . . by the time they got the white man, they had someone who by nature hated everything that was darker than he was" (1971, pp. 56–57).

White people are so far removed from the black humanity out of which they were rendered that they do not even warrant a humanizing pronoun: "You're not using the right language when you say the white man," Malcolm urges.

> You call it the devil. When you call him devil you're calling him by his name, and he's got another name—Satan; another name—serpent; another name—snake; another name—beast. All these names are in the Bible for the white man. Another name—Pharaoh; another name—Caesar; another name—France; French; Frenchman; Englishman; American; all those are just names for the devil. (1971, p. 57)

The newly created white race eventually emerged from the island of Patmos with instructions from Yacub in the science of "tricknology," which whites then used to "divide and conquer" the rest of the world. "You see," explains Malcolm, the white man is "an underdog. He's a minority, and the only way a minority can rule a majority is to *divide* the majority. This is the trick that the white man was born to execute among the dark mankind here on this Earth" (1971, p. 58). He created divisions among the Native Americans, "South Korea–North Korea, South Vietnam–North Vietnam" and elsewhere. "He always discourages unity among others but he encourages unity among his own kind" (1971, p. 59).

A worldview more strictly bifurcated between black good and white evil would be difficult to imagine. The white race literally embodies evil, with all vestiges of goodness bred out. The white race is the snake in the garden, disrupting the dark-skinned Eden that prevailed before whites' hellish and unnatural emergence. Because all white people share a common ideology of lies and trickery, and a common purpose of division and conquest, they are irredeemable. This speech also illustrates to its audience the way that foundational texts—whether the words of Elijah Muhammad or the Bible—are to be interpreted within that bifurcated frame. The tone is relentlessly concrete and realistic, so that narratives such as the Exodus story, which might otherwise be understood as providing instructive, or inspirational, symbolic parallels to the experiences of African Americans, are instead understood as historical records. Malcolm presents an authorized exegesis, so that the interpretive practice being modeled is not animated by the goal of exploring complexity but instead by a practice that eliminates alternative readings.

The Ballot or the Bullet

"The Ballot or the Bullet" became the standard text that Malcolm delivered many times between his split with the NOI and his journey to Mecca, and because he generally spoke extemporaneously, the specific wording varied. I take as my text a transcript of the version most often anthologized, which was delivered to a predominantly black audience at the Cory Methodist Church in Cleveland, Ohio, at a meeting sponsored by the local chapter of the Congress of Racial Equality (CORE).

The speech provides a vivid contrast with "Black Man's History," indicating both the evolution of Malcolm's thought and the way that he adapted his public address to suit the occasion and the audience. The most obvious difference is that Malcolm's focus is political rather than spiritual. This is a public speech given to an audience who has not come to hear Malcolm X explicate NOI doctrine, but to hear him comment on culture and politics. Accordingly, Malcolm shows his audience how to "read" recent world events rather than how to interpret mythological or religious narratives. The worldview presented in this speech is not characterized by a simple bifurcation, perhaps because such neat and stable divisions are difficult to reconcile with actual world events. Significantly, the interpretive practice that Malcolm X is modeling for his audience, here, is not designed to eventuate in a single authorized version of events to which all members of a community are expected to adhere, but instead in a mode of interpretation that questions the limitations and expectations that have been imposed by others.

Structurally, the speech divides into three sections. The first third pushes against the boundaries that limit African American behavior and self-evaluation within the United States; the second third parallels the first, except that the scope is broadened to a global perspective. Then, in the final third of the speech, working within the broadened circumference that he has established, Malcolm begins to explicate the antifoundationalist mode of interpretive judgment that would come to characterize many of his last speeches and statements.

The three sections of the speech can be traced by attending to different referents for the speech's key terms, the "ballot" and the "bullet." As the speech opens, they refer to domestic voting rights and to the threat of urban violence. Malcolm demonstrates that African American political power is severely limited as long as it is understood as operating primarily or exclusively within the United States, and that by expanding affiliations and identifications beyond North America, African Americans can augment their influence. Analyzing the "ballot" from this domestic perspective, in other words, entails understanding both the potential political power of the black vote and the structural constraints that are placed on that power.

Malcolm indicates the potential power of the African American vote by explaining that "it was the black man's vote that put the present [Kennedy-Johnson] administration in Washington, D.C." "Your vote, your dumb vote, your ignorant vote, your wasted vote," he continues, "put in an administration in Washington, D.C., that has seen fit to pass every kind of legislation imaginable, saving you until last, then filibustering on top of that" (1965, pp. 26–27). He is referring to the Senate filibuster that was keeping the Civil Rights Act of 1964 from coming to a vote.

"Look at it the way it is," Malcolm urges his audience. "They have got a con game going on, a political con game, and you and I are in the middle." This introduces one of the key motifs of the speech, and of Malcolm's speeches throughout his last year: recurrent references to *sight*. For Malcolm X, *seeing* things in a certain way is a substantive political act: African Americans, he says, are "beginning to see what they used to only look at. They're becoming politically mature." African Americans need to be able to "let them know your eyes are wide open. And let them know you got something else that's wide open, too. It's got to be the ballot or the bullet. The ballot or the bullet." The "bullet," here, refers to some "new thinking coming in" that entails the possibility that "it'll be Molotov cocktails this month, hand grenades next month, and something else next month. It'll be ballots, or it'll be bullets. It'll be liberty, or it will be death" (1965, pp. 31–32).

Malcolm is not telling his audience to throw Molotov cocktails at the police; he never advocated violence in any of his speeches, though, of course, he did not endorse nonviolence either. "I don't mean go out and get violent," he tells his audience, "but at the same time you should never be nonviolent unless you run into some nonviolence" (1965, p. 34). He is presenting a concrete visual vignette to illustrate a justifiable possibility, one that lies clearly beyond the norms established by the dominant culture but one that nevertheless should be included within the widening scope of possible actions contemplated by his audience.

In the second section of the speech, the "ballot" and the "bullet" are reframed in an international or global context. "When we begin to get in this area," he says, "we need new friends, we need new allies. We need to expand the civil-rights struggle to a higher level—to the level of human rights." The shift from "civil" to "human" rights is another common theme throughout the speeches of Malcolm's last year, and entails not only taking a broader perspective but transcending domestic limitations. "Whenever you are in a civil-rights struggle," Malcolm argues, "whether you know it or not, you are confining yourself to the jurisdiction of Uncle Sam" (1965, p. 34).

The broader scope of this international perspective would support bringing "Uncle Sam before a world court" represented by the United Nations. Though this plan never came to fruition, Malcolm does exploit the possibilities for more flexible and imaginative identifications within the broader sphere represented by the UN. He urges his audience, for example: "You'd get farther calling yourself African instead of Negro," because "they don't have to pass civil-rights bills for Africans. . . . Just stop being a Negro. Change your name to Hoogagagooba." Malcolm also relates the story of "a friend of mine who's very dark [who] put a turban on his head and went into a restaurant in Atlanta before they called themselves desegregated," and was served.

Again, Malcolm is not advocating that his audience put on turbans and enter segregated southern restaurants. Rather, his purpose here seems to be to provide an illustration of the sort of thinking and acting that is made possible when drawing upon the resources present in a wider frame of reference. The legal system of the United States is not the only one available; the "Negro" identity is unstable and arbitrary and thus open to subversion; and seemingly impermeable racial barriers are ridiculed when exposed to the light of a broader perspective.

Paralleling the pattern of the first part of the speech, Malcolm next shifts his attention to the "bullet" by approvingly discussing guerrilla tactics. Dark-skinned people "who just a few years previously were rice farmers got together and ran the heavily-mechanized French army out of Indochina," he points out, and the "Algerians, who were nothing but Bedouins, took a rifle and sneaked off to the hills, and de Gaulle and all of his highfalutin' war machinery couldn't defeat those guerrillas. Nowhere on this earth does the white man win in a guerrilla warfare" (1965, p. 37).

Once again, in what by now is a recognizable pattern, it is clear that Malcolm X is not recommending that his audience in the Cory Methodist Church begin a guerrilla war armed only with "a rifle, some sneakers and a bowl of rice" (1965, p. 37). But thinking like a guerrilla, or perhaps thinking that being a guerrilla is a viable potential identity, can show his audiences that the great white nations can successfully be challenged through inventive tactics. The broadened scope of the international "bullet" expands the palette of identities and actions from which his audience might choose.

This expanded palette is suggested near the end of the speech, for example, when Malcolm calls for a "black nationalist convention." This never materialized, but its most prominent feature was to have been a radical flexibility. He promises, "We become involved with anybody, anywhere, any time and in any manner that's designed to eliminate the evils, the political, economic and social evils that are afflicting the people of our community." "We will hold a seminar," he continues, "we will hold discussions, we will listen to everyone," and "at that time, if we see fit then to form a black nationalist party, we'll form a black nationalist party. If it's necessary to form a black nationalist army, we'll form a black nationalist army. It'll be the ballot or the bullet" (1965, p. 41). Thus two key terms of this speech—the "ballot" and the "bullet"—mark the extremes of a wide range of options, most of which may be well outside the range accepted by the white dominant culture, but all of which must remain on the table as live possibilities.

In Rochester

Some of the themes from "The Ballot or the Bullet" are further developed in his speech at the Corn Hill Methodist Church in Rochester, New York, on February 16, 1965. Both speeches toggle between domestic and international perspectives, for example. But in this speech, the international context does not offer an antidote for the oppression of the domestic context. Malcolm does not invite his audience to abandon a domestic perspective for an international one, because neither perspective offers an unproblematic escape from the corruption and complexities of the other. Instead, all of the categories and perspectives are impure, so that no group of people or place in the world is entirely innocent or thoroughly guilty. The most productive perspective, then, seems to be one that rejects the limitations of any of them. In this way, Malcolm and his audience might harness some of the broader context offered by the international perspective without ever fully losing touch with the obstacles and oppression they face each day.

Early in the speech, Malcolm signals his intention to focus on the relationships between the domestic and the international perspectives, urging his audience that "we have to not only know the various ingredients involved at the local level and national level, but also the ingredients that are involved at the international level," because racial oppression has "become a problem that is so complex . . . that you have to study it in its entire world, in the world context or in its international context, to really see it as it actually is" (1992a, p. 144). His phrasings continue the emphasis on sight, warning his audience that "if you only try and look at it in the local context, you'll never understand it. You have to see the trend that is taking place on this earth" (1992a, p. 147).

The "racism practiced by America," for example, is the same racism that is involved in "a war against the dark-skinned people in Asia . . . a war against the dark-skinned people in the Congo, the same as it involves a war against the dark-skinned people in Mississippi, Alabama, Georgia, and Rochester, New York." And a key technique of this practice of racism is, as Malcolm puts it, "a science that's called image making" designed to make it "look like the victim is the criminal, and the criminal is the victim" (1992a, p. 150).

Malcolm provides a pair of examples to illustrate this theory, one in the United States and the other in Africa. The domestic example concerns the press coverage of the Harlem riots of the previous summer, 1964. "During these riots," Malcolm notes, "the press, very skillfully, depicted the rioters as hoodlums, criminals, thieves, because they were busting up property." But Malcolm invites his audience to "look at it from another angle," and to see that actually the inner-city African American is "a victim of economic exploitation, political exploitation, and every other kind." The apparent victims, on the other hand, are revealed to be "landlords who are nothing but thieves, merchants who are nothing but thieves, politicians who sit in the city hall and who are nothing but thieves in cahoots with the landlords and the merchants" (1992a, p. 153). The allocation of good and evil implied by the media, Malcolm suggests, does not hold up under scrutiny.

Similarly, "just as this imagery is practiced at the local level, you can understand it better by an international example," such as the US-supported bombing of rebels in newly independent Congo. The American press "refer to the villages as 'rebel held,'" for example, "as if to say, because they are rebel-held villages, you can destroy the population, and it's okay"; the pilots were called "'Anti-Castro Cuban,' that makes them okay"; and "they're able to do all of this mass murder and get away with it by labeling it 'humanitarian,' 'an act of humanitarianism'" (1992a, pp. 153–54). In this way, a criminal act at the international level—bombing villages—is remade into a heroic act.

Malcolm's audience is not asked to view one of these examples from the point of view of the other; that is, neither example is privileged, and the audience is not asked to identify fully with either the domestic or the global position. They are both corrupt. Malcolm's audience, then, is encouraged to critique each of these two perspectives without becoming aligned with either, and thus is positioned to exploit the interpretive potentials of both perspectives while avoiding the constraints of either.

The speech proceeds with another pair of parallel examples, but this time moves in the opposite conceptual direction: Malcolm begins with a global perspective and then moves back toward the domestic. Again, however, the lesson is about the methods consistently used by the white oppressor to keep dark-skinned people in check. He begins by noting that at the conference of emerging postcolonial states held in Bandung, Indonesia, in 1955, people found that they were bound together by a common oppressor. As Malcolm tells it, this realization "fed the flames of nationalism" in Asia and Africa, causing the colonial powers to turn to the United States for assistance. And this inspired the United States to develop a new approach to oppression, which Malcolm calls "benevolent colonialism" or "philanthropic imperialism" (1992a, p. 160).

The link back to the domestic perspective is through a Pan-Africanist militant awakening. Malcolm explains that as "the Black man in Africa got independent" and became "master of making his own image," the "Black man throughout the Western Hemisphere, in his subconscious mind, began to identify with that emerging positive African image." As African Americans were inspired by this new image and began to identify more closely with the Africans, the United States began to use on African Americans the same strategies of oppression that had been developed to deal with the Africans. As Malcolm explains, "Just as [the Americans] had to change their approach with the people on the African continent, they also began to change their approach with our people on this continent. As they used tokenism and a whole lot of other friendly, benevolent, philanthropic approaches on the African continent … they began to do the same thing with us here in the States" (1992a, pp. 161–62).

In "Black Man's History" Malcolm X encouraged his followers to reject one frame of reference (secular, or Christian) and to adopt a new one (that represented by the NOI). Similarly, in "The Ballot or the Bullet" he asked his audience to reject one perspective (one limited to the United States) and to adopt a new one (an international perspective). But at Rochester he is advocating something more complex. He is not suggesting that the domestic frame be rejected and an international frame be adopted in its stead, but rather that his listeners craft a new frame that encompasses some aspects of both the domestic and the international perspectives. In this speech, when he describes his plan to bring the United States before the World Court of the United Nations on charges of human rights grievances, he does not present the UN as an opportunity to effect a clean break from the domestic sphere, but instead as a venue wherein the international and the domestic spheres might interact, and where the domestic civil rights issues can "be discussed by people all over the world" (1992a, p. 170). In other words, Malcolm is working here to position his audience in between the domestic and international spheres, where they can engage in processes of critical judgment unbound by the limitations of the first but yet not so thoroughly absorbed into the second that they lose contact with the United States.

In speeches during his last year, as exemplified by his speech at Rochester, Malcolm worked to break his audiences free from the limitations of the dominant white culture, to broaden the scope within which they perceived their own situation and, thus, to bring to their minds and hands resources that would not otherwise be available. Malcolm was modeling for his audiences a *way of thinking*—his point was not that his listeners should now take action based on his analysis, but that they should engage in their own analysis using the interpretive strategies he had performed. Just as Malcolm X is able, at will, to expand or constrict the stage upon which he reasons, critiquing both the domestic and international spheres without fully rejecting the productive potentials of either, so too should his audiences become similarly perspicacious, unaligned, and empowered.

In some of the speeches Malcolm delivered after he returned from Mecca, he gave this untethered, nomadic critical stance a name: "positive neutrality." On December 20 in Harlem's Audubon Ballroom—where he would be assassinated about two months later—he explained "what this positive neutrality means":

> If you want to help us, help us; we're still not with you. If you have a contribution to make to our development, do it. But that doesn't mean we're with you or against you. We're neutral. We're for ourselves. Whatever is good for us, that's what we're interested in. That doesn't mean we're against you. But it does mean we're for ourselves. (1992b, p. 132)

An attitude of "positive neutrality" carries tremendous emancipatory potential for Malcolm's audiences. Suspended between dangerous sites of power and oppression, they can engage in practices of judgment and critique that are not otherwise available; under no obligation to become aligned with preexisting norms or categories, they are free to innovate and invent extravagantly.

These three speeches provide the outline of a three-part rhetorical narrative: While an NOI minister speaking to the NOI faithful, as in "Black Man's History," Malcolm delivers a prophetic discourse characterized by a narrow interpretive practice well suited to a worldview simply divided between absolute good and absolute evil; after leaving the NOI but before his journey to Mecca, and addressing a more diverse and politically engaged audience, in "The Ballot or the Bullet" he offers an enlarged international perspective as a source of possibilities for resistance and identity not available within the narrow confines of the domestic sphere; finally, in his speech at Rochester after he returns from Mecca and just days before his death, Malcolm presents neither the domestic context, nor the international context, nor any other context or ideology, as politically pure, and instead develops a radically flexible perspective characterized by a suspicion of all stable definitions and stances.

Conclusion

In this brief essay, I have set two narratives of the life of Malcolm X next to one another. The first, the biographical narrative, divides Malcolm's life into identifiable phases, with the transformations and reinventions between each phase relatively clearly marked. First, he transforms from a poor boy from a small Midwestern town into a petty criminal; then he experiences a religious conversion to join Elijah Muhammad's Nation of Islam; and finally he splits with the NOI and commits to Sunni Islam. The second narrative, which I refer to as his rhetorical narrative, shows that Malcolm's public address evolved over time, as he addressed more diverse audiences, from the relatively narrow and well-defined, bifurcated worldview generally allotted to ministers of the NOI toward a broader, more complex perspective better fitted to the impure politics of global race relations.

Placing these two narratives alongside one another emphasizes what is missed by attending to only one or the other. While the biographical narrative presents Malcolm's identity as versatile and malleable, for example, to the extent that he periodically reinvents himself, it does not draw our attention to the perspective that his speech and statements invite his followers to adopt. In other words, while Malcolm the man is a study in personal transformation, limiting our focus to his biographical arc omits the political transformation being advocated by Malcolm the orator. While the *Autobiography of Malcolm X* is a powerful story of transformation, it was through the act of performing his public address that Malcolm invented and modeled the modes of critical political engagement that he would have his audiences emulate. Most significantly, the biographical narrative presents Malcolm's life as a series of relatively discrete moments when he shifted from one relatively stable and well-defined identity to another, while the rhetorical narrative, in contrast, shows Malcolm evolving out of the relatively stable binaries of NOI doctrine and into a position characterized by a rejection, or at least suspicion, of stable binaries, clear boundaries, and codified ideologies.

Neither of these two narratives is the "correct" one, and neither should be dismissed at the expense of the other. Rather, they should be taken together, because by allowing each narrative to illuminate the other a far richer and more complex portrayal of Malcolm X emerges. His life was one of constant transformation, as many of his biographers have noted, and as such it demonstrates an incredible capacity for reinvention that provides a valuable model for people anywhere who face rapidly changing contexts and relatively limited resources. Seemingly unable to have much effect on his circumstances, Malcolm changed himself and, as a result, his circumstances did change. The rhetorical narrative, on the other hand, shows us that Malcolm is capable not only of changing himself, but also of inviting his audiences to change. He first invited them to adopt the strictly Manichaean worldview of the NOI, in which all whites are evil and all blacks are saints, and then, toward the end of his life, a more complex and nuanced perspective. But in either case, his public address demonstrated an unfailing faith that his followers, like himself, were capable of transforming themselves. Taking both of these narratives together, then, shows us that Malcolm X, through both his biography and his rhetoric, presented a powerful discourse of transformation.

■ References

Breitman, G. (1988). *The assassination of Malcolm X.* 2nd ed. New York: Pathfinder.

DeCaro, L. A., Jr. (1996). *On the side of my people: A religious life of Malcolm X.* New York: New York University Press.

Epps, A. (1968). *Malcolm X and the American Negro revolution: The speeches of Malcolm X.* London: Peter Owen.

Essien-Udom, E. U. (1962). *Black nationalism: A search for identity in America.* Chicago: University of Chicago Press.

Evanzz, K. (1992). *The Judas factor: The plot to kill Malcolm X.* New York: Thunder's Mouth.

Friedly, M. (1992). *Malcolm X: The assassination.* New York: Carroll & Graf / Richard Gallen.

Goldman, P. (1973). *The death and life of Malcolm X.* New York: Harper & Row.

Lee, S., & Wiley, R. (1992). *By any means necessary: The trials and tribulations of the making of Malcolm X.* New York: Hyperion.

Lincoln, C. E. (1994). *The Black Muslims in America.* 3rd ed. Grand Rapids, MI: William B. Eerdmans Publishing.

Lomax, L. E. (1964). *When the word is given: A report on Elijah Muhammad, Malcolm X, and the Black Muslim world.* New York: Signet Books.

Malcolm X. (1965). The ballot or the bullet. In *Malcolm X speaks.* G. Breitman (ed.). New York: Pathfinder Press, 23–44.

———. (1971). Black man's history. In *The end of white world supremacy: Four speeches by Malcolm X.* B. Karim (ed.). New York: Little, Brown, 23–66.

———. (1992a). Not Just an American Problem, but a World Problem. In *February 1965: The Final Speeches.* S. Clark (ed.). New York: Pathfinder, 143–70.

———. (1992b). There's a worldwide revolution going on. In *February 1965: The Final Speeches.* S. Clark (ed.). New York: Pathfinder, 120–42.

Malcolm X & Haley, A. (1964). *The autobiography of Malcolm X*. New York: Ballantine.

Marable, M. (2011). *Malcolm X: A life of reinvention*. New York: Viking.

Muhammad, E. (1965). *Message to the blackman in America*. Chicago: Muhammad's Temple No. 2.

Perry, B. (1991). *Malcolm: The life of a man who changed Black America*. Barrytown, NY: Station Hill.

Wolfenstein, E. V. (1981). *The victims of democracy: Malcolm X and the black revolution*. Berkeley: University of California Press.

Stokely Carmichael and the Rhetorical Articulation of Black Power

Richard D. Besel and Bernard K. Duffy

On October 29, 1966, the outspoken civil rights leader Stokely Carmichael delivered his "Black Power" address to "a throng of ten thousand spectators, mostly whites, gathered in the Greek Theatre" on the University of California, Berkeley, campus (Leeman & Duffy, 2012, p. 297). Invited by the Students for a Democratic Society (SDS) as part of a conference on black power, the occasion was much anticipated, but not without its critics. Within the university there was disagreement about whether or not Carmichael and other prominent civil rights leaders should even broach the subject of black power when addressing white audiences. The Afro-American Student Union was especially vocal in its objections to the SDS conference, believing the topic should be reserved for black audiences only. The university administration also feared a potential riot that would cause an unprecedented level of physical damage and embarrassment. Given Carmichael's presence at a recent Atlanta riot following one of his speeches, the scenario seemed plausible (Leeman & Duffy, 2012, pp. 297–98). The political climate in the state of California was equally turbulent. Incumbent governor Pat Brown and challenger Ronald Reagan attempted to leverage race concerns in their respective campaigns. Less than one week before the event, many political observers noted that Governor Brown might need to "bring in the troops" should the event get out of hand (Reston, 1966, p. E8). Given the political and cultural volatility of the time, one could find it reasonable that a speaker would choose to skip the conference altogether. Carmichael did not.

Stokely Carmichael's black power rhetoric stands out as a unique contribution to the chorus of civil rights voices. According to public address scholars James R. Andrews and David Zarefsky, of those drawing attention to the plight of blacks in the United States, "few were more vocal than Stokely Carmichael" (1989, p. 100). Larry Richardson concluded that "His oratory has now become the 'Magna Charta' of a protest movement which has affected the destiny of America" (1970, p. 212). The influence of Carmichael's black power rhetoric is undeniable and is still easily found in modern-day discourse. Social movement scholar Charles Stewart notes how Carmichael's rhetoric of black power "forever replaced 'Negro' with black and African-American." Indeed, "The word black instilled a new identity, pride, and cultural association among black Americans while the word Negro vanished from the American lexicon" (1991, pp. 443–44). One may even argue that the title of this collection is, in some ways, indebted to Carmichael's speeches. While Carmichael's black power rhetoric as a whole is significant, the speech he delivered on the Berkeley campus in particular is worthy of our attention. According to Andrews and Zarefsky, the "Black Power" address was "the forerunner of what became his standard speech" (1989, p. 101).

We turn to Carmichael's "Black Power" speech not only as an important historical repository of civil rights era ideas, but also as a text that may inform contemporary understandings about current race relations. After offering a brief history of the phrase "black power" and Carmichael's role in popularizing it, we investigate three important themes that emerge from a close reading of his speech. First, Carmichael believed not only that blacks should participate in defining themselves but also that *articulating* their own definition was an important exercise of agency. Second, although it has been noted often that Carmichael did not really have much to say to whites, this speech stands out as a notable exception. Finally, we explore what Carmichael had to say about war and its connection to race relations and economics. From its philosophical beginning to its aggressive end, Carmichael's speech is an integral cornerstone of twentieth-century civil rights rhetoric.

The Origins of "Black Power"

The notion of black power did not originate with Stokely Carmichael. It is connected to notable black spokesmen such as Frederick Douglass, Marcus Garvey, and Richard Wright. The term came to attention during the civil rights movement in the title of Richard Wright's autobiographical account of a trip to Africa (Wright, 1954; Peller, 2011). It was later used by US congressman and civil rights advocate the Reverend Adam Clayton Powell Jr. in a commencement address at Howard University and also at a rally just before John F. Kennedy was nominated for the presidency (Stewart, 1991, p. 443). Although Powell breathed new life into the expression, "It was Carmichael who made it famous, especially as a counter to 'freedom now' and 'we shall overcome,'" slogans that were dominating other strands of the civil rights movement (Andrews & Zarefsky, 1989, p. 100). In stark contrast to the words of leaders like Martin Luther King Jr. and Roy Wilkins of the National Association for the Advancement of Colored People (NAACP), Carmichael's rhetorical posture was better aligned with nationalism, militancy, confrontation and with what King referred to as the "fierce urgency of now" rather than gradualism or integration. According to Stewart, Carmichael "associated 'integration' with failure, apathy, shame, begging, tokenism, and subservience and 'black power' with real change, commitment, pride, taking, and self-determination—all mainline American values." Ultimately, "Carmichael's militant black power rhetoric provided his generation with a new dream of a more perfect order" (1991, p. 439).

Stokely Carmichael was born in Port of Spain, Trinidad and Tobago on June 29, 1941, making him only twenty-five years old when he delivered the "Black Power" address. Despite his young age, Carmichael had no problem providing his bona fides if pressed. For Stewart, Carmichael "had paid his dues literally and figuratively. He had been active in the mainstream civil rights movement for six years, since he was a high school student, and had been in the front lines of sit-ins, marches, freedom rides, and demonstrations" (1991, p. 434). While a student at Howard University, Carmichael spent summers registering voters. In 1964, he began working with the Student Nonviolent Coordinating Committee (SNCC) in Mississippi. Two years later, in May 1966, he assumed the SNCC chair position and shifted the organization's focus from nonviolence and civil disobedience to a more militant and separatist outlook. The moment could not be more opportune: "Stokely Carmichael was the right person, at the right time, and in the right place to foment an evolution of the civil rights movement" (Stewart, 1991, p. 443).

By the time Carmichael arrived at Berkeley, his activism across the country had already been reported by numerous national media outlets. It was not only the radical substance of his message that mesmerized the press, but also his versatile style and delivery. Carmichael was a tall, charismatic speaker who was "built like a basketball guard, dark, handsome, and virile," someone his associates called the "Magnificent Barbarian" (Stewart, 1991, p. 435). Carmichael seemed to adapt to his situations and audiences with ease, sometimes highlighting his intellectual magnificence, and at other times delivering street knowledge with a barbarous vernacular: "He was an actor-showman with a gift for histrionics. At one moment he was a sophisticated and soft-spoken academic explaining the economics or philosophy of black power; at another he was a poor old southern boy with a southern drawl; at another he was a shouting, threatening militant" (Stewart 1991, p. 435). Versatile as he was, his approach did not fit into the category of the preacher-like style of his more moderate counterparts.

Although by 1966 he had already earned a name for himself, not all of the attention was positive. Carmichael's advocacy for black power led Martin Luther King to declare that "black supremacy would be equally as evil as white supremacy." Fearing that the black power slogan would fan the flames of racial unrest, King maintained that blacks should share power with whites ("Dr. King Deplores 'Black Power' Bid," 2016). Historian Simon Hall notes the slogan "black power" had "created a political firestorm within both the civil rights movement and the broader body politic. For its critics, Black Power symbolized a dangerous new force and conjured up images of 'Black Jacobinism' and the 'Mau Mau . . . coming to the suburbs at night'" (Hall, 2007, p. 50). Rhetoric scholars Wayne Brockriede and Robert Scott capture the sentiment differently: "One meaning and one image thoroughly has engulfed the public mind and has dominated the attitudes of most white liberals: Black Power is violent racism in reverse, and Stokely Carmichael is a monster" (1968, p. 4). Regardless of what one thought of Carmichael by the time he delivered his "Black Power" speech, one could not help but listen.

The "Black Power" Speech

The opening sentences of Carmichael's "Black Power" speech accomplish much of what is expected in an introduction. After thanking his audience and noting that "it's a privilege and an honor to be in the white intellectual ghetto of the West," Carmichael adopts a philosophical tone as he establishes the warrant for the remainder of the speech. Following existentialist philosophers Camus and Sartre, Carmichael asks, if the relations between blacks and whites are unjust, is it possible "for a man to condemn himself"? For an answer, he turns to Frantz Fanon and argues a "man could not." Thus, "In a much larger view, SNCC says that white America cannot condemn herself. So black people have done it—you stand condemned" (2012, p. 304). But Carmichael's speech is not one of condemnation alone. By using three questions, Carmichael previews the arguments developed in the remainder of his speech: "How can black people inside this country move? How can white people who say they're not a part of those institutions begin to move? And how then do we begin to clear away the obstacles that we have in this society, to make us live like human beings?" In other words, Carmichael offers advice to black people about how they can define and articulate their own identities, advice to nonracist whites about what roles they should adopt in the civil rights movement, and, although it is not as clear from the preview, a humanist critique of US imperialism (Carmichael, 2012, p. 305).

Definition and Articulation

In addressing the question, "How can black people inside this country move," many scholars suggest Carmichael focuses on the need for blacks to define their own identities in their own ways, as opposed to the definitions assigned to blacks by whites. For example, Brockriede and Scott observe: "Foremost among the implications of his ideology is his insistence that black people, as a matter of personal pride, must assume the right to define their own identity, their relation to the total society, and the meaning of such important terms as Black Power" (1968, p. 5). Andrews and Zarefsky agree: "Perhaps most significantly, the Black Power slogan raised the issue of blacks' right to define their own identity; it was a demand for control of one's own self-concept. Carmichael argued that blacks would always be in a dependent relationship as long as whites could determine their identity" (1989, p. 101). This act was revolutionary in the sense that it no longer identified blacks as "less than" or "inferior" to whites. As Carmichael noted on a different occasion: "If we allow white people to define us by calling us Negroes, which means apathetic, lazy, stupid, and all those other things . . . then we accept those definitions" (qtd. in Stewart, 1991, p. 437). Not surprisingly, "Like other young leaders of social movements in the 1960s, Carmichael understood the importance and power of words, that whoever controls language controls the world" (Stewart, 1991, p. 439).

Our reading of Carmichael's "Black Power" speech does not contradict the observations about the importance of definition made by other scholars. Indeed, there is plenty of evidence in the text to suggest this is an accurate interpretation, such as when Carmichael states:

"We are now engaged in a psychological struggle in this country, and that is whether or not black people *will have the right to use the words they want to use* without white people giving their sanction to it" (2012, p. 307; emphasis added). The act of defining, according to B. Scott Titsworth, is a "starting point for arguments" (1999, p. 171). However, these starting points do not merely appear when called forth by a speaker; they are often tethered to and reliant upon already existing networks of power relations and ideologies. For argumentation scholar Douglas Walton, definitions are "deployed to serve the interest of the definer" (2001, p. 117). Thus, it should come as little surprise that it is with the act of definition that Carmichael begins the "strategic maneuvering" of his speech (Zarefsky, 2006, p. 399).

Although the act of defining is important, there is a second and often overlooked element to Carmichael's rhetoric, one in which definition alone is not enough to reclaim a sense of agency or control over one's identity. In addition to emphasizing that blacks needed to define concepts, Carmichael also stressed the importance of being able to *articulate* those definitions. If "the first step toward Black Power was for blacks to redefine themselves," the second was for blacks to articulate that definition to others (Andrews & Zarefsky, 1989, p. 101).

The concept of articulation has several meanings. For rhetoric scholar Nathan Stormer, many believe "articulation typically refers to enunciation or clear speech that produces intelligible sounds or, in a more general sense, when a speaker expresses an idea with eloquence and lucidity" (2004, p. 263). However, there is a second, less well-known meaning, one in which articulation refers to the joining or coming together of what are often seen as disparate parts. Feminist rhetoric scholar Tasha Dubriwny argues articulation is a form of "strategic linking" (2005, p. 396). Similarly, Stormer claims articulation "refers to the linkage between parts"; it brings "together the material world, language, and spatial arrangement into one act. Articulation deals with form and construction, connections and disjunctions, substance and discourse" (2004, p. 263). In other words, an articulate orator is not just someone who is capable of speaking with clear enunciation and lucidity, but is also someone who is capable of connecting and joining together different material conditions, ideas, and words in such a way that they appear as a coherent whole that is greater and more palatable than its divergent constituents. It is through this act of articulation, the reimagining of how things may and should "fit together," that new realities may form. For Carmichael, it was not enough for blacks to define their own identities; they also had to articulate what it meant to weave their new self-definition into the social and cultural tapestry of 1960s America.

The word "articulate" appears in some form no fewer than nine times throughout Carmichael's speech. These variations are scattered throughout the speech and often reference a variety of topics. For example, when referring to the psychological state of blacks when confronted by whites who are "showing them how to do" a particular task, Carmichael states: "Black people must be seen in positions of power, doing and articulating for themselves, for themselves" (2012, p. 310). If whites continue to occupy solely leadership and instructional positions, they are the ones who will determine the "proper" way to accomplish certain tasks; in essence, Carmichael is commenting on white articulation as much as he is pointing out the need for empowered black role models. This is not to say Carmichael is advocating a removal of all whites from positions of power; but rather that he is concerned with giving power to those who have had little to none. The repetition of "for themselves" further underscores the importance he assigned to blacks exercising agency.

In another section of the speech, Carmichael asks: "How do you begin to articulate the need to change the foreign policy of this country—a policy that is decided upon race, a policy on which decisions are made upon getting economic wealth at any price, at any price" (2012, p. 315)? Here the notion of "strategic linking" becomes relevant. While some may argue foreign policy is determined in a color-blind manner, Carmichael clearly disagrees. Thus, Carmichael not only attempts to express his ideas about foreign policy, but also joins his understanding of racial tensions and profit motives with the change he and others demanded. Whether speaking about one's ability to accomplish a task or taking a position on foreign policy, Carmichael seems to ask continuously: "How do we articulate those positions?" (2012, p. 316). It is worth noting that Carmichael is not asking, "What do we articulate?" For him, before one articulates the substance of a speech, one must first be recognized as a speaker who may articulate at all. For Carmichael, this is the problem of legitimacy: "Who has power? Who has power to make his or her acts legitimate? That is all. And in this country, that power is invested in the hands of white people, and they make their acts legitimate. It is now, therefore, for black people to make our acts legitimate." While much of what Carmichael says is addressed to blacks, he did not forget that his Berkeley audience was mostly white. The second theme in the "Black Power" speech thus focuses on Carmichael's advice to whites.

Advice for Whites

If the repetition of phrases such as "for themselves, for themselves" was meant to encourage blacks to take control of their own identities and actions, it was equally suggestive that the converse must also be true: that whites should not interfere with the emergence of organic black identities and concerns. In this sense Carmichael had a message for white members in the audience and beyond. However, he was not concerned with asking whites for permission; instead, the speech positioned blacks as already authorized to control their own fates. According to Andrews and Zarefsky, Carmichael faced a tricky rhetorical situation: "To 'explain' Black Power, in a sense, presumes that it must be made comprehensible *to whites*, but that assumption perpetuates the very dependency relationship that Black Power seeks to change. On the other hand, to threaten whites might provoke a strong backlash." This leads Andrews and Zarefsky to conclude: "Carmichael sought largely to *proclaim* Black Power in a way that rendered whites irrelevant to the attainment of blacks' goals. They could understand and sympathize, but there was little they could do to help" (1989, p. 101). Although we generally agree with Andrews and Zarefsky's reading of the situation, Carmichael had much to say about what whites could do to help in this particular speech. Rhetoric scholar Victoria Gallagher argues that Carmichael "did not appeal to white audiences for assistance or civic hand-outs but instead attempted to tell them what they needed to do to correct *themselves* and their civic culture" (Gallagher, 2001, p. 155).

Thus, early in the speech he admonishes his white critics to "dig yourself." Whether dispensing advice to blacks or whites, Carmichael's philosophical underpinnings were always connected to a spirit of self-control and introspection. What could blacks do to define and articulate for themselves? What could whites do to allow that to happen without becoming paternalistic? And what do all of these combined actions do for larger systems of power?

As Gallagher notes, Carmichael's key message to white audience members was that they did not need to, and should not attempt to, assist blacks directly; blacks did not need help to understand power, or definitions, or racism. Carmichael is clear on this point: "And we're never going to get caught up in questions about power. This country knows what power is. It knows it very well." Instead, whites were encouraged to focus on other whites so that they might work "within their own communities to tear down racist institutions" (Gallagher, 2001, p. 149). Carmichael's goal was not simply one of reformation, but one of transformation: "If he could get whites to be reflexive about their own positions within society, then he could open up possibilities that would change the world around him, that would ultimately pull people together rather than splitting them apart" (Gallagher 2001, 154).

Carmichael's advice to whites is buttressed by at least three basic assumptions: blacks have inherent human rights, those rights have been violated, and moral responsibility for stopping those violations rests with whites. While it seems obvious to most readers that all people possess basic human rights, Carmichael needed to make this explicit. For example, in his discussion of the civil rights bill, he argues: "I am black. I know that. I also know that while I am black I am a human being, and therefore I have the right to go into any public place. White people didn't know that. Every time I tried to go into a place they stopped me. So some boys had to write a bill to tell that white man, 'He's a human being; don't stop him.' That bill was for that white man, not for me. I knew it all the time. I knew it all the time." However, Carmichael also insists that bills aimed at curbing discrimination did not mean whites were the ones manifestly empowered to grant blacks their rights. Only by recognizing blacks as already free could things be set right: "Now, then, in order to understand white supremacy we must dismiss the fallacious notion that white people can give anybody their freedom. No man can give anybody his freedom. A man is born free." Taken to its ultimate conclusion, Carmichael later claims: "You may enslave a man after he is born free, and that is in fact what this country does. It enslaves black people after they're born, so that the only acts that white people can do is to stop denying black people their freedom; that is, they must stop denying freedom." Similarly, Malcolm X had asked: "How can you thank a man for giving you what is already yours?" (Leeman & Duffy, 2012, p. 284).

While Carmichael's commentary on the civil right bill makes his position clear, this is not the only example he offered when addressing whites. He also addressed what he perceived to be the problem with integration as its advocates conceived of it at the time. For Carmichael, integration could not work because there were too many people in power who did not commit to it fully. "That is what is called in this country . . . integration: 'You do what I tell you to do and then we'll let you sit at the table with us.'" Carmichael used housing to illustrate his point. Simply having one black family move into a white neighborhood and calling it "integrated" was not enough. This was merely geographic tokenism at its worst. Black power included authentic integration in the sense that it advocated for both blacks and whites the freedom to live where they wanted. Carmichael pointedly insisted that true integration was not just about a handful of blacks moving to white neighborhoods, but also involved whites moving to black neighborhoods: "We must now set up criteria and that if there's going to be any integration, it's going to be a two-way thing. If you believe in integration, you can come live in Watts. You can send your children to the ghetto schools. Let's talk about that. If you believe in integration, then we're going to start adopting us some white people to live in our neighborhood." Of course, Carmichael probably realized some white audience members would wince at this suggestion, but that made his point more poignant and effective. If whites said no to a "two-way" form of integration, then perhaps they needed to rethink their positions on whether or not blacks truly had access to the same resources and opportunities provided to whites.

Perhaps Carmichael's clearest expression of advice to whites was that they should build coalitions with blacks. For whites to become genuine allies to blacks required an alliance between progressive whites and empowered blacks, not racial paternalism. The white activist needed to be a person "who's willing to move into the white community and start organizing where the organization is needed." Indeed, Carmichael posed questions to both whites and blacks while suggesting potential pathways forward: "We have developed a movement in the black community. The challenge is that the white activist has failed miserably to develop the movement inside of his community. And the question is, can we find white people who are going to have the courage to go into white communities and start organizing them? Can we find them?" Whites had a role to play in Carmichael's black power movement, but it was a defined and limited role. Progressive whites needed to dismantle the mechanisms of racism within white communities and then act as partners to those in black communities. Carmichael asks: "If they're going to move inside that structure, how are they going to organize around a concept of whiteness based on true brotherhood and based on stopping exploitation, economic exploitation, so that there will be a coalition base for black people to hook up with?"

In one of the more inflammatory sections of the speech, Carmichael argues that there is much more whites can do to foster positive social and political relations between all groups of people. Even if the basic human rights of blacks were recognized, and even if housing practices were equal, there is still the problem of naming. Whether one references black or white organizations, Carmichael demanded symmetrical naming practices. Speaking of the Lowndes County Freedom Organization, he noted that the press called them the "Black Panther Party," after their emblem, "a black panther, a beautiful black animal which symbolizes the strength and dignity of black people, an animal that never strikes back until he's back[ed] so far into the wall." However, when referencing the Alabama Democratic Party, which has as its emblem "a white rooster and the words 'white supremacy,'" he playfully suggests consistency would compel the press to call them the "White Cock Party." Ultimately, he continues, "It is now white America that is going to deal with those problems of sex and color." Although Carmichael's view of "color" primarily focuses on black and white, his views are more cosmopolitan. His sharp insights regarding domestic racial oppression also spilled over into commentary about America's place in the world at large.

Vietnam and the Specters of Colonialism

For many black civil rights leaders, including Carmichael and Malcolm X, the Vietnam War was a synecdoche of American cultural and economic imperialism. The white majority, according to Carmichael, has never made democracy "work," not in the United States, and not in Vietnam. The missionaries, he said sardonically, had come with their Bibles to places where "we had the land, when they left, they had the land, and we still had the Bible" (Carmichael, 2012, p. 307). He criticizes Peace Corps volunteers as "modern day missionaries," "the sons of Kennedy" who appear to do good while the United States plunders the natural resources of underdeveloped countries and sells what is produced from them back to those countries for a profit (Carmichael, 2012, p. 316). That's been the "rationalization for Western civilization as it moves across the world—stealing, plundering and raping everybody in its path" (Carmichael 2012, p. 307). In a way, Carmichael contrasts the power of "the wealthiest nation in the world," which in World War II and its aftermath arose as a "world power," with the ethical power of the individual to say no to the war (Carmichael 2012, p. 314). There is, he says, a "higher law" than that of Secretary of Defense Robert McNamara and Secretary of State Dean Rusk, or "the law of a buffoon named Johnson. It is the law of each of us. . . . It is the law of each of us saying that we will not allow them to make us hired killers." In a phrase: "Hell no, we ain't going" (Carmichael, 2012, p. 311).

In 1966, student draft deferments were still firmly in place for those who could afford full-time enrollment in colleges and universities. Legal deferments, and morally questionable ones based on fabricated or exaggerated physical and mental disabilities, were far more available to those who came from prosperous families. As a result, in the 1960s, draft boards conscripted 30 percent of eligible blacks and only 14 percent of eligible whites. Moreover, many blacks enlisted in the military. It is not surprising, therefore, that in 1967, the 14 percent black representation in combat units exceeded their 11 percent representation in the US population. More sinister, however, is the fact that blacks accounted for 23 percent of all combat casualties. The indictment of the Civil War, "a rich man's war, poor man's fight," was recast for Vietnam as "a white man's war, black man's fight." Black civil rights leaders, including Carmichael, Malcolm X, and Martin Luther King Jr., echoed this sentiment, and were outraged by the injustices toward blacks who fought in Vietnam and the carnage of a war fought against other people of color. Fortunately, their voices were heard. By the war's end the total combat casualties among blacks were only roughly 1 percent higher than those suffered by whites (Krewasky, 2003, p. 116).

Carmichael realized that his immediate audience, largely comprised of UC Berkeley students, had not been able to take the peace movement beyond the campus walls, where it would resonate with those most likely to be drafted. The vast majority of Berkeley students also had coveted 2-S student deferments. They needed, he said, to go into the "white ghettos of this country" to "articulate a position for those who do not want to go" (2012, p. 311). The Student Nonviolent Coordinating Committee, which he headed, was not positioned to do it. Ironically, peace groups accused SNCC of being violent, when "in fact we are the most militant organization [for] peace or civil rights or human rights against this war in Vietnam in this country today" (2012, p. 311). SNCC opposed both the war and the draft. However, Carmichael intimated violence in his rhetorical opposition of the Vietnam War. While saying that the administration would not make them "hired killers," he added provocatively: "We will not kill anybody they say [to] kill. And if we decide to kill, we're going to decide who we going to kill" (2012, p. 311). This comment was, of course, very much in the vein of Malcolm X's rhetoric, which advocated reciprocal violence upon whites who enacted violence against blacks. However, it also reclaimed a sense of agency that many blacks had been denied.

Carmichael asserts provocatively that blacks who fight in Vietnam are "black mercenaries," fighting on behalf of a corrupt system. His discussion is a study in irony that exposes the hypocrisy of the system. He says scathingly: "Any time a black man leaves the country where he can't vote to supposedly deliver the vote to somebody else, he's a black mercenary" (Carmichael, 2012, p. 312). They are not fighting a just cause for a moral nation, but an "illegal and immoral war," for "a nation of thieves," embodied not only in its capitalism and imperialism, but also its history of slavery and black oppression. "It stole everything it has, beginning with black people" (Carmichael, 2012, pp. 311–12). The Vietnam War was simply another example of American rapacity and greed. Carmichael refused "to be part of the American pie," by which he meant the economic wealth of the country stolen by "raping South Africa, beating Vietnam, beating South America, raping the Philippines, raping every other country you've been in." He wants neither "the American pie" nor the "blood money" that created it (2012, p. 314). In his autobiography, Carmichael would reflect that "sending young black men to be cannon fodder in the Vietnam atrocity . . . was the crowning insult. The Vietnam war ain't nothing but white men sending black men to kill brown men to defend, so they claim, a country they stole from red men" (Carmichael & Thelwell, 2003, p. 546).

Carmichael chafes at the idea that his opponents have labeled him and his followers "reverse racists" because he and they do not want to be part of that system of corruption (Carmichael, 2012, p. 314). Rather, he represents himself as an "anti-racist racist" (Carmichael, 2012, p. 310). He also sees the Johnson administration's admonitions against violence as hypocritical. Following Malcolm X, Carmichael points out that "nonviolence" is a term invoked only when "black people move to defend themselves against white people." Punctuating his thought three times with the anaphora (repeated word or phrase) interspersed as a refrain: "Don't nobody talk about non-violence," he then amplifies the irony that "Lyndon Baines Johnson is busy bombing the hell out of Vietnam" while "White people beat up black people every day" (2012, p. 318).

The day before Carmichael spoke at Berkeley, he had undergone a two-day preinduction physical examination that involved an overnight stay at Saint Albans Naval hospital in New York. His current classification was 1-Y, a temporary deferment predicated upon one of three conditions—that he did not "meet mental, moral, or physical induction standards." As the *New York Times* pointed out, his draft board was silent on the issue of which of these standards was in question. For his part, Carmichael used the opportunity to assert his opposition to being drafted: "I'll go to Leavenworth [Federal Penitentiary] first." While Carmichael in his speech emphasized the hypocrisy of the government urging nonviolence, while engaged in a violent war, the *Times*, which labeled Carmichael "the militant advocate of black power," wryly contrasted his declaration in August that he would not fight in Vietnam with his repeated statement that he was "not personally opposed to violence" (Johnson, 1966, pp. 1, 9).

Carmichael's antiwar rhetoric was consistent with SNCC's protests, which found expression in a formal statement in 1965 and in demonstrations and a vigil in August 1966 (Anti-War Protests, SNCC Digital Gateway, nd). The SNCC antiwar, antidraft statement played upon the hypocrisy of drafting blacks to lay down their lives on behalf of freedom in a nation that did not accord freedom to blacks. Although hitting the same targets, its jabs were more subdued than the blistering antiwar comments Carmichael made in the "Black Power" speech:

> We are in sympathy with, and support, the men in this country who are unwilling to respond to a military draft which would compel them to contribute their lives to United States aggression in Vietnam in the name of "freedom" we find so false in this country. We recoil with horror at the inconsistency of a supposedly "free" society where responsibility to freedom is equated with the responsibility to lend oneself to military aggression. We take note of the fact that 16 percent of the draftees from this country are Negroes called on to stifle the liberation of Vietnam to preserve a "democracy" which does not exist for them at home. We ask, where is the draft for the freedom fight in the United States?" (SNCC Statement on Vietnam, January 6,1966, SNCC Digital Gateway, nd)

SNCC-sponsored demonstrations were intended to highlight this position. In the first demonstration in Atlanta at the Twelfth Army Corps and Induction Center demonstrators held up placards with the declaration: "The Vietcong never called me a nigger." Another placard featured a picture of a 1919 lynch murder of a black chained to a log and captioned: "Did the Vietcong do this?" Whites responded with taunts: "Kill the Black sons-of bitches," "Send all Niggers to Vietnam." During another demonstration at the same induction center twelve protestors were arrested and dragged into police wagons to be taken to the city jail. The remaining demonstrators chanted, "Racism runs this country," and "Die in Vietnam to support racism at home," and were also threatened with arrest. The arrest of the twelve protestors on the charge of insurrection led to a vigil for their release, of which SNCC wrote: "The psychological effect that the vigil is having on the power structure is fantastic" (Report on Draft Program, 1966).

Charles Stewart notes that attacking the Vietnam War and cultural imperialism "linked black power with the anti-Vietnam War, student and counter culture movement," and shows that SNCC realized also that the message that had been articulated in the South needed to be expressed in urban areas (Stewart, 1991, p. 439). The antiwar movement had also not pervaded the social groups most likely to be drafted, the poor, both white and black. In the 1960s, social movements overlapped issues—Gloria Steinem blamed the continuation of the war on what she termed the "male mystique" and Richard Nixon's unwillingness to admit defeat; John Kerry, on behalf of Veterans Against the War, argued powerfully that the war was racist, both in the weapons used against an Asian foe and the disproportionate number of black casualties and the 33 percent of blacks veterans who were unemployed (Steinem, 1978, p. 48; Kerry, 1978, pp. 10–11). Carmichael was not drafted, nor did he serve in Vietnam, although to the chagrin of the US government he did visit the war-torn country.

Conclusion

Without doubt, Stokely Carmichael "was the ideal charismatic leader of the black power struggle within the civil rights movement" (Stewart, 1991, p. 434). Although he was not the first to use the phrase "Black Power," he was its most effective popularizer. Turning to Carmichael's 1966 "Black Power" speech delivered at Berkeley, we have pointed out three themes that we believe are useful touchstones for contemporary students and scholars of the civil rights movement. In addition to commenting on Carmichael's use of definition, we have also noted the important role articulation plays in his rhetoric, a perspective not yet emphasized by other scholars. Turning to his advice to whites, Carmichael's rhetoric was also contextualized in a way that does not position black power as antithetical to whites. Carmichael asked whites to look inward as they worked to build communities with which blacks could build meaningful coalitions. Finally, we also explored Carmichael's position on war and economics given the speech's historical context.

While students of rhetorical history may find our comments on the three themes of Carmichael's speech of interest, history also has a way of informing the present. We do not believe that Carmichael's speech is a relic of some past movement, the details of which many have forgotten. Carmichael's words are still salient for today's audiences, audiences that are confronted with questions of police violence against Michael Brown in Ferguson, Missouri, or the shooting of high school student Trayvon Martin in Sanford, Florida. Gallagher has made a similar observation when she calls Carmichael's speech "a kind of blueprint for contemporary approaches to issues of civil rights and racial equality" (2001, p. 154). And how could it not be? Ethics and public affairs professor Peniel E. Joseph has recently noted: "The [black power] movement's panoramic critique of institutional racism anticipated the Black Lives Matter protests." Just as Carmichael had demanded over fifty years ago, Black Lives Matter movement participants have argued that "demanding human rights for all means claiming audacious power bold enough to declare that black lives matter in a world that has too often asserted that they do not." Carmichael's words must not be viewed as separate from a larger, broader conversation about race, a conversation that has proven both long and lasting. Instead, Carmichael's words are just one of many important articulations that ask all of us to reflect on what it means to be a black American, a white American, and a human being concerned with the wellbeing of others.

In 1969, three short years after the "Black Power" speech in Berkeley, Carmichael left the United States to live in the Republic of Guinea, changing his name to Kwame Ture and ultimately agreeing to head the African Peoples' Revolutionary Party. Perhaps Carmichael's decision to change his name should not come as a surprise to observers. He was also aware of the importance attached to names and the definitions that followed. Whatever he decided to call himself, he remained always the articulate and outspoken advocate of black power.

■ **References**

Andrews, J., & Zarefsky, D. (eds.). (1989). *American voices: Significant speech in American history, 1640–1945*. White Plains, NY: Longman.

Anti-War Protests by SNCC's Atlanta Project. Https://snccdigital.org/events/anti-draft-protests-snccs-atlanta-project/.

Brockriede, W. E., & Scott, R. L. (1968). Stokely Carmichael: Two speeches on black power. *Central States Speech Journal 19*, 3–13.

Carmichael, S. (2012). Black power. In *The will of a people: A critical anthology of great African American speeches*, R. W. Leeman & B. K. Duffy (eds.). Carbondale: Southern Illinois University Press, 295–303.

Carmichael, S. with E. M. Thelwell. (2003). *Ready for revolution: The life and struggles of Stokely Carmichael (Kwame Ture)*. New York: Scribner.

DeLuca, K. (1999). Articulation theory: A discursive grounding for rhetorical practice. *Philosophy and Rhetoric 32*, 334–48.

Dubriwny, T. A. (2005). Consciousness-raising as collective rhetoric: The articulation of experience in Redstockings' abortion speak-out of 1969. *Quarterly Journal of Speech 91*, 395–422.

"Dr. King deplores 'black power' bid." *New York Times*, 21 June 1966, p. 30.

Gallagher, V. J. (2001). Black power in Berkeley: Postmodern constructions in the rhetoric of Stokely Carmichael. *Quarterly Journal of Speech 87*, 144–57.

Hall, S. (2007). The NAACP, black power, and the African American freedom struggle, 1966–1969. *Historian 69*, 49–82.

Johnson, Thomas A. (1966). "Carmichael Says He Won't Go if Drafted," *New York Times*, 29 October, pp. 1, 9.

Joseph, P. E. (2016). Commentary: 'Black and proud': From black power to black lives matter. Reuters, June 16. Http://www.reuters.com/article/us-social-race-blackpower-commentary-idUSKCN0Z7329.

Kerry, J. (1978). Speech before the Senate Foreign Relations Committee. In *Critical anthology of public speeches*, K. H. Jamieson, (ed.). Palo Alto, CA: SRA, 9–12.

Krewasky, A. Salter. (2003). *Combat multipliers: African American soldiers in four wars*. Fort Leavenworth, Kansas: Combat Institute Press.

Leeman, R. W., & Duffy, B. K. (eds.) (2012). *The will of a people: A critical anthology of great African American speeches*. Carbondale: Southern Illinois University Press.

Peller, Gary. (2011). *Critical race consciousness: Reconsidering American ideologies of racial justice*. Boulder: Paradigm Publishers.

Report on draft program. (1966). Student Nonviolent Coordinating Committee. Http://www.crmvet.org/docs/6608_sncc_draft-resist.pdf.

Reston, J. (1966). Berkeley, California: The university and politics. *New York Times*, October 23, E8.

Richardson, L. S. (1970). Stokely Carmichael: Jazz artist. *Western Speech 34*, 212–18.

Salter, K. A. I. (2003). *Combat multipliers: African-American soldiers in four wars*. Fort Leavenworth, KS: Combat Studies Institute Press.

SNCC Statement on Vietnam, January 6,1966. Https://snccdigital.org/inside-sncc/policy-statements/
        vietnam/.Steinem, G. (1978). Speech to the U.S. Naval Academy. In *Critical anthology of public
    speeches*, K. H. Jamieson (ed.). Palo Alto, CA: SRA, 46–50.

Stewart, C. J. (1991). The evolution of a revolution: Stokely Carmichael and the rhetoric of black power.
        Quarterly Journal of Speech 83, 429–446.

Stormer, N. (2004). Articulation: A working paper on rhetoric and taxis. *Quarterly Journal of Speech 90*,
        257–84.

Titsworth, B. S. (1999). An ideological basis for definition in public argument: A case study of the
        individuals with disabilities in education act. *Argumentation and Advocacy 35*, 171–84.

Walton, D. (2001). Persuasive definitions and public policy arguments. *Argumentation and Advocacy 37*,
        117–32.

Wright, Richard. (1954). Black power: A record of reactions in a land of pathos. New York: Harper.

Zarefsky, D. (2006). Strategic maneuvering through persuasive definitions: Implications for dialectic
        and rhetoric. *Argumentation 20*, 399–416.

Barack Obama, the Rhetoric of Racial Reconciliation, and Donald Trump's Audience

Realizing the Promise of the "A More Perfect Union" Address

David A. Frank

The election of Donald Trump as president of the United States in 2016 reflected and deepened divisions in the nation's polarized electorate. In the wake of the election, divisions of race, gender, class, education, and a host of other distinguishing factors seemed to widen. These divisions were due, in part, to a lack of engagement between and among members of various identity groups and their tendency to seek out information to confirm preexisting ideologies and opinions (Rothwell & Diego-Rosell, 2016). There is also a history to these divisions that has yet to be fully excavated and worked through with public discourse, communal dialogue, argument, and interpersonal efforts that interrogate the color lines in the United States. Illustrating the power of the past to haunt the present, William Faulkner, in *Requiem for a Nun*, writes that the "past is never past. It's not even past" (1975, p. 80). Barack Obama, in his March 18, 2008, address in Philadelphia, quoted Faulkner's passage and then confronted the nation's racial past, doing so in a speech that is widely, but not universally, acknowledged as a masterpiece (Obama, 2016; Frank, 2009; Terrill, 2015; Rowland and Jones, 2011).

I suggest that the template for future efforts to create an effective rhetoric of racial reconciliation can be constructed from Obama's speech. This template, designed to help Americans work through what Obama called the nation's original sin of slavery, recognizes the significance of institutional racism, interrogates the meaning of white privilege, and encourages genuine argument in search of racial rapprochement. As Terrill writes, Obama's speech marks an inventional breakthrough on the topic of race, as he presented to his audience a "duality" that

pairs points of view, within which one viewpoint is not intended to dominate or supplant the other and whose tensions or contradictions are to be neither transcended nor synthesized; Obama's audience is invited to inhabit them both and to understand both as comparable in terms of reasonableness yet never collapsible into homogeneity. (2015, p. 144)

With his analysis of Obama's address, Terrill seeks to develop our democracy's capacities of intentional criticism, which are on display in Obama's race speech.

Unfortunately, the promise of Obama's template of racial reconciliation in the "A More Perfect Union" address was not fully realized, as "most of Obama's other discourses about race . . . throughout the campaign and into his first term, did not invite his audiences" to participate in the same expression of reason in his race speech. "They were mostly concerned with positioning Obama . . . as an extension of a peculiarly narrow conception of the civil rights movement" (Terrill, 2015, p. 144). The speech stands as an undeveloped model of thinking and speaking about race. Yet, with all its strengths, the template did not challenge the status of race as a biological concept, address the nation's other original sins (including the dehumanization of the Native American by European colonists, the creation of a class-based society founded on the backs of African American slaves and poor Scots-Irish, the disenfranchisement of women, etc.), and separate the aspiration of a postracial country from the concrete realities of racism. I seek to revisit Obama's race speech and make use of inventional criticism to imagine how its template might been used to launch new and novel approaches to battle racism.

I intend, using what Karlyn Kohrs Campbell and Kathleen Jamieson term "touchstone criticism," to expand the template Obama introduced in his March 18, 2008, address by including Kimberlé Crenshaw's principle of intersectionality, America's multiple original sins, and the development of a prophetic postracial outlook as set forth by Paul Taylor (Campbell and Jamieson, 1979; Crenshaw, 1989; Taylor, 2016).

Touchstone Criticism of Obama's Race Speech

Campbell and Jamieson invite critics of public discourse to juxtapose speeches that were delivered by speakers with those that the critic imagines might have better addressed the rhetorical situation and the historically situated audience faced by these speakers. The critic's imagined speech then becomes a touchstone used to evaluate the speech that was delivered (1979, p. 23). There are, of course, constraints placed upon the speaker's imagination if persuasion is a goal; namely, the speaker will need to present arguments the audience deems worthy of action. Campbell and Jamieson, in their analysis, tap a concept central to rhetorical theory: imagination. To illustrate how critics might carry out touchstone criticism, they study Barbara Jordan's keynote speech to the Democratic National Convention on July 12, 1976, and then imagine a speech she might have delivered. Jordan's presence, as a black woman, "incarnated the argument" and served as "the proof of the truth" of what she said. As the first African American to serve as a keynote speaker, her act of speaking enacted an argument that the Democratic Party best represented diversity and the American dream (p. 6). However, Campbell and Jamieson are disappointed by the address, as it "was a rather ordinary speech that like many others, returned to basic principles" (p. 6). Jordan spoke about the Constitution and launched an attack on the positions taken by the Republican Party; nothing in the address was said about race or gender.

The speech, Campbell and Jamieson conclude, would "not be memorial except as a speech *given by* Barbara Jordan" (p. 6). Campbell and Jamieson then imagine Jordan offering a different address. Jordan's speech, as imagined by Campbell and Jamieson, launched from Jordan's actual introduction:

> A lot of years (have) passed since 1832, and during that time it would have been most unusual for any national political party to ask a Barbara Jordan to deliver a keynote address. But tonight here I am. (p. 11)

What followed, in Campbell and Jamieson's imaginary address, deviated significantly from the speech as delivered:

> They did not make keynote addresses, nor indeed addresses of any sort, the Barbara Jordans of those days. They were not welcomed into this, or any other, political party. Surely some of them, some of those blacks, some of those women, were able as I . . . They died, often in poverty and pain, and always without the fulfillment that America promised them. There were many in number, these women and blacks and minorities. (p. 11)

In the Campbell and Jamieson rendition, Jordan would speak directly about her status as a black and a woman, pairing the two identities as separate but interacting, with race and gender as factors that help explain the historic oppression of blacks, women, and minorities.

Campbell and Jamieson draw on Jordan's empathy and imagination to include an expansive community and vision of concern: that Barbara Jordan stands as a symbol for other Barbara Jordans who have struggled and died in pain. "It is for that other Barbara Jordan, for all the blacks, and women, and minorities and poor of yesterday and tomorrow that I ask for your support" (p. 11). Their imagined speech takes Jordan's ordinary address and transforms it into a prophetic message transcending the moment and broadening the vision of the speech to include the facts of race, gender, class, and those who are minorities. While undeveloped, Campbell and Jamieson's imagined address foreshadows Crenshaw's theory of intersectionality.

In contrast, Barack Obama's "A More Perfect Union" address was no ordinary speech. Like Barbara Jordan, Obama "incarnated the argument" advanced in the speech; that as a biracial man he could cross over both sides of the color line and view the world the world through the lens of both black and white America (Frank, 2009; Terrill, 2015). Unlike Jordan, Obama faced a rhetorical situation very different from a keynote address: he was under attack for his association with Jeremiah Wright, his pastor at University Trinity Church in Chicago. Wright, in a series of sermons, indicted America for its hypocrisy and condemned the nation for its gratuitous support of racism. When Wright's sermons were taken out of context and replayed incessantly on American television, Obama was forced to deliver what many would call his "race speech" on March 18, 2008.

Obama's race speech, limited as it was to the black-white divide, reflected a robust imagination of his audience. The conservative columnist and former speechwriter for Ronald Reagan, Peggy Noonan, wrote that the "speech assumed the audience was intelligent," as it gave presence to truths about race in America. "We've never had a major-party presidential front-runner who is black, or rather black and white, who has given such an address," Noonan concluded. The distinguished African American historian John Hope Franklin agreed (Scott, 2008). The address set forth a template for racial reconciliation in which Obama attempted to establish four commonplaces in which he paired contraries of slavery and the Constitution, black and white, compassion and despair. First, Obama joined the nation's Constitution with the "nation's original sin of slavery" to suggest that the Constitution, an imperfect document open to improvement, provides the ground rules for progressive change. The Constitution had "embedded within" it the capacity to confront and overcome the moral degradation of slavery and other ills as it establishes the glide path to a "more perfect union." With the Constitution as the value guide, the government, Obama argued, is the agent that should ensure equal treatment under the law.

In this speech, Obama placed himself among the black racial optimists in opposing the black racial pessimists. "Racism is an integral, permanent, and indestructible component of this society," Bell and other black pessimists argue (1992, p. ix). Black racial pessimism places racism beyond the reach of history and time, rendering naive those who believe the disease can yield to treatment. By placing the country's racial trauma in history rather than out of time, Obama called the country to confront its racial past with the expectation that it could yield to reason.

A second commonplace established by Obama, one that requires empathy, is an expectation that America's white audience understand that "the path to a more perfect union means acknowledging that what ails the African-American community does not just exist in the minds of black people; that the legacy of discrimination—and current incidents of discrimination, while less overt than in the past—that these things are real and must be addressed." Whites must move beyond claims of "white innocence" to a recognition that the sin of slavery left in its wake intergenerational barriers to progress; that 250 years of slavery, 90 years living under the Jim Crow regime, and the appearance of adaptive racism, which rejects overt expression of racism in favor of dog whistles and coded phrases, significantly constrain blacks.

In turn, Obama identifies a third commonplace: White privilege is not granted to all whites. Obama observed, 'Most working and middle-class white Americans don't feel that they've been particularly privileged by their race. . . . As far as they're concerned, no one handed them anything; they built it from scratch." This audience, the white working class, was Donald Trump's primary audience during the 2016 presidential campaign, and he played to their anger and fear. Obama recognized in his race speech that when whites

> are told to bus their children to a school across town, when they hear that an African-American
> is getting an advantage in landing a good job or a spot in a good college because of an injustice
> that they themselves never committed, when they're told that their fears about crime in urban
> neighborhoods are somehow prejudice, resentment builds over time.

Obama acknowledged white as well as black suffering without equating the two, but recognizing their separate realities.

The fourth commonplace Obama outlined was the expectation that the United States should "work through" its racial trauma. Obama embraced here a therapeutic approach to racial trauma and the nation's racial future. Obama observed that "the issues that have surfaced over the last few weeks reflect the complexities of race in this country that we've never really worked through, a part of our union that we have not yet made perfect." Obama places the trauma suffered by blacks in historical time, refusing to vest American racism with a transcendent and an immutable reality. He also called for whites and blacks to engage one another, to leave their "hush harbors" in which each race stays within its own rhetorical enclave to rehearse grievances and to discover or invent arguments that reinforce preexisting beliefs about the self and others.

Obama celebrated the power of engagement and rhetoric to affect racial reconciliation, that it was possible for whites and blacks to achieve a degree of communion. As proof, Obama, like Jordan before him, drew from his own history and biography: he was a biracial man who had succeeded in the American culture. He pointed to the votes he won from white citizens in rural areas that helped secure his election as senator from Illinois. Racial trauma, Obama insisted, could yield to racial understanding through acts of interracial engagement.

Obama's speech was well received by political players across the political spectrum. The speech, Michael Eric Dyson suggests, "justly won wide acclaim" (2016, p. 89). Noonan writes that the speech prompted "talking, [with] pundits left and right, black and white, about what they'd experienced of race in America." The speech, with its commonplaces, offers a prototype for a rhetoric of reconciliation. Regrettably, Obama did not fully develop these commonplaces. In the years after his race speech, Obama would often speak in universal terms about issues of race. However, in the latter stages of his second term, he did speak more directly to the need for racial reconciliation. He did, with eloquence, highlight the problem of race in his 2015 eulogy for Reverend Clementa C. Pickney and his January 10, 2017, farewell address.

Obama's farewell address did capture themes deserving development during the eight years of his presidency. In this address, Obama called for empathy, an appreciation of the racism faced by blacks and the suffering of the white working class. In what follows, I engage in touchstone criticism to imagine the commonplaces and rhetoric Obama might have used to better inoculate against the racial polarization prompted by Donald Trump and to use inventional criticism to suggest the trajectories a rhetoric of racial reconciliation might take. I imagine three commonplaces that could help realize the promise of Obama's race speech.

Intersectional Consilience and Race

Campbell and Jamieson's imagined address has Jordan listing her identities as a black and a woman. However, they do not have Jordan explaining why listing both was necessary or how alone and together they were important. Crenshaw, some ten years after Campbell and

Jamieson's contribution on Jordan's keynote speech, offered a theory of intersectionality that explained why it is essential to consider both race and gender in an analysis of oppression. Intersectionality "is a way of understanding and analyzing the complexity of the world, in people, and in human experiences" in which no one factor can explain social and political life (Hill Collins & Bilge, 2016, p. 2).

> When it comes to social inequality, people's lives and the organization of power in a given society are better understood as being shaped not by a single axis of social division, be it race or gender or class, but by many axes that work together and influence each other. Intersectionality as an analytic tool gives people better access to the complexity of the world and of themselves. (p. 2).

A single-axis framework designed to explain historic oppression that only considers race, writes Crenshaw, "erases Black women in the conceptualization, identification and remediation of race and sex discrimination" (1989, p. 14).

The notion of intersectionality, Crenshaw continues, establishes a framework wherein a number of factors such as gender and race intersect. When both race and gender are included in the analysis of the oppression of black women, "the intersectional experience is greater than the sum of racism and sexism, [and] an analysis that does not take intersectionality into account cannot sufficiently address the particular manner in which Black women are subordinated" (p. 14). Studies of intersectionality have flourished since Crenshaw's original statement. Obama's admirable attempt to effect racial reconciliation in his Philadelphia speech was limited to the topics of race, class, and religion. An intersectional commonplace for the address would invite a much broader definition of the audience's identity and interrogate the foundational assumptions of race.

If an intersectional commonplace is in use, then a rhetoric of consilience, equipped to build from and acknowledge the many axes of identity, would be a good fit. A rhetoric of consilience begins with the separate and interlinking experiences and histories of a composite audience made up of individuals and groups holding sometimes similar and sometimes conflicting values (Perelman and Olbrechts-Tyteca, 1969). The speaker then builds up and from these separate experiences to values the individuals and groups would share in common. I have described a rhetoric of consilience in an early study of Obama's rhetoric, conducted in collaboration with Mark McPhail (Frank & McPhail, 2016). The inventional task of a speaker seeking racial reconciliation would be to begin with an understanding of the historical experiences of the many identities, such as race, gender, class, religion, and educational backgrounds represented by the members of an audience and then to bring them into the space of communion on issues of common cause. A truly intersectional analysis would acknowledge that "many Americans continue to view race as biologically real and racial categories as meaningful divisions in the population" (Khanna & Harris, 2009, p. 370; Johnston-Guerrero & Tran, 2016). An important first step in using the intersectional commonplace would be to challenge the notion of race as an essential biological fact, let alone the most essential biological fact.

In his depiction of race in the Philadelphia address, Obama established black and white races as real and discrete, and attempted to bridge them with the constitutional principle of equality in the Constitution and mutual empathy. In *Dreams from My Father*, Obama describes himself as biracial, a function of his "mixed blood" (1995, p. xv). When Obama limits his race talk to black and white and mixed blood, he makes it appear that race is a biological truth. As Yudell et al. observe in a recent *Science* article, "Language matters, and the scientific language of race has a considerable influence on how the public (which includes scientists) understands human diversity" (2016, p. 565). Scientists are in consensus that the word "race" does not describe something essential to human biology or identity. The "twentieth-century revolutions of population and quantitative genetics, molecular genetics, cellular biology, bioinformatics, and genomics," writes Graves, "have produced enough new knowledge to forever banish [the ideology of racism] to the dustbin of history" (2015, p. 412).

Indeed, beginning with Lewinton's research in 1972 and continuing to the genome project (Bonham, Warshauer-Baker, & Collins, 2005) and beyond, scientists have marshaled powerful evidence that there is a need to take "race out of human genetics" (Yudell et al., 2016). Scientists are moving away from the language of race and toward "terms like 'ancestry' or 'population' to describe human groupings in genetic studies" (p. 565), which helps guide thinking away from biological essentialism. Following the lead of the best scientific knowledge on race and the insights offered by scholars of intersectionality (Hancock, 2016; Bright, Malinsky, & Thompson, 2016), race should be described as a social rather than an essential biological fact, one of many axes used to describe the social world.

What, then, would an address building from Obama's race speech and from the commonplace of intersectional consilience yield? Race, gender, class, religion, and a number of other interacting axes would be key factors in an audience analysis designed to achieve reconciliation. I imagine something as follows:

> I am a man of mixed ancestry and understand what it is like living in Kansas and Hawaii. I cherish my Christian heritage and honor my maternal grandfather, Stanley Armour Dunham, who lived in Wichita, served in the 1830th Ordnance Supply and Maintenance Company during World War II. My great-uncle Ralph was deployed to France six weeks after D-Day. Like many Americans, I am the son of immigrants. My father was from Kenya, and I honor the value of education he prized. With a mother from Kansas and a father from Kenya, I represent a population of Americans that is proud of its layered history and tradition and sustains a passionate commitment to the values that make the United States the greatest nation in the world.

With good reason, a critic might find Obama's original text far better as the use of the terms "ancestry" and "population" might sound stilted and fail to replace racial vocabulary (Atkin, 2016). The intent of this effort of imagination is to offer a passage to racial reconciliation that departs from the language of biological race toward the shared experience of ancestry and population. In this rendition, Obama is not of mixed blood or mixed race—characteristics that might reflect essential, biological features—but rather a member of a population cluster with a common history of experiences. An intersectional commonplace prompting the use of consilient rhetoric would invite a recognition that race is socially constructed and acknowledge the origins of trauma and stress affecting multiple audiences, ancestries, and populations clusters.

America's Original Sins

In his Philadelphia speech, Obama targeted the "nation's original sin" of slavery, a legacy that he argued helped explain the status of blacks in the United States. Given that his speech was responding to his status as a black and the role he could play in fostering black-white rapprochement, his choice to limit the number of the nation's original sins to one is understandable. However, as television talk show host Tavis Smiley argues, Obama erred in his race speech by using a constricted definition of original sin. Smiley observes, "America's original sin is not [Black] slavery. America's original sin is its treatment . . . of indigenous people." America's true original sin, Smiley notes, was the dehumanization of indigenous people. Historians confirm Smiley's claim, for the "Age of Discovery, with its expansions of empires and exploitations of New World natural resources, was accompanied by the seizure and forced labor of human beings, starting with Native Americans" (Nabokov, 2016).

The treatment of the New World's land and indigenous people by European-based Christian colonists was founded on a misreading of Hebrew Scripture that defined the land and people of North America as a wilderness inhabited by heathens that God wanted conquered and controlled (Newcomb, 2008). European Christian colonists believed it was their right to hold Native American and African slaves and justified their claims with race-based reasoning. While the enslavement of Africans was a prominent outcome of the European Christian colonial worldview, Native Americans and the Scots-Irish were also ensnared in its toxic web. In her book *White Trash: The 400-Year Untold History of Class in America*, Nancy Isenberg explains the original sin committed against poor "whites" in American history.

Affluent European Christians created a class and caste system in the new land. Native Americans and Africans were treated as chattel and put in service to creating an economy that served the ends of the wealthy (Isenberg, 2016). Poor men and women of European ancestry from Ireland, Scotland, and England were imported to till the land. The affluent, using racial reasoning, defined the poor with white skin as a separate "breed." This "breed" of white people was inferior. The skin of this inferior breed was seen by the affluent as possessing a "ghastly yellowish white complexion, which was clearly the result of bad food and poverty" (Isenberg, 2016, p. 150). The breed was defined as "white trash," with its descriptors being lazy, ignorant, queer, and loathsome. As Isenberg observes, this "breed," this underclass, has "been with us since the first European settlers arrived on these shores. It is not an insignificant part of the vast national demographic today" (p. 151). And it is this national demographic, one that is in pain, that yielded to the rhetoric of Donald Trump (Case & Deaton, 2015).

Members of this demographic do not see themselves as benefiting from white privilege, as Obama explains in his race speech, and, as individuals or a population cluster, do not see themselves as responsible for systemic racism or its results. They also believe they have been treated unfairly by the elites and that the future is in deep peril (Dreher, 2016; Vance, 2016). The deep stories they use to define their lives hold that people of color, immigrants, have benefited at their expense, which they see Barack Obama supporting (Hochschild, 2016). They hold a deep resentment (Cramer, 2016). This demographic has experienced, since the founding of the United States, an intergenerational transfer of poverty and pain, which has yet to be addressed. Eric Alterman rightly observes that after eight years as president,

> Obama never even came close to solving the problem[:] . . . What to say to the white working-class people whose way of life was being destroyed by the vagaries of global capitalism coupled with a political system that responded first and foremost to the wealthy? This, too, is part of his legacy. And it has helped to give rise to a billionaire demagogue, who has answered Obama's question with a combination of racism, xenophobia, false promises, and threats of violent reprisals.

Obama's race speech might have offered the beginnings of a solution.

Imagine him declaring in his race speech:

> The Constitution our founding fathers produced was eventually signed, but ultimately unfinished. It was stained by this nation's original sins, which was due to a system of government based on race and class that we have struggled to repair and improve. Because of our imperfect and unfinished constitution, Native Americans, Africans, and poor whites of European ancestry were mistreated and viewed by the affluent as less than human. Native Americans and Africans were enslaved, and many of Irish and Scottish ancestry were condemned to involuntary servitude. Our nation still suffers from the consequences of these and other original sins, and our Constitution hosts within it the capacity to address these ills.

Obama's race speech displays the history of black oppression; my imagined embellishment seeks to provide the same for Native Americans and poor working-class whites. By providing a historical explanation, the speech could have outlined the different but interrelated trajectories of these populations to the present. Without question, America's "white trash" had it better than the slaves of African ancestry, but they were still treated as pariahs. A full acknowledgment of African American trauma is not diminished when the trauma of America's "white trash" is also on the agenda for repair.

To summarize, the commonplaces highlighting intersectional consilience and original sins expand the framework of Obama's race speech to include the assumption that race is a biological reality and that there are many original sins the nation must confront. A third commonplace, which I suggest could be the polar star of a rhetoric of reconciliation, is the need for a prophetic postracial commonplace. Obama has made clear on numerous occasions that his election and presidencies did not mark the outbreak of a postracial present. However, some of his pronouncements, beginning with his 2004 keynote address before the Democratic National Convention, have been interpreted as suggesting the country had solved its race problem. A prophetic postracial commonplace should offer a foothold for a rhetoric of reconciliation that avoids the problems of racial pessimism and the dangers of translating a postracial aspiration into a claim that the dream of a postracial society is at hand.

PROPHETIC POSTRACIALISM

Mark McPhail and I offered different interpretations of Obama's 2004 keynote address that revealed the split between the empirical existence of racism and the aspiration of postracism. With good evidence, McPhail argued that Obama's 2004 address suggested the empirical arrival of the postracial moment; I suggested that the speech was an attempt to bring members of his composite audience together around common values and goals. Obama's 2008 race speech was different because he was forced to deal with the realities of racism. He addressed these realities with a clear and compelling explanation of black trauma and ended the address with a splendid conclusion featuring a black man expressing empathy and concern for a white woman. The speech did pair the realities of racism blacks face with the hopeful act of racial compassion at its end. However, the speech did not spell out a commonplace that might be used to join a pragmatic and grounded critique of racist practices with the aspirations of racial justice and reconciliation.

Paul Taylor, in his *On Obama*, suggests that prophetic postracialism might yoke the universal values of equality and justice to the realities of racism. Building from the work of Cornel West on the role of the prophetic in racial politics, Taylor sees the value in identifying a future "still in the making" (2016, p. 32) that refuses to use race as a barrier to social justice. This is what he would define as the prophetic stance, that current racial thinking would mutate, allowing racial consciousness to evolve beyond its status as an essential human feature. Prophetic postracialism is clear-eyed and pragmatic about the empirical reality of socially constructed racism and challenges it with inspired universal values and visions of alliance and collaboration between and among citizens representing different ancestries.

Taylor, for good reason, is cautious about advancing prophetic postracialism as a useful approach to the problems of racism, fearing it would be used to justify a "color-blind" approach to both the analysis of and solution to problems of race (2016, p. 33). With this caution in mind, a prophetic postracialism need not limit our imaginations of the future; it could provide the equipment necessary to work through historic trauma by nesting the social realities of racism with a vision of a society that does not use race to deny equal opportunity. Taylor is right to highlight the capacity of the prophetic approach to leave the future open, which offers spiritual and policy alternatives to black pessimism.

Dominic LaCapra has developed the most complete secular theory of historical trauma, which invites a rhetoric of racial reconciliation that seeks to avoid the nihilism of pessimism and the naïveté of unrestrained optimism (Lacapra, 2014, 2016). Historical trauma, LaCapra argues, can be worked through with compromises, partial solutions, and small steps in the right direction. To illustrate, South Africa has successfully confronted its racist past. South Africa has reconstructed its society in the wake of apartheid through its South African Truth and Reconciliation Commission (Arthur, Issifu, & Marfo, 2015). A study conducted by the South African Institute of Race Relations found:

> Far from being hostile towards one another, most South Africans, black and white, occupy a pragmatic middle ground on race relations. White South Africans understand and support the need for redress. Black South Africans do not believe that their white compatriots should be treated as second-class citizens. The overwhelming majority of both groups believe that they need each other for progress to be made. (2016, p. 2)

John Campbell affirms this conclusion and observes that the "institutional and ideological props of white supremacy [in South Africa] are gone" (2016, p. 14). This progress is due, in large part, to the use of the ubuntu principle, the South African expression of prophetic postracism (Arthur, Issifu, & Marfo, 2015). This principle accounts for the need to address historical trauma while building toward a future of reconciliation.

Cornel West, author of *Democracy Matters: Winning the Fight against Imperialism*, describes similar success in the United States that resulted when populations defined by skin color and class collaborated: "The uniqueness of Lyndon Johnson was that he recognized that the interests of poor whites were the same as those of the vast majority of black people in America. . . . Under Roosevelt the organized power of working people was made legitimate and under Johnson one-half of all black people and elderly citizens (of all colors) were lifted out of poverty" (2004, p. 34). In this instance, the prophetic aspiration was the reduction of poverty achieved in part by a social movement that bridged class and race.

I imagine Obama, drawing on the notion of prophetic postracism, stating:

> We have made progress on the problem of race in the United States and we have much more to do. Our future progress will require working through the traumas of the past and creating in the present alliances and collaborations of those representing all the ancestries and populations in our country. We can point to the progress made in post-apartheid South Africa. The people of South Africa, following the leadership of Bishop Desmond Tutu and the South African Truth and Reconciliation Commission, are no longer hostile to each other; citizens of European ancestry recognize that their brothers and sisters of African ancestry may need redress; and all South Africans, irrespective of ancestry, understand that all the people of South Africa will need to join forces if progress is to be made.
>
> We can look at our own history as well. Presidents Roosevelt and Johnson recognized that poor people and those who have suffered because of their racial heritage have common interests because of the actions of the civil rights movements and advocates for the poor. We must remember that because of policies President Johnson initiated, some 50 percent of our African-American and elderly citizens were lifted out of the horrific state of poverty. We can have a grand vision of a society at ease with its kaleidoscope of ancestries and populations while insisting that we address the realities of race, gender, and class discrimination.

The establishment of prophetic postracialism as a commonplace along the lines outlined here might help address the problems Taylor identifies in the approach. Race, in this vision, becomes an accidental rather than an essential feature of the human being, and alliances of people from different ancestries will allow for the creation of policies that reduce inequality.

Touchstone Criticism and the Rhetoric of Racial Reconciliation

Barack Obama's 2008 race speech has entered the pantheon of great orations. The speech, beautifully written and delivered, does stand as an exemplar of rhetorical excellence. Using Campbell and Jameson's insights on touchstone criticism, I have attempted to imagine how the speech might have been buttressed and embellished to address the recurring need for racial reconciliation and the rise of Donald Trump. Toward this end, I have suggested the development of three commonplaces that forthrightly challenge the biological fact of race that Obama seems to assume, his restrictive sense of America's original sin, and the slippage between the realities of racism and the dream of a color-blind society. Emulating Campbell and Jameson's effort to imagine what Barbara Jordan might have said in her keynote address, I image what Obama might have argued in his race speech, building from these three commonplaces, while anticipating the concerns of Donald Trump's audience.

I would fully understand the objections that Obama and others might offer to my imaginaries, beginning with the commonplace of intersectional consilience. Our social world is more easily understood with one or two rather than multiple axes of identity (Atkin, 2016). Donald Trump's success was due to his ability to mobilize one axis: the white Republican audience. Yet the rhetorical challenge posed to those who seek racial reconciliation is to understand rather than to demonize this audience. The evidence suggests that the Clinton-Trump 2016 election cycle primed this audience to think in racial terms (Klein, 2016), an unfortunate outcome given that Trump won 194 of the 207 counties that had voted for Obama in 2008 or 2012 (Uhrmacher, Schaul, & Keating, 2017). Economic rather than racial issues were emphasized in the campaigns of 2008 and 2012. This audience of Obama-Trump voters, as the theory of intersectionality explains, has overlapping identities of race, gender, class, nationality, religion, and so on, that might harbor racist attitudes but vote for a candidate who is of color if economic arguments are featured. Those who speak to the white working class would need a rhetoric that recognizes and addresses its historic and economic traumas while binding all audiences to values it shares with other audiences (Vance, 2016).

The terms "ancestry" and "population clusters" that I have used in this chapter, which admittedly sound awkward, constitute my effort to collaborate with scientists to change the public language of race (Yudell et al., 2016). And the use of race language in social descriptions will continue irrespective of the biological and genetic research. To illustrate, Obama is a self-identified black man. In *Dreams from My Father*, Obama rejected the declarations made by his mixed-race friend "Joyce" that she did not need to choose to be black, or any other race, because she was multiracial (Obama, 1995, pp. 159–62). He made the choice to self-identify as black because of his concrete and striking experiences as a black man and to honor his ancestry and that of the civil rights movement. This is understandable given the prominent role race currently plays in our society. Over time, a rhetoric of racial reconciliation will need to deconstruct race as a biological reality, which would then liberate our thinking from the biologic essentialism at the heart of racism and embrace the truths of intersectionality.

Some might object to the expansion of America's original sin to include treatment of the white working class. This objection is reasonable given the historic trauma experienced by African Americans. Tavis Smiley, I believe, offers a proper corrective that places African American trauma both in perspective and alongside Native American trauma. In turn, the historic trauma suffered by poor whites, I argue, belongs in a rhetoric intended to foster racial reconciliation. The three traumas are different, but to recognize that they share the same origin, dehumanization, and then have taken different trajectories is to take in the full panorama of American history and oppression. By doing so, those who seek to create a rhetoric of reconciliation can reach out to multiple audiences at the same time. Obama was justly praised for addressing both black and white trauma in his speech, refusing to equate them and doing so on their own terms (Terrill, 2015); my criticisms and imagined improvements build from his humane insights.

Finally, the notion of prophetic postracialism introduces treacherous language. "The very idea of post-racialism," observes Taylor, "both presupposes and reinforces a racially circumscribed vision of race in the United States" (2016, p. 33). It can be used retrospectively, as John Roberts has done from the bench of the Supreme Court, to declare that all existing government programs must be color-blind, which elides the country's history of racism. And it can reinforce racism by stipulating, with the election of Obama and other advances, that the United States has conquered the problem of race. These are reasonable objections. Yet the adjective "prophetic" rules the noun "postracialism," and a host of African American scholars believe it is an adjective with power (Barnes & Robinson, 2014). At its best, prophetic postracialism juxtaposes the realities of racism with the promise of a society that does not make race essential to render justice and seek the remedies of legislation.

The tricky problem that prophetic postracialism does not directly address is class. In the aftermath of Donald Trump's election as president, the Democratic Party continued to struggle with the relationship between race and class (Levitz, 2016). Ultimately, it appears that a rhetoric and social policies designed to address race and class both separately and together will be needed. If so, the definition of prophetic postracialism will need to broaden to include an intersectional framework. Regardless, prophetic postracialism offers an avenue to racial reconciliation, which will require a coherent rhetoric and serial engagements between and among the various populations in this country. Both laboratory and field studies demonstrate that engagement, based on mutual understanding and contact with others, can reduce conflict and promote community (Lemmer & Wagner, 2015; Pettigrew & Tropp, 2006).

Obama ended his race speech with the story of Ashley and an elderly black man who were helping the Obama campaign, a story underscoring the importance of engagement and direct contact. Ashley, as Obama relates, attended because she had a parent who had suffered from cancer and wanted to support a candidate who would extend health insurance throughout the nation. When an elderly black man heard Ashley's reason, he told the gathering that he was there "because of Ashley." Obama concluded, "By itself, that single moment of recognition between that young white girl and that old black man is not enough . . . But it is where we start." And Obama's 2008 Philadelphia speech and his 2016 farewell address provide scholars and orators with commonplaces for the development of a rhetoric of racial reconciliation.

■ References

Alterman, E. (2016). The hole in Obama's legacy. *New Yorker*, August 12. Http://www.newyorker.com/news/news-desk/the-hole-in-obamas-legacy.

Arthur, D. D., Issifu, A. K., & Marfo, S. (2015). An analysis of the influence of ubuntu principle on the South Africa peace building process. *Journal of Global Peace and Conflict 3*, 63–77.

Atkin, A. (2016). Race, definition, and science. In *The Oxford handbook of philosophy and race*. N. Zack (ed.). Oxford: Oxford University Press, 139–49.

Barnes, S. L., & Robinson, Z. F. *Repositioning race: Prophetic research in a postracial Obama age*. Albany: State University of New York Press, 2014.

Bell, D. (1992). *Faces at the bottom of the well*. New York: NY Basic Books.

Bonham, V. L., Warshauer-Baker, E., & Collins, F. S. (2005). Race and ethnicity in the genome era: The complexity of the constructs. *American Psychologist 60*, 9–15.

Bright, L. K., Malinsky, D., & Thompson, M. (2016). Causally interpreting intersectionality theory. *Philosophy of Science 83*, 60–81.

Campbell, J. (2016). *Morning in South Africa*. Lanham, MD: Rowman & Littlefield.

Campbell, K. K., & Jamieson, K. M. (1979). *Form and genre: Shaping rhetorical action*. Falls Church, VA: Speech Communication Association.

Case, A., & Deaton, A. (2015). Rising morbidity and mortality in midlife among white non-Hispanic Americans in the 21st century. *Proceedings of the National Academy of Sciences 112*, 15078–83.

Cramer, K. J. (2016). *The politics of resentment: Rural consciousness in Wisconsin and the rise of Scott Walker*. Chicago: University of Chicago Press.

Crenshaw, K. (1989). Demarginalizing the intersection of race and sex: A black feminist critique of antidiscrimination doctrine, feminist theory and antiracist politics. *University of Chicago Law Forum 1*, 139–67.

Dreher, R. (2016). Trump: Tribune of poor white people. *American Conservative*, July 22. Http://www.theamericanconservative.com/dreher/trump-us-politics-poor-whites/.

Dyson, M. E. (2016). *The black presidency: Barack Obama and the politics of race in America*. Boston: Houghton Mifflin Harcourt.

Faulkner, W. (1975). Requiem for a nun. New York: Vintage Books.

Frank, D. A. (2009). The prophetic voice and the face of the other in Barack Obama's "A More Perfect Union" address, March 18, 2008. *Rhetoric & Public Affairs 12*, 167–94.

Frank, D. A., & McPhail, M. L. (2006). Barack Obama's address to the 2004 Democratic National Convention: Trauma, compromise, consilience, and the (im)possibility of racial reconciliation.

Rhetoric & Public Affairs 8, 571–93.

Graves, J. L. (2015). Great is their sin: Biological determinism in the age of genomics. *Annals of the American Academy of Political and Social Science 661*, 24–50.

Hancock, A.-M. (2016). *Intersectionality: An intellectual history*. New York: Oxford University Press.

Hill Collins, P., & Bilge, S. (2016). *Intersectionality*. Malden, MA: Polity Press.

Hochschild, A. R. (2016). *Strangers in their own land: Anger and mourning on the American right*. New York: New Press.

Isenberg, N. (2016). *White trash: The 400-year untold history of class in America*. New York: Viking.

Johnston-Guerrero, M., & Tran, V. (2016). Born this way? U.S. college students make sense of the biosocial underpinnings of race and other identities. *International Journal of Multicultural Education 18*, 107–24.

Khanna, N., & Harris, C. A. (2009). Teaching race as a social construction: Two interactive class exercises. *Teaching Sociology 37*, 369–78.

Klein, E. (2016). The hard question isn't why Clinton lost—it's why Trump won. *Vox*, November 11. Http://www.vox.com/policy-and-politics/2016/11/11/13578618/why-did-trump-win.

Lacapra, D. (2014). *Writing history, writing trauma*. Baltimore: Johns Hopkins University Press.

———. (2016). Trauma, history, memory, identity: What remains? *History and Theory 55*, 375–400.

Lemmer, G., & Wagner, U. (2015). Can we really reduce ethnic prejudice outside the lab? A meta-analysis of direct and indirect contact interventions. *European Journal of Social Psychology 45*, 152–68.

Levitz, E. (2016). What Bernie Sanders gets right about identity politics. *New York*, December 1. Http://nymag.com/daily/intelligencer/2016/12/what-bernie-sanders-gets-right-about-identity-politics.html.

Lewontin, R. C. (1972). The apportionment of human diversity. In *Evolutionary Biology*. New York: Springer, 381–98.

Nabokov, P. (2016). Indians, slaves, and mass murder: The hidden history. *New York Review of Books*, November 24. Http://www.nybooks.com/articles/2016/11/24/indians-slaves-and-mass-murder-the-hidden-history/.

Newcomb, S. T. (2008). *Pagans in the promised land: Decoding the doctrine of Christian discovery*. Golden, CO: Fulcrum Publishing.

Obama, B. (1995). *Dreams from my father: A story of race and inheritance*. New York: Times Books.

———. (2016). A more perfect union. Http://www.americanrhetoric.com/speeches/barackobamaperfectunion.htm.

———. (2017a). Presidential farewell address. Http://www.americanrhetoric.com/speeches/barackobama/barackobamafarewelladdress.htm.

———. (2017b). Eulogy for Clementa Pinckney. Http://www.americanrhetoric.com/speeches/barackobama/barackobamaclementapinckneyeulogy.htm.

Perelman, C., & Olbrechts-Tyteca, L. (1969). *The new rhetoric: A treatise on argumentation*. Notre Dame, IN: University of Notre Dame Press.

Pettigrew, T. F., & Tropp, L. R. (2006). A meta-analytic test of intergroup contact theory. *Journal of Personality and Social Psychology 90*, 751–83.

Rothwell, J. T., & and Diego-Rosell, P. (2016). Explaining nationalist political views: The case of Donald

Trump. Http://dx.doi.org/10.2139/ssrn.2822059.

Rowland, R. C., & Jones, J. M. (2011). One dream: Barack Obama, race, and the American dream. *Rhetoric & Public Affairs 14*, 125–54.

Scott, J. (2008). Obama chooses reconciliation over rancor. *New York Times*, March 19. Http://www.nytimes.com/2008/03/19/us/politics/19assess.html.

Smiley, T. (2016). Author Jim Wallis. February 16. Http://www.pbs.org/wnet/tavissmiley/interviews/author-jim-wallis/.

South African Institute of Race Relations. (2016). *Race relations in South Africa: Reasons for hope.* Johannesburg, SA.

Taylor, P. C. (2016). *On Obama: Thinking in action.* New York: Routledge Taylor & Francis Group.

Terrill, R. (2015). *Double-consciousness and the rhetoric of Barack Obama: The price and promise of citizenship.* Columbia: University of South Carolina Press.

Uhrmacher, K., Schaul, K., & Keating, D. (2017). These former Obama strongholds sealed the election for Trump. *Washington Post*, November 9. Https://www.washingtonpost.com/graphics/politics/2016-election/obama-trump-counties/.

Vance, J. D. (2016). *Hillbilly elegy: A memoir of a family and culture in crisis.* New York: Harper.

West, C. (1993). *Race matters.* Boston: Beacon Press.

———. (2004). *Democracy matters: Winning the fight against imperialism.* New York: Penguin.

Yudell, M., Roberts, D., DeSalle, R., & Tishkoff, S. (2016). Taking race out of human genetics. *Science 351*, 564–65.

 VIGNETTE

History teaches Black men that they are nothing more than uneducated savages, and American systems often set them up for failure. Ronnie almost became a statistic because of this mentality. Many of his family members made fun of him when he spoke "like a White person." Despite being ridiculed for acting White, Ronnie knew that he wanted to go to college. However, when he was older, Ronnie was stuck in a place where he couldn't advance to more than a minimum wage job, and had to work multiple minimum wage jobs to be able to go to school full time and make ends meet. Born into an environment that told him, historically, Black men are set up to fail, Ronnie almost fell into this type of thinking. However, he met a teacher named Mr. Spencer, who helped him reset his focus on many things. Mr. Spencer became a mentor and provided Ronnie with advice he did not get elsewhere. Today, because someone stepped in and offered support, Ronnie has an advanced degree and has moved onto a comfortable and happy life and career.

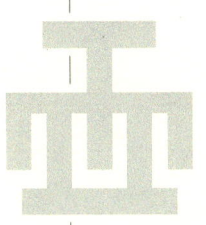

PART 2

Research and Research Trends

INTRODUCTION

Darryl B. Holloman and Corey D. Givens

In a seminal poem, Paul Laurence Dunbar intones that Black Americans wear masks. He reflects, "We wear the mask that grins and lies, / It hides our cheeks and shades our eyes" (1898, p. 167). Dunbar implies that Black Americans during the nineteenth century guarded aspects of their identities to protect themselves from the harsh realities of their lived experiences. These aspects of hidden identities, which are shielded by opulent masks, can be viewed as applicable to the experiences of Black men in America today. Scholars and researchers have found that capturing the experiences of Black men can be troublesome. Attempts to investigate the journeys of Black men, whether in, between, or outside of school settings, provide complex investigative outcomes. These layered outcomes, or the lack of specific answers to the continued questions that arise from these investigations, have led to even more scholarly inquiry. Hence, the need to continue lines of inquiry that not only raise questions concerning the experiences of Black men but provide answers that seek to address the societal challenges that these men face. This part of the Handbook, "Research and Research Trends," seeks to investigate and expose the multiplicity found within the Black male diaspora in America.

The intent of this part, in conjunction with the overall goals of the Handbook, is to highlight how varied the experiences of Black men can be. Within empirical research, homogeneity has its benefits. Homogeneity provides a snapshot of a group of subjects in order to apply meanings that are applicable across broad spectrums of those being investigated. Homogeneity allows for a clearer means to generalize research findings in attempts to answer questions on large scales. Research, however, should also be conducted that serves to do the opposite. There are moments when we raise investigative questions that explore the spaces inhabited myopically by the individual. The goal of this part is to combine both of these approaches in the difficult task of addressing what it means to be Black, male, and American.

This part encompasses works that move toward investigating why Black men think, react, and respond in the ways that they do. The contributors to this part have written chapters that work toward dismantling the social construct of Black masculinity. Each contributor chose topics and explored research that provides insight into how complex and incongruent the varied experiences of Black men are.

The chapter by Michell Temple, Teresita Warren, and Michael Anderson expands on the multiplicity found within the Black male experience by challenging us to rethink how disabilities, or the lack of research on this topic, encompass the varied dynamics of Black Male identity. This chapter reveals that although there is a plethora of research on Black males and research on individuals with disabilities each class of inquiry conducted independently of the other, few researchers have worked to cross-tabulate these two critical areas. With the significant challenges often presented in reference to education and Black males, investigating the intersection of Black males who may have a disability could provide answers in addressing those challenges. Such an approach to this combined inquiry would support the research of scholars, such as Terrell Strayhorn and Shawn Harper, who have challenged researchers to examine Black male identities and spaces in more complex ways.

The chapters by Jeffrey Coleman and by Robert Bryant and Georj Lewis present research on Black men, a group on which research continues to expand. Researchers since the seminal works of Jaqueline Fleming and Michael J. Cuyjet have challenged us to understand that Black men continue to be a group that needs extensive investigation. For the last thirty years, scholars have presented research that has raised multiple questions concerning the impact of education on the experiences of Black men. What we now see emerging in the scholarship are skilled scholar-practitioners who seek to not only raise their own set of questions, but provide practical, applicable solutions to address those questions. This practical approach is found in the work of these scholars. Coleman seeks not only to contribute to the literature on Black men but, through his investigation of a program targeting this group, to identify implications that impact the retention, progression, and graduation of these men. Coleman also examines how institutional commitment, or the lack thereof, hinders the progression of Black men at our colleges and universities. Coleman challenges institutions to understand the societal importance of ensuring that they invest in these men and their success within higher education. Bryant and Lewis examine the significance of Black men who work as either diversity professionals or senior executives within higher education. These scholars explore how these professionals often endure various levels of being marginalized not only as Black men but as men whose roles in their chosen fields are often devalued. Through the narrative of Black men who serve as chief diversity officers (CDOs), these researchers reveal the journeys of men who themselves are often the champions, and sometimes the only bastions, of diversity on their campuses. Bryant and Lewis discuss how these Black male CDOs find place and purpose within work that is important to their campuses but often underfunded, devalued, and under constant threat of being eliminated. The men who serve as senior-level administrators are often challenged to demonstrate the scope and impact their work has on their campuses. These men speak of being "second-guessed" routinely and feel compelled to develop coping strategies that help them navigate unwelcoming political, social, and emotional environments. The investigation of CDOs and senior executives reveals the journey of men who often face isolation within their careers. These researchers reflect the experience of men who are often the only senior Black male executives on their campuses. They reveal how Black men, even as university presidents, are unable to establish networks or find mentors in their efforts to be successful in their work.

Tomeka Davis and Theodore Greene in their respective chapters examine the experiences of Black men outside the sphere of higher education. One of our purposes as the editors of this part was to seek scholars who conducted work outside of colleges and universities because we believe that only through an investigation of the Black male continuum do we effectively resolve the challenges faced by Black men in America. To undertake a cradle-to-grave approach in the investigation of Black men provides insight into how these men develop and respond to their existence over time. Many things influence Black men before, after, and outside of higher education, and those things need to be investigated without isolated parameters that are set by only investigating men who have attended college. Tomeka Davis challenges the assumptions that Black boys do not thrive in school because of their behaviors. Using data from the Early Childhood Longitudinal Study, Davis analyzes data through growth curve modeling to examine the impact of family, school, and neighborhoods on the academic achievement of Black boys. Using such a comprehensive approach to examine the educational lives of Black boys provides insight into how they develop, and how that development, good and bad, has an influence on their classroom engagement. Davis further compares these factors on the academic trajectories of other race-gender groups, which similar to Martell's work, does not hold Black male experiences in isolation of other groups. Utilizing research methodologies and designs that compare the results of Black men and boys with other groups situates their experiences within a framework that helps to diminish a sense of "victim" status and provides opportunities to delve further into the complexity of the Black male experiences in relations to the others that share Black male spaces.

Theodore Greene delves into discussions surrounding Black male sexuality that few researchers broach. Greene, through ethnographic methods, explores the lived experiences of gay, bisexual, and queer (GBQ) men of color in gay neighborhoods. This work is critical to the continuation of the discussion concerning exposure to the myriad of experiences that shape the lives of Black men, but more importantly it exposes us to the lived experiences of men who sleep with men. This perceivedly taboo topic is oftentimes completely absent from the discussions on the sexuality of Black men. The discussion of gay, bisexual, and queer Black men is most times discussed in generalities with heterosexual Black men, but few researchers, outside of Terrell Strayhorn's work, have specifically situated Black men directly within the LGBT realm on their own terms. Such illustrious work on the specific experiences of LGBT Black men is important because it not only highlights the experiences of these men but humanizes them. Research such as the study done by Greene removes the caricatures that at times have materialized in contemporary pop culture on the topic of LGBT men of color. Much like the misnomers associated with the "mammy" caricatures that were prevalent at the turn of the century and their distorting influence on the lived experiences of Black women, these pop culture mediums have fit Black men into spheres that may not fully represent this group. These mediums, which reflect LGBT Black men as overly effeminate, or hypersexual, or overtly masculine, images that are probably evident within aspects of the Black LGBT community, should not be the only viable descriptions presented. Greene's work shows Black LGBT males as vibrant members of their social and political communities, as Dunbar exclaims, "Masters of their own destinies" (1898, p. 167). Greene further examines and presents the idea that gay men are a monolithic group as he discusses the racial tensions and systemic racisms that can exist between Black and White members of the LGBT communities. Through rich and descriptive language that captures the spirit of his participants, Greene's discussion of race and place within the LGBT communities explores a topic that few researchers have the inclination (or skill) to expound upon.

This was a very meaningful journey for us in pulling together such intense and varied contributors, who research the lived experiences of Black men. In keeping with our academic practices, where we attempt to provide a platform for a wide range of voices within academia, you will find a range within this chapter that spans from budding researcher to seasoned scholar. It is important to explore a range of academic talent because our field often only seems to rely on the information purported by advanced scholars, which although informative, does not always bring a fresh, new perspective to research paradigms.

We personally would like to thank each of the contributors for agreeing to take this journey to present their work in such a comprehensive way.

This collection of work elevates the discussions of Black men and their lived experiences because the work demonstrates their lives on a continuum. The works collectively examine Black men and boys through lenses that takes them out of isolation and position them, through research method, research design, or research methodology, in a worldview. Taking this bird's-eye view of the Black male experience helps to highlight the multiplicity of Black male experiences and forces us to think of Black men in ways other than tangential approaches. Only through viewing Black men in holistic ways can we ever hope to fulfill the prophesy of Paul Dunbar, who concluded, "Why should the world be over-wise, / In counting all our tears and sighs? / Nay, let them only see us, while we wear the mask" (1898, p. 167).

■ **Reference**

Dunbar, P. (1898). *Lyrics of Lowly Life*. New York: Dodd, Mead.

Black Male College Students with Disabilities

The Role of Self-Determination in College Completion

Michell L. Temple, Teresita Warren, and J. Michael Anderson

The research presented in this chapter was the result of the authors' desire to improve their practices as disability services professionals in higher education. The inquiry into current literature begins with the intent to answer the primary research question: How does self-determination influence the college completion rates of Black males with disabilities?

After a thorough search by the authors of available literature, it was discovered that there is sparse research available on the subject concerning the college completion of Black males with disabilities. Studies that focus on the retention, persistence, and graduation rates among Black males or among people with disabilities in colleges and universities were plenteous. Moreover, research that described and explored self-determination with these groups was also readily available. A closer review of the literature focusing on persons with disabilities in higher education determined that studies were likely to include Black men because studies typically reported demographics of participants by race, gender, diagnosis, or type of disability. A similar review of the demographic descriptions of participants was conducted on the literature that targeted Black men. The authors noted that these studies described participants by race, age, and academic characteristics, but not disability status. Consequently, the authors concluded that they could not conduct a literature review that would result in an answer to the overarching selected research question.

To continue this course of inquiry, the authors selected as their framework "intersectionality," as coined by Crenshaw in 1989. Intersectionality synthesizes and draws inferences from the review of categorical research about the role of self-determination in the ability of Black males with disabilities to complete college. Intersectionality proposes that "human beings are shaped by the interaction of different social locations, such as race/ethnicity, indigeneity, gender, class, sexuality, geography, age, disability/ability, migration status, religion" (Hankivsky, 2004, p. 2). Based on the use of intersectionality, two additional research questions were added:

1. What are the barriers to college completion for Black males and people with disabilities?
2. What role does self-determination have in the ability of Black males and people with disabilities to complete college?

The review of relevant research begins by providing a demographic overview and then defining self-determination and its researched relevance to higher education generally, and groups specifically. Next, we identify the barriers to college completion for Black males and people with disabilities. Then comparisons are made between the perspectives of self-determination, the barriers to college completion, and the role of self-determination by group through the lens of intersectionality to answer the primary research question.

Overview of the Demographic and Graduation Landscape of Higher Education

The term *diversity* on college campuses has broadened to include race, ethnicity, sex, nation of origin, and disability (Temple, 2015). The total fall enrollment of all degree-granting institutions from 2000 to 2014 reflects a dramatic shift in enrollment numbers, with Hispanics showing the largest percentage increase, 119 percent. Black enrollment increased by 57 percent during the same period. The lowest percentage increase was for Caucasians or Whites, 7 percent (Kena et al., 2016).

The shift in enrollment based on gender from 1976 to 2012 and the inclusion of people with disabilities also illustrate the changing demographic landscape. The percentage of eighteen- to twenty-four-year-olds attending college increased from 19.2 percent of women and 33.1 percent of men in 1976 to 44.5 percent of women and 37.6 percent of men in 2012. However, students with disabilities were not identified as such in 1976. In 1978 only 3 percent of undergraduate college students self-identified as having a disability, and by 1998 that number had tripled to 9 percent (Kober, 2002). The number increased again in 2003 to 11 percent, decreased slightly in 2008 to 10.9 percent. Then in 2012, the number returned near its 2003 level at 11.1 percent (US Department of Education, 2016). Graduation rates from postsecondary education are vastly disparate based on gender, race, and ethnicity.

Graduation Rates

GENDER
Women exceeded men in the percentage of degrees attained regardless of institutional type. DeAngelo et al. (2011) analyzed 2004 Cooperative Institutional Research Program (CIRP) Freshman Survey National Student Clearinghouse (NCS) data and found that women who graduated

from four-year public colleges and religious four-year colleges at rates of 52.7 percent and 62.4 percent, respectively, while men graduated from these same types of colleges at rates of 45.3 percent and 52.1 percent. Additionally, Kena et al. (2016) found that 50 percent of women who were between the ages of twenty-five and twenty-nine had earned their associates degree or higher, compared to 41.9 percent of males in the same age group.

RACE AND ETHNICITY

Research shows that Asian American and White students earn an associate or a bachelor's degree in four years at double the rate of Blacks (DeAngela et al., 2011). Asian American and Caucasian students had the highest rate of four-year degree completion (44.9 percent and 42.6 percent respectively), whereas the rates for Latino/a (25.8 percent), Black (21.0 percent), and American Indian (16.8 percent) students were considerably lower (DeAngelo et al., 2011). A similar gap was noted by Kena et al. (2016): in 2015, 31 percent of Blacks between the ages of twenty-five and twenty-nine had earned an associate's degree or higher, compared to 54 percent of Caucasians.

BLACK'S GRADUATION RATES BY GENDER

Based on current research it is evident that Blacks as a group lag behind other underrepresented groups in terms of college enrollment and completion. Harvey (2008) indicated that of the 73.7 percent of Black males who finished high school in 2000, only 33.8 percent enrolled in college. Among Black females in this period, 79.7 percent completed high school, and 43.9 percent of this group enrolled in college. Using information acquired from Mortenson Research Seminar in 2001, Strayhorn (2012) indicated that Black males made up 4 percent of the total undergraduate population and that only 30 percent attained their college degree. Specifically, Harper (2006) found that two-thirds of Black males enrolled in four-year institutions do not graduate within six years.

DISABILITY STATUS

According to the US Department of Education (2013), more students with disabilities are enrolling in college after they graduate from high school. In 2003, among persons with disabilities ages fifteen to twenty-three, nearly 47 percent were attending college. Then, in 2008–9, the enrollment of the age group with disabilities increased to over 52 percent, an increase that substantially closed the gap between students without disabilities, with a college enrollment rate of 59 percent. Yet, as noted earlier, people with disabilities comprised approximately 11 percent of students in postsecondary education in 2003, 2008, and 2012.

Students with disabilities are still underrepresented in postsecondary settings, but it is predicted that college enrollment of students with disabilities will continue to increase (Mamiseishvili & Koch, 2010). However, Mamiseishvili and Koch (2010) did not report the graduation rates of people with disabilities separately. According to the American Community Survey of 2013, of the 3.5 million possible working-age (eighteen to sixty-four) respondents who completed the survey, only 13.5 percent of people with disabilities reported earning a bachelor's degree or higher, compared to 32.1 percent of people without disabilities (Erickson, Lee, & von Schrader, 2014). These statistics are in stark contrast to the reported percentages of persons with disabilities and those without disabilities who attained some college or an associate's degree, 30.4 percent and 32.3 percent, respectively with a margin of error of 9% for all data (Erikson et al., 2014). These data suggest that the graduation rates from bachelor's degree programs for students with disabilities is significantly lower than for students without disabilities, whereas rates of attending college are relatively similar for the two groups..

Although more persons from diverse backgrounds are entering and graduating from college, the research suggests that there are barriers to degree attainment for Black males and people with disabilities. In the next section, we will define self-determination, describe its purpose, and review relevant research. We then discuss the categorical literature available about self-determination in higher education as well as the barriers to college completion for Black men and people with disabilities.

What Is Self-Determination?

Self-determination is a lifelong developmental task that represents the skills and attitudes that empower people to choose (Ryan & Deci, 1985). Research indicates that self-determination serves as a source of human motivation and empowerment that can be used to explain the purpose of a person's behaviors, thoughts, and feelings about himself and the social and physical environment (Wehmeyer, 1999; Ryan & Deci, 2000). As a macrotheory of human motivation, self-determination theory (SDT) addresses such basic issues as personality development, self-regulation, universal psychological needs, life goals and aspirations, energy and vitality, nonconscious processes, the relations of culture to motivation, and the impact of social environments on motivation, affect, behavior, and well-being (Deci & Ryan, 2008).

Ryan and Deci (2000) describe the scale of human motivation as a continuum from motivated to amotivated that is influenced by two distinct types of motivation: intrinsic and extrinsic. Intrinsic motivation (IM) reflects the innate affirmative propensity of people to expand and apply their capacities to explore and to learn. IM embodies the cognitive behavioral measure of "free choice" that can be facilitated or undermined by social and environmental factors. Extrinsic motivation (EM) refers to an action that is done to secure a result that is external from the person. The person does not perceive the action or activity as innately enjoyable, but engages in the activity to obtain some other outcome. EM relates to an "other," whether human or thing. Intrinsic and extrinsic motivation are catalyzed into action by an essential desire to meet three basic psychological needs of autonomy, competence, and relatedness. Autonomy defines a person's perception of his or her behaviors as self-selected or chosen. Competence describes a person's capacity to think, feel, and behave within social contexts, through rewards, communication, and feedback. Relatedness refers to a person's sense of belonging to a community based on similar goals or desired behaviors.

Research suggests that a person's ability to behave in a self-determined manner is influenced by opportunity (Deci et al., 1991; Ryan & Deci, 2000; Reeves, 2002) and disability (Murray, Lomardi, & Kosty, 2014; Garrison-Wade, 2012; Getzel, 2008; Wehmeyer, 1999; Field, Sarver, & Shaw, 2003). Specifically, the person's default belief about his ability to control or manage his life and resultant behaviors appear to be a product of environments that either thwart or cultivate self-determination through satisfying or depleting a person's desire to meet the three basic psychological needs (Ryan & Deci, 2000). Beliefs about self-efficacy influence motivation and a person's ability to achieve selected goals (Reeves, 2002; Ryan & Deci, 2000).

How Might a Person Behave According to SDT?

Self-determination research consistently proposes that a person who has experienced a social environment that nurtured his self-determination may exhibit more autonomous behavior as well as integrated or identified self-management behaviors. Integrative regulatory behaviors are those that are integral to a person's sense of self. Identified regulatory behaviors are more congruent with one's personal values and identities, but not fully internalized (Deci et al., 1991; Ryan & Deci, 2000; Jenkins-Guanrieri, Vaughn, & Wright 2015).

Conversely, research suggests that individuals who have experienced a social environment that inhibited the development of self-determination may lack self-direction and may exhibit an introjected or external regulation style. Introjected regulatory behavior refers to a person's desire to engage in a behavior or goal to affirm himself or receive accolades. Similarly, external regulation reflects the perception that activities are performed with a feeling of pressure, for example, to avoid guilt or anxiety or to build a sense of self-worth (Deci et al., 1991; Ryan & Deci, 2000, Jenkins-Guanrieri et al., 2015).

Why Does Self-Determination Matter in Higher Education?

When applied to educational settings, SDT is primarily concerned with the promotion of students' interest in learning and the valuation of education. Additionally, SDT implemented within educational settings cultivates the students' confidence in their own capacities and attributes (Deci et al., 1991).

Reeves (2002) cites twenty years of empirical research on the reliable and valid application of SDT in K–12 settings, and Jenkins-Guanrieri, Vaughn, and Wright (2015) in their development of a self-determination measure for college students cite fifteen years of empirical research within postsecondary educational settings. The two conclusions about SDT and educational settings that may be drawn from these bodies of research state that (1) students' intrinsic motivation influences their ability to achieve academically, thrive socially, manage challenges, and be creative, and (2) students' extrinsic motivation appears to resemble integrated or identified regulatory style when academic and social environments support their autonomy. The research described in this chapter focused on the first conclusion.

What Are Perspectives on Self-Determination in Black Males?

Two perspectives on self-determination in Black males were identified in the relevant research, "somebodiness" (Johnson, 2016) and "cult of anti-intellectualism" (Cokley, 2003). The first perspective, "somebodiness, is an innate desire in the psychological functioning of Black men; without a deep sense of somebodiness, the feeling of being incapable may rise to full maturity (Johnson, 2016). Johnson (as cited by White and Cones, 1999), indicated that somebodiness is concerned with self-determination, self-definition, self-acceptance, and self-love that the subject needs in order to feel like everyone else (2016). The second perspective investigated what McWhorter identified as a cultural trait among Blacks that he called a "cult of anti-intellectualism," which associates academic achievements and learning for learning's sake as "acting White" (Cokley, 2003). This victimhood ideology, according to McWhorter, leads Black students to not try as hard as students from other ethnic groups because they believe they are victims of discrimination.

What Are the Perspectives on Self-Determination in People with Disabilities?

Wehmeyer's (1999) functional model of self-determination appears prominently in the relevant research (Getzel & Thoma, 2008; Zheng et al., 2014). The model has been used as a framework for educators and counselors to develop and implement interventions to promote self-determination for people with and without disabilities. Wehmeyer defined self-determination as "acting as the primary causal agent in one's life and making choices and decisions regarding one's quality of life free from undue external influences or interference" (p. 56). Moreover, his research described self-determined behavior as a person's perceived freedom and intent behind the action. Wehmeyer indicated that acting autonomously, under one's control and desire, and with purposeful intent to interact with one's environment, is an essential characteristic of self-determined behavior. Wehmeyer operationalized these dispositional characteristics into component elements that include but are not limited to "choice-making, goal-setting, self-advocacy and leadership, internal locus of control, positive attributions of efficacy and outcome expectancy" (p. 59). Research has suggested that Black men and people with disabilities who are self-determined are more successful in college (Field, Sarver, & Shaw, 2003). However, research has also identified barriers to degree attainment for these groups.

What Are Barriers to Degree Attainment for Black Men and People with Disabilities?

Researchers have postulated many factors that serve as barriers that impede Black males from enrolling in higher education institutions and subsequently earning their degrees. Black male college students are labeled in the literature as disengaged (Harper, 2012) and academic underachievers (Wood & Ireland, 2014; Bush & Bush, 2014). Descriptors such as endangered, dysfunctional, lazy, and uneducable are often used to describe members of this group. When these negative stereotypes are internalized, research suggests, a sense of self-doubt and lower self-esteem results, which impacts Black males' ability to persist toward college completion (Palmer et al., 2010; Majors & Billson, 1992; Parham & McDavis, 1987; Jackson & Moore, 2006, 2008; Strayhorn, 2008).

Strayhorn (2012) argued that many Black males are academically unprepared for postsecondary education. He also indicated that as a result of their low socioeconomic status, Black males have financial responsibilities that differ from their counterparts, compromising their education commitment.

What Will People Say about Me and My Disability?

According to Kowalsky and Fresko (2002), students with disabilities are faced with a plethora of difficulties in college, such as low self-esteem, lack of content preparation, and not mastering efficient learning strategies needed to perform academically. Seemingly, these challenges create conditions that have lowered peers' and faculty's expectations of what students with disabilities will contribute to their social and academic environments (Garrison-Wade, 2012).

Moreover, Murray and Naranjo inferred (as cited by Luthar, 2006; Wagner, Newman, & Cameto, 2004; US Census Bureau, 2013) that American youth with disabilities from low-income backgrounds are vulnerable to a range of negative outcomes that can be further exacerbated by exposure to additional factors such as risks within the family, deviant peer affiliations, and poor-quality schools (2008).

How Are Some Black Men and People with Disabilities Able to Complete College?

Because of the broad experiences that these two subgroups of college students encounter, research has not assigned one set of factors to achievers, but research implies that self-determination has contributed to these two groups' successful college completion. Self-determination appears to explain the strategies of Black men and people with disabilities to manage the barriers encountered in college.

The Role of Self-Determination in Black Males' Ability to Complete College

Research suggested that Black males who demonstrated self-determination from the "somebodiness" (Johnson, 2016) perspective and were able to reject the cult of anti-intellectualism (Cokley, 2003) were more likely to attain a college degree. Black males who behaved in a self-determined manner appeared to have opportunities to act autonomously, practice and learn strategies needed to navigate a variety of social settings, and relate to a community that has goals and desires that are aligned with their own. A review of relevant research reveals three themes that reflect the role of self-determination in Black males' ability to complete college: those who succeeded identified and utilized support systems, got involved on campus, and benefited from an engagement with faculty.

SUPPORT SYSTEMS

Parental and familial guidance to purse a college education attributed to the success of Black male college students (Harper, 2012). The study findings suggest that the participants chose particular institutions based upon family members who attended a particular institution and teachers and other educational professional who took a personal interest in their success. Additionally, a group of the participants also credited their success in college to connecting with same-race peers.

Similarly, the results of a qualitative 2015 study completed by Harrison, Martin, and Fuller framed within the tenets (competence, autonomy, and relatedness) of SDT suggested that Black male student-athletes who demonstrated high levels of autonomous behavior concerning their own college experience demonstrated a tenacity that helped them to excel academically. The study found that these students recognized that interactions with college resources such as fraternities, teammates, classmates, and members of the campus community at-large played a pivotal role in the facilitation of their autonomous demeanor and fulfillment of their aspirations.

INVOLVEMENT ON CAMPUS

In Harper's (2012) *Black Male Student Success in Higher Education: A Report from the National Black Male College Achievement Study*, the participants indicated that their ability to successfully traverse campus environments that were racially intense, participation in opportunities to become involved on campus and assume leadership roles, and their affiliation with pre-college programs were all contributing factors they utilized to navigate their course toward degree attainment and success. Additionally, participating in college from the "somebodiness" perspective seemed to allow participants in Harper's (2012) study to respond productively to racism because they were able to choose to use those moments constructively to dispel negative stereotypes or biased assumptions.

Becoming engaged on college campus is widely accepted as one of the contributing factors that leads to persistence. "We know one thing for certain: Students who are actively engaged in educationally purposeful activities and experiences, both inside and outside the classroom, are more likely than are their disengaged peers to persist through graduation" (Harper & Quaye, 2009, p. 4).

ENGAGEMENT WITH FACULTY

In a study completed by Wood and Turner (2010), they discovered that Black male college students attributed their academic success to having a positive engagement with faculty. The participants in the study indicated that the personal attention exemplified by faculty who were concerned for their overall academic success, actively listened to students' concerns, assisted with problem-solving their issues surrounding academic performance, and encouraged and believed in their ability to be successful contributed to their willingness to approach faculty and seek help when needed. Faculty's friendly demeanor contributed liberally to the students' willingness to engage with faculty and provided the students with a sense that someone was concerned about them and was invested in seeing their dream of a college degree realized. Moreover, Harper (2012) found that Black males perceived that opportunities to interact with faculty promoted an internal drive to be academically successful. Participants in the study indicated that those interactions placed them in positions to network with other academically talented students, which further supported their academic success.

The Role of Self-Determination on the Ability of People with Disabilities to Complete College

Study findings suggests that people with disabilities who are able to perceive themselves as self-determined and then demonstrate self-determined behaviors complete college. College students with disabilities who exhibit the essential behaviors of self-determination persisted in college in a study by Getzel and Thoma (2008). Getzel and Thoma found that postsecondary education students who registered with the disability services office in two- and four-year college settings perceived the following self-determination skills were imperative as they progressed and persisted to graduation: problem-solving, understanding one's disability, goal setting, and self-management. The study further revealed that effective self-advocacy skills played a critical role as students sought needed support services.

Another study conducted by Zheng, Erickson, Kingston, and Noonan (2014) concluded that for students with learning disabilities, self-determination was a predictor of academic achievement. Specifically, Zheng et al.'s study determined that study participants were more likely to sustain intensive efforts to learn challenging academic content, capitalize on their strengths, and take ownership of their actions. The study also found that male students with learning disabilities who were self-determined had higher academic achievement than their female counterparts.

A final study by Murray et al. (2014) concluded that college students with disabilities who were categorized as average and highly adjusted students demonstrated a greater capacity to self-advocate. The study also proposed that these students held positive beliefs about their ability to complete college, and were able to engage in meaningful relationships with family, peers, and other figures of authority. Research seemed to conclude that a self-determined perspective and behaviors motivated college students with disabilities to self-advocate, request and use accommodations and academic supports, and establish and sustain familial and peer relationships to achieve their educational goal.

SELF-ADVOCACY

The ability to speak up for what you want and need and is an expectation in college (Schreiner, 2007; Murray et al., 2014). It is also an essential skill for students with disabilities. Those students who are not able to advocate for themselves face challenges that could have been avoided if they had developed self-advocacy skills at an earlier age. Schreiner (2007) and Murray et al. (2014) noted that self-advocacy begins when students understand their strengths, abilities, and needs.

ACCOMMODATIONS AND ACADEMIC SUPPORTS

As Kowalsky and Fresko note (2002), support services are being provided to students with disabilities in many institutions of higher education. Enabling students to gain access to and make progress in the education curriculum has become a core requirement of federal laws governing educational services for students with disabilities. As described by Wade and Lehmann (2009), federal laws such as the Individuals with Disabilities Education Act of 2004, Section 504 of the Rehabilitation Act of 1973, and the Americans with Disabilities Act (1990 and 2004) have been influential in creating more opportunities for students with disabilities to enter into and complete postsecondary education. These federal mandates require support for disabled students to implement their future educational goals.

Peer tutoring has generally resulted in positive outcomes for disability students in academia (Zheng et al., 2014). As stated by Kowalsky and Fresko (2002) a review of peer tutoring in higher education has shown different forms of tutoring to be effective with respect to achievement gains, reduced stress, graduation outcomes, and dropout rates.

SUPPORT SYSTEMS

Having family and friends as part of their supports systems contributed to the success of students with disabilities. According to Wade (2009), a family provides care, warmth, protection and support. Parental support was found to be an effective protective factor (Wade, 2009). Families played a major influence in the creation of a vision for the student's future. Family involvement in the transition-planning process also had an impact on the student's self-determination.

Another support system for students with disabilities was friendship. Besides parents, friends were considered potential resources because adolescents tend to seek peer support when they encounter troubles (Getzel, 2008). Maintaining a steady circle of friends while in college helped create a sense of belonging. Having friends made college easier for students with disabilities because it made them feel like everyone else, gave them a sense of determination to do well in classes, and allowed them to compete as peers with other students.

The research literature has identified perspectives of self-determination, barriers to college completion, and the role of self-determination in the ability of Black men and people with disabilities to complete college. However, there appears to be limited research on the subgroup of Black male college students with disabilities. To provide a description of the Black male college student with a disability, we conducted a comparative summary of the research findings through the lens of intersectionality (Hankivsky, 2004) to provide an answer to the primary research question: How does self-determination influence the college completion rates of Black males with disabilities?

Thinking of Black Males with Disabilities in College

Black males and people with disabilities are capable of self-determined thoughts, feelings, and actions. The relevant research implied that the developmental of self-determination in these two groups results from the influence of the social environments' cultivating opportunities that promoted a capable perception of self and others.

Research suggested that Black males could exhibit a productive or unproductive manifestation of self-determination, somebodiness (Johnson, 2016) or a cult of anti-intellectualism (Cokley, 2003). The vantage point by which a Black male perceived his ability to choose his behaviors seemed contingent upon the social environment that nurtured his beliefs about self-efficacy and people from a different race.

Somebodiness (Johnson, 2016) appeared to be linked to allowing Black males to behave autonomously, demonstrate competence, and relate to community. Additionally, the perspective of self-determination seemed to promote and sustain intrinsic motivation in Black males. Conversely, the cult of anti-intellectualism (Cokely, 2003) perspective did not appear to allow Black males to satisfy the three basic psychological needs that drive self-determination. Black males could competently "try less hard at their academics" to avoid "acting White" to relate to a group of Blacks who believe that historical discrimination is fought by refusing to behave like a Caucasian person. The basis of the perspective hinged on a perception of discrimination, which indicated an "other" group of people motivated the behavior or extrinsic motivation. The resultant behaviors from these two perspectives suggest polar outcomes for Black male college students' preparation, admission, progression, and graduation.

In comparison, the primary self-determination perspective identified in the research about people with disabilities in higher education was an instructional model (Wehmeyer, 1999). The perspective resembled the general tenets of self-determination theory as described by Ryan and Deci (1985, 2000, 2008). Both perspectives indicated that self-determination is motivated behavior that results from a person's internal desire to experience choice with limited interference. Ryan and Deci research focused on the psychological impact of the social environment's ability to impede or cultivate the development of self-determination, meaning people's perceptions of "free choice" and their capacity to effectively act to achieve desired results are developed through opportunities to self-selected behaviors, demonstrate capacity to think, feel, and act, and was emotionally connected to a community. People who lacked sufficient opportunity were less motivated, intrinsically and extrinsically. However, Wehmeyer (1999) provided K–12 educators with descriptive characteristics of self-determined behavior such as goal setting, decision-making, problem-solving, and self-management to develop instructional material. These two perspectives suggest that people with disabilities in college who are able to demonstrate self-determination had an opportunity and direct instruction in the K–12 grades that allowed them to learn and practice self-determined behaviors.

Applying the construct of intersectionality on the categorical findings suggests that behavior manifestations of self-determination by Black male college students with disabilities are reflective of the continuum of motivation, with the motivated and amotivated and the two poles (Ryan & Deci, 2000), as related to opportunity and disability within the academic environment. Specifically, Black male college students with a disability who have experienced social environments that nurtured their self-determination may exhibit more independent behavior as well as self-efficacy, for example, integrated or identified regulatory behaviors. These students might have experienced instruction in K–12 grades on specific self-determination skills with opportunities to practice and obtain feedback on their efforts to master those skills.

For example, a Black male college student with a disability may have difficulties in a specific course or a social setting. In response to the challenge, the student would demonstrate self-awareness by acknowledging his strengths and weaknesses within the course or social setting openly, for example, integrated or identified regulatory behaviors. He would then seek the most effective outside support because he has learned to accept those abilities and inabilities. The student, in response to the same challenge, might acknowledge that he needs support, but limit the resources he contacts to those that are specific to students that he perceives are most similar to him. Both actions of self-determined behavior are based on the goal of persisting in college.

Conversely, Black male college students with a disability who have experienced social environments that inhibited the development of self-determination may have difficulty articulating strengths within a course or social settings, but have the capacity to describe an exhaustive list of weaknesses, or seek external affirmation of their abilities from peers, for example, introjected and external regulatory behaviors. Using the same example from above, the student might appear too indecisive and worrisome about his decision to seek assistance because of fear about others' perception of him. The student might seem to blame others, such as the course instructor or group of peers, for his difficulties. He might also perceive that he does not have a choice about the resources he contacts for support in areas of need. He might believe that he must contact the course instructor for help or the counseling center for social support.

Generally, the Black male college students with disabilities might seem to need ongoing encouragement and assistance to sustain his motivation to persist in college.

Barriers to College Completion

The barriers to college completion identified for Black males and people with disabilities were related to negative perceptions of "others" about their disengaged behaviors and limited abilities in the academic setting (Harper, 2012, Wood & Ireland, 2014; Bush & Bush 2014; Kowalsky & Fresko, 2002). Similarly, research indicated that the lack of academic preparation resulted in these groups reporting lower self-esteem and self-doubt, which influenced their belief that "others" had lower expectations of them socially and academically (Palmer et al., 2010; Majors & Billson, 1992; Strayhorn, 2008; Garrison-Wade, 2012). Moreover, both groups experienced financial stressors due to their socioeconomic status and responsibilities to aid the family financially while in college, which regularly interfered with academic progression (Murray & Naranjo, 2008; Luthar, 2006; Jackson & Moore, 2006, 2008; Parham & McDavis, 1987).

The similarities that emerged from the literature seem to postulate that Black male college students with disabilities would have experiences with college completion that are comparable to those of both Black males and students with disabilities. Black males with disabilities in higher education are likely to experience any combination or the majority of the above barriers as they progress through college. They may struggle with self-doubt and low self-esteem, which could be compounded by others who perceive them as disengaged , or as engaged but unable to contribute to the academic and social environment. Additionally, Black males with disabilities may enter college academically unprepared and find themselves performing poorly in their courses. These challenges coupled with financial stressors could make college completion extremely difficult for this subgroup.

The Role of Self-Determination on College Completion

Black men and people with disabilities who have formed and used social support systems are likely to graduate from college (Getzel, 2008; Wade, 2009; Harper, 2012; Wood & Turner, 2010). Members of both groups' social support systems were found to include faculty, friends, family, and college personnel. Specific to Black males, those who had developed a sense of "somebodiness" were found to persevere and overcome the barriers they encountered in college (Johnson, 2016; White & Cone, 1999; Cokely, 2003). People with disabilities, however, needed specific skills and support services such as self-advocacy (Schreiner, 2007) and peer tutoring to complete college (Kowalsky & Fresko, 2002).

Similarly, Black males with disabilities increase their likelihood to attain a college degree if they develop a sense of somebodiness, or a sense of self-definition, self-acceptance and self-love (Johnson, 2016). They also might need to demonstrate relevant self-advocacy skills and use available academic support services to access legally mandated accommodations and learn course material. Moreover, formation and utilization of a support system comprising family members, college personnel, faculty, and significant others may provide Black males with disabilities the needed social support to navigate the various obstacles that may arise during the college years.

Reeves's (2002) and Jenkins-Guanrieri et al.'s (2015) conclusions about SDT within educational settings appear to align with the studies identified for this research and the inferences that were drawn via intersectionality. Black male college students with disabilities who are intrinsically motivated demonstrate the ability to achieve academically, acclimate to and navigate the social terrain of college, and effectively manage a variety of barriers while progressing toward graduation.

Conclusion

Current literature abounds with information concerning Black male college students that addresses their postsecondary experience, but there is a paucity of research pertaining to the experiences of Black male college students with disabilities in the postsecondary setting. The role of self-determination on Black male college students' ability to graduate from college appears equally relevant to the categorical groups. Consequently, postsecondary institutions are encouraged to develop programs and services that respond to the multi-identities that students present within the context of intersectionality.

Further research is needed to provide Black male college students with disabilities a voice in the literature. Qualitative studies would benefit the field by either substantiating, refuting, or clarifying the conclusions drawn in this chapter. Moreover, quantitative studies would benefit the field by articulating the progression of Black male college students with disabilities while considering the academic and financial barriers that inhibit their ability to complete college. It was our intent through this chapter to provide future researchers with a foundation to address this complex and challenging issue.

■ **References**

Bush, E. C., & Bush, V. L. (2010). Calling out the elephant: An examination of Black male achievement in community colleges. *Journal of Black Males in Education 1*(1), 40–62.

Cokely, K. O. (2003). What do we know about the motivation of Black students? Challenging the "anti-intellectual" myth. *Harvard Educational Review 79*, 524–58.

DeAngelo, L., Franke, R., Hurtado, S., Pryor, J., & Tran, S. (2011). *Completing college: Assessing graduation rates at four-year institutions.* Los Angeles: Higher Education Research Institute, UCLA.

Deci, E. L., & Ryan, R. M. (1985). *Intrinsic motivation and self-determination in human behavior.* New York: Plenum Press.

———. (2008). Self-determination theory: A macrotheory of human motivation, development, and health. *Canadian Psychology 49*, 183–85.

Deci., E. L., Vallerand, R. J., Pelletier, L. G., & Ryan, R. M. (1991). Motivation and education: The self-determination perspective. *Educational Psychologist 26*, 325–46.

Erickson, W., Lee, C., & von Schrader, S. (2014). 2013 Disability status report: United States. Ithaca, NY: Cornell University Employment and Disability Institute. Http://www.disabilitystatistics.org/StatusReports/2013-PDF/2013-StatusReport_US.pdf.

Field, S., Sarver, M., & Shaw, S. (2003). Self-determination: A key to success in postsecondary education for students with learning disabilities. *Remedial and Special Education 24*, 339–49.

Garrison-Wade, D. (2012). Listening to their voices: Factors that inhibit or enhance postsecondary outcomes for students with disabilities. *International Journal of Special Education 27*(2), 113–25.

Getzel, E. E. (2008). Addressing the persistence and retention of students with disabilities in higher education: Incorporating key strategies and supports on campus. *Exceptionality 16*, 207–219.

Getzel. E. E., & Thoma, C.A. (2008). Experiences of college students with disabilities and the importance of self-determination in higher education settings. *Career Development for Exceptional Individuals 31*, 77–87.

Hankivsky, O. (2004). Intersectionality 101. Institute for Intersectionality Research & Policy. Https://www.sfu.ca/iirp/documents/resources/101_Final.pdf.

Harper, S. R. (2006). *Black male students at public flagship universities in the U.S.: Status, trends, and implications for policy and practice.* Washington, DC: Joint Center for Political and Economic Studies.

———. (2012). *Black male student success in higher education: A report from the national Black male college achievement study.* Philadelphia: University of Pennsylvania, Center for the Study of Race and Equity in Education.

Harper, S. R. & Quaye, S. J. (2009). *Student engagement in higher education: Theoretical perspectives and practical approaches for diverse populations.* New York: Routledge.

Harrison, K. H., Martin, B. E., & Fuller, R. (2015). "Eagles don't fly with sparrows": Self-determination theory, Black male scholar-athletes and peer group influences on motivation. *Journal of Negro Education 84*(1), 80–93.

Harvey, W. B. (2008). The weakest link: A commentary on the connections between K–12 and higher education. *American Behavioral Scientist 51*, 972–83.

Jackson, J. F. L. & Moore, J. L., II (2006). Black males in education: Endangered or ignored. *Teachers College Record 108*, 201–5.

——— (2008). The Black male crisis in education: A popular media infatuation or needed public policy response. *American Behavioral Science 51*, 847–53.

Johnson, P. D. (2016). Somebodiness and its meaning to Black men. *Journal of Counseling and Development 94*, 333–43.

Kena, G., Hussar W., McFarland, J., de Brey, C., Musu-Gillette, L., Wang, X., . . . Dunlop Velez, E. (2016). The Condition of Education 2016 (NCES 2016–144). US Department of Education, National Center for Educational Statistics. Washington, DC. nces.ed.gov/pubsearch.

Kober, N. (2002). *Twenty-five years of educating children with disabilities: The good news and the work ahead.* Washington, DC: American Youth Policy Forum and Center on Education Policy.

Kowalsky, R., & Fresko, B. (2002). Peer tutoring for college students with disabilities. *Higher Education Research and Development 21*, 259–71.

Luthar, S. S. (2006). Resilience in development: a synthesis of research across five decades. In D. Cicchetti & D. J. Cohen (eds.), *Developmental psychopathology: Risk, disorder, and adaptation 3*, 739–95. New York: John Wiley and Sons.

Majors, R. & Billson, J. (1992). *Cool pose: The dilemmas of Black manhood in America.* New York: Touchstone.

Mamiseishvili, K., & Koch, L. C. (2010). First-to-second-year persistence of students with disabilities in postsecondary institutions in the United States. *Rehabilitation Counseling Bulletin 54*(2), 93–103.

Murray, C., Lombardi, A., & Kosty, D. (2014). Profiling adjustment among postsecondary students with disabilities: A person-centered approach. *Journal of Diversity in Higher Education 7*, 31–44. doi:10.1037/a00035777.

Murray, C. &, Naranjo, J. (2008). Poor, Black, learning disabled, and graduating: An investigation of factors and processes associated with school completion among high-risk urban youth. *Remedial and Special Education 29*, 145–60.

Palmer, R. T., Davis, R. J., Moore, J. L., & Hilton, A. A. (2010). A nation at risk: Increasing college participation and persistence among Black males to stimulate U.S. global competitiveness. *Journal of Black Males in Education 1*(2), 105–24.

Parham, T. A. & McDavis, R. J. (1987). Black men, an endangered species: Who's really pulling the trigger? *Journal of Counseling and Development 66*, 24–27.

Reeves, J. (2002). Self-determination theory applied to educational settings. In E. Deci & R. Ryan (eds.), *Handbook of self-determination research*, pp. 183–203. Rochester, NY: University of Rochester Press.

Ryan, R., & Deci, E. L. (2000). Intrinsic and extrinsic motivations: Classic definitions and new directions. *Contemporary Educational Psychology 25*, 54–67.

Schreiner, M. B. (2007). Effective self-advocacy: What students and special educators need to know. *Intervention in School and Clinic 42*, 300–304.

Strayhorn, T. L. (2008). The role of supportive relationships in supporting Black males' success in college. *NASPA Journal 45*, 26–48.

———. (2012). Satisfaction and retention among Black men at two-year colleges. *Community College Journal of Research and Practice 36*(4), 358–75. doi:10.1080/10668920902782508.

Temple, M. (2015). From process to outcomes: An evaluation of a university's student affairs' cultural program. Doctoral dissertation. Available from ProQuest Dissertation and Theses database. UMI No. 3718990.

US Census Bureau. (2003). Poverty in the United States: *2002*. Washington, DC: Author.

US Department of Education, National Center for Educational Statistics. (2013) *Digest of Education Statistics, 2012* (NCES 2014-015), Table 269.

———. (2016). *Digest of Education Statistics, 2014* (NCES 2016-006), Table 311.10.

Wade, G. D. F., & Lehmann, J. P. (2009). A conceptual framework for understanding students with disabilities transition to community college. *Community College Journal of Research and Practice 33*, 417–45.

Wagner, M., Newman, L., & Cameto, R. (2004). Changes over time in the secondary school experiences of students with disabilities: A report from the national longitudinal transition study-2 *(NLTS2)*. Menlo Park, CA: SRI International.

Wehmeyer, M. L. (1999). A functional model of self-determination: Describing development and implementing instruction. *Focus on Autism and Other Developmental Disabilities 14*, 53–62.

Wood, J. L., & Ireland, M. (2014). Supporting Black male community college success: Determinants of faculty-student engagement. *Community College Journal of Research and Practice 38*, 2–3, 154–65. doi:10.1080/10668926.2014.851957.

Wood, J. L., & Turner, C. S. (2010). Black males and the community college: Student perspectives on faculty and academic success. *Community College Journal of Research and Practice 35*, 1–2, 135–51. doi:10.1080/10668926.2010.526052.

Zheng, C., Erickson, A. G., Kingston, N. M., & Noonman, P. M. (2014). The relationship among self-determination, self-concept, and academic achievement for students with learning disabilities. *Journal of Learning Disabilities 47*, 462–74.

Educational Emancipation

Liberating African American Male Students at PWIs

Jeffrey K. Coleman

The issue of persistence and graduation is not just something that only I have had to confront, but it is a phenomenon that African American students have had to deal with since public schools were established during the nineteenth century (Spring, 2005). Our primary and secondary educational system seems to fail African American males by not being sensitive to the various cultural backgrounds that lend themselves to diverse learning styles. There is a process in the K–12 educational system that uses standardized tests to determine a student's placement in academic courses (Weaver, 2011). These methods are used to define a student's learning ability or inability. African American males are most likely at a disadvantage in these situations because of the stereotype threat that Steele (1997) describes when they are in test-taking situations. Steele defines it as a threat that has an adverse effect on a group that carries socially negative stereotypes. He suggests that it is possible for members of these groups to internalize a fear of being minimized to that stereotype, which could ultimately become personally threatening. Steele says,

> Negative stereotypes about women and African Americans bear on important academic abilities. Thus, for members of these groups who are identified with domains in which these stereotypes apply, the threat of these stereotypes can be sharply felt and, in several ways, hampers their achievement . . . if the threat is experienced in the midst of a domain performance—classroom presentation or test-taking, for example—the emotional reaction it causes could directly interfere with performance. (1997, p. 614)

In many low-income and ethnic minority communities, students and parents often have scant knowledge about how to approach test preparation and the implications of these tests. This was my experience throughout my schooling. My parents and I were not made aware of how they could prepare me for these tests at a young age and how the results of these tests would affect my academic placement through high school and into college.

Standardized test-taking and its implications impact African American male students differently than other students due to external demographic factors coupled with stereotype threat (Steele, 1997). Many times minority and low-income parents who are not college educated are not knowledgeable about the level of math and English their students should be placed in through school so that they will not be at an academic disadvantage when they enter college. Additionally, parents have not been engaged by the school and provided information on how to prepare their children to earn standardized test scores that will place them on track for successful preparation, transition, and persistence in college (Viadero & Johnston, 2000). It is also common that many African American parents do not have bachelor's degrees or careers that require graduate degrees, and therefore may not be knowledgeable about how to advocate for ways the school system should prepare their children for college. Their economic status may lead them to vote to reduce the amount of tax dollars spent on educational costs instead of investing more funding in the educational system (Leachman & Mai, 2014).

My study examines the issues and factors that impact the college retention and graduation of traditional-aged African American male undergraduate students at predominantly White institutions (PWIs) in the United States. Currently, the structure of education is one that separates the successful from the unsuccessful, which benefits those from privileged backgrounds, who have had a state-of-the-art, generously financed educational preparation provided in their school systems (Gibson, 1986). Often the factors that impact success for African American males are related to race, class, family support, and other non-school-related demographics (Delpit, 1998). Carla O'Connor, Jennifer Mueller, R. L'Heureux Lewis, Deborah Rivas-Drake, and Seneca Rosenburg (2011) argue that Black students tend to underachieve due to an overrepresentation of them in lower-level classes and under-representation in higher-level courses. This divide is partially caused by limited advanced course offerings at predominantly Black schools compared to predominantly White schools. However Black students are not well represented in higher-level courses at predominantly White schools. O'Connor et al. draw on Oaks's (2005) description of this as a second-generation segregation that limits access Black students have to resources of academic support. O'Connor et al. believe that this structure for schooling proves that tracking has a negative influence on Black achievement, as these racially stratified academic hierarchies produce racial tensions that make it difficult for Black students make positive progress toward academic success (O'Connor et al., 2011).

One way to examine this issue is to compare college retention and graduation rates of traditional-aged African American males to the general population using national, regional, and institution-specific data. According to the 2012 report of the National Center for Education Statistics, the most current national enrollment rate of first-time, full-time, degree-seeking African American male college students is 12 percent, compared to 62 percent of White male college students (National Center for Education Statistics, 2012a). A 2013 report indicates that the most current five-year national graduation rate of first-time, full-time, degree-seeking African American male college students is 16.3 percent, compared to 36.6 percent of White male college students (National Center for Education Statistics, 2013). My belief is that PWIs fail to provide African American male students with an environment that encourages their retention and graduation because they inadequately support the academic and social needs of this population. This chapter will identify issues and factors that can influence college retention and graduation rates of traditional-aged African American male students at PWIs in the southeast region of the United States.

I will use data collected from my work as a multicultural affairs practitioner coordinating the Rites of Passage program, which supports the retention and graduation of African American male students at a public research university (which I will call "PRU"). This study rests on some fundamental assumptions. The first is that the process of earning a bachelor's degree at a PWI is inherently not conducive to the success of African American males. I argue this is because mainstream institutions of higher education embrace elements of a privileged White culture and do not pay much attention to the need for academic support, financial support, or multicultural services for their African American students, particularly African American men. Michael Brooks, Christopher Jones, and Isaac Burt (2012) reference research by David Harmon (2002), Gloria S. Bourte (1992), Rose E. Huff et al. (2005), and Donna Y. Ford (1996), who identify three specific challenges that threaten Black male retention at PWIs: (1) students' reflections of their social-emotional needs, including relationships involving culturally and linguistically diverse (CLD) students, their classmates, and their teachers; (2) concerns of CLD families that relate to their children's level of happiness and sense of belonging to the institution; and (3) the ability of CLD students to attain acceptable levels of academic success.

The second assumption is that the White privileged culture has influenced the development of barriers throughout the schooling process that have hindered African American male students in their quest to become educated. This disparity and preparation begins with the K–12 educational system and continues through the university experience. Primary and secondary schools in underprivileged areas, for example, have fewer resources to devote to individual student ambitions (Berg, 2010). At the university level, there are some faculty who do not feel that African American male students are capable of successfully completing the curriculum of study and discourage them from taking their courses. Other times these students do not receive the appropriate academic advising that takes into consideration their quality and level of precollege preparation. The ultimate goal of undergraduate education should be to prepare students with skills and knowledge for careers and lifelong pursuits. However, it seems that this is a battle in which many African American male students have not been equipped to fight.

Background

Research indicates that African American male students do not graduate from college at significant rates (Hoston, Graves, & Fleming-Randle, 2010; Journal of Blacks in Higher Education,

2012; Robertson, 2012). According to the 2011 report of the National Center for Education Statistics, the national graduation rate of first-time, full-time, degree-seeking African American male college students is 15 percent and the national enrollment rate is 12.5 percent (National Center for Education Statistics, 2011). According to the PRU Office of Institutional Research, the current four-year retention rate for African American male students is 72.2 percent, and the current four-year graduation rate is 18.8 percent.

The retention rate for Rites of Passage program participants increased to 80.7 percent in the 2012–13 academic year. In addition, there was a higher four-year graduation rate (26.8 percent) for Rites of Passage participants than the rate (17.6 percent) for non-participants who were African American male. This suggests there was a positive correlation between participation in Rites of Passage during the 2009–10 year and graduation from PRU (PRU Office of Institutional Research, email communications, January 30, 2014).

PRU has been recognized as the most diverse institution in the state university system, which makes work around supporting minority populations more relevant. Rites of Passage is a program formerly developed by the PRU Office of Multicultural Affairs out of a need to address low retention and graduation rates of African American males at the university. It was designed to support the educational and professional aspirations of incoming freshmen and transfer male students from historically underserved populations. The goal of the program was to develop a community of support to help students succeed academically and persist toward graduation, fully immerse themselves in college life, and enhance their life management skills.

During its tenure, the program evolved into a learning community focusing on minority male mentoring. The program required students to participate in at least two (2) concurrent courses with integrated learning assignments and at least one planned cocurricular activity linked to course material and the goals of the Rites of Passage program during the school year. Students also had the option to participate in a yearlong service-learning project to enhance skills in leadership, civic engagement, and personal development. Rites of Passage workshops occurred monthly during each semester to address topics including academic enhancement, career exploration, civic engagement, personal development, and leadership development. Rites of Passage peer mentors were recruited to stay in touch with program participants through academic and social events, and check in with them to make sure they were finding everything they needed to be successful. Finally, students participated in a group coaching component during monthly Rites of Passage workshops to help them connect the information they were learning in their life management workshops to their individual identity transformation throughout the whole process.

Case Study

The purpose of this study was to analyze the impact Rites of Passage had on the academic success of its participants. This study was guided by the following central research question: *What are the conditions that lead to the success or failure among African American undergraduate male students at predominantly White institutions?* There were three subresearch questions: (1) How was success defined among African American male undergraduate students enrolled at a PWI during the 2009–13 academic years? (2) During this time frame, what did African American male undergraduate students articulate as the factors that contributed to their success at a PWI? (3) What did African American male undergraduate students experience as challenges and barriers to success at PWIs?

In response to the purpose of this study and the central research question and subsidiary research questions, I administered a qualitative interview-based case study to examine the factors that impacted the intent and success of former participants of the Rites of Passage program to remain enrolled at PRU and complete their bachelor's degree within a period of four years. A random sample of ten of the program's past participants were selected for this study. The individuals in this study included five African American males who were past participants in Rites of Passage and graduated from PRU in four years, and five African American males who were past participants in Rites of Passage but did not graduate from PRU in four years. These former students were selected and divided into these categories to identify common themes within similarities and differences that lead toward success or failure in college among each group.

Scholars like Brooks, Jones, and Burt (2012) have studied the effect these issues have on Black male retention. Their work is based on Tinto's (1999) definition of retention, which is the principle of keeping students enrolled, focusing "on maintaining several factors including a welcoming environment, high member morale, and organizational processes" (Brooks, Jones, & Burt, 2012, p. 1). Brooks, Jones, and Burt reference research by David Harmon (2002), Gloria S. Bourte (1992), Rose E. Huff et al. (2005), and Donna Y. Ford (1996), who identify three specific challenges that threaten Black male retention at PWIs. The first is when their social and emotional needs of developing relationships with students, faculty, and staff from diverse backgrounds are not met. The second is when their level of happiness and sense of belonging to the institution are affected by family concerns (i.e., financial challenges, medical challenges, and child care/child custody issues) that take their attention away from school. The third challenge is their ability to achieve acceptable levels of academic success. Being that academic ability did not surface as major theme in this case study, the focus rested on social and emotional needs of students as well as their sense of belonging to the institution.

I will present a discussion of the major research findings, along with implications for future research and practices. The discussion has been arranged into the following categories, which will also serve as subtopics: (*a*) conditions that lead to success or failure of African American male undergraduate students at PWIs; (*b*) implications of an education and schooling process that is emancipating for African American males; and (*c*) creating curricular and cocurricular emancipating experiences for African American males at PWIs. Finally, I will conclude with recommendations for practice.

Major findings of this study showed that (*a*) success is defined by time management, being a well-rounded student, and becoming involved in activities outside of class, degree completion, cocurricular involvement, and building a network of students, faculty, and other individuals;

(*b*) factors that contributed to success at a PWI focused on the ability to develop and recognize personal identity, build a community of support, manage priorities, and utilize academic resources such as professors, academic advisers, and tutoring services; (*c*) financial challenges as barriers to success included exercising wisdom when spending refund checks they received each semester for unused student loan money, and the need to work to take care of physical and intellectual needs when coming from families experiencing financial difficulties; (*d*) racial challenges were barriers to success when they surfaced in the classroom or in an environment connected to their academic major, developed as students were socially adjusting to the campus climate, defined a perception of them, and challenged their individual identity development; and (*e*) gender challenges were barriers to success when they created a stereotypical depiction and educational limitations for them as African American males.

Many of the challenges and barriers to success that African American male undergraduate students experienced at PRU are aligned with those in current research literature on what Black males experience at PWIs. At the same time, some unique findings surfaced through the challenges and barriers that participants shared. Furthermore, Rites of Passage offered academic and cocurricular experiences to address the challenges and barriers participants shared.

Conditions That Lead to Success or Failure of African American Male Undergraduate Students at PWIs

Participants who graduated in four years defined success as finding personal identity, being a well-rounded student, and becoming involved in activities outside of class, whereas participants who did not graduate in four years defined success as degree completion, cocurricular involvement, and building a network of students, faculty, and other individuals. Considering both of these definitions, it can be concluded that an environment that fosters self-discovery, networks of support, and motivation toward degree completion, and provides opportunity for cocurricular involvement equips students with the ingredients for success. To address this, the Rites of Passage program offered curricular and cocurricular experiences in the form of a learning community that focused on skill development and education in the areas of academic achievement, time management, career development, financial management, presentation of self, civic engagement, and leadership development. Moreover, it appears that none of the research participants specified a grade or grade point average requirement in their definition of success, but focused on environmental fit, as supported by Tinto (1987). His retention theory focuses on maintaining several factors in a student's experience, which includes a welcoming environment, high member morale, and organizational processes.

Those individuals who graduated in four years suggested that their ability to develop and recognize personal identity, build a community of support, and manage priorities were factors that contributed to their success at a PWI. On the other hand, individuals who did not graduate in four years also felt that the utilization of academic resources such as professors, academic advisers, and tutoring services were the factors that contributed to their success at a PWI. This suggests that the participants who graduated in four years viewed the management and development of human relation skills, interpersonal skills, and practical competence as factors contributing to success. However, those participants who did not graduate in four years viewed the use of academic resources as factors contributing to success. This suggests a positive association between experiences offered through Rites of Passage such as building human relation skills, interpersonal skills, and practical competence, and graduating from a PWI in four years. It also supports research (Cuyjet, 1997; Edelin-Freeman, 2004; Palmer & Young, 2010; Robertson, Mitra, & Delinder, 2005; and Robertson & Mason, 2008) that suggests positive social adjustment and personal development are the best determinants of good academic performance among African American males at PWIs.

Participants who graduated in four years reported that their ability to meet and manage financial demands was a barrier to success for them when they were not able to receive support in this area from their family. These demands included financial expenses associated with an academic major, as well as acquiring material possessions to combat the perception of being stereotyped as a societal failure who did not belong in college. The financial aid refund enabled some individuals to change their outward appearance, challenge this stereotype, and develop an internal peace that resulted from not fighting a negative identity placed on them as a Black male but instead embrace a new positive perception that created a sense of belonging for them. Many of the participants who did not graduate in four years reflected on how they too did not have financial support from their families and therefore had to work their way through college. Some discussed how working to make ends meet became a priority over school. In response to these challenges, a component of the Rites of Passage program included workshops focusing on managing finances. In addition, the program fostered a community of support consisting of faculty, staff, and students focused on equipping African American males to successfully overcome societal stereotypes facing them. These findings support Cuyjet's (1997) research that financial challenges may be a leading reason why only 38 percent of Black college students are males. This also relates to Palmer and Young's (2010) theory that when campus administrators create an environment that fosters a culture of care and a sense of belonging, it has a positive impact on Black male retention. This includes providing an educational environment that is nonintimidating and nurturing of their academic success, and deconstructing stereotypical negative perceptions of African American males.

Individuals who graduated in four years identified the racial identity and stereotypes associated with being a Black male as a barrier to success. This barrier manifested itself in classroom interactions and interactions with peers outside of class, and influenced the formation of a new Black male identity that established a sense of belonging on a predominantly White campus for these students. Those individuals who did not graduate in four years also reported racial identity associated with being a Black male as a barrier to success as they were stereotyped as poor and low achieving. This barrier became magnified in settings where they were the only one or one of a few African Americans present. Moreover, this negative stereotype and feeling of isolation became intimidating for them. In an effort to address this issue, a component of the Rites of Passage program included group coaching sessions facilitated by African American male university faculty and staff, which provided students the opportunity for candid conversations with African American male role models to reinforce their sense of belonging with the institution and develop mentoring experiences. This also supports the research of Harper (2009) which suggests that PWI campus administrators should address the racism and structural barriers to achievement and justice that occur on their campuses because they are of major importance to African American male students, who are more at risk for attrition than other minority groups, as Palmer and Young (2010) explain.

Participants who graduated in four years identified their gender as a barrier to success in the way it defined their individual identity according to societal norms. This barrier was intertwined with racial challenges and a societal view of how masculinity and male identity are defined for African American males. It is also comparable to the previously mentioned racial barrier in how it substantiates a perception and educational limitations placed on African American males. Participants who did not graduate in four years also reported that gender was a barrier to success and agreed that it was reflective of these societal stereotypes placed on African American males. Whereas the group that graduated in four years took the approach of overcoming this barrier by redefining their identity in outward appearance and interactions, the group that did not graduate in four years was not able to do so because they wrestled with carrying the burden of isolation. The group coaching sessions offered through Rites of Passage created a safe space for African American men to deconstruct the Black male stereotype, reinforce their sense of belonging with the institution, and develop mentoring experiences. This supports the findings of Robertson and Mason (2008) that Black males experience isolation and challenges with academic performance when they feel that the climate of the larger White society, and the university environment in particular, is not welcoming. Furthermore, it substantiates the analyses shared by Allen and Haniff (1991), Feagin, Hernan Vera, and Imani (1996), Pascarella and Terenzini (2005), Rankin and Reason (2005), and Tinto (1987) showing that Black students who attend PWIs often struggle with alienation and tend not to involve themselves in cocurricular experiences.

Therefore, personal identity development, environmental fit, positive social adjustment and personal development, management of financial demands, and being in an environment where there is a shared commitment from faculty and staff to foster a culture of care and a sense of belonging are all conditions that lead to success or failure of African American male undergraduate students at PWIs. The key factor that emerges among members of the group that graduated in four years was that they had a determination to challenge the perception that they knew had been placed on them by defining who they were going to be at PRU and how they were going to fit into this particular predominantly White campus. Moreover each of the conditions described above were incorporated in the Rites of Passage program, as it encouraged an environment that motivated determination for success. However, the program was met with resistance from the university and consequently was eliminated over the course of time. I will return to this in the conclusion. This is relevant to the challenges facing African American men in our society as their structures of support are dismantled to maintain an imbalanced social structure because addressing this concern compromises the class and power status of the dominant race and class.

Creating Curricular and Cocurricular Emancipating Experiences for African American Males at PWIs

As it currently stands, PWIs do not always provide African American male students with an environment that is emancipating for them, which is why they persist and graduate at low rates. In order for this to change, these institutions must reestablish their campus environment so they support, cultivate, and enhance the academic and social needs of this population. As educators, we must change the focus from preparing students to contribute to consumerism and profit making, to preparing them to contribute to a national democratic citizenship (Giroux, 2010). According to bell hooks (1994), a citizenship that builds as a democracy is one where African American males have an equal opportunity for social equality and economic self-sufficiency instead of being restricted to specific social and economic groups even when they go to college and work hard to graduate. As Freire (1998) discusses, education is not a neutral process, as it differs from person to person, and therefore one approach and one environment will not be sufficient for everyone. Aronowitz (1997) explains that the way one person defines his or her identity differs from how other persons define theirs and is based on each individual's cultural practices and beliefs that impact the way the individual receives education. Harper (2009) suggests that equality in education requires acknowledgment of racial and social class disparities and equitable responses. This is not desired by the dominant race and class because it compromises their class and power status. Harper and Kuykendall (2012) note that racial equality is not going to evolve on its own; key university stakeholders must spearhead a social movement to make this a priority for those in power. Each of these theories supports the establishment of a program such as Rites of Passage that creates an emancipating environment that acknowledges social and class inequities, but reinforces equal opportunity for social equality and economic self-sufficiency.

In consideration of climate challenges facing African American males at PWIs, there are eight characteristics that should be present in such an environment to foster emancipating experiences for this population. These eight characteristics include: establishing an equity scorecard, collaboration in initiatives, involvement in the strategic planning process, confronting barriers, use of high achieving peers, acknowledgement of racist stereotypes, institutional ladders of accountability, and intergenerational mentoring.

Equity Scorecard

First, the Equity Scorecard process is an excellent example of acknowledging social and class inequalities in student success and reinforcing equitable responses. Harper and Kuykendall

(2012) discuss how key transparency and data-guided institutional activities are supportive in this environment. Through this process, faculty, administrators, and institutional research staff work together to interpret data that are separated by race and gender. This process brings key stakeholders to the table to develop ways to provide equitable responses to race and gender imbalances in student achievement. This was a valuable approach in the development of Rites of Passage as it identified the retention and graduation rates of African American males as a significant concern and provided a starting point to address the issue.

Collaboration in Initiatives

African American male students in a supportive environment at a PWI are engaged in meaningful collaboration and viewed as experts in designing, implementing, and assessing campus initiatives. Oftentimes the Black males invited to participate in these efforts are the well-known student leaders. "Lower-performing undergraduates also should be actively sought, as this opportunity could be a turning point in their college trajectories" (Harper & Kuykendall, 2012, p. 26). These types of experiences can be emancipating being that they motivate a low-achieving student toward academic success. Involving African American male students in such collaboration can also provide the institution with a core group of students to continually provide feedback on the needs, experiences, and what would be appealing for the majority of their same-race male peers. This was another component of Rites of Passage, as workshops were open to all students regardless of academic ability and their feedback was solicited in assessing program effectiveness and future initiatives.

A Strategic Plan

A strategic plan that is collaboratively developed by institutional stakeholders, ranging from students to the president, can be a valuable resource as it guides university-wide initiatives. It is important for faculty and staff at all levels (including the president, provost, and tenured White professors) and African American male undergraduate students to collaboratively develop a strategic action plan to address institutional barriers to student success. "The document should clearly convey that the institution, not just its Black culture center or employees of color, assumes responsibility for employing a coordinated set of strategies to improve Black male student success" (Harper & Kuykendall, 2012, p. 26). The strategic plan should hold stakeholders accountable for fostering emancipatory educational experiences by articulating the institution's responsibility in developing an environment conducive to the success of Black male students and how the success of these students is a priority. Unfortunately, this was not incorporated in the strategic plan at PRU and therefore poses a concern for how the challenges facing African American men in society are reinforced at the university level by not being considered a priority.

Confronting Barriers

Campuses must place priority on learning, academic success, student development, and increasing graduation rates over social programming by helping students successfully manage challenges or barriers to success.

> Architects of the strategy document [strategic plan] and subsequent initiatives should prioritize programs and services that will help Black male students adjust smoothly to the academic demands of college, learn how to effectively study and manage their time, resolve identity conflicts that undermine academic achievement, respond productively to racist stereotypes, and learn how to ask for help well before they find themselves on the brink of failing a course or—even worse—dropping out. (Harper & Kuykendall, 2012, p. 26)

There is a need to develop initiatives that proactively prepare students to appropriately handle the barriers that lead to low academic achievement and college dropout. Rites of Passage consisted of initiatives designed to help students successfully overcome barriers that negatively impact academic success.

Use of High-Achieving Peers

Institutions should use high-achieving Black male students as a resource for creating an educational experience that is emancipating for African American males on their campuses and help them be successful. There are Black males who are doing well academically and are involved in cocurricular activities. According to Harper and Kuykendall (2012), approximately one-third of this group of students completes their bachelor's degree. "Hence, institutional stakeholders should better understand the conditions and institutionalize the factors that enable current achievers to thrive and that helped Black male alumni to persist when they were enrolled" (p. 27). The best way for institutions to find out how to create an environment that fosters academic achievement of African American male students is to ask current achievers and alumni to share the motivational influences in their retention and graduation. This element was also incorporated in Rites of Passage workshops facilitated by alumni and mentoring relationships with upper-class peers who were doing well academically and involved in cocurricular experiences.

Acknowledgment of Racist Stereotypes

Key agents at the institution must have those difficult, yet honest discussions about racism and its harmful impact on the academic achievement of Black male students. When initiatives overlook these issues, they are more likely to experience limited success. "Acknowledging the existence of racism and racial stereotypes is a necessary first step in strategically addressing their harmful effects on Black men's educational outcomes and sense of belonging" (Harper & Kuykendall, 2012, p. 28). A main ingredient in creating an environment that is emancipating to the academic and social needs of African American students is to acknowledge the existence of racism and racial stereotypes and address them. It is not clear that this was a common practice at PRU, and therefore it is assumed that it did not take place. In addition, it also raises concern for how the challenges facing African American men in society are reinforced at the university level by not being considered a priority.

Ladders of Accountability

Faculty and administrators at all levels should be held accountable for improving African American male persistence, academic achievement, campus involvement, and degree attainment. The president should be accountable to the trustees, executive administrators should be accountable to the president, units should be accountable to deans and other institutional leaders, and individual educators must hold themselves accountable for meeting institutional strategic goals related to the success of African American male students. This kind of accountability requires reflection that is individual and collective, transparency of assessment data, proof of educational effectiveness, and appropriate steps toward adjusting professional practices that produce inequity. Institutions should offer professional development opportunities and resources for faculty and administrators who do not know how to effectively engage African American males or provide culturally responsive instruction in the classroom. "Furthermore, these educators should be challenged to confront the implicit biases that lead them to have low expectations for and racist stereotypes about these students" (Harper & Kuykendall, 2012, p. 28). In order to create an environment that yields an educational experience that is emancipating for African American male students at PWIs, faculty and administrators must be challenged to work through their personal biases that cause them to have low expectations and racist views of students from this population. This is another practice where it was not clear if and how it was implemented at PRU. It suggests that the university supported societal inequities facing African American males and the historical process of schooling that reinforced race, class, and gender divisions.

Intergenerational Mentoring

Finally, intergenerational mentoring initiatives where peers, faculty, staff, and alumni serve in the capacity of mentoring are great ways to establish an environment that embraces students' cultural identity and fosters a freeing experience for them to be academically successful. Learning communities that are made up of African American males and focused on African American male identity create wonderful environments that allow African American males at PWIs to embrace the culture and identity. This means that students are having educational experiences outside of class such as trips to museums, attending conferences on Black culture, participating in experiential educational team-building programs, attending lectures on campus, and so on together and reflecting on them in classes they have together, such as was the case in the Rites of Passage mentoring and learning community. Education in this form becomes emancipating as it motivates academic achievement for students while giving them space to "act Black" in order to be academically successful. It appears that we need to do more research in how to develop more environments at PWIs where mentoring groups, leadership opportunities, and African American male learning communities can be established within academics, career aspirations, and personal interests.

Educational emancipation becomes a significant challenge for African American males at PWIs. Many of them become subject to the practice that Harper (2009) refers to as "Niggering," when their institutions talk about supporting them but never develop any systematic practices to undo racism or break down barriers to success. A successful institutional model is one where faculty, administrators, and students develop a strategic plan and implement activities to address institutional barriers to student success. The strategic plan includes activities guided by data on inequities; initiatives designed, implemented, and assessed in collaboration with African American male students; actions developed through collaboration of institutional stakeholders ranging from students to the president; a structure where academic success, student development, and degree completion are prioritized over social programming; initiatives based on research in college male, masculinity, and African American male theory; input from Black male student achievers; honest discussions among influential faculty and staff about racism and its effects on Black male student achievement; and a description of how all faculty and staff will be held accountable for increasing retention, academic achievement, campus involvement, and graduation rates of African American male students. In order for emancipating experiences for African American males to take place, Black male student success must be an institutional priority while faculty and administrators on all levels are held accountable for Black male student success. These practices, along with a program like Rites of Passage, are an ideal model for PWIs to implement, as it recognizes past institutional failures and offers a way to address the democratic promise of political, economic, and social justice in the United States. The implications of a model such as this include increased retention, academic achievement, campus involvement, and degree completion at PWIs.

Recommendations and Conclusions

The findings in this study revealed a number of promising practices at predominantly White institutions, as well as expanding current research literature on factors impacting the retention and graduation of African American male undergraduate students. Furthermore, several patterns and themes surfaced that allowed for a discussion of conditions that lead to the success or failure among African American undergraduate male students at PWIs. Findings also identified common themes, with similarities and differences that lead toward success or failure in college among former Rites of Passage participants who graduated from PRU in four years and those who did not. The findings also showed that the Rites of Passage program had a direct impact on the success of its participants by offering experiences that addressed the conditions leading to success. These findings are critical for identifying, defining, and advancing efforts toward increasing the persistence and graduation of African American male undergraduate students now and in the future. It can also be argued that the findings in this study contribute to the premise that creating participatory experiences on a college campus that are inclusive of the cultural identity of African American male students can become fully emancipatory, resulting in a citizenry that is built on the principle of a collective responsibility for fulfilling America's promises for democracy, equality, and social justice.

The intention of this study is to impact higher education by providing a framework for creating a campus environment at PWIs that is conducive to success and graduation of African American male students. It proposes practical solutions to increasing retention and graduation rates of this demographic population on the campuses of PWIs. Related to this notion of emancipatory education, Wolk (2007) suggests higher-education environments should respect the identity of its diverse student populations. Therefore, this study also offers an adaptable model for colleges and universities to use to address ways to improve retention and graduation rates of other demographic populations, resulting in an increase in overall degree attainment. It is intended to make these institutions more attractive to prospective students, increase enrollment and income from tuition, and position them as leaders in higher education.

The research presented shows us that in order to move toward educational emancipation, we must create environments at K–12 schools and colleges and universities that are inclusive of the culture and identity of African American males. The atmosphere inside and outside the classroom must send the message that success is equated with each individual's cultural identity. Therefore I would like to recommend research on how educational leaders can design experiences and activities for students to be able to see personal and cultural relationships that draws their participation. In the case for African American males, we as university practitioners must design our curricular and cocurricular experiences to be inviting of the cultures and identities of students from this population. This is a springboard to developing an education experience that becomes a liberating truth for students, freeing them from a historic cycle of discriminating schooling practices.

There are some practical ideas we as educators can use to contribute to creating educational experiences that are emancipatory by implementing this research at PWIs. Intergenerational mentoring initiatives where peers, faculty, staff, and alumni serve in the capacity of mentoring are great ways to establish an environment that embraces a student's cultural identity. Approaches such as mentoring give students freedom to equate "acting Black," or proudly embracing their cultural identity, with being academically successful. Learning communities that are made up of African American males and focused on African American male identity create wonderful environments that allow African American males at PWIs to embrace their culture and identity. This means that students are having educational experiences outside of class such as trips to museums, attending conferences on Black culture, participating in experiential educational team-building programs, attending lectures on campus, and so on, together and reflecting on them in classes. This is motivational in their academic achievement as it gives them space to "act Black" in order to be academically successful. It appears that we need to do further research in how to develop more environments at PWIs where mentoring groups, leadership opportunities, and African American male learning communities can be established within academics, career aspirations, and personal interests.

Although oppressive practices related to race and class have evolved over time, there is that critical hope that we can strive toward social change by embracing practices and learning approaches that promote equity. We also need to adopt the concept of sociological mindfulness by making a conscious effort to understand how past beliefs and practices influence the privileged or powerful status quo of one group over another and begin to take steps toward ending these attitudes and behaviors. In the context of schools, this requires we understand the systems of power and privilege that exist in schools and how these systems put some groups of students at an advantage and others at a disadvantage. It also requires us to take strides to end these oppressive practices through approaches that lead to educational emancipation. This will allow us as educators to develop teaching strategies that complement the diversity and the uniqueness that exist among the students we serve.

■ **References**

Allen, W. R., & Haniff, N. Z. (1991). Race, gender, and academic performance in U.S. higher education. In W. R. Allen, E. G. Epps, and N. Z. Haniff (eds.). *College in black and white: African American students in predominantly White and in historically Black public universities* (pp. 95–109). Albany: State University of New York Press.

Aronowitz, S. (1997). Between nationality and class. *Harvard Educational Review 67*(2), 188–207.

Berg, G. (2010). *Low-income students and the perpetuation of inequality: Higher education in America.* New York: Routledge.

Bourte, G. S. (1992). Frustrations of an African-American parent—a personal and professional account. *Phi Delta Kappan 73*, 786–88.

Cuyjet, M. J. (1997). African American men on college campuses: Their needs and their perceptions. *New Directions for Student Services 80*, 5–16.

Delpit, L. D. (1998). The silence dialogue: Power and pedagogy in educating other people's children. *Harvard Educational Review 58*(3), 280–98.

Edelin-Freeman, K. (2004). African American men and women in higher education: "Filling the Glass" in the new millennium." In A. McDaniel and O. McDaniel (eds.). *21st century African American cultural issues: A reader* (pp. 123–37). Mason, OH: Thomson Publishing.

Feagin, J. R., Vera, H., & Imani, N. (1996). *The agony of education: Black students at white colleges and universities.* New York: Routledge.

Ford, D. Y. (1996). *Reversing underachievement among gifted Black students: Promising practices and programs.* New York: Teachers College Press.

Freire, P. (1998). *Pedagogy of freedom: Ethic, democracy, and civic courage.* Oxford: Rowman & Littlefield.

Gibson, R. (1986). *Critical theory and education.* London: Hodder and Stoughton.

Giroux, H. A. (2010). *Politics after hope: Obama and the crisis of youth, race, and democracy.* Boulder, CO: Paradigm Publishers.

Harmon, D. (2002). *In light of our differences: How diversity in nature and culture makes us human.* Washington, DC: Smithsonian Institution Press.

Harper, S. R. (2009). Niggers no more: A critical race counternarrative on Black male student achievement at predominantly White colleges and universities. *International Journal of Qualitative Studies in Education 22*(6), 697–712.

Harper, S. R. & Kuykendall, J. A. (2012). Institutional efforts to improve Black male student achievement: A standards-based approach. *Change 44*(2), 23–29.

hooks, b. (1994). *Teaching to transgress: Education as the practice of freedom.* New York: Gloria Watkins.

Hoston, W., Graves, S., & Fleming-Randle, M. (2010). Individual practices to increase the graduation rate of African American students at predominantly White colleges and universities. *Journal of College Orientation and Transition 18*(1), 69–77.

Huff, R. E., Houskamp, B. M., Watkins, A. V., Stanton, M., & Tavegia, B. (2005). The experiences of parents of gifted African American children: A phenomenological study. *Roeper Review 27*, 215–21.

Journal of Blacks in Higher Education. (2012). The huge racial gap in college graduation rates. Https://www.jbhe.com/2012/04/the-huge-racial-gap-in-college-graduation-rates/.

Leachman, M. & Mai, C. (2014). Center on Budget and Policy Priorities. *Most states still funding schools less than before the recession.* Http://www.cbpp.org/research/most-states-still-funding-schools-less-than-before-the-recession#_ftn1.

O'Connor, C., Mueller, J., Lewis, R., Rivas-Drake, D., & Rosenberg, S. (2011). "Being" Black and strategizing for excellence in a racially stratified academic hierarchy. *American Educational Research Journal 48*(6), 1232–57.

Palmer, R. & Young, E. (2010). How a supportive campus climate promotes student success. In T. L. Strayhorn, and M. C. Terrell (eds.). *The evolving challenges of Black college students: New insights for policy, practice, and research* (pp. 138–60). Sterling, VA: Stylus.

Pascarella, E. T., & Terenzini, P. T. (2005). *How college affects students: A third decade of research.* 3rd ed. San Francisco: Jossey-Bass.

Rankin, S. R., & Reason, R. D. (2005). Differing perceptions: How students of color and White students perceive campus climate for underrepresented groups. *Journal of College Student Development 46*(1), 43–61.

Robertson, R. V. (2012). A qualitative examination of what Black males say about their experiences at a predominantly White college. In A. Simpson, Jr. (ed.). *Ain't nobody worryin': Maleness and masculinity in Black America* (pp. 145–58). San Diego, CA: Cognella.

Robertson, R. V., & Mason, D. (2008). What works? A qualitative examination of the factors related to the academic success of African American males at a predominantly White college in the south. *Challenge 14*(2), 67–89.

Robertson, R. V., Mitra, A., & Delinder, J. V. (2005). The social adjustment of African American females at a predominantly White Midwestern university. *Challenge 8*(4), 31–45.

Spring, J. H. (2005). *The American school, 1642–2004*. 6th ed. Boston: McGraw-Hill.

Steele, C. M. (1997). A threat in the air: How stereotypes shape intellectual identity and performance. *American Psychologist 52*(6), 613–29.

Tinto, V. (1987). *Leaving college*. Chicago: University of Chicago Press.

———. (1999). Taking retention seriously: Rethinking the first year of college. *NACADA Journal 19*(2), 5–9.

US Department of Education, National Center for Education Statistics. (2012a). *The condition of education 2011* (NCES 2012–045). Http://nces.ed.gov/programs/digest/d11/tables/dt11_347.asp.

———. (2012b). *Digest of education statistics, 2011* (NCES 2012-001). Http://nces.ed.gov/programs/digest/d11/tables/dt11_237.asp.

———. (2013). *Digest of education statistics, 2013* (NCES 2013-037). Retrieved from Http://nces.ed.gov/programs/digest/d12/tables/dt12_376.asp.

Viadero, D., & Johnston, R. C. (2000). Lifting minority achievement: Complex answers. *Education Week*, April 5.

Weaver, K. (2011). Standardized testing: Measurement of academic achievement. Liberty University. Https://files.eric.ed.gov/fulltext/ED525158.pdf.

Wolk, S. (2007). Why go to school? *Phi Delta Kappan 88*(9), 648–58.

Qualitative Research Approach When Studying Black Males

Robert G. Bryant and Georj Lewis

It can be said that Black men are an anomaly among senior administrative leadership positions in the professional world that includes, but is not limited to, K–12 school systems, postsecondary educational institutions, business, and industry. Often chief executive officers, presidents, and other senior administrative positions (vice presidents, executive directors, etc.) in organizations have a dismal representation of Black professionals, especially males, suggesting that corporate executives or their subordinates make little effort to hire Black professionals. The data further evidences this perspective. Whites represent 96 percent of all Fortune 500 company CEOs. Less than 1 percent of fortune 500 CEOs are Black, and 93 percent of the CEOs are white men (Feagin, 2014). The low representation of Black male and other minority chief executive officers is similar on college and university campuses; as of 2006 only 13.5 percent of college and university presidents identified belonging to a minority population (ACE, 2007).

According to Jones (1986), corporations and educational organizations have been giving thousands of Black managers and leaders the background to move up to more responsible positions, but the access to senior administrative positions has been limited. According to Lewis (2007), Black males must overcome systemic barriers and have internal fortitude if they are to reach the senior administrative (also called executive) ranks in the academy. Bryant (2015) specifically highlights the importance of context and systemic issues that support or impede the work of Black male chief diversity officers (CDOs), who are campus senior diversity administrators in higher education. Current narratives of Black males who reach senior administrative positions in higher education provide insight into the contextual factors impacting those who are senior administrators. Both Lewis (2007) and Bryant (2015) used qualitative research designs to collect narratives and analyze the words, feelings, and descriptions from current Black males who are senior administrators at colleges and universities. In each study, their participants had some understanding about the process and value for research in general. This chapter outlines some of the factors that Black men encounter on their trajectory to becoming a senior administrator at colleges and universities in the United States.

Both researchers used a qualitative research design to understand the lived "real world" perspective of Black males who have reached the senior administrative ranks within their institution. Each participant shared his experiences using rich descriptions so that a reader could understand the challenges and other concerns attached to the respondent's career trajectory. Findings from Lewis (2007) and Bryant (2015) indicate that a deeper understanding of one's lived experience can be obtained from qualitative research. Qualitative strategies offer researchers a unique framework for research. Qualitative research is an in-depth inquiry method used to examine or understand a specific phenomenon and to make a hidden reality visible (Denzin & Lincoln, 2008). Merriam and Associates (2002) refer to qualitative research by stating:

> Qualitative research lies with the idea that individuals in interaction with their world socially construct meaning. The world, or reality, is not the fixed, single, agreed upon, or measurable phenomenon that is assumed to be in positivist, quantitative research. Instead, there are multiple constructions and interpretations of reality that are in flux and that change over time. Qualitative researchers are interested in understanding what those interpretations are at a particular point in time and in a particular context. (pp. 3–4)

The primary endeavor of qualitative research is not to verify a predetermined idea, but to uncover findings that may lead to new insights into how people think or feel in relation to a given topic and enable the researcher to talk with people about events that happened in the past and those that are yet to happen (Sherman and Webb, 2001). Qualitative research focuses on the constructed nature of reality, the relationship between the researcher and what is studied, and the situational constraints that shape the research (Denzin & Lincoln, 2008). Qualitative researchers seek answers to how an experience occurs and what meaning these experiences have. Through the use of techniques such as interviewing and observation, the qualitative researcher can capture participants' perspectives (Denzin & Lincoln, 2008).

Lewis (2007) and Bryant (2015) used qualitative research to understand the experiences of Black men who are senior administrators in higher education, using their words to construct findings. Throughout the chapter there are references to Black males in senior administrative roles. The term "senior administrator" can be found in the literature to refer to one being an "executive," which is the case for this chapter. We selected the term "senior administrator" due to the context of higher education and language used in the profession. Black male senior administrators and their experiences in higher education are the topic for the chapter, which highlights a population with a limited voice in academic writings. Qualitative research brings the voice of Black male senior administrators alive through research and other writings to end the silence of a population that speaks about resilience.

Researching Black Male Executives

Research on Black male students as well as minority executives exists; but the list of studies is sparse concerning Black male senior administrators in higher education. This chapter contributes to a growing conversation about Black male administrators at institutions of higher education. Qualitative research is valuable for this particular topic because the outcomes feature the authentic voice of the population being studied. Additionally, the cultural setting can be shared through the descriptions shared by the participants, which adds additional information about other individuals, issues, and the environment. Cultural settings are frameworks to better understand the connected pieces of the participants' lived experience (Johnson-Bailey, 2002). When participants share their narratives about an experience, multiple details that are otherwise hidden become visible. The details within individual narratives provide various examples and nuggets of information about the challenges and successes within a particular lived experience. An example of such a detail is how racism still impacts Black male senior administrators who work in higher education (Lewis, 2007). Faculty of color still confront discrimination, which affects the number of Black faculty members on college and university campuses (Branch, 2001). Living as Black males in these social contexts presents another challenge. Additionally, the successes that come from being a Black male in these spaces provide insight about what is favorable about the experiences of these men.

Resilience

Qualitative research is used in social science research to gather information from participants who have firsthand information about a phenomenon. This chapter is about Black men senior administrators who discussed the impact of their lives and the issues that created challenges during their journey. One challenge mentioned in Lewis's 2007 study was as attempt to intentionally exclude a participant from significant decision-making and networking situations. This participant experienced a peer's attempt to exclude him from a regularly scheduled cabinet meeting with a simple and piercing phrase, "We haven't decided if you are going to be a member of this group" (Lewis, 2007, p. 90). Furthermore, this participant was not extended an invitation to the local country club, as were his white peers. According to Lewis's study, the rationale provided to the participant was, "They already had enough people from the university there" (2007, p. 79). Bryant (2015) discovered that Black males who became senior diversity administrators (specifically a CDO) experience challenging moments as well. Having to "prove their worth" despite a strong background as a higher education professional was a normal encounter. Black men must often overcome obstacles to be accepted and noticed when they reach the senior administrative rank in higher education, according to Bryant (2015). It was their learning that helped propel them into a space to effectively navigate the terrain, a learning process that is mostly self-directed rather than encouraged. Additionally, learning to overcome challenges and the ability to persevere helped these Black men to be resilient in their quest to be senior administrators in higher education.

Resilience and Personal Factors

Historically, Black men were designated as an "endangered species" (Brunswick et al., 1988). Today many Black males are forced to navigate the challenges and barriers of the professional arena without much guidance. Survival in any professional arena for Black males is consistently characterized by the pressure of myths and stereotypes, dealing with accusations of being unqualified, enduring pressures to maintain a cultural identity while also "fitting in," and progressing without assistance from a professional mentor (Dey & Thompson, 1998). In Lewis's 2007 study, qualitative inquiry was used to access the perspectives that Black males hold on their resilience as senior administrators in higher education. This form of inquiry provided the opportunity to capture unfiltered examples from the perspectives of the participants. The qualitative methodological strategies used illustrated the absurdity and severity of the challenges for the participants.

Existing within a healthy work environment, meaning are there resources, like networks, available to support success, has an impact on resilience. Data from both studies suggests that healthy environments likely to be conducive to success are those environments that support diversity. Lewis (2007) reported the following based on statements from current Black male senior administrators:

> If you can be a Black administrator where there are other people of color in leadership positions, those people can provide an environment that is more supportive than one that does not have people of color in the administration. (p. 99)

Another participant said, "I think one of the healthiest environments is at an institution where in its mission statement, it embraces those things that create a sense of welcoming a diverse environment, etc.," and finally, "I think it's critically important that the upper administration sets the tone for the type of environment that will be expected" (Lewis, 2007, p. 99).

In addition to context, Lewis's study also identified other items that are likely to support the long-term success of a Black male president. One participant addressed search committees, system offices, and campus board's role in the hiring process: "My point is that sometimes search committees or the campus communities have to take a risk with us and with the proper mentoring and leadership skills, one can be successful" (Lewis, 2007, p. 98). Other participants identified mentoring programs (both formal and informal), and one encouraged the use and knowledge of history as an inspiration that can assist in being resilient. For example, one participant recommended the Harvard Institutes for Higher Education, and another responded, "Mentoring is really critical . . . having people who have been there and done that, who can help you pave the way." (2007, p. 86). However, others in the study did not have the experience of formal mentoring programs but were motivated in other ways, specifically one participant said:

> You should use your personal history as a guide. . . . You can actually pull on that history and that experience, whether you select somebody that grew up in slavery or you select someone who grew up and became a role model that you can seek support from as a frame of reference from time to time. (Lewis, 2007, p. 97)

Lewis's study also identified personal and professional characteristics that would likely lead to success for a Black male. Some of these characteristics are common for any demographic group with aspirations of ascending to the presidency and having a tenure filled with success in that role. For example, the following comments were captured: "You have to have personal and professional integrity. You have to be able to communicate. Both written and oral communication is very important" (Lewis, 2007, p. 101). However, as the probing questions deepened and discussions became more specific to Black males, more nuanced differences were eventually suggested. One participant reported, "In my opinion it is even more important that Black males have a very good grounding in self-perception." He went on to say, "You can't allow people who, basically who don't support you in the first place, to undermine the way you feel about yourself" (Lewis, 2007, p. 101). All of the participants specifically addressed the ability to recognize and embrace the fact that Black men are scrutinized at a higher level than their other professional colleagues. After mentioning the necessity to possess basic skills such as budget, organizational skills, time management, and so on, participants said the following: "I think it's especially important for Black males at White institutions to understand there is a tendency for us to be a bit more scrutinized," "When you make an error . . . they are not likely to give you a second chance so that's even more of a reason why you want to be fully aware of where you are," and "Black men are heavily scrutinized when it comes to spending the budget" (Lewis, 2007, p. 92).

Lewis's study also helped uncover coping skills the participants deemed to be important to Black male senior administrators' success in higher education. One participant said, "Well, my coping skills are a sense of work, a sense of self-esteem, a sense of knowing that God has given me a talent and that talent has been developed" (p. 102). Another participant spoke of being conditioned to deal with certain things as a result of where he grew up: "I don't think it was as difficult for me and I say that because of my coming out of place and growing up at a time where I was almost an expert at dealing with racism and oppression because I saw it every day as I grew up" (p. 102). One participant even identified an "intuition" or additional sense that enabled him to be safe in the environment: "As a result of my experience, I know, I have an antenna you know when a person is interacting with me because of my color, but I don't play into that but I definitely know when a person is interacting with me, not as a president of a university but as a Black person" (Lewis, 2007, p. 102).

Context and Supportive Factors

Black males experience moments when understanding the institutional culture isn't enough (Bryant, 2015). As CDOs, people of color, especially Black males, must identify allies and have the support of the president to move a diversity agenda forward. Without the proper connections, moving a diversity agenda forward proves to be an unmovable challenge. The challenges that Black males encounter may not always be uncovered using a quantitative research approach. Qualitative data, however, uncovered details about factors within academic environment and the support found by Black males working as senior administrators in higher education.

Black male senior administrative officers relied on their individual learning to be effective in their role (Bryant, 2015). Transitioning into an executive role occurred without a manual or formal training; hence, overcoming barriers through trial and error was one method that led to success for some executives. Understanding how to leverage support systems on campus is a priority for Black males who enter senior administrative roles. A participant in Bryant's study mentioned "injection points" to describe how he influenced campus constituents in certain areas of the university to recognize diversity as a resource:

> When you have a forward thinking president, that's always a resource even if they don't know the diversity game because that's why they hired you, you're supposed to be the expert so they hired you for your job. But then . . . there is the Centers, like the Center for Faculty Teaching and Learning, they should be strategic partners, Institutional Research, a strategic resource human resources as well and then leadership, Faculty Senate, Academic Leadership Council should be areas where you can go and inject certain diversity initiatives to make them real. Over in Student Affairs, certain areas of that like the Greek system . . . there is a huge injection point if you use it the right way. And even the athletic system, a relationship with the coaches is critical as well to the extent that you have active organizations in the community that aren't afraid to come on campus and make something happen. (Bryant, 2015, p. 127)

Given the larger social context, Black male senior administrators encounter contested spaces that require the president's support, according to Bryant's findings. Our nation continues to struggle with social issues that position Black men to be perceived in ways that vary depending on the individual. If one were to take a quick scan, it would be no surprise to notice the low number of Black men in senior administrative roles at colleges and universities. Black men who become CDOs, like others in senior administrative roles, rely on the president's power to move the diversity issues forward on campus (Bryant, 2015). Leveraging support from constituents and other senior leaders, as well as networks, is a strategy that most Black males use to be effective if they become a senior administrators within higher education (Bryant, 2015).

Themes found by Bryant (2015) about context also surfaced in Lewis's discussion on the factors that impact resilience. The participants in Lewis's study addressed context by responding to several questions designed to identify organizational factors that contribute to the resilience of Black senior administrators on campus. One participant stated:

> I think if you can have a diverse upper administration, I think that's the best environment for one to do his or her best . . . it has to be an institution that values diversity and values the importance of having a diverse faculty, staff, administration, and students on campus. (Lewis, 2007, p. 97)

Context matters and should be acknowledged because individuals, tools, and the setting are examined in concert to have a comprehensive understanding. Bryant (2017) discovered that context mattered when discussing Black males who become senior diversity administrators. Additionally, Bryant found that participants discussed their passion for diversity work and "living" social justice in the day-to-day life. In one instance, a participant talked about his upbringing, where he realized that some populations did not get the same opportunities as others. Bryant used contextual factors to describe the participants' background and when scaffolding data to understand an authentic representation of the participants' experiences. Lewis described how the pre-senior administrative social settings had an impact on how Black males cognitively approached perceptions and realities about senior administrative leadership. A participant discussed how segregation and early failures propelled him to be resilient—a piece of what he carries today as a senior leader in the academy. In both cases, the cultural setting is a force that shapes the participants' lived experience.

Institutions of higher education present support as well as challenges for Black men who enter senior administrative roles. The setting of a college or university campus depends on contextual factors, including the people, artifacts, culture, as well as other causes. Navigating the successes and challenges is necessary for CDOs to "move the needle" on diversity, which suggests the ability to be effective (Bryant, 2015). Understanding the context takes an administrator one step closer to noticing the support and challenge points on campus. To have support allows Black males an opportunity to navigate through campus cultural issues. On the contrary, the challenges faced by these men diminished the ability of Black males to be effective in their role.

A contributing factor for the success of Black male executives was the ability to build and sustain credibility on their respective campus. Credibility is important because it can be an additional step toward being accepted or being seen as authentic, according to Bryant (2015). It is not common for White male executives to discuss the idea of building credibility, a reticence that could be attributed to the normalcy of White males as the litmus test in the larger social context. In one case, a participant mentioned that "students as well as administrators, community members can kind of sense whether or not you're committed and authentic in the work that you do" (Bryant, 2015, p. 135). That phrase connects to the notion that Black men must prove they are capable and knowledgeable to do the work they were hired to lead. This also ties to Lewis's claim that the historical misrepresentation of Black men as inferior presents a challenge. The reality of "proving oneself" was a hurdle that must be overcome in the process of Black male executives garnering support.

Allies were also seen as beneficial to Black male executives, who sought to understand the campus milieu and understand the intricacies of the university. Developing key relationships with power brokers and other colleagues is essential for the success of Black male senior administrators, but it is equally important for them to develop and identify allies. It is vital to network to know how and when to leverage supports, as one CDO stated:

> You've got to be prepared because you're going to have to put your neck out there, you're going to have to challenge some things and sometimes it can be a lonely existence and so certainly that's one, being courageous and being politically savvy . . . you've got to know how to negotiate the institution and you've got to learn how to tap into not just the formal but also the informal opinion leaders. I think you've got to know how to leverage people. I think you've got to know how to tap and engage in community. (Bryant, 2015, p. 126).

Engaging networks throughout the campus community opens a lens to better understand the university, especially to negotiate systemic matters and learn how to understand what it means to be a Black male executive.

Systemic and Learning Factors

The findings of Bryant's and Lewis's studies, along with the previous contents of this chapter, clearly indicate that barriers and challenges are common for Black males seeking senior administrative positions in higher education. While examples of successful Black males leading institutions can be observed throughout the United States, one would be naive to project a significant elimination of the barriers to success (Lewis, 2007). This situation calls for efforts from the target population, their families, as well as decision-makers in the environment found in higher education, which can assist in the improvement of Black males' position in higher education.

According to Bryant (2015), context is important to how various systemic factors are situated within the organization. Organizational factors that can contribute to the effectiveness of Black male senior administrators include environments that embrace support of professional growth, the creation of formal and informal mentoring networks, and an emphasis on diversity throughout the mission of college campuses. Although the personal characteristics that contribute to the target group's resilience seem similar to that of any person or population, the state of being a Black man makes the success-facilitating characteristics much more complex. Black men should understand that professional skills and attributes such as integrity, persistence, perseverance, and organizational skills should be part of their portfolio; this, however, is not an exhaustive list. If a Black male administrator does not have the ability to cope in a hostile environment, garner the support of Black faculty and administrators as well as that of White colleagues, and treat people with respect and dignity regardless of whether that treatment is reciprocated, and does not possess a special skill that enables him to respond to and protect himself from the underlying racist behaviors of others, he will not be successful (Lewis, 2007).

Institutional and organizational politics is just one major systemic concern that impacts how most professionals accomplish their work, including Black male senior administrators. Political constructs will be found in most organizations, but each college or university presents unique bureaucratic issues because a shared governance approach permeates many campuses. In one case, Bryant (2015) discovered how Black males use their learning and networks to understand the political structures on campus. The idea of being a person from a diverse group offers another layer of politics that Black men will likely encounter (Lewis, 2007). Political structures position Black male executives to rely on the supportive networks and successes in order to work in the trenches effectively. One executive described overcoming challenges by knowing what to negotiate and how to leverage relationships with power brokers.

Implications and Additional Thoughts

The participants' voices must be presented at all times in qualitative research, and that requires an effort to eliminate the researcher's voice when interpreting and presenting the data. Johnson-Bailey (2002) highlights the importance of representing the authentic voice of the participant when collecting and constructing narratives. Often researcher tell themselves, "I get it" or "I really understand what that person means," and these are moments when such assumptions must be suspended to avoid inserting biases. Additionally, one must negotiate the insider/outsider influence that accompanies the role of "being the research instrument." Merriam et al. (2001) discuss insider and outsider status as a complex issue that researchers should explore through their positionality, power, and representation. At the same time, outsider status can be attributed to a lack of executive-level experience, a limited role due to one's position in the organizational structure, and a less broad professional background in comparison to a seasoned executive. When conducting qualitative research, it is vital for the researcher to avoid muting the participant's voice; hence; using strategies to ensure authenticity is a priority.

Transparently, we admit that we identify as Black males who have a combined forty years of experience in higher education. Our experiences and positionality made it important to identify strategies to suspend bias or judgement, especially during the data analysis process. Multiple scholars reviewed the findings, discussion, and themes in this chapter to determine relatability, as well as verify accuracy. For instance, interpretations that did not connect to the research questions were removed. There are multiple resources available to understand validity and reliability, which vary depending on the scope and design of a study.

Bogdan and Biklen (2003) define subjectivity as biases that are introduced through the opinions, prejudices, and experiences of the researcher, a serious concern that must be constantly monitored. A researcher's subjectivity is like a nonremovable garment that must be attended to throughout the research process (Peshkin, 1988). The "nonremovable garment" is real because we all live in a larger context that creates thoughts or judgements based on individual experiences. As researchers, we must take appropriate steps to avoid inserting a perspective that incorrectly represents the authentic meanings of participants. Despite the attempts of objective researchers, Peshkin (1988) argues that we must be conscious of subjectivity at all phases of the research design. It is essential for Black males who study other Black males to understand the "nonremovable garment." If interviews are used to collect data, then it is important to monitor nonverbal or verbal cues. A simple "Oh yes" on the part of the interviewer has the potential to suggest agreement with a situation the participant mentions. During the data analysis process, avoiding the interference of personal experiences is equally important. Interpreting a negative or positive exert could be misunderstood if researchers allow their thoughts or beliefs to become involved.

■ References

American Council on Education. (2007). *The American college president.* Washington, DC: Author.

Bogdan, R. C., & Biklen, S. K. (2003). *Qualitative research for education: An introduction to theories and methods.* 4th ed. Boston: Pearson.

Bryant, R. G. (2015). The professional learning narratives of chief diversity officers. Doctoral dissertation. The University of Georgia.

Brunswick, A. F., Connor, M. E., Dembo, R., Gibbs, J. T., Larson, T. E., Reed, R. J., & Solomon, B. (eds.). (1998). *Young, Black, and male in America: An endangered species.* Westport, CT: Auburn House.

Denzin, N. K., & Lincoln, Y. S. (2008). *Collecting and interpreting qualitative materials.* 3rd ed. Los Angeles: Sage.

Dey, E. L., & Thompson, C. J. (1998). Pushed to the margins: Sources of stress for African American college and university faculty. *Journal of Higher Education* 69(3), 324–45.

Feagin, J. R. (2014). *Racist America: roots, current realities, and future reparations.* New York: Routledge.

Johnson-Bailey, J. (2002). Dancing between the swords: My foray into constructing narratives. In S. B. Merriam & Associates, *Qualitative Research in Practice: Examples for Discussion and Analysis,* 323–26. San Francisco: Jossey-Bass.

Jones, E. W., Jr. (1986). Black managers: The dream deferred. *Harvard Business Review* (May–June), 84–93.

Lewis, G. L. (2007). African-American male senior administrators in predominantly white institutions: A study on resilience. Doctoral dissertation, Georgia Southern University.

Merriam, S. B., & Associates. (2002). *Qualitative research in practice: Examples for discussion and analysis.* San Francisco: Jossey-Bass.

Merriam, S. B., Johnson-Bailey, J., Lee, M. Y., Kee, Y., Ntseane, G., & Muhamad, M. (2001). Power and positionality: Negotiating insider/outsider status within and across cultures. *International Journal of Lifelong Education* 20(5), 405–16.

Peshkin, A. (1988). In search of subjectivity—one's own. *Educational Researcher* 17(7), 17–21.

Sherman, R. R., & Webb, R. B. (eds.). (2001). *Qualitative research in education: Focus and methods.* London: Routledge Falmer.

How Schools Fail Black Boys (and Girls Too)

Race, Gender, and Academic Trajectories from Kindergarten through Eighth Grade

Tomeka Davis

For many years, sociologists and other scholars have studied the academic gap between Blacks and Whites (Berends, Lucas, & Penaloza 2008; Fryer & Levitt 2004, 2006; Hanushek & Rivkin 2009; Jenks & Phillips 1998). More recently, scholars have begun to examine the emerging reverse gender gap in educational achievement and attainment (Buchman & DiPrete 2006; DiPrete & Buchman 2013; Owens 2016), as historical trends favoring men's educational attainment has shifted to favor women. While the gender advantage in education among Blacks has always favored women, little of the emerging research on the gender gap has addressed the problems facing Black male youth specifically (Buchman & DiPrete 2013; Ferguson 2002; Grant 1985; Noguera 2003). Given the severe problems Black males face in many facets of life—disproportionate levels of incarceration as well as poor employment and economic opportunities—traditional wisdom leads even the most seasoned reasoned researchers to expect that the Black gender gap in educational achievement would also be to the disadvantage of Black male youth. Yet there is a growing body of research that indicates that Black girls may not be faring better than Black boys in school, and in fact may be struggling in similar ways, possibly even worse, both socially and academically (Blake et al. 2011; Ispa-Landa 2013; Jones 2009; Morris 2007; Morris, 2016; Smith-Evans, George, Graves, Kaufman, Frohlich 2014).

Worrisome findings indicate rather than decreasing the disadvantages Black students bring from home, schools increase the gap between Black and White students. Downey, Broh, and von Hippel (2004) compared differences in seasonal learning rates (school year versus the summer) along class, gender, and race lines. The researchers found that although the class gap among students in reading and math is reduced during the school year, the gap in

169

math and reading scores *increases* between Black and White students during the school year. Similarly, Fryer and Levitt (2004) find net of all other characteristics, the gap in reading and math skills between Black and White students grows between kindergarten and third grade. However, none of this research has examined how and whether gender affects the growth of these deficits.

Existing scholarship on the academic problems of Black boys in schools has varied in its approach and direction. Although sociologists have been concerned with many of the problems facing Black men like incarceration, violence, and joblessness (Anderson 2000; Pettit and Western 2004; Royster 2003; Young 2006), few have focused specifically on the academic trajectories of Black male youth. Given the limited opportunities available to Blacks in past eras, academic achievement was less likely to impact their occupational attainment and income. With the removal of many, though not all, of the discriminatory barriers that impeded Black advancement over the last few decades, academic achievement has potentially grown in importance in predicting occupational outcomes and mobility. Yet sociological research has lagged in researching the educational trajectories of Black male youth. Most of the sociological literature on gender inequality in education in the last few decades focused on White women's disadvantage compared to White men (Buchman and DiPrete 2013; Jacobs 1996; Mickelson 1988). With regard to race, for many years much of the sociological discussion on racial inequality in education involved oppositional culture. Though much of this research was intended to debunk myths about low academic achievement being attributable to youth culture and racial identity (Ainsworth-Darnell and Downey 1998; Carter 2005; Downey and Ainsworth-Darnell 2002; Robinson and Harris 2007; Mickelson 1990; Tyson 2002, 2011), the inordinate focus on oppositional culture served to direct attention away from the macro- and meso-level institutional causes of low achievement and viable policy solutions to improve achievement. Consequently, only a handful of sociologists, mostly working in the qualitative tradition (Carter 2005; Ferguson 2002) weighed in with rigorous empirical research investigating or reflecting on the causes of low achievement among Black male youth specifically.

Over the last few decades, the academic achievement of Black male youth has grown in importance for a number of reasons. First, in earlier eras, racism and discrimination limited the educational and economic opportunities Blacks could avail themselves of, making it less likely that Black men could attain a good job with high levels of education or that they would have gained the skills from subpar schools to attend college (Katznelson 2005). Second, increasing rates of incarceration among men since the 1970s have hit Blacks, particularly Black men with low levels of education, especially hard. Thus, net of changes in the criminal justice system, low levels of educational achievement and attainment make it more likely that Black men will end up in prison (Pettit and Western 2004). Finally, structural changes in the American economy since the 1970s have made a college education increasingly important for success in the labor market (Wilson 1979; Waldinger 1996).

In this chapter, I use data from the Early Childhood Longitudinal Study (ECLS) to examine how individual correlates of disadvantage (i.e., poverty), teacher characteristics, and institutional characteristics affect gender differences in academic growth among Black children.

Ultimately, I find that although Black boys are disadvantaged compared to their White peers, Black girls are not doing much better.

Literature Review

The relatively large literature on academic differences between Blacks and Whites pinpoints three primary factors that potentially explain the role race plays in the school achievement of Black youth—culture, parental socioeconomic status, and school context. As previously mentioned, culture has loomed large in sociological studies of the racial gap in academic achievement. While some scholars cite a rejection of mainstream values in favor of behaviors that match racialized identities for the causes of the lower educational achievement of African American youth (Farkas, Lleras, & Maczuga 2002; Loury 1985; Thernstrom & Thernstrom 2003), many sociologists have spent a great deal of energy directly challenging the notion that cultural differences explain lower levels of achievement among Black youth (Ainsworth-Darnell & Downey 1999; Tyson 2002, 2011) or have somehow attempted to redirect the arguments about culture and identity by emphasizing the functional and situational nature of those behaviors (Carter 2005; Harris & Robinson 2007; Mickelson 1989). While putting cultural explanations regarding the Black-White gap to rest was necessary, the focus on culture nevertheless took valuable time and energy away from understanding other more policy-malleable causes of the Black-White achievement gap in schools. Thus, sociologists are only now getting around to examining other aspects of racial inequality in schooling.

For the most part, sociologists argue that much of the Black-White gap can be attributed to structural disadvantages faced by Blacks that increase their likelihood of poverty and expose them to poorer (economically) school conditions. Family background and socioeconomic status are probably the most significant predictor of lower educational outcomes for Black youth (Berends, Lucas, & Penazola 2008; Duncan & Magnuson 2005; Lee & Burkham 2002). For example, Berends, Lucas, & Penazola (2008) found that economic gains by Blacks since the 1970s played a significant role in reducing the Black-White achievement gap, even greater than improvements in school climate and economic context brought on by school integration efforts. Others find that the early cognitive and achievement deficits Black children face are significantly reduced altogether erased after controlling for poverty (Fryer & Levitt 2004).

Recent scholarship focused on the "boy crisis" (Barnett & Rivers 2009) and recent socio-logical research focusing on "the rise of women" has directed attention toward the differences between male and female youth, and in doing so, has paid some attention to the factors influencing attainment for Black men and boys (Buchman & DiPrete 2006; DiPrete & Buchmann 2013). Generally, this line of research argues that social and behavioral skills matter a lot for the achievement deficit boys in general suffer in relation to girls. DiPrete and Jennings (2012) found girls outperformed boys academically in the early grades because girls started school with more advanced social and behavioral skills, an advantage that the authors found grew over time. A recent study by Owens (2016) finds that behavioral differences as early as ages four and five help explain gender gaps in schooling as late as ages twenty-six to twenty-nine. Similarly, DiPrete and Buchman (2013) find that a primary explanation for boys' lower level of academic achievement is that they tend to put forth less effort in school; they conclude that boys are hurt by tacit cultural beliefs and socialization practices that characterize schoolwork as a feminine endeavor. As we will see, behavior and perceived social skills play a major part in the academic achievement and evaluations of Black male youth especially. Titus (2004) notes that

> since the advent of mass schooling in the 19th century, there have been charges that by merely being female, women teachers harm their male students. . . . The complaint now is that boys are victims of female teachers who allegedly dominate the profession, create a feminized culture in the school, design curriculum for the female's learning style, and cater to and reward female patterns of behavior. (152)

Similar sentiments remain today, as current scholars contend that curricular materials disadvantage boys, who are more likely to "prefer reading texts based on action, nonfiction, scary fairy tales, super heroes, video games, and humor" and texts with male characters (Husband 2012) and that "children's literature used in most early childhood and elementary classrooms doesn't embody the themes and characters that correspond with boys' preferences" (Husband 2012, p. 24) or that Black boys' learning style in particular requires more movement and energy (Webb-Johnson 2000).

A common theme among the existing researchers investigating racial inequality in schools but not necessarily academic achievement is teachers' sensitivity to Black boys' behavior. In an early examination of Black boys in desegregated classrooms, Grant (1985) found that teachers evaluated Black boys as having poorer behavioral skills. Interestingly, Grant noted that teachers viewed Blacks males as "mysterious." Teachers maintained that some of the Black male students were high achieving in the previous grade or classroom but regressed the following year and the reason for the fallback was unclear. Other teachers noted that Black male students were "unpredictable," or that they had difficulty understanding what "made them tick," or that they seemed to be "wearing a mask." Grant notes that this perceived unpredictability threatened teachers' sense of control over their classrooms and Black male students in particular. Carter (2005) found that boys' school behaviors were influenced by gender identities and constructions of masculinity; boys felt that they had to project an image of "hardness" and masculinity in order to successfully traverse neighborhood and school social contexts that were often characterized by violence. Ferguson's (2002) ethnography of Black boys in an integrated California elementary school paints a much more insidious image of schooling for Black boys. Ferguson found that the school was characterized by a racial order and a punishment system that resulted in Black boys being more likely to be labeled as "troublemakers" and sent to in-school suspension than children from other groups, including Black girls. Ferguson argues that as a result, Black boys do poorly in school and develop their identities through the lens of punishment. She concludes that school disciplinary policies and teacher bias that lead to time out of the classroom and the development of identities associated with failure and punishment help to funnel young Black men into the criminal justice system.

Many scholars outside of sociology are also critical of how school disciplinary structures unfairly target young Black boys, and have written extensively about how Black boys are disproportionately surveilled and punished. Like Ferguson, these scholars highlight the bias Black boys face in schools and classrooms from teachers and institutional arrangements that criminalize them, even at the youngest ages. Ladson-Billings (2011) argues that young Black boys are only perceived as "cute" for a short time before they are seen as "adult" and therefore dangerous. A recent report by The US Department of Education Office of Civil Rights (2016) showed that Black children are 3.6 times more likely to be suspended in *preschool* than White children. Moreover, the report also indicates while Black boys represent only 19 percent of male preschool enrollment, they make up 45 percent of male preschool children receiving one or more out-of-school suspensions (US Department of Education 2016). Researchers at Yale studied the implicit bias of preschool teachers using technology that tracked teacher eye movements while they watched video footage of preschool students engaged in a group activity. The researchers found that when teachers were told to expect misbehavior from one of their students, they watched the Black children, especially the Black boys longer (Gilliam et al. 2016). Other scholars highlight school disciplinary policies like zero tolerance that result in higher rates of suspension and expulsion for Black boys. Using disciplinary data from nineteen Indiana middle schools, Skiba et al. (2002) found that Black students were more often sent to the office for subjective offenses like disrespect or perceived threat while White students were more often referred for "objective" events like smoking or vandalism. Gregory, Skiba, and Noguera (2010) argue that the "discipline gap," that is, the disproportionate sanctioning of Black and Hispanic youth in schools, contributes to racial gaps in achievement. Consequently, biased evaluations and disproportionate sanctions for behavior for boys of color result in lower levels of achievement among them.

The Impact of School Context and Teacher Characteristics

Of course, school context matters a great deal for how well children do in school. Many scholars have devoted attention to school racial composition and the economic disparities that result from it. School poverty is probably the most important school context factor. Economically poorer schools have fewer physical, fiscal, and human resources to increase student achievement. Poorer schools are also less likely to attract the most talented and experienced teachers, who can command better salaries in more affluent districts (Darling–Hammond 2004; Hanushek & Rivkin 2009), and fewer high-achieving peers (Davis & Welcher 2013; Hanushek & Rivkin 2009) than more affluent schools. Fryer and Levitt (2004) conclude that growth of the Black-White deficit over the course of schooling may be a result of the fact that Black students are more likely to attend lower-quality schools (measured in part as schools with more poor students, more problems like gang participation, larger class sizes, more teacher turnover, etc.) than White students.

Moreover, even within schools, differences in teacher characteristics also affect the performance of Black students compared to their White counterparts. A great deal of research (Darling-Hammond 2004; Darling-Hammond et al. 2005, 2007; Hanushek & Rivkin 2009; Lubienski, Lubienski, & Crane 2008; Rivkin, Hanushek, & Kain 2005) indicates that minority students are more likely to have teachers who lack full certification, have fewer years of experience, and are exposed to higher teacher turnover rates, all of which negatively impact achievement.

How Are Black Male and Female Youth Different?

One of the problems associated with focusing attention on the inequalities experienced by Black men is that oftentimes, and depending on the domain of research, Black women are experiencing only marginally better outcomes, if they are doing any better at all. More generally, many scholars have challenged the "boy crisis" with a variety of critiques, including arguments that focus on the small magnitude of the academic differences between boys and girls (Davis & Keese 2015; Husain & Millimet 2009), that schools are very masculine spaces (Pascoe 2012), or that White suburban boys are still very privileged compared to boys of color or rural boys (Rivers & Barnett 2006).

While some existing work reveals that some means of marginalization may be gendered, for example by shaming Black girls for not adhering to norms of femininity (Morris 2007) while sending Black boys to the punishing room (Ferguson 2002), other research reveals that Black girls are marginalized equally, sometimes even more so, and by the same means as Black boys in school. Black et al. (2011) find that Black girls were twice as likely to receive in-school and out-of-school suspensions than other female students. Murphy, Acosta, and Kennedy-Lewis (2013) find an academic component to Black girls' behavior and treatment at school. These authors found that Black middle school girls acted out in school because they did not receive the academic support they needed from teachers. Grant (1984) found that Black girls were less likely to be assigned academic roles in classrooms and were more likely to be assigned social roles, especially as "enforcers" of teacher disciplinary norms. Ispa-Landa (2013) and Wells et al. (2009) found that Black girls experience more social isolation than Black boys in racially integrated school settings, while Morris (2016) finds that Blacks girls "are also directly impacted by criminalizing policies and practices [in schools] that render them vulnerable to abuse, exploitation, dehumanization, and under the worst circumstances, death" (p. 2). Thus, activists and scholars have begun to question the specific focus on Black men and male youth that seemingly render invisible the challenges faced by Black women and female youth. The heavy focus on Black men and their policy needs at the expense of focus devoted to all Black youth regardless of gender and, as I demonstrate in the next section, a failure to take the intersections of race and gender and other identities into account raise theoretical questions about inequality and social justice that sociologists and feminist theorists have tried to address (Choo & Ferree 2010; Collins 2005; McCall 2005).

Using Intersectionality Theory to Frame the Academic Trajectories of Black Boys and Girls

Scholars working in the intersectionality tradition view race, class, and gender as "mutually constructing systems of power" (Collins 2005, p. 11) and maintain that ranking oppressions or regarding one to be more important that the other is problematic (Crenshaw 1989; Collins 2000, 2005; King 1988). Key to scholars working in this field is the "complexities" of intersecting identities (McCall 2005). Black women, the group whose oppression intersectionality theory was intended to address, experienced forms of subjugation different from Black men and White women. For example, McCall (2005) notes that in the earliest treatments of intersectionality, Black feminist scholars argued that new ways of approaching Black women's oppression was necessary:

> It was not possible, for example, to understand a black woman's experience from previous studies of gender combined with previous studies of race because the former focused on white women and the latter on black men. Something new was needed because of the distinct and frequently conflicting dynamics that shaped the lived experience of subjects in these social locations. To take just one example from the earliest explorations, Black women seemed to achieve greater equality with men of their race relative to White women because the conditions of slavery and white supremacy forced them to work on par with black men, yet black women also were more vulnerable to sexual violence because whites did not consider them worth protecting "as women." The potential for both multiple and conflicting experiences of subordination and power required a more wide-ranging and complex terrain of analysis. (p. 1780)

Consequently, intersectionality scholars argue that these "multiple" and "conflicting" identities must be considered not only in the ways scholars and activists understand racial inequality but also in the approaches used to ameliorate it. Moreover, while the theory was initially intended to "demarginalize" Black women's experiences (Crenshaw 1989), it has been applied to other groups, including Black men (Collins 2005). In the context of this chapter, intersectionality is a useful way of framing race- and gender-based deficits in academic achievement because it embraces the potential complexities of outcomes. Thus, while the egregious attacks on Black boys and men in some domains like the criminal justice system are coming to light more and more, intersectionality theory suggests that (1) academic outcomes for Black girls should not be marginalized (2) untangling the effects of mutually constructed systems of power is difficult (Collins 2005), and (3) provides a framework for understanding why taking intersectional identities into account is important, regardless of whether the observed gender differences between Black boys and Black girls are "statistically significant."

In the next section, I present a complex analysis that takes these intersecting identities into account. As scholars working within the intersectionality framework contend, quantitative analyses that use an intersectional rather than additive approach are often complicated (McCall 2005). The analyses that follow are in fact very detailed. I model the effects of race, gender, and time, as well as a series of student-level and school-level variables to see how all of these factors combine to disadvantage Black boys and girls academically.

Methods

I use data from the Early Childhood Longitudinal Study–Kindergarten (ECLS-K) to examine the factors that impact the academic trajectories of Black boys and girls. ECLS-K is a nationally representative, longitudinal survey conducted by the National Center for Education Statistics under the authority of the US Department of Education that follow students over time. The survey collects data on students, family, teacher, and school characteristics from students across the country and US territories including Guam, Puerto Rico and the US Virgin Islands. ECLS uses a complicated design in obtaining its sample; the sample includes children from different racial/ethnic and socioeconomic backgrounds. The survey takes special care in making sure that some racial and ethnic groups are oversampled to ensure that enough students of this race/ethnicity are in the survey to make estimates derived from any analysis more accurate. ECLS began collecting data on children who were in kindergarten in the fall of 1998 and conducted follow-ups in the spring of kindergarten and fall and spring of first grade, followed by the spring of their third-, fifth-, and eighth-grade years. The original wave of data collection consisted of twenty thousand kindergartners, but as a result of attrition and other analytic considerations, my analytic sample consists of approximately eleven thousand students.

Key Variables

I use math and reading IRT (item response theory) test scores to assess academic achievement. These assessments were administered as part of the ECLS-K survey at each wave of data collection. Race is a binary variable coded 1 to indicate that a student is Black. Female is also binary and coded 1 to indicate that a student is female. To assess behavior, I use a variable in ECLS that assesses acting-out behaviors such as the frequency with which a child argues, fights, gets angry, acts impulsively, and disturbs ongoing activities. The frequency of these behaviors is measured on a four-point scale (1 to 4) where 4 indicates greater frequency of the behaviors. Family poverty is a dichotomous variable coded 0 if a family was in poverty in a given wave and 1 if a family was at or above the federal poverty threshold in the survey year. Teacher experience is a continuous variable that indicates how long the teacher responding to the survey had been teaching the grade currently assigned. School poverty is a continuous variable that reports the percentage of students in a school who are eligible for free lunch. Unfortunately, all of these key variables were not available in every wave of data collection. More specifically, years teaching current grade and behavior were only available through the fifth-grade wave of ECLS-K. Consequently, I was forced to restrict the descriptive and multivariate analyses including these variables to fifth rather than eighth grade.

Analyses

In addition to basic descriptive analyses, I utilize multilevel modeling methods to examine changes in reading and math achievement over time. My analysis contains three different analytic levels: The level-1 unit of analysis is time, that is, the various waves of the ECLS-K data, the level-2 analysis models differences between children and therefore contains explanatory variables at the individual level, while the level-3 model contains school-level variables. The level-1 model is formulated as

$$Y_{ijk} = \pi_0 + \pi_1(\text{WAVE}_{ijk}) + e_{ijk},$$

where Y_{ijk} represents the reading/math score at time i for student j in school k and π_{0ijk} represents the average reading/math score at the start of kindergarten and π_{1ijk} represents the linear rate of growth for reading scores across each wave of data. The full level-2 model consists of time-varying and time-invariant child-level explanatory variables along with interactions among these variables. In the level-2 model, π_0 and π_1, are outcome measures. The level-2 model is specified as

$$\pi_{0jk} = \beta_{00k} + \beta_{01k}(\text{BLACK}_{jk}) + \beta_{02k}(\text{FEMALE}_{jk}) + \beta_{03k}(\text{FAMILY POVERTY}_{jk}) + \beta_{04k}(\text{BEHAVIOR}_{jk})$$
$$+ \beta_{05k}(\text{TEACHER EXPERIENCE}) + \beta_{060k}(\text{BLACK}_{jk} \cdot \text{FEMALE}_{jk}) + \beta_{07k}(\text{BLACK}_{jk} \cdot \text{BEHAVIOR}_{jk})$$
$$+ \beta_{080k}(\text{BLACK}_{jk} \cdot \text{TEACHER EXPERIENCE}_{jk}) + r_{0k}$$

$$\pi_1 = \beta_{10k} + \beta_{11k}(\text{BLACK}_{jk}) + \beta_{12k}(\text{FEMALE}_{jk}) + \beta_{13k}(\text{FAMILY POVERTY}_{jk}) + \beta_{14k}(\text{BEHAVIOR}_{jk})$$
$$+ \beta_{15k}(\text{TEACHER EXPERIENCE}_{jk}) + \beta_{16k}(\text{BLACK}_{jk} \cdot \text{FEMALE}_{jk}) + \beta_{17k}(\text{BLACK}_{jk} \cdot \text{BEHAVIOR}_{jk})$$
$$+ \beta_{18k}(\text{BLACK}_{jk} \cdot \text{TEACHER EXPERIENCE}_{jk}) + r_{0k}$$

Finally, the level-3 model represents the effect of school poverty on initial reading and math scores at the start of kindergarten as well on reading and math score growth. The level-3 equation is represented as

$$\beta_{00k} = \gamma_{000} + \gamma_{001}(\text{SCHOOL POVERTY}_k) + u_{00k}$$
$$\beta_{10k} = \gamma_{110} + \gamma_{111}(\text{SCHOOL POVERTY}_k) + u_{11k}{}^{[1]}$$

Results

As figures 1 and 2 show, Black student test scores are relatively close to White students at the start of kindergarten. Black boys and girls begin kindergarten virtually tied with White girls and boys, though there is some disadvantage (the regression coefficient for the Black effect on the intercept will tell us exactly how much). But there is a notable divergence over time—Black boys and girls begin to fall behind their White counterparts. Black girls have no real advantage over Black boys in reading or math. The racial differences grow over time and appear larger than within-race gender differences.

Table 1 displays descriptive statistics for the key variables in the analysis. The patterns for reading and math scores in Table 1 mimic the patterns seen in figures 1 and 2. Like the figures, Black and White student test scores are closest in the fall of kindergarten, and grow over time such that by fifth grade, Black children's math and reading test scores resemble the test scores of White third graders. The within-race gender gap does not grow nearly as much and appears relatively steady over the time period covered here (between two and five points). Black and White girls outpace their male counterparts in reading but only by two to five points at each test period; similarly, Black and White boys outpace their female counterparts in math by a similar margin at each test period. The regression models will indicate whether these differences are statistically significant (holding other factors constant).

Table 1 displays the means for other key variables from kindergarten through fifth grade. Family poverty status is a binary variable coded 1 if a family is not in poverty at the time of data collection. Since the variable is binary, the mean indicates the proportion of families (Black families, White families, Black boys' families, Black girls' families, etc.) that were nonpoor at each wave. Poverty is much higher among Black families in the ECLS-K data. Roughly 60 percent of Black families were nonpoor while 90 percent of White families were nonpoor. Black students also experienced higher exposure to school poverty, almost two to three times more than White students. Teachers rated Black children higher with regard to externalizing than White children at each wave of data collection. Black boys were rated as exhibiting the most negative behaviors, followed by White boys and Black girls. White students also tend to have slightly more experienced teachers than Black students, though only by about a year. Mean externalizing behavior scores tend to grow over time, but it does not appear that they grow at different rates for any particular group. Thus although Black boys are rated as acting out in class and school more than other students, the growth in these ratings over time does not appear to be specific to them.

Table 2 displays regression estimates of the impact of the child- and school-level variables on reading and math scores. Before I present the findings from the models, the layout of the table requires some explanation. First, the first set of results under the label "Intercept" shows two things. The estimates for the "Intercept-intercept" term, γ_{000}, represents the average reading and math score when all of the covariates are set to zero, that is, reading/math score in the fall of kindergarten for a White male student whose family lives below the poverty line, has average behavior rating scores, and has a teacher with no experience teaching the student's current

Figure 1. Kindergarten through Eighth Grade Reading Trajectories by Race and Gender

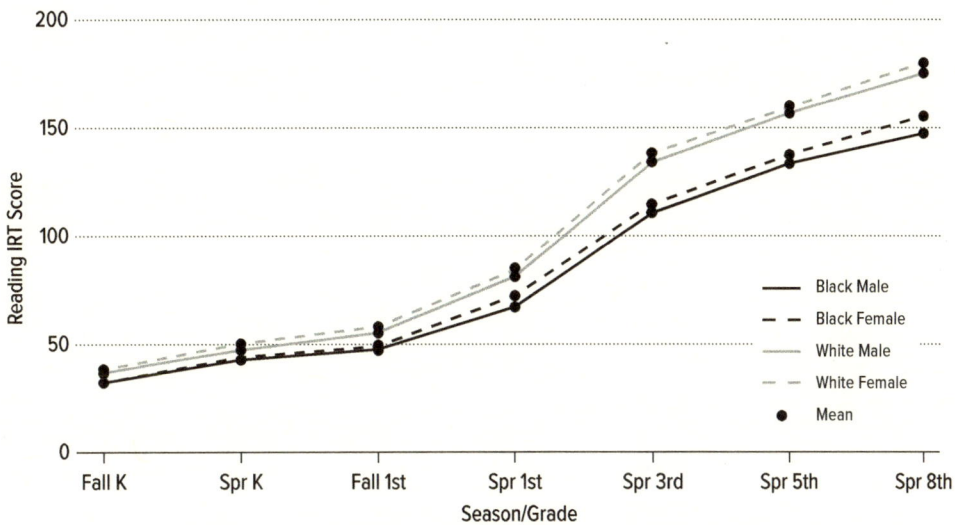

Figure 2. Kindergarten through Eighth Grade Math Trajectories by Race and Gender

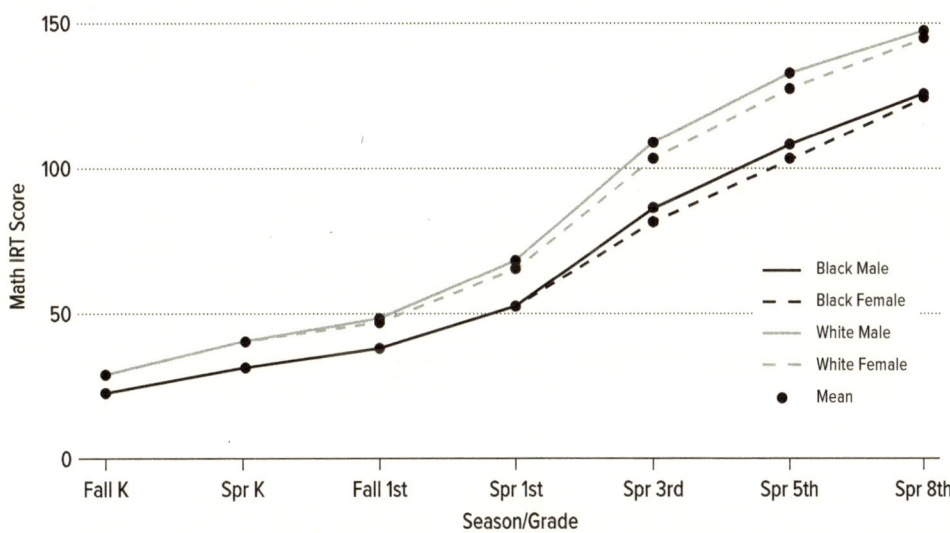

grade. The various child- and school-level covariates listed below γ_{000} represent the effect of the child and school-level covariates on "initial status," that is, reading and math scores in the fall of kindergarten. For example, the estimate for γ_{010} represents the difference between Black and White students on reading and math scores in the fall of kindergarten. The estimates in the second portion of the model under the "Linear Slope for Wave" represent, first, the impact of time on reading of math scores (γ_{100}) followed by the effect of the child- and school-level

Table 1. Means for Key Variables by Race and Gender

	BLACKS	WHITES	BLACK BOYS	BLACK GIRLS	WHITE BOYS	WHITE GIRLS
Reading scores						
Fall kindergarten	32.577	36.609	32.222	32.936	35.897	37.324
Spring kindergarten	42.597	48.234	41.971	43.210	46.954	49.535
Fall 1st grade	48.560	55.407	47.822	49.361	53.645	57.195
Spring 1st grade	70.798	82.060	68.774	72.744	80.036	84.074
3rd grade	112.884	132.963	110.337	115.214	130.449	135.508
5th grade	135.024	151.832	132.917	137.271	150.060	153.628
Math scores						
Fall kindergarten	22.518	28.372	22.627	22.408	28.578	28.163
Spring kindergarten	31.033	39.286	31.454	30.621	38.634	38.932
Fall 1st grade	38.761	46.796	38.735	47.209	46.377	53.423
Spring 1st grade	53.423	65.814	54.169	52.706	67.036	64.599
3rd grade	84.049	104.127	85.481	82.740	106.490	101.737
5th grade	106.329	126.497	108.114	104.427	129.060	123.900
Family poverty						
Fall kindergarten	0.580	0.904	0.594	0.568	0.907	0.900
Spring kindergarten	—	—	—	—	—	—
1st grade	0.586	0.893	0.597	0.575	0.897	0.889
3rd grade	0.565	0.871	0.572	0.559	0.868	0.874
5th grade	0.579	0.823	0.598	0.558	0.825	0.822
Externalizing behaviors						
Fall kindergarten	1.762	1.554	1.906	1.616	1.670	1.436
Spring kindergarten	1.818	1.560	1.958	1.675	1.700	1.462
1st grade	1.808	1.576	1.954	1.670	1.707	1.446
3rd grade	1.917	1.630	2.044	1.801	1.747	1.512
5th grade	1.899	1.605	2.033	1.757	1.741	1.478
Teacher experience						
Fall kindergarten	7.899	9.704	7.793	8.006	9.719	9.689
Spring kindergarten	7.904	9.748	7.843	7.967	9.758	9.738
1st grade	8.078	8.939	7.484	8.649	8.846	9.031
3rd grade	7.381	8.247	7.490	7.281	8.183	8.313
5th grade	6.301	7.859	6.264	6.400	7.870	7.848
School poverty						
Fall kindergarten	57.167	22.373	56.660	57.681	22.232	22.514
Spring kindergarten	—	—	—	—	—	—
1st grade	48.030	20.820	47.792	48.255	21.154	20.487
3rd grade	54.289	24.009	54.444	54.147	23.992	24.027
5th grade	60.977	34.022	61.103	60.842	33.478	34.573

Table 2. Multilevel Maximum Likelihood Results for Reading and Math Trajectories (Coefficients Only)

	READING				MATH			
	MODEL 1	MODEL 2	MODEL 3	MODEL 4	MODEL 1	MODEL 2	MODEL 3	MODEL 4
Intercept								
Intercept: γ_{000}	7.485c	7.764c	7.501c	7.792c	8.530c	8.121c	8.598c	8.121c
Black: γ_{010}	−5.478c	−0.681	−5.653c	−1.135	−7.653c	−1.041	−8.449c	−1.031
Female: γ_{020}	2.652c	1.975c	2.704c	2.067c	−2.583c	0.333	−2.694c	0.259
Family Poverty: γ_{030}	6.979c	1.237	6.981c	1.223	4.529c	0.313	4.535c	0.311
Behavior: γ_{040}	−2.609c	−0.092	−2.633c	−0.250	−2.346c	−0.256	−2.406c	0.298
Teacher Experience: γ_{050}	0.021	0.079	0.016	0.067	−0.007	0.093b	−0.009	0.100c
Black · Female: γ_{060}			−0.546	−1.052			1.124	0.840
Black · Behavior: γ_{070}			0.158	1.165			0.453	0.371
Black · Teacher Experience: γ_{080}			0.053	0.132			0.020	−0.050
School Poverty: γ_{001}	−0.064c	0.084c	−0.064c	0.085c	−0.019b	0.022c	−0.019b	0.021a
Linear Slope for WAVE								
Intercept: γ_{100}	27.484c	27.496c	27.483c	27.475c	22.222c	22.515c	22.222c	22.533c
Wave · Black: γ_{110}		−1.892c		−1.703c		−2.798c		−3.078c
Wave · Female: γ_{120}		0.287		0.264		−1.300c		−1.327c
Wave · Family Poverty: γ_{130}		1.867c		1.872c		1.508c		1.511c
Wave · Behavior: γ_{140}		−0.882c		−0.877c		−0.781c		−0.827c
Wave · Teacher Experience: γ_{150}		−0.019		−0.015		−0.033c		−0.034c
Wave · Black · Female: γ_{160}				0.244				0.245
Wave · Black · Behavior: γ_{170}				0.244				0.314
Wave · Black · Teacher Experience: γ_{180}				−0.042				0.009
Wave · School Poverty: γ_{101}		−0.047c		−0.047c		−0.012c		−0.012c
Log–Likelihood	−112158.2	−112157.63	−111877.04	−111875.03	−108195.83	−107943.31	−108194.93	−107939.71
N	11,253				11,314			

a p < 0.05, b p < 0.01, c p < 0.001

covariates on reading and math trajectories. The latter of these are "cross-level interactions" and are therefore shown as interaction terms in the tables. For example, the estimate γ_{110} for the wave × Black interaction is the effect of race on reading and math score growth.

I present four models. The first model is a "main effects" model, which does not include any cross-level or within-child interactions. In this model, race is a significant predictor of math and reading test scores. Black students have reading scores that are roughly five points lower than White students and math scores that are almost eight points lower. Behavior also has a significant negative effect on scores, as does school poverty. Family poverty has a positive impact on scores, meaning that being from a family that has an income above the poverty line is associated with a seven- and five-point increase in reading score and math scores respectively. Surprisingly, teacher experience has no significant impact on scores. This may be a consequence of the fact that teacher experience is operationalized as experience in teaching the present grade and not overall time teaching. School poverty has a significant negative effect on reading and math scores. The variable "wave" in Model 1 indicates the impact of time on test scores. The effect is positive and significant, indicating that scores increase with each successive wave of data collection, around twenty-seven points with each wave.

Model 2 of table 2 includes cross-level interactions for wave- and child-level time-variant and time-invariant characteristics. The coefficient for the wave × Black indicates that being Black reduces the impact of a wave on math and reading score increases. In other words, Black students' scores increase at lower rates over time than do White students. The cross-level interaction between wave and gender is significant only for math, indicating that girls' math scores rise at a slower rate over time than do boys', but not for reading. Behavior also tends to dampen the effect of time on student learning. Again, students who are rated as exhibiting negative classroom behaviors have lower rates of test score growth than students who are rated as exhibiting less of these behaviors. Although I include no direct tests indicating evaluation bias on the part of teachers toward Blacks students, coupled with established research, this finding suggests that any racial bias in evaluating the behavior of Black students has an apparent negative impact on their achievement.

Model 3 of table 2 examines the interactions between the child-level covariates. Surprisingly, none of these interactions are significant. For the present purposes, the key interaction in these models are between race and gender. The lack of a race × gender significant interaction in these models mimics the pattern seen in figures 1 and 2: The absence of a significant interaction coefficient indicates that the gap in the lines between Black male and female students is not statistically significant, meaning that Black boys are not scoring significantly worse than Black girls in reading and vice versa for math. Instead, the biggest and most meaningful gap appears to be between Black and White students. Model 4 combines Models 2 and 3. The results in Model 4 largely resemble the outcomes in the previous models. None of the three-way interactions in the model are significant. This indicates that, for example, being female has no special effect on math and reading growth over and above the impact of race on math and reading growth. The same is true for the wave × Black × behavior and wave × Black × teacher experience interactions. Behavior and teacher experience add no additional deficit or improvement to the effect that race alone has on reading and math growth.

Discussion

My goal in this chapter was to examine how race and gender, along with other factors, impact the academic achievement of Black boys and girls. Although the abysmal treatment and outcomes of Black men in many other facets of life might lead many to assume that Black boys are the most academically disadvantaged group, the results presented here indicate that Black girls experience similar outcomes. In line with previous research to some degree (Brooks-Gunn et al. 2003), racial deficits upon entering kindergarten were relatively small, but they increased over time. In the descriptive analysis, Black girls and Black boys were virtually equal in reading and math at the start of kindergarten, and over time the differences between them amounted to only a few points, which in the multivariate models proved to be meaningless. However, racial disadvantage proved robust, even after controlling for family and school poverty. As predicted, behavior ratings did have a strong effect on reading and math growth, though this factor did not compound the racial disadvantage. This may not necessarily matter; since Black boys had the most negative behavior ratings anyway, the interaction between race and behavior may have been redundant.

So how should policymakers think about approaching the racial gap in achievement? In keeping with the intersectionality framework outlined earlier in the chapter, Collins (2005) notes that an antiracist social justice agenda cannot ignore other identities like gender, class, age, and so on. While it is important to confront the problems facing Black boys and men, scholars and activists should not overlook the challenges facing Black girls and women. Family and poverty had a similarly robust effect on academic disparities in my analytic models, indicating that these variables matter too. Thus, while racial deficits proved to have a stronger impact on academic disparities here, future research should explore the intersecting identities of race, class, and gender on other outcomes and experiences in schools.

■ **Note**

1. This translates into the following mixed model: $Y_{ijk} = \gamma_{000} + \gamma_{001}(\text{SCHOOL POVERTY}_k) + \gamma_{010}(\text{BLACK}_{jk})$
   $+ \gamma_{020}(\text{FEMALE}_{jk}) + \gamma_{030}(\text{FAMILY POVERTY}_{jk}) + \gamma_{040}(\text{BEHAVIOR}_{jk}) + \gamma_{050}(\text{TEACHER EXPERIENCE}_{jk})$
   $+ \gamma_{060}(\text{BLACK}_{jk} \cdot \text{FEMALE}_{jk}) + \gamma_{070}(\text{BLACK}_{jk} \cdot \text{BEHAVIOR}_{jk}) + \gamma_{080}(\text{BLACK}_{jk} \cdot \text{TEACHER EXPERIENCE}_{jk})$
   $+ \gamma_{100}(\text{WAVE}_{ijk}) + \gamma_{101}(\text{WAVE}_{ijk} \cdot \text{SCHOOL POVERTY}_k) + \gamma_{110}(\text{WAVE}_{ijk} \cdot \text{BLACK}_{jk}) + \gamma_{120}(\text{WAVE}_{ijk} \cdot \text{FEMALE}_{jk})$
   $+ \gamma_{130}(\text{WAVE}_{ijk} \cdot \text{FAMILY POVERTY}_{jk}) + \gamma_{140}(\text{WAVE}_{ijk} \cdot \text{BEHAVIOR}_{jk}) + \gamma_{150}(\text{WAVE}_{ijk} \cdot \text{TEACHER EXPERIENCE}_{jk})$
   $+ \gamma_{160}(\text{WAVE}_{ijk} \cdot \text{BLACK}_{jk} \cdot \text{FEMALE}_{jk}) + \gamma_{170}(\text{WAVE}_{ijk} \cdot \text{BLACK}_{jk} \cdot \text{BEHAVIOR}_{jk}) + \gamma_{180}(\text{WAVE}_{ijk} \cdot \text{BLACK}_{jk} \cdot$
   $\text{TEACHER EXPERIENCE}_{jk}) + e_{ijk}.$ In order to obtain more interpretable estimates of the intercepts

(γ_{000}, interpreted as reading and math scores at the Fall of Kindergarten, and γ_{110}, the average growth rate of math and reading scores across each wave of data collection), I grand mean center behavior (which has no meaning when set to zero in its uncentered form) and recoded wave to be wave minus 1. Thus, the estimates for γ_{000} is math or reading score at the Fall of Kindergarten for a White male student whose family lives below the poverty line, has average behavior rating scores, and has a teacher with no experience teach the student's current grade.

■ **References**

Ainsworth-Darnell, J. W., & Downey, D. B. (1998). Assessing the oppositional culture explanation for racial/ethnic differences in school performance. *American Sociological Review 63*(4), 536–53.

Anderson, E. (2000). *Code of the street: Decency, violence, and the moral life of the inner city*. New York: Norton.

Barnett, R., & Rivers, C. (2009). *Same difference: How gender myths are hurting our relationships, our children, and our jobs*. New York: Basic Books.

Berends, M., Lucas, S. R., & Penaloza, R. V. (2008). How changes in families and schools are related to trends in Black-White Test Scores. *Sociology of Education 81*(4): 313–44.

Blake, J., Butler, B. R., Lewis, C., & Darensbourg, A. (2011). Unmasking the inequitable discipline experiences of urban Black girls: Implications for urban educational stakeholders. *Urban Review 43*, 90–106.

Brooks-Gunn, J., Klebanov, P., Smith, J., Duncan, G., & Lee, K. (2003). The Black-White test score gap in young children: Contributions of test and family characteristics. *Applied Developmental Science 7*(4), 239–52.

Buchmann, C., & DiPrete, T. (2006). The growing female advantage in college completion: The role of family background and academic achievement. *American Sociological Review 71*(4), 515–41.

Carter, P. L. (2005). *Keepin' it real: School success beyond Black and White*. New York: Oxford University Press.

Choo, H. Y., & Ferree, M. M. (2010). Practicing intersectionality in sociological research: A critical analysis of inclusions, interactions, and institutions in the study of inequalities. *Sociological Theory 28*(2), 129–49.

Collins, P. H. (2000). *Black feminist thought: Knowledge, consciousness, and the politics of empowerment*. New York: Routledge.

Crenshaw, K. (1989). Demarginalizing the intersection of race and sex: A Black feminist critique of antidiscrimination doctrine, feminist theory, and antiracist politics. *University of Chicago Legal Forum 1989*(1), 139–67.

Darling-Hammond, L. (2004). Inequality and the right to learn: Access to qualified teachers in California's public schools. *Teacher's College Record 106*(10), 1936–66.

———. (2007). Race, inequality and educational accountability: The irony of "no child left behind." *Race, Ethnicity, and Education 10*(3), 245–60.

Darling-Hammond, L., Holtzman, D. J., Gatlin, S. J., & Vasquez Heilig, J. (2005). Does teacher preparation matter? Evidence about teacher certification, Teach for America, and teacher effectiveness. *Education Policy Analysis Archives 13*(42), 1–42.

Davis, K. (2008). Intersectionality as buzzword: A sociology of science perspective on what makes a feminist theory successful. *Feminist Theory 9*, 67–85.

Davis, T., & Keese, T. (2015). Parental expectations, family structure, and the Black gender gap in educational and occupational attainment: An intersectional approach to the social psychological model of status attainment. In E. Wright & E. Wallace (eds.), *Black sociology: Contemporary issues and future directions* (pp. 92–114). Farnham, UK: Ashgate.

Davis, T., & Welcher, A. (2013). School quality and the vulnerability of the Black middle class: The continuing significance of race as a predictor of disparate schooling environments. *Sociological Perspectives 56*(4), 467–93.

DiPrete, T., & Buchman, C. (2013). *The rise of women: The growing gender gap in education and what it means for American schools.* New York: Russell Sage Foundation.

DiPrete, T., & Jennings, J. (2012). Social and behavioral skills and the gender gap in early educational achievement. *Social Science Research 41*(1), 1–15.

Downey, D. B., & Ainsworth-Darnell, J. W. (2002). The search for oppositional culture among Black students. *American Sociological Review 67*(1), 156–64.

Downey, D. B., Von Hippel, P., & Broh, B. (2004). Are schools the great equalizer? Cognitive inequality during the summer months and the school year. *American Sociological Review 69*(5), 613–35.

Duncan, G. J., & Magnuson, K. A. (2005). Can family socioeconomic resources account for racial and ethnic test score gaps? *Future of Children 15*(1), 35–54.

Farkas, G., Lleras, C., & Maczuga, S. (2002). Does oppositional culture exist in minority and poverty peer groups? *American Sociological Review 67*(1), 148–55.

Ferguson, A. A. (2001). *Bad boys: Public schools in the making of Black masculinity.* Ann Arbor: University of Michigan Press.

Fryer, R., & Levitt, S. (2004). Understanding the Black-White test score gap in the first two years of school. *Review of Economics and Statistics 86*(2), 447–64.

———. (2006). The Black-White test score gap through third grade. *American Law and Economics Review 8*(2), 249–281.

Gilliam, W., Maupin, A., Reyes, C., Accavitti, M., & Shic, F. (2016). Do early educators' implicit biases regarding sex and race relate to behavior expectations and recommendations of preschool expulsions and suspensions? Yale Child Study Center. Http://ziglercenter.yale.edu/publications/Preschool%20Implicit%20Bias%20Bias?%20Policy%Preschool%20Implicit%20Bias%20Policy%20Brief_final_9_26_276766_5379.pdf.

Grant, L. (1984). Black females' place in desegregated classrooms. *Sociology of Education 57*(2), 98–111.

———. (1985). Uneasy alliances: Black males, teachers, and peers in desegregated classrooms. ERIC Number ED262115.

Hanushek, E., & Rivkin, S. (2009). Harming the best: How schools affect the Black-White achievement gap. *Journal of Policy Analysis and Management 28*(3), 366–93.

Harris, A. L., & Robinson, K. (2007). Schooling behaviors or prior skills? A cautionary tale of omitted variable bias within oppositional culture theory. *Sociology of Education 80*(2), 139–57.

Husain, M., & Millimet, D. L. (2009). The mythical "boy crisis"? *Economics of Education Review 28*(1), 38–48.

Husband, T. (2012). Why can't Jamal read? *Phi Delta Kappan 93*(5), 23–27.

Ispa-Landa, S. (2013). Gender, race, and justifications for group exclusion urban Black students bussed to affluent suburban schools. *Sociology of Education 86*(3), 218–33.

Jacobs, J. (1996). Gender inequality and higher education. *Annual Review of Sociology 22*, 153–85.

Katznelson, I. (2005). *When affirmative action was White: An untold history of racial inequality in twentieth-century America.* New York: Norton.

King, D. (1988). Multiple jeopardy, multiple consciousness: The context of a Black feminist ideology. *Signs 14*(1), 42–72.

Ladson Billings, G. (2011). Boyz to men? Teaching to restore Black boys' childhood. *Race, Ethnicity, and Education 14*(1), 7–15.

Lee, V., & Burkham, D. (2002). *Inequality at the starting gate: Social background differences in achievement as children begin school.* Washington, DC: Economic Policy Institute.

Loury, G. (1985). The moral quandary of the Black community. *Public Interest 79*, 9–22.

Lubienski, S., Lubienski, C., & Crane, C. (2008). Achievement differences and school type: The role of school climate, teacher certification, and instruction. *American Journal of Education 115*(1), 97–138.

McCall, L. (2005). The complexity of intersectionality. *Signs 30*(3), 1771–1800.

Mickelson, R. (1989). Why does Jane read and write so well? The anomaly of women's achievement. *Sociology of Education 62*(1), 47–63.

———. (1990). The attitude-achievement paradox among Black adolescents. *Sociology of Education 63*(1), 44–61.

Morris, E. W. (2007). "Ladies" or "Loudies"? Perceptions and experiences of black girls in classrooms. *Youth & Society 38*(4), 490–515.

Morris, M. 2016. *Pushout: The criminalization of Black girls in schools.* New York: The New Press.

Murphy, A. M. A., & Kennedy-Lewis, B. (2013). "I'm not running around with my pants sagging, so how am I not acting like a lady?": Intersections of race and gender in the experiences of female middle school troublemakers. *Urban Review 45*(5), 586–610.

Owens, J. (2016). Early childhood behavior problems and the gender gap in educational attainment in the United States. *Sociology of Education 89*(3), 236–58.

Pascoe, C. (2012). *Dude, you're a fag: Masculinity and sexuality in high school.* Berkeley: University of California Press.

Pettit, B., & Western, B. (2004). Mass imprisonment and the life course: Race and class inequality in U.S. incarceration. *American Sociological Review 69*(2), 151–69.

Phillips, M., Crouse, J., & Ralph, J. (1998). Does the Black-White test score gap widen after children enter school? In C. Jencks & M. Phillips (eds.), *The Black-White test score gap* (pp. 229–72). Washington, DC: Brookings Institution.

Rivers, C., & Barnett, R. (2006). The myth of "the boy crisis." *Washington Post,* April 9, p. B01.

Rivkin, S., Hanushek, E., & Kain, J. (2005). Teachers, schools, and academic achievement. *Econometrica 73*(2), 417–58.

Royster, D. (2003). *Race and the invisible hand: How White networks exclude Black men from blue-collar jobs.* Berkeley: University of California Press.

Smith-Evans, L., George, J., Graves, F., Kaufmann, L. S., & Frohlich, L. (2014). *Unlocking opportunity for African American girls: A call to action for educational equity.* Http://www.naacpldf.org/files/publications/Unlocking%20Opportunity%20for%20African%20American%20Girls_0.pdf.

Thernstrom, A., & Thernstrom, S. (2003). *No excuses: Closing the racial gap in learning.* New York: Simon and Schuster.

Titus, J. (2004). Boy trouble: Rhetorical framing of boys' underachievement. *Discourse: Studies in the Cultural Politics of Education 25*(2), 145–69.

Tyson, K. (2002). Weighing in: Elementary-age students and the debate on attitudes toward school among Black students. *Social Forces 80*(4), 1157–89.

———. (2011). *Integration interrupted: Tracking, Black students, and acting White after* Brown. New York: Oxford University Press.

Waldinger, R. (1996). *Still the promised city? New immigrants and African-Americans in post-industrial New York.* Cambridge, MA: Harvard University Press.

Wells, A. S., Holme, J., Revilla, A., & Atanda, A. (2009). *Both sides now: The story of school desegregation's graduates.* Berkeley: University of California Press.

US Department of Education, Office of Civil Rights. (2016). Key data highlights on equity and opportunity gaps in our nation's public schools: 2013–2014 civil rights data collection. Http://www2.ed.gov/about/offices/list/ocr/docs/crdc-2013-14.html.

Wilson, W. J. (1987). *The truly disadvantaged: The inner city, the underclass, and public policy.* Chicago: University of Chicago Press.

Young, A. A. (2006). *The minds of marginalized Black men: Making sense of mobility, opportunity, and future life chances.* Princeton, NJ: Princeton University Press.

Aberrations of "Home"

Gay Neighborhoods and the Experiences of Community among GBQ Men of Color

Theodore Greene

Travyon (twenty-six, African American, gay) lives on the South Side of Chicago with Cedric (twenty-four, African American, gay), his boyfriend of five years. Both college-educated professionals, they prefer a hip-hop presentation outside of working hours: dark, oversized T-shirts that obscure their sinewy, muscular frames; baggy jeans hanging low enough to reveal a streak of brightly colored boxer shorts; brightly colored leather sneakers so polished they glisten in the sunlight. Throughout our interview, both peppered their eloquent comments with various Black colloquialisms, demonstrating their extensive exposure to and knowledge of street culture (Anderson, 1994) and a mastery of linguistic code-switching (Gilyard, 1991; Pattillo-McCoy, 1999). On weekends, they typically prefer hanging out with friends in black nightclubs and entertainment venues closer to home; however, on occasion, they also enjoy a night out with some of Cedric's college friends in Boystown. "I can't help it," Cedric explained, laughing. "Sometimes, I want a little [Lady] Gaga or Taylor Swift with my Nicki Minaj."

Although neither has experienced any open hostility for being gay, they have expressed discomfort in displaying open affection toward one another when walking down Halsted Street (Boystown's main strip). "We get the strangest looks when [Cedric] and I are walking down Halsted together," Trayvon described. "I mean I don't think we're doing anything *too* crazy—sometimes, we hold hands, and every so often, we might peck each other on the lips. Once, we were walking along real close, and I had my had in his back pocket. [This] white dude approaches us on the street and flat out asks whether we are a couple. I'm like, 'Dude, I'm palming his ass—what the fuck you think we doin'!" "I don't know," Cedric immediately followed, "I guess dudes don't expect two guys dressed like homo-thugs to put our business like that out on the street. But what do we have to fear? We know who we are."

Trayvon's and Cedric's experiences in Boystown mirror those of many of the gay, bisexual, and queer (GBQ) men of color featured in this chapter. In theory, nothing about Trayvon's and Cedric's behavior seems out of the ordinary. While political gains and increasing social acceptance have indeed expanded the residential imagination of gays and lesbians beyond iconic gay neighborhoods like Boystown (Collins, 2004; Collins & Drinkwater, 2015; Ghaziani, 2014; Ruting, 2008), many respondents identified iconic gayborhoods among the few places within cities where gays could openly express their sexuality without fear of homophobic retribution. As gay neighborhoods diversify sexually, everyday practices like public displays of affection among same-sex couples reinforce cultural norms consistent with the area's local character as a queer-friendly space (Greene, 2014). Yet Trayvon's and Cedric's "hip-hop" presentation renders their displays of affection illegible in the context of the gayborhood. Bystanders experience cognitive dissonance reconciling two perceptually oppositional cultural performances; not only does Trayvon's and Cedric's presentation makes them vulnerable for hypercriminalization by local residents in a predominantly white neighborhood (Anderson, 2012; Lacy, 2002; Rios, 2011), but the hypermasculinity also attributed to this aesthetic conjures the common (mis) perceptions of black men as homophobic (McCune, 2014). Ultimately, the controlling images of black male criminality (Collins, 2004) preclude Trayvon's and Cedric's sexuality, calling any legitimate claims to community in gay neighborhoods into question.

Despite the increasing visibility of LGBTs of color in queer spaces, iconic gay neighborhoods persist largely as what sociologist Elijah Anderson (2015) refers to as "white spaces"—places that may appear racially diverse yet privilege normative whiteness. Although people of color must navigate white spaces as a condition of their existence, they nevertheless find themselves subjected to the controlling images (Hill Collins, 2004) of race held by whites. As anonymous persons moving through the white space, Trayvon's and Cedric's presentation yields cultural images seen in mutual opposition.

Additionally, the role of iconic gay neighborhoods as sexual fields (Green, 2008) privileges white desire. Gay men of color who do not embody the Eurocentric standards of beauty that structure the cultural and sexual life of gay neighborhoods must somehow conform to sexualized fantasies of white gay men. Thus, GBQ men of color who fail to perform sexual stereotypes that fulfill white sexual desire often find themselves invisible in gay spaces, even in contexts outside of sexual interaction. The invisibility that many GBQ men of color experience often alienates them from a sense of community within iconic gay neighborhoods, whether they seek symbolic community through their participation, or whether they identify as local residents who may legitimately claim community membership through their material ties to the neighborhood.

Drawing primarily on interview, archival, and ethnographic data collected from gay neighborhoods in Washington, DC (Dupont Circle, Logan Circle, and Shaw / U Street) and Chicago (Boystown), this chapter explores the lived experiences of gay, bisexual, and queer men of color in iconic gay neighborhoods. Not all GBQ men of color search for community within these white gay spaces, nor do they experience their sexual identities in the same way (see Hunter, 2010). However, those who do actively privilege their sexual identities as salient to their self-perceptions as gay, bisexual, or queer often circumscribe their public sexual identities to spaces within the gayborhood. Many live outside gay neighborhoods, priced out of or displaced from housing markets in the local area. Others choose to live within their racial or ethnic enclaves, living closeted lives locally to access the social and cultural bonds they associate with their personal histories. Irrespective of residential choice, many GBQ men of color seek gay neighborhoods as asylums from the potential threats of ostracism and violence that arise out of their sexual orientation. Subjected to sexual objectification and hypercriminalization (Rios, 2011) at the hands of local residents (including white gay men), GBQ men of color nevertheless identify themselves as vital parts of an area's local LGBT community, defending their legitimate claims of "ownership" and investment against internal and external threats to their perceptions of authentic community. And as popular and academic scholars of gay neighborhoods argue the declining salience of gay neighborhoods in a "postgay" era (Brown, 2007; Collins, 2004; Collins & Drinkwater, 2015; Ghaziani, 2011, 2014; Ruting, 2008), the limited participation of GBQ men of color ultimately contributes to the persistent value of iconic gay neighborhoods as safe spaces where public forms of gender and sexual expression are affirmed and supported.

Gay Neighborhoods as White Spaces

Although recent scholarship on the people and practices associated with the postindustrial city have renewed scholarly interest in iconic gay neighborhoods, much of this research focuses on the notion that widespread acceptance of sexual minorities has rendered iconic gay neighborhoods "passé" as sites of political, cultural, and physical communities (Brekhus, 2003; Brown, 2007; Collins, 2004; Collins & Drinkwater, 2015; Ghaziani, 2010; Ruting, 2008). Scholars largely attribute three sociological phenomena to the "de-gaying" (Ghaziani, 2014) of gay neighborhoods. First, scholars highlight the attraction of these amenity-rich communities for an emerging class of moneyed, heterosexual cosmopolitans (Anacker & Morrow-Jones, 2005; Black et al., 2000; Cooke & Rapino, 2007), who also value places with perceptually high thresholds for tolerance (Florida, 2002, 2003, 2008). Second, scholars draw on a panoply of demographic data now available from the US Census Bureau to highlight both the residential decline of gay households in iconic gay neighborhoods and the residential dispersion of LGBT residents in cities, suburbs, and rural areas throughout the United States (Black et al., 2000; Gates, 2007; Gates & Ost, 2004a; Ghaziani, 2014; Hayslett & Kane, 2011; Simmons & O'Connell, 2003). These data demonstrate the expanding "residential imagination" of LGBT citizens, who prefer a panoply of lifestyles that mirror their heterosexual counterparts to living "distinctly gay lifestyle[s]" (Barrett & Pollack, 2011; Pew Research Center, 2013).[1] Finally, studies focus on how the rise of Internet and mobile app technologies have supplanted the need for the physical institutions that once anchored gay life in cities (Brown, 2007; Kunerth, 2007; Smith, 2008; Sullivan, 2007; Thomas, 2011; Usher & Morrison, 2010; Williams, 2007).

This emphasis on the sexual diversity of gay neighborhoods elides their conspicuous absence of racial and ethnic diversity. Scholars who briefly acknowledge the overwhelming whiteness of iconic gay neighborhoods attempt to disavow structural and interactional racism in favor of alternate explanations. In their studies connecting gay residential actors to gentrification, Lauria and Knopp (1985), for example, argue that while homosexual desire crosses boundaries of race, class, and gender,

> the self-identification of individuals as gay is more of a white, middle-class phenomenon. This is because it is easier, economically and otherwise, for middle-class white males to identify and live lives openly as gay people than it is for women, non-whites, and non-middle-class people. (cf. Knopp, 1990, p. 339)

In recent years, scholars like Amin Ghaziani (2014) have not only identified "emerging gay enclaves" in black and Hispanic neighborhoods as evidence of a diffusive queer residential landscape, they have also celebrated these residential settlements as examples of dynamic place-making by queer communities of color. Reflecting on the "paradox" presented by cultural studies scholar Charles Nero (2005) in his now classic essay "Why Are the Gay Ghettos White?" (in which Nero questions the overwhelming whiteness of gay enclaves despite the fact that homosexuality is considered multiclassed and multiracial), Ghaziani (2014) observes,

> Charles Nero was right to wonder, "Why are the gay ghettos white?" Fortunately, however, his paradox does not mean that the lives of queer people of color are casualties of racism. On the contrary, what we are witnessing in Chicago and New York illustrates the powerful agency that they have in creating their own spaces and shaping their own destinies. (p. 230)

Although Ghaziani correctly recognizes the development of gay microenclaves in iconic ghettos (Anderson, 2012) and ethnic enclaves, this analysis also oversimplifies the complex political, economic, and cultural dynamics that necessitated their existence in the first place. Dating back to the early twentieth century, many gay neighborhoods in the United States flourished through a variety of practices that systematically excluded or limited the participation of gay people of color (Armstrong, 2002; Beemyn, 1997; Chauncey, 1994; Clendinen & Nagourney, 1999; Conerly, 1996; DeMarco, [1983] 1999; Drexel, 1997; KQED Inc., 1997). Discriminatory housing and commercial practices made it particularly difficult for black gays and lesbians to participate in the sociocultural and political life of gay neighborhoods. In his pointed critique of Knopp's history of the Farbourg-Marigny as a gay neighborhood, Nero (2005) highlights how the racially exclusive hiring practices of the University of New Orleans in the 1960s, which hired many of the early settlers in Marigny, played a pivotal role in the racial homogeneity of the neighborhood. "Racially segregated workplaces," Nero notes, "made it highly unlikely that middle-class black and white gay males would create" the kind of informal networks that made gentrification in Marigny possible (2005, 232). Additionally exclusionary practices, like informal bar policies that require racial minorities to produce additional forms of ID at the door for entry, persist in gay neighborhoods, as evidenced in the 2005 investigation of a Castro gay bar (Hegranes, 2005), or in the recent efforts of gay bars in Philadelphia's gayborhood to implement "dress codes" that prohibit attire commonly worn by African American gay men (Colletta, 2015).

Gay Communities in the Black Metropolis

Contrasting contemporary depictions of black gays and lesbians living on the "down-low" (Boykin, 2006; McCune, 2014), gay community historians note how racial exclusion precluded many from living closeted, anonymous lives. Beemyn (1997), for example, recounts that the prevalence of racism among whites kept gay and lesbian African Americans living in Washington, DC, closely linked to the city's black communities. "Because Black lesbians, gay men, and bisexuals often remained in or near the Washington neighborhoods in which they were raised, they lived out their sexual preferences within the confines of their home communities, making it difficult to conceal their same-sex sexual attraction from families and friends" (Beemyn, 1997, p. 202). Given how racism forced black gays and lesbians to turn to their racial communities to find community, we know very little about how sexuality is negotiated among black gays and lesbians—what concessions are necessary in order to participate as members of the black community.

Gay community studies have also been integral in showcasing how black gays and lesbians created a vibrant and highly visible culture in black urban centers. Private house parties (Beemyn, 2015), nightclubs, and drag balls (Cabello, 2012a, 2012b; Chauncey, 1994; Drexel, 1997; Heap, 2009) were integral spaces for developing a gay black community in large urban centers such as the South Side of Chicago, Harlem in New York, and the Shaw / U Street neighborhoods in Washington, DC. Not only were these events successful in attracting gay black men and lesbians from around the country, but they also provided the few opportunities in which gay blacks and gay whites socialized in Jim Crow America. Both in New York's Harlem and on the South Side of Chicago, gay white communities found a haven to explore their sexuality openly, as drag balls, gay speakeasies, and tearooms provided the few opportunities in which racial mixing occurred.

By midcentury, drag balls were also successful in attracting mainstream black audiences. Among heterosexual blacks, Drexel (1997) explains how the drag bars on Chicago's South Side attracted as many straight as gay spectators; the events were promoted extensively throughout the community, and were covered by the black press, including *Ebony, Jet,* and the *Chicago Defender.* While we cannot take these stories to indicate a widespread acceptance of homosexuality among the black community, it does serve to suggest, "in some respects at least, that black gay men were in fact more fully accepted within the city's black working-class and poor communities prior to the 1960s than they have been in more recent decades" (Drexel 1997, p. 127).

Two movements seem critical to the "closeting" of black gay and lesbian life. The rise of the Black Power movement in the 1960s proved extremely detrimental, as movement leaders promoted homosexuality "as a 'white disease' that had 'infected' the black community" (Johnson & Henderson, 2005, p. 4). Leaders such as Eldridge Cleaver argued that homosexuality undermined the power and authority of black masculinity. Claiming that black gay men "are outraged and frustrated because in their sickness they are unable to have a baby by a white man," Cleaver consigned homosexuality among black men to a new form of slavery, whereby black gay men willingly enabled their emasculation by allowing white gay men to penetrate them: "The cross th[at gay black men] have to bear is that, already touching their toes for the white man, the fruit of their miscegenation is not the little half white offspring of their dreams" (Cleaver, [1968] 1991, p. 128). Although this framing of homosexuality as a "white disease" was not new to the black community,[2] scholars have attributed the rhetoric of black power in transforming black consciousness in the latter part of the twentieth century and in shaping the discourse of homophobia that remains associated with "the black community" (Clarke, 1999; Cohen, 1999; Collins, 2000; Johnson & Henderson, 2005).

The second contributing factor to the "closeting" of black gay and lesbian culture is the series of riots that devastated urban centers across the United States in the 1960s. Scholars have given considerable attention to how the political unrest of the late 1960s furthered the economic decline of urban black neighborhoods, which began with the out-migration of middle-class blacks during the previous decade (Klinenberg, 2003; Massey & Denton, 1991; Pattillo-McCoy, 1999; Wilson, 1996). As businesses and institutions were pushed out, forced out of business, or burned down during the unrest (Wilson, 1996), black churches remained one of the few remaining institutions that residents could turn to satisfy their sense of community, "act[ing] simultaneously as a school, a bank, a benevolent society, a political organization, a party hall, and a spiritual base" (Pattillo-McCoy, 1998, p. 768).

The black church has always played a pivotal role in criticizing the homosexual cultures displayed in black communities, dating as far back as the fiery sermons of Adam Clayton Powell in 1920s Harlem (Chauncey, 1994). As black religious leaders continue to criticize openly homosexuals and their pursuit for acceptance (Bennett & Battle, 2001; Monroe, 1999), scholars have given greater attention to the discrepancies surrounding what is practiced and what is preached. Keith Boykin (1999; 2006) argues that there exists a paradox in the black church; it is the most homophobic institution in the black community, yet it is also among the most tolerant. Boykin continues to argue that black churches operate under a "don't ask, don't tell" policy. Gays and lesbians are often visible in the leadership of the church (e.g., deacons, choir leaders, organists), and while their sexuality may be no secret to members of the church, the issue remains largely unspoken. Battle and Bennett (2001) argue that the hostile reception of homosexuality in the black church might have contributed to a culture where homosexuality was implicit, but never openly discussed. "Given that the black church is so important to the African-American community, the church's attitude toward sexuality becomes a unique and oppressive vessel for limiting the acknowledgement and openness for members of African-American families, further enforcing a heteronormative model of black life" (Bennett & Battle, 2001, p. 59).

As sociologist Elizabeth Armstrong argues, "Gay men of color [continue to face] a hard choice. They could live with the racism in the gay world, or they could reject participation in the gay community and lose access to the only spaces in which they could be safely gay" (2002,

p. 147–8). Even as gay white gentrifiers enter and become a visible presence in historically black neighborhoods like Shaw in Washington, DC (McChesney, 2005; Vargas, 2006), many GBQ men of color prefer to keep their sexual lives private within their local communities. This lack of visibility bears serious consequences for new generations of LGBT citizens, whose decision to live more open lives results in ostracism and violence (Trice, 2009). As a result, many GBQ men of color who cannot turn to networks within their local communities often turn to iconic gay neighborhoods to find that sense of safety and community. Despite the fact that those who seek asylum in gay neighborhoods may find themselves incapable of accessing the sociocultural, political, and economic life of gay neighborhoods, many nevertheless defend a right to participate in these neighborhoods, ultimately reaffirming the utility of gay neighborhoods as cultural and political safe spaces that foster the safe exploration of gender- and sexual-queer expression.

Not in (or near) My House

Keith (fifty, African American, gay) has been a lifelong resident of Shaw, a historically black neighborhood in Northwest Washington, DC. As a boy, he attended one of the area's local churches with his middle-class parents, who served in leadership positions within that church for nearly a half-century. When his parents died, leaving their townhouse to Keith and his two siblings, he bought out his siblings in order that he could stay in Shaw. As white gay residents began moving into the neighborhood, he has served in the community as an unofficial middleman (Pattillo, 2007), welcoming newcomers and promoting the neighborhood's economic growth while also protecting the interests of the lingering old-timers, many of whom he continues to think of as family. "I ran in and out of these houses with my friends," he recalled, laughing. "Their mothers treated us all the same. If we were hungry, they fed us. If we got into trouble, they would discipline us, then tell our parents so they could have *their* turn. These people are my family."

Although Keith has been out since college, his sexuality remains what he calls a "nonsecret." He will honestly answer questions about his sexuality, and he believes his neighbors know (or have some inkling) about his perpetual bachelorhood, his long-term roommates, and the occasional "bachelor" parties he threw that also attract the neighborhood's white lesbian couples. However, despite the increased gay visibility in Shaw, Keith remains reluctant to live as openly as his white gay neighbors. When not entertaining guests in his home, Keith prefers to spend his time in gay spaces far removed from his community. When asked why he never chooses to participating in the neighborhood's burgeoning queer culture, he simply answered: "Oh no. You never shit where you eat."

Keith's succinctness provides one possible explanation to a question that many gay white men asked over the course of my research: *why won't gay black men create their own queer spaces?* The realities of GBQ men of color who live in racial or ethnic enclaves reveal more complicated dynamics. In Shaw, for example, many black gay men believe that the demonstrations of tolerance that many of their white LGBT counterparts enjoyed from old-timers do not apply to them. "There are a lot of old attitudes that thinks [*sic*] of homosexuality as a 'white thing,'" Trent (forty-five, African American, gay) explained. "Some of the mothers within the community have a live-and-let-live attitude for [our white residents]. However, for many of [the black gay men] who grew up around here, we are so close to people here . . . there's just too much to lose to take that kind of chance." Carlos (fifty-five, mixed, gay) echoed that statement. Although he no longer frequents the church of his youth, he maintains close ties to many family friends who worship there, and remains fearful of their disapproval should his sexuality be discovered. "There are way too many eyes in this hood," he commented. "The last thing I need is for somebody to step up to me and tell me my business." When he is not socializing in the privacy of his own home, he also "gay[s] it up" in a different neighborhood.

Keith, Trent, and Carlos each speak to the ways that, as gay men, they segregate their sexual activities in different parts of the city when they are outside the privacy of their homes. Each of these men find a sense of "home" in this community, which for each of them grew out of connections made through the black church. The centrality of the black church to the lives of African Americans in Shaw makes it difficult to completely escape for many gay black men, even if they no longer affiliate with a local church. However, they each maintain that the ties they have cultivated and maintained among old-timer residents are important enough to protect at any cost, even if that means "concealing" their sexual lives from those they value and respect as extended family.

The alliances they have cultivated within their local communities often shape their local political participation; few felt any real investment to political issues that protected or promoted queer community in their neighborhoods. In 2006, plans emerged for a gay bar to open in Shaw across the street from a historically black church. As newcomers championed the bar as bringing much-needed economic investment into the neighborhood, black church leaders and their parishioners mobilized a campaign to prevent the bar from gaining the necessary liquor license to open its doors (Lynsen & Chibbaro, 2006; Marzullo, 2006; O'Bryan, 2006). In a letter to the DC Alcohol and Beverage Regulation Administration, one church leader argued that a gay bar would "undermine the moral character of the Shaw community, stain its tradition and send the wrong message to children and families," and "only promote an alternative lifestyle that runs counter to the values" of the neighborhood (Naff, 2006). While the bar's opening generated passionate debate from gay white newcomers and black old-timer residents, many of the local black gay residents actively abstained from the discussion. Those who discussed the bar in interviews reasoned that since they would likely never patronize the bar anyway due to its proximity to the neighborhood, they saw no reason to, as Keith said, "put their neck out for no good reason." "Many of us just didn't see how it mattered," Julian (thirty-seven, African American, gay) explained.

Those without the social and affective ties to their local communities often spoke of keeping their sexual lives private in order to protect their property. Some respondents, like Barry (fifty-five, African American, gay) who bought a home in the up-and-coming NoMA neighborhood (DC) described their home as a safe space that they did not wish to see disturbed: "I get a little nervous sometimes when I get out of my car. There are these kids hanging out on the street corner, and when I walk to my porch, they give me the funniest looks. I don't know whether they are looking at my car, the [professional] way I dress, or if they have figured me out, but I try not to draw attention to myself, especially—this is my home, man. The one place where a person should feel safe. And I can't have anything happening to give me pause about that, you know?" Others, like DeShaun (thirty-three, African American, bisexual), who recently moved into a black middle-class neighborhood on the South Side of Chicago, spoke of his home as an investment that he wanted to protect. "I moved [to this neighborhood] because I wanted to be around other black people," he explained to me during our interview. "But since I don't know the people too well, I don't want to put my life out there in a way where I can be a target. I put in my life savings to have a place on my own. I can't afford having anything happen to my house, especially over something stupid like whom [I'm sleeping with]."

Both Barry and DeShaun gesture to the potential of violence arising out of being too conspicuous about their sexual lives in their own neighborhoods. While academic and popular scholars have successfully challenged the perceptions of African Americans as being more homophobic than other communities (Boykin, 1996, 2006; Cannick, 2008; Hunter, 2010a; Monroe, 1999), violence in black communities for living openly as sexual subjects remains a reality for many LGBT citizens. In recent years, black and Latino queer youth have sought asylum in iconic gay neighborhoods like Boystown to escape the violence and homophobia that many have experienced in their own communities. Jorge (nineteen, Latino, gay) described how he could not remember a day when the neighborhood kids in his Humboldt Village neighborhood didn't call him names. "When I was in middle school, there were these guys who would follow me home, calling me 'faggot' and throwing shit at me," he recalled. "I tried to ignore them, man, I didn't want them to see my cry 'cuz I knew that shit would be so much worse." Sammy (twenty-four, African American, gay) grew up on the South Side of Chicago with his father and four brothers. Growing up, he not only experienced violence from the other neighborhood children, but also from his father and brothers. "My dad used to always say to me, 'If someone threatened your shit, you've got two choices: you fight them, or you fight me.' I hated fighting. I was small, and I couldn't throw a punch for shit, so whenever someone came up to me, I would try to run . . . but they would always catch me. Then, when I came home, and my dad found out what happened, he would take me outside and have his turn. If I cried—and I always did—it would get worse." When his father discovered he was gay at the age of fifteen, his father threw him out of the house. Sammy tearfully recalled the last conversation he had with his father: "He called me a fucking disgrace, and said he would rather kill me than have a faggot for a son. I was out in the street at fifteen with nowhere to go."

Of those living in racial or ethnic enclaves, nearly all of the gay and bisexual black men I interviewed expressed a preference to keep their sexual lives private in their local communities. Despite the widespread sociopolitical acceptance that LGBT citizens now enjoy in the United States, many GBQ men of color still find coming out and living openly as gay or queer in their own residential communities too great a risk. Many have negotiated ways for living some kind of gay life while maintaining social ties with family and friends; others have suffered violence and rejection from their families. What these respondents share, however, is the necessity to seek outside spaces to explore their sexuality and find a sense of queer community. Some have found this sanctuary in iconic gay neighborhoods, and even though they experience rejection and hypercriminalization at the hands of local residents, many nevertheless defend their right to be in these spaces in ways they do not imagine possible in their residential communities.

A Conditional (and Alienating) Acceptance

While respondents generally agree that iconic gay neighborhoods like Dupont Circle and Boystown have increasingly diversified racially over the last decade, many gay men of color see their presence and acceptance by the mainstream gay community as conditional. Despite possessing the necessary cultural capital to navigate gay white spaces successfully, many GBQ men of color identified themselves as cultural "outsiders-within" (Collins, 1986), where their race always creates an invisible boundary between themselves and their white gay counterparts. Even when playing a visible role within these spaces (e.g., as bartenders, bouncers, DJs), respondents not only described the pressures they faced to assimilate their embodiment and practices to standards of white gay male cultural norms, but also the sense of invisibility, ostracism, and open hostility they experienced when they failed to do so.

Given the production of gay bars as sexual fields (Green, 2008), respondents noted how they often confront the controlling images of racialized sexuality held by gay white men. Troy (twenty-eight, African American, gay) is a tall, muscular black man with a Harvard law degree and a conservative presentation. Despite his educational background and impeccably neat preppy attire, he nevertheless encounters white gay men who expect him to play out their fantasies of the hypersexual black buck. "I'm constantly accosted by these men who say the craziest things to me. Once, I was at this [gay bar in Dupont Circle] just minding my business when this white guy—he had to be in his early forties—just walked up to me, grabbed my crotch, and whispered in my ear, 'I'd love for you to rape me with that big black dick of yours.' That's all they see when they look at me—a walking, talking, fucking black dick." Despite the significant attention Javier (twenty-five, Latino, gay) receives from white men in gay establishments, he often finds himself frustrated by the stereotypes he encounters by "well-meaning" white men. "Guys approach me all the time with 'Hola, papi,' or why they love 'spicy Latin men,' or how much they love uncut dick, and that shit drives me crazy. And when I go off on them, they think I'm crazy!" Regardless of the attention that guys like Troy and Javier receive in these spaces, both experience a sense of alienation from the reactions they receive from other patrons, raising questions whether they can ever find a sense of community.

Black men who do not fit white men's black stereotypes often find themselves completely invisible in these spaces. Joey (twenty-two, African American, gay), a slender, effeminate man, described one occurrence when he was hanging out with his white boyfriend at the bar of a Boystown night club: "We were chilling out at the bar—we had just ordered our drinks—and we were just talking. All of a sudden, this [white guy] approaches us and literally wedges himself between us. I mean, the bitch stepped on my foot! With his back turned to me, he started telling my boyfriend how cute he was and how his friend wanted to meet him. When [my boyfriend] told him that he was taken, gesturing to me, he said, 'Oh,' turned around, served me stink face, and walked away. He was lucky that my man handled it, because I was literally a half-second off his ass." Joey's vignette also highlights another microaggression that many GBQ men experience in these white spaces. Despite the fact that Joey expressed a willingness to respond aggressively toward the transgression, many of the GBQ men of color work actively to disavow any associations with the iconic ghetto (Anderson, 2012), where their actions might confirm white patrons' stereotypes of criminality and violence traditionally associated with GBQ men of color, especially black and Latino gay men. Joey's boyfriend operated as a white gay broker in this situation, mediating the conflict before Joey had the opportunity to escalate the situation himself. This offers another way in which GBQ men of color feel they lack a voice in the white space. "[My boyfriend] and I talk about this quite a bit," Joey explained to me when I asked him about resolving moments like these himself. "You know that the moment I might start something, *I* would be the one getting my ass kicked out of the club, even though I didn't start shit. So if it isn't too serious, I take a breath and let [my boyfriend] handle it."

The limited visibility of black gay men in Boystown or Dupont Circle establishments makes interracial dating (GBQ men of color dating white men) expected or compulsory. Respondents often express frustration at dispelling assumptions that their presence in the white space either signals their attraction to gay white men or their sexual availability to them. Jayson (twenty-four, African American, gay) grew up in Southeast Washington, DC, but now lives in the trendy U Street neighborhood in Northwest DC. On a given Friday or Saturday night, he often finds himself as one of a handful of black men in the bars he frequents, which produces assumptions among patrons about his preference for sexual partners. "Most men believe that if you're a black gay man hanging out in a place like JR's [in Dupont Circle]," he observed, "then you must be looking for some white man to date." This perception is so pervasive that many gay black men approach other black men at gay bars in iconic gay neighborhoods with some caution. In white gay bars, a GBQ man of color will rarely approach another man of color he finds sexually attractive out of fear that he does not prefer "their own kind." "Some of the gay Asian men I encounter [in gay bars] are just as racist as white gay men," Jeffrey (twenty-six, Asian, gay), a Boystown resident explained. "I would never approach them in the gay bars around here. I'm tired of hearing guys say they are not "into sticky rice" (Asian gay men who date other Asian gay men). The kind of fatigue that Jeffrey describes often lead GBQ men of color to look at each other with suspicion, undermining the very efforts to create community among GBQ men of color that many respondents identified craving. Rashad (thirty-nine, African American, gay), who grew up on Chicago's South Side and now spends a significant amount of time in Boystown, explained that his encounters with other gay black men in gay bars elicit one of two responses. "Don't get me started on black gay men [at bars] in Boystown," he began. "Either they think of you as competition, so they will try to undercut you—especially if you are talking with a white guy—or they just come out and assume you are into white guys. I'm always baffled by the fact that the first question I am asked when a black man would approach me is whether I dated other black men." The common belief among gay black men, that bars operate as white spaces, constrains their ability to seek each other out for mutual support.

Many respondents quickly pointed out that they cannot really let their guard down in these spaces, for the moment they do is when they become reminded of their status as outsiders. At a popular Boystown bar one Saturday evening, Frank (thirty, African American, gay) overheard a group of white men expressing their frustration over the "overrepresentation" of black men. "I grabbed my drink and went to this corner," he observed, "and there was this group of white guys who had to be in their twenties who were complaining about how there were too many black guys there, saying shit like, 'It's getting too dark in here,' and 'Why do they have to come in a ruin our clubs?' I was like, 'What the fuck do you mean! I could count the black guys that night on one hand!' Seriously, when did a handful of black guys in a gay bar on some random Friday night all of a sudden mean that it's becoming a black bar [*laughs*]?"

The perception of a critical mass of black gay men in traditionally white bars can create divisions that manifest themselves spatially. When the city's decision to build a baseball stadium along DC's Anacostia River forced the closure of a number of gay black bars in the area, many of the black patrons found a new hangout in Halo, a gay bar in the heart of Logan Circle. Opened in 2004, the chic, yet predominantly white gay lounge Halo became popular among many Dupont and Logan residents as the first nonsmoking gay bar in the city. However, a critical mass of gay black men on Friday nights diminished its popularity among many of its gay white patrons, resulting in a situation that many in the city described by several respondents as "gay apartheid," where black patrons congregated on the first floor, while white patrons would almost exclusively hang out upstairs on the second floor. Colin (thirty, white, gay), who worked as a barback at Halo during that period, described his disappointment in seeing how "the white boys would walk into the room, see the sea of black, and walk right upstairs." "It was one of the nights that my coworkers dreaded," Colin remembered. "It was sad to see my coworkers being the typical hater in terms of the room full of black guys." The situation became so pervasive that CNN and ESPN columnist L. Z. Granderson referred to the phenomenon in response to a 2008 *Advocate* article claiming how "gay [was] the new black": "There is a bar at the heart of the nation's capital that might as well rename itself Antebellum," he writes, "because all of the white patrons tend to stay upstairs and the black patrons are on the first floor" (Granderson, 2009).

Some of the effects that gay men of color experience in iconic gay spaces spill out into their daily (Logan & Molotch, 2007) and nightly (Hunter, 2010b) rounds; for local residents, the sense of alienation they experience by completing their daily activities within the gayborhood makes them feel like strangers in their own community. Daniel (thirty-four, black, gay) consciously chose to move to Boystown seven years ago because he wanted to be more connected to the gay community. While he has never had encountered any overt racism, he does encounter a variety of microaggressions in his daily life that he attributes to being black in a predominantly white neighborhood. "When I'm walking down the street to the grocery store or whatever," Daniel explained, "and despite the physicality of skin color—which makes you hypervisible because you stand out—people still seem to look right through me. At my gym a lot, I feel people often don't hold doors for me, even though I'm like, right behind them. Or at bars, even when I am going out of my way to chat someone up, or be friendly or engage in small talk, which is not really my sort of inclination—and they turn their back toward me. It's not even that I want to be desired, but I want recognition—to be treated with dignity."

Of course, Daniel's experiences may have very little to do with his race. However, his "definition of the situation" (Thomas, 1923) has led him to believe that his social location as a black man makes him an outsider to Boystown's gay community, despite his status as a local resident. He expressed his frustration over the fact that white gay-vicarious citizens from other parts of the Midwest feel more "at home" in Boystown than he does: "It really becomes . . . I would use the word *painful* . . . during these sort of big events, like Pride, Market Days, or whatever. Because these people come in from places like Michigan, Wisconsin, and Iowa, and they often . . . the rhetoric they use to describe these events—homecoming, you know, whatever—it's offensive to me. Because, they'll come in, and it feels like they are coming home to their family . . . and strangers sleeping with all their cousins if you want to play the metaphor out . . . slutting it up for the weekend, and treating me like shit. And I'm like, wait a minute: I live here! I don't know—that's just like very upsetting to me. I don't pay taxes in this neighborhood, but I spend a lot of money in this neighborhood . . . and it's my neighborhood!"

Daniel's reflections speak to the ways that many gay black men feel like cultural impostors in iconic gay neighborhoods (Nero, 2005), where their participation somehow seems inauthentic compared to their white gay counterparts. His inability to associate his local community with the same images of "home" and "homecoming" that extralocal white gay men use often makes him feel like a stranger in his own community, where his identity as a gay man is always called into question by those with an easier time of assimilating into the mainstream gay culture.

Not in *My* Gayborhood!

Despite being often themselves unwelcome in iconic gay neighborhoods, many GBQ men of color nevertheless exercise a right to participate as legitimate stakeholders within the community. For many, this often necessitates fighting two fronts simultaneously; not only must GBQ men of color challenge the invisibility and racism they endure from the gay white community, they must also contend with the increasing presence of white heterosexual gentrifiers, whose presence and values threaten the production of queer space within iconic gay neighborhoods.

Just as coming out became a central strategy in the creation of gay neighborhoods and mobilizing the contemporary gay rights movement (Armstrong, 2002; Castells, 1983; Escoffier, 1998; Ghaziani, 2008), visibility remains the most effective strategy that GBQ men of color deploy to challenge their exclusion from community in iconic gay neighborhoods. Consider the example of Trayvon and his boyfriend Cedric above. Despite the complex readings that their "hip-hop" presentation elicit when they express affection in Boystown, they recognized the value in making black queer love visible. "We get that folks don't see it too often," Cedric explained. "But we ain't got shit to be afraid of. We don't need some white man to make us feel good about who we are [as gay people]. Black gay love is something worth celebrating." Even as many GBQ men of color recognize how white gay men stigmatize their presence within these spaces, respondents also realize how their presence can constitute revolutionary acts. Ritchie (thirty-two, African American, gay) lives on the far north side of Chicago. Although he expressed no desire to live in the Boystown neighborhood, he wanted to live in an affordable neighborhood where he could easily access Boystown. He spends a lot of his time frequenting the gay bars in his own neighborhood because he enjoys the diversity of the patrons. "On rare occasion, when I'm feeling particularly brave or particularly drunk," he says, laughing at himself, "I will hold my date's hand [while walking down the street of his neighborhood] as a form of resistance." However, he remains cautious about being too "conspicuously affectionate" in areas outside of Boystown: "I know that there is a risk when two men walk down the street holding hands in Rogers Park. And if there is a group of six or seven guys, I would probably not hold a guy's hand, especially at night . . . whereas I have no problem doing that in Boystown."

Sometimes, this visibility requires drawing on unfamiliar spatial practices to make their claims to community known. While iconic gay neighborhoods like Boystown have become increasingly popular destinations for queer youth of color, many find themselves both symbolically and structurally excluded from the cultural and economic life of the gayborhood. Much of what anchors the material culture of gay neighborhoods (e.g., bars, bathhouses, bookstores) is age-restrictive and depends economically on their patrons, formally limiting the avenues of participation for LGBT youth. Thus, in order to make a claim to community, many transport spatial practices indigenous to their own residential communities to the gayborhood; queer youth of color forge "street families" (Anderson, 1999) in public spaces around key institutional anchors (outside bars, community centers, and cultural iconography). Being on the sidewalks and in public spaces in the gayborhood exposes the youth to the area's cultural and sociopolitical community through casual and peripheral contact with other LGBT-identified individuals. At the same time, large clusters of black and brown bodies on street corners late at night in a white neighborhood also raises concerns among local residents, who argue their presence constitutes a potential threat to neighborhood safety (Barlow, 2011; Sosin, 2011a). In fact, when crime spiked in Boystown during the summer of 2011, the queer youth became easy targets of residents' ire. As one local resident posted on the neighborhood's "Take Back Boystown" page, "Boystown was created by gay whites with hard earned money years back to make the neighborhood that it is today . . . It's sad that Boystown has been taken advantage of by these savage monkeys" (Take Back Boystown, 2011).

Yet the negative attention presented a political opportunity for the queer youth to articulate their own claims to community. When "Take Back Boystown" cocreators organized and advertised a "positive loitering walk" through their Facebook page on July 2, 2011, GenderJUST advocates organized a counterprotest that same evening, confronting the fifty "positive loiterers" with megaphones accusing them of "policing queer youth of color outside the neighborhood" (Sosin, 2011b). Clubgoers who filled the Halsted Street that Saturday night witnessed the standoff between the two groups at the 7-Eleven parking lot on the corner of Roscoe and Halsted, which culminated in the arrest of two people. These altercations provided a legitimate platform for LGBT youth to openly challenge racial profiling at the hands of local residents. At a press conference held one week later, several representatives of the queer youths shared experiences of racial profiling and harassment by local residents and the police. Describing his own experiences of being called the "n-word" by local residents, twenty-one-year-old South Side Chicago resident Joshua McCool emphasized the difficulties that he and many like him faced every day in Boystown. "We have issues already on the south and west sides that we are dealing with as queer youth," McCool told the crowd, encouraged by his comrades. "But when you go to [Boystown] that is supposed to be this gay-friendly place, you realize, 'Oh, I forgot. I'm of color. Now where do I go to?' Boystown is supposed to be the gay place for Chicago, but I always say that it seems to be more like white Boystown." As the queer youth defended their right to community in Boystown, highlighting the racial tensions within the local community provided a fruitful avenue to articulate and demand recognition as legitimate community members.

Equally, many GBQ men of color create visibility by mobilizing in solidarity with the local LGBT community. "[Gay people] are like your siblings," Danté (twenty-one, black, queer) explained to me. "Sure, they piss you the fuck off sometimes. But when the chips are down, you got their backs." Danté recalled a time when he was walking in Boystown with some of his friends when they fell upon a gay white man being harassed by a couple of "straight dudes." "They had this guy cornered up, and they looked like they were about to pounce," he said. "But then we rolled upon those dudes—there were about ten of us—and you should have seen them shitting their pants. Suddenly, they realized that these 'faggots' were going to tear him up."

Threats of violence perpetrated by straight interlopers seems to transcend generation, age, race, class, and gender. When the manager of a drug store chain in a DC kicked out a black Maryland gay couple for showing affection in the store, local residents organized a "hug-in," where same-sex couples lined up in front of checkout lines and hugged each other for about a minute. Organizers promoted the event through Facebook and local neighborhood blogs after reading about the incident in a local gay paper. None of the organizers knew the couple prior to the incident, nor was the drug store even considered a gay institutional anchor. Rather, organizers mobilized to challenge action they found inconsistent with the character of the neighborhood. "I'm not one to sit around and say, 'Oh well' when I hear about people's rights being violated," one organizer, a gay white male, explained to the *Washington Blade* in an interview, "especially when it happens to gay couples and especially in my neighborhood" (Cavanaugh, 2007). One of the evicted men expressed his pride and surprise in the community's response. "It was a bit of a shock for the most part, since I didn't realize I had a support system," he explained. "I didn't know that the incident reached a lot of people . . . I was more than glad to see that . . . people in general were standing up for our rights, and it's about time" (Cavanaugh, 2007).

This chapter examines some of the various challenges that GBQ men of color experience in their search for community in iconic gay neighborhoods. Despite the recent attention that iconic gay neighborhoods like Boystown and Dupont Circle have received in popular and academic scholarship, the experiences of gay, queer, and bisexual men of color in these spaces remain vastly underexplored. As these studies present the growing influx of straight residents as evidence of the high threshold for tolerance and acceptance for LGBT Americans broadly (Florida, 2002, 2003, 2008; Ghaziani, 2014), gay neighborhoods persist as white spaces where GBQ men of color feel they do not belong. When it comes to their participation in gay neighborhoods, many gay men of color have a complex, perhaps contradictory relationship to the community contained therein. On the one hand, many of them face rejection, objectification, and invisibility at the hands of white gay men, and yet many GBQ men of color find enough value within the sociocultural and political life of gay neighborhoods to protect these safe spaces from external threats that may compromise their role as safe spaces. As gay neighborhoods remain white spaces in the popular imagination, GBQ men of color will face myriad challenges to gain the kind recognition that would fully incorporate them as legitimate stakeholders within the community.

However, as LGBT identities gain greater political and social acceptance, a few respondents, like Dominic, express some optimism that as more gay black men become visible, the cultural imagination iconic gayborhoods like Boystown will also expand to accommodate them. "Sure," he begins, "these places are still racially divided. But you are beginning to see changes happen. I see places like the Center on Halsted [Boystown's LGBT community center] open their doors and provide a safe place for black queer youth, and people are beginning to mix and mingle, and all of a sudden, there is an opening of the mind of what gay is. Then all of a sudden, gay neighborhoods aren't these lily-white places anymore. And the more folks realize that, we will finally begin to see places like Boystown be more reflective of the diversity we find in cities all over the country."

■ Notes

1. Since 1990, the Census Bureau includes "unmarried partner" among the relationship categories item "to measure the growing complexity of American households and the tendency for couples to live together before getting married" (Simmons and O'Connell, 2003, p. 2). Scholars designated a household as a "same-sex unmarried-partner household" based on whether the householder identified another adult of the same-sex as his or her unmarried partner (Gates & Ost, 2004a, p. 20). Gates and Ost (2004a, 2004b) have used this information to argue the presence of same-sex couples in 99.3 percent of all counties in the United States.

2. Chauncey (1994) describes how middle-class blacks mobilized against the visible homosexual culture in Harlem during the 1920s. Alongside arguments that homosexuality was a "white influence," middle-class blacks believed that homosexuality threatened middle-class black values and efforts for respectability.

■ References

Anacker, K. B., & Morrow-Jones, H. A. (2005). Neighborhood factors associated with same-sex households in U.S. cities. *Urban Geography 26*(5), 385–409.

Anderson, E. (1994). The code of the streets. *Atlantic Monthly 273*, 80–94.

———. (1999). *Code of the streets: Decency, violence, and the moral life of the inner city.* New York: Norton.

———. (2012). The iconic ghetto. *Annals of the American Academy of Political and Social Science 642*, 8–24.

———. (2015). The white space. *Sociology of Race and Ethnicity 1*(1), 10–21.

Armstrong, E. (2002). *Forging gay identities: Organizing sexuality in San Francisco, 1950—1994.* Chicago: University of Chicago Press.

Barlow, G. (2011). Speakers clash on crime, race, age issue at Boystown CAPS meeting. *Gay Chicago*, 7.

Barrett, D. C., & Pollack, L. M. (2011). Testing a typology of adapting to same-sex sexual orientation among men. *Sociological Perspectives 54*(4), 619–40.

Beemyn, B. (1997). A queer capital: Race, class, gender and the changing social landscape of Washington's gay communities, 1940–1955. In B. Beemyn, (ed.), *Creating a place for ourselves: Lesbian, gay, and bisexual community histories* (pp. 183–210). New York: Routledge.

Beemyn, G. (2015). *A queer capital: A history of gay life in Washington, DC.* New York: Routledge.

Bennett, M., & Battle, J. (2001). We can see them, but we can't hear them. In M. Bernstein & R. Remain (eds.), *Queer families, queer politics* (pp. 53–67). New York: Columbia University Press.

Black, D., Gates, G. J., Sanders, S. G., & Taylor, L. (2000). Demographics of the gay and lesbian population in the United States: Evidence from available systematic data sources. *Demography 37*(2), 139–54.

Boykin, K. (1996). *One more river to cross: Black and gay in America.* New York: Doubleday.

———. (2006). *Beyond the down low: Sex, lies, and denial in black America.* New York: Carroll and Graf.

Brekhus, W. (2003). *Peacocks, chameleons, and centaurs: Gay suburbia and the grammar of social identity.* Chicago: University of Chicago Press.

Brown, P. L. (2007, October 30). Gay enclaves face prospect of being passé. *New York Times.* Http:// www.nytimes.com/2007/10/30/us/30gay.html/ei=5070&en=22520eb6996396dc&ex=1194494400 &adxnnl=1&emc=eta1&adxnnlx=1193889647-Ghee4TP7bC3CeCNjLAgyIw.

Cabello, T. (2012, February 29). "Queer Bronzeville: A history of African American LGBTs on Chicago's South Side, 1900–1985, Part I: The emergence of African-American queer cultures on Chicago's South Side, 1920–1940. *Windy City Times.* Http://www.windycitymediagroup.com/lgbt/Queer-Bronzeville-African-American-LGBTs-on-Chicagos-South-Side-1900–1985/36389.html.

———. (2012, March 13). "Queer Bronzeville: A history of African American LGBTS on Chicago's South Side, 1900–1985, Part II: Being black and queer in 1940s Bronzeville: Race, class and queer identities in Black Chicago, 1940–1950. *Windy City Times.* Http://www.windycitymediagroup. com/lgbt/Queer-Bronzeville/36615.html.

Cannick, J. (2008, November 8). No-on-8's white bias. *Los Angeles Times.* Http://www.latimes.com/ news/opinion/commentary/la-oe-cannick8–2008nov08%2C0%2C3669070.story.

Castells, M. (1983). *The city and the grassroots.* Berkeley: University of California Press.

Cavanaugh, A. (2007, November 2). Gays stage "hug-in" to protest couple's eviction from Rite Aid. *Washington Blade*, 6.

Chauncey, G. (1994). *Gay New York: Gender, urban culture, and the making of the homosexual.* New York: Basic Books.

Clarke, C. (1999). The failure to transform: Homphobia and the black community. In E. Brandt (ed.),
 Dangerous liasons: Blacks, gays, and the struggle for equality (pp. 31–44). New York: New Press.

Cleaver, E. ([1968] 1991). *Soul on ice.* New York: Delta Books.

Clendinen, D., & Nagourney, A. (1999). *Out for good: The struggle to build a gay rights movement in
 America.* New York: Simon & Schuster.

Cohen, C. (1999). What is this movement doing to my politics? *Social Text 61, 17*(4), 111–18.

Colletta, J. (2016, October 6). Protests, meetings address racism in the
 gayborhood. *Philadelphia Gay New.* Http://www. epgn.com/news/
 local/1119-protests-meetings-address-racism-in-the-gayborhood.

Collins, A. (2004). Sexual dissidence, enterprise, and assimilation. *Urban Studies 41*(9), 1789–1806.

Collins, A., & Drinkwater, S. (2015). Fifty shades of gay: Social and technological change, urban
 deconcentration and niche enterprise. *Urban Studies,* 1–21. doi:10.1177/0042098015623722.

Collins, P. H. (1986). Learning from the outsiders within: The sociological significance of black feminist
 thought. *Social Problems 33*(6), S14–S32.

———. (2000). Gender, black feminism, and black political economy. *Annals of the American Academy
 of Political and Social Science 568*(8), 41–53.

Conerly, G. (1996). The politics of black lesbian, gay, and bisexual identity. In B. Beemyn, and Mickey
 Eliason (eds.), *Queer studies: A lesbian, gay, bisexual, and transgender anthology* (pp. 133–45). New
 York: New York University Press.

Cooke, T. J., & Rapino, M. (2007). The migration of partnered gays and lesbians between 1995 and 2000.
 Professional Geographer 59(3), 285–97.

DeMarco, J. ([1983] 1999). Gay racism. In M. J. Smith (ed.), *Black men / white men: Afro-American gay life
 and culture* (pp. 109–18). San Francisco: Gay Sunshine Press.

Drexel, A. (1997). Before Paris burned: Race, class, and male homosexuality on the Chicago South Side,
 1935–1960. In B. Beemyn (ed.), *Creating a place for ourselves: Lesbian, gay, and bisexual community
 histories* (pp. 119–44). New York: Routledge.

Escoffier, J. (1998). *American homo: Community and perversity.* Berkeley: University of California Press.

Florida, R. (2002). *The rise of the creative class.* New York: Basic Books.

———. (2003). Cities and the creative class. *City & Community 2*(1), 3–19.

———. (2008). *Who's your city? How the creative economy is making where to live the most important
 decision of your life.* New York: Basic Books.

Gates, G. J. (2007). *Geographic trends among same-sex couples in the U.S. census and the American
 Community Survey.* Los Angeles: University of California Los Angeles.

Gates, G. J., & Ost, J. (2004a). *The gay and lesbian atlas.* Washington, DC: Urban Institute Press.

———. (2004b). Getting us where we live. *Gay and Lesbian Review,* 19–22.

Ghaziani, A. (2008). *The dividends of dissent: How conflict and culture work in lesbian and gay marches
 on Washington.* Chicago: University of Chicago Press.

———. (2010). There goes the gayborhood? *Contexts 9*(3), 64–66.

———. (2011). Post-gay collective identity construction. *Social Problems 58*(1), 99–125.

———. (2014). *There goes the gayborhood?* Princeton, NJ: Princeton University Press.

Gilyard, K. (1991). *Voices of the self: A study of language competence.* Detroit: Wayne State University

Press.

Granderson, L. (2009, July 16). Commentary: Gay is not the new black. *CNN*. Http://www.cnn.com/2009/POLITICS/07/16/granderson.obama.gays/index.html.

Green, A. I. (2008). The social organization of desire: The sexual fields approach. *Sociological Theory 26*(1), 25–50.

Greene, T. (2014). Gay neighborhoods and the rights of the vicarious citizen. *City & Community, 13*(2), 99–118.

Hayslett, K. L., & Kane, M. (2011). Out in Columbus: A geospatial analysis of the neighborhood-level distribution of gay and lesbian households. *City & Community 10*(2), 131–56.

Heap, C. (2009). *Slumming: Sexual and racial encounters in American nightlife, 1885–1940*. Chicago: University of Chicago Press.

Hegranes, C. (2005, June 29). Badlands confidential: Is there a race problem at a Castro gay bar—or a propriety problem in a city supervisor's office? *SF Weekly*. Http://www.sfweekly.com/content/printVersion/391713.

Hill Collins, P. (2004). *Black sexual politics: African Americans, gender, and the new racism*. New York: Routledge.

Hunter, M. A. (2010a). All the gays are white and all the blacks are straight: Black gay men, identity, and community. *Sexuality Research and Social Policy 7*(2), 81–92.

———. (2010b). The nightly round: Space, social capital, and urban black nightlife. *City & Community 9*(2), 165–86.

Johnson, E. P., & Henderson, M. G. (2005). *Black queer studies: A critical anthology*. Durham, NC: Duke University Press.

Klinenberg, E. (2003). *Heat wave: A social autopsy of disaster in Chicago*. Chicago: University of Chicago Press.

Knopp, L. (1990). Some theoretical implications of gay involvement in an urban land market. *Political Geography Quarterly 9*(4), 337–52.

KQED Inc. (Writer). (1997). *The Castro. Neighborhoods: The hidden cities of San Francisco*. KQED.

Kunerth, J. (2007, September 16). For a number of gay bars, it's last call—a changing society might not need the bars as cultural centers today. *Orlando Sentinel*. Http://articles.orlandosentinel.com/2007-09-16/new/gaybars_1_gay-bar-bars-in-orlando-gay-nightclub.

Lacy, K. (2002). Black spaces: Strategic assimilation and identity construction in middle-class suburbia. *Ethnic and Racial Studies 27*(6), 908–30.

Lauria, M., & Knopp, L. (1985). Toward an analysis of the role of gay communities in the urban renaissance. *Urban Geography 6*(2), 152–169.

Logan, J. R., & Molotch, H. ([1987] 2007). *Urban fortunes: The political economy of place*. 20th anniversary edition. Berkeley: University of California Press.

Lynsen, J., & Chibbaro Jr, L. (2006, April 21). Be bar liquor license fight goes before board. *Te Washington Blade*, 10.

Marzullo, G. (2006, March 17). Church leader challenges D.C. gay bar: ANC protests be bar license after anti-gay pastor complains. *Washington Blade*. Http://www.washblade.com/print.cfm?content_id=7870.

Massey, D. S., & Denton, N. (1991). *American apartheid: Segregation and the making of the underclass.* Cambridge: Harvard University Press.

McChesney, C. (2005). Cultural displacement: Is the GLBT community gentrifying African American neighborhoods in Washington, DC? *Modern American 1,* 24.

McCune, J., Jr. (2014). *Sexual discretion: Black masculinity and the politics of passing.* Chicago: University of Chicago Press

Monroe, I. (1999, December 9). The garden of homophobia. *Advocate 9,* 9.

Naff, K. (2006, April 21). Blade blog: Where is the outrage over black pastor's homophobia? *Washington Blade.* Http://washblade.com.

Nero, C. I. (2005). Why are the gay ghettos white? In E. P. Johnson & M. G. Henderson (eds.), *Black queer studies: A critical anthology* (pp. 228–45). Durham: Duke University Press.

O'Bryan, W. (2006, April 20). Be bar faces off with opponents. *MetroWeekly.* Retrieved from Http://www.metroweekly.com/news/?ak=2086.

Pattillo, M. (2007). *Black on the block.* Chicago: University of Chicago Press.

Pattillo-McCoy, M. (1998). Church culture as a strategy of action in the black community. *American Sociological Review 63*(6), 767–84.

———. (1999). *Black picket fences: Privilege and peril among the black middle class.* Chicago: University of Chicago Press.

Pew Research Center. (2013). *A survey of LGBT Americans: Attitudes, experiences and values in changing times.* Http://www.pewsocialtrends.org/2013/06/13/a-survey-of-lgbt-americans.

Rios, V. M. (2011). *Punished: Policing the lives of black and latino Boys.* New York: New York University Press.

Ruting, B. (2008). Economic transformations of gay urban spaces: Revisiting Collins' evolutionary gay district model. *Australian Geographer 39*(3), 259–69.

Simmons, T., & O'Connell, M. (2003). *Married-couple and unmarried-partner households: 2000.* Washington, DC: US Department of Commerce, Economics and Statistics Administration, US Census Bureau.

Smith, S. V. (2008, April 25). Gay bars adjusting to a new reality. *Marketplace.* Http://www.marketplace.org/topics/life/gay-bars-adjusting-new-reality.

Sosin, K. (2011a, July 13). Hundreds pack Boystown violence forum. *Windy City Times,* 8.

———. (2011b, July 6). Lakeview "loitering" event turns into dramatic showdown with queer youth organizers. *Windy City Times.* Http://www.windycitymediagroup.com/gay/lesbian/news/ARTICLE.php?AID=32608.

Sullivan, R. D. (2007, December 2). Last call—why the gay bars of Boston are disappearing, and what it says about the future of city life. *Boston Globe,* E1.

Take Back Boystown. (2011). Https://www.facebook.com/TakeBackBoystown.

Thomas, J. (2011). *The gay bar: Its riotous past and uncertain future.* Washington, DC: Slate Magazine.

Thomas, W. I. (1923). *The unadjusted girl.* Boston: Little, Brown.

Trice, D. T. (2009, November 30). Some black youth feel more at home in Boystown, but get a chilly reception. *Chicago Tribune.* Http://articles.chicagotribune.com/2009-11-30/news/0911290242_1_gay-bars-same-sex-partner-youth.

Usher, N., & Morrison, E. (2010). The demise of the gay enclave, communication infrastructure theory, and the transformation of gay public space. In C. Pullen & M. Cooper (eds.), *LGBT identity and online new media* (pp. 271–87). New York Routedge.

Vargas, J. A. (2006, April 20). In Shaw, pews vs. stools. *Washington Post*, C01.

Williams, G. (2007, September 19). 10 businesses facing extinction in 10 years. *Entrepreneur*. Http://www.entrepreneue.com/article/184288.

Wilson, W. J. (1996). *When work disappears: The world of the new urban poor.* New York: Vintage Books.

VIGNETTE

In graduate school, Ronnie was a residential life professional in New Mexico, where he noticed several gaps and issues in diversity and education among the students with whom he worked. Ronnie also taught courses at the institution and noticed those gaps in that area as well. A small percentage of African American students in the college, especially African American males, were getting in trouble more, falling behind in class, and not developing the necessary skill sets to be successful following graduation. Ronnie helped to develop the first Afro-American studies course on the campus to reach those students and provided them not only with history but life skills that would be transferrable. After the first year, he saw improvement in the campus climate and more students becoming involved. The course continues to this date, and continues to help students find their way and become innovators in the industry.

PART 3

Health

INTRODUCTION

Brent E. Johnson

One ever feels his twoness—An American, a Negro; two souls, two thoughts, two unreconciled strivings; two warring ideals in one dark body, whose dogged strength alone keeps it from being torn asunder.

—DuBois, *The Souls of Black Folk*, 1903

In the American classic *The Souls of Black Folk,* W. E. B DuBois described the psychological, cultural, and social struggle existing both in civil society and in black bodies. Disillusioned with the lack of progress, DuBois moved to Ghana, where he lived the remainder of his life. The literature and life of W. E. B. DuBois serve as a shining example of the "dis-ease" Black males live with in the United States of America.

Recently, February 3, 2017, after watching the critically acclaimed, *I Am Not Your Negro,* the documentary based on an unfinished manuscript by James Baldwin, a friend and colleague stated the following:

Maybe difficult is the wrong word to describe it. Perhaps, "extremely heavy" is more appropriate. It was heavy because you are surrounded throughout the whole film with the perplexing words and acute analysis of James Baldwin. The film is kind of centered around the deaths of Medgar Evers, Malcom X, and Martin Luther King, Jr. I guess the difficult part was hearing/seeing a large majority of white people in the audience clapping and cheering at the end of the film. It made me sad and angry, as if they had not watched the same film that I had. It literally almost made me vomit. (personal correspondence, 2017)

What W. E. B. DuBois and Jonathan Hamilton are describing is the social and cultural dissonance in which Black males exist and the effects manifested by this lived experience.

For decades, critical voices have been screaming about the onslaught of the neoliberal agenda in all aspects of social life. And Black voices have been interpreting how this agenda affects us. Whether it was Marable (1983) examining how capitalism has underdeveloped Black America, West (1994) telling us that race matters, or Gause (2008) and Billings (1995) advocating for a more culturally relevant pedagogy, our chorus has been singing about how two groups of people occupy one space inequitably.

However, the election of Donald Trump as president has finally lifted the veil from the eyes of many Americans who thought we were moving toward a postracial America. I heard someone once say that when America catches a cold, Black people get the flu. In other words, Black people have been the canary in the mine.

What is health? What does it mean to be healthy? According to the *Miller-Keane Encyclopedia and Dictionary of Medicine, Nursing, and Allied Health* (2003), health is defined as a relative state in which one is able to function well physically, mentally, socially, and spiritually in order to express the full range of one's unique potentialities within the environment in which one is living. In the words of René Dubos, "Health is primarily a measure of each person's ability to do and become what he wants to become" (1978, 74).

According to the theory of health as expanding consciousness put forth by Margaret Newman, health can be viewed as the undivided wholeness of the person in interaction with the environment (Endo, 2017). If health is primarily a measure of each person's ability to do and become what he wants to become, what happens when variables beyond the person's control inflict their influence on that person? If health is viewed as the undivided wholeness of the person or group in interaction with the environment, what is the outcome if the environment is either unsuitable or even hostile toward the person or group?

This part of the Handbook interrogates the topic of Black males and health within the United States of America. Through various lenses, the authors of this part interrogate some of the structures and systems causing and contributing to the Black male health issue, as well as offering methods and modalities to combat these structural health impediments.

The first chapter in this part, Rana Walker's "I Can Breathe," offers a holistic approach to the Black male health crisis. Focusing on the mind, body, and soul, this chapter invokes modalities from the ancient world to restore internal sanctity as well as offer tools to resist external pressures unique to Black men. Understanding the long-term effects of sustained individual and systemic attacks on black males, such as poor physical health and a compromised psychological mental state, the calls for sustenance with nutritional value, yoga, and meditation are not only healthy options, but, for Black males, revolutionary options that preserve the physiological and reenergize the intellectual.

The second chapter, Taura Taylor's "Fatherhood, Resilience, and Black Men's Mental Health," examines the provider role strain experienced by Black homeschooling fathers. Homeschooling, a form of school public choice in many states, is being chosen by an increasing number of Black families instead of risking the systemic harm often applied to students of color in public schools. Told through the lens of their wives, this chapter contributes to the growing body of literature that reflects how systemic inequities create stress to middle-class Black fathers, who are customarily seen as evidence of progress made by an integration of civil rights gains and American values. To counter social injustices, the concepts of role resilience and microresistance are helping articulate the ways Black families are navigating issues of race, class, and gender associated with role strain to reclaim parental empowerment.

The third chapter, "Improved Health Care for Black Males as a Function of Increased Graduation Rates," by Brent E. Johnson, investigates the relationship between Black male graduation rates and health care. Utilizing a combination of historical and critical frameworks, Johnson interrogates the idea of poor health as a by-product of an educational system that is contentious toward Black boys, and manifested in poor self-esteem, a brainwashing by culture, and increased dropout rates. However, a pedagogy of scholar-servanthood is offered as a potential onto-epistemological process, idea, and ideal as a response to the current educational framework, potentially improving the health of Black males.

The fourth chapter in this part, "The Epigenetics of Being Black and Feeling Blue," by Darron Smith, chronicles the effects of historical trauma on the life outcomes of Blacks in America that can be traced epigenetically. It provides an overview of the Black experience from before slavery to modern times. This chapter makes a compelling argument and gives language to account for the lower life outcomes of Black males, including heart disease and stress, traced to chronic exposure to hate crimes as well as other racial mistreatment.

The final chapter, James H. Campbell's "Djangos Chained," uses critical race theory as a lens to investigate the competing, cooperative, and tension-filled intersectionality between Black male Division I athletes, the National Collegiate Athletic Association, labor, objectification, and wealth. As Black male student-athletes produce billions of dollars of revenue for their institutions, coaches, and leagues, the glaring inequality of labor exerted versus the wealth (or lack of wealth) received by the players themselves represents a psychological and emotional tension an increasing number of Black males are experiencing.

Employing a bricolage of frameworks, holistic ideas, and other alternative methodologies, this part examines the health of Black males as a function of living in a society that privileges and protects whiteness. Spaces such as elementary and high schools, universities, and city streets can be hostile spaces for young Black males, while corporate spaces produce microaggressive attacks on middle-class Black males that may only appear to be living the American Dream.

Black males, if treated at all, are given medication that only masks the issues and dulls the pain. In other words, symptoms are treated, with very little time and analysis given to root causes. This part and these contributors strive to accomplish two goals. The first is to examine the social, cultural, political, historical, and economic causes that often undergird the physical and psychological ailments afflicting Black makes. The second is to offer strategies, pedagogies, and methods that result in providing direct counterhegemonic action or add to the discourse that produces agency in the future.

■ **References**

Du Bois, W. E. B. (1996). *The souls of Black folk.* New York: Random House.

Dubos, R. (1978). Health and creative adaptation. *Human Nature 1* (January), 74–82.

Gause, C. P. (2008). *Integration matters: Navigating identity, culture, and resistance.* New York: Peter Lang.

Ladson-Billings, G. (1995). Toward a theory of culturally relevant pedagogy. *American Educational Research Journal 32*(3), 465–91.

Marable, M. (1983). *How capitalism underdeveloped Black America: Problems in race, political economy, and society.* Boston: South End Press.

West, C. (1994). *Race matters.* Boston: Beacon Press.

I Can Breathe

Transforming the Mind, Body, and Spirit of Black Males

Rana Walker

Black men are constantly being bombarded with labels that describe them as 'less than,' and the images that dehumanize them at every turn via the media have warped the perception of Black men into a criminalized distortion (Page, 1997; Jackson, 2006). According to the documentary *13th* by Ava DuVernay (2016), the justice system is disproportionally biased against Black men in that one in three Black men will encounter jail at some point in their lifetime, while only one in seventeen white men will face jail time (Mauer, 2011). Black men are incarcerated for misdemeanors, while their White counterparts only receive a slap on the wrists. Judicial inequities are just one type of discrimination that is glaring and real for Black men, yet very little is being done to address daily coping mechanisms for Black men, and the stress of their reality is damaging to them, their families, and their communities (Smith, Hung, & Franklin, 2011). Considering that Black men are squarely in the center of the reality of contending with the effects of negative societal perceptions of their personhood, it is easy to see how taking the time for self-care may not be the highest priority when Black men are merely trying to survive.

As a therapist for over twenty years and a client several times throughout my own life following traumatic and transitional events, I understand soul searching and defining one's own image for oneself is not easy and requires a great deal of courage. As a Black woman, I also know that fighting the internalization of societal negativity requires personal effort and conscientious dedication to self-care. To combat society's negativity, Black men must tell their own positive stories about themselves and change their self-talk in order to begin seeing themselves as fully alive, authentic, and deserving to be living their lives fully and as creatively as possible with no excuses (Watkins & Jefferson, 2013). Connecting to the inner self and to the world is necessary for Black men to die to their false selves so they can be reborn to their true, authentic, selves. As men become liberated, they experience the emotional freedom to live purposefully as they pursue their passions.

This chapter presents information, advice, and exercises grounded in empirical research to address how Black men can practice self-care to enhance their personal progress. Connecting the mind, body, and spirit through yoga, deep breathing, nurturing their chakras, receiving sufficient nutrition and adequate sleep is a must for total well-being.

Your Self-Care

Self-care is any voluntary activity that consists of taking care of one's self, that is, mind, body, and spirit (Good Therapy, 2017). Self-care can create a space in life which will allow you to feel more in tune with yourself and help you learn to value yourself in a way like never before. The key to self-care is to recognize and be grateful for the diamonds in your backyard and cultivate them with the same care and love as you would a baby. Black men can use various positive and healthy methods of self-care to manifest their authentic selves, realize their maximum fullness, and mine the diamonds in their lives.

One effective method of self-care and catharsis is written expression, such as a journal or video diary and using stream-of-consciousness writing, poetry, and prose.

Another easy way to practice self-care is visualization. For example, visualize a strong, clear green light filling up your heart center, which is located in the center of your sternum and below your shoulder blades (Chopra, 2015), or experience the world by going for a walk, taking a hike, riding a bike, swimming, or simply sitting on a park bench and looking at the beauty of nature. Sleep is also important in maintaining mind, body, and spirit health; approximately seven to nine hours of sleep per night is essential, and ideally you should make certain that you are sleeping by 10:00 P.M. because that is the time when the body repairs itself and the liver detoxes (Thiessen, 2013). Black men can greatly enhance their lives by learning to express their feelings, taking time to visualize positive thoughts, experiencing the world around them, and allowing their minds to rest with adequate sleep so they can maintain their mental, physical, and emotional strength for the benefit of themselves and others.

Connecting the Mind, Body, and Spirit

Your Mind: Meditation

Meditation's benefits have been scientifically proven and recently embraced by the medical profession; it improves the quality of your life in that it reduces stress, improves sleep quality, extends life span, improves concentration and focus, creates balance, brings more peace to your daily life, and enables you to surrender to the things in life over which you have no control (Fortune & Taylor, 2010). Meditation also allows you to cope with life's challenges in a much more optimistic way. Sitting or still meditation, now popularly called mindfulness meditation, is another way to get in touch with your breath. One modality of mindfulness is Vipassana meditation (Gunaratana, 2017). In the Buddhist tradition Vipassana means insight into the true nature of reality. The Vipassana journey is a ten-day silent process when there is no talking and participants practice mindful eating, sitting for hours at a time, contemplating, raising awareness, scanning the body for any sensations, and observing them briefly as they dissipate and move on (Chiesa, 2010). Vipassana meditation has been used in the penal system to help prisoners cope with being within the confines of a six by nine prison cell, and the results were astonishing; the men learned to contend with being imprisoned, were more peaceful and felt more purposeful in their everyday routines, and were less stressed and could handle life behind closed doors in a healthier and more empowered manner (Perelman et al., 2012).

My business partner, Gerri H. Walker, first introduced Vipassana meditation to me as she completed the entire ten-day journey and shared in vivid detail how it impacted her life:

> Vipassana meditation made me aware of the connection between mind and body. Gave me a tool to scan my body, notice and pinpoint finite areas of tension/tightness, irritation in different parts of my body and through merely noticing them for 20 to 30 seconds attaching no judgment, dissolve them. After every session despite sitting in one position for over an hour, I felt better, lighter. Of course it was difficult at first, but easier around day 5 of the 10-day silent retreat.

Your Body: Yoga

As a mental health therapist for over twenty years, a licensed spiritual practitioner who has researched the importance of the mind, body, and spirit connection for many years, I am aware of what it takes to maintain total health. My current yoga teacher training immerses me in the mind, body, and spirit connection that reveals itself in my life in many ways: in my relationships with myself and others, and through my emotions and thoughts. Yoga is not only breathing techniques or a series of body poses, it is also an ancient spiritual philosophy that is centered on the practice and application of its definition; yoga means "union with God," which is both a definition and a call to action in the practice of yoga (Satchidananda, 2017). As you practice yoga both physically and philosophically and move closer to unite with the soul force within, you have to shed, release, and reinvent aspects of the self that no longer serve you.

The alignment of the mind, body, and spirit through the practice of yoga is important to the well-being of human beings and integral to the holistic health and self-care of men from the African diaspora (Caslin, 2017). Practicing yoga can enable Black men to remain in the present and can yield a host of health benefits such as helping to relieve chronic lower back pain, reducing stress, and improving sleep quality (Stephens, 2017). Yoga has also been proven to enhance heart health (Pullen et al., 2010). Changa Bell, executive director of the Black Male Yoga Initiative, shared the following in *Rolling Out* magazine:

Put simply Black males of all ages are dying prematurely over very solvable challenges. Anger management for youth dying in senseless violence, high blood pressure, hypertension, type 2 diabetes, cancer, heart disease, ADHD, mental health issues and more. Not to mention the physical challenges of life such as arthritis, injuries from athletics and car accidents. All these challenges of life are ameliorated or completely prevented with a committed yoga practice. Women are very open to and benefit greatly from the practice of yoga its secondary and tertiary outcomes, so I wanted to be clear in my messaging so that men of color felt welcomed and would know from the outset that in our space their needs would be met and they could feel comfortable in an unknown and unfamiliar learning space. (Caslin, 2017)

According to *Men's Fitness* magazine (2017), yoga breathing exercises activate the parasympathetic nervous systems and decrease cortisol levels in the body, a hormone that causes the body to store fat in the belly and increases the chance of heart attacks. As yoga can be considered a moving meditation, more simple practices like walking, cooking, creating artistically are also moving meditations. Research studies have shown that practicing yoga as a physical exercise contributes to behavioral and psychological changes as well as physiological changes in the body that promote weight loss (Yadav et al., 2016; Ross et al., 2016; Bernstein et al., 2014).

Although pro athletes practice yoga (Capouya, 2003), such as LeBron James, who was named America's Favorite Athlete (Conway, 2014), and the members of the Denver Broncos football team (Denver Broncos, 2017), yoga is not as widely practiced among men as it is among women in the United States. According to Niiler (2013), men comprise only 18 percent of the 20.4 million yogis in the United States, and even fewer Black men practice yoga. Some men refrain from practicing yoga by claiming that yoga is feminine and they are not flexible enough, and some men feel intimidated initially because they may not be able to do all of the poses, a limitation that affects their ego (Zolotow, 2017). In much of conventional medicine, most patients are passive recipients of care. However, in yoga, it is what you do for yourself that matters. Yoga encourages self-care and gives you the tools to help you change, and you might start to feel better even after the first time you try practicing (Walkiewicz, 2017). The more you commit to practicing yoga, the more you will benefit. This results in three things: you become actively involved in your own self-care, you will discover that your involvement gives you the power to effect change, and seeing that you can effect change will give you hope—and, hope itself can be healing.

Yoga increases your self-esteem, and many of us, particularly Black men, suffer from chronic low self-esteem. Black men who handle low-esteem negatively and have unhealthy lifestyles (e.g., taking drugs, overeating, working too hard, acting promiscuously) may pay the price in poor health physically, mentally, and spiritually (Royster et al., 2006). Black men who take a positive approach and perform yoga as both a philosophical and physical practice will gradually sense that they are worthwhile or, as yogic philosophy teaches, that they are a manifestation of the divine. Practicing yoga regularly with an intention of self-examination and betterment and not just as a substitute for an aerobic class will reveal a different side of

yourself; you will experience feelings of gratitude, empathy, and forgiveness, as well as a sense that you're part of something bigger.

Yoga can give you inner strength and can help you make changes in your life; in fact, that might be its greatest strength. *Tapas* is the Sanskrit word for "heat"; it is the fire, the discipline, that fuels yoga practice and that regular practice builds (Habash, 2012). The *tapas* you develop can be extended to the rest of your life to overcome inertia and change dysfunctional habits. You may find it without making a particular effort to change things: you start to eat better, exercise more, or finally quit smoking after years of failed attempts. Yoga builds awareness for transformation. And the more aware you are, the easier it is to break free of destructive emotions like anger. Studies suggest that chronic anger and hostility are strongly linked to heart attacks (O'Donnell et al., 2016; Heart Disease Weekly, 2015). Yoga appears to reduce

anger by increasing feelings of compassion and interconnection and by calming the nervous system and the mind. It also increases the ability to step back from the drama of your own life and breathe, to remain steady in the face of bad news or unsettling events. Yoga speeds reaction time, and you can still react quickly when you need to, but you can take that split second to choose a more thoughtful approach and reduce suffering for yourself and others. While better health is not the goal of spirituality, research shows it is often a by-product (Carmody et al., 2008).

Love may not conquer all, but it certainly can aid in healing. I have found that cultivating the emotional support of friends, family, and community has improved my own physical health and emotional healing. Yoga also benefits relationships: a regular yoga practice helps develop friendliness, compassion, and greater equanimity (ReShel, 2016). Your relationships may be improved by following the yogic philosophies of avoiding harm to others, telling the truth, and taking only what you need.

Yoga helps you serve others. Karma yoga (i.e., service to others) is integral to yogic philosophy (Reder, 2007). And while you may not be inclined to serve others, your health might improve if you do. A research study found that volunteering in service to others had a protective effect on the mortality of the older people who participated in the longitudinal research study (Musick, Herzog, & House, 1999). Serving others can give meaning and length to your life, and your problems may not seem so daunting when you see what other people are dealing with.

The aforementioned benefits are a few of the many ways that yoga improves your mind, body, and spirit connection, and there is a lot of overlap because they are intensely interwoven. This is one of the great lessons of yoga: everything is connected. Your hip bone is connected to your anklebone, you to your community, your community to the world. This interconnection is vital to understanding yoga. This holistic system simultaneously taps into many mechanisms that have multiplicative effects. This energy may be the most important way of all that yoga heals (McCall, 2007).

In the 1970s, Kemetic yoga became popular both as a physical yoga form and as a philosophy based upon the ancient Egyptian Kemetic systems of self-development that spawned Western science, philosophy, and religion (Hotep, 2016). Kemetic Yoga was developed by studying, translating, and interpreting the commonly called hieroglyphic texts of Kemet (ancient Egypt) and images of yogic postures that are clearly pictured on the walls of the Kemetic temples (Tang, 2017). Hatha yoga is a path toward creating the balance of uniting opposites in our physical bodies; we develop a balance of strength and flexibility, and balance our effort and surrender in each pose (Pizer, 2017). Hatha yoga can be translated in two ways: as willful or forceful, or the yoga of activity; and as "sun" (*ha*) and "moon" (*tha*), the yoga of balance. Hatha yoga is a powerful tool for self-transformation; it asks us to bring our attention to our breath in order to still the fluctuations of the mind, and it helps us be more present in the unfolding of each moment.

EXERCISES: YOGA ASANAS (POSES)

For well over five thousand years, various types of yoga (e.g., Ashtanga, vinyasa, Iyengar, power, yin, and aerial) have concentrated primarily on the performance of physical exercises known as "asanas," which are postures designed to align your skin, muscles, and bones (Do Yoga with Me, 2017). The sequences of postures of those physical yoga styles open the many channels of the body, especially the main channel (i.e., the spine) in order for energy to flow freely (Yoga Journal, 2017). Here are several yoga poses or asanas to help you open your heart:

- Upward-facing dog (Urdhva Muka Svanasana) has a host of health benefits, such as strengthening the mind, arms, and wrists and stretching the chest and lungs, shoulders, and abdomen. Upward-facing dog also firms the buttocks, stimulates abdominal organs, and helps relieve mild depression, fatigue, and sciatica. Upward-facing dog is also therapeutic for asthma.
- Camel pose (Ustrasana) helps to reduce fat on your sides, open up your hips as you stretch deep into your hip flexors, and stretch and strengthen the shoulders and back. Camel pose is an excellent heart opener and expands the abdominal region that improves digestion and elimination. It is also good for improving posture, opening the chest, and improving respiration. Camel pose also loosens up the vertebrae and relieves lower-back pain.
- The health benefits of eagle pose (Garudasana) are stronger arms, legs, knees, and ankles. It opens the shoulder joints, creating space between the shoulder blades, opening the hips and the iliotibial band, and increases circulation to all joints. Eagle pose is also helpful in improving digestion and elimination, balance, and focus. All of these health benefits are achieved when eagle pose is done properly and consistently.
- Bridge or wheel or any other back-bending pose also opens up the heart. Whenever you feel yourself closing off your heart, chant the word "YAM," which is the vibrational sound associated with the heart chakra to reopen your heart and send love to everyone and everything with which you come in contact.

Your Spirit: Breathing

Sufficient oxygen reaching the brain determines the outcome of myriad things, such as clear thinking, the ability to relax and be fully present in one's body, and the body operating at its highest level. Deep, diaphragmatic breathing provides oxygen to your entire being and improves cell regeneration so that they function at the highest level possible (Sovik, 2013). Diaphragmatic breathing slows down your heart rate, promotes better blood flow, allows you to think clearly, induces calmness by clearing uneasy feelings from your body, makes your heart stronger, relieves pain, massages your organs, and helps you make decisions by encouraging you to be proactive instead of reactive. Deep abdominal breathing, also known as "pranayama," is a fundamental part of the study of yoga and is one the limbs of Patanjali's eight-limbed path (Wilson, 2014). Yogic breathing is defined as the "control of life force" (i.e., the spirit) and is aimed at increasing vital energy in the body and mind (Wilson, 2014).

EXERCISES: DEEP BREATHING

When you change your posture, you change the way you breathe, and your breathing changes your nervous system. The four-square breathing technique is designed to balance and cleanse the entire nervous system, thereby reducing anxiety. This meditation technique only takes a few minutes and will reduce anxiety while sitting at your desk, riding the train, or waiting for your date to return from the ladies room:

- Think of breathing deeply. Inhale for a count of four, hold for a count of four, and exhale for a count of four. Repeat this for a minimum of five breath cycles.
- When inhaling, focus on each sip of air, and when exhaling focus on releasing each sip of air.

The most important rule of thumb is for Black men to listen to their bodies and honor their limitations. As a result of leading groups for over twenty years, I know that when the right environment is set in motion, a safe harbor is created for Black men to remove their masks and the labels foisted upon them and are finally able to breathe. Black men require love and deserve to be able to breathe.

Connecting to Yourself and to the World

Nutrition

Keeping the mind clear and focused and ensuring that the body operates at an optimal level means we cannot overlook the importance of the emotional, mental, spiritual, and physical impact of what we eat and drink. Nutrition is an essential component of the total mind, body, and spirit journey (Brookover, 2017). Studies suggest that a diet that is primarily plant-based can stave off certain cancers, such as prostate cancer (American Institute for Cancer Research, 2008; Nguyen et al., 2006). As a breast cancer survivor for the last nine years, I understand the importance of consuming live foods to increase energy levels and improve and maintain overall health. I had the most energy, felt and looked my best, achieved the most mental clarity, and was the happiest when I was a raw foodist and vegan and I fed my body live foods. In addition to conscientious food consumption, it is critical to drink water every day in order to maintain hydration, reduce fogginess of the mind, release waste and other toxins, increase energy, and assist in weight control. The human body is 60 percent water, and the recommended amount of water consumption for men is thirteen cups per day (Mayo Clinic, 2017), and it is important to replenish the water that has been lost after exercising.

Chakras

Men of African descent have buried their true essence and have been taught to hate themselves and to mask their self-loathing with unending promiscuity, alcoholism, substance abuse, domestic violence, and gluttony in the way of excess materialism. Many behave and navigate their way through this maze called life with a chip on their shoulder and bars across their hearts just to survive, just to stay alive, and never reach the point of being able to truly thrive. Consequently, destructive behaviors, suppressed emotion, outbursts of anger, and the inability to share their innermost thoughts and fears can increase the risk of Black men suffering detrimental conditions such as cardiovascular disease and heart attacks (Mostofsky, Penner, & Mittleman, 2014). Black men who take time to be centered, calm, and in touch with their chakras through the practices of self-care, yoga, deep breathing, good nutrition, and adequate sleep can strengthen their mind, body, spirit connection, and thus improve their quality of life.

It is the mind, body, spirit connection that allows us to understand that we are more than just human beings, that we are spiritual beings having a human experience. Knowing the truth is what sets us free, sets us apart from the false beliefs that attempt to bear down on us, to crush us, to tell us who we are and who we are not. We are the physical manifestations of God and we are greater than we can imagine. Black men are love personified in the forms of fathers, sons, brothers, husbands, cousins, and uncles. Therefore, the centers of the spiritual strength of Black men (i.e., chakras) must be maintained to ensure that the frailties of the human condition do not suppress their inner power and their connection to themselves and to others whom they influence and with whom they share their heart chakra.

EXERCISE: CHAKRA ENHANCEMENT

The area that gets to the heart of the matter involves one of the chakras in our body and is directly in the middle of the three lower chakras that connect to the earth and the three higher chakras that connect to the sky. The fourth primary chakra is the heart chakra, or *anahata*, according to Hindu yogic, Shakti, and Buddhist tantric traditions (Snyder, 2015). In Sanskrit, *anahata* means the heart that is unhurt and unbeaten and implies that, deep beyond these personal stories of suffering and pain, lies boundless love and compassion (Fondin, 2017).

It is important to recognize when the heart or *anahata* is blocked and identify ways to unblock it, which is something akin to an emotional/spiritual colonic. Some of the signs that the heart chakra (i.e., *anahata*) may be blocked include feelings of shyness and loneliness. If you find yourself unable to forgive or you have a tendency to lack empathy, then you may be using your head more than your heart. If so, breathe deeply into your heart space and imagine that you are breathing in love and expelling love. This can become a part of your daily routine, and can take as little as three to five minutes. As a result, you will begin to feel more loving and compassionate toward yourself and everyone else you encounter. It is great to know that no matter what we look like on the surface, deep down within us there is pure love and nothing else (Smith, 2014).

On the other side, having an overpowering chakra can lead to feelings of codependency and looking outward for love and acceptance or self-fulfillment. If you are experiencing intense jealousy or harsh judgment of others, that is also a red flag. So if you realize that you fall into the blocked category, rebalancing your chakras means releasing repressed emotions, which all of us embody. Whether it is a traumatic event stemming from childhood that you cannot remember or a grudge you are holding onto tightly from last week that you cannot get out of your head, when you choose to ignore these feelings, your heart chakra is going to be imbalanced. Set five intentions to rid yourself of your repressed emotions:

1. Be open with your emotions. You may want to write them down, write a letter to yourself, write a letter to someone who has upset you, or write a letter and burn it. It's up to you just as long as you get it out of you in a healthy way. Even though this may only be an exercise that we elect to do in the privacy of our home, it will still be challenging and painful to be honest with yourself and to face the truth of what is eating at you, what is causing you to shut down, and what is causing you to close your heart off from the world.

2. Create a new story by refusing to cling to your feelings. Envision the life you desire, not expending energy on the undesired life that brought you pain, dissatisfaction, and regret. This is why the practice of yoga is a great tool because it is a mind, body, spirit practice that keeps you in the present moment. All three must be in harmony for you to remain balanced, focused, and present. Yoga does not create space for you to dwell in the past or to run to the future because, as we know, neither one of them really exists.

3. Practice the art of acceptance, surrendering to situations over which you have no control.

4. Think of five things you're grateful for every day. List them in your journal and date them so that you can go back at the end of each week to see how much you have to be thankful for.

5. Be of service to someone other than yourself. Do a good deed, smile at someone, give of your time, help someone with something that was difficult for him or her but easy for you, be there for someone when it's not convenient for you, be a good listener, be a mirror, and laugh every day.

So, in life as we move through and encounter different people in different situations that don't turn out the way that we would have liked or imagined, we begin to close off our heart. The most important aspect of allowing your heart to open is to forgive yourself and others who you believe have wronged you (Smith, 2014).

Communication

In the Black community, it is taboo to speak about or acknowledge mental health concerns, so masking becomes a way of life perpetuating pervasive dysfunction. Communicating thoughts and feelings is important because it allows you to get your story out, discuss it, evaluate it, and perhaps even choose to create another story that manifests the life you wish to experience. As a trained mental health therapist and an Emmy Award–winning life coach, I am an advocate for individual and group therapy as a tool for everyone, but especially for Black men since they seek counseling less often than Black women (Watkins & Jefferson, 2013).

Black men, in particular, have not been given permission to be free to just be. Society's overarching depiction of Black men as the embodiments of negative, terroristic threats to humankind have subconsciously seeped into the minds of Black men. This brainwashing and crippling of the Black man's sense of self began in slavery and is still very much alive to this present day. The media and our patriarchal society dictate how men should handle their masculinity and ignore their femininity. They have been taught to believe that their femininity is a weakness and must be discarded or at the very least repressed. However, without the yin and the yang, the masculine and feminine, the anima and the animus, there is no balance. For centuries men have been taught not to express themselves, to hold in anything that would appear to be less than masculine, while being encouraged to always present as the alpha male. As a result, men are dying of heart attacks, strokes, cancer, and other debilitating diseases because they're always in a state of incarceration whether it be mental, physical, spiritual, or literal.

Patriarchy promotes that the idea that men should not be emotionally available; therefore, there should be a limit to emotional engagement. It's helpful to have a safe space that celebrates men, especially Black men, being their whole selves.

COMMUNICATION IN THE HUDDLE: A TIME FOR MEN

In 1999 I created Diamond Cutter, a wellness company dedicated to enhancing mind, body, and spirit. One of the communal exercises we designed is called "The Huddle," which evolved from my research that showed men felt that their voices were not heard unless they demonstrated anger. The Huddle was designed specifically for Black men, who are frequently disenfranchised and require safe spaces to share emotions. At one session for the Huddle, a group of ex-felons convicted of murder, armed robbery, crimes of passion, and other anger-induced deviant behavior participated in the therapy program as a communication exercise. The session was a time for these imprisoned Black men from all walks of life to come together and be supported in their individual and collective healing. For these Black men, the Huddle was a sacred space where they could remain men or recall the emotions they had as little boys and feel comfortable crying or reliving painful moments from their childhoods. The men were allowed to let the masks fall away so their vulnerabilities could be revealed and addressed. The value of that Huddle was that each man respected the others as men and allowed them to share the stage while they provided informative and supportive feedback to each other. The men were free to reexamine their macho beliefs and immature actions and determine whether or not they were willing to get in touch with their innermost feelings.

The Huddle technique was also used during a counseling session with a group of Black males, a mixture of blue-collar workers, college graduates, and entrepreneurs who did not know each other. Although the men's chosen career paths were varied, they faced similar challenges in their day-to-day existence. Navigating the onslaught of racism in their personal and professional lives was a popular topic during the session, and the men shared their stories about being viewed as threatening and being seen as lesser professionals than their White counterparts. During the counseling session, the group brought to light childhood traumas that the men still carried with them as adults. Ground rules were established for the Huddle, the most important of which was confidentiality; the Huddle was an environment where dialogue remained confidential and conversation that could not happen anywhere else was in a free zone. The Huddle participants were asked key questions: Who are you? What do you want for your life? What do you want your legacy to be? How do you want your family to view you? The session gave the men the opportunity to explore what sharing feels like and then opened their minds to the possibility of considering individual therapy sessions. The Huddle participants were listened to, mirrored in affirmation, and allowed to voice their anger, disappointment, sadness, hopes, and desires. Some of the men were so moved by the experience that they cried freely with the realization that they were being supported and surrounded by men who knew their journey intimately and did not judge them for being human.

Greg Corbin, spoken-word poet and founder of the Philadelphia Youth Poetry Movement who is also a graduate of Lincoln University (a historically black university), said that the Huddle impacted him in this way:

> The Huddle impacted me by providing a space where I could show up as a human being first. Often, men are so busy being men we behave through that lens of thought and interaction. Men need safe spaces just as much as any other gender. Healing and restoration will benefit everyone, every human being. Slavery taught Black people to desensitize themselves as a means of survival. Black men have been taught a toxic masculine perspective that is perverted through entertainment and industry and systemic patriarchy. Communication and dialogue are needed to bridge the gaps among Black people to create community; vulnerability is a super power of healing and isn't possible without courage, humility, and kindness.

What I discovered, which was rather surprising to me as a therapist, was that I had to let go of an old paradigm from my childhood conditioning and acknowledge that men actually do have feelings and hurt just as much as women but are less likely to share with anyone. They are less likely to be honest with themselves and others about how they truly feel, what matters the most to them, and the things that don't really matter but men pretend do. The discoveries that I made by acting as a midwife for the men's emotional births have been life affirming for the participants and for me; all human beings desire to be loved, and Black men are no exception.

In addition to group therapy exercises, participating in journaling, individual therapy, and self-help books are also excellent tools and ways of conveying to the outer world what is transpiring in your inner world. Reginald E. Walker is a teacher, life coach, and spiritual guide who developed a program called "Mind Power," which was the first of its kind offered at his alma mater, the University of Pennsylvania. In 2016, Walker authored a book entitled *Life Is Funny, but It Ain't No Joke* that chronicles his spiritual journey and is filled with wise and thought-provoking insights that are transformative for all of humankind and are specifically impactful for Black men who are seeking to expand their consciousness as they look within themselves. Referring to the odds he faced while striving to lead a life that is meaningful, Walker (2016) profoundly stated, "What you believe can move a mountain or put one in your way." Walker's insights are reminders of the power of belief and are useful tools for Black men to use on a daily basis as they endeavor to overcome challenges in their lives.

An Exercise in Self-Care: Michael's Story

Walker's words perfectly exemplify the story of one of my clients, Michael[1] as it relates to the necessity of Black men's communication of their feelings in order to connect with themselves and others. Michael was adopted when he was two years old, and his feelings of being treated differently than his siblings by his adoptive family and not knowing his biological parents caused him to suffer from low self-esteem. Michael knew that he was depressed, emotionally damaged, and required counseling, but he procrastinated about seeking help, which was most likely due to his fear that he would tap into emotional and mental distress from which he might not recover. After being encouraged and persuaded, Michael decided that counseling would help him in different areas of his life. During our sessions, I asked Michael how depression had affected his life and his willingness to be open to exploring uncharted territory while endeavoring to find his parents. He responded by saying that although focused on the end goal, he repeatedly questioned why his parents had chosen not to raise him and left his care in the hands of others. I encouraged and reassured him that there is a light at the end of the tunnel and that everything is in divine order. I shared with Michael that taking the first step towards self-help demonstrates that he values himself, and desires to have better relationships with others, and most importantly, himself.

Michael began to believe that it was worth facing the unknown in order to begin to gain some stability in his life and trust that the whole world was not going to abandon or reject him as his parents had. I admired Michael's level of resilience and the determination it took for him to locate his parents and begin to develop a relationship with them, thus dealing with the void in his life that had perpetuated his depression. Although he was nervous, Michael was clear that seeking therapy would positively impact his relationships with the people most important to him. Michael shared that completing DNA testing and meeting his parents as an adult after searching for them for many years helped him to piece his life together. As our time together progressed, Michael exclaimed in personal triumph, "Now that I know who I am, I feel better about myself. My self-esteem is so much stronger." All he needed do was leap and the net would appear.

Michael sought counseling which unblocked his *anahata* (heart chakra) and enabled him to accept his past and live his authentic life in truth. I share Michael's story in hopes that other men of African descent will break the cycle and no longer allow society or their egos to hold them hostage or to believe that in order to be a real man you must solve your own problems. The truth is that a real man acknowledges that seeking help and having someone listen is one of the most priceless gifts he can give himself. It gives him permission to breathe.

Conclusion

So as we move through life and encounter different people in situations that do not turn out the way that we would have liked or imagined, we begin to close off our hearts. The most important aspect of allowing your heart to open is to forgive yourself and forgive others who you believe have wronged you. Those of us who are brave enough to seek help, commit to helping ourselves, and then stand in the midst of our stories ready to deal with what may come our way are truly able to move forward in our lives.

Black men can become the love that they wish to experience in their own lives by practicing self-care and giving love to others with authentic intent. Living authentically is to live your life on your own terms without apology and in defiance of negative societal connotations. Life is for the living, so live your life out loud, with purpose, and with joy.

■ Notes

All of the images were taken by photographer Amy Goalen.

1. Michael is a pseudonym.

■ References

American Institute for Cancer Research. (2008). Still your best bet: A varied plant based diet. *American Institute for Cancer Research Newsletter 100*, 8.

Bernstein, A. M., Bar, J., Ehrman, J. P., Golubic, M., & Roizen, M. F. (2014). Yoga in the management of overweight and obesity. *American Journal of Lifestyle Medicine 8*(1), 33–41. doi:10.1177/1559827613492097.

Brookover, A. (2017). What is the definition of nutrition? Http://www.healthguidance.org/entry/9975/1/What-Is-the-Definition-of-Nutrition.html.

Capouya, J. (2003). *Real men do yoga*. Deerfield Beach, FL: Health Communications, Inc.

Caslin, Y. (2017). Yogi Changa Bell on benefits of yoga; talks God and Black male yoga initiative. Http://www.rollingout.com.

Chiesa, A. (2010). Vipassana meditation: Systematic review of current evidence. *Journal of Alternative and Complementary Medicine 16*(1), 37–46. doi:10.1089/acm.2009.0362.

Chopra, D. (2015). Deepak Chopra's 7-step meditation to open your heart. *Yoga Journal*. Http://www.yogajournal.com/meditation/deepak-chopras-7-step-meditation-to-open-your-heart.

Conway, T. (2014.) LeBron James passes Michael Jordan as America's favorite athlete in Harris Poll. *Bleacher Report*. Http://bleacherreport.com/articles/2133370-lebron-james-passes-michael-jordan-as-americas-favorite-athlete-in-harris-poll.

Carmody, J., Reed, G., Kristeller, J., & Merriam, P. (2008). Mindfulness, spirituality, and health-related symptoms. *Journal of Psychosomatic Research 64*(4), 393–403. doi:10.1016/j.jpsychores.2007.06.015.

Denver Broncos. (2017). *Yoga in the fieldhouse* (video). Http://www.denverbroncos.com/multimedia/videos/Yoga-in-the-Field-House/b93f5004–2242–4714-a27b-05dbf3a8774d.

Do Yoga with Me. (2017). 14 different yoga styles and their benefits to your health. Https://www.doyogawithme.com/types-of-yoga.

DuVernay, A. (2016). *13th*. Netflix.

Fondin, M. (2017). Open yourself to love with the fourth chakra. *The Chopra Center*. Http://www.chopra.com/articles/open-yourself-to-love-with-the-fourth-chakra--sm.0013jylg7118cdbcqsw20wq17vcos.

Fortney, L., & Taylor, M. (2010). Meditation in medical practice: A review of the evidence and practice. *Primary Care: Clinics in Office Practice 37*(1), 81–90. doi:10.1016/j.pop.2009.09.004.

Goalen, A. (2017). *Inside the warrior: The masculine side of yoga*. Amy Goalen Photography. Https://www.amygoalen.com/.

Good Therapy. (2017). *Self-care*. Http://www.goodtherapy.org/learnabout-therapy/issues/self-care.

Gunaratana, B. H. (2017). What exactly is Vipassana meditation? *Tricycle*. Https://tricycle.org/magazine/vipassana-meditation/.

Habash, C. (2012). Igniting tapas (discipline). *Awakening Self*. Https://www.awakeningself.com/writing/igniting-tapas-discipline/.

Heart Disease Weekly. (2015). Intense anger associated with high risk of heart attack.

Hotep, Y. R. (2016). Kemetic yoga: Resurrection of an African legacy. *Gaia*. Https://www.gaia.com/article/kemetic-yoga.

Jackson, R. L., Project Muse, & Ebrary Academic Complete Subscription Collection. (2006). *Scripting the Black masculine body: Identity, discourse, and racial politics in popular media*. Albany: State University of New York Press.

Mauer, M. (2011). Addressing racial disparities in incarceration. *Prison Journal 91* (3_suppl). 87S-101S. doi:10.1177/0032885511415227.

Mayo Clinic. (2017). *Water: How much should you drink every day?* Http://www.mayoclinic.org/healthy-lifestyle/nutrition-and-healthy-eating/in-depth/water/art-20044256.

McCall, T. (2007). 38 health benefits of yoga. *Yoga Journal*. Http://www.yogajournal.com/lifestyle/

count-yoga-38-ways-yoga-keeps-fi.

Men's Fitness. (2017). *The Beginner's Guide to Yoga for Men.* Http://www.mensfitness.com/training/pro-tips/beginners-guide-yoga-men.

Mostofsky, E., Penner, E., & Mittleman, M. (2014). Outbursts of anger as a trigger of acute cardiovascular events: A systematic review and meta-analysis. *European Heart Journal 35*(21), 1404–10. doi:10.1093/eurheartj/ehu033.

Musick, M. A., Herzog, A. R., & House, J. S. (1999). Volunteering and mortality among older adults: Findings from a national sample. *Journals of Gerontology—Series B Psychological Sciences and Social Sciences 54*(3), S173–S180. doi:10.1093/geronb/54B.3.S173.

Niiler, E. (2013). Why yoga is still dominated by women despite the medical benefits to both sexes. *Washington Post*, October 21.

Nguyen, J. Y., Major, J. M., Knott, C. J., Freeman, K. M., Downs, T. M., & Saxe, G. A. (2006). Adoption of a plant-based diet by patients with recurrent prostate cancer. *Integrative Cancer Therapies 5*(3), 214–23. doi:10.1177/1534735406292053.

O'Donnell, M., Yusuf, S., Lamelas, P., Teo, K., Smyth, A., & Rangarajan, S. (2016). Physical activity and anger or emotional upset as triggers of acute myocardial infarction. *Circulation 134*(15), 1059.

Page, H. (1997). Black male imagery: Anti-media containment of African-American men. *American Anthropologist 99*(1), 99.

Perelman, A. M., Miller, S. L., Clements, C. B., Rodriguez, A., Allen, K., & Cavanaugh, R. (2012). Meditation in a Deep South prison: A longitudinal study of the effects of Vipassana. *Journal of Offender Rehabilitation 51*(3), 176–98. doi:10.1080/10509674.2011.632814.

Pizer, A. (2017). What is hatha yoga? *Very Well.* Https://www.verywell.com/what-is-hatha-yoga-3566884.

Pullen, P. R., Thompson, W. R., Benardot, D., Brandon, L. J., Mehta, P. K., Rifai, L., & Khan, B. V. (2010). Benefits of yoga for African American heart failure patients. *Medicine and Science in Sports and Exercise 42*(4), 651–57. doi:10.1249/MSS.0b013e3181bf24c4.

Reder, A. (2007). Karma yoga: Do yoga, do good. *Yoga Journal.* Http://www.yogajournal.com/yoga-101/do-yoga-do-good.

Reshel, A. (2016). How yoga can improve your relationships. *Uplift.* Http://upliftconnect.com/yoga-and-relationships/.

Ross, A., Brooks, A., Touchton-Leonard, K., & Wallen, G. (2016). A different weight loss experience: A qualitative study exploring the behavioral, physical, and psychosocial changes associated with yoga that promote weight loss. *Evidence-Based Complementary and Alternative Medicine 2016*, Article 2914745. doi:10.1155/2016/2914745.

Royster, M. O., Richmond, A., Eng, E., & Margolis, L. (2006) Hey brother, how's your health? A focus group analysis of the health and health-related concerns of African Americans in a southern city in the United States. *Men and Masculinities 8*(4), 389–404. doi:10.1177/1097184X04268798.

Smith, T. A. (2014). Is your heart chakra blocked? Here's how to open it. *Mind, Body, Green.* Https://www.mindbodygreen.com/0-12236/is-your-heart-chakra-blocked-heres-how-to-open-it.html.

Smith, W. A., Hung, M., & Franklin, J. D. (2011). Racial battle fatigue and the miseducation of Black men: Racial microaggressions, societal problems, and environmental stress. *Journal of Negro Education 80*(1), 63–82.

Snyder, S. (2015). Chakra tune-up: Intro to the anahata. *Yoga Journal.* Http://www.yogajournal.com/
    yoga-101/intro-heart-chakra.

Sovik, R. (2013). Diaphragmatic breathing in 3 key yoga poses. *Yoga International.* Https://
    yogainternational.com/article/view/diaphragmatic-breathing-in-3-key-yoga-poses.

Stephens, I. (2017). Medical yoga therapy. *Children 4*(2), 12. doi:10.3390/children4020012.

Tang, K. (2017). Kemetic yoga poses. *AZ Central.* Http://healthyliving.azcentral.com/kemetic-yoga-
    poses-15173.html.

Thiessen, T. (2013). The connection between sleep and the liver. *Naturmend.* Https://www.naturmend.
    com/blog/2013/04/09/the-connection-between-sleep-and-the-liver/.

Townsend, T. (2017). Passion to purpose: Changa Bell talks inspiration, Black male yoga initiative
    & more. *Black Enterprise.* Http://www.blackenterprise.com/bemodernman/2017/04/25/
    changa-bell-black-male-yoga/.

Walker, R. (1999). President and founder, Diamond Cutter, LLC. *Wikipedia.* Https://en.wikipedia.org/
    wiki/Rana_Walker.

———. (2012). One survivor to another. *Funtimes: Celebrating Africa and the diaspora.* September–
    October, 31–37.

Walker, R., & Walker, G. H. (2004). The Huddle™: A time for men (therapy program). Diamond Cutter,
    LLC., Philadelphia.

Walker, R. E. (2016). *Life is funny, but it ain't no joke: A journey of awakening through wisdom sayings.*
    Philadelphia: Harmanity Press.

Walkiewicz, S. (2017). A first-time yoga experience. *Men's Fitness.* Http://www.mensfitness.com/
    training/workout-routines/first-time-yoga-experience.

Watkins, D., & Jefferson, S. (2013). Recommendations for the use of online social support for African
    American men. *Psychological Services 10*(3), 323–32. doi:10.1037/a0027904.

Wilson, A. (2014). Yogic breathing: The physiology of pranayama. *Huffington Post.* Http://www.
    huffingtonpost.com/kripalu/yoga-practice_b_4762303.html.

Yadav, R., Yadav, R. K., Pandey, R. M., & Kochar, K. P. (2016). Effect of a short-term yoga-based lifestyle
    intervention on health-related quality of life in overweight and obese subjects. *Journal of
    Alternative and Complementary Medicine 22*(6), 443–49. doi:10.1089/acm.2015.0268.

Yoga Journal. (2017). *Yoga poses.* San Francisco: Yoga Journal.

Fatherhood, Resilience, and Black Men's Mental Health

Exploring the Contributions of Black Homeschooling Fathers

Taura Taylor

Occasions to assess the accomplishments of black fathers are often eclipsed by the preponderance of scholastic investigations into the fragility of the black family (Allen, 2015; Connor & White, 2007, 2012; Jayakody & Kalil, 2002; Lu et al., 2010; McAdoo, 2007; McLoyd, 1990). However, beyond the absenteeism of black fathers and the economic adversities of poor black Americans is a growing collective of financially stable black households that are modeling the traditional family ideal, the family configuration consisting of a male breadwinner and a female homemaker. While a small but emerging body of research has drawn attention to the changing dynamics of motherhood for middle-class black women—emphasizing their shifting roles with their professions, parenting strategies, and stay-at-home statuses (Barnes, 2009, 2015; Crowley & Curenton, 2011)—for middle-class black fathers, their narratives remain conspicuously overlooked (Allen, 2015; Barnes, 2015; Crowley & Curenton, 2011; Haynes, 2000; Vincent, Rollock, Ball, & Gillborn, 2012).

This chapter reflects upon the provider role strain experienced by black homeschooling fathers as told from the perspective of their wives. Role strain refers to difficulty or inability to meet the demands, obligations, or desired goals in valued social roles (Bowman, 1990; Goode, 1960; Lois, 2006). Black homeschooling families, like other American homeschooling families, are customarily two-parent, middle-class households with adequate access to financial, emotional, and social networking resources. However, intersecting inequalities related to class, race, and gender impress upon the experiences of black mothers *and* black fathers as they sacrifice, time, income, and occasionally parental mental health to provide their school-aged children with an academic curriculum and environment consistent with their family beliefs, morals, and standards.

Drawing from existing literature on the black family, role strain, and participant accounts, this chapter illuminates the relationship between the breadwinner role and mental health among middle-class black fathers. In addition, the author introduces the novel concept *role resilience* to explain how black families navigate race-, gender-, and class-associated role strain to achieve parental empowerment.

Background and Theoretical Framework

Homeschooling is the parent-directed education of school-aged children at home rather than in private and public school environments. Considered an unconventional school choice, for a number of black families concerned with the academic and social welfare of their children, homeschooling is an endearing undertaking and source of parental empowerment. Researchers have advanced that homeschooling mitigates educational disparities found in public school settings, many of which disproportionately affect black children. Amid increasingly amiable responses toward homeschooling, black families of varying socioeconomic backgrounds have shown interest in becoming home educators.

Current data suggest that the homeschooling community is diverse, varying demographically in terms of race, religion, socioeconomic status, and beliefs. However, over 68 percent of the homeschooling population is non-Hispanic white (Redford, Battle, & Bielick 2012), two-parent, and middle class, and typically employs a gendered division of labor as it relates to financial provision, parenting, and teaching roles. Although homeschooling may appeal to black families across socioeconomic status, homeschoolers are ordinarily nuclear households with a male breadwinner and female homemaker—a family configuration that researches refer to as "traditional" and "ideal," but is anthologized as uncharacteristic of *average* black families (Connor & White, 2007). Historically, black families have been characterized as unconventionally matrifocal and egalitarian with regards to family roles and duties. While politicians, scholars, and members of the black community have glorified the benefits and privileges of the two-parent family model as the response to many social ills affecting black families—prompting upwardly mobile black families to aspire to or adopt the ideal family model—research establishes that increased socioeconomic status is not a firewall against race-related challenges (Haynes, 2000; Jayakody & Kalil, 2002). In addition, family, feminist, and black feminist scholars present critiques that the ideal family model, also referred to as the Standard North American Family (SNAF), presents distinct discriminatory psychological and social consequences for women and black families in particular (Haynes, 2000; Staples, 1971).

Intertwined with the privileges of the ideal family are complex interconnecting stratifications of multiple social institutions. The dynamic nature of stratification privileges white males and systemically perpetuates privilege and marginalization within the intersecting institutions of family, labor force, and education (among other social institutions) (Collins, 1998; Staples, 1971). Furthermore, black families are consigned to *controlling images*—racist, constructed stereotypes that project socially marginalizing, derogatory, and objectifying race-, gender-, and class-specific depictions of black men and black women as well as their children. Collins (2000) and Smith (1993) offer descriptions of the socially constructed and normalized image of family as portrayed in American society. The SNAF is described by Smith (1993) as the conceptualization of family as a "legally married couple sharing a household" in which "the adult male is in paid employment; his earnings provide the economic basis of the family household. The adult female may also earn an income, but her primary responsibility is to the care of the husband, household, and children."

In Collins's and Smith's characterization, family needs are provided for from within the family unit, based upon the assumption that the father earns an adequate salary that will allow the wife to withdraw from the public work sector and manage private domestic responsibilities. Although the ideal image of family often positions the wife as a stay-at-home mother, children are expected to attend traditional forms of schools—such as public or private schools. Homeschooling, shading the family brown, adding extended family members, or depicting two mommies or two daddies immediately distorts the "recognizable" and normalized image of family. The ideal family is one such construct that can have marginalizing consequences for black homeschooling families. Collins specifies that the American normalized image of the ideal family is intersectional—meaning it is raced, gendered, classed, and sexed.

Studies have shown that although the black middle class is typically better off than their lower-income-earning black counterparts, black American families typically earn depressed wages compared to white American families, and live in or around central urban areas that are routinely segregated and disadvantaged (Johnson 2006; Omi & Winant, 1994; Shapiro, 2004). Such areas are overwhelmed with inadequate housing, meager resources, and deficient social services, and are typically the bottom rung on the socioeconomic ladder (Massey, 2001). According to 2012 reports from the National Center for Education Statistics, 37 percent of black children were living in households that were below the poverty level, highest percentage for children of any racial category.

Gendered Division of Labor

The combining of parent, worker, and spousal roles has different gendered consequences for individuals' mental health. Simon (1995) explores the meaning that men and women attach to their multiple roles. Role strain among married couples has been attributed to structural encumbrances, such as institutionalized gender inequality in work and home spaces. Research on role strain has repeatedly confirmed that women experience greater amounts of mental distress stemming from role strain. Role strain is distress associated with balancing or managing multiple role responsibilities (Bowman, 1990; Lois, 2006). In contrast, in this chapter I introduce *role resilience*, a concept that describes and accounts for the ways in which black homeschooling families achieve their homeschooling and parenting goals.

Men construct their identities as good fathers around their abilities to provide economically for their families. Previous research has found that men and women perceive work outside the home as either assisting in accomplishing family goals or competing against efforts and thus compromising time as well as physical and mental wellness (Bowman, 1990). The 1980s saw an emergence of research on role strain related to increasing number of women entering the workforce. Whereas black women always worked, feminist and gender research turned its focus to the gendered dynamics of the division of labor in households and changing family dynamics for workforce mothers. For black families, middle-class status granted an opportunity to aspire and simulate the ideal family ideal; however achievement is forever thwarted, as the ideal is grounded in racial and gendered constructions unobtainable by mothers and fathers racialized as black.

Research Design/Methodology

Data from this chapter comes from an exploratory study emphasizing the role of intersectionality upon black homeschooling families' abilities to meet their homeschooling goals. By asking, "What types of support do black families need to homeschool their children?" the author originally set out to examine the tangible and intangible resources and interactions that black American homeschooling families at different social locations either explicitly or implicitly identified as substantive to sustaining their homeschooling efforts. Consistent with the literature, the homeschooling families in the study were most often two-parent, middle-class households, who cited pedagogical, ideological, and cultural reasons as their motives for homeschooling. Participants' accounts substantiated findings from previous studies on black homeschoolers by Fields-Smith and Williams (2009), and Mazama and Lundy (2012), who advanced that black families often homeschooled as an assertion of their parental empowerment to avoid adverse experiences associated with "school-related racism" (2012, p. 723). In addition, candid admissions regarding spousal support yielded unanticipated yet significant findings that provide the focal point of this chapter.

Utilizing a nonprobability, purposive sampling to access participants, the author selected twenty households from three "general" regions and their greater surrounding areas: Atlanta, Georgia; Washington, DC, and Maryland; and Raleigh, North Carolina. Respondents participated in a single tape-recorded interview. The three locales were selected primarily for their diversity and renowned black homeschooling populations. Half of the interviews were face-to-face, and the other half were via telephone. The interviews typically lasted at least one hour, with the shortest lasting about thirty minutes and the longest lasting an hour and a half. To ensure confidentiality, all participants were assigned pseudonyms using numbers (such as L1, L2, A1) on interview files to avoid using participants' names as identification.

The narratives come from the primary homeschooling parent, all of whom were black women and the biological mother of at least one homeschooled child (see table 1). The twenty mothers interviewed all identified as either African American or black, with one mother identifying ethnically as Nigerian American. The average age for the primary caretaker/homeschooling parent was forty-two, with ages ranging from thirty-one to forty-eight. The average age of the

Table 1. Demographics of Characteristics of Respondents

	HOUSEHOLD TYPE	NUMBER OF CHILDREN	RESPONDENT'S AGE	MARITAL STATUS	RESPONDENT'S EDUCATION	INCOME	CHILDREN'S AGES
Cassandra	MSE	3	38	M	M.B.A	120+	5–13
Ruby	MSE	3	38	M	M.A.	20–40	4–8
Yvonne	MSE	2	46	M	M.A.	120+	7/7
Marie	MSE	2	31	M	B.S.	0–20	5–6
Nora	MSE	4	42	M	B.A.	120+	1–10
Ife	MSE	3	31	M	High School	20–40	3–8
Odessa	MSE	4	47	M	M.A.	120+	7–19
Sonia	MSE	2	41	M	M.A.	120+	6–9
Jackie	MSE	3	45	M	B.A.	120+	8–14
Abiona	MSE	3	34	M	B.S.	90–120	3–8
Fatima	MSE	3	34	M	B.A.	60–90	5–12
Phylicia	MSE	5	44	M	B.S.	40–60	3–18
Amaya	MSE	3	37	M	B.A.	90–120	10–14
Dina	Ret	2	45	M	M.A.	120+	14–19
Simone	DE	2	44	M	B.S.	60–90	4–10
Miriam	DE	2	39	M	High School	60–90	10–18
Beah	SF	2	47	D	M.A.	90–120	7–9
Kitt	SF	3	48	D	High School	0–20	8
Ella	SF	2	31	D	B.A.	20–40	9–13
LaDonna	SF	3	43	S	High School	20–40	8–17

Household Type=MSE:Married Single Earner; RET: Married Retired; DE: Married Dual Earner; SF: Single Female

secondary caretaker, when present, was forty-one, with a range from twenty-nine to fifty-three. The average number of children in the family was three, ranging from prekindergarten age to high school / college age. Sixteen of the twenty participants were married, whereas two participants were divorced, one participant was legally married but separated from her spouse, and another was married in a spiritual tradition, however legally was considered a domestic partner. Thus, from participant accounts, the households were categorized into five types—*married, single-earner; married, dual-earner; retired; single female, head of household; and extended family*. Four of the twenty mothers reported having graduate degrees, two held bachelor's degrees, one held an associate's degree, and the remaining four obtained their high school diploma (with two of the four working on college degrees at the time of the interview). The biological father was often the secondary caretaker and most often provided the sole financial support. Four of the fathers had graduate or professional degrees, a PhD, MBA, MA, or MD. Two fathers held bachelor's degrees, and one father held a high school diploma only. Most often fathers did not contribute substantially to the direct teaching of children. The average income was $73,000, with one family reporting an income below $20,000. Most households reported an income of $120,000 or higher. According to the National Center for Educational Statistics, two-parent households make up 89 percent of the homeschooling population; 54 percent of homeschooling households include two parents, with one parent in the labor force (Redford,

Battle, & Bielick, 2012). In 2007, families earning between $25,001 and $75,000 homeschooled at higher rates than families earning $25,000 or less.

In the interest of broadening what we know about homeschoolers and black families, the focus of this chapter is on black fatherhood. Whereas prevailing literature has a proclivity to focus on the pathology of black families or homeschoolers' motivations for choosing home-schooling, this analysis takes into account the idea that the social situations in which people are embedded affect their motivations, beliefs, and actions and are determinants of mental health.

Findings

Described as the ultimate privatization of education, homeschooling means that parents forfeit their entitlement to public schools and assume all costs, commitments, and responsibilities associated with educating their children. To sustain their homeschooling commitments, families in this study depended upon three broad types of assistance: *emotional, instructional,* and *financial.*

Simone, a married mother of two, shared that operating a homeschool and teaching one's own child led to a host of dynamics rarely required of a conventional teacher in a conventional classroom or conventional family:

> You would need support on just a trustworthy curriculum on what to do, support on how to set up your day for your children, how to understand what type of learner your child is, how to bal-ance your household with your schooling and your children and your life, how to balance your finances, because usually what happens is you typically have . . . one family income, one primary income, and so that is something that you almost have to create your own science based on all the needs that still remain. Even [if] there are two people working, you consider that something [has] to balance out.

Not surprisingly, socioeconomic status and interpersonal relationships were the most sig-nificant determinants upon which tangible and intangible resources were either readily available from within the home or sought outside of the home. In a similar thought, Amaya, a married mother of three, who had experiences homeschooling her children abroad and in the United States, shared this perspective about the significance of having adequate resources and support:

> I feel, obviously, not everyone can homeschool, and there are different circumstances that make that [homeschooling] not a reality or viable or even healthy because obviously . . . it [homeschool-ing] cannot be a positive experience. By that I mean . . . if you have a lack of resources or the person who is giving the instruction or facilitating the learning is not doing what they need to be doing, then the child is obviously at a disservice. It has the potential, just like anything, to be a really great way to learn, but it has its own downfalls. . . . I think a large part of it is about resources and being

able to plug in and get help in the things that you're weak in or being able to just provide what you're not able to personally provide.

Outside of rudimentary competence, the "different circumstances" mentioned by Amaya are attributable to matters of social location and abilities and inabilities to emulate the traditional family ideal. As participants elaborated on the rewards and encumbrances associated with the responsibility of homeschooling, their perceptions of their access to "resources" and ability "to plug in" were most often discussed in reference to constraints or privileges related to race, gender, income, and marital status.

Some families shared that they were able to meet all their material and emotional needs within their nuclear household—relying upon others simply for organized recreation and casual social interactions—while others relied upon extended family, friends, and formal support groups to supplement their lack of financial, instructional, and recreational resources, or to provide empathy and encouragements (*resilience*). Differences and similarities in participants' accounts draw attention to spousal support and the role of black fathers as providers of conspicuous and inconspicuous benefits and privileges. Through role resilience, families negotiated role strain as well as conventional and stratified boundaries.

I Guess He Helps: Role Strain and Invisible Labor (Overlooked Contributions)

The frequency and candidness with which participants discussed their homeschooling needs in reference to their marital and income-generating status drew attention to participants who did not mention their partners' contributions. For example, several married participants shared that their spouses earned annual salaries above $60,000 and yet they often did not mention how his salary contributed to their abilities to homeschool. Black fathers' contributions as financial providers were unmarked, not as an act of contempt, but as taken for granted. The ideal-family model undervalues the financial accomplishments of both black women and black men. A common adage for black parental responsibility is, "You don't get a pat on the head for what you're supposed to do." True and yet, considering the social obstacles that often deter or inhibit some black men and women from achieving prescribed parental standards (ideals set by the mainstream) there are disproportionate health implications related to the encumbrances of racial and gendered inequality.

If Anybody Should Homeschool Their Children in America, It Should Be Black People

Teaching as a parenting responsibility may be socially differentiated from teaching professionally, but for participants such as Ruby and Beah, homeschooling is perceived as evolving "naturally" because, in spite of social conventions, all aspects of education are continuous impositions of habits and behaviors onto children (Handel, Cahill, & Elkin, 2007). Although we learn and naturalize cultural categories—lumping and splitting the natural world into conventional boundaries such as home and school, and parent and teacher, to the point of internalizing their borders as essential—meanings and borders are not stagnant or fixed and can be rearticulated through interaction (Zerubavel, 1991). Berger and Luckmann's social construction of reality theory (1966) is useful in understanding how the homeschooling mothers in my study experienced both an objective and subjective reality through their social interactions, habitualizations, and internalizations of themselves as products of their social and cultural worlds and as producers of sociocultural experiences. However, due to stratification and power differentials (Richardson, 1988), some individuals and even social groups must contend with their modifications being perceived as social deviations. Whereas some social actors occupy social positions that afford them the institutionalized power to redefine social conventions and social systems of powers, others occupy marginalized statuses in which they must contend with resistance and opposition to their rearticulated reality. Some families reported similar incomes and yet their experiences reflected different middle-class status. Several nuclear households were able to accommodate their families' educational experiences, whereas others were dependent upon extended family and various social support networks to supplement the resources they could not obtain from their family income. Questions about accumulated wealth would have helped me to discern between varying socioeconomic dynamics.

Resilience

Many of the participants were proud to assert their agency—believing they were overcoming structural inequalities by homeschooling. Yet findings suggest that although the context had changed and the families believed they were able to provide their children with better educational experiences than their public schools could provide, they still faced structural inequalities, often based in the racial wealth gap. Several participants were unable demonstrate American values such as individualism and meritocracy because they were dependent upon outside sources for many basic resources. The few who appeared to have accumulated wealth were able to meet their educational goals by purchasing educational resources that others looked for from their family, friends, and community.

It was not uncommon for participants to form instrumental relationships with individuals and support groups to further their homeschooling goals and enhance their experiences. According to American values of individualism and meritocracy, such groups threaten the ideal of being firmly middle class and financially independent but for many of the participants common goals of parental empowerment allowed them to construct community and social supports as contributes to resilience. Via role resilience, social allowances such as *sense of empowerment* (interpretation of agency) and access to resources incurred by homeschooling households in spite of structural constraints and differential power determinants related to intersecting social statuses allowed social actors to create new sociopolitical perspectives and identities by rearranging and reassigning meaning from existent knowledge, information, and social phenomena—most often through the infusion of their own culture (Omi and Winant, 1994; Collins, 2005). Both sense of accomplishment and sense of empowerment are contingent upon whether households perceived homeschooling as a disruption to their standard of living, as an improvement in their standard of living, or as a positive indicator of their standard of living.

Role Resilience and Mental Health

Although we should not lose sight of homeschooling as occurring within the context of a growing trend toward a family configuration of husband as breadwinner and wife as home-maker, black women choosing to stay at home highlight participants' abilities and inabilities to access resources as emanating from personal dispositions but more importantly, social claims of unequal distribution of materials and resources as well as unequal recognition of subaltern and marginalized identities. Furthermore, black men's contributions in the model are underrepresented in scholastic discussions of distributive politics and identity politics, the paradigms of redistribution and recognition critical to understanding that homeschooling boundaries are social injustices related to broader, intersecting social stratifications and un-equal power differentials (Apple, 2000; Fraser, 1997; Richardson, 1988). Through empowerment and role resilience, homeschooling families in my study demonstrated their resourcefulness by negotiating conventional and stratified social boundaries. Breadwinners, stay-at-home mothers, and homeschoolers function within social inequalities related to systemic social stratifications and gendered unequal power differentials—present sociocultural obstructions to equal opportunities critical to parenting. Literature on mental health informs us that men's and women's emotional and psychological well-being is affected by broad sociocultural factors such as work conditions and gendered roles as providers and caregivers. For black Americans, well-being is further compromised by systemic, gendered racism.

Problematic is the inattention to black fathers' psychological well-being as breadwinners. Lacy (2007) establishes that middle-class black families assert family values that are not variant from either black low-income families or middle-class white families, both of which have been constructed as their race and class counterparts. The effects of race and gender stratification on black middle-class parents' willingness to sacrifice for their children, whether to provide for their children at all costs or to temper their own financial needs, is often influenced by their construction of parenting. Likewise, or similarly, participants in my study engaged in a similar consideration, although indirectly revolving around money but more specifically exchange of their labor with their family in order for their wives and children to have specific experiences, such as opportunities for psychological well-being. By protecting their children from racist environments, via division of labor, black homeschooling fathers and mothers asserted a form of resilience that had positive consequences for their self-esteem and sense of purpose as parents. Research demonstrates that the breadwinner role is related to psycho-logical distress. However, other studies argue that working wives are also related to spousal distress with regard to gendered power dynamics and household negotiations. Participants in this study shared narratives that reflected unequal as well as equal distributions of labor but, most important, equally committed goals for their children's education and well-being. The primary homeschooling parents are aware of how their spouses' income supports their ability to homeschool, but they distinguish their financial contributions from direct instruction.

> IFE: I am the primary. My husband works, it feels like twenty-four hours. It's a sacrifice, but he does it. He does it (laughter). [Interviewer: Does he contribute to any of the homeschooling education?] Yes. I want to say once a week. That's me making sure he gets in there and does something (laughter).
>
> IFE: Because money is not an issue in our household, but my husband and I know that if both of us were working, it would be so much easier. . . . We didn't think what would happen if the money that you're making is no longer enough and you have to work. . . . My husband, he's like I do this because I want you to homeschool our children, but I see the stress on him. I see the stress on him. He teaches extra classes and stays at the glass studios longer to make more pieces to sell. It's like we have no social life with each other, literally. When we do, it's so at the last minute. It's like, I really don't want to go out, would you rather kind of get some sleep, but we do get a babysitter.
>
> KITT: Public school hasn't always around. Initially everyone homeschooled. It just got, public school is, it's not new but it's not old either, and I guess we kind of got out of the idea of homeschooling because it was more convenient for people when, especially when the women started going into the job force, more convenient to put their children in an environment and let somebody else take care of their education.

Gendered ideology about teaching, childcare, and women's participation in the labor force is evident in some of the interviewees' comments.

> BEAH: I think the number one difference is that I'm a single parent. So the onus is on me to provide, other than God, who I see as the provider. The onus is on me to see that the financial needs of the family are met. The onus is on me to make sure the home is taken care of, getting food, their clothes are getting washed, those typical wife duties are getting done. The onus is on me to teach everything—or I won't say teach everything—be responsible for teaching everything. I don't have to be the one that teaches them, [but] I am the only one available to say what they get taught and how. Other homeschool families, they have a husband and a wife. The wife may be the primary teacher, but the husband can step [in]: "I'm comfortable with physics, I'll teach a piece." "I'll find the guitar tutor or the Latin instructor." There's a shared responsibility and a lifestyle. I don't know of many homeschool families, I can't think of a one, where the husband or the wife aren't in agreement that the children should be homeschooled and where the father is involved, maybe not directly on a daily basis.

Fatima commented on oversight and instruction as needed:

FATIMA: My husband was supportive, because I asked him before as I was thinking about it and he was like "Yeah, I think you should go for it." Once I had his support, I was like, "OK, good," I was all right. The way that he was supportive, he was like, "Yeah, it's a good idea." When I showed him a few things that I was doing with our youngest daughter, he was like, "Wow!" He was just really got all gung ho, like "OK!. Anything that will make his girls smart, he's like "Oh yeah, I'm all for it." That's what really got him on board. Now, he stays out of my way. I was talking to some other homeschool moms: "I hate when my husband's home. He's kind of in our way." But he stays out of our way. I guess he helps with gas money and stuff like that, our memberships and stuff like that. Yesterday I told him we need help with our art museum membership, its coming around for renewal, different things like that.

Nation building is an incentive for homeschooling among African Americans families.

KITT: The majority of the people who are homeschooling and are familiar with the homeschool environment are Caucasian. One of the reasons why they are more free to homeschool [is] because [in] a lot of them the wife doesn't have to work, so she's able to stay home and homeschool, and honestly had I not gotten sick, I would have to work, and my daughter would be in public school. I was, honestly, just blessed that I got sick and became disabled to the point where . . . I can't work a full-time job, so I can homeschool her.

Kitt's comments demonstrate how race and marital status intersect to impact one's parental empowerment and resilience in homeschooling.

The more that families perceived their homeschooling endeavors as a resilient response to structural inequality, the more often they perceived their own roles and mental stresses as an act of resilience, perseverance, and empowerment.

- They had the resources to navigate disinterested, discriminatory schools, and even biased and discriminatory homeschooling organizations and supplemental groups (resource driven).
- They used unconventional methods and framings of their behaviors and actions to achieve their goals, such as kinship ties, cooperatives, bartering, and self-sufficiency (process driven).

In response to stratification and white normativity, many black households experience marginalization within various contexts of everyday life. What is learned from the participant accounts in this study is that, through the interactive and interpretative processes of role resilience, participants mobilized material and human resources to transcend stratified social boundaries that otherwise would have narrowed or restricted their educational progress. Black homeschooling families were able to proclaim propriety over their definitions of family and education. From my analysis of participant accounts, I eventually hypothesized that the effectiveness of homeschooling was directly linked to homeschooling families' ability to negotiate cultural categories and mobilize on behalf of their interests.

Without considering the unique social and historical events of mothering and parenting among black families, it could be presumed that homeschooling mothers who narrate their inclinations to homeschool as natural are engaged in affirming or assimilating gender scripts based upon the ideal notions of family. However, as Collins (2000, p. 57) asserted, "Motherhood as an institution occupies a special place in transmitting values to children about their proper place"; therefore, homeschooling mothers are in an instrumental and empowering position to contribute to their child's oppression or liberation. Several of the participants' spouses articulated their willingness to endure the burdens of provider role strain in resilient efforts to empower their families. Ruby's account is a demonstration of role resilience:

> In America from our history, we always took care of someone else's children, so I think being able to take care of your own, that's unique about it. Being able to pour directly into your children. I think that's why I am so adamant about, why I want to be at home. I was pouring into other children. Now, they were other black children, so I saw the value in that. I don't want my children to miss out on anything that I can give, that I bring as their mother. . . . That is why I knew I was going to come home. Part of [what happened] when my husband and I were dating [was] we worked that out. . . . I'm coming home and you're going to work. He was like. "I want that for our children."

Perspectives about family and education are created in the larger society, reinforced, and sometimes reconstructed within intimate contexts. How reality is experienced and known is through interaction. Whereas multiple participants relied upon formal support groups for social and recreational activities, almost all participants expressed some dependency upon either their spouse or immediate family members for their financial, emotional, and instructional needs. Through daily interactions and conversations, attitudes and routines related to homeschooling were shaped, modified, and eventually internalized as resilience or resistance. As a result of the accounts shared by several participants, we learn how their spouses facilitated their changed perspectives about parenting, teaching, working, time management, and resource allocation. When we consider that stress and esteem are signifiers of unstable and stable mental health respectively, we come to understand how the habits, behaviors, and attitudes that are institutionalized in our society impress upon mental well-being. Participants' accounts demonstrate how black fathers were engaged in interactive and interpretive processes that contributed to their ability to transform their reality and mental dispositions.

Conclusion

The prevalence of the presumed pathology of black families and absence of black fathers often overshadows not only complex racialized and gendered structural obstacles that impose on black families' internal dynamics but also black women's and men's adaptive fortitude to withstand such obstacles (Allen, 1995; Collins, 2000; Davis-Sowers, 2006; Mosley-Howard & Evans, 2000). Concurrently, most studies on the black family only tangentially include the narratives of black fathers, often omitting their voices entirely (McDowell, Sanchez, & Jones, 2000; Fields-Smith & Williams, 2009). Whether deliberate or not, generalizations, silence, and invisibility contribute to marginalization and subsequently subordinate black fathers' contributions and challenges within the family. Considering the social positionality of black homeschoolers offers an opportunity for inclusion, as middle-class homeschooling mothers reflect upon the role of their marital status and impart insights about their marital partners' efforts. Their narratives bring to light black fathers' motivations, socioeconomic status, and breadth of sociomental consequences within their homeschooling efforts.

Previous research on homeschooling populations has substantially contributed to what is known about American families, education, and sociopolitical reform. From parental involvement and emotional role strain, to time management and political activism, homeschooling research has magnified the ways in which social actors assert their agency in determining their children's educational experiences. Though multiple studies have reiterated that homeschoolers are not a homogenous group and that homeschooling is not a monolithic movement, black homeschoolers' identities, interests, and experiences are routinely overlooked or minimized within the homeschooling literature. In the exceptionally few studies that have chronicled black homeschoolers' experiences, the role of the secondary parent, black fathers, remains clandestine. They are the critical focus of this chapter. As with most preliminary endeavors, this work accentuates the need to broaden both the homeschooling discourse and family literature with additional inquiries, critical dialogue, and analysis. Researching the needs of black homeschoolers utilizing an intersectionality framework will yield information about the effects of race, gender, and class status upon families' ability to achieve their educational goals. Furthermore, homeschooling among black households represents an opportunity to examine how the role of the black father is situated via race, gender, and class and affects black men's mental health as providers. Through role resilience, the fathers in this chapter changed their minds and the minds of others about the institutions of education and family and most importantly about the values, behaviors, and options available to black families.

■ **References**

Allen, Q. (2015). They think minority means lesser than: Black middle-class sons and fathers resisting microaggressions in the school. *Urban Education 48*(2), 171–97. doi:10.1177/0042085912450575.

Aud, S., Hussar, W., Johnson, F., Kena, G., Roth, E., Manning, E., Wang, X., and Zhang, J. (2012). The

Condition of Education 2012 (NCES 2012-045). U.S. Department of Education, National Center for Education Statistics. Washington, DC.

Barnes, R. (2009). Race, class, and marriage: Black women, social mobility and the companionate marriage ideal. Doctoral dissertation, Emory University.

———. (2015). *Raising the race: Black career women redefine marriage, motherhood, and community.* New Brunswick, NJ: Rutgers University Press.

Bowman, P. J. (1990). Coping with provider role strain: Adaptive cultural resources among black husband-fathers. *Journal of Black Psychology 16*(2), 1–21. doi:10.1177/00957984900162002.

Collins, P. (1998). Intersections of race, class, gender, and nation: Some implications for black family studies. *Journal of Comparative Family Studies 29*(1). Http://www.jstor.org/stable/41603544.

Connor, M. E., & White, J. L. (2007). Fatherhood in contemporary black America: An invisible presence. *Black Scholar 37*(2), 2. doi:10.4324/9781410617026.

——— (eds.). (2012). *Black fathers: An invisible presence in America.* 2nd ed. New York: Routledge.

Crowley, J. E., & Curenton, S. (2011). Organizational social support and parenting challenges among mothers of color: The case of mocha moms. *Family Relations 60*(1), 1–14. doi:10.1111/j.1741-3729.2010.00629.x.

Goode, W. (1960). A theory of role strain. *American Sociological Review 25*(4), 483–96.

Haynes, F. E. (2000). Gender and family ideals: An exploratory study of black middle-class Americans. *Journal of Family Issues 21*(7), 811–37. doi:10.1177/019251300021007001.

Jayakody, R., & Kalil, A. (2002). Social fathering in low-income, African American families with preschool children. *Journal of Marriage & Family 64*(2), 504–16. doi:10.1111/j.1741-3737.2002.00504.

Lois, J. (2006). Role strain, emotion management, and burnout: Homeschooling mothers' adjustment to the teacher role. *Symbolic Interaction 29*(4), 507–29. doi:10.1525/si.2006.29.4.507.

Lu, M. C., Jones, L., Bond, M. J., Wright, K., Pumpuang, M., Maidenberg, M., . . . Rowley, D. L. (2010). Where is the F in MCH? Father involvement in African American families. *Ethnicity & Disease 20*(1–2), 49–61. Http://www.pop.ishib.org/journal/20-1s2/ethn-20-01s2-s49.pdf.

McAdoo, H. P. (2007). *Black families.* 4th ed. Thousand Oaks, CA: Sage.

McLoyd, V. (1990). The impact of economic hardship on black families and children: Psychological distress, parenting, and socioemotional development. *Child Development 61*(2), 311–46. doi:10.1111/j.1467-8624.1990.tb02781.

Redford, J., Battle, D., & Bielick, S. (2016). *Homeschooling in the United States: 2012.* NCES 2016-096. National Center for Education Statistics.

Staples, R. (1971). Towards a sociology of the black family: A theoretical and methodological assessment. *Journal of Marriage and the Family 33*(1), 119–38.

Vincent, C., Rollock, N., Ball, S., & Gillborn, D. (2012). Being strategic, being watchful, being determined: Black middle-class parents and schooling. *British Journal of Sociology of Education 33*(3), 337–54. doi:10.1080/01425692.2012.668833.

Improved Health Care for Black Males as a Function of Increased Graduation Rates

A Scholar-Servanthood Pedagogical Approach

B etween me and the other world there is an unasked question: unasked by some through feelings of delicacy; by others through the difficulty of rightly framing it. All, neverthe-less, flutter round it. How does it feel to be a problem? (DuBois, 1996, p. 15).

In 1903, W. E. B. DuBois asked the above question in his literary American classic, _The Souls of Black Folk_. In this same treatise, he wrote of the Black man,

> He simply wishes to make it possible for a man to be both a Negro and an American, without
> being cursed and spit upon by his fellows, without having the doors of Opportunity closed
> roughly in his face. This, then, is the end of his striving: to be a co-worker in the kingdom of
> culture, to escape both death and isolation, to husband and use his best powers and his latent
> genius. (DuBois, 1996, p. 17)

One hundred thirteen years ago, DuBois answered the question as well as issued a challenge. The question is this: "Can Black people live in the United States of America and be treated as fair as white males in all aspects (both interpersonally and organizationally, both public and private) in society?

Even with the election of our first Black president and the claims of living in a more equitable society, racism and other types of oppression are alive and well in the United States. Microag-gressions toward difference, social assumptions accepted as "norms," and institutional policies have successfully maintained the conditions that slavery, Jim Crow, forced immigration of in-digenous populations, and legal terrorism of citizens created over the last four hundred years. The majority of public schools have served as conduits to ensure societal inequity continues.

With the election of Donald Trump and the appointment of prochoice and privatization advo-cate Betsy DeVos as the Secretary of Education, Black and Brown children will find themselves even more vulnerable and victimized by structurally racist and classist policies. With a history of separate and unequal education, the recent rise of public displays of white nationalism, and the control of the state apparatus being placed in the hands of fascist neocons, what can realistically be implemented to improve the educational quality of Black males?

The aim of this chapter is to arm critical and/or humanistic educators with tools to help Black male students grow academically while learning to advocate for their human rights. By utilizing a scholar-servanthood pedagogical framework, teachers and students will grow in their critical awareness and ability to transform ideas into action, the result of which will hopefully be increased graduation rates, improved life circumstances, and better health.

This chapter will examine graduation rates and health as a function of educational success. Applying the ideas of Derrick Bell's racial realism theory (Bell, 1992), this chapter discusses the reality that racism is endemic and will always be integrated into American education. Next, we will introduce the idea of scholar-servant pedagogy and how this pedagogy has the potential to improve graduation rates and subsequently improve Black male health. Shortcomings of scholar-servanthood pedagogy will be discussed, as well my vision and hope for this pedagogy.

Health and Education

According to Freudenburg and Ruglis (2007), good education predicts good health, and dis-parities in health and education are closely linked (p. 1):

> First, the more schooling people have the more money they earn, enabling them to purchase better housing in safer neighborhoods, healthier food, better medical care and health insurance, and more education; each one of these factors is associated with improved health. Each one allows individuals to move up the occupational and income ladder, giving them more prestige and power, both of which are associated with better health. High school completion is also the gateway into college, which offers even greater benefits than high school alone. Second, education facilitates healthier behavior choices by offering learners access to health information and tools to acquire help and resources such as smoking cessation programs. Third, education helps people to social support, strengthen social networks, and mitigate social stressors. The more education people have the more social support they have. Education helps people to gain a sense of control over their lives, an outcome associated with better health. (Freudenburg & Ruglis, 2007, p. 2)

If education is a predictor of health, and if more education equates to improved health, how do education and health impact persons on the basis of race, class, gender, sexual orientation, religious affiliation, and other markers of difference? What does this mean for Black males?

Graduation Rates and Race

According to the *2015 Schott 50 State Report on Public Education and Black Males* (Schott Foundation for Public Education, 2015), the national graduation rate for Black males in the 2012–13 school year was 59 percent. The national graduation rate for Latino males and white males was, respectively, 65 percent and 80 percent (Schott Foundation for Public Education, 2015, p. 7).

The reasons why differences in graduation rates occur are systemic, personal, social, cultural, and political. This author does recognize personal responsibility and the importance of hard work, sacrifice, and "grit." However, the overwhelming evidence of inequitable treatment of people living within the borders of the United States of America based on race is not only ever present in our educational system but is a result of racism's being one of the foundational pillars on which our country was established.

> From the very inception of the Republic to the present moment, race has been a profound determinant of one's political rights, one's location in the labor market, and indeed one's sense of "identity." The hallmark of this history has been *racism*, not the abstract ethos of equality, and while minority groups have been treated differently, all can bear witness to the tragic consequences of racial oppression. The U.S. has confronted each racially defined minority with a unique form of despotism and degradation. The examples are familiar: Native Americans faced genocide, blacks were subjected to racial slavery, Mexicans were invaded and colonized, and Asians faced exclusion. (Omi & Winant, 1994, p. 1)

Racism and Education: A Brief History

Since the 1600s, and with very little exception, Africans brought to America and born in America have been situated in a secondary status. Compromises originally written into the US Constitution, the refusal to relinquish the practice of slavery in the southern colonies after England abolished slavery (which was a major reason why the original colonies, ironically, decided to emancipate themselves from England) firmly established American racism. Post–Civil War, Confederate-friendly concessions, a brief period of Reconstruction (eleven years), Jim Crow (legal segregation solidified by *Plessy v. Ferguson*), and widespread, acceptable, and constant terrorist acts (by individuals and the very systems designed to protect its citizens) represent the historical lived-experience timeline of Black people in America. Unfortunately, the history of the American schooling system for African Americans mimics and reinforces much of the same.

The history of education for Black people in America, with few exceptions, has operated to maintain control and compliancy. With chattel slavery being the practice in the southern colonies, education was forbidden for slaves. There were instances where slaves received vocational training and even training in plantation management, but this was to reduce the work of the owner or make the slave more valuable in the marketplace (Spring, 1994). However, reading was strictly forbidden. According to Henry Bullock (1970) in *A History of Negro Education in the South: From 1619 to Present*, there was a "general fear that literacy would expose the slaves to abolition literature."

In northern colonies, slavery did not exist, but there were laws, "Black Codes," that forbade Black people to participate in certain activities of civil life. According to historian Leon F. Litwack (1961, 72): Ohio "provided a classic example of how anti-immigration legislation could be invoked to harass Negro residents." The state had enacted Black Laws in 1804 and 1807 that compelled blacks entering the state to post bond of $500 guaranteeing good behavior and to produce a court paper as proof that they were free.

Although the abolitionist movement held a much stronger political position than that in the south, the Black Codes ensured that Black people received an education separate from their white counterparts, one that was most often inferior. Attempts to integrate schools were met with legal, social, and physical opposition.

The outcome of the American Civil War presented the question of incorporating roughly four million newly freed slaves into American civil society. To respond to this issue, the Freedman's Bureau was formed. Overseen by former Union general Oliver Otis Howard (founder of Howard University), schools were created to begin the process of educating newly freed slaves. However, the process of creating another method of controlling Black people also began.

Despite the best efforts of those such as W. E. B. DuBois and Carter G. Woodson, who believed that education should be a conscious-raising and thus political activity that moves people toward full citizenship and "humanship" through social struggle, ideologies advocating vocational training and delaying full citizenship for Black people was the preferred educational direction (Watkins, 2005). Former Union general Samuel Chapman Armstrong, founder of the Hampton Institute, and his protégé, Booker T. Washington, were the most ardent advocates of this type of education. With Hampton teachers spread across the South, Armstrong believed, African Americans would be "civilized" and brought to accept their subordinate place in society (Spring, 1994, p. 170).

With the prevalent pedagogy being vocational training, schools for Blacks became producers of laborers whose pathways were destined to uphold the vision described by General Samuel Chapman Armstrong. Jim Crow laws served as a reminder of one's place. Even with the landmark Supreme Court decision of *Brown v. Board of Education* in 1954, ruling against the "separate but equal" doctrine and subsequently making Jim Crow laws unconstitutional, the racists ideas held by many white people were too entrenched to begin the process of integration. (For the purposes of this chapter, desegregation and integration are not the same and not interchangeable. I believe and argue that integration has never been realized. However, desegregation has occurred, and the actions taken have been, as Derrick Bell theorized in his idea of interest convergence [Delgado & Stefancic, 2001], beneficial to Blacks only if the action benefited whites as well.)

With the system of schooling used as a tool to perpetuate human inequity, I argue that the ideas put forth in Bell's theory of racial realism can be used as a lens to examine the current climate of the schooling environment. Black males, the group systemically dehumanized by this system, will require teachers and spaces that teach and encourage these students utilizing a type of advocacy pedagogy. For this to take place, teachers have to incorporate a pedagogy of scholar-servanthood.

Racial Realism

Racial realism, an idea coined by Derrick Bell, states that Black people should acknowledge the permanence of their subordinate status. That acknowledgment enables us to avoid despair, and frees us to imagine and implement racial strategies that can bring fulfillment and even triumph (Bell, 1992). Bell in putting forth racial realism prefaces this philosophy with the following claim:

> Black people will never gain full equality in this country. Even those herculean efforts we hail as successful will produce no more than temporary "peaks of progress," short-lived victories that slide into irrelevance as racial patterns adapt in ways that maintain white dominance. This is a hard-to-accept fact that all history verifies. (Bell, 1992, p. 373)

When examining the historical and current landscape of k–12 education in the United States in order to prove or reject Bell's claim, the evidence supports the former. Even changes that were considered tremendous movements toward educational equality, such as the landmark decision *Brown v. Board of Education*, have been undermined by state-level segregation laws and unconstitutional funding formulas, both of which deprive predominantly Black and Brown schools of an education equitable to their white counterparts. The social and cultural terrorist practices of many whites in political and economic power (especially in southern and Midwestern states) were actions that further oppressed and depressed the educational aspirations of Black people as well as other people of color. With an onslaught of educational human inequity, including teacher preparation programs that ignore or issues of race, class, and gender; reforms such as NCLB (No Child Left Behind); zero-tolerance discipline policies; charter schooling reforms (used to hypersegregate on the basis of race and access); and Black administrators and teachers who have bought into the American "white supremacist" ideology (referred to by Dr. Nathan Hare [1965] as "Black Anglo-Saxons or "Oreos"), the system of public education especially in urban conclaves is under attack. Now, with the recent appointment of Betsy DeVos as the Secretary of Education (a billionaire who was born into wealth, never held a position in a school building or school system, and advocates for vouchers and charter schools with little oversight [Zernike, 2017]), the future outlook of public education has the potential to become more ominous for students of color, especially Black male students.

Scholar-Servanthood Pedagogy

Scholar-servanthood pedagogy is one idea that may move our students from passive receptors of misinformation to active, educated agents in the betterment of their lives, which includes health care. Scholar-servanthood pedagogy is a fluid, ongoing, onto-epistemological process of lifelong critical self-reflection, the recognition of structural and social variables that promote and maintain asymmetrical power relations, the acknowledgment and acceptance of complexity and discomfort, and an expertise that is subjective, situational, and provided primarily by those organically connected to that which agency requires (Johnson, 2016).

Scholar-servanthood pedagogy originated from and is closely connected to scholar-servanthood theory. Scholars Shawanee Howard-Baptiste and Moise Baptiste, disenchanted with traditional theories of leadership that were often employed with study-abroad programs and mission work, were desirous to shift the focal point of leadership from those in power to those traditionally situated in the margins (Howard-Baptiste and Baptiste, 2013). While discussing other applications of this theory, a question was posed of its possibilities in traditional educational settings (Johnson, 2014). Shortly after, the term *scholar-servanthood pedagogy* was coined.

The conceptual scaffolding of scholar-servanthood pedagogy is based on the idea of critical self-reflection. According to Dantley,

> Critical self-reflection takes place as leaders engaged what has been termed their sacred selves or their genuine personhood. This entails leaders' grappling with issues such as their personal predispositions and belief systems on matters of race, class, and gender and their individual sources of motivation and purpose, as well as their coming to grips with the social construction of their individual identities. Critical self-reflection does not occur until leaders have forthrightly embraced the totality of themselves. (2005, pp. 503–4)

Not a linear or fixed onto-epistemology, scholar-servanthood pedagogy is guided by five tenets: (1) Sschool personnel acknowledge their privileges (especially teachers, administrators, and school counselors); (2) expertise is shared between school personnel and students (personnel might be trained and may have credentials but students, especially students of color, understand their contexts and lived experience best); (3) school personnel must relinquish control (the pedagogy and curriculum must be relevant; this may mean that some curriculum will develop out of oppressive issues faced by students); (4) school personnel must realize and accept being uncomfortable for change to occur (issues that cause human inequity and oppression will often be interrogated and examined to discomforting levels in order to produce agency and provide real change); and (5) accepting that this is a never ending process. Because the process of oppressing humans is continual and can be dynamic and multiple, so must be agency.

A teacher who becomes proficient in delivering a scholar-servanthood pedagogy will understand the importance of encouraging students to speak their "truth" as well as assist them in understanding the power of advocacy. Teachers employing this pedagogy do as much learning as teaching. One is more of a facilitator than a traditional teacher. A space such as this becomes a welcoming place. It is transformed from a space that oppresses and dehumanizes Black males to a space where agency is learned and practiced. A classroom such as this and a school such as this become places where Black males will attend and graduate.

An Example of How Scholar-Servanthood Pedagogy Can Improve Health Care for Black Males

A saddened student, Darryl, walked into his science class. His teacher, Mr. Franklin, noticed the sullen look on the student's face and inquired as to why. Darryl, through his tears, began to explain that his favorite uncle was diagnosed with prostate cancer and the prognosis looks dim. Another student, overhearing the conversation, added that his grandfather died of prostate cancer. Two other students began to share their stories. Within minutes, the entire class was sharing stories of male relatives who had either died of prostate or colon cancer or had been diagnosed. Mr. Franklin, understanding that a teachable moment had arrived, posed the following question: "Is there anything we can do about this?" One student said, "We are not doctors. We can't examine them." Another student said excitedly, "We can tell them to go to the doctor." Excitedly, other students began making suggestions and adding ideas. Mr. Franklin quickly assigned two students to begin writing down these ideas. By the end of the period, there was a list of ideas.

The following day, Mr. Franklin presented the class with a project generated from various ideas. Students were placed into groups and given the task to research the causes of colon and prostate cancer as well as preventive measures. One of the student groups went to their neighborhood clinic to retrieve more information. While at the clinic, they articulated their purpose to the receptionist, who decided to inform the nurse and doctor on duty. The doctor and nurse decided to not only provide information but ask to speak with the teacher and principal about presenting their projects at the clinic.

A month later, Mr. Franklin's class presented their projects at the clinic. While students were discussing their projects, the doctor and nurse were speaking with various members of the community and passing out literature. As a result, more Black men in the community educated themselves on the topic as a well as made appointments to undergo prostate exams. What began as a saddened student expressing himself in a science classroom blossomed into community project focused on improving the health of Black Males.

This example illustrates the possibility of using scholar-servanthood pedagogy in multiple and overlapping ways that ultimately result in increasing graduation rates and improving the health care of Black males. First, the curriculum moved from teacher-led to student-led. Student-led topics interest students. Thus, students were not made to come to class, they chose to come to class. The teacher moved from expert to facilitator. The students were becoming the experts. The topic was relevant and personal not only to the students but to the community as well. The immediate outcome of the project was increased awareness. The potential long-term effect of the project is both teachers and schools shifting their curriculum and instruction to address, more directly, the issues faced by the students and community. The possible result is more (Black male) students remaining in school and graduating.

Health Care as a Function of Education

How does this translate into improved health care? Research indicates that more educated people are healthier people (Robert Wood Johnson Foundation, 2009). According to David Williams, the director in charge of the cited study:

> A poor education can lead to limited job options, lower incomes, and greater work related stress. Down the road, that can limit a family's chances of living in a healthy home and neighborhood, increasing exposure to harmful conditions and further emotional stresses that can lead to illness. (Williams, 2009 as quoted in Hitti, 2009)
>
> In contrast, better-educated people are more likely to have jobs that provide health insurance coverage, to be more knowledgeable about their health, and have more time to attend to their health. We cannot separate education from health (Williams, 2009).

As multiple studies have indicated, education is closely related to quality health care. Since the public school system is the primary mechanism used to educate Black males, it is imperative that this system undergo a transformation that identifies its Black male students as human beings worth educating instead of "others" who either assimilate into a schooling environment hostile to Black and Brown culture or are expelled entirely.

Conclusion

According to the literature, obesity, high blood pressure, strokes and other cardiovascular diseases, sexually transmitted diseases, colon and prostate cancer, and a litany of other ailments disproportionately affect Black males at a higher rate than white males. The reasons this occurs are multiple. Systemic racism, economic inequality, poor housing, a history of legal and illegal injustices against people of color, and the relational constructions stemming from such hegemonic deployments of these structures are just a portion of the rationale. The process of how American school systems educate Black males is another important variable.

Improved health care for Black men is a function of education. As the literature suggests, the more educated one is, the more likely it is that one will receive high-quality health care services. If Black males continue to graduate from high school at a lower rate than their white counterparts, Black males will continue to suffer the health effects that correlate with less education.

Schools play a very important role in this process. Historically, Black students have traveled a tumultuous road when it comes to being educated in the United States of America. From being totally excluded to receiving separate and unequal education both legally and socially, Black students continue to be marginalized, dehumanized, and "othered" by the execution of the dominant assimilationist ideology permeating the vast majority of schools and school districts in the United States of America.

Scholar-servanthood pedagogy is one method to counter the assimilationist movement of our school system. Guided by a critical reflective framework and the tenets of privilege-acknowledgment, shared expertise, becoming comfortable with discomfort in order to learn, and relinquishing control, teachers, counselors, and administrators can progress from agents of assimilation to agents of transformation. Such a paradigm shift will create the type of environment necessary to improve the graduation rates of Black males. Improved graduation rates result in improved health care.

■ References

Baptiste, M. & Howard-Baptiste, S. (2014). Echoes of a not so distant summer: Scholar-servants as humble leaders. In A. H. Normore & N. Erbe (eds.), *Collective efficacy: Interdisciplinary perspectives on international leadership*. Bingley, UK: Emerald Group Publishing.

Bell, D. (1992). Racial realism. *Connecticut Law Review 24*, 363–79.

Bullock, H. A. (1970). *A history of Negro education in the South: From 1619 to the present*. New York: Prager.

Dantley, M. (2005). The power of critical spirituality to act and reform. *Journal of School Leadership 15*(5), 500–518.

Delgado, R. & Stefancic, J. (2001). *Critical race theory: An Introduction*. New York: New York University Press.

Du Bois, W. E. B. ([1903] 1996). *The souls of Black folk*. New York: Random House.

Freire, P. (1970). *Pedagogy of the oppressed*. Trans. M. B. Ramos. New York: Continuum.

Freudenberg, N. & Ruglis, J. (2007). Reframing school dropout as a public health issue *Preventing Chronic Disease 4*(4). Http://www.cdc.gov/pcd/issues/2007/oct/07_0063.htm.

Hare, N. (1965). *The Black Anglo-Saxons*. New York: Macmillan.

Hitti, M. (2009). More education, better health: People with more education report better health, study shows. Http://www.webmd.com/20090506/more-education-better-health.

Johnson, B. (2016). Disrupting zombie production: Using scholar-servanthood pedagogy to help humanize our students. Center of Excellence in Teaching and Learning Workshop, Gordon State College.

Litwack, F. (1961). *North of Slavery: The Negro in the Free States, 1790-1860*. Chicago: The University of Chicago Press.

Omi, M., & Winant, H. (1994). *Racial formation in the United States from the 1960s to the 1990s*. 2nd ed. New York: Routledge.

Spring, J. (1994). *The American school, 1642–1993.* 3rd ed. New York: McGraw Hill.

Watkins, W. (2001). *The white architects of Black education: Ideology and power in America, 1865–1954.* New York: Teachers College Press.

Zernike, K. (2017). DeVos' knowledge of education basics is open to criticism. *New York Times*, January 19.

The Epigenetics of Being Black and Feeling Blue

Understanding African American Vulnerability to Disease

Darron Smith

Black Americans have endured four long centuries of unimaginable hardships ever since twenty Africans set foot in Jamestown, Virginia, in 1619. For almost 90 percent of US history, white elite men and their subordinates devised and successfully implemented federal and state-sponsored[1] policy initiatives to undermine democracy. This was accomplished by denying black Americans full social, economic, and political equality. Over a period of 250 years, enslaved black labor was exploited under backbreaking conditions in the warm southern sun on stolen Native American lands. Enslaved African labor plowed the fields and harvested cash crops (among other task) to be exported around the world during the Industrial Revolution, which gave rise to massive wealth and wealth-generating opportunities for mostly white people. Though the ratification of the Thirteenth Amendment officially abolished slavery in 1865, it did not end the persistence of black peonage. Half-hearted measures aimed at transforming the South during the Reconstruction era were modest, as Presidents Abraham Lincoln and Andrew Johnson were more concerned about quick repatriation of an unrepentant southern polity than the plight of four million mostly illiterate, newly emancipated freed people. For the nation's capital, this meant yielding to racist bigotry and turning a blind eye to state-sanctioned racial violence against blacks who attempted to challenge white resolve at the ballot box and in the workplace.

Even those that did not challenge the status quo were subjected to violence and brutality; the Ku Klux Klan, a white domestic terror organization, would ride through the night committing barbaric acts of cruelty, instilling fear and trepidation. The message was clear that black life in America was tenuous at best. Chief Justice Roger Taney did not mince words regarding his feelings toward black people in the infamous *Dred Scott* case of 1857, as he prophetically intoned that black people possessed "no rights which the white man was bound to respect" (Finkleman, 1997, p. 1).

Just as the procrustean justice predicted, the black freedom struggle for social justice and equality, as guaranteed in the Constitution, has been sadly and deliberately weakened. And although the last civil rights law was passed in 1968 to bring about much-needed reform in the housing market, white resistance to black advancement is stubbornly defiant and resolute. The unrelenting white efforts to control blacks' access to good neighborhoods and decent schools for their children, gainful employment and good wages, health care and housing, has nearly eliminated the chance of black upward mobility in a white supremacist society, particularly after generations of bondage (Washington, 2006). In the United States today, as in other Western cultures, black people live with persistent discrimination in the form of racial microaggressions reinforced within white culture and its institutions (Perez & Solorzano, 2015). The existential inequality of people of African lineage has much to do with the white American ego complex—an inflated sense of unjust and unearned group position. Central to this complex is the deployment of defensive measures that whites use to deny and convince themselves that they are neutral to matters of race—the new racism of color-blind ideology (Bonilla-Silva, 2017).

Humankind has survived millions of years (in part) through negativity bias, knowing when to fight, flee, or freeze in the face imminent danger (Cacioppo, Cacioppo, & Gollan, 2014). Modern humans have evolved with the same negativity bias our ancestors relied upon as they wandered the Serengeti plains, but what has been passed down in the last four hundred years are racist attitudes and beliefs, casting black men in particular as violent, lazy, unintelligent, dangerously brutish, and animal-like in character and habit merely on the basis of skin tone. In this regard, a racial superhumanization bias formed toward black men and boys, inducing white fear as a way to control competition and stifle advancement as people (Smith, 2013; Kempley, 2003).

This negative framing of black males is evident in many recent and deadly high-profile shootings witnessed in media where mostly white law enforcement officials routinely anthropomorphize their black male suspects long before unloading a hail of bullets at them (Swaine & McCarthy, 2017). Take Darren Wilson, for example, the former white cop who shot and killed eighteen-year-old Michael Brown in the middle of a hot Ferguson street in the late summer of 2014. He stated in his testimony that Brown looked like a "demon" during their supposed altercation (Mendes et al., 2002). Wilson then went on to describe how he believed Brown was "bulking up to run through the shots," a superhuman feat in itself (Sanborn, 2014, p. 1). This type of vivid narrative around black bodies is not new. The racist depictions of black males would have you believe that white folk should flee in terror before them, but the opposite is true. Given the long-standing unequal and unjust relationship between black Americans and their white oppressors, including the very men and women who swore an oath to serve and protect them, blacks have good reason to be wary (Akinola & Mendes, 2012).

The degree of angst that black Americans carry around inside their body over whether or not they might be the next victim of a random act of white racial violence is real (Zimmerman et al., 2000). Recent FBI crime statistics clearly highlight that the disproportionate number of hate crimes reported were directed at African Americans, with white Americans being the usual offenders (US Department of Justice, Federal Bureau of Investigation, 2015). For black Americans, the accrual of centuries-old racial oppression and the current state of racial tension in the United States has been described as "racial battle fatigue," a state of keeping the bodies of stigmatized minorities hypervigilant in anticipation of the next white racial insult (Smith, Allen, & Danley, 2007; DeSantis et al., 2015). Racial battle fatigue affects human biology and physiology at the cellular level, leaving the bodies of the poor, the impoverished, and the targeted more vulnerable to mental and physical health decline (Smith, Hung, & Franklin, 2011).

Threats to self, in which some aspect of our identity is singled out and adversely evaluated, are one of the most injurious pathways to psychological distress (Dickerson, Gruenewald, & Kemeny, 2004). The day-to-day tussle with white anti-black sentiment has the potential to seep into the neurobiology of the brain, where subcortical neural circuits that are wired together fire in ways that keep the limbic system—an area where emotion is deciphered and processed for action—of African Americans dysregulated, overly twitchy, and hypervigilant. Consequently, the damage to the body is not always visually apparent, as it happens silently beneath the skin invisible to the naked eye (Allison, 1998). Since the explosion of brain research in the 1990s, the scientific literature has captured the significance how sensitive our brains are to the social environment. This discovery has provided new clues into understanding the etiology of white racial bias and the lack of empathy for black Americans (Waytz, Hoffman, & Trawalter, 2015; Goff et al., 2014; Gutsell & Inzlicht, 2010).

Racism, discrimination and other types of preventable social deprivations are enormously toxic psychosocial stressors that subsist beyond the veil in the future offspring of the victimized (Iacoboni, 2009; Aronson et al., 2013). Put differently, living with the pain of hate in America does not end with death but is carried forward to generations of black Americans through a process known in biomedical research as epigenetics (Non & Gravlee, 2015). Environmental epigenetics is the study of how the social world affects gene regulation in DNA molecules, which can alter its expression and function and, in turn, be heritable. Our genes listen for cues from the environment, such as the food we eat, the kind of communities where we live and work, the circumstances of our birth, and the race- and class-based divisions we share with one another. Social inequities in life may cause biochemical modifications, or "tags," that mark specific genes within the intricate DNA complex. Imagine a tag as a volume control knob that signals the gene to turn up or down its respective programmed function—influencing our biology in deleterious ways.

Environmentally induced cellular modifications increase the vulnerability to disease for populations exposed to trauma. For example, the seminal longitudinal Dutch Famine Birth Cohort study that began shortly after World War II captures the complexity of environmental factors on our genes (Stein & Lumey, 2000). Researchers examined the long-term physical and emotional effects in children who were exposed to maternal malnutrition in the fetal environment. The mothers' cells reacted to stressors in the social structure at crucial developmental times in the womb. Through this study, scientist found that nutrition deficits lead to epigenetic changes in the fetus and its developing biological systems, which predisposes cells to certain diseases of slow accumulation that include obesity, kidney disease, lung problems, cardiac disease, breast cancer, and a host of additional physical and mental health disorders (Baccarelli, Rienstra, & Benjamin, 2010).

Human wars, famines, droughts, plagues, physical, mental, and emotional abuse, and other forms of traumatic events not only leave their mark on society in unproductive ways, but also wreak havoc within the cells of our bodies that have an influence on health later in adult life. As such, the body becomes more sensitive and more susceptible to lifestyle-related disease in which the disenfranchised members are more likely to engage in high-risk behaviors to cope or ease the burden of worry and concern.

In social epidemiology and other closely related social science disciplines, it has been well established that class position is inversely linked to health (Espelt et al., 2008). Further, it is well known that race and class are closely aligned; therefore, race-based disease frequencies mirror class-based frequencies. Intersectional dimensions of social inequalities like race, class, and gender, for instance, intensify insults to the bodies of African Americans to a much greater degree.

Empirical research over the last four decades has mounted strong statistical evidence that racial discrimination on the basis of physical attributes (i.e., hair, bone, lips, skin color, eye shape, etc.) takes a heavy toll on black people, not only in the social, political, and economic spheres, but also in the body. Mistreatment is a type of distress that keeps levels of the hormone cortisol elevated longer in African Americans, which is slower to return to baseline (Djuric et al., 2008). Biological activities that regulate these functions can be epigenetically altered to increase the physiological stress response at a rate longer than what is considered normal (Zota, Shenassa, & Morello-Frosch, 2013). This, in turn, can impact the normal function of a cluster of differing cells that regulate blood pressure, kidney function, and cardiac function. Thus, this long-term activation of the stress response can disrupt normal physiology, increasing the risk for disease. Just as nutritional deficits early in life can lead to epigenetic alterations, racial prejudice, discrimination, daily microaggressions and overwhelming bias can likewise produce considerable health-related sequelae (Bratter & Gorman, 2011).

African Americans are constantly relegated to the margins of society, where they are exposed to mundane discrimination in virtually all areas of life in the United States. Within this space, many African Americans withstand daily hassles and sustained assaults for being black in a patriarchal capitalistic white supremacist society. The science of epigenetics is unlocking significant clues as to how our genes operate under these conditions, thus providing us a richer understanding as to how racial discrimination can trigger weathering changes to the expression of genes that can linger. Health and disease are no longer purely infectious in nature; instead, exposure to conditions in the social milieu accounts for most chronic disease. This dynamic interaction between our genes and environment should serve as reminder that human beings thrive in the absence of war, famine, and other manufactured discord.

Conclusion

Black Americans and their descendants have found no justice in the United States. This is indicative in the number of black Americans locked up and shut out of society, and in the consistency of under- and unemployment and low educational expectation and college completion rates for black men.

The election and reelection of the nation's first black president, Barack Obama, in 2008 and 2012, respectively, brought a renewed since of hope and optimism to black people.

However, during the Obama administration's eight years in the White House, the fantasy was short lived as the United States witnessed a precipitous rise in hate (Rushin and Edwards, 2018). Unarmed Black men and boys were especially at risk to this uptick in a number of police shootings across the country, where most of the officers were acquitted of any wrongdoing. Persistently elevated stress from chronic exposure to black antipathy exemplified in this chapter have been shown to be physiologically and mentally corrosive to human health and emotional well-being. The result is dysregulation of gene expressions through epigenetic tags. Thus, in the absence of sweeping governmental reforms that place human rights over property rights, black people must take greater accountability in their own health care by becoming informed on effective ways to reduce psychological stress—to the extent possible given the maintenance of white supremacy as a system of domination. In the end, health literacy may be the only way to positively improve the quality of black life.

■ Note

1. Racism should be understood as an organized system of white domination predicated on the ranking of human beings on the basis of physical characteristics (i.e., bone, hair, skin, eye shape), which devalues, demeans, and disempowers the black body. This oppressive system of white supremacy was historically put in place to differentially allocate resources and opportunities for white Americans and their descendants at the expense of those deemed inferior.

■ References

Akinola, M., & Mendes, W. B. (2012). Stress-induced cortisol facilitates threat-related decision making among police officers. *Behavioral neuroscience 126*(1), 167.

Allison, K. (1998). Stress and oppressed social category membership. In J. K. Swim & C. Stangor (eds.), *Prejudice: The target's perspective.* New York: Academic Press.

Aronson, J., Burgess, D., Phelan, S. M., & Juarez, L. (2013). Unhealthy interactions: The role of stereotype threat in health disparities. *American Journal of Public Health 103*(1), 50–56.

Baccarelli, A., Rienstra, M., & Benjamin, E. J. (2010). Cardiovascular epigenetics. *Circulation: Cardiovascular Genetics 3*(6), 567–73.

Bratter, J., L., & Gorman, B. K. (2011). Is discrimination an equal opportunity risk? Racial experiences, socioeconomic status, and health status among black and white adults. *Journal of Health and Social Behavior 52*(3), 365–82. DOI: 10.1177/0022146511405336.

Bonilla-Silva, E. (2017). *Racism without racists: Color-blind racism and the persistence of racial inequality in America.* Rowman & Littlefield.

Cacioppo, J. T., Cacioppo, S., & Gollan, J. K. (2014). The negativity bias: Conceptualization, quantification, and individual differences. *Behavioral and Brain Sciences 37*(3), 309–10.

DeSantis, A. S., Adam, E. K., Hawkley, L. C., Kudielka, B. M., & Cacioppo, J. T. (2015). Racial and ethnic differences in diurnal cortisol rhythms: Are they consistent over time? *Psychosomatic medicine 77*(1), 6–15.

Dickerson, S. S., Gruenewald, T. L., & Kemeny, M. E. (2004). When the social self is threatened: Shame, physiology, and health. *Journal of Personality 72*(6), 1191–216.

Djuric, Z., Bird, C., Furumoto-Dawson, A., Rauscher, G., Ruffin, M., Stowe, R., Tucker, K., & Masi, C. (2008). Biomarkers of psychological stress in health disparities research. *Biomark Journal 1*(1) 7–19.

Espelt, A., Borrell, C., Rodríguez-Sanz, M., Muntaner, C., Pasarín, M. I., Benach, J., & Navarro, V. (2008). Inequalities in health by social class dimensions in European countries of different political traditions. *International Journal of Epidemiology 37*(5), 1095–105.

Goff, P. A., Jackson, M. C., Di Leone, B. A. L., Culotta, C. M., & DiTomasso, N. A. (2014). The essence of innocence: Consequences of dehumanizing Black children. *Journal of personality and social psychology 106*(4), 526.

Gutsell, J. N., & Inzlicht, M. (2010). Empathy constrained: Prejudice predicts reduced mental simulation of actions during observation of outgroups. *Journal of Experimental Social Psychology 46*(5), 841–45.

Iacoboni, M. (2009). *Mirroring people: The new science of how we connect with others.* New York: Macmillan.

Kempley, Rita (2003). Movies magic Negro saves the day, but at the cost of his own soul. *Black Commentator* 49, reprint from *DVRepublic*, July 3. Http://www.blackcommentator.com/49/49_magic.html.

Mendes, W. B., Blascovich, J., Lickel, B., & Hunter, S. (2002). Challenge and threat during social interactions with white and Black men. *Personality and Social Psychology Bulletin 28*(7), 939–52.

Non, A. L., & Gravlee, C. C. (2015). Biology and culture beyond the genome: Race, racism, and health. *American Anthropologist 117*(4), 737–38.

Pérez, H. L., & Solorzano, D. G. (2015). Racial microaggressions as a tool for critical race research. *Race Ethnicity and Education 18*(3), 297–320.

Rushin, S., & Edwards, G. S. (2018). The Effect of President Trump's Election on Hate Crimes. Service Subscription Research Network. http://dx.doi.org/10.2139/ssrn.3102652.

Sanborn, J. (2014, November 25). All the ways Darren Wilson described being afraid of Michael Brown. *Time*. Http://time.com/3605346/darren-wilson-michael-brown-demon/.

Smith, D. T. (2013). Images of Black males in popular media. *Huffington Post*, March 14. Http://www.huffingtonpost.com/darron-t-smith-phd/Black-men-media_b_2844990.html.

Smith, W. A., Allen, W. R., & Danley, L. L. (2007). "Assume the position . . . you fit the description" psychosocial experiences and racial battle fatigue among African American male college students. *American Behavioral Scientist 51*(4), 551–78.

Smith, W. A., Hung, M., & Franklin, J. D. (2011). Racial battle fatigue and the miseducation of Black men: Racial microaggressions, societal problems, and environmental stress. *Journal of Negro Education 80*(1), 63–82.

Stein, A. D., & Lumey, L. H. (2000). The relationship between maternal and offspring birth weights after maternal prenatal famine exposure: The Dutch famine birth cohort study. *Human Biology 72*(4), 641–54.

Swaine, J., & McCarthy, C. (2017, January 8). Young black men again faced highest rate of US police killings in 2016. *Portside.* Http://portside.org/2017-01-16/young-black-men-again-faced-highest-rate-us-police-killings-2016.

US Department of Justice, Federal Bureau of Investigation. (2015, November). Hate crime statistics, 2015. Https://ucr.fbi.gov/hate-crime/2015.

Washington, H. A. (2006). *Medical apartheid: The dark history of medical experimentation on Black Americans from colonial times to the present.* New York: Harlem Moon.

Waytz, A., Hoffman, K. M., & Trawalter, S. (2015). A superhumanization bias in whites' perceptions of Blacks. *Social Psychological and Personality Science 6*(3), 352–59.

Zimmerman, M. A., Ramirez-Valles, J., Zapert, K. M., & Maton, K. I. (2000). A longitudinal study of stress-buffering effects for urban African-American male adolescent problem behaviors and mental health. *Journal of Community Psychology 28*(1), 17–33.

Zota, A. R., Shenassa, E. D., & Morello-Frosch, R. (2013). Allostatic load amplifies the effect of blood lead levels on elevated blood pressure among middle-aged US adults: A cross-sectional study. *Environmental Health 12*(1), 1–11.

Djangos Chained

The Struggle for Freedom

James H. Campbell

Using critical race theory (CRT) as a conceptual foundation, this work examines the struggle and unique tensions encountered by African American males participating in Division I basketball in the United States. Particularly, it examines those tensions associated with the inequities these athletes experience as a result of eligibility requirements, their experience of otherness, and the lack of agency. The primary research question is: How do Division I African American male intercollegiate basketball players narrate their university experience and what do those narratives reveal about their understanding of the material conditions of their labor? This question aims at understanding how the players cope with the stresses of their experiences at their university both on and off the basketball court. The work also addresses black masculinity, "otherness," and persistence as it is related to higher education for the black male. These stresses manifest themselves in a variety of ways including but not limited to mental health concerns, physical manifestations of chronic illnesses, and social isolation. This work also provides a brief history of black male intersectionality with the National Collegiate Athletic Association.

The primary question for this work was, "How do Division I African American male intercollegiate basketball players narrate their university experience and what do those narratives reveal about their understanding of the material conditions of their labor?" In addressing this question I explored the social, emotional, personal, academic, and athletic tensions associated with participation of intercollegiate athletics at the Division I level by African American male basketball players?" This piece may also touch on other issues such as economic exploitation of student-athletes in revenue producing sports, feelings of otherness felt by these students, and experiences of racism on campus. This question aimed at understanding how these tensions are understood by the players themselves as revealed in the narratives they tell and will likely examine issues that arise far from the basketball court, but, primarily, in their narratives of their experiences in their academic life.

The research will provide a road map for the landscape of the intersection of higher education and Division I collegiate male basketball. When speaking of the two, there is usually a disconnect as if the two are not intertwined. Sport is separated from academia; however, the narrative is that of the student-athlete. In my findings the inverse seems to be more true. The athlete-student is the more accurate and prevalent measure of the nature of the existence of these young black men at predominantly White Institutions (PWIs). When we add the issues that race brings to bear into the quagmire that exists in high-level academia and big-time collegiate athletics, it gets even murkier. There is substantial research that supports the notion of the black male being underserved and underrepresented on the campuses of the PWI. A considerable portion of this research speaks to what insight the understanding of black masculinity can offer in understanding what it means and does not mean to be a black male.

Black Masculinity

In this section a brief summary of the notion of Black masculinity is provided. The purpose of examining Black masculinity is to provide a foundation for the disparity in understanding the tensions of "being a Black male" and the common misconceptions and beliefs about the capabilities of Black males. The Black male form was commodified in the United States for many years prior to the formation of the country. Sport, according to Hoberman (1997), "is the point where it is embraced as a foundation of Black identity" (p. 4). Matthew Henry states that

> Black masculinity—one defined mainly by an urban aesthetic, a nihilistic attitude, and an aggressive posturing—has made its way into the cultural mainstream in the last two decades. Though there are numerous contributing factors, this image of Black masculinity has developed largely as a result of the commodification of hip-hop culture, and the ubiquity of rap music and the "videomercials" that sell it. More specifically, it is the result of the popularity of the urban "gangsta." (2004, p. 1)

In contemporary times the Black male is viewed as a dominant physical specimen both athletically and socially. As discussed in earlier sections the Black male has not been given the benefit of being thought of as an intellectual being. Harry Edwards (1984) states:

> They must contend, of course, with the connotations and social reverberations of the traditional "dumb jock" caricature. But Black student athletes are burdened also with the insidious racist implications of the myth of "innate Black athletic superiority," and the more blatantly racist stereotype of the "dumb Negro" condemned by racial heritage to intellectual inferiority . . . [u]nder circumstances where there exists a pervasive belief in the mutual exclusivity of physical and intellectual capability. (p. 8)

The frameworks for Black masculinity are positioned with negative overtones. The overwhelming sentiment is that the Black man has a beastly personality and an exaggerated performative sense of machismo. This style is described by Rhoden (2006): "Black style is a state of mind; something felt something seen and immediately identified as one's own" (p. 143). Bell hooks (1992) writes that the masculinity of the Black man is represented as violent, misogynistic, sexist, phallocentric, and homophobic. According to Lewis (2008),

> Black masculinity has historically been framed in notions of Brute Negro, Stud, noble savage, Uncle Tom, and Bad Nigger. In the modern world, sports culture and music frame Black masculinity as Hustler, Militant/Bad Nigger, Super Jock or Womanizer, lazy, flashy, greedy, violent and dumb. (p. 7)

Another of the narratives of Black masculinity is the notion of the Black man as a well-endowed individual. Collins states that "White elites reduced Black men to their bodies, and identified their muscles and their penises as their most important sites" (2005, p. 57). Many Black men have embraced the concept of Black masculinity as being tied to their penises. By embracing this stereotype, some Black men have helped create the illusion that the stereotype is true. This embracement seems to straddle the realms of stereotype and fact. According to Staples (1982),

> Black males have traditionally had a strong sexual orientation because the sexual conquest of women was considered a masculine trait. Since other symbols of masculinity have been denied them in the society, sexual prowess became a partial substitute for achievement in other areas. (p. 81)

In keeping with the notions of CRT, Black masculinity in sport is a microcosm of the broader culture. Mary Jo Kane (1996) writes, "Sport consists of a set of ideological beliefs and practices that are closely tied to traditional power structures" (p. 95). These power structures often are attached to a notion of Black males as possessing an "animal-like nature, emphasizing their sexuality, aggressiveness, and physical power" (Ferber, 2007, p. 19). This ideology of what constitutes The athletic abilities of Black men are viewed as God given, while White men are viewed as having "fortitude, intelligence, moral character, strategic preparation, coachability and good organization" (Coakley, 2006, p. 288). The paradigm of Black man as athlete or entertainer further perpetuates the dynamics of White supremacy in that the Black man is viewed as a safe individual if he can be controlled by the White man. Thus, the "coach is similar to the White male father figure" (Ferber, 2007, p. 20).

Collins states that the image of Black men is viewed as naturally violent.

> This combination of violence and sexuality made Black men inherently unsuitable for work until they were trained by White men and placed under their discipline and control. To explain these relations, White elites created the controlling image of the buck. Unlike images of African natives who roam their wild homelands like beasts untamed by civilization (colonialism), the representations of the buck described a human animal that had achieved partial domestication through slavery (2005, p. 56).

However, when there is a Black man that does not conform to the narrative of being a child under the control of his White father figure, he is viewed as a troublemaker. The troublemaker is ostracized and made an example of by the media, especially when an athlete is involved in an altercation that stems from what is assumed to be the primitive nature of the Black man. Violators of the safe Black man role have very public interactions with the law. Some of these violators have been O. J. Simpson, Aaron Hernandez, Ray Lewis, Plaxico Burress, Ron Artest, Stephen Jackson, Michael Vick, Rae Carruth, Allen Iverson, Kobe Bryant, Tiger Woods, and Latrell Sprewell. Collins (2005) states that Latrell, who was suspended by the National Basketball Association for an altercation in which he attached and choked his head coach, P. J. Carlesimo, received an undue amount of scrutiny from the media that may be indicative of the ways in which Black masculinity is depicted as oversexed, aggressive, violent, confrontational, and reckless.

Black masculinity in the United States has been directly associated with criminal activity. Black men are arrested and convicted at a disproportionate rate compared to other racial groups. Weathersbee shows that one-third of Black men from the age of maturity to age forty will have an encounter with the legal system including probation, incarceration, or parole (Weathersbee, 2006). Feagin, Vera, and Batur (2001) state that "a majority of Whites still stereotype Black people as violence-prone, inclined to live on welfare, and disinclined to hard work, and a substantial majority still stereotype Black Americans as unintelligent" (p. 188).

Black masculinity is a subjective notion that has very little validity in the depiction of the lived existences of Black men. It might be considered a cloak spread over the Black man to subjugate him to conform to the notions that the dominant society perpetuates as its narrative of what constitutes Blackness.

CRT, in general, and interest convergence, in particular, provides a compelling framework for the experiences of Black male basketball players at institutions with Division I athletic programs. Through this lens, racial tolerance at the Division I level may be shown as a mechanism for maximizing the material rewards to society's elites while sustaining and maintaining the racial status quo. The practices and concessions of the university to attract and retain the student-athlete should make an individual wonder why institutions bend as much as they do to accommodate these young men. Surely, we must consider the possibility that interest convergence plays a role in actions that might appear, on the surface, to promote racial equity.

In education, American liberalism, with its emphasis on formal equality rather than substantive equality, has led to color-blind policies that refuse to recognize that people exist in social and cultural intersections. Liberal formalism has required the application of sameness to individuals. This favoring of formal equality rather than substantive equality has led liberalism to proceed with the assumption that sameness of schooling,, with the assumption that treating everyone as an individual unlinked from social positions, provides equal opportunity in life. This assumption, based on the principle of meritocracy, has been claimed through the repeated telling of success stories. As Zamudio et al. explain, "CRT challenges the liberal doctrine that equates individual political rights with equality" (2010, p. 19).

CRT can provide a lens to examine the lived existence of the Black male student-athletes that participate in Division I intercollegiate basketball at a PWI. A critical lens can provide these student-athletes a chance to share their stories as they see fit without the overbearing gaze of the institution upon them. I agree with Zamudio et al. when they state that "CRT has a tradition of interrogating or questioning ideologies, narratives, institutions and structures of society through a critical lens" (2010 p. 11). As such, CRT provides an excellent foundation for this narrative.

Predominantly White Institutions

We have been introduced to the PWI. Let us take a closer look at this social structure. The PWI is the label placed on institutions of higher education that have an enrollment consisting of majority White students. In terms of athletics these colleges and universities comprise the overwhelming majority of Division I institutions. According to the NCAA (2011), there are 335 institutions that participate in men's basketball at the Division I level. Of the 335, only 23 institutions are majority Black or historically black colleges and universities. There are 13 institutions that participate in Division I men's basketball from the Mid-Eastern Athletic Conference and another 10 institutions in the Southwestern Athletic Conference.

According to the NCAA (2013), Black males comprise 58.9% of Division I men's basketball teams. In the arena these men are the majority; however, at their respective institutions they are overwhelmingly underrepresented in enrollment numbers. The Black male is the person who earns the wealth in college athletics. According to Hawkins (2010), this reality will impact several components of the lived existence of these student-athletes, including but not limited to, their social lives, educational experiences, a sense of self, feeling of otherness, and varying levels of feelings of disenfranchisement or empowerment.

Scholarship at the PWI

The Black male at a PWI has the unenviable status of frequently having the moniker placed upon him of "dumb jock." According to Hawkins, this dumb jock label is more likely to be placed on the Black athlete than his White counterpart. Hawkins writes, "Despite his academic credentials, his race, gender, and athletic identity constrained him to historical stereotypes and images that sustain the system of White supremacy" (2010, p. 119).

The Black male athlete occupies a space at the PWI that is very distinctive. It is one of being a minority on campus yet a majority on revenue-generating teams within the athletics department. This positioning situates him in space that further creates a separation between himself and the nonathlete Black male.

> Black males and Black male athletes share race and gender in common and this commonality occasionally causes them to occupy the same space, however, their experiences vary significantly when athletic identity cloaks the racial identity of the Black male athletes. Therefore, a Black male

means one thing and a Black male athlete means something different in the context of PWIs. (Hawkins, 2010, p. 120)

Black males struggle to navigate the landscape of PWIs because they were not designed with Black males in mind. According to Chavous et al. (2004), Black males are seen as being over-represented in college athletics, and this causes them to be experience pressure to perform academically as well as athletically. These men have the burden of being the representatives for their race in these spaces.

According to *Minorities in Higher Education*, among all Black students matriculating in higher education, nearly 80 percent attend a PWI (Cook & Córdova, 2007). Even with this high level of enrollment at PWIs, Fleming (1985) states that the White institution has an environment that is not welcoming to athlete or nonathlete Blacks. There is this sense of not having a social framework that is conducive to the manners in which Blacks commune. Most PWIs have events geared toward Blacks and other people of color; however, these events are few and far between. The most notable are Black History Month activities and any cultural diversity events.

The statistic that receives the most attention in regard to Black male athletes is their graduation rate in comparison to their counterparts. According to the NCAA (2012b), the graduation rate for the freshman class of 2005 at Division I institutions for Black students was 38 percent, compared to 60 percent by their nonathlete cohort. This statistic leads one to believe that the Division I environment may be beneficial to Black student-athletes—until one views the converse of the statistic: the graduation rate for the freshman class of 2005 at Division I institutions for White students was 63 percent, compared to 80 percent by their student-athlete cohorts. So when viewed in this dynamic it can be seen that the environment of the PWI is more beneficial to the White student and student-athlete. This calls into question the Black student's ability to prosper within these social structures at a rate that yields similar results as their White counterparts. There is a significant differentiation in the levels of persistence between the two groups. Many would argue that the two groups are not even on the same playing field, so to speak.

Persistence

Persistence is a student's continuation behavior leading to a desired goal; in this instance the goal is graduation from a four-year institution of higher education. The significance of persistence to this study is these student-athletes have historically had lower graduation rates than their White counterparts. Factors that generally affect persistence are grouped into cognitive, noncognitive, and environmental. Cognitive factors relate to the intellectual factors that contribute to persistence. Noncognitive factors relate to the motivational factors that contribute to persistence. Environmental factors are grouped into the categories of internal and external (Astin, 1975; Tinto, 1993). These factors may work independently or in conjunction to influence the student-athlete to discontinue his education.

I supply an example of each of the factors that affect the retention of the Black male student-athlete that participates in Division I intercollegiate basketball. The first is an example of a cognitive factor, which is when student-athletes have the pressure of remaining in good standing academically with the university. This is not unlike the general student body population. The only difference is that the student-athlete must maintain a minimum grade point average and complete a certain portion of the core curriculum for a degree program to remain eligible to participate in athletics. These regulations could potentially add higher levels of pressure to these individuals to perform academically.

An example of a noncognitive factor is that graduation eludes many African American men's basketball players at a substantial rate compared to their White counterparts. Some recent data indicates that African Americans' graduation success rate (GSA) is 23 percent less than their White counterparts. African American males have a GSA of 61 percent, compared to the GSA of White males of 84 percent (NCAA, 2011, p. 11). A primary variable that affects this statistic is the ability to forgo collegiate participation for the pursuit of a career as a professional athlete.

As an environmental factor, pursuit of a career as a professional athlete contributes greatly to the lack in retention of male basketball players at Division I institutions. This is because these athletes are permitted to forgo their amateur status after the age of nineteen once they have been removed from high school for a year or completed one year at the collegiate level (NBAPA, 2009, p. 225).

There are many different factors that contribute to persistence for the student-athlete. I have put them into four categories; academics, athletics, social factors, and personal factors. Some academic factors include becoming eligible, choosing a major, scheduling classes, maintaining satisfactory progress, entertain the possibility of transferring schools, and working toward graduation.

Some athletic factors include abiding by NCAA regulations, staying eligible, practice schedule, playing schedule, travel schedule, injury, rehab, recovery, playing time, exposure, draft potential, professional development, agents, time management, and building relationships with teammates.

Some social factors include peer group, relations with the public, relations with faculty, relations with staff, relations with the student body, assimilation, race relations, an adjustment to weather, and adjustment to the climate of the university.

Some of the personal factors that affect persistence are family, friends, children, significant others, finances, housing, working, transportation, drugs, alcohol, mental health, and physical health.

With the multitude of contributing factors that affect persistence, there is a necessity for the institution to assist in the retention of students. Tinto (1993) states, "The key to successful student retention lies with the institution, in its faculty and staff, not one formula or recipe" (p. 4). Assessment, planning, implementation, evaluation, and reformation are key components to an institutional retention plan. These components need to be coupled with multiple levels of commitment, including administrative and institutional commitment (Tinto, 1993). According to Person and LeNoir:

> One initiative institutions can take . . . is to hire more staff of color to serve as role models. The lack
> of representation in the main office and coaching staffs mirrors the minimal numbers of African
> American faculty and staff at institutions; this often leaves the student with very few mentors and
> adds to their feelings of marginality. (1997, p. 84)

These remedies to this issue need to be investigated for the overall well-being of the African American student-athlete. It is imperative to improve persistence in this group of college students.

Student-athletes must have a sense of connection to the institution. Along with this connection, these students must also have a goal commitment. According to Astin (1975), a student's level of dedication to the goals is measured by the commitment to entering college and obtaining a degree. It can be stated that all student-athletes have the expectation of receiving an education when attending college. What cannot be measured is the level of goal commitment. This may serve to be the determining factor when looking at persistence.

The Black student-athlete, a minority socially and numerically, stands out on the PWI like a raisin in a bowl of milk, as the old saying goes. The visibility that engulfs his existence contributes to the sense of otherness that many Black student-athletes feel during their time at the PWI.

Otherness

The African American male is deemed to be an outsider in several ways at the institution where he participates in athletics. I identify five ways in which the African American male is Othered: as a member of a revenue-generating sport team, as a participant in the sport of basketball, as an African American male, as a community icon and celebrity with vast earning potential, and finally as a catered-to student matriculating in a degree program without a substantial amount of rigor.

Edward Said popularized the term "other" in his book *Orientalism* (1978); the roots of othering are entrenched in philosophy. The evolution of the concept of othering indicates that there are a vast variety of connotations and implications. A sampling of the areas that are impacted by othering are politics, economics, education, social interactions, and psychology. "Marginalized groups often gain a status of being an 'other'" (Collins, 1986, p. S18). In essence, you are "an other" if you are different from what Audre Lorde calls the mythical norm.

> "Others" are virtually anyone who differs from the societal schema of an average White male. The
> sociological term for this is "othering" or specifically attempting to establish a person as unacceptable based on a certain criterion that fails to be met. (Ritzer, 2007, p. 205)

As a member of a revenue-generating sports team, the student is viewed as an outsider to the rest of the athletic teams. The reason for this is that typically at the Division I level there are only two sports, football and men's basketball, that generate revenue, whereas the other fifteen to twenty-five do not (Fulks, 2002). For schools where other sports do generate revenue, the amounts pale in comparison to the totals of the primary two sports teams. So, what this means is that as a member of the revenue-generating sports team, you are afforded better facilities, a plusher locker room, apparel sponsored by marquee athletic corporations, television exposure, and merchandising opportunities (Fulks, 2002).

Finally, revenue-generating sports participants have the opportunity to be selected to compete professionally for huge sums of money. Although this is not exclusive to revenue-generating sports, these are the only sports that require an athlete to participate at the collegiate level to be considered eligible to be selected for professional participation (Hawkins, 2010). In men's basketball there are some exceptions to this standard. To be eligible to compete in the National Basketball Association, an individual must be over the age of nineteen, have completed a year at a collegiate institution, or have international competition experience (NCAA 2009, p. 63). These opportunities may cause members of other programs to become envious toward the members of revenue-generating sports programs.

As participants in the sport of men's basketball, these individuals are Othered on the campuses of Division I institutions. This is due to the fame that accompanies participation in this sport. There are campus rituals that give men's basketball players more exposure than other sports programs on campus. The most notable of these rituals is Midnight Madness, which opens the basketball season's practices (Hawkins, 2010). At many Division I institutions Midnight Madness is televised nationally. As opposed to football, basketball players do not have their faces covered for the majority of the time that they are participating in the sport. This gives them an edge in exposure, in that they are very visible at competitions and on television. Another important ritual that accompanies the sport of men's basketball is March Madness. This is the annual basketball tournament that begins at the end of the regular season and conference tournaments. This tournament determines which team will be crowned national champion for Division I men's basketball. Among many nuances of the tournament is the selection show. The selection show is where the governing committee decides which teams qualify to participate in the tournament. At many Division I institutions, the student bodies have pep rallies and viewing parties to witness if their school is selected to the tournament and where they will play.

African American male basketball players are also Othered due to race. African American males at a Division I institution are in the minority. According to US Census (2005), African Americans males constitute 5.5 percent of the college population in the United States. African American males participate in percentages upwards of 40 percent in intercollegiate athletics at Division I institutions and on average comprise less than 3 percent of the undergraduate population on Division I campuses (NCAA, n.d.). This reinforces the notion that African American males are represented at very low levels at Division I institutions.

The African American male is Othered in terms of being a community icon and celebrity. These athletes are separated from other students because of their participation in athletics. For many institutions the identity of the school is forged through athletics, especially the sports of football and basketball. Coupled with this, marketing of the sport usually includes the advertisement of the athletes in printed materials, including but not limited to posters, pocket schedules, television commercials, billboards, Internet postings, newspaper ads, magazine articles, game programs, and media guides. The level of exposure contributes to the amount of attention that these athletes garner from the public. As a component to foster good public relations, many members of the athletics department participate in community outreach opportunities. Habitat for Humanity is one of the major organizations that benefit from participation of athletes in activities such as building homes for underprivileged families. "There is a thin line between admiration and resentment by the university community" (Leach & Conners, 1984, p. 36). Premiere athletes also have the opportunity to have merchandise sold that replicates their presence on the team, usually in the form of a jersey with their number.

The assumption that athletes, especially African American male athletes, are enrolled at the university for their athletic prowess and not there for their intellectual acuity prompted Anton L. Allahar to state,

> An ideology, once having taken root in a concrete context, can develop a life of its own and spread to encompass different individuals and groups in different situations that are far removed from the original context in which the ideology developed. (1993, p. 341)

For the African American male athlete, this is grounding for how they will experience a predominantly White institution. Too frequently, the sentiment is that the African American athlete does not have the ability to compete in the classroom. African American male athletes are stereotyped by classmates and faculty as low academic performers (DeFrancesco, 1996). This leads to the assumption that in order to be at the university, the athlete must be receiving additional academic help. This help, many believe, exists outside of the permissible academic tutors and study tables that athletes have at their disposal. According to Hawkins (2010),

> In sports, the dumb jock belief has functioned to cast a veil over athletes in general, and Black athletes specifically. The dumb jock belief is a means of typecasting and racial profiling that, once internalized, reveals the power that works to set parameters and socially control Black athletes. (p. 79)

The aforementioned parameters lead to these athletes being placed in academic programs of lesser rigor to promote successful completion of a degreed program. This is done with little regard to the athletes' ability to generate any level of professional development for a working career as opposed to an athletic career. According to Hoberman (1997),

> The entrapment of the African Americans in the world of athleticism is the result of a long collaboration between Blacks seeking respect and expanded opportunity and Whites seeking entertainment, profit, and forms of racial reconciliation that do not challenge fundament assumptions about racial difference. (p. 4)

The immutable factor of being African American creates a landscape in which these young men must learn to navigate. This study provides a glimpse of how the academic tensions they experience intersect with their identities. The social ramifications of these stresses are played out not only on the court but in the hallways of higher education, in the dorm rooms, and within the public sphere of the larger university community. The African American male basketball player is familiar to all those who applaud his accolades on the television screen and on floors of arenas, but he is very unfamiliar when viewed making the trek across campus to an 8:00 A.M. course after an extremely early morning of weight training, film sessions, and team breakfast or after a late night of travel to return to the university from an away contest at some distant university. Perhaps we gain some understanding of the pressure of performing in front of strangers uttering and yelling obscenities while attempting to win a competition for the benefit of his home institution and within a twelve-hour window returning to the classroom to compete intellectually against the star pupil, who merely watched the game.

The African American male basketball player who participates in Division I basketball has been commodified in a multitude of fashions, including his body, race, athletic ability, and intellect. These individuals also have to accept that even though they are sacrificing themselves for the reputation and prestige of the university, they may not be accepted authentically as stakeholders in the institution. Being a member of a racial minority at a PWI increases the visibility that you will receive from the college community.

These students are fighting for their emancipation from the governance of institutions and organizations that view them as a product to be marketed, used, and thrown to the wayside after its value has been exhausted. The similarities to the plantation culture that our great country once knew as a standard way of life are startling. Without authentic mentorship that truly wants to see these young men succeed as men and not just athletes, and without advocacy within the institutions that hold these individuals as voluntary captives, there is not much hope in the form of social justice for these individuals. These chained Djangos will continue to struggle for freedom.

■ **References**

Allahar, A. L. (1993). When Black first became worthless. *International Journal of Comparative Sociology* 34(1–2), p. 341.

Astin, A. W. (1975). *Preventing students from dropping out.* San Francisco: Jossey-Bass.

Chavous, T., Green, L., Harris, A., Helarie, L., & Rivas, D. (2004). Racial stereotypes and gender in context: African Americans at predominantly black and predominantly white colleges." *Sex Roles* 51(1–2), 1–16.

Coakley, J. (2006). *Sports in society: Issues and controversies.* New York: McGraw-Hill.

Collins, P. H. (1986). *Learning from the Outsider Within: The Sociological Significance of Black Feminist Thought. Social Problems* 33(6) Special Theory Issue. (Oct.–Dec. 1986), S14–S32.

Collins, P. H. (2005). *Black sexual politics: African-Americans, gender and the new racism*. New York: Routledge.

Cook, B. J., & Córdova, D. I. (2007). *Minorities in Higher Education: Twenty-Second Annual Status Report. 2007 Supplement*. Washington, DC: American Council on Education.

DeFrancesco, C. (1996). Support services for African-American student athletes: A case study analysis. *College Student Journal, 30*, 2–18.

Edwards, H. (1984). The black dumb jock: An American sports tragedy. *College Board Review 131*, 8–13.

Ferber, A. (2007). The construction of Black masculinity: White supremacy now and then. *Journal of Sport and Social Issues 31*(1), 20.

Fleming, J. (1985). *Blacks in college: A comparative study of students' success in Black and in White institutions*. San Francisco: Jossey-Bass.

Fulks, D. (2002). *Revenues and expenses of Divisions I and II, intercollegiate athletics programs: Financial trends and relationships*. National Collegiate Athletic Association. Http://www.science.smith.edu/ exer_sci/ESS200/Ed/Fulk2003.pdf.

Hawkins, B. C. (2010). *The new plantation: Black athletes, college sports, and predominantly White NCAA institutions*. New York: Palgrave Macmillan.

Henry, M. (2004). He is a "Bad Mother*$%@!#": "Shaft" and contemporary Black masculinity. *African American Review 38*(1), 119–26. doi:10.2307/1512235

Hoberman, J. (1997). *Darwin's athletes: How sport has damaged Black America and preserved the myth of race*. New York: Houghton Mifflin.

hooks, b. (1992). *Black looks: Race and representation*. Boston: South End Press.

Kane, M. J. (1996). Media coverage of the post Title IX female athlete: A feminist analysis of sport, gender and power. *Duke Journal of Gender Law and Policy 3*(1), 95–127.

Leach, B., & Conners, B. (1984). Pygmalion on the gridiron: The Black student-athlete in a White university. In A. Shriberg & F. R. Brodzinski (eds.), *Rethinking services for college athletes* (pp. 31–48). San Francisco: Jossey-Bass.

Lewis, T. (2008). The modern athlete, hip-hop, and popular perceptions of Black masculinity. *Ameriquests 6*, 1.

NBAPA. (2009). Collective Bargaining Agreement. Http://www.nbpa.org/cba/2005/ article-x-player-eligibility-and-nba-draft.

NCAA: College athletes breaking records in graduation rates. (n.d.). Retrieved February 21, 2018, from https://collegefootball.ap.org/article/ncaa-college-athletes-breaking-records-graduation-rates

NCAA (2011, December 7) Who we are. Divisions. Http://www.ncaa.org/wps/wcm/connect/ public/NCAA/About+the+NCAA+OLD/Who+We+Are/Differences+Among+the+Divisions/ Division++III/About+Division+III.

NCAA (2012a, June 17). Finances. Revenue. Http://www.ncaa.org/wps/wcm/connect/public/NCAA/ Finances/Revenue.

NCAA (2012b, October 25). Academics. Resources. Http://www.ncaa.org/wps/wcm/connect/public/ ncaa/pdfs/2012/d1gradrateaggregatepdf.

NCAA Division I Manual (2009). NCAA Academic and Membership Affairs Staff.

NCAA Research Staff (October 2011). Trends in graduation-success rates and federal graduation rates at NCAA Division I institutions.

Person, D., & LeNoir, K. (1997). *Retention issues and models for African-American male athletes: New Directions for student services.* San Francisco: Jossey-Bass.

Rhoden, W. C. (2006). *40 million dollar slaves: The rise, fall, and redemption of the Black athlete.* New York: Random House.

Ritzer, G. (2007). *Contemporary sociological theory and its classical roots: The basics.* Boston: McGraw-Hill.

Said, Edward W. (1978). *Orientalism.* New York: Pantheon.

Tinto, V. (1993). *Leaving college.* Chicago: University of Chicago Press.

Weathersbee, T. (2006, May 16). Putting Blacks in prison is the latest legacy of slavery. *Florida Times Union.*

Zamudio, M. M. & Russell, C., Rios, F. A. & Bridgeman, J. L. (2010). Critical race theory matters: Education and ideology. *Critical Race Theory Matters: Education and Ideology.* New York: Routledge.

 VIGNETTE

Ronnie was nineteen the first time he mentioned to an instructor that his moods would often change steadily. He informed the professor that he could be really happy and in a great mood, and then out of nowhere he would be sad and feel alone. Ronnie thought he might have depression. The instructor told him, "Black people don't get depressed." Ronnie, shocked by the answer he received and the lack of support, decided not to tell anyone else about the struggles he had with his mental health until years later when he discovered that depression was prevalent within the Black community. Today, after receiving therapy, he has a better hold on his situation and educates others on mental illness in the Black community.

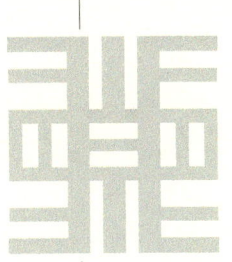

PART 4

Education

INTRODUCTION

Theodore S. Ransaw

I f someone from another planet came to Earth and wanted to know everything there was to know about Black males and education, that being could do no better than to start with Dr. Jawanza Kunjufu. His name is so synonymous with Black males and education, that if you wrote a dissertation, report or book about Black boys and schooling without mentioning his name, no one would take you seriously. It is for this reason the education part of the handbook starts with Kunjufu.

I first met Kunjufu at an education conference in Las Vegas, Nevada. He was a keynote speaker and later that day a copanelist with Dick Gregory. I went up to him afterward to shake his hand. He gave me a hug instead. Kunjufu is from Chicago, as I am. When I met him I mentioned that he and my father went to college together. I didn't know that growing up. I found out in my twenties about their connection when I showed my father a book called *To Be Popular or Smart: The Black Peer Group* by Kunjufu. It was then that my father told me stories about how Kunjufu had a printing press and that many people in the movement went to him to make pamphlets and fliers. A year or so later after I met Kunjufu, I did a phone interview with him for a magazine. Kunjufu gave me so many facts and statistics that I could barely write them down fast enough. Currently, Kunjufu has been writing and publishing about Black males and education for over forty years. A short time later, I emailed Kunjufu a paper I had written for a class in my doctoral program about the school-to-prison pipeline. He read it and gave me feedback within hours the same day I emailed it. He suggested I consider his publishing company, African American Images, if I ever wanted to expand my paper into a book. When I graduated with my PhD, I did. He published my first academic book. *The Art of Being Cool: The Pursuit of Black Masculinity.*

Kunjufu is like that—warm and gracious. He encourages, supports, and provides opportunities for Black males. Not just me, but literally thousands of Black males have been inspired by Kunjufu. Put simply, he believes in Black males. It is more than fitting to start with a chapter from Kunjufu for the education part of *The Handbook of Research on Black Males*. Kunjufu's chapter, "Understanding Black Male Learning Styles," makes the case that it is not enough to know that boys and girls are different, but you have to do something about it. Kunjufu also encourages readers to remember that Black boys are just that—Black and boys—more than capable of success with proper guidance and appropriate teacher pedagogy.

Next follows "The Black Male Founders of Emancipatory Education," a chapter that highlights the brilliance of eight Black male thought leaders who have guided and continue to illuminate the field of education: Frederick Douglass, W. E. B. DuBois, Booker T. Washington, Carter G. Woodson, Molefi Asante, Jawanza Kunjufu, William Cross, and Richard Majors. The first luminary in the chapter, Frederick Douglass, was born a slave and went on to become an international speaker. But his inspiring life began when he sold his meager rations of food for lessons to read from other White students. W. E. B. DuBois is known for his theory of double consciousness. However, DuBois was one of the first researchers to academically analyze Blacks in the United States. Booker T. Washington, a counterpart of DuBois, was a prominent speaker and also a prolific fund-raiser for Black educational institutions. Carter G. Woodson penned one of the most influential books in American education history, *The Mis-education of the Negro* in 1933, and it is still in reprint today. An innovator in the field of cultural ethics, Molefi Asante is a well-known advocate of people of African descent to keep the ethnic teachings of Africa at the center of their hearts and minds. William Cross helped to articulate the cognitive and emotional process that African Americans went through in their quest to define themselves as Black instead of Negro. The chapter ends with a summary of Richard Majors's contribution to Black male cultural intellectualism, *Cool Pose*. *Cool Pose* helps educators to translate Black male behavior and frustration in terms that reinforce that Black boys are human and deal with oppression by means of stoic resolve.

The next chapter is by emerging scholar Anindya Kundu, who is on his way to immensity. His chapter, Agency and Grit: Fostering the Growth of Black Male Students to Achieve Greatness, is full of enthusiasm, focus, and language precision. Kundu accurately articulates that the aims of educators to recognize and encourage all students to be successful often miss males of color because of, well, colorism. The perspective that achievement in America is based on how hard one works and the desire to get ahead leaves those who are not successful in school portrayed as unmotivated and undeserving. This perspective ignores that fact that skin color, and the assumptions that surround it, is more of a predictor of success in America than determination. Black males, because of their generational history of achieving through adversity, including gender and skin color discrimination, already have agency and grit. Kundu's chapter answers the question, "What would happen if educators built on the inherited strengths of Black males and supported them?" The answer: Black males would achieve greatness!

While Robert Berry and Kateri Thunder were not aware of Kundu's focus on agency and grit, they synonymously focus on a similar innate power of Black male resolve, persistence, in their chapter. Berry and Thunder's "Black Learners' Perseverance with Mathematics: A Qualitative Metasynthesis," jumps right into the heart of an issue affecting Black boys in school—misguided assumptions. For example, despite assumptions, Black learners who take advanced mathematics courses are more likely to have high scores, enroll in college, and complete bachelor degrees. Former math teachers, Berry and Thunder are a dynamic duo that fights against criminalization of low expectations for Black males. They examine equity issues that affect student math achievement, especially Black males, in ways that maximize instructional time. If you add perseverance to understanding Black male mathematic achievement without subtracting the effects of deficit thinking, then the numbers add up. Black males can achieve.

What I like most about this part of the Handbook is that it leaves the reader with the belief that Black makes can achieve anything, no matter the obstacles. The next chapter, "We Real Cool," by David Kirkland and Austin Jackson, focuses on Black male literacy achievement. The energy of this chapter is pleasantly infectious. In real life, the lead author walks and talks like a character out of a contemporary Black Hollywood movie. What is more surprising is that he actually did. Son of a single mother, Kirkland spent time on the streets until he walked into a classroom one day and demanded they give him a quality education. And they did, all the way to a PhD.

I first met Kirkland when he was reading a chapter from one of his books to a captive audience. Not a captive audience of students who had to come to class for a grade, but to an adoring mix of assorted academics from various disciplines. Appeasing and enthralling such a diverse group was no small feat on a college campus. In that reading session, David gave what I came to find out was his signature style, a Shakespearian prose laced with street language that juxtaposed accepted academic language with vivid everyday realness. Oftentimes punctuated with an "Unnngh, Da na na naa," David always gives a nod and a grin to let those of us in the audience know which language use he prefers. David's chapter is cowritten with Austin Jackson, a quiet and stoic counterpoint to David. Austin also remixes teaching practices and concepts related to literature into a remix that is known as hip-hop pedagogy. By looking at ways to implement cultural patterns and symbols in fresh new ways that make learning cool, Kirkland and Austin crafted a chapter that gives the students authentic voice.

Raven Jones Stanbrough is a former Detroit classroom teacher who loves all her students but also, and as equally important, teaches them to love themselves. Raven can recite Langston Hughes's prose as well as she can rap Chance the Rapper lyrics. Not afraid to rap with the kids in her classroom, but when she does, she can flow as well they can. She is the perfect match of structure and creativity to the audacity and bravado that the Black males bring to her school. Her chapter, "Culturally Sustained Debaters: Understanding the Legacy Learning Literacies of Young Black Men," details that structured oral communication can positively affect cognition but also build a sustainable learning community.

Stuart Rhoden provides another perspective on perseverance with "Perseverance Will Prevail: Three Young Black Males Whose Lives Matter." Rhoden's chapter is a qualitative analysis of three Black males who graduated from the same predominantly Black charter high school and who were interviewed during their sophomore year in college. The three Black males all attended predominantly White institutions. One was bullied in high school for being too nerdy; another was a first-generation college student from a large family with a single mother, a brother in jail, and constantly surrounded by negative peer influences; and the other was raised by both his mother and his grandmother and was a high school jock as well as a decorated scholar. Together these three Black males represent a composite of many Black males who are on target to graduate from college. However, each of these young Black men exemplifies what is imaginable when institutional trust manifests itself in positive individual achievement.

"Examining Campus Climate for African American Males at Predominantly White Universities" by James Bridgeforth investigates whether African American male college students differ from Caucasian males and females regarding feelings of being targeted at a predominantly White university. While there are numerous research articles that detail the experience of K–12 Black male student experiences, Bridgeforth's contribution is novel because it not only looks at Black males' levels of comfort in college, but also looks at feelings toward relationships with professors and experiences in residence halls.

This part ends with a word from Louis Napoleon straight from a jail cell. Napoleon's writing style is both gritty and polished. It is a reflection of a man who took the hard knocks that life afforded him and used those experiences to transform himself and other formally incarcerated Black men into refined and smooth Black marble statues of fortitude through sheer force of will and endurance. While incarcerated for thirty years, Napoleon educated himself in prison libraries, attended AA meetings, went to counseling, and listened to other bright minds that just happened to be incarcerated. Napoleon eventually was so successful as a self-educated man he wound up teaching GED courses in two correctional facilities and developed an accredited correctional high school curriculum, all while incarcerated himself.

Today Napoleon provides resources and support for the formally incarcerated through literacy programs. His chapter "No Positive Role Models" elucidates an often-neglected aspect of the school-to-prison pipeline, juveniles who are sentenced as adults. From Napoleon's firsthand account, juveniles who spend time incarcerated with adults have little opportunities to be educated by positive male influences. A reader can expect a plea to treat young Black males not with forgiveness, but with compassion for their humanity and with guardianship of their innocence.

The education part of the Handbook contains issues related to Black males and K–12 education as well as in higher education. This part also has the benefit of comprising a broad spectrum of authors, from tenured professor to emerging scholars. The breadth of authors provides a wide spectrum from various fields of education. The authors in this part are also scholars, publishers, and activists. I am proud to know them and I am sure you will be pleased to read what they have shared.

Understanding Black Male Learning Styles

Jawanza Kunjufu

Understanding how boys and girls learn differently may be the most important issue. With such a disproportionate percentage of males placed in special education—almost a two-to-one ratio between White males and White females and almost a four-to-one ratio between African American males and African American females—it is obvious that we have not fully understood male learning styles and gender differences.

In my workshops for teachers I always ask if they know that boys and girls are different. Teachers will say yes, we know boys and girls are different.

If you know boys and girls are different, then . . .

1. How do you allow for those differences in the classroom? Do you teach to only one learning style or many?
2. Have you ever taken a course in male learning styles? Have you ever taken a course in *African American male* learning styles?
3. What are some of the differences between the ways boys and girls learn?
4. How do gender differences in behavior and cognitive ability affect learning?

Listed below are some general characteristics of boys that differentiate them from girls:

- More aggressive
- Higher energy
- Shorter attention span
- Slower maturation rate
- Less cooperative
- Physically larger
- Influenced more by peer group
- Greater interest in math than reading

- Not as neat as girls
- Louder
- Distinctive walk
- Larger, more sensitive ego

- Hearing inferior to that of girls
- Gross motor skills more developed than fine motor skills

- If boys are more aggressive than girls, how do we allow for that difference in the classroom?
- If boys have a shorter attention span, what should we do differently when constructing our lesson plans?
- Boys mature more slowly than girls. How do we respond to that difference in our classrooms?
- If boys are more competitive, how does that change our pedagogy?
- If boys are more influenced by their peer group, do we discipline them differently around their peers? How do we deal with the large, sensitive egos of boys?
- If, on average, boys are not as neat as girls, should we allow for any differences in their notebook organizational skills?
- If girls hear better than boys, how should we change our seating arrangements?
- How do we allow for the fact that boys are more advanced in gross motor skills and girls are more advanced in fine motor skills?

In his book *Boy Writers: Reclaiming Their Voices*, Ralph Fletcher devotes an entire chapter to the issue of handwriting, fine and gross motor skills, and the differences between boys and girls (Fletcher, 2006). Recalling his own boyhood, Fletcher says that when it came to handwriting, his teachers made no distinction between *what* he wrote and *how* he wrote it. Many years later, he conducted a survey of boys and asked them to answer the following question: "For me, the hardest part of writing is . . ." He thought the boys would talk about "the sheer drudgery of writing" (p. 73). Instead they gave the following enlightening answers:

- My hand hurts.
- My hand gets sore (fourth-grade boy).
- My fingers burn (third-grade boy).
- Hand aches. (p. 73)

A fifth-grade teacher told Fletcher, "The first, most obvious thing I notice is that boys have a harder time writing neatly and quickly. . . . Many boys comment that their hands hurt" (p. 73). It is not enough to theoretically know that boys and girls are different and not allow for those differences. If we are cognizant of gender differences, it is incumbent upon us to make the necessary adjustments (other than disproportionately placing males of all races and ethnic groups in special education). Whether gender differences are genetic or caused by environmental factors (family upbringing, socioeconomic status, etc.) is being hotly debated and researched across many disciplines, including education. What do you

Table 1. Brain Gender Differences

PART OF BRAIN OR HORMONE	FUNCTION AND DIFFERENCES	SIMILARITIES	IMPACT
Arcuate Fasciculus	Curving bundle of nerve fibers in the central nervous system	Likely develops earlier in girls as evidenced by their earlier speed capabilities	Females speak in sentences earlier than males
Broca's Area	Motor area for speech process; grammatical structure for word production	More highly active in females	Improved verbal communication skills in females
Cerebellum and corpus callosum	Contains neurons that connect to other parts of the brain and spinal cord; connects the two hemispheres of the brain	Larger in females	Females have superior language and fine motor skills; helps females coordinate the two sides of the brain better
cerebral cortex	Contains neurons that promote highly intellectual functions and memory; interprets impulses	Thicker in males on the right side of the brain; thicker in females on the left side	Males tend to be right-brain dominant; females tend to be left-brain dominant
Estrogens	Several female sex hormones that shape female brain	Much more present than in males	In females, lowers aggression, competition
Testosterone	Male steroid sex hormone	Much more present and functional in males	Increases aggression and competition

Source: Gurian, 2001.

think? Are gender learning differences due to nature or nurture? How much is genetic and how much is cultural?

Gender Learning Differences

An excellent article by Dr. Francis Wardle, "The Challenge of Boys in Our Early Childhood Programs," cites the following:

PHYSICAL ACTIVITY. In general, boys are more physical than girls. Far more boys engage in rough-and-tumble play than do girls. Boys also tend to enjoy physical activity on the playground, which is also cultural, as men in our culture engage in physical sports. Our boys' need for more physical activities is probably due to culture. It is neurological as well. The brains of boys develop slower than those of girls, even before birth. Further, on average, boys tend to be more aggressive than girls, a trend that appears in many cultures. Not only is this due to brain development, but also due to male sex hormones.

SPACE. Boys simply take up more space than girls in their daily activities, both indoors and out. From the teacher's perspective they seem to spread out, use the far reaches of the playground, want to push the limits on field trips. Maybe this is one reason boys love to play and work on the floor.

KINESTHETIC LEARNING. Learn through movement. Boys seem to thrive using kinesthetic learning, which fits well with the use of space needs for physical activity and their aggressive behavior. They love outdoor projects, gardens, building with units and hollow blocks, field trips, and games.

HANDS-ON LEARNING. Boys are more advanced than girls in mathematical reasoning, spatial ability, and mechanical ability, while girls score higher on memory, perceptual accuracy, verbal fluency, and language tasks. (Wardle, 2000)

Janice Hale further explains why there may be a greater number of Black boys in special education, more than even White males. She offers the following:

> African American children are generally more kinesthetic than White children and have a higher level of motor activity. There is also medical evidence that African American males have a higher testosterone level than White males. African American children, particularly boys, should not be required to sit for long periods of time without an opportunity to spend energy. (Hale, 2001, p. 118)

In my book *Countering the Conspiracy to Destroy Black Boys*, I use the graphs shown in Figures 1 and 2 to measure attention span (Kunjufu, 1995; McGuinnes, 1986).

A psychologist and I were walking through a school and she commented, "Which boy is just being a boy and which one has ADD or ADHD, because I can't tell the difference." What a profound observation! They were just being boys.

For many boys, the trouble starts as young as five, when they bring to kindergarten a set of physical and mental abilities very different from girls'. Boys tend to have better hand-eye coordination, but their fine motor skills are less developed, making it a struggle for some to control a pencil or a paintbrush. Boys are more impulsive than girls; even if they can sit still, many prefer not to—at least not for long (Tyre, 2006).

I never will forget the kindergarten boy who, after his first week, told me in frustration, "You can't do anything in this class." He felt totally restricted in a classroom designed for females. He was looking for briefcases and empty boxes and hard hats and hammers and balls and trucks, but his teacher had not provided any of those things. I wonder if this boy's frustration will lead to behavioral issues in the classroom that the teacher can't control. Will she refer him to special education? Will she retain him? Some school districts retain almost 20 percent of their kindergarten students, most of whom are male. While I am against social promotions, boys should not be retained because they mature academically at a slower rate than girls—yet kindergarten retention rates are increasing (Chicago Public Schools, 2007; Elkind, 1981, p. 68).

Students that are behind are not equally behind in all things. So if one of the areas here is reading, then interventions like one-on-one tutoring in reading or early literacy does not mean that they need a whole grade reclassification. They need reading instruction reclassification (King, 2010).

Figure 1. Hyperactivity: A Diagnosis in Search of a Patient

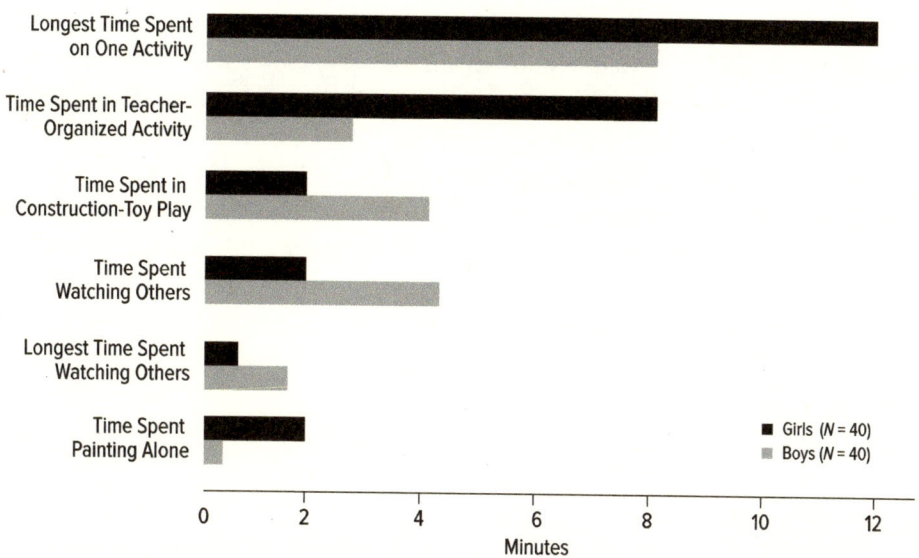

Longest Time Spent on One Activity

Time Spent in Teacher-Organized Activity

Time Spent in Construction-Toy Play

Time Spent Watching Others

Longest Time Spent Watching Others

Time Spent Painting Alone

■ Girls (*N* = 40)
■ Boys (*N* = 40)

0   2   4   6   8   10   12

Minutes

Figure 2. Hyperactivity: Unraveling the Evidence

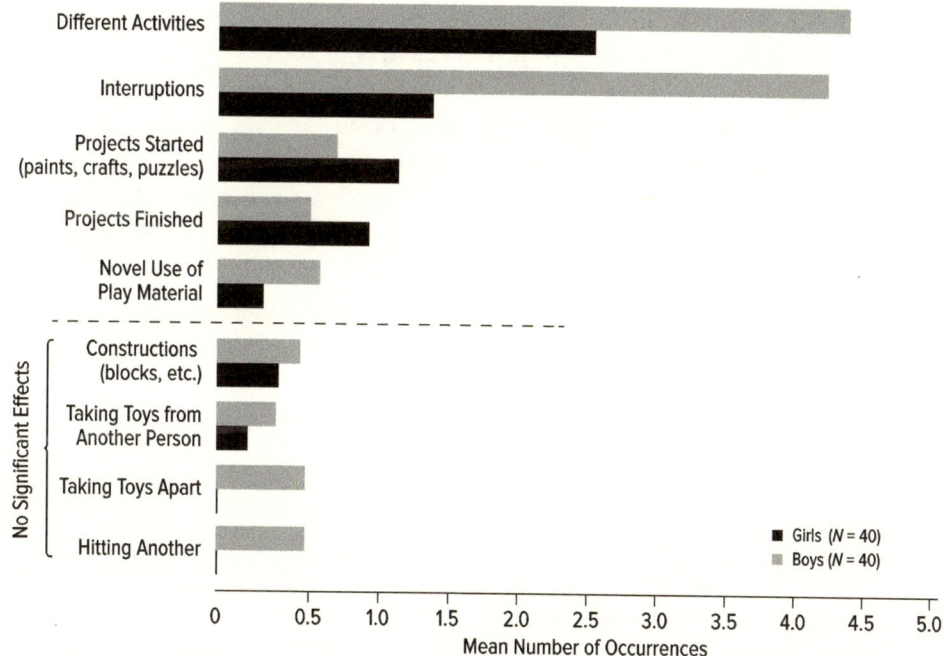

Different Activities

Interruptions

Projects Started (paints, crafts, puzzles)

Projects Finished

Novel Use of Play Material

No Significant Effects
- Constructions (blocks, etc.)
- Taking Toys from Another Person
- Taking Toys Apart
- Hitting Another

■ Girls (*N* = 40)
■ Boys (*N* = 40)

0   0.5   1.0   1.5   2.0   2.5   3.0   3.5   4.0   4.5   5.0

Mean Number of Occurrences

Attention Span

In an hour-long class, boys' attention span will average about twenty-two minutes. So what are the consequences of giving a thirty- to fifty-minute lesson to a student with a twenty-two-minute attention span? Should boys be placed in special education because the lecture is too long, or should the teacher shorten the lecture to create more alignment with the child's learning style? The attention span of boys is short because of low serotonin levels (Coleman, 1971). So why are we forcing them to increase their attention span? Why not shorten the lecture or make the lesson more interesting and relevant? Reduce the use of ditto sheets and textbooks. When boys study subjects that interest them—sports, adventure, technology, automobiles, and so on—their attention span increases.

Maturation

What can we learn from the fact that boys mature more slowly than girls? From kindergarten through twelfth grade, there is almost a three-year difference. Some schools are experimenting with putting eight-year-old boys in classes with six-year-old girls. In Germany, Switzerland, Belgium, and Hungary, the entrance of boys into elementary school is delayed until age six or seven. Unfortunately, in America parents use schools as a babysitting service, so I am not suggesting that we delay the entrance of boys into school because many parents would not know what to do with their sons. American schools can either allow for the maturation difference, place six-year-old boys in classrooms with five-year-old girls, or provide single-gender classrooms.

Maturation differences between boys and girls are expressed in many ways. Schools do not value how well boys can hold and manipulate big toys such as trucks and balls. They do value fine motor skills, such as the ability to manipulate pencils, pens, and crayons. Unfortunately, many schools expect five- and six-year-old boys to have the same level of penmanship as five- and six-year-old girls. Boys who are unable to write or color as well as girls are threatened with special education. Since we know that on average girls hear three times better than boys, teachers should change their seating charts and put boys in the front of the class. The hearing issue, in addition to testosterone, helps explain why boys are so loud and why they respond better to a strong voice.

In the excellent book *Equity in the Classroom*, edited by Patricia Murphy, the following insight is provided:

- Males tend to extract information from context while females tend to pay attention to context in a study of a problem.
- In considering male reasoning or other male problem solving, males tend to take analytical-rule-based approaches while females tend to take holistic approaches and emphasize empathy.
- Males tend to be more hasty, impulsive, and willing to take risks while females exercise more care and deliberation.

- Males tend to attribute success to their own efforts and failure to external factors while females do the reverse. The perception of personal failure may inhibit subsequent performance.
- Interactions among males, including their discourse, are marked by competition while females appear to prefer to work in cooperation. Their discourse is relational, the reference made to the previous speaker.
- Girls work in a concentrated way. Subject matter is worked through in half the time used by boys. Girls are well prepared.
- Girls keep strictly to the subject.
- Girls see the lesson as a shared venture.
- Girls listen and show respect when others speak.
- Girls are helpful to each other.
- Boys are active in an anarchistic way.
- Boys have a low degree of preparation.
- Boys broaden subjects and include new angles and points of view.
- Boys see the lesson as an individual matter.
- Boys constantly interrupt each other.
- Boys compete with each other in getting the teacher's attention.
- (Murphy, 1996, pp. 5, 178–79)

Before we continue, I am in no way suggesting that these differences are 100 percent universal. Not all boys are aggressive, have shorter attention spans, show slower maturation rates, exhibit more advanced gross motor skills, are less verbal, or can't hear as well as girls. But on average these are some of the gender differences. More importantly, it is obvious from the disproportionate percentage of boys in special education how teachers respond to these differences. Being different is not synonymous with being deficient. Boys and girls simply are different. Boys and girls each have unique strengths and unique challenges to deal with.

Other Differences

To serve boys in the classroom, teachers must be aware of and understand gender learning differences. Teachers must allow for those differences and make adjustments without resorting to putting boys in special education.

Boys have larger and more sensitive egos than girls. Boys with ADD or ADHD tend to be more oppositional and aggressive than girls and thus are more of a discipline problem with instructors, custodians, and referral agents. While 67 percent of boys with ADHD are diagnosed with defiant disorder (ODD), only 33 percent of girls are so labeled (Biederman, 2008). Boys possess a greater propensity for rebelling against authority and engaging in conflict than girls, who are more likely to comply with authority and a hierarchical structure. The oppositional style of boys is seen as early as kindergarten; in contrast, females tend to avoid conflict and seek to preserve harmony. In the book *Bad Boys*, Ann Ferguson makes the following observations:

African American boys are not accorded the masculine dispensation of being naturally "naughty." Instead, the school reads their expression and display of masculine naughtiness as a sign of an inherent injudicious, insubordinate nature that is a threat to order that must be controlled. Consequently, school adults view any display of masculine mettle on the part of these boys, through body language or verbal rejoinders, as a sign of insubordination.

In confrontation with adults, what is required from them is a performance of absolute passivity that goes against the grain of masculinity. Black boys are expected to internalize the ritual obeisance in such exchanges so that the performance of docility appears to come naturally. This is not a lesson that all children are required to learn, however. The disciplining of the body within school rules has specific race and gender overtones. For Black boys the enactment of docility is a preparation for adult racialized survival rituals of which the African American adults in the school are especially cognizant. For African American boys, bodily forms of expressiveness have repercussions in the world outside the chain linked fence of the school. The body must be taught to endure humiliation in preparation for future enactments of submission. (Ferguson, 2001, pp. 86–87)

When I was writing *Keeping Black Boys Out of Special Education*, I shared my ideas, concerns, and research with my colleagues. One of them very succinctly said, "The major problem in American schools is that we have not found positive ways to channel Black male energy."

That statement resonated with me because the percentage of Black boys in special education is simply too high and unacceptable. This is a major issue that needs to be resolved. The Montessori teaching method uses a rich kinesthetic and experiential environment that helps children learn to learn. The emphasis is placed on manipulating materials, which certainly taps into the strength of the tactile learner. Unfortunately, Montessori schools are private and expensive and out of the price range of many African American students. Fortunately, there has been an increase in the number of charter schools that use the Montessori method, and I encourage more founders to consider implementing the method in their schools. But because a large number of African American students will not attend a charter school, traditional schools should consider utilizing the Montessori method as well.

Physical Education

One of the important outcomes of Leave No Child Behind is that not only have art and music been virtually wiped out in schools, we have reduced, if not eliminated, physical education. These subjects are critical for right-brain learners, yet according to the Centers for Disease Control, only 3.8 percent of elementary schools, 7.9 percent of middle schools, and 2.1 percent of high schools offer PE on a daily basis (Physical Education, 2006).

For kinesthetic learners, and in fact all children, it is crucial that we provide PE on a daily basis. If you are concerned that offering PE will put reading and math scores in jeopardy, then you have not read the research. Eleven published studies analyzing data from approximately fifty-eight thousand students have found positive correlations between participation in physical activity and improved academic performance (Robert Wood Foundation, 2007).

A study conducted by the California Department of Education showed a significant relationship between academic achievement and the physical fitness of public school students. In another study where reading and math scores were matched with fitness scores of 353,000 fifth graders, 322,000 seventh graders, and 279,000 ninth graders, high achievement was associated with higher levels of fitness in each of the three grade levels. Studies done in Australia and Korea also found that PE improved academic achievement (Castelli, 2007; Grissom, 2005; Kim, 2003).

According to various international ranking systems (e.g., Organization for Economic Cooperation and Development), America's academic performance has dropped significantly among industrialized nations (World University Rankings, 2010). In one list, the United States didn't even place among the top twenty-five countries in reading, math, or science (World University Rankings, 2010). I believe the reduction of P. classes in public schools is a major culprit. Exercise must once again become a regular part of school programs.

There are now schools being built without playgrounds. Can you imagine a school without a playground? Can you imagine the impact that has on all students, especially kinesthetic learners? How can we build schools without playgrounds in light of the research showing that as you increase PE, you increase academic achievement? Research shows that if time is taken away from reading instruction to allow for PE, students still score higher in reading and math. As much as I am an advocate of time on task, here is evidence that says you cannot force students, especially kinesthetic learners, to stay focused only on reading and math for the six-hour school day to the exclusion of physical education.

Not only have PE programs been reduced, many schools have eliminated recess. The least we can do is provide periodic stretch breaks throughout the day. Research shows that when teachers provide recess or stretch breaks, students improve academically.

Investigators in Georgia studied the effects of an activity break on classroom behavior in a sample of forty-three fourth-grade students. Students exhibited significantly more on-task classroom behavior and significantly less fidgeting on days when an activity was scheduled than on nonactivity days (Physical Education, Physical Activity, 2007).

A research project in North Carolina evaluated the effects of providing 243 students in kindergarten through fourth grade with a daily ten-minute activity break. Researchers found that the daily break increased on-task behavior by an average 8 percent. Among the least on-task students, the activity breaks improved on-task behavior by 20 percent (Physical Education, Physical Activity, 2009).

In a New Jersey study with 177 elementary students, researchers compared concentration test scores after students completed either a classroom lesson or a fifteen-minute physical activity session. Fourth-grade students exhibited significantly better concentration scores after completing the physical activity (Physical Education, Physical Activity, 2009). I commend the large numbers of affluent White families who demand the return of morning and afternoon recess and greater PE or they will remove their children from the school. I am still waiting for African American parents to demand the same.

Single-Gender Classrooms

In 1985, at the NABSE (National Alliance of Black School Educators) conference in Portland, Oregon, I recommended implementing single-gender classrooms in schools in my keynote address. I received tremendous opposition. It has only been in the last decade that our society has seen the need to provide single-gender classrooms for boys. One major reason is because White feminists have found that if single-gender classrooms are provided for females, their chances of pursuing careers in math and science are increased. For years, feminists have been frustrated by the fact that White females outperform White males K–12, yet White males still earn more money.

For two decades I have been recommending that schools implement more right-brain classrooms. I now want to go on record with the following statement: Less than 8 percent of American schools provide PE on a daily basis. Clearly traditional schools are not equipped to meet the needs of kinesthetic learners. We need to provide schools exclusively for kinesthetic learners that offer PE on a daily basis.

The solution for kinesthetic learners is not Ritalin. The solution is providing movement, allowing activity, providing on a daily basis. Movement will help positively channel Black male energy.

Cooperative Learning

We have discussed the value of cooperative learning at length, so now I'd just like to stress that boys and girls are different when it comes to learning either independently or cooperatively. Girls tend to learn independently, and boys tend to thrive when they are in a cooperative learning environment. Nature or nurture? I would say both. Now that's not to say that girls can't thrive in a cooperative learning group and that boys can't do well by themselves. But the research is clear on gender learning preferences.

Classrooms are oriented to the independent female learner, not the cooperative/competitive male learner. We would improve the academic performance of boys if we tapped into their cultural strengths and created more cooperative and competitive learning activities for them.

Homework

There's been a lot of discussion about the importance of homework. Some teachers believe that the more you give reflects the quality of the school. Others believe that homework should not be busywork.

Research shows that 84 percent of males either turn their homework in late or not at all. In contrast, only 4 percent of females turn their homework in late or not at all (Coates & Draves, 2006).

Let me paint a clear picture. A male student receives an A on the midterm and a B on the final exam but receives a D on his report card. How can that be? An A on the midterm, a B on the final, and a D for the final grade. Not doing the homework was the culprit. On the other hand, doing the homework was not a precursor to doing well on the tests. Do you feel disrespected when your male students do not turn in their homework? If they do well on in-class assignments, quizzes, and tests and the only problem is not turning in homework, should their report cards be used against them?

If boys are given homework that is not intellectually stimulating, they will take hours to complete it. They will view it as busywork, especially if they're earning As and Bs on exams. This kind of homework insults their intelligence. In contrast, if you give them a more challenging homework assignment, they will be more focused on completing it within a reasonable time frame.

If we really want to maximize the academic achievement of African American male students, we must become more cognizant of homework and its gender implications for male students. I strongly recommend that teachers consider implementing the following homework policies:

- Do not use low report card grades as a way to penalize boys for not turning in homework assignments. Let report card grades reflect the work students have done in class and at most, major assignments and special projects that have to be completed after hours.
- Let daily homework assignments serve as a way for students to earn extra credit points.
- Give less homework.
- Give more intellectually challenging homework.
- Give homework exercises that are based on lessons that were covered in class. Never give students homework that they don't understand, that they didn't learn about first in class. One reason why African American scores decline after fourth grade is because teachers expect parents to serve as their assistant teachers at home. This is a middle-class concept that does not take into account the fact that for many African American students, the at-home playing field is not always level. For example, to expect an illiterate parent to tutor a child in algebra, geometry, or trigonometry, biology, chemistry, or physics is unreasonable and extremely unfair.
- A peer-learning approach would be to let students create homework assignments that interest them. Let your students know that this is how doctoral candidates in college earn their PhDs. They create their own program of research and study. Imagine your African American male students asking if they can write a music video or develop a business plan. Your job would be to help him develop the elements that would go into the assignment.

■ **References**

Biederman, Joseph, et al. (2008, December). The longitudinal course of comorbid oppositional defiant disorder in girls with ADHD: Findings from a controlled, five-year prospective longitudinal follow-up study. *Journal of Developmental Behavioral Pediatrics*, 501–7.

Castelli, D. M., et al. (2007). Physical fitness and academic achievement in third- and fifth-grade students. *Journal of Sport & Exercise Psychology 29*, 239–52.

Chicago Public Schools Flunk Black Students. (2007, August 13). *Chicago Reporter.*

Coates, J., & Draves, W. A. (2006). Smart boys, bad grades. *Learning Resources Network.* Http://www.smartboysbadgrades.com/smartboys_badgrades.pdf.

Coleman, M. (1971, June). Serotonin concentrations in whole blood of hyperactive children. *Journal of Pediatrics 78*(6), 985–90.

Elkind, D. (1981). *The hurried child.* DaCapo Press.

Ferguson, A. (2001). *Bad boys.* Ann Arbor: University of Michigan Press.

Fletcher, R. J. (2006). *Boy writers: Reclaiming their voices.* Portland: Stenhouse Publishers.

Grissom, J. B. (2005). The relationship between physical fitness and academic achievement. *Journal of Exercise Physiology 8*(1), 11–25. Http://asep/org/files/Grissom.pdf.

Gurian, M. (2001). *Boys and girls learn differently.* San Francisco: Jossey-Bass.

Hale, J. (2001). *Learning while black.* Baltimore: Johns Hopkins University Press.

Kunjufu, J. (1995). *Countering the conspiracy to destroy black boys.* Chicago: African American Images.

Kim, H-Y., et al. (2003). Academic performance of Korean children is associated with dietary behaviours and physical status. *Asia Pacific Journal of Clinical Nutrition 12*(2), 186–92.

King, R. (2010, October 10). IPS kids repeat kindergarten at a high rate, but does it help? IndyStar.com. Http://www.indystar.com/article/201010100245/LOCAL/10100393.

McGuinnes, D. (1986). *When children don't learn: Understanding the biology and psychology of learning disabilities.* New York: Basic Books.

Murphy, P. (1996). *Equity in the classroom.* New York: Routledge.

Physical Education. (2006). *School health policies and programs study.* Centers for Disease Control. Http://www.cdc.gov/HealthyYouth/ spps/2006/factsheets/pdf/FS_PhysicalEducationSHPPS 2006.pdf.

Physical Education, Physical Activity and Academic Performance. (2007, Fall). *Active Living Research.* Http:// www.activelivingresearch.org/files/Active.Ed.pdf.

Physical Education, Physical Activity and Academic Performance. (2009, Summer). *Active Living Research.* Http://www.rwjf.org/files/research/20090925a/ractive education.pdf.

Robert Wood Foundation. (2007, Fall). *Active Education.*

Tyre, P. (2006, January 30). The trouble with boys. *Newsweek.* Http://www.newsweek.com/2006/01/29/the- trouble-with-boys.html.

Wardle, F. (2000). The challenge of boys in our early childhood programs. *Early Childhood News*, Fall, 4–12. Http://www.earlychildhoodnews.com/earlychild hood/article_view.aspx?ArticleID=414.

World University Rankings 2010–2011. (2010, September). Organization for Economic Cooperation and Development. Http://www.community.oced.org.

The Black Male Founders of Emancipatory Education

Frederick Douglass, W. E. B. DuBois, Booker T. Washington, Carter G. Woodson, Molefi Asante, Jawanza Kunjufu, William Cross, and Richard Majors

Theodore S. Ransaw

The concept of America as a nation and the use of the word *freedom* are intrinsically intertwined, so much so that the phrase "justice, freedom and the American way" is conceptualized as the fabric of the United States. But what does it mean to be free in America? Do Blacks in America experience liberty the same way as others do? History tells us that the path of Black males in the United States is obstructed by a peculiar set of barriers while at the same time paved with clear signposts of alacrity that serve to navigate oppressive terrains for all Americans.

For example, for Black males in particular, who have historically been recipients of gender-based subpar and unaffirming education, the use of generative words such as *freedom, justice, liberty*, and *emancipation* has been of particular importance to the formation of identity. A generative word is one that has the capacity to confront the social, cultural, and political reality in which the people live (Ojokheta, 2007). Identity development is particularly interwoven with racial mindfulness and consciousness. Sometimes called *Negro*, sometimes called *colored*, sometimes called *Black*, and sometimes called *African American*, Blacks in America have undergone many name changes that are reflections of how they see themselves and how others see them. Consequently, what we know to be true is often culturally framed, and knowledge combines self-reflection as well as an examination of the social environment in which we live to make meaning. Thus, what we know to be true is generative, as malleable and fluid as the way Black males define themselves in different situations, just as Americans have redefined their use and understanding of the words *freedom* and *liberty*. For both Black and White Americans, much of what we know of the world is based on our adaptive perspectives gleaned from education.

Overview

Eight African American scholars and activists who have been influential in the field of education, Frederick Douglass, W. E. B. DuBois, Booker T. Washington, Molefi Asante, Carter G. Woodson, William Cross, Jawanza Kunjufu, and Richard Majors, will be used to examine the manner in which emancipation is interpreted by African Americans in terms of their self-reflectiveness, culturally conscious identity, and critical examination of society.

Douglass, DuBois, Washington, Woodson, Cross, Asante, Kunjufu, and Majors are by no means exhaustive of all Black male influential leaders in education. However, collectively, all eight of the aforementioned thought leaders experienced a liberating educational event that reinterpreted their identity, both in terms of how they saw themselves and how others perceived them; experienced a culturally conscious self-reflective process that informed their writing; and encouraged critical examination of social conditions to reinterpret society's way of knowing the world. Identity, the first theme, is crucial to understanding these Black male founders of education because "the first function of education is to provide identity" (Akbar, 1998, p. 2). Identity formation and learning can be formal as well as informal, and both methods require a process of self-reflection (Freire, 1995). Culturally conscious self-reflection, the second theme, was important to Douglass, DuBois, Washington, Woodson, Cross, Asante, Kunjufu, and Majors because identity and self-reflection are best achieved with dialogue (Freire, 1972). All of these eight founders discussed their ideas frequently and freely through speeches, debates, writings, and lectures. The last theme, critical examination (Freire, 1972; Bell, 1992), is the key to consciously informed social action that changes the world for the better. Combined, these thought leaders have advanced the field of education not just for Black males but for us all.

The next section offers sketches of Douglass, DuBois, Washington, Woodson, Asante, Kunjufu, Cross, and Majors. Each narrative portrait includes a brief bio, origin story (every superhero has an origin story), and a historical perspective that reveals both a liberating educational event and a culturally conscious self-reflective process that sparked a critical examination of social conditions that informed their activism. However, the theoretical framework that grounds the chapter will first be discussed.

Theoretical Framework

As a method for organizing a brief sample of Black male intellectuals and their contribution to the field of education, this chapter will utilize the framework of emancipatory education. Emancipatory education "frees people from personal, institutional, or environmental forces that prevent them from seeing new directions, from gaining control of their lives, their society, and their world (Apps, 1985, p. 151). Internal and self-reflective in nature at first, emancipatory education also inspires action through social change. In short, emancipatory education changes a person's way of being by liberating the person's from oppression.

The word *liberating* is fitting here, as Freire (1995) proposed using language and dialogue as a means of transforming the consciousness of the oppressed through reflection. Freire was a social activist who informed much of the thinking behind emancipatory education; he conceptualized the term "conscientization," which enables the oppressed a way to perceive themselves individually while simultaneously seeing their place in society (Freire, 2007).[1] Consciousness—derived from a critical awareness to inform actions—is a form of activism that allows the oppressed the freedom to enact change by combining both theory and praxis (Freire, 2007). Derrick Bell was a social activist that advocated for a critical examination of policies that legally oppress people both racially and economically; he understood that critical awareness is necessary to understand where true oppression lives.[2] For the purpose of this chapter, oppression is defined as both a state of being that restricts opportunities and a process with historical implications (Watts, Griffith, & Abdul-Adil, 1999).

Freire (2007) believed that only by combining critical self-reflection with active participation in the struggle to end oppression can an oppressed people find freedom. The following section begins with Frederick Douglass—one of the first Black male intellectuals to use self-reflection and education to become internationally recognized as an educator and social activist.

Frederick Douglass

Self-educated, Frederick Douglas was born a slave in 1818 under the name Frederick Augustus Washington Bailey in Talbot County, Maryland. He did not change his last name to Douglass until 1838. He did so to avoid being recaptured by patty rollers—runaway slave capturers. Douglass was raised by his grandmother after members of his family were sold to other plantations; he had no memories of his mother after the age of seven. He ate corn meal out of a trough and slept on the floor with no bed and no blanket (Douglass, 1845). He was sold to the Auld home, where Mrs. Auld used to read the Bible aloud to him. When Mrs. Auld noticed his enthusiasm for the written word, she started to teach young Douglass to read. His lessons were abruptly stopped in 1827 when he heard Mr. Auld tell his wife, "If you teach that nigger how to read, there would be no keeping him . . . [he will] become unmanageable, and of no value to his master" (Douglass, 1845, p. 33). From that moment on, Douglass knew that education would be his key to freedom.

Douglass taught himself to read when he could find the time and sometimes paid for his lessons from White students with pieces of bread. By the time he was seventeen, Douglass had taught fellow slaves to read in secret meetings on Sundays. When he moved to Baltimore in 1837, he and other free Negroes formed a debate team called the East Baltimore Mental Improvement Society (Lampe, 1998). By the time he died in 1895, Douglass had become a nationally and internationally renowned lecturer for the Anti-Slavery Society, served as a Zionist minister, was involved in the Underground Railroad, attended the first women's rights convention, met with President Abraham Lincoln to discuss the treatment of Negro soldiers during the Civil War, met with President Andrew Johnson to discuss Negro suffrage, was an editor of the *North*

Star and the *New National Era*, and served as the president of the Freedman's Savings and Trust Company. He also worked as a US marshal, lectured on Scandinavian folklore, worked in Washington, DC, as a recorder of deeds, and was appointed American consul general to Haiti.

This brief biography of Douglass is important because it shows how self-reflection can be combined with action as a powerful means of instigating ethical and social change beyond mere self-improvement. Douglass (1964) once said, "The moral growth of a great nation requires reflection" (p. 1).

Humble as he was well spoken, Douglass described his success as a lecturer in this way: "Fugitive slaves were rare then, and as a fugitive slave lecturer, I had the advantage of being the first one out" (Douglass, 1892, p. 8). However, his humbleness does not overshadow the fact that Douglass made his living as a lecturer based on his ability of making his self-reflection relevant to others. Take, for example, this excerpt from his best-known speech, "What to a Slave Is the Fourth of July?"

> What, to the American slave, is your 4th of July? I answer; a day that reveals to him, more than all other days in the year, the gross injustice and cruelty to which he is the constant victim. To him, your celebration is a sham; your boasted liberty, an unholy license; your national greatness, swelling vanity; your sound of rejoicing are empty and heartless; your denunciation of tyrants brass fronted impudence; your shout of liberty and equality, hollow mockery; your prayers and hymns, your sermons and thanksgivings, with all your religious parade and solemnity, are to him, mere bombast, fraud, deception, impiety, and hypocrisy—a thin veil to cover up crimes which would disgrace a nation of savages. There is not a nation on the earth guilty of practices more shocking and bloody than are the people of the United States, at this very hour. (Douglass, 1852)

In the seventy-six years between the original reading of the Declaration of Independence and Douglass's rereading, Independence Square and the famous Liberty Bell had increased both in national meaning and in public sentiment. Douglass exploited the cultural and historical significance of Independence Square to underscore the disparity in the meaning of freedom between Whites and Blacks in America. For White Americans, freedom meant liberty—freedom from British imperialism to be self-reliant and independent. For Negroes, freedom meant emancipation—freedom from slavery. Douglass's word "savages" in this passage is the exact term the writers of the Constitution of the United States used to describe Native Americans. Racism becomes most apparent when analyzed through language. As the word "savages" is examined through the eyes of the oppressed, the real savage is revealed to be those who celebrate their liberation from oppression at the expense of those whom they in turn oppress.

Calling on his abilities as an AME Zion minister, Douglass delivered his speech with the same discursive power and eloquence as the Declaration of Independence. The self-reflection of a Black man's place in the Declaration of Independence by Douglass, an escaped slave who eventually purchased his freedom, resulted in a dialogue that awakened a different consciousness of America and its association with the word "freedom."

When he delivered his "What to a Slave Is the Fourth of July?" speech, Douglass had split from the Anti-Slavery Society and his association with its leader, William Lloyd Garrison. The Anti-Slavery Society helped publish Douglass's first autobiography, *The Narrative of the Life of Frederick Douglass*. In a meeting in May 1965 with the Anti-Slavery Society, one month after the end of the Civil War, Douglass stepped away from Garrison and the society when Garrison proposed the organization be disbanded now that its goal had been achieved. Douglass responded by adopting yet another self-reflective analysis of what it meant to be a Negro male in America. He said: "Slavery is not abolished until the Black man has the ballot" (Douglass, 1965, p. 83). From that moment on, Douglass was an agent of change by using his abilities as an orator to persuade Americans to allow Blacks to vote.

Douglass was forty-seven years old in December 1865, when the Thirteenth Amendment to the US Constitution abolished slavery. However, Blacks were not able to vote until Douglass was fifty-two with the passage of the Fifteenth Amendment in 1870. During that time, Douglass worked diligently toward obtaining the rights that allowed Blacks the right to vote. Douglass thought that American social conditions were largely about power and that, through language and action, power could be abated.

> Power concedes nothing without a demand. It never did, and it never will. Find out just what people will submit to, and you have found out the exact amount of injustice and wrong which will be imposed upon them; and these will continue till they have resisted with either words or blows, or with both. The limits of tyrants are prescribed by the endurance of those whom they suppress. (Douglass, p. 1, 1857)

Thus, America used resistance through action—the Revolutionary War showed resistance through language in the Declaration of Independence. Douglass also used dialogue as a form of action and used reinterpretation of language to wrestle a positive form of African American identity from the oppressor. Douglass's voice of freedom in the form of social justice was just as sharp and clear as the Liberty Bell that hung in Independence Square when he delivered his "What to a Slave Is the Fourth of July?" speech. Douglass was a clarion for emancipation from slavery and the right for African Americans to vote. One note singing out alone has little impact, but many notes ringing in unison can create a symphony of change. Other African American voices joined in the revolutionary spirit of Douglass's voice. One of the voices came from W. E. B. DuBois.

W. E. B. DuBois

William Edward Burghardt DuBois was highly influenced by Douglass. He was twenty-six when Douglass died in 1895. DuBois quoted Douglass extensively and referred to his "What to a Slave Is the Fourth of July?" speech often. In fact, DuBois commented that "Frederick Douglass [was] the noblest slave that ever God set free" (DuBois, 1935, p. 15). Despite his affection for Douglass, DuBois's background differed greatly from Douglass's.

DuBois was born in 1868 in Massachusetts to African American parents whose ancestors had been free for over one hundred years. This produced a view of freedom slightly different from Blacks who were born as slaves, such as Douglass. DuBois's family and personal experience with emancipation set in motion his work to free all African Americans through education. His life largely advocated for African Americans to use their intelligence for the good of others. Emancipation, for DuBois, meant the freedom provided by a good education; the freedom to learn and to help others (DuBois, 1949).

DuBois pronounced his name Doo Boiz; "Du with u as in Sue; Bois, as oi in voice. The accent is on the second syllable" (cited in Berkshire Publishing Group, 2007), perhaps in rejection to his European heritage (DuBois 2007). The son of a biracial union, DuBois had some advantages, but was hardly well off. Church members collected offerings to help pay for his college education at Fisk University. While attending Fisk, DuBois developed a sincere and honest wish to use his knowledge to help others. A few years later, DuBois traveled to Europe to attend graduate school at the University of Berlin; he then returned to the United States to become the first African American to obtain a PhD from Harvard.

Shortly afterward, early in his career as an educator, DuBois became the first person in the United States to conduct a social survey of African Americans. Spending almost eighteen months in Philadelphia studying African Americans, DuBois published his findings in an 1899 report he called *The Philadelphia Negro*. Using interviews and observations, he detailed close to forty thousand people of African descent in America living in Philadelphia (DuBois, 1967). Subsequently, DuBois felt that the burden of advancing Blacks in the United States was to be borne on the shoulders of the top 10 percent of college-educated African Americans (later amended to the guiding one-hundredth) whom he believed should become leaders in the Black community (Johnson, 1976). This view enhanced his work in higher education.

DuBois served as an educator in the United States when African Americans made up 20 percent of the population in the South (DuBois, [1903] 1994). This was during the late 1800s when both African Americans and White Americans were just starting to look for solutions to improve White and Black relations. When he died in 1963, DuBois was also known internationally as a proponent of social change through education.

The most widely recognized writings of DuBois stem from his suggestion that African Americans have a double consciousness; this argument was espoused in his 1903 publication, *The Souls of Black Folk*. The idea of double consciousness is rooted in the belief that African Americans can look at the American experiences with a divided self; they are able to see the world through multiracial eyes (DuBois, [1903] 1994). This intuitiveness enables the oppressed to see society from a unique moral perspective. This double consciousness, which is an outcome of slavery, empowered those who struggled with the residual impact of being in bondage; this double consciousness is a critical perspective of African American identity. DuBois saw the critical reflection that double consciousness provided as a way of looking at the world though both the eyes of the oppressor and the oppressed.

DuBois's life was filled with the rumblings of the oppressed combined with the echoes of the drums of war. DuBois lived during both World War I and II. He was well aware of the disappointment and deafening "wail of poisoned souls within the veil and the mounting fury of shackled men" (DuBois, [1903] 1994, p. 57). DuBois knew that African Americans did not find relief from their anguish from unrecognized sacrifice to the American dream after they sacrificed their lives for freedom in the Revolutionary War, the Civil War, or either of the two world wars. Regarding the Civil War, DuBois said:

> The nation has not yet found peace from its sins; the freed man has not yet found in freedom his promised land. Whatever of good may have come in these years of change, the shadow of a deep disappointment rests upon the Negro people—a disappointment all the more bitter because the unattained ideal was unbounded by the simple ignorance of a lowly people. ([1903] 1994, p. 4)

Despite his disappointment in the conditions of Black after emancipation, a feeling that was echoed by many others, DuBois did not falter in his steps toward making progress, He continued to advocate for dogged activism by sharing with others his opinion that social change required not only the self-reflection that double consciousness provides but also the very real hard work of praxis. True change requires a little less complaint and whining, and a little more hard work (DuBois, 1967). DuBois knew that for African Americans to be recognized as a people, they needed to work hard at educating themselves in all areas related to human development—socially, economically, and politically. Freedom brought about by education was a form of respected cultural capital that could be used to barter away the barriers of racism that blocked African American progress. DuBois encouraged African Americans to beat the wings of freedom against all barriers including "barriers of caste, of youth, of life; at last, in dangerous moments, against everything that opposed [one] even a whim" (DuBois, [1903] 1994, p. 42). DuBois used the metaphorical image of a bird beating its wings in its flight toward freedom as an allegory of praxis and resistance that could be symbolically achieved by African Americans who resisted oppression.

DuBois ([1868] 1999) referred to the barrier of race as a veil. However, DuBois's veil was an unseen metaphorical barrier that separated Blacks and Whites socially as well as legally that he wished could be lifted to enable a man to be both a "Negro and an American without being cursed and spit upon by his fellows" (DuBois, [1903] 1994, p. 3). DuBois's definition of the word *freedom* was later expanded to mean freedom from the oppressive veil of racism. As an educator during two global wars, DuBois knew that true freedom meant the end of oppression not just in America but around the world.

DuBois's perspectives and encouragement for Americans to look critically at the function of racism resonated with many Blacks and Whites of his day. One such person was Booker T. Washington; he was viewed as DuBois's counterpart on issues of race relations. Washington was the other face of the drum that played a steady beat for change in America; sometimes it was in sync with DuBois, but sometimes not.

Booker T. Washington

Booker Taliaferro Washington was born a slave in 1856, in Halle's Ford, Virginia. However, Washington was unarguably a success by the time he died in 1915 in Tuskegee, Alabama. By the time he passed away, he had graduated from Hampton College in 1875 and became a board member of Fisk University, the founder of Tuskegee University, and a towering intellectual of his day. In fact, Washington was regarded as the best public speaker since Frederick Douglass, and was even called the Negro Moses for his ability to draw a crowd (Creelman, 1895). DuBois ([1903] 1994) referred to Washington as "the most distinguished Southerner since [former president] Jefferson Davis and the one with the largest following" (p. 26).

Washington's life as a child was very different from DuBois's, who was born to free parents. Washington worked in a salt mine as a boy for meager wages. He was inspired one day at work when he overheard two miners talk about a school for colored people somewhere in Virginia that accepted worthy students who were poor; they allowed them to work for room and board. In his book *Up from Slavery* ([1901] 1995), Washington describes his inspiration that propelled him out of the oppressive dark cave mines toward the bright light of emancipation. Discussing the conversation he heard between the two miners, he wrote,

> As they went on describing the school, it seemed to me that it must be the greatest place on earth, and not even Heaven presented more attractions for me at that time than did the Hampton Normal and Agriculture Institute in Virginia, about which these men were talking. I resolved at once to go to that school, although I had no idea where it was, or how many miles away, or how I was going to reach it; I remembered only that I was on fire constantly with one ambition, and that was to go to Hampton. The thought was with me day and night. (Washington, [1901] 1995, p. 21)

Shortly after overhearing that it was possible for a Negro to obtain an education, Washington went to work for a Mrs. Ruffner to earn money for school. Mrs. Ruffner was a stern and strict woman who taught him how to clean meticulously and allowed him to go to school for an hour a day during the winter. Eventually, Washington saved what he thought was enough money to travel to West Virginia, the location of Hampton. After several misadventures, Washington made it to Hampton, disheveled, unbathed, exhausted, and, worse, broke. He had spent all his money just to get to Hampton. Talking his way through the door of Hampton, but not quite fully admitted, the head teacher asked him to sweep a recreation room to see if he would be a worthy janitor. "Never did I receive an order with more delight. I knew that I could sweep, for Mrs. Ruffner had thoroughly taught me how to do that" (Washington, [1901] 1995, p. 25). Washington did more than an adequate job and was allowed to attend Hampton as a janitor in exchange for room and board. "I have passed many examinations since then, but I have always felt that this was the best one I passed" (Washington, [1901] 1995, p. 25).

Although *Up from Slavery* was well received, Washington was equally well known for his Atlanta Exposition address delivered on September 15, 1865. Also known as the "Atlanta Compromise" speech, it was recited before a predominantly White audience at the Cotton States and International Exposition in Atlanta. For many, both Black and White, it was the first time they had witnessed a Black mean speak with no one to interrupt him (Creelman, 1895). Encouraging Black and Whites to recognize that Black labor could sustain the Black community while not threatening White economic interests, Washington stated:

> To those of my race who depend on bettering their condition in a foreign land or who underestimate the importance of cultivating friendly relations with the Southern white man, who is their next-door neighbour, I would say: Cast down your bucket where you are—cast it down in making friends in every manly way of the people of all races by whom we are surrounded. (1895)

Washington continued:

> As we have proved our loyalty to you in the past, in nursing your children, watching by the sick-bed of your mothers and fathers, and often following them with tear-dimmed eyes to their graves, so in the future, in our humble way, we shall stand by you with a devotion that no foreigner can approach, ready to lay down our lives, if need be, in defence of yours, interlacing our industrial, commercial, civil, and religious life with yours in a way that shall make the interests of both races one. In all things that are purely social we can be as separate as the fingers, yet one as the hand in all things essential to mutual progress.... There is no defense or security for any of us except in the highest intelligence and development of all. If anywhere there are efforts tending to curtail the fullest growth of the Negro, let these efforts be turned into stimulating, encouraging, and making him the most useful and intelligent citizen. Effort or means so invested will pay a thousand per cent interest. (1865)

Because of the racial tensions that existed at the time, Washington was of the opinion that Whites were fearful of Blacks' political, social, and economic progress. The perspective that Whites lose if Blacks gain is a view that still prevails today. Washington was very conscious of the precarious position Blacks had in the South of the perception that Black advancement disadvantaged Whites, but he was determined to speak the truth. Much of Washington's work, including public speaking, was undertaken with a frame of mind that he would speak his mind, not say anything in the North that he would not say in the South, and that he would give credit to Whites that supported Negroes, thereby helping America. It was easier to work with others when you praised them for noteworthy actions than when you tore them down. Washington felt that Whites would financially support Negroes who learned trades and received an education because they would, in turn, become skilled workers for Whites, thereby not posing a threat to White jobs. This purposeful strategy was especially relevant for an exposition in the South that was designed to showcase southern social and industrial progress. Washington's nonthreatening strategy also and had the added benefit that it made the Negro more acceptable because Whites were already more comfortable supervising Negro workers than foreigners and immigrants. The polysemic metaphor of casting buckets where you are meant that southern Whites could remain in their comfort zones by employing local workers and that southern Blacks did not have to travel to the North for jobs.

Those who opposed Washington, many of whom were aligned with DuBois, felt that Washington's overtures to accommodate White interests in the name of Negro economic prosperity teetered on racial and moral compromise, hence the reason the Atlanta Exposition address is also known as the "Atlanta Compromise." The result of differing points of view toward what was best for progress for Blacks was oversimplified as follows: DuBois was an advocate of higher education for the improvement of the Negro race, while Washington was only a proponent for trade schools for the betterment of Negro people. DuBois and Washington had many publicized and well-attended public debates about their differing perspectives. The great debates between DuBois and Washington were often described as being contentious and occasionally hostile. But in fact, DuBois and Washington, at least initially, had a close friendship and merely presented two sides of an argument to get Blacks talking about many issues, including postsecondary school, in essence to raise their consciousness about multiple possibilities for the future (Johnston, 1976). Washington sponsored many public debates between himself and DuBois to stimulate thought as well as action to uplift Negroes. DuBois and Washington both agreed that America would never spend more money for educational institutions that empowered former slaves with opportunities enabling them to compete with Whites unless it benefited them in some way (Johnson, 1976). In essence, an education does not do any good unless society is willing to hire those who are educated. What good does it do for a Black man to be educated if he cannot find employment? DuBois and Washington wanted Negros to create their own businesses and employ one another whether formally educated or not.

Other contemporaries of DuBois and Washington also saw that poverty and a lack of employment were barriers to the freedom of financial independence and self-reliance. Another Black male intellectual, Carter G. Woodson, who was a contemporary of DuBois and Washington, was in agreement with the idea that Negroes should be self-reliant.

Carter G. Woodson

Carter Godwin Woodson asserted that one of America's biggest failures was that Negroes had not "learned to make a living" (Woodson, 1990, p. 88). Woodson advocated that both educational and professional development were keys for success for Negroes. Because of his tireless efforts as a historian, Woodson is known as the Father of Black History. Woodson founded Black History, the precursor to Black History Month. He is also known for his influential book, *The Mis-education of the Negro*. Woodson was born in New Canton, Virginia, in 1875 and lived until 1950. Woodson received both his AB (bachelor's degree) and his AM (master's degree) in 1908 from the University of Chicago and his PhD in history from Harvard in 1912. Woodson was the second Negro to obtain a PhD from Harvard, after DuBois. Woodson was also a high school teacher in Washington, DC, a school supervisor in the Philippines, and a dean of the College of Arts and Sciences at Howard University.

Although typically not associated with the debate between trade schools and postsecondary education, Woodson's views resonated with those of DuBois and Washington, as he was highly critical of the fact that far too many Negroes were concerned with attaining degrees and working in White intuitions and White business sectors instead of establishing ground-level business in the Black community; he argued that American Whites opened business in Negro communities and became rich from Black dollars. He was highly conscious of the fact that "Negros of the District of Columbia have millions of dollars deposited in [White] banks downtown, where women are not allowed in the ladies' rest room" (Woodson, 1990, p. 163).

Woodson typically referred to Whites in America as American Whites and Blacks as Negroes, perhaps as a way to highlight there was a different racialized experience for Blacks in America; this is still the case now. For Woodson, the color line was divided between being a full-fledged American who was empowered (read White) and being a Black American, who was only allowed to come close to being a full participant in society: "While being a good American, he must above all things be a good Negro. He must know his place" (Woodson, 1990, p. 6). Throughout most of his writing, Woodson was aware of both what it means to be a Negro and what it means to be an American, and the racial as well as the economic divide between them. Woodson witnessed White faculty members at White institutions support other Whites to get into college who needed help through lenient admissions or by sending them to additional schooling to prepare them for graduate school, while more suitable Black applicants were denied admission or only allowed to teach in Negro communities when they graduated. Frustrated by oppressive double standards in education, Woodson stated that when a Negro has a college education

> and has been equipped to begin the life of an Americanized or Europeanized White man, but before he steps from the threshold of his alma mater, he is told by his teachers that he must go back to his own people from whom he has been estranged by a vision of ideals which in his disillusionment he will realize that he cannot attain. He goes forth to play his part in life, but he must be both social and biosocial at the same time. While he is a part of the body politic, he is in addition to this a member of particular race to which he must restrict himself in all matters social. (Woodson, 1990, p. 75)

Similar to DuBois, Woodson felt the veil in America was racism, but a particular type of academic racism that restricted Blacks from achieving based on a lack of affirming education that permeated their progression all the way from formative schooling until graduate school. In fact, Woodson (1990) said: "White presidents of these intuitions are often less scholarly than Negroes who have to serve under them" (p. 26). While Woodson did not feel that White teachers should not be allowed to teach Black children, Woodson did feel that knowledge of the historical contributions of Negroes in America was either misinformed or nonexistent, leaving many students, White and Black, to feel that Blacks were unimportant and insignificant in the classroom (Woodson, 1990).

Then disenfranchisement of the Negro through the school curriculum had effects outside of the classroom as well. White Americans, the ones most likely to be allowed to own businesses, never learned that Blacks were important to the construction of America and frequently saw no reason to hire them irrespective of whether Whites were racist or not. Consequently, Blacks of Woodson's day often felt despair about employment opportunities. "Negroes have learned from their oppressors to say to their children that there are certain spheres into which they should not go because they would have no chance therein for development" (Woodson, 1990, p. 75).

Woodson argued that the failure of schools to acknowledge the Negro contribution in America affected Blacks in many ways, including Whites feeling that Blacks were unworthy to be employed, so much so that Blacks sometimes resented their own Blackness and heritage. In his appendix in *The Mis-education of the Negro* (1990), after looking at an attractive Black woman, Woodson recalls a tribe in Africa that "feels unusually proud of being Black" (p. 202), even to the point of sometimes dying their skin the darkest dye they can find to be even darker. Woodson encourages the reader to wonder what would happen if Negroes embraced their cultural heritage in everything that they do.

Molefi Asante several years later encouraged African Americans to embrace the Blackness given to them by the sun-kissed continent of Africa.

Molefi Kete Asante

Asante's views resonated with those of his predecessors. He acknowledged the importance of Douglass, DuBois, and Woodson, writing that Douglass was one of the one hundred greatest African Americans. He stated that DuBois "stands at the helm of intellectual and political advancement in the contemporary world" (Asante, 2008a, p. 22), and that Woodson was the "principal impetus" for his Afrocentric approach (Asante, 2003, p. 22).

Born Arthur Lee Smith Jr. in Valdosta, Georgia, in 1942, Asante was twenty-one when DuBois died in 1963. Asante graduated from Oklahoma Christian College in 1964 with a BA in communication. He completed his MA in communication at Pepperdine University in 1965. He was awarded his PhD in communication in 1968 from UCLA. Asante was eventually appointed full professor at the State University of New York at Buffalo. While there, he chaired the Communication Department from 1973 to 1980. He worked in Zimbabwe as a trainer of journalists from 1980 to 1982. In the fall of 1984, Asante became chair of the African American Studies Program at Temple University, where he created the first PhD program in African American studies in 1987. Asante has even been named an honorary African chief by the Asante tribe. He changed his name to Molefi Kete Asante in rejection of what he called his slave name in 1973 while visiting the University of Ghana. For Asante, freedom meant the ability to look at the world and oneself critically through the lens of culture and heritage.

Asante is most famously known for his work on the theoretical framework called Afrocentricity. Afrocentricity is an African and African American construct that continuously places Black consciousness at the center of its ideology. A trope of both thought and action, Afrocentricity is dedicated to resisting oppression, and the idea that African consciousness should be the force behind Black political and social actions (Asante, 2003). Similar to emancipatory education,

Afrocentricity is a theory that enables a person to reject European-framed knowledge systems in favor of other types of truths. In other words, African and African Americans can become the subjects rather than the objects of European education (Asante, 1991). Looking at those of African descent as active participants in history instead of merely as oppressed individuals creates a consciousness that is both self-reflective and empowering.

When oppressive discourses are adjusted to recognize the contribution of the oppressed, new opportunities are created for self-discovery and the freedom to use words that have new meaning. These discourses create a language that changes the way oppressed individuals relate to themselves and one another. Asante asserted, "There can be no freedom until there is freedom of the mind. The first rule for freedom of the mind is the freedom of language" (2003, p. 41). Asante proposes freedom from oppression whenever he mentions the liberating language that Afrocentricity provides.

Asante studied how the French Revolution used words such as "*liberté, egalité,* and *fraternité* and made them instruments for a collective will to power" (Asante, 2003, p. 41). Asante asserted that African Americans were denied their traditional language during slavery; he argued that "language serves as an instrument of social restrain" (Asante, 2003, p. 43). Thus, if Blacks reinterpret the oppressor's language in favor of an Afrocentric view, racial barriers can be lifted when the oppressed learn the truth about themselves. This truth is based on the knowledge that Africans are more than a people who are oppressed worldwide and have a hidden place in history.

Like Douglass and DuBois, Asante also made references to consciousness by suggesting that those of African descent have an unconscious inheritance of language that needs to be awakened. "I seek a language [through Afrocentricity] whose axiological basis resides in history, but those pragmatic manifestations are in our present reality" (Asante, 2003, p. 45).

DuBois also referred the barrier of race a veil (DuBois, [1868] 1999). However, DuBois's veil was an unseen barrier that separated Blacks and Whites that he wished could be lifted away to enable a man to be both a "Negro and an American without being cursed and spit upon by his fellows" (DuBois, [1903] 1994, p. 3). DuBois's version of the word *freedom* was later expanded to mean freedom from the oppressive veil of racism. As an educator during two global wars DuBois know that true freedom meant the end of oppression around the world.

Another African American intellectual took the term *veil*, in yet another example of reinterpretation, and saw it in terms of his African American heritage. Molefi Kete Asante saw the veil as a symbol of power when his parents told him that he was born with a veil over his face, "which is a[n African] symbol of luck and intelligence" (Asante, 2008a, p. 1). Building upon the language and words of your ancestors, such as *veil* and *freedom*, is a traditional African tradition that Asante calls ancestral strides (Asante, 2008b). It is a way of honoring the heritage of those who have come before you.

By drawing on the rich and colorful knowledge of African culture, African Americans can rewrite and engage discourse to reclaim the contributions of their history that have been hidden and erased. "All oppressor nations attempt to create taboos or legal prohibitions to block languages that might change the way people think" (Asante, 2003, p. 45).

For Asante, freedom takes the form of Africans and African Americans using education to reclaim their knowledge of self that has been hidden from them. Although he was not the creator of Afrocentricity, Asante is the most recognizable author on the topic. His name is synonymous with Afrocentricity, and his writing on the subject has influenced scholars from all over the world. One such scholar is Jawanza Kunjufu.

Jawanza Kunjufu

Arguably the most cited author with regard to Black males and education, Jawanza Kunjufu was born in Chicago on June 15, 1953. Kunjufu attended Illinois State University at Normal and received a BS in economics in 1974. He received a PhD in economics in 1984 from the Union Graduate School. Kunjufu was also a teacher at an Afrocentric school from 1974 to 1980. Kunjufu is the owner of African American Images, one of the largest publishing companies and bookstores in the United States; he is best known for his book *Countering the Conspiracy to Destroy Black Boys*, first released in 1982. This book was so popular that Kunjufu created a second volume in 1986, a third volume in 1990, and a fourth volume in 1994.

Kunjufu strongly believes that public schools dehumanize Black boys because they are the greatest threat to White supremacy (Kunjufu, 1985). Kunjufu is also vehemently opposed to the increasing number of Black males placed into special education tracks, which he refers to as a new form of segregation. Based on data that he collected, Kunjufu became an advocate for the need for more Black male teachers, especially in the fourth grade, and has inspired more than a hundred Black males become classroom educators. Additionally, talking about what we now know today as the school-to-prison pipeline, Kunjufu (1986) was one of the first educators to recognize that the age where Black men are at their peak physically, between eighteen and twenty-five, is when they are most likely to be incarcerated.

> We must develop programs and organizations to protect and develop African American boys because a conspiracy exists to destroy African American boys. The motive of the conspiracy is racism, specifically European American male supremacy. The conspiracy has become more complex as often the perpetuators reside in the home and in the classroom. It is most destructive in the primary grades. The method is to eliminate positive role models, discourage emotional and spiritual development; de-emphasize academics while the technology becomes more complex. (Kunjufu, 1985, p. 32)

The trend to disregard the education of Black males is a key issue for Kunjufu. Kunjufu's frustration with American policies toward education is highlighted by the fact that governors used his reading data for Black males as an excuse to build more prisons instead of putting money into literacy interventions as he suggested. Since then, many states decide how many prisons to build based on Black male fourth-grade reading scores.

Since the American educational system is a reflection of society, Kunjufu has been vocal about his disappointment in the way racism outside of the classroom affects Black male motivation to be successful inside of the classroom.

> It becomes very frustrating for me to travel from city to city and encounter White males who are fresh out of college and the day before were involved in frat bashing and beer fights, and now earn $30,000 plus as sales representatives. This is a very popular position for assertive, aggressive males who did not perform academically in college. They are members of the buddy/buddy club with unlimited income. I really don't see a great difference between a 21-year-old White male and an African American male except privilege and a safety net. A salary net that allows White males to matriculate into the larger economy and forces African American males to choose between the military, McDonalds, drugs, and crime. For many African American males, that's how they see their options. If African American men can sell drugs, they can sell Fortune 500 products if given the opportunity. (Kunjufu, 1990, p. 67)

Here Kunjufu is conscious of the fact that African American males are aware of both their potential and the barriers they face to fully participating in the American dream. Kunjufu echoed Douglass and DuBois's perspective that ethnic and national identity harmony is a dream deferred.

> Du Bois and Douglass remind us that we are not one self but two selves and we are frequently reminded of the tension between the two selves when we are confronted with symbols of nationhood. This tension—brought on by America's refusal to admit its racism and then to eliminate it—causes African Americans a great deal of ambivalence about our American identity. (Kunjufu, 1988, p. 27)

Since academic achievement has become synonymous with being White as well as American, there is an internal identity struggle for Black males regarding their relationship to both America and education (Kunjufu, 1988). African American male contributions including intellectual identity are not commonly reinforced, depicted, or encouraged in U.S. schools, while African American males' athletic ability is. Keenly aware of America's racism and genderism, Black boys have internalized the fact "that a White male with a high school diploma will make more than anyone of another gender and race with a college degree" (Kunjufu. 1988, p. 95). *To be Popular or Smart*, the title of another book by Kunjufu, argues that the internal questions asked by many Black boys leave them with the decision to be either an athlete or to be popular and cool (or both), (Kunjufu, 1988). This definition of Black masculinity is often conceptualized as a cool pose (Majors & Billson, 1992), or withdrawal from study and immersion in sports to be popular.

In *To Be Popular or Smart*, Kunjufu tells educators and parents that being American implicitly means there is a Black and White duality in America that often goes undiscussed. Many Black students resent having to work twice as hard for half as much, and realize that American society does not create spaces where they can participate in the American dream equally (Kunjufu, 1988). "They have consciously or unconsciously created another 'cultural frame of reference' of activities and standards" (Kunjufu, 1988, p. 29). What is worse for Kunjufu, is the fact that many parents have *not* told their children there are racial and economic barriers related to success, and that their children are free to achieve as long as they work hard. For those children who were raised from a meritorious perspective, the words "struggle, liberation, and freedom are not part of their vocabulary" (Kunjufu, 1988, p. 29). Therefore, Black males who are raised from a race less perspective are often unprepared when confronted with barriers based on their gender and ethnicity in schools from both their peers and teachers.

Kunjufu asserts that Blacks must understand their circumstances, so they do not use the same value system of the oppressor. Oppression is oppression whether it is administered by a European or a Negro (Kunjufu, 1988). Kunjufu (1988) advocates for a new definition of Blackness that allows individuality without being individualistic, and encourages self-determination rather than the binary choice of being popular or smart that many Black males face.

To alleviate Black male peer pressure to act cool, Kunjufu suggests schools implement cooperative learning environments. Typical U.S. classrooms are structured so that when a teacher asks Jerome to spell a word out loud and a gets it wrong, she asks the class if anyone can help Jerome answer it correctly. If Jerome is one of the few Black males in the class, this instructional strategy becomes a racially oppositional situation for all the students. Instead, Kunjufu recommends that educators

> imagine that the structure of this classroom has been changed. Billy and Sam have been asked to work together. Now their goal is to see how many points the two boys can earn together when they take their spelling tests. In this situation, Sam will want to make sure not only that he knows his spelling words, but also that Billy knows his. Billy will feel the same responsibility for Sam's learning. Sam and Billy want to help each other study and will encourage continued support. (Robert Slavin, quoted in Kunjufu, 1990, p. 79)

Even before differentiated learning was a popular pedagogical approach, Kunjufu was an advocate for it as a viable strategy to teach Black males. Differentiated learning and unique instructions for individual students (Tomlinson, 2007) can also include students working in groups. Encouraging students to work collaboratively and inclusively helps Black males to counter peer pressure. Because of social conditioning, African American students are more likely to seek help from small cooperative groups where they are comfortable challenging explanations and requesting justifications, and are supported with challenging engagement (Nelson-Le Gall & Jones, 1991). African American students who are high achievers typically do so as members of peer groups (Faqs.org, 2014).

In other words, peer pressure can influence student outcomes both positively and negatively. The affirming effects of positive peer pressure are one of the reasons why Kunjufu (1985) suggests single-gender classrooms as one solution to help Black males succeed in school. In fact, peer pressure can be more influential than ethnicity, gender, or income (Johnson, 2000). In addition to highlighting innovative thinkers, such as Slavin, Kunjufu also highlighted William Cross, a Black male educator from Chicago who has influenced the way educators understand Black males.

William E. Cross Jr.

William E. Cross Jr., or "Bill" Cross, was born in 1940 in Chicago to Margaret Cross (a maid) and William E. Cross (a Pullman porter) on the South Side of Chicago. Bill attended McCosh Elementary School in Chicago, but his formative years were grounded in Evanston, where he graduated from Evanston Township High School. Cross received his BA in psychology from Denver University in 1963, and attended Roosevelt University in Chicago for graduate school in clinical psychology. Although he did not finish his master's degree, Cross obtained his doctorate in psychology from Princeton University in 1976. While at Princeton, Cross was an assistant to the chair of Afro-American Studies. Cross was also a member of the American Black Psychologists, who believed that as practitioners in the field of Black mental health they were Black people *first* and *psychologists* second (Vandiver et al., 2002). Cross is best known for his African American Identity Model, also known as the Nigrescence Model, which he first articulated in 1971. Cross's African American Identity Model provided the context behind the creation of his book *Shades of Black*.

Written in 1991, *Shades of Black* critically picks up after the 1970s research trend that often oversimplified and uncritically analyzed African Americans between the years leading up to the Civil War and ending shortly after desegregation. Cross felt that much of the previous research about African Americans asserted that Blacks suffered from low self-esteem, anti-Blackness, and self-hate, perspectives that we would call a deficit mind-set today. What is most significant about *Shades of Black* is the scholarly exploration and expansion of *nigrescence*, a term that describes the "process of becoming Black" (Cross, 1991, p. x). In *Shades of Black*, Cross explains how he and his fellow graduate students investigated the process and formation of Black identity and Black consciousness that occurred in the 1960s. In addition to the change of the cultural and political mind-set where African Americans began to refer to themselves as Black instead of Negro, the 1960s also saw the implementation of the Fair Housing Act. The Fair Housing Act allowed Blacks to move into White neighborhoods and was implemented close to the same time as the War on Poverty; despite the best of intentions, it set the stage for the criminalization of males of color. The 1960s also saw the Cuban Missile Crisis, which escalated nuclear tensions between the United States and Russia, the assassination of President John F. Kennedy, the assassination of his brother, Senator Bobby Kennedy, the assassination of Black nationalist Malcolm X, the assassination of Rev. Dr. Martin Luther King Jr., and the US moon landing. In short, the 1970s witnessed a whirlwind of political, social, and cultural change that impacted both American and African American consciousness. Cross's research moved away from the idea that being a Negro was a debilitating pathology and suggested that embracing Blackness in all of its forms was a process of identity development that was necessary for a healthy state of mind. Cross and his fellow doctoral students at Princeton theorized that Blacks were part of humanity and to be human by definition has to be complex, and thus an accurate analysis of Black psychological functioning would be multidimensional and would include positive as well as negative themes, functional and dysfunctional proclivities, and strengths in addition to weaknesses and vulnerabilities (Cross, 1991, p. xii).

Cross's (1991) African American Identity Model occurs in five stages: (1) pre-encounter, (2) encounter, (3) immersion/emersion, (4) internalization, and (5) internalization-commitment. Kunjufu (1988) in his book *To Be Popular or Smart* conceptualizes Cross's African American Identity Model as Malcolm X's journey from the hip pimp and smooth criminal Detroit Red with processed hair (pre-encounter), to the incarcerated Black male prisoner (encounter), which led him to the (immersion) of a positive and alternative Afrocentric Black culture based on the teachings of Elijah Muhammad; this gave Malcolm an alternative frame of reference, a consciousness (internalization) and finally led him to (internalization-commitment) a praxis of well-being where Malcolm was at peace with himself and his environment, and committed to building positive institutions and communities.

Clearly, the importance of Cross's African American Identity Model lies in the fact that it highlights that identity formation is a self-reflective process that occurs in identifiable stages. The African American Identity Model is both a conscious and an unconscious way of understanding one's role, and the actual part one plays is not always related. Because the finale stage requires internalization and commitment, the full-immersion African American Identity Model allows Black males to be authors of their own stories and not mere actors.

Richard Majors

Richard Majors was born in Ithaca, New York in 1954. He received his PhD in counseling psychology from the University of Illinois, Champaign-Urbana in 1987. He is an honorary professor at University of Colorado–Colorado Springs. He undertook postdoctoral work at the University of Kansas from 1987 to 1989 and was a clinical fellow in psychiatry at Harvard Medical School from1989 to 1990. Majors is also the founder and former editor of the *Journal of African American Men*, the first referred journal in the United States on Black males, known today as the *Journal of African American Studies*. Majors was appointed to a ministerial education advisory group under Tony Blair's administration in the United Kingdom. He has taught a short course at Cambridge University and he was invited to do a lecture at Oxford University. Dr. Majors was also invited to the White House in Washington, DC, in 1994, to meet with members of the Clinton administration to discuss youth policy. While at Harvard, Majors founded the National Council of African American Men (NCAAM), one of the first umbrella groups in the United States for African American males. The Illinois chapter is still very active.

He is the recipient of two prestigious Transfer of Innovations (TOI) awards from the European Union for his work on emotional literacy and psychological well-being among teachers. He is the founding director of the, Applied Centre for Emotional Literacy & Research. Dr. Majors also has been used as an expert legal psychologist on a number of high profile legal cases in both the United States and the United Kingdom. In 2011 he wrote the expert psychological legal statement for the landmark case in the British High Courts *G. vs St. Gregory's Catholic Science College*, which granted Black children in the United Kingdom the right to wear their hair in culturally specific styles without being punished.

He is the author (with Jacob Gordon) of the *American Black Male: His Present Status and Future*, one of the first analogies ever written about Black males. One of the major contributions of this book was to document and chronicle the importance and rise of the Black male moment or Black male renaissance that we are witnessing today. He is also the author of the influential book *Educating Our Black Children: New Directions and Radical Approaches*. However, he is best known for his bestselling book *Cool Pose: The Dilemmas of Black Manhood in America*, one of the most-cited books in race relations and gender. *Cool Pose* has generated and inspired many publications, debates, articles, reports, studies, and doctoral dissertations by other scholars and community leaders.

As a trained psychologist, Majors is a keen observer of the human condition, especially Black males. For example, inspired by a conversation with "Phil," a Black male janitor in an elevator, his subsequent interviews with Phil served as the majority of the data for his dissertation that eventually became the book *Cool Pose*. This book is based on the premise that one of the ways Black males resist oppression is by appearing to be aloof, detached, and silent; namely, they adopt a cool pose (Majors & Billson, 1992).

The word *cool* has roots in Africa, especially the Yoruba tribe in Nigeria and Benin (Thompson, 1973). In fact, the cool aesthetic stems from *ewuare*, a Yoruba term in West Africa that is often assigned to one who is crowned king (Majors & Billson, 1992). Cool, frozen, masklike facial expressions appear in many African warrior sects' rituals and dance performances.

> Playing it cool protects one's chance of survival and enhances self-esteem. A cool pose can be used as a form of protection against White authorities. The man—police and other symbols of White authority—can be thrown off balance by a carefully staged cool performance. *Cool Pose* serves as a guide for behavior under the kind of pressure that might occur during an encounter with the police or a boss. (Majors & Billson, 1992, p. 38)

The word "cool," which is defined as intersecting race, class, and gender (Wilkins, 2008). and its inclusion in cool behavior has been the spark that has inflamed many negative interactions between Black males and teachers as well as police officers, which have contributed to the school-to-prison pipeline (Majors and Billinson, 1992). Black males specifically are removed from classrooms for nonviolent behavioral offenses (Majors & Billson, 1992) such as talking back, scowling, and not sitting still. Black students, in general, are more likely to be suspended for nonviolent offenses such as disruption or truancy (Fabelo et al., 2011); moreover, the overrepresentation of Black students in suspensions can start as early as preschool (Office of Civil Rights, 2015; CBS, 2014). The suspension rates of African American males are a reason for concern because school suspensions frequently lead to underachievement, juvenile detentions, and future arrests.

The quiet stoicism offered by a cool pose that includes a straight face and piercing stares is often interpreted as challenging and, even worse, insubordinate by teachers, most of whom are White females, as well as by police officers (Kunjufu, 1986). Nonviolent offenses, such as noncompliance, create many microaggressions between White teachers and Black male students even when they are not suspended or expelled, making school uncomfortable for both students and teachers (Majors, Cook, & Read, 2011). For this reason, many African American males feel that school is not a welcoming place and immerse themselves in a state of being that affirms their cool pose identity and increases disengagement in school (Majors & Billson, 1992). Distancing themselves from uncool activities can have negative implications for how Black males fare in the formal structures of school. Activities that are perceived as uncool are likely to include studying, going on field trips to museums, and relating positively to teachers (Majors & Billson, 1992).

To counter negative reactions to the cool pose, Majors and Billson suggest Afrocentric socialization that encourages teaching children "values emphasizing cooperation, mutual respect, commitment, and love of family, race, community, and nation" (Majors & Billson, 1992, p, 111). An Afrocentric ideology is not anti-White, but advocates an African-centered consciousness that is the antithesis of anything that does not improve the life and well-being of people of African descent (Majors & Billson, 1992). The impetus for Afrocentricity in *Cool Pose: The Dilemmas of Black Manhood in America* stems from the premise that if Black males and White teachers both knew more about African and African American history, school would become a more amenable place.

Analysis and Discussion

The intention of this study was to provide an overview of eight Black males who have influenced the field of education using the framework of emancipatory education. Emancipatory education is a process that liberates a person mentally and encourages socially conscious action. The results suggest that Douglass, DuBois, Washington, Woodson, Asante, Kunjufu, Cross, and Majors in some way (1) experienced a liberating educational event that reinterpreted their identity—both in terms of how they saw themselves and how others perceived them; (2) experienced a culturally conscious self-reflective process that informed their writing; and (3) encouraged critical examination of social conditions to reinterpret society's way of understanding the world. These three themes are all examples of an emancipatory educational experience. The journey of self-reflection, critical consciousness, and praxis is not always an individual experience. Knowledge is a process of inquiry that "emerges only through invention and re-invention . . . human beings pursue in the world, with the world, and with each other" (Freire, 1972, p. 58). Each of these founders, to borrow a phrase from James Baldwin (2017), "banged against and reveal each other."[3] For example, many of these founders mentioned one another in their writings, and they all in some way reflected on the particular notion of what it means to be Black and American.

Summary of Findings

Douglass was consistent with Freire (2007), who believed that only by combining critical self-reflection with active participation in the struggle to end oppression can oppressed people find freedom. Douglass sounded the drum for both an emancipatory life and an emancipatory education. After learning how to read, Douglass was able to critically analyze his world and ask the question: "What to a slave Is the Fourth of July?" A former slave, he realized that Blacks in his day were not considered American; he worked for and encouraged others to abolish slavery and allow Blacks to vote. Douglass used the guilty conscious of Americans who fought during the Revolutionary War and the Civil War to expand their language to include slaves in the term "American" because Black Americans fought in both wars and should be free from slavery, and should have the right to vote. For Douglass, emancipatory education meant an educated Black man could find emancipation from slavery through literacy.

As the first African American to graduate from Harvard with a PhD, DuBois was keenly aware that Blacks looked at the world through a type of double consciousness of being both Black and African American. DuBois used double consciousness as a lens to recognize African American oppression and to change it. For DuBois, emancipatory education meant full social access through education and informed social action (Freire, 1971).

Washington learned that education had the ability to elevate a Black man and saw racism as intrinsically tied to economics. He felt that progress for Blacks required that they work together with Whites because they controlled the money, and until Blacks had financial stability, they would not be free. This perspective was congruent with Bell (1992), who called the phenomenon where Whites only supported Black progress if it benefited White needs "interest convergence." For Washington, emancipatory education meant Black progress that stemmed from economic independence.

Witnessing favoritism in colleges based on biased assumptions of Black people's competency, Woodson saw firsthand that both Blacks and Whites were misinformed about Black people in America. Woodson knew that by teaching Black people their true history he could raise their consciousness and encourage them to continue to find greatness (Freire, 1972). Woodson also encouraged African Americans to educate themselves whenever possible to enact social change. For Woodson, emancipatory education meant education in the form of higher education as well as self-sustainability through understanding Black history.

Asante felt that being both African and African American was not enough. Blacks in America needed to acknowledge their spiritual heritage to achieve a complete state of elevated consciousness. By focusing on African thought in both words and action, Asante knew that history needed to be taught with a lens completely free of any perspective other than being African centered. Freire (1972) also advocated for people to be the narrators and participants in their own lives, utilizing their own experiences and worldviews. Asante used the hidden cultural consciousness of Africa to awaken a newly framed African American heritage. For Asante, emancipatory education meant liberation from the captivity of racist language and culture.

Kunjufu advocated for Blacks to be liberated from dehumanizing conditions in the classroom. Far too many Black boys suffer from far too few choices in school. Bell (2005) asserted that lack of equitable resources led to Black males who gravitate to the cultural resources of both Black and White social acceptance by being a popular athlete. Teachers and parents need to acknowledge the dilemma that social pressures force many Black males to choose between being popular or smart. For Kunjufu, emancipatory education meant that Black boys needed to realize that there were more opportunities in life than just playing sports or dropping out of school.

Cross reviewed previous literature about African American identity and concluded that most of the perspectives were neither objective nor very nuanced. Based on personal experiences, he knew that Black identity encompassed more than various forms of self-hatred. Cross discussed the difference between the awareness of self as conceptualized in the White man's eye and the realization of who you really are as a Black male in your mind and truly embracing yourself. The tension between knowing who you are and understanding the perception of how others see you is a struggle that can lead to informed social activism (Freire, 1972). For Cross, emancipatory education meant understanding the journey of transition from Negro to Black.

Majors was attuned to misalignments between student and teacher expectations that often resulted in Black males being suspended or expelled more than other groups. Many of the offenses were for nonviolent offenses that where often racially subjectively interpreted. Majors realized that many Black makes adopted the cool pose as a means of protection against cultural and gender assimilation or regulation. Additionally, Freire (1972) argued that the cool pose was a form of resistance to embrace the behavior of the oppressor. For Majors, emancipatory education meant accepting the fact that the Black male adopted the cool pose as a means of emotional and physical protection as well as psychological resistance against oppression.

Education alone is not transformative, but a critical self-reflective education does start the journey towards liberation. Douglass, DuBois, Washington, Woodson, Asante, Kunjufu, Cross, and Majors each experienced a self-reflective process that influenced his way of making authentic meaning for himself. Consequently, they were centered in their understanding of self and embraced their identity-shifts as they interfaced with the world around them. The result of their self-reflections allowed them to critically examine society and advocate for change through speeches, debates, writings, and lectures. Freire (2007) referred to this form of emancipatory education as conscientization—raising people's consciousness and praxis—reflection linked to political action. By combining conscious self-reflection and dialogue with active participation in the struggle to end oppression, oppressed people can find the freedom to be active participants in their own stories.

In this chapter, emancipatory education was the most salient factor for analysis. Emancipatory education liberates people from oppression and empowers them to change the world through informed action (Apps, 1985). The results of this research suggest that the self-reflective and critical awareness that Douglass, DuBois, Washington, Woodson, Asante, Kunjufu, Cross, and Majors experienced allowed them to perceive their realities in a way that enabled them to enact change for the betterment of their society; these are key elements of emancipatory education. Self-identity and reflection are influential elements for both student and teacher development and social justice. Therefore, Frederick Douglass, W. E. B. DuBois, Booker T. Washington, Molefi Asante, Carter G. Woodson, Jawanza Kunjufu, William Cross, and Richard Majors are suitable founders to study in the field of education.

■ Notes

1. Freire was born in 1921 in Recife, Pernambuco, Brazil. He graduated from Recife's school of law in 1947 and completed his doctorate at the University of Recife in 1947. When Freire died in 1997, he had traveled and worked extensively in both Latin American and Africa. Freire's work as an educator in rural farm areas and exposure to Marxism, combined with his Christian beliefs, heavily influenced his views on education of the oppressed. Freire was uncommonly successful at raising the literacy rate of farmworkers. Freire believed the ability to change oneself and one's situation for the better is brought about by the freedom language gives people to narrate their own lives.

2. Bell was born in 1930 in Pennsylvania and died in 2011. Bell was the first one in his family to go to college, receiving his AB in 1952 from Duquesne University and his LLB (in 1957 from the University of Pittsburgh School of Law. An officer in the air force and head of the NAACP Legal Defense and Educational Fund, Bell was the first tenured Black professor at Harvard Law School and eventually became dean. Bell advocated for the voices of people of color to be included in conversations that affect them, especially in matters related to positive educational outcomes for African Americans.

3. This is taken from an audio recording of James Baldwin in the film *I Am Not Your Negro* and has no page number.

■ References

Akbar, N. (1998). *Know thy self.* Tallahassee, FL: Mind Productions.

Apps, J. W. (1985). *Improving practice in continuing education: Modern approaches to understanding the field and determining priorities.* San Francisco: Jossey-Bass.

Asante, M. (1991). The Afrocentric idea in education. *Journal of Negro Education 60*(2), 170–80.

———. (2002). *100 greatest African Americans: A biographical encyclopedia.* Amherst, NY: Prometheus Books.

———. (2003). *Afrocentricity: The theory of social change.* Chicago: African American Images.

———. (2008a). *Afrocentricity. World Ages Archives.* Http://www.worldagesarchive.com/Reference_Links/Afrocentricity.htm.

———. (2008b, November). DuBois and Africa: The convergence of consciousness. Lecture delivered at the University of Northern British Columbia, Prince George British Columbia.

Baldwin, J. (Writer), Peck. R. (Director). (2017). *I am not your Negro.* Berlin: Velvet Films.

Bell, D. (1993). *Faces at the bottom of the well: The permanence of racism.* New York: Basic Books.

———. (2005). *Silent covenants:* Brown v. Board of Education *and the unfulfilled hopes for racial reform.* New York: Oxford University Press.

Berkshire Publishing Group. (2007). Du Bois: How to spell it how to say it. *W. E. B. Du Bois Global Resource Collection.* Http://www.duboisweb.org/.

CBS News. (2014, March 21). Black students more likely to be suspended—even in preschool. Http://www.cbsnews.com/news/education-department-Black-preschoolers-more-likely-to-be-suspended/.

Creelman, J. (1865, September 19). The effect of Booker T. Washington's Atlanta speech. *New York World.* Http://digital.archives.alabama.gov/cdm/ref/collection/voices/id/6603.

Cross, W. E. (1971). Negro-to-Black conversion experience: Toward a psychology of Black liberation. *Black World 20*(9), 13–27.

———. (1991). *Shades of black: Diversity in African-American identity.* Philadelphia: Temple University Press.

Douglass, F. (1845). *Narrative of the life of Frederick Douglass.* Boston: Anti-Slavery Office.

———. (1852). The meaning of July Fourth to the Negro. History is a weapon. Http://www.historyisaweapon.com/defcon1/douglassjuly4.html.

———. (1857, August 3). The significance of emancipation in the West Indies. Speech, Canandaigua, New York. In J. W. Blassingame (ed.). *The Frederick Douglass papers*, Series 1: *Speeches, debates, and interviews*, vol. 3: *1855–63*. New Haven: Yale University Press.

———. ([1865] 2007). In what new skin will the old snake come forth? In J. W. Blassingame (ed.), *The Frederick Douglass papers*, Series 1: *Speeches, debates, and interviews*, vol. 4. New Haven: Yale University Press.

———. (1892). *The life and times of Frederick Douglass.* Boston: De Wolfe & Fiske.

DuBois, W. E. B. ([1868] 1999). *Darkwater: Voices from within the veil.* New York: Dover Publications.

———. ([1899] 1967). *The Philadelphia Negro: A social study.* New York: Benjamin Bloom.

———. ([1903] 1994). *The souls of Black folk.* New York: Dover.

———. (1935). *Black reconstruction: An essay toward a history of the part which Black folk played in the attempt to reconstruct democracy in America, 1860–1880.* New York: Russell & Russell.

———. (1949) The freedom to Learn. *Midwest Journal 2*, 9–11.

Fabelo, T., Thompson, M., Plotkin, M., Carmichael, D., Marchbanks, M., & Booteh, E. (2011). Breaking schools' rules: A statewide study of how school discipline relates to students' success and juvenile justice involvement. Public Policy Research Institute, Texas A&M University.

Faqs.org. (2014). Peer pressure. Http://www.faqs.org/health/topics/76/Peer-pressure.html.

Freire, P. ([1992] 2007). *Pedagogy of the oppressed.* New York: Continuum.

———. (1972). *Pedagogy of the oppressed.* New York: Penguin Books.

———. (1995) *Pedagogy of hope: Reliving "Pedagogy of the Oppressed".* New York: Continuum.

Johnson, A. (1976). A history and interpretation of the William Edward Burghardt Du Bois–Booker Taliaferro Washington higher educational controversy. Doctoral dissertation, University of Southern California.

Johnson, K. (2000, May 26). *The peer effect on academic achievement among public elementary students.* CDA Report No. 00-06. Heritage Center for Data Analysis, Heritage Foundation, Washington, DC.

Kunjufu, J. (1985). *Countering the conspiracy to destroy Black boys.* Vol. 1. Chicago: African American Images.

——— . (1986). *Countering the conspiracy to destroy Black boys.* Vol. 2. Chicago: African American Images.

——— . (1990). *Countering the conspiracy to destroy Black boys.* Vol. 3. Chicago: African American Images.

Lampe, G. (1995). *Frederick Douglass: Freedom's voice, 1818–1845.* East Lansing: Michigan State University Press.

Majors, R., & Billson, J. M. (1992). *Cool pose: The dilemmas of Black manhood in America.* New York: Lexington Books.

Ojokheta, J. (2007). Paulo Freire's literacy teaching methodology: Application and implications of the methodology in basic literacy classes in Ibadan, Oyo State, Nigeria. *Adult Education and Development 69*(10), 111–20.

Tomlinson, C., A. (2007). *How to differentiate instruction in mixed-ability classrooms.* 2nd ed. Alexandria, VA: Association for Supervision and Curriculum Development.

Thompson, R. T. (1973). An aesthetic of the cool. *African Arts, 7*(1), 40–49.

Vandiver, B., J., Cross, W. E., Worrell, F., C., & Fhagen-Smith, P. E. (2002). Validating the cross racial identity scale. Journal of Counseling Psychology 49(1): 71–85.

Washington, B. T. (1895, September 18). Address of Booker T. Washington, principal of the Tuskegee Normal and Industrial Institute, Tuskegee, Alabama, delivered at the Opening of the Cotton States and Industrial Exhibition, at Atlanta, Ga., September 18, 1895. Http://digital.archives.alabama. gov/cdm/singleitem/collection/voices/id/6602/rec/1.

——— . ([1901] 1995). *Up from slavery.* New York: Dover.

Watts, R. J., Griffith, D. M., & Abdul-Adil, J. (1999). Sociopolitical development as an antidote for oppression: Theory and action. *American Journal of Community Psychology 27*(2), 225–40.

Wilkins, A. C. (2008). *Wannabes, goths, and Christians: The boundaries of sex, style and status.* Chicago: University of Chicago Press.

Woodson C. G. (1990). *The mis-education of the Negro.* Washington, DC: African World Press.

Agency and Grit

Fostering the Growth of Black Male Students to Achieve Greatness

Anindya Kundu

The United States celebrates "rugged individualism" (a term coined by Herbert Hoover during his presidency, associated with social Darwinism) as a cultural value believed to be tied to success. This long-standing notion implies that Americans reap what they sow and that individual effort is the key determinant for one's future outcomes. Relatedly, recent research in psychology has introduced "grit" as an important characteristic observable in successful students (Duckworth, 2016). Grit highlights the importance that "passion and persistence toward long-term goals" can have to help students overcome difficulties. Some popular interpretations of this framework reinforce the idea that the onus of achievement should rest upon the individual student (Tough, 2012), which can lead failure to be considered a result of a deficiency on the student. An example of this is quickly assessing underachievement as the result of coming from a culture of academic disinterest, rather than problems with the system (McWhorter, 2000; Patterson, 2015).

Surely individual aptitude, determination, and grit are important to scholastic success and mobility, but should they be viewed as the primary components necessary for greatness? If schools are gardens, such a narrow focus on American individualism might impede the process of growing as many roses as possible. Instead of standing alone, we may be surrounded by plenty of rosebuds that simply need more fertilizer to bloom. Accordingly, it remains critical to acknowledge that systems of support are also needed for success.

In particular, Black male students often find themselves on the short end of the stick when it comes to societal perceptions. Contemporary evidence continues to show that people of color, especially Black and Latino men, have much poorer life outcomes in education, health, income expectancy and more (Noguera, 2009; Patterson, 2015). Men of color are further marginalized from a social-psychology lens because societies tend to conjure up phobias and fetishes toward groups that are disenfranchised (Bhabha, 1994; Noguera, 2009). Black men are twenty-one times more likely to be fatally shot or involved in violent altercations with police than White men (Gabrielson, Sagara & Jones, 2014).

Thus, sociologically, certain *applications* of grit can be limited when working to understand the academic achievement of Black male students: (1) they do not address the social contexts (families, networks, demographics) or structural challenges of the young people whose achievements they assess; and (2) they are not necessarily rooted in a dynamic understanding of these students' cultures, which can change and adapt under different environmental contexts. It is important to realize that Black male students in poverty may have setbacks that keep them from realizing what goals they might be passionate about and persistent toward in their lives.

This chapter is based on a larger research study that applies a social frame to grit research, through locating and recognizing *agency*, to then more broadly understand factors that constitute the success of students of color from low-income households. Agency may be more context-sensitive than grit in understanding how individuals can impact their own lives, especially in the social context of education. This chapter offers the following definition for agency, adopting and synthesizing the work of scholars in sociology and psychology: Agency must be context-specific. While it can manifest through action and outcome, agency can also be promoted by internalized qualities like self-efficacy (Bandura, 1982). Agency can exhibit resistance, as a means of expressing individualism (Genovese, 1976; Kelley, 1996, but more importantly, *successful* agency benefits from critical thinking on one's social position and deliberate efforts taken to change one's circumstances for the better (Freire, 1970; MacLeod, 1987; Kundu, 2016). It is related to the unique circumstances and social position of each person assessing his specific capacities for change (Giroux, 1983; Kundu, 2016).

The larger qualitative study from which this chapter is derived consists of interviewing students ($n = 40$) who have increased their personal agency through experiencing high levels of academic and/or professional success. A subset of Black males ($n = 10$) is extracted from the larger study and examined for the purpose of this chapter. Empirical evidence in social sciences indicates that structural inequalities faced by students with disadvantaged circumstances can make it more difficult for them to succeed than for those from more advantaged backgrounds (Bourdieu & Passeron, 1977; Bowles & Gintis, 2011; Fruchter et al., 2012; Duncan & Murnane, 2014). This implies that successful students from troubled backgrounds likely benefit from both personal and social factors that facilitate their upward mobility.

The "strivers" in this research are not meant to be considered outliers, but rather representatives of possibility for all students. These individuals should not be thought of as *exceptions*, but rather *exceptional*. Also, the term "disadvantage" in this study is not meant to be used in a derogatory or sympathetic manner, but rather a simple admission of the fact that some students in the American educational system are less privileged than others, with race and socioeconomic status being the main characteristics of interest in this research frame. Accordingly, this work will also attempt to use "person-first language" to respect the dignity of participants, for instance, using "students with disabilities" in place of "disabled students" (Blaska, 1993).

This chapter offers contemporary hypotheses on the interplay between grit and agency, which if fostered can increase the achievement of Black male students. To unlock this interplay, the guiding question in this study has been *How do students with initial social and economic disadvantages, who experience levels of success, describe the factors that allow them to navigate obstacles to success?*

Significance in Existing Literature

There is an ongoing debate about whether structural conditions or individuals' abilities are more influential upon one's educational outcomes. Within sociology, structure versus agency can be considered the classic disciplinary dilemma. In the context of education, some scholars emphasize that schools provide enough opportunity for disadvantaged students to achieve, attributing students' failures to exhibiting cultures that reject academics or to individual lack of effort (Ogbu, 1992; McWhorter, 2000). Cultural deficit models have been widely used to explain underachievement, with popular outlets sometimes claiming that low performers are prone to self-sabotage and victimization (Henry, 2015; McWhorter, 2000; Tough, 2012).

Other camps, focused primarily on structural inequalities, contend that social origin and socioeconomic status (SES) trump schooling effects in predicting educational attainment and SES returns (Bourdieu & Passeron, 1977; Bowles & Gintis, 2011). Structural and neo-Marxian accounts often find that within the capitalist ideology and economic system of American societies, schools can serve to reproduce inequity and maintain the status quo (Giroux, 1983; Bowles & Gintis, 2011). And micro-level, interactionist accounts show that disciplinary measures and teacher expectations are often shaped by race and class biases, which can negatively affect the academic tracks that students are on, as well as their likelihood for attending college (Oakes & Guiton, 1985; Delpit, 2012). Furthermore, society can now be considered in more blurry state of "liquid modernity," with less obvious boundaries between institutions, like schools, and groups, like families (Bauman, 2013). With these shifting spheres, there is a greater need for novel approaches to make sense of pedagogy that can shape the sense of self and subsequent achievement of Black males.

Demographic characteristics continue to be dominant predictors of college-readiness levels—with students' race, home zip code, and income levels at the top of the list (Fruchter et al., 2012; Sharkey, 2013; Duncan & Murnane, 2014). In nineteen of New York City's poorest neighborhoods, only 10 percent of seniors graduate from high school college-ready (Fruchter et al., 2012). These neighborhoods are made up of close to 100 percent Black or Latino residents. In contrast, in the wealthiest neighborhoods of Manhattan, the vast majority of students are college-ready. Less than 10 percent of the residents in these neighborhoods are Black or Latino (Fruchter et al., 2012). Furthermore, the graduation rate for Black males in New York City is only 28 percent, which is more than 25 percent lower than the graduation rate for White males. This is increasingly troubling when considering that New York City educates more Black males than any other American city (Superville, 2015).

In education, research to bridge various perspectives and disciplines is needed to expand the understanding of achievement. This chapter reconciles these divided discourses by expanding upon grit research to include the voices of young adults who make for exceptional cases, *experiencing levels of success* in their lives *despite initial disadvantages*. Exceptional cases sometimes serve to substantiate deficit models, viewing achievers as outliers and ostracizing the wider spectrum of underachievers. This research rejects such a narrow view of achievement culture, aiming to show instead that success is possible over wide variability in disadvantages.

Methodology and Data

This chapter adds two components to grit-related considerations through characteristics associated with agency: (1) observing how individuals can learn to navigate opportunity structures (schools, higher education, and enrichment programs) and exhibit help-seeking behavior; and (2) investigating the role of support systems through identifying the role of social and cultural capital in these individuals' lives (Bourdieu, 1986), and hypothesizing how other students can learn to acquire them. Social capital (or resources gained through networks and relationships) and cultural capital (the behavior, knowledge, and skills that are gained and signaled through membership in different groups) are used together as the main theoretical framework for this study to understand how Black males can increase their social mobility.

This study follows sociological methods and student-level analysis of qualitative data that focuses on achievement mind-sets and mobility. The data in this chapter come from face-to-face, semistructured interviews with a sample of mostly young adult participants (ages eighteen to twenty-five) and a few adult participants (ages twenty-five to forty), 10 percent of the sample, who became college students later in life. This chapter pulls quotes from a subset of Black males ($n = 10$) from this study. Students were interviewed with the intention of learning about the individual and social factors that may have fostered their characteristics of grit and agency, while remaining open-ended enough for participants to direct the conversation about their lives and disclose what they felt comfortable. The semistructured method allowed the interviewer to probe at emerging themes when necessary. Interviews were chosen as a data source because the research intended to learn about their life from childhood to present day, including formative events and individuals.

Participants and Sampling

All students voluntarily opted-in to be interviewed, learning about this project from programs that assisted in recruitment. The programs included two after-school enrichment programs in New York City, which select participants through need-based considerations that fit the researcher's selection criteria, and one selective honors program at a New York City community college where the majority of students also are from low-income, and often immigrant, households. All participants grew up in poverty. This selection process located young adults who exhibited grit-mindsets and levels of success amid adversity through the help of support systems. They are all on a path of upward social mobility. By exhibiting these characteristics, these participants also demonstrate agency and improvement of circumstances in their lives.

Data Analysis

Table 1 shows three of the major themes uncovered during the coding process, pertinent to the success of Black male students. These include mental health, networking, and goal formation, all of which were also found important for helping the broader set of students in poverty to succeed academically and professionally. Within each theme, categories were created based on the most prevalent concepts mentioned by participants as important. While the larger research project uncovered more than six overarching themes (yielding more categories and subcategories), this chapter focuses on three themes and six categories that present a more succinct overview for educators and mentors on factors that help youth in poverty or in "at-risk" situations succeed and attain socially mobility.

Findings

The themes and categories in table 1 present some factors, influences, and considerations that facilitate the success of Black male students. The last column includes real quotations from participants in the research project. The first theme, "Mental Health," indicates that Black male students can have a keen awareness of their emotions as well as ability to monitor happiness and depression. Emotional awareness is a finding that serves to contradict the idea that Black boys are less emotional and cold in school settings, and suggests rather that they are emotionally complex (Way, 2011). This may be the result of dealing with many responsibilities from early ages, including taking care of siblings while parents work, helping to pay the family's rent, and overcoming drug addictions or traumatic experiences. Taking one's own mental health-temperature is related to resilience, knowing that negative feelings are fleeting, but also letting them run their course. If educators are not able to form close and genuine relationships with their Black students, they may be less likely to notice mental health issues because students may be less likely to open up.

The "Networking" theme highlights how Black males from poor communities have to learn this skill for themselves, compared to more advantaged students who are often parented in ways that explicitly teach networking (Lareau, 2011). As different networks helped these students receive rewards, the value of networking became apparent. Networks were the most frequently mentioned theme in the larger research project when participants were asked about important life-lessons. These students grew up with access to a very small network of family and peers who shared their social class. Through the help of various mentors (educators and other

Table 1. Three Primary Themes: Mental Health, Networking, Goal Formation

THEME	CATEGORY	DEFINITION	SAMPLE QUOTATION
Mental health	Optimism and contentedness	A sense of hope rooted in having overcome unimaginable circumstances already in life. A steady recognition that even the most difficult of times are transient, especially with the right forward-thinking attitude. This was often accompanied by an ability to put oneself in others' shoes and show empathy and charity toward those in disadvantaged situations.	I haven't had the hardest road to travel, when compared to other people. Who am I to complain? There's always solutions—everything has a solution. Even when I'm weak or I feel like I didn't do enough and failed, I feel like it's okay because I'll do better tomorrow. I got air in my lungs, I'm breathing. I got my kid next to me and family. That's what I focus on if I have negative thoughts. Obstacles make you stronger. The tougher the obstacle, the stronger you come out on the end.
	Trauma	A burden that continues to linger long after traumatic experiences are experienced. Participants stated that there is no completely overcoming such trauma; just learning to acknowledge one's mental health and learn ways to practice being uninhibited. A form of grit and resilience, knowing that depression will pass, and not to act impulsively on sad emotions.	I've seen the strongest guy in the room, lifting four or five hundred pounds, becoming weak at seeing his little girl, on a visiting floor. Or when he's sentenced to forty years. And then, the opposite, being able to do five, ten years in solitary confinement, and walk out of there with your head up. Although you can't lift the eight hundred pounds in the yard, there is strength there. That resilience, that ability to bounce back, despite the fact that life has beaten you up and tried to hammer you down, and you still wake up every day.
Networks	Circle-jumping	Learn to navigate from one network to another. Through signaling cultural capital gains from one group, students can "jump" into other circles comfortably, thereby also increasing their social capital and ability to formulate future goals, from meeting new people. This is a reproductive phenomenon.	I learned things about myself and learned what I didn't know. When you first go in they help you fine-tune skills: time management, email etiquette, communication. I learned I was good at it. Especially good at relationship building. My instructor told me that I was great at networking.
	Value realized over time	The value of networks and networking was stated as a lesson learned over time. The more that networks benefited participants, the more they learned to use networks to their advantage. Once results of networking are positively reinforced by rewards, networks are seen as critical to mobility.	I actually draw my network out. I put "network" in the middle and then put little lines to say, "I know this person that works here." It's something that I use as a tool. The goal is to add two to three people every year.
Goal formation	Horse to water	The concept that students need to be made aware of the vast array of potential opportunities in front of them. Still, this realization cannot be forced and requires guided, firsthand experiences. Sometimes goals are hard to visualize, if students can't imagine themselves in other shoes.	They say you can lead a horse to water, but you can't make it drink. But it's even more scary when you lead a horse to water and they say, "What water?" I was the horse who didn't see the ocean in front of them. You tell me to drink, it's not a conscious decision that I'm making. I really am ignorant to the fact that what is in front of me is water. In every story, we have to understand that the person may not see that this is a good option. They may not understand that this is water that they're looking at. So when we say, "Drink the water, go to college, don't commit crime, listen to your parents," they're like, "What? What water? I don't get it."
	Passion related to origin	Students are more able to form goals to be passionate toward, if they are somehow relatable to their origin and heritage. Helps with the visualization necessary in "Horse-to-water theme."	We'd have students from NYU teach us the SATs. They were students of color. They looked like us, they sounded like us, and they were in college, doing big things. They were adults, they were cool, they were suave, and we wanted to be just like them. And we didn't see that. I didn't see any kids from college or anything like that. So just seeing these kids was amazing.

influencers), these students were able to expand their networks. In particular, circle-jumping, a phenomenon coined in this study, highlights how social and cultural capital can tangibly be used to navigate from one network to another, as individuals pick up skills and characteristics, like using proper email etiquette, to propel themselves toward various goals. The student whose quotation is used in this category recalls how he used tools from his first internship to eventually land his current position doing compliance work for a major private bank.

"Goal Formation" is particularly important when considering the grit and effort Black males put toward achieving goals. As illustrated in the "Horse to Water" category and example, it can sometimes be hard for these students to set reasonable goals from lack of experience and understanding of available opportunities available. At the same time, when Black male students are provided clearer pathways for striving, they can realize their importance quickly, and remain diligent until a goal is achieved. These opportunities and pathways become clearer and most effective to students when they are associated with the student's background, making them easier to relate to. The themes in this study will be elaborated further in the "Discussion" section, which provides concrete takeaways for educators.

Discussion

Through studying these students' increased agency, this research framework generated hypotheses on how to understand the success of Black males from disadvantaged backgrounds, and how they can critically think about challenges in their lives. The stories heard explained how students from low-income households learned to first be aware of systemic problems that directly affected their lives, and then how they conceptualized strategies for navigating around them. This is closely related to Freire's (1970) "praxis": students reflect on their limit situations in the process of becoming emancipated from them, while also expanding their worldview. This can influence their future thinking and action in new circumstances as they strive for mobility in their lives.

Attempting to understand students' views and actions on a dynamic scale implies respecting their unique personhood. Each person's social origin is important to consider and address when crafting scaffolded, effective strategies for growing grit and agency toward specific goals. This can be a particularly important perspective to have in educational contexts, where teaching and learning are social processes between students and teachers (Freire, 1970). Black students in poverty do not simply underperform because of socioeconomic factors and because wealthier students attend wealthier schools. Rather, there is also an intricate interexchange of lifelong knowledge, skills, and social networks and other factors, between schools, families, and students that contributes to the disparate outcomes, manifest through hidden curriculum in schools and societal constructs in the outside world (Noguera, 2003; Patterson, 2015).

There are specific takeaways for educators and other stakeholders in the lives of youth from the three themes mentioned in this chapter. "Mental Health" and categories of "Optimism & Contentedness" and "Trauma" intend to show how complex the socioemotional lives of these students can be. Black males from poor backgrounds tend to be resilient, having faced a number of challenges at home early on, like hunger, but at the same time can keep feelings to themselves at young ages. Educators should try to understand their emotional states, but not from an overbearing perspective. Being a soundboard is seen as immensely valuable to these students. If possible, school leaders should work to avoid excessive disciplinary punishment, but focus on increasing access to mental health resources for at-risk youth. In general, students of minority backgrounds have been found disproportionately tracked toward suspension, expulsion, and eventual dropping out (Ransaw & Majors, 2016).

For "Networking" it is important to remember that teachers are often a first link for students with disadvantages to expand their network. Teachers, whether they realize it or not, have opportunities to connect their students to other networks. Teachers can work to connect students to resources that align with their interests, using academic motivators and incentives. One participant in this study mentioned that his English teacher started his "circle-jumping" process, whereby she connected him to an internship after he turned in all of his homework for her class.

Students benefit from being connected to other adults who can serve as mentors and role models, or structured environments like after-school programs, which can be immensely beneficial for students' positive behavior adjustments and academic performance (Durlak & Weissberg, 2007). If Black male students are able to see their network expand, they can be quick to work harder to keep growing their list of contacts and subsequent skills. Through mentors and new opportunities students can increase their social and cultural capital, signaling cues that tend to be rewarded by greater society.

Finally, "Goal Formation" may be the closest concept associated with grit and agency, and the subsequent mobility of students. The manners in which educators craft curricula can have an influence in students being able to form realistic yet challenging goals, as well as follow through with them. Even though Black male students may actually believe schools work for most students, they may have trouble seeing education benefiting their own lives (Mickelson, 1990). To resolve this discrepancy and also foster their feelings of self-worth, educators should try to incorporate relatable subject material into their lessons. For instance, Black students are found to benefit greatly from learning about historical Black figures across disciplines to be able to envision themselves succeeding in different fields (Kafele, 2009). Also, as indicated by the quotation in the "Passion related to origin" category, when students are provided access to mentors who resemble them (by race and background), they are more likely to form academic goals and mind-sets.

Conclusion

This research highlights strategies that can be used to help young Black male scholars achieve agency, increasing their ability to enact their own free will toward success. This is different from popular applications of research on grit that sometimes argue that students who fail lack "gritty" resiliency (Tough, 2012). On the contrary, this chapter serves to show that success is possible for Black students who face a range of disadvantages, including but not limited to low-income and single-parent households; parents who have struggled with substance abuse, or participants who themselves have struggled with substance abuse; and subjects who have been previously been homeless or incarcerated or have suffered from ongoing trauma from very sensitive life experiences, such as traumatic violence.

Accordingly, the males in this study possess high levels of grit, yet their grit toward certain goals was found to increase over time as they learned to navigate success in different settings. This is important for educators and adults in the lives of Black male students to acknowledge; instead of explaining underachievement primarily as the result of individual-level factors such as laziness or lack of motivation, we can argue that with the right systems of support, all students can learn to thrive.

Finding commonalities among students who defy expectations is a fairly unique approach in sociology. In fact, much existing research takes a strong structural viewpoint, asking why students with disadvantages fail, not how they are able to succeed (Bowles & Gintis, 2011). Within existing research that seeks to address what makes academic success possible, relatively few projects synthesize both social and individual factors by allowing them to build off each other. This project has aspired to synthesize these factors and present a more holistic understanding of what factors constitute scholastic success of Black males within educational environments.

The importance of structured school-environments for Black males growing up in poverty cannot be overstated. These students are in greater need for safe spaces that facilitate their developmental growth and provide enriching resources like adult supervision (Noguera, 2003; Ransaw & Majors, 2016). While it is true that schools in low-resource communities have a plethora of factors that make the jobs of educational leaders very challenging, they should take solace in recognizing the potential for their schools and classrooms to positively benefit the lives of many youth. By focusing on increasing the agency and grit of Black males, educators can meet these students' needs on a more direct and individualized basis, as well as foster students' abilities to achieve goals and increase their social mobility.

The egalitarian hope is that all students will develop into contributing citizens through education. But for education to work for Black males, educators must respect and try to understand their individual empirical realities, and the circumstances of their origin, to then be able to foster their unique growth. Because students who are increasingly marginalized—those of color from low-income backgrounds—experience the greater threats to forming their academic identities, grit alone is unlikely to account for increased upward mobility (Hanselman et al., 2014; Ransaw & Majors, 2016). Grit is immensely necessary in the formula for achievement; however, the ability to fire on all cylinders is not fully possible without also considering agency. Without agency, students cannot realize their *purpose* for setting certain goals, and their reasons for reaching them. If grit is the water that allows flowers to show bursts of growth, agency might be the sunlight needed to regularly nourish hope and fulfillment.

And if our options are between wilting separately or learning to grow together, the choice should be an easy one. Hope is the best motivator to realize our collective responsibilities to try harder for each student.

■ **References**

Bandura, A. (1982). Self-efficacy mechanism in human agency. *American Psychologist 37*(2), 122.

Bauman, Z. (2013). *Liquid modernity*. New York: John Wiley & Sons.

Bhabha, H. (1994). The postcolonial and the postmodern. *The Location of Culture*. New York: Routledge.

Blaska, J. (1993). The power of language: Speak and write using "person first." In M. Nagler (ed.), *Perspectives on disability: Text and readings*, 25–32. Palo Alto: Health Markets Research.

Bourdieu, P. (1986). The forms of capital. In J. Richardson (ed.), *Handbook of theory and research for the sociology of education*, 241–58. New York: Greenwood.

Bourdieu, P., & Passeron, J. C. (1977). *Reproduction in education, culture and society*. Thousand Oaks, CA: Sage/

Bowles, S., & Gintis, H. (2011). *Schooling in capitalist America: Educational reform and the contradictions of economic life*. Chicago: Haymarket Books.

Carter, P. L. (2005). *Keepin' it real: School success beyond Black and White*. Oxford University Press.

Coleman, J. S. (1988). Social capital in the creation of human capital. *American Journal of Sociology 94*, S95–S120.

Delpit, L. D. (2012). *"Multiplication is for White people": Raising expectations for other people's children*. New York: New Press.

Duckworth, A. L. (2016). *Grit: The power of passion and perseverance*. New York: Simon and Schuster.

Duckworth, A. L., Peterson, C., Matthews, M. D., & Kelly, D. R. (2007). Grit: Perseverance and passion for long-term goals. *Journal of Personality and Social Psychology 92*(6), 1087.

Duncan, G. J., & Murnane, R. J. (2014). *Restoring opportunity: The crisis of inequality and the challenge for American education*. Cambridge, MA: Harvard Education Press.

Durlak, J. A., & Weissberg, R. P. (2007). *The impact of after-school programs that promote personal and social skills*. Collaborative for Academic, Social, and Emotional Learning.

Freire, P. (1970). *Pedagogy of the oppressed*. Trans. M. B. Ramos. New York: Continuum.

Fruchter, N., Hester, M., Mokhtar, C., & Shahn, Z. (2012). Is demography still destiny? Neighborhood demographics and public high school students' readiness for college in New York City. A research and policy brief. Annenberg Institute for School Reform at Brown University.

Gabrielson, R., Sagara, E., & Jones, R. G. (2014). Deadly force, in black and white. ProPublica, October 10. Https://www.propublica.org/article/deadly-force-in-black-and-white.

Genovese, Eugene D. (1976). *Roll, Jordan, roll: The world the slaves made*. New York: Vintage.

Giroux, H. (1983). Theories of reproduction and resistance in the new sociology of education: A critical analysis. *Harvard Educational Review 53*(3), 257–93.

Hanselman, P., Bruch, S. K., Gamoran, A., & Borman, G. D. (2014). Threat in context: School moderation of the impact of social identity threat on racial/ethnic achievement gaps. *Sociology of Education 87*(2), 106–24.

Henry, W. A., III. (2015). *In defense of elitism*. New York: Anchor.

Kafele, B. K. (2009). *Motivating Black males to achieve in school & in life*. Alexandria, VA: ASCD.

Kelley, R. (1996). *Race rebels: Culture, politics, and the Black working class*. Simon and Schuster.

Kundu, A. (2016). Roses in concrete: A perspective on how agency and grit can foster the success of all students, especially those most disadvantaged. *Journal of School & Society 3*(2), 18–31.

LaCapra, D. (1972). *Émile Durkheim: Sociologist and philosopher*. Ithaca, NY: Cornell University Press.

Lareau, A. (2011). *Unequal childhoods: Class, race, and family life*. 2nd ed. Berkeley: University of California Press.

MacLeod, J. (1987). *Ain't no makin' it: Leveled aspirations in a low-income neighborhood*. Boulder, CO: Westview Press.

McWhorter, J. H. (2000). *Losing the race: Self-sabotage in Black America*. New York: Simon and Schuster.

Mickelson, R. A. (1990). The attitude-achievement paradox among Black adolescents. *Sociology of education 63*(1), 44–61.

Noguera, P. A. (2003). *City schools and the American dream: Reclaiming the promise of public education*. New York: Teachers College Press.

———. (2009). *The trouble with Black boys . . . and other reflections on race, equity, and the future of public education*. New York: John Wiley & Sons.

Oakes, J., & Guiton, G. (1995). Matchmaking: The dynamics of high school tracking decisions. *American Educational Research Journal 32*(1), 3–33.

Ogbu, J. U. (1992). Understanding cultural diversity and learning. *Educational Researcher 21*(8), 5–14.

Patterson, O. (2015). *The cultural matrix: Understanding Black youth*. Cambridge, MA: Harvard University Press.

Ransaw, T. S., & Majors, R. (eds.). (2016). *Closing the education achievement gaps for African American males*. East Lansing: Michigan State University Press.

Seligman, M. E. (2002). Positive psychology, positive prevention, and positive therapy. In C. R. Snyder & S. J. Lopez (eds.), *Handbook of Positive Psychology*, 3–12. New York: Oxford University Press.

Sharkey, P. (2013). *Stuck in place: Urban neighborhoods and the end of progress toward racial equality*. Chicago: University of Chicago Press.

Superville, D. R. (2015). Graduation rates rise; gap between black and white males grows, report says. *District Dossier*, February 11. Http://blogs.edweek.org/edweek/District_Dossier/2015/02/as_nation_graduation_rate_grew.html.

Tough, P. (2012). *How children succeed*. New York: Random House.

Way, N. (2011). *Deep secrets*. Cambridge, MA: Harvard University Press.

Black Learners' Perseverance with Mathematics

A Qualitative Metasynthesis

Robert Q. Berry III and Kateri Thunder

Black learners who take advanced mathematics courses are more likely to earn high achievement scores, enroll in college, pursue STEM majors in college, and complete bachelor's degrees (National Science Board [NSB], 2012). The literature on the course enrollment patterns of Black learners shows that the percentage of Black learners enrolled in high-level mathematics courses has not significantly changed over time. Moreover, Black learners are more likely to report enrollment in lower-level courses and less likely to report studying higher-level courses than students of other ethnicities (NSB, 2012). Data from the 2011 National Assessment of Educational Progress for eighth-grade mathematics indicate that Black learners, who make up 16 percent of the overall eighth-grade population, were overrepresented in the lowest quartile of score bands, comprising 28 percent of this group, and grossly underrepresented in the highest quartile, comprising just 5 percent of this segment (Snyder & Dillow, 2012). Despite the highly documented underachievement and low-level course enrollment patterns of Black learners, not all of them achieve at low levels. In fact, many do quite well and stand in opposition to the literature documenting failure and underachievement. There is limited research, however, that focuses on Black learners in mathematics education who experience success. For these reasons, the purpose of this chapter is to present findings of a qualitative metasynthesis focused on Black learners' perseverance in negotiating the K–12 mathematics experiences that contributed toward their mathematics identities over time.

Much of the research related to Black learners focuses on the gap in achievement between Black and White learners. Focusing on an achievement gap often drives research agendas that situate Black children as deficient. The implicit message is that Black children are not worth studying in their own right and that a comparison group is necessary. Such framing situates whiteness as the norm and positions Black learners and Black culture as deviant (Gutierrez, 2008). However, there is a growing body of research that positions Black learners as capable of achieving in mathematics at high levels (Berry, 2008; Berry, Thunder, & McClain, 2011; Jett, 2011; Martin, 2006, 2008; Noble 2011; Stinson, 2008; Thompson & Lewis, 2005). This body of research considers issues of race, racism, contexts, identities, agency, and perseverance as variables that impact the mathematical experiences of Black learners. This growing body of research is relatively small but an important contribution that challenges the dominant discourse and pushes the field of mathematics education to consider sociological, anthropological, and critical theories.

Since the late 1990s, there has been significant growth in the use of qualitative research methodologies for examining the mathematical experiences of Black learners; however, little is known about how this body of work contributes toward providing evidence for supporting positive mathematics experiences for Black learners (Berry, Pinter & McClain, 2013). There is insufficient work on how to integrate or synthesize findings across qualitative studies related to the mathematical experiences of Black learners. This chapter uses qualitative metasynthesis to discuss Black learners' perseverance in negotiating the K–12 mathematics experiences that contributed toward their mathematics identities over time. This chapter is organized as follows: We first describe our theoretical framework. Second, we describe qualitative metasynthesis by providing a definition and rationale for using qualitative metasynthesis. Third, we describe the methods for conducting a qualitative metasynthesis. Fourth, we describe our findings. Finally, we reflect on the findings by answering the following research question: In what ways do Black learners negotiate their experiences to persevere with mathematics across time?

Theoretical Framework

Conceptualizing mathematics learning and participation as "racialized forms of experience" provides space for a research approach that frames learning and participation as the intersection between race, identities, agency, and perseverance for Black learners (Martin, 2009). *Racialized forms of experience* are defined as "experiences in which the socially constructed meanings for race in society emerge as highly salient in structuring (1) the way that mathematical experiences and opportunities to learn unfold and are interpreted, and (2) the manner in which mathematics literacy and competency are framed, including who is perceived to be mathematically literate and who is not" (Martin, 2009, p. 324). Within race-based frameworks, it is necessary to consider discriminatory experiences as potentially subjugating Black learners; many Black learners resist subjugation by utilizing agency-related behaviors based on a belief that mathematics knowledge is important to helping understand and change the circumstances of their lives and communities. Thus, a high sense of agency can be conceptualized as perseverance.

Martin (2009) argues that what is needed in mathematics education are theoretical frameworks and research methods that move beyond static notions of race to acknowledge that mathematics participation can be viewed as *racialized forms of experience*. In conceptualizing *racialized forms of experience*, Martin (2009) conceptualizes issues of identity—racial, cultural, gender, mathematical identity—and agency as centrally important when seeking to better understand how learners make sense of, and respond to, their mathematical experiences. Martin (2009) proposes a theory that conceptualizes *racialized forms of experience* as an approach to informing research, policy, and practices in mathematics education based on four constructs:

1. Conceptualizations of race: Race as a sociopolitical construction; historically contingent nature of race; and consideration of racism and racialization
2. Conceptualizations of learners: Consideration of the negotiated nature of identity with respect to mathematics
3. Research, policy, and practice orientations to race: Consideration of everyday institutional and structural racism
4. Aims and goals of mathematics education research, policy, and practice: Empowerment and liberation from oppression for marginalized learners

Within these four constructs, identity, agency, and perseverance are central to understanding how learners make sense of and respond to ways they learn and participate within their mathematical experiences. While identity is overtly mentioned, agency and perseverance can be conceptualized in the way marginalized learners garner a sense of empowerment and liberation from oppression. That is, as Black learners encounter resistance, how might they use agency and perseverance relative to the resistance they encounter? Using *racialized forms of experience* as a framework allows researchers to use learner-centered and identity-related conceptions of race and participations (Martin, 2009). This chapter uses this framework to understand Black learners' interwoven identities and how these learners exhibit agency to develop a sense of control for self-exploration. This chapter also uses this framework to examine how these learners assert their own identities to consciously make decisions about ways to persevere and engage in mathematics.

Identities

Knowing the stories of learners provides the context for understanding, feeling, and interpreting the identities to which they give voice. Voice is identity—having a sense of self, a sense of purpose, and a sense of relationship to others. Learners announce to the world who they think they are, who they see themselves becoming, how others see them, and how they act as a result of these understandings, feeling, and interpretations. Identity is a dynamic and context-driven construct that changes, grows, and evolves over time (Aguirre, Mayfield-Ingram, & Martin, 2013). Identities include early identifications with college attendance and careers, such as doctors, scientists, teachers, engineers, or mathematicians. Such identification is important because it serves as a source of strength and motivation for explaining why some learners persevere and do well in school, and specifically in mathematics (Martin, 2008). For example, in Berry (2008, p. 482), Andre, a Black learner, stated, "I want to go to the Air Force Academy and become a pilot. You have to be good at math to get into the Academy." This short example, along with other interviews and observations, reveals that Andre negotiates several interwoven identities (e.g., academic identity, mathematics identity, racial identity, and future occupational identity) that are important to him and that these identities serve as motivations for him to persevere and do well with mathematics. When learners identify themselves as participatory and doers of mathematics, they make positive connections and are motivated to achieve at high levels (Martin, 2009). This understanding of learners' identities gives insights into how and why some learners might make positive connections with mathematics, while others do not (Aguirre et al., 2013).

Mathematics identity includes beliefs about oneself as a mathematics learner, one's perceptions of how others perceive one as a mathematics learner, beliefs about the nature of mathematics, engagement in mathematics, and perception of self as a potential participant in mathematics (Solomon, 2009). For example, in Berry (2008), seven of the eight Black boys in this study expressed a strong mathematics identity indicating that they were "good at mathematics." These boys were confident about their mathematics ability, and they perceived that their abilities allowed them to be among the "smart kids." By identifying themselves as being "smart kids," these boys positioned themselves as members of a particular group with certain behavioral and social expectations. From their perceptions, smart kids do their work, answer questions and participate in class, and are good at mathematics. These behaviors are identity-affirming by teachers, peers, and families and influenced the ways in which these boys participated in mathematics and how they saw themselves as doers of mathematics. Clayton, a Black boy in Berry's study, stated, "I like being with the smart kids because that means I am one of the smartest . . . since I answer all of the questions in math that means I am the smartest of the smart kids." Learners who have a positive mathematics identity exhibit behaviors similar to Clayton's description. Conversely, learners who have a negative mathematics identity may not participate in mathematics, limit their participation, or remain silent due to the fear of being judged. Furthermore, in mathematics teaching and learning, we see identity-affirming criteria emerging as learners are labeled as "smart," "gifted," "proficient," "at risk," or "on grade level" (Aguirre et al., 2013). Learners will come to see themselves in particular ways relative to others in their mathematics experiences.

Identity-affirming behaviors influence perseverance with school mathematics by impacting learning experiences and social relations among learners, teachers, and family members (Cornell & Hartmann, 2007). Learners who are identified and behave as "gifted" receive identity-affirming feedback from teachers and peers on the perceived ways gifted learners should behave and interact in their mathematical experiences. These learners are more likely to engage in problem-solving tasks requiring explanation and justification, to work in small groups with peers, to use mathematical tools and technologies, and to be active participants in their mathematics experiences (Ellis, 2008). Teachers cultivate and affirm mathematical behaviors by providing opportunities for learners to make sense of and persevere in challenging mathematics. Consequently, this kind of teaching uses identity-affirming practices, such as differentiated tasks, flexible groupings, and publicly praise of perseverance, to cultivate and affirm mathematical participation (National Council of Teachers of Mathematics, 2014). On the other hand, learners who are identified and behave as "at risk" receive identity-affirming feedback from teachers and peers that is often focused on standardized testing preparation because these learners are perceived as being at risk of not passing standardized tests (Ellis, 2008). At-risk learners often receive identity-affirming instruction that situates them as passive in their mathematics experiences; this instruction is focused on recalling facts or definitions and executing procedures and algorithms. These learners often have limited opportunities to develop conceptual understanding, to engage as active participants by explaining and justifying their thinking, or to explore problem-solving tasks; the focus of their experiences is to pass a standardized test that others perceive them as being at risk of not passing.

Many influences shape learners' mathematical identity—some are directly related to in-school activities and others are occur in out-of-school contexts. According to Martin (2007), mathematics identities do not develop in isolation from other identities learners construct (e.g., racial, cultural, ethnic, religious, athletic, gender). Berry (2008) discussed three interwoven identities that support the mathematics and academic identities of Black boys: (1) cocurricular and special academic program identity, (2) religious identity, and (3) athletic identity. Nasir (2002) examined how Black males learn mathematics through out-of-school experiences and how those experiences help to facilitate the development of identities, goals, and learning. Berry and McClain (2009) found that parents of Black boys engaged in racial socialization practices designed to help their sons manage in a world where racial prejudice and discrimination are likely to be aimed at them. These identities are interwoven with their mathematics identity and contribute to learners' sense of agency.

Agency

Agency is the behavioral aspect of identity that is the behavioral aspect of identity that focuses on participation and performance (Aguirre et al., 2013). Agency is identity in action, and it explains why learners persevere or do not persevere in mathematics. One's sense of agency can be either high or low. A high sense of agency is associated with self-exploration and self-direction in determining one's life course (Côté & Schwartz, 2002). Learners with a high sense of agency make decisions about their participation in mathematics in pursuing mathematical experiences that provide them with the broadest academic options, such as being in advanced mathematics groups, seeking additional cocurricular and special programs, choosing to participate in positive community activities, and being associated with the smart kids. Simply put, high agency can be conceptualized as perseverance with mathematics. The boys in Berry's (2008) study chose actions and behaviors that supported perseverance, success, and participation with mathematics. For example, Bilal showed a high sense of agency by stating, "I gotta excel in everything I do. Be the best that I can be . . . being the best means doing your work, asking questions, and being involved in class." A high sense of agency can be resistant to negative identities while at the same time supporting perseverance. Learners rely on identify-affirming feedback in order to be active participants in their mathematics experiences and to maintain a positive mathematics identity.

Conversely, a low sense of agency is defined as a low degree of self-exploration that is translated into a low level of control over one's life course. Learners with a low sense of agency have limited participation in their mathematics experiences and may perceive that participation will not change their situation. These learners are passive recipients in their mathematical experiences, perhaps due to negative structural and institutional forces. Learners with a low sense of agency might make a statement such as, "Why should I do my work? It won't matter anyway." The qualitative metasynthesis presented in this chapter uses *racialized forms of experience* as a framework positioning learning and participation as the intersection between race, identity, agency, and perseverance for Black learners.

Methods

Qualitative metasynthesis is a procedure for qualitative research synthesis that produces interpretative results from integrating, comparing, and interpreting patterns and insights systematically across qualitative research studies while maintaining the integrity of the individual studies (Erwin, Brotherson, & Summers, 2011). A qualitative metasynthesis is not a review of literature; it is an analysis and interpretation of the findings of a selected pool of studies. Researchers conducting qualitative metasynthesis use a deliberate process of selecting studies and focus on synthesizing, analyzing, and interpreting findings across the selected studies.

Qualitative metasynthesis first emerged in the 1970s and has gained considerable attention in the field of nursing (Finlayson & Dixon, 2008). Qualitative metasynthesis is sometimes referred to as "meta-ethnography" (Noblit & Hare, 1988), "metasynthesis" (Sandelowski, Docherty, & Emden, 1997), or "metastudy" (Paterson et al., 2001). Although some focused synthesis work has been conducted in the areas of educational leadership and desegregation (Noblit & Hare, 1988) and coteaching in the special education literature (Scruggs, Mastropieri, & McDuffie, 2007), to date there has been only one (Berry & Thunder, 2012) qualitative synthesis of mathematics education research. Noblit and Hare (1988) were one of the first to introduce qualitative metasynthesis to the broader field of education research by describing a method they identified as meta-ethnography, or "the synthesis of interpretive research":

> A meta-ethnography seeks to go beyond single accounts to reveal the analogies between the accounts. It reduces the accounts while preserving the sense of the accounts through the selection of key metaphors and organizers. The senses of different accounts are then translated into one another. The analogies revealed in these translations are the form of the meta-ethnographical synthesis. (Noblit & Hare, 1988, p. 13)

Through a process of qualitative metasynthesis, our knowledge base can be broadened to provide insights into attitudes, perceptions, interactions, structures, and behaviors relevant to mathematics education.

Six discrete steps were followed for this qualitative metasynthesis: (1) identify a specific research question; (2) conduct a comprehensive search; (3) select initial relevant studies; (4) appraise the quality of initially selected studies; (5) synthesize findings of selected studies; and (6) present findings across the studies. Our research question was: In what ways do Black learners, who have been successful with mathematics, negotiate their experiences in order to persevere with mathematics across time? In our research question, we use the language "across time" to differentiate between research that is focused on a narrow period of time and research that focuses on a broad period of time. We define "across time" as studies in which learners reflect on their experiences by, for example, describing how experiences from early time periods contributed to their current position with mathematics. This approach contrasts with studies that focus on a finite period of time, such as a specific grade level or time spent in a mathematics club. Studies with in-school and out-of-school settings were included for this qualitative metasynthesis.

Sample

We used EBSCO to simultaneously search the following databases for peer-reviewed journal articles: (*a*) Academic Search Complete, (*b*) Education Research Complete, (*c*) ERIC, (*d*) Teacher Reference Center, and (*e*) Education Full Text (H. W. Wilson). For a detailed description of our search terms and special limiters, please see appendix 1. Our initial search using the five EBSCO databases produced 531 documents, and the Sociological Abstracts database produced 310 documents. The inclusion/exclusion protocol from table 1 was used to determine which documents met the criteria to be used to investigate the research question. After reviewing and subjecting each document to the inclusion/exclusion protocol, we identified sixty peer-reviewed articles.

We recognize that qualitative research cannot be treated as a unified field due to the plurality of methodological approaches (Dixon-Woods et al., 2004); however, qualitative research studies should include basic criteria of quality for methodological aspects, such as research problem/purpose/question, data collection techniques, data analysis, report of findings, and implications/conclusions. To appraise the quality of the sixty articles, we adapted an appraisal checklist reported by Erwin, Brotherson, and Summers (2011). Table 2 shows the adapted checklist, providing points for each indicator with a maximum of fifteen points.

Table 3 provides a summary of the thirteen qualitative articles we ultimately used for this qualitative metasynthesis. These thirteen articles scored in the high range (eleven to fifteen points) on the appraisal checklist. It should be noted that while there are thirteen articles, there are only ten distinct studies. The Berry (2005) is a case study of two boys that builds upon the larger Berry (2008) study about the mathematical identities of eight Black boys. Similarly, Jett (2011) is a case study that derives from a larger study by Jett (2010), and McGee and Martin's

Table 1. Inclusion and Exclusion Criteria

INCLUSION CRITERIA	EXCLUSION CRITERIA
Empirical qualitative research	Quantitative methods
PreK–12	Mixed methods
Mathematics (STEM)	Review of literature or summaries of research
Black and/or African American	Policy documents
Setting/context United States	Calls for research
Additional permissible inclusion criteria	Book reviews
Longitudinal qualitative with learners older than PreK–12 is included but the article had relevance to PreK–12 educational experiences (i.e., reflections)	Op-ed pieces
While a study focused on learners other than learners (i.e., parents and teachers), the research had to be central to in-school and out-of-school experiences of learners	Not United States setting/context
Studies focused on additional learning opportunities and out-of-school programs	Pedagogical/practitioners articles describing implementation of teaching, tools, and/or practice with learners
Most of the learners are identified as Black in cases with non-Black learners.	Multiple publications using the same data

Table 2. Appraisal Criteria for Assessing Quality of Qualitative Research Process

CRITERIA	POSSIBLE POINTS	POINTS GIVEN
Research problem, purpose, and/or question	2	
Problem is stated clearly and related to the research literature		
There is a clear statement of research purpose and/or question		
Method: Data collection and analysis	6	
Study is methodology qualitative		
Sample plan and data collection are appropriate to the question		
Data analysis plan is consistent with design and purpose		
Describes the learners of the study and how they were selected		
Researchers show an awareness of their influence on the study and its learners (describe experiences and/or assumptions with which the researchers enter the research)		
Data collection procedures are fully described		
Steps/process of the data analysis are clear with examples		
Techniques for credibility and trustworthiness are described and used correctly		
Findings	5	
Interpretations of data are plausible and/or substantiated with data		
Overall findings address the purpose of the study		
Ideas (themes, categories, concepts, etc.) are precise, well developed, and linked to each other		
Results offer new information about or insights into the targeted phenomenon		
Quotes provide support/evidence for each theme/concept presented		
Discussion and implications	2	
Returns to the research questions/purpose proposed at the beginning and discusses interpretation and significant findings		
Recommendations for intended audience and future research issues		
Total points	*15*	

High overall standards of quality and credibility = 11–15 points. Moderate overall standards of quality and credibility = 6–10 points.
Low overall standards of quality and credibility = 0–5 points

Table 3. Qualitative Studies Used for This Qualitative Metasynthesis (January 2004 to January 2014)

1	Berry, R. Q., III, Thunder, K., & McClain, O. L. (2011). Counter narratives: Examining the mathematics and racial identities of black boys who are successful with school mathematics. *Journal of African American Males in Education 2*(1), 10–23.
2	Berry, R. Q., III (2005). Voices of success: Descriptive portraits of two successful African American male middle school mathematics students. *Journal of African American Studies 8*(4), 46–62.
3	Berry, R. Q., III (2008). Access to upper-level mathematics: The stories of successful African American middle school boys. *Journal for Research in Mathematics Education 39*(5), 464–88.
4	Ellington, R. M., & Frederick, R. (2010). Black high achieving undergraduate mathematics majors discuss success and persistence in mathematics. *Negro Educational Review 61*(1–4), 61–84.
5	Jett, C. C. (2010). "Many are called, but few are chosen": The role of spirituality and religion in the educational outcome of "chosen" African American male mathematics majors. *Journal of Negro Education 79*(3), 324–34.
6	Jett, C. C. (2011). "I once was lost, but now am found": The mathematics journey of an African American male mathematics doctoral student. *Journal of Black Studies 42*(7), 1125–47.
7	Martin, D. B. (2006). Mathematics learning and participation as racialized forms of experience: African American parents speak on the struggle for mathematics literacy. *Mathematical Thinking and Learning 8*(3), 197–229.
8	McGee, E. O., & Martin, D. B. (2011a). "You would not believe what I have to go through to prove my intellectual value!": Stereotype management among academically successful black mathematics and engineering students. *American Educational Research Journal 48*(6), 1347–89.
9	McGee, E., & Martin, D. B. (2011b). From the hood to being hooded: A case study of a black male Ph.D. *Journal of African American Males in Education 2*(1), 46–65.
10	Noble, R. (2011). Mathematics self-efficacy and African American male students: An examination of models of success. *Journal of African American Males in Education 2*(2), 188–213.
11	Stinson, D. W. (2008). Negotiating sociocultural discourses: The counter-storytelling of academically (and mathematically) successful African American male students. *American Educational Research Journal 45*(4), 975–1010.
12	Thompson, L. R., & Davis, J. (2013). The meaning high-achieving African-American males in an urban high school ascribe to mathematics. *Urban Review 45*(4), 490–517.
13	Thompson, L. R., & Lewis, B. F. (2005). Shooting for the stars: A case study of the mathematics achievement and career attainment of an African American male high school student. High School Journal 88(4), 6–18.

(2011a, 2011b) articles also used the format of a case study drawn from a larger study. Each of these articles was included within the data analysis, however, because they each reported unique qualitative data. In other words, although the articles overlapped in some respects, they did not report repetitive data.

Data Analysis

The findings from each article were treated analogously as informants; consequently, the findings were extracted into a single document to be coded. A grounded theory approach was used to code, categorize, and constantly compare data to develop a general theory (Strauss & Corbin, 1997). The researchers open-coded the findings independently and then negotiated those independent codings to reach a single shared set of codes and definitions. It should be

Table 4. Findings from Data Analysis

First finding	Learners developed identities based on values, which were affirmed by others with whom they interacted; these values were identity-affirming and supported perseverance in mathematics.
Second finding	Learners negotiated their own definitions of success; perseverance was anchored by meeting learners' new and evolving definitions of success across time.
Third finding	Learners encountered issues of awareness and access along their experience pathways and persevered in order to overcome these issues.
Fourth finding	At the intersection of academic and racialized images, learners negotiated ways to persevere in mathematics.
Fifth finding	Learners with a high sense of agency persevered with mathematics across time; they chose to pursue their own pathways to success sustained by the work ethic of practice and perseverance.

noted that the theoretical framework provided the framing for the development of the initial codes: race/racism, identities (mathematics, academic, athletic, religious, gender, and racial), identity-affirming (behaviors, actions, and policy), and agency. The initial codes were then categorized. We reread and recoded to refine and verify coding and to ensure consistency. After this, we sorted the data by codes and reread, looking for themes within each code to see if there were dimensions that required the data to be further discriminated. Through this process, themes emerged from the data. From this categorization and classification of the data, we provide and describe the findings.

Findings

Our qualitative metasynthesis produced five findings about the ways in which Black learners who have been successful with mathematics negotiated their experiences in order to persevere with mathematics across time. Table 4 presents the five findings.

These findings describe defining qualities of the complex, nonlinear experience pathways unique to the learners across the studies. Appendix 2 presents a sampling of data across the thirteen articles to support the findings from this metasynthesis. While all thirteen articles were coded, going forward we will frame our discussion around ten studies due to the overlaps of the three pairs of studies discussed earlier. The following sections discuss our five findings and the representativeness of the data.

Finding 1: Values as Identity-Affirming and Supporting Perseverance

All ten studies had learners who identified and embraced particular values early in their experiences with mathematics and continued to do so throughout their lives. The learners valued (*a*) caring about their church, communities, and families; (*b*) being revered, well regarded, and admired; and (*c*) mathematical knowledge. The sources of these values were (*a*) the ways church, community, and family members held high expectations for the learners, (*b*) the ways the learners experienced being revered academically and in athletics, and (*c*) the ways the learners developed an early understanding that mathematics is important from parents and teachers.

The learners developed early identifications and affirmation with mathematics, college, and careers. Additionally, several specific identities—mathematical, academic, and religious identities—emerged in these learners' experiences. These identities were based on values affirmed by others with whom they interacted, including family, neighbors, church members, coaches, teammates, teachers, club members, and peers. In the Berry (2005, 2008) study, Cordell, a Black boy in middle school, stated:

> My grandmother and aunts help my mother by encouraging me to make good decisions and make sure that I stay on the right track. My grandmother and mother talk to me about doing well in school and make sure I do my work. My mother is always saying I better do well in school if I plan on going to school. (Berry, 2008, p. 473)

We see identity development and identity-affirmation in Cordell's statement in the ways his relatives discussed the value of doing well and making good decisions. Roger, a Black man in Jett's (2010, 2011) studies of the mathematics journeys of Black male doctoral students, valued the role of God in his life and valued following God's will. Below, Roger discusses issues of race and racism at his job when he was not considered for advancement:

> But I see right now that's not in God's plans for me to do. So at that point in time I was kind of frustrated, but right now I'm glad that it didn't go through. So I don't have a problem with it because they cutthroat. When it comes to hiring up in the company, they cutthroat. And as a Black man, I already know I'd a got cut. (Jett, 2011, p. 1138)

Roger's statement represents the kind of everyday institutional and structural racism (perceived and real) that could potentially impact the identity of a man who identifies himself as competent and a doer of mathematics. Roger's religious identity and the associated values mediated the potential belief that God did not allow him to secure the position.

Learners valued knowledge as a means for improving or maintaining their financial situation and for earning the reverence and admiration of others by gaining status. Valuing knowledge led to a value of future options, including access to higher levels of education and mathematics-related careers. Nathaniel, a Black high school student from Stinson's (2008) study of academically and mathematically successful males, saw academics as possibly improving his financial situation. Nathaniel stated, "I got a sense [from my parents] that learning was something important, it was something that . . . put food on our plate, and eventually led us to moving up in social standing" (Stinson, 2008, p. 988). McGee and Martin (2011a, 2011b) studied Black college students who had successfully negotiated the mathematics pipeline and documented the way values and interwoven identities support perseverance. They stated:

The majority of the students in this study admitted to gravitating toward mathematics and engineering to be perceived as smart. The respondents recognized that excelling in mathematics meant being the beneficiary of privileged status and having access to the educational opportunities they need to get ahead. (McGee & Martin, 2011a, p. 26)

Finding 2: Negotiating Definitions of Success to Persevere

It should be noted that all of the studies in this metasynthesis focused on learners who were successful or high-achieving in academics in general and in mathematics specifically. Studies that focused on success were not intentionally part of our search criteria for this metasynthesis. The finding that the collection of thirteen articles focuses on success is interesting because it suggests that research on the identity and agency of Black learners is focusing on a narrow group of learners who are successful. In all the studies, the researchers' definition of success was used as selection criteria for participation. As we coded the data, however, we found that learners defined success in ways different from researchers.

Learners defined success based on their values in two areas: academics (specifically in mathematics) and life. The definition of success in academics was conceptualized as (*a*) outperforming peers, (*b*) enrollment in gifted and advanced courses of study, (*c*) college attendance, and (*d*) achieving career goals. The definition of success in life was conceptualized as (*a*) taking care of families, (*b*) giving back to community, (*c*) being a role model, and (*d*) keeping a spiritual and religious grounding.

Some learners' definitions of success were based on the achievement of certain outcomes. In school, Alfred (Noble, 2011) and all of the learners in the Berry (2005, 2008) study negotiated success as outperforming peers through class participation, grades, and testing, and as being labeled as gifted, enrolling in advanced courses, and attending college. Alfred, a Black man in Noble's (2011) study of Black men who excelled in mathematics, stated:

> I always scored a perfect score in the math section . . . I took this as a sign that I was a pretty good mathematician in my younger years. As the years progressed I took these scores plus my many A's that I got in my math classes as something to be proud of. (Noble, 2011, p. 197)

Berry (2008) reported:

> Seven boys [out of eight] reported feeling successful in the elementary grades because they knew their multiplication tables before their peers, were grouped with the smart kids for mathematics, or were challenged during their pre-fourth-grade years with assignments that were above their grade level. (Berry, 2008, p. 477)

We see that Alfred defined success as doing well in mathematics and that this definition was affirmed by scores and grades that allowed him to persevere with mathematics. Derrell, a Black boy in middle school in Berry, Thunder, and McClain's (2011) study, defined success outside of the school context but within his familial context by stating, "I realized I was good at math when my mom, brother, sister, or grandparents were doing bills or taxes and everyone asked me, 'How did you know this and that?' That made me feel very happy" (Berry, Thunder, & McClain, 2011, p. 16).

Success for some learners was connected to their interwoven identities as being Black and being members of the Black community. In Ellington and Frederick's (2010) study, Anita, a high-achieving Black college student, defined success as meeting career goals in which they gave back to their community and became role models. Anita stated:

> There's the social obligation [to stay in the mathematics program]. Where, you know, you feel like, as a Black female in the program, one of few, that, if you don't stay in the program, then nobody else will. And what happens to the little Black girl who wants to be a math major, and doesn't see anyone who's one, and then she doesn't become one.... And so that's something I feel has motivated me. (Ellington & Frederick, 2010, p. 74)

In Anita's statement, we see the interwoven mathematics, racial, and gender identities. She appears to be motivated to be successful and persevere through her sense of obligation to Black girls. Similarly, Raheem, a participant in Martin's (2006) study, expresses his sense of obligation:

> That's why I decided to become a teacher, because I want to help too . . . If I demonstrate to children that a Black person is intelligent and they know what they are talking about, that will help them have more confidence in themselves and their own people. (Martin, 2006, p. 218)

Both young learners in the midst of their elementary education and adult learners reflecting back on their experiences, like those in the Stinson (2008) study, identified their successes as acquiring knowledge that enabled them to take care of their families. Stinson stated:

> No matter how participants conceptualized success, implicitly or explicitly stated throughout their conversations was the undisputed need for education, whether it was to pass knowledge on or to ensure that one could financially care for loved ones. (Stinson, 2008, p. 988)

Although these outcome-based definitions of success permeated the data, the learners' definitions of success were not static. Rather, across these studies and within the learners' stories, the definitions of success appear to be under negotiation and to evolve over time. Consequently, as learners' identities evolved, their definitions of success evolved and contributed to their perseverance. In short, perseverance appeared to be anchored by meeting new and evolving definitions of success across time.

Finding 3: Persevering to Overcome Issues of Access

Across all ten of the studies, learners encountered issues of access along their experience pathways. These issues included access to gifted programs, advanced mathematics courses, rigorous curriculum, role models, and high-quality teaching. Across these studies, gatekeepers worked to limit learners' access while advocates worked to expand the learners' options. As they reflected on their experiences, some learners realized critical points along their pathways that appeared to be analogous to a crossroads. These crossroads impacted learners' experiences and opportunities. For some, the learners' reflections suggest an awareness that they may not have understood in the midst of the encounter. For others, reflection helped them to understand the presence of barriers and the lack of awareness in the midst of the encounters, which resulted in restricted access. Raheem's story represented awareness through reflection, as when he stated:

> I remember Ms. Berks at the end of the school year telling me that she made a mistake not putting me in the algebra class in the 8th grade. And I remember her telling me this and not realizing what algebra was and I was just, "Oh well, no big deal to me" . . . that's to me an example of the fact that Black children, even when you do well, your educational future is not planned out properly for you . . . I was bored as hell in that class . . . by the time I got to algebra in 9th grade, I had kinda lost interest in math. (Martin, 2006, pp. 210–11)

Similarly, Cordell, a Black boy identified as successful in Berry's (2008) study, described his encounter with the issue of access to a gifted program. Identification with the gifted program is an important crossroads in Cordell's experience because not being in the program could have negatively impacted his participation and perseverance with mathematics. Cordell stated:

> My mother thought I was not being challenged enough and that that is why I got into trouble. The teacher and principal did not want me tested because they felt I was not gifted. My mother thinks the reason they did not want to test me was because I am Black. She stayed on the teachers and principals until I was tested. I did well enough to be placed in the AG [gifted] program. (Berry, 2008, p. 473)

Malik, a Black boy in Thompson and Lewis's (2005) case study, gained access to advanced mathematics courses by serving as his own advocate to alter course offerings. Malik stated:

> I want to go to one of the best colleges. I want to be something . . . I was looking at the required classes [for college] and I realized that where I stand right now as a junior, I don't have what it takes to succeed at that type of college . . . I knew I had to try to find a way to better prepare myself. So I went to Mr. King and asked him if there's any way we could add more advanced math classes to the schedule. (Thompson & Lewis, 2005, p. 11)

It should be noted that Malik exhausted the mathematics course offerings at his high school. We see in his statement both academic identity and a sense of agency. He enacted a sense of agency to prepare himself for the best colleges.

Access to high-quality teaching, "smart peers," enriching academic programs, and quality curricula was evident in all ten studies. The challenge for many learners was the ways in which they gained access through support and advocacy. Wynn, a Black boy in middle school, contended that access matters: "At my school, really it matters what classes I'm in . . . I was the only African American who was in there the whole year . . . It's better in the gifted classes because personally I think the teachers are nicer" (Berry, Thunder, & McClain, 2011, p. 18). Stinson's (2008) description is representative of what access meant to the experiences of the learners across the ten studies:

> Each of the participants had been tracked into honors programs early in his education, providing him with access to enriched schooling experiences and academic programs and access to the most credentialed and experienced teachers. (Stinson, 2008, p. 996)

Advocacy was evident across all ten studies. Advocacy came from parents, as in Cordell's case, and from peers and teachers, as in Malik's case. Alfred described peer support by stating, "When I have friends who I know are good at math, then a lot of times we'll work together. And so they help me learn more and become better" (Noble, 2011, p. 201). Karen, an undergraduate mathematics major, described the significance of teacher support and teacher quality in her experience:

> Our teachers expected a lot out of us . . . I told my teacher I couldn't do it at first. I was like, no, I'm not smart enough to do it. She's like: *yes you are!* I'm like, *no, I'm really really not.* She's like, *yes you are.* So she made me do it and I did it.
>
> Yeah, it was no problem, but I didn't think I could at first. (Ellington & Fredrick, 2010, p. 69)

Tinesha, a doctoral mathematics education student, discussed managing access by overcoming the lack of support from teachers and peers, stating:

> I came to realize, like, these people [teachers and her peers] don't expect too much of me in this class. . . . If you tell me that I can't do something, then I want to prove to you that I can. And so for the rest of the time in all my upper-level classes, that was my goal. . . . I took that attitude from that point on in all my math classes. . . . I sat at the front of the class. Like, I didn't come in and come to the back of the class. I sat at the front of the class. (McGee & Martin, 2011a, p. 19)

It should be noted that context is important to Karen's and Tinesha's experiences. Karen reflected on her elementary grades experiences. This early experience contributed to her identity development. Tinesha reflected on her undergraduate experiences in which she had a sense of isolationism. Her early, strong academic and mathematics identity helped her to persevere and overcome the isolation.

Finding 4: Using Images to Persevere

In this metasynthesis, images are defined as learners' self-identities, learners' perceptions of others' identities, and learners' perceptions of how they themselves are perceived. In the studies we synthesized, earners used image-based criteria in conjunction with their values to negotiate their experience pathways. This negotiation considered two categories of images that are highly interwoven and are not mutually exclusive: academic images and racialized images. Academic images are defined broadly to include (*a*) the ways learners see themselves relative to their previous academic performances, (*b*) their perceptions of peers' academic performances, (c) leaners' performance relative to perceived standards, and (*d*) role models of doers of mathematics. Racialized images are defined as (*a*) images of Black learners of mathematics as anomalies, (*b*) stereotypes from the media, (*c*) role models and non-role models, (*d*) perceptions of peers' identities, and (*e*) perceptions of self by others. Central to both categories are the ways learners negotiate images of themselves as doers of mathematics; this negotiation is always under construction.

Malik, Dexter, and David are examples of learners using the images of others, perceived standards, and academic performances of others to compare with their own performance. Malik, a Black boy who attends an urban high school, compares himself to others by stating:

> When you're at Garvey High School, the competition may not be as great as maybe some of the other schools . . . you're on this false sense of confidence. But once you start to compare yourself to kids nationwide, you're like oh, I'm kinda weak compared to these guys . . . so when I was going into my senior year I was like, I gotta do something now. (Thompson & Lewis, 2005, p. 7)

Dexter, a Black man in Noble's (2011) study, is an example of a learner using academic images of others relative to his own performance. He stated:

> I never really felt like somebody that's in the same class as me is smarter than me. I've never really felt that way. So, when they succeed, I feel like that shows me that I could have succeeded if I didn't succeed. I realize that I should have set the bar higher. (Noble, 2011, p. 201)

Similarly, David, a mathematics major in Ellington and Fredrick's (2010) study, stated,

> This is what I've been searching for all my life—I'm in a group now, I'm surrounded by a bunch of people just like me. So, now I'm not the outcast so to speak. . . . Now I've found that niche where I'm surrounded by people who are just as competitive. (Ellington & Frederick, 2010, p. 70)

In contrast, Spencer, a Black boy in high school, used image comparison to show that he was worthy of his status by stating, "I make sure that I raise my hand to answer the questions early . . . I try to prove my worth, show that I belong" (Stinson, 2008, p. 994).

Raheem, Phillip, Keeshawn, and Antonio are examples of learners discussing racialized images as having an impact on the construction of their identities of self and as doers of mathematics. Raheem discussed the lack of Black teachers:

> I can count on one, just about one hand the Black teachers that I had. I look back and reflect on the way I thought, in the way I perceived things. That had an impact on the way I felt about my own people. I saw people that were not Black as my teachers. So that made me self-consciously come on with the thought that Black people are just not that smart. (Martin, 2008, pp. 209–10)

Phillip, a boy in middle school, discussed resisting and combating negative images of Black boys by saying:

> Unfortunately, many of the African American boys at my school set bad examples and make bad reputations for African American boys. I work hard to carry myself in a mature manner all day, every day. My dad has talked to me and other African American boys at my church about the importance of being a positive role model for younger boys. (Berry, 2008, p. 476)

Likewise, Keeshawn, a boy in middle school, discussed his resistance to the dominant discourse and images that situate Black boys negatively:

> I know that African American males . . . don't achieve too well in math and stuff. But I feel that just because like statistics show that African Americans don't do as well in math, don't achieve more, I still feel that we can do good . . . that kind of gives me a boost. (Berry, Thunder, & Mc-Clain, 2011, p. 19)

Antonio, a high school student, discussed the lack of Black images in mathematics by stating, "There ain't nobody out there for us, you know, no black males with math and all that in their heads. All we see is gang bangers on TV, rapping and sports" (Thompson & Davis, 2013, p. 510).

At the intersection of academic images and racialized images, many learners negotiated ways to persevere in mathematics. This perseverance is seen in several ways: (*a*) through comparisons to meet the image of academic success, (*b*) combating negative images of Black males, and (*c*) proving themselves worthy of access. Images include role models but should be understood as something more than role models; rather, both positive and negative images motivated these learners positively to engage and persevere academically and mathematically.

Finding 5: High Sense of Agency as Perseverance

As stated in the theoretical framework, agency is identity in action, and a high sense of agency can be can conceptualized as perseverance. Learners' enactment of agency across contexts is highly connected to issues of awareness, access, and images. As a result, learners either surrendered to or rejected forms of participation in mathematics. Learners with a low sense of agency followed a default pathway; for many Black learners, this meant being placed in low-tracked mathematics courses. Learners with a high sense of agency asserted their identities to make decisions about their participation in mathematics. In other words, these learners chose a pathway based on their values and negotiated definitions of success. Phillip's and Elijah's voices are representative of learners with a high sense of agency. Phillip, a boy in middle school, described his interwoven identities and images to enact agency by stating, "I think God tells us to be achievers, so anything I set my mind to I can achieve. Church keeps me encouraged to do what is right, and my church has many positive Black Christian male role models" (Berry, 2008, p. 50). Elijah's mathematics identity allowed him to persevere to take mathematics courses beyond requirements; he stated, "I've taken more math courses than I've actually had to, which is something I don't mind doing. . . . I've taken some of the more difficult classes as electives, some of the classes that people generally try to stay away from" (Noble, 2011, p. 199).

Learners with a high sense of agency chose to pursue their own pathways to success sustained by the work ethic of practice and perseverance. At decision markers across time, learners negotiated their paths or patterns of participation in varied settings. Malik and Roger shared representative stories of such decision markers along their paths; these served as moments when Malik and Roger enacted their high agency by choosing to change paths and patterns of participation. Malik described a critical point in his experience to focus on mathematics:

> I had always wanted to be part of the in crowd and do what was cool; and what was cool was to play sports. So I never really focused on the books. . . . When I got to high school, I started to make a change. Math class really changed everything for me because I started seeing myself putting the kind of effort into the classroom that I put into the field and I was dominant. . . . It made me realize that this is where I compete, this is my passion and it can be just as fun as sports. This is where I can make a difference. (Thompson & Lewis, 2005, pp. 6–7)

Similarly, Martin (2008) described Roger's pathway:

> Roger mentioned that he did not think that he would achieve so much as it pertains to school. . . . He made reference to the fact that he was "lost" as it pertains to his educational goals. . . . He was going through the motions as a football player, not contemplating the ramifications of his own education his life. He now, however, has a clear vision of his future in mathematics, one that includes attracting more African American male students to the mathematics pipeline. (Martin, 2008, p. 1140)

Encounters with nonsuccess were defining markers along each learner's pathway. Learners with a high sense of agency demonstrated perseverance and resiliency to transform these encounters with nonsuccess into opportunities to increase their awareness of options and opportunities, to reevaluate their choice of pathway, and to renegotiate their identities and definitions of success. David's, Rob's, and Amber's stories are representative of the learners' descriptions of encounters with nonsuccess. Each of these learners was resilient and persevered in the face of nonsuccess. David, a mathematics major, experienced non-success and struggle:

> I had faith that I could get it [mathematics]. I wasn't going to quit, [be]cause I had a bad feeling when I dropped that computer science class and I switched majors.
>
> And it was very much a feeling that I didn't want again . . . I didn't feel like God brought me to my junior year to have me fail a class. I just had to ultimately say that everything was going to be okay, and that it was just only a matter of time. (Ellington & Frederick, 2010, p. 73)

Similarly, McGee and Martin (2011a) described Rob's experiences of self-doubt and being perceived by others as an "affirmative action case" at a predominantly white school:

> In order to preserve his racial self-esteem, he dropped out of Science Tech and moved back to the safe haven of his childhood neighborhood, taking an entire year off from school. . . . He has no regrets about leaving Science Tech because that year was critical to rebuilding his racial self-esteem. Rob eventually received three master's degrees . . . as well as his PhD in applied mathematics. (McGee & Martin, 2011a, p. 56)

While David and Rob resolved to continue their chosen experience pathway, Amber refused to follow the default pathway being forced onto her. Instead, she chose a new pathway that was not in conflict with her negotiated identity and definition of success. Amber thought that her schooling was being stunted and that the best learning opportunities were being reserved for White and Asian American students, despite the fact that she transferred from a private high school to a public school in which she was one academic year ahead of her peers. Amber stated:

> I knew it right away. They do that because they want to push them along and keep us back. A lot of minority students knew this but they accepted it. I hated it. Why should I accept this, just because I'm a Black person? This is not fair.
>
> You're advancing them and letting them advance. . . . So that's why I said forget it. I hate this, I'm leaving. I checked out, getting a GED and went ahead and did what I needed to do. (Martin, 2006, p. 216)

Many of the learners had a forward vision and chose to continue on or redirect their experience pathways. Their pathways can be described as complex, nonlinear experience pathways

Figure 1. The Defining Qualities of a Learner's Experience Pathway

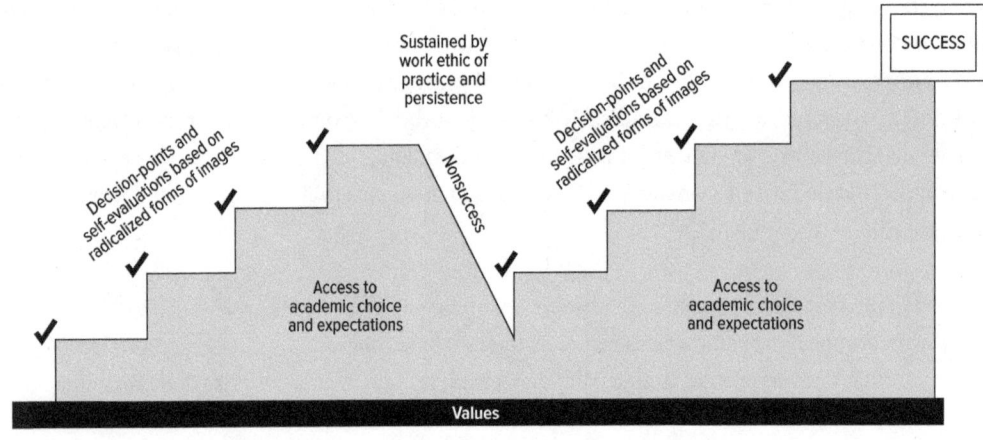

that represent the ways Black learners negotiated their experiences in order to persevere with mathematics across time.

Figure 1 is a representation of one such experience pathway and its defining qualities.

Conclusion

The research question that guided this metasynthesis was: In what ways do Black learners negotiate their experiences in order to persevere with mathematics across time? The answer to this research question is found in the ways the learners enacted their sense of agency. For the learners, a sense of agency was not mutually exclusive from race and identity. Through self-exploration, these learners negotiated values, perceptions of success, awareness of and access to opportunities, and various forms of images to enact their sense of agency. This negotiation informed their participation with mathematics—or in other words, patterns of participation in mathematics were connected to learners' sense of agency.

Learners with a high sense of agency were able to negotiate and interpret participation with mathematics as a means to access opportunities, fulfill social obligations, and understand the consequences of differential forms of participation. When we consider the resources of the learners' communities and families, we find strong contributions of value, faith, and support. It is these contributions that were foundational to the high sense of agency that supported resiliency and perseverance with mathematics.

The Black learners who persevered with mathematics across time were students with a high sense of agency. Their identity in action was characterized by self-exploration associated with a high degree of self-direction in making choices along their experience pathways. They chose actions and behaviors that embodied an active pursuit of success based on their own definitions of success. These actions and behaviors enabled them to select from the broadest academic options, particularly in mathematics, and to meet their goals for success. In order to support Black learners with a high sense of agency, educators, family members, community members, and peers should use actions and words that affirm positive, persevering mathematical identities and values. The choice of language and practices also holds the potential to shift learners with a low sense of agency to a high sense of agency by facilitating their movement from passive to active learners.

In order to support a high sense of agency and perseverance in mathematics, educators must have an effective mind-frame combined with effective instructional practices (Hattie, 2012). A mind-frame is the set of assumptions, expectations, and beliefs that guide behavior and interactions. Effective mind-frames are growth mind-frames, while ineffective mind-frames are fixed (Sousa & Tomlinson, 2010). Educators with growth mind-frames believe that all students can succeed, that students' success depends on the effectiveness of educators' instructional decisions, and that students can change their achievement.

Educators with growth mind-frames avoid static labels, such as "at risk," which can be identity-affirming language that develops a low sense of agency. Educators who support perseverance in mathematics also implement effective instructional practices that affirm a high sense of agency. These practices include goal-setting; self-monitoring; self-evaluation; differentiated tasks; problem-solving tasks that require explanation and justification; use of mathematical tools and technologies; flexible grouping; public praise of perseverance; and cultivation and affirmation of participation by orchestrating productive mathematics discussions (Hattie, 2012; Smith & Stein, 2011). These instructional practices facilitate students' self- exploration and self-direction, encourage students to define and pursue success in mathematics, and cultivate identities with positive self-efficacy.

These practices also require students to move from passive to active roles as learners in order to shift learners with a low sense of agency to a high sense of agency. Learners with a low sense of agency typically participate in limited ways, perceive that participation will not change their situation, and do not persevere to overcome negative structural and institutional forces. Educators who implement these effective instructional practices will grow students with high sense of agency by requiring all students to participate in multiple, active ways and by facilitating students' active participation to positively change their achievement. In addition, educators in all roles (teachers, guidance counselors, administrators, and policymakers) can grow students with a high sense of agency by serving as advocates rather than as gatekeepers when students encounter structural and institutional obstacles. As advocates, educators can help all students to have access to the broadest academic options and to select challenging academic options that lead to their definitions of success.

Appendix 1. Conducting a Comprehensive Search

To create the sample for our metasynthesis, we used EBSCO to simultaneously search the following databases for peer-reviewed journal articles: (*a*) Academic Search Complete, (*b*) Education Research Complete, (*c*) ERIC, (*d*) Teacher Reference Center, and (*e*) Education Full

Text (H.W. Wilson). We conducted subject term searches within the selected databases with this protocol: mathematics in SU Subject Terms; AND (Black or "African American") in SU Subject Terms; NOT ("black holes") in SU Subject Terms. We also conducted a search using the Sociological Abstracts database with this protocol: mathematics in All field (no full text)—ALL; AND (Black or "African American") in All field (no full text)—ALL. Previous work suggested that qualitative research on Black learners has increased since the mid to late 1990s (Berry, Pinter, & McClain, 2013); thus, we limited the dates of the search from January 2004 to January 2014. The following special limiters were used:

- Academic Search Complete database, Publication Type: Periodical and Document Type: Article.
- ERIC database, Journal or Document: Journal Articles (EJ) and Publication Type: Journal Articles.
- Education Research Complete database, Publication Type: Academic Journal and Document Type: Article.
- Education Full Text (H. W. Wilson) database, Publication Type: Academic Journal and Document Type: Article.
- Sociological Abstracts database, Source Type: Scholarly Journals and Document Type: Journal Article.

Appendix 2. A sampling of Data Across the 13 Articles

The following sections discuss findings of metasynthesis and the representativeness of the data that frames our discussion to help the reader follow along.

FINDING	BERRY, THUNDER, & MCCLAIN (2011)	BERRY (2005, 2008)	ELLINGTON & FREDERICK (2010)
Learners developed identities based on values, which were affirmed by others with whom they interacted; these values were identity-affirming and supported perseverance in mathematics.	Jamal: What I like about math is it's kind of complicated. . . . I want my work to be complicated so I can actually do better when I get to higher grades. And it feels like I finished something. It's like when it's hard, like when we were doing an engineering project, I feel like I finished something really good (p. 17).	Cordell: My grandmother and aunts help my mother by encouraging me to make good decisions and make sure that I stay on the right track. My grandmother and mother talk to me about doing well in school and make sure I do my work. My mother is always saying I better do well in school if I plan on going to school (p. 473).	Karen: My mom taught us how to count and everything like that. And every time we went someplace, oh, what's 1 + 2? And what's 2 + 2? . . . I know before [age] 5, I know I could add (p. 67).

Learners negotiated their own definitions of success; perseverance was anchored by meeting learners' new and evolving definitions of success across time.	Derrell: I realized I was good at math when my mom, brother, sister, or grandparents were doing bills or taxes and everyone asked me, "How did you know this and that?" That made me feel very happy (p. 16).	Seven boys reported feeling successful in the elementary grades because they knew their multiplication tables before their peers, were grouped with the smart kids for mathematics, or were challenged during their pre-fourth- grade years with assignments that were above their grade level (p. 477).	Anita: There's the social obligation [to stay in the mathematics program]. Where, you know, you feel like, as a Black female in the program, one of few, that, if you don't stay in the program, then nobody else will. And what happens to the little Black girl who wants to be a math major, and doesn't see anyone who's one, and then she doesn't become one. . . . And so that's something I feel has motivated me (p. 74).
Learners encountered issues of awareness and access along their experience pathways and persevered in order to overcome these issues.	Wynn: At my school really it matters what classes I'm in. . . . I was the only African American who was in there the whole year. . . . It's better in the gifted classes because personally I think the teachers are nicer (p. 18).	Cordell: My mother thought I was not being challenged enough and that that is why I got into trouble. The teacher and principal did not want me tested because they felt I was not gifted. My mother thinks the reason they did not want to test me was because I am Black. She stayed on the teachers and principals until I was tested. I did well enough to be placed in the AG program (p. 473).	Karen: Our teachers expected a lot out of us. . . . I told my teacher I couldn't do it at first. I was like, no, I'm not smart enough to do it. She's like: yes you are! I'm like, no, I'm really really not. She's like, yes you are. So she made me do it and I did it. Yeah, it was no problem, but I didn't think I could at first (p. 69).
At the intersection of academic and racialized images, learners negotiated ways to persevere in mathematics.	Keeshawn: I know that African American males . . . don't achieve too well in math and stuff. But I feel that just because like statistics show that African Americans don't do as well in math, don't achieve more, I still feel that we can do good . . . that kind of gives me a boost (p. 19).	Phillip: Unfortunately, many of the African American boys at my school set bad examples and make bad reputations for African American boys. I work hard to carry myself in a mature manner all day, every day. My dad has talked to me and other African American boys at my church about the importance of being a positive role model for younger boys (p. 476).	David: To maintain [your scholarship], you must maintain a certain standard and it's very competitive. . . . This is what I've been searching for all my life— I'm in a group now, I'm surrounded by a bunch of people just like me. So, now I'm not the outcast so to speak. . . . Now I've found that niche where I'm surrounded by people who are just as competitive (p. 70).

| Learners with a high sense of agency persevered with mathematics across time; they chose to pursue their own pathways to success sustained by the work ethic of practice and perseverance. | Tinashe: I think [being Black] hasn't affected me because it doesn't really matter what color I am. . . . I'm addicted to math (p. 19). | Phillip: I think God tells us to be achievers, so anything I set my mind to I can achieve. Church keeps me encouraged to do what is right, and my church has many positive Black Christian male role models (p. 50). | David: I had faith that I could get it [mathematics]. I wasn't going to quit, [be]cause I had a bad feeling when I dropped that computer science class and I switched majors. And it was very much a feeling that I didn't want again. . . . I didn't feel like God brought me to my junior year to have me fail a class. I just had to ultimately say that everything was going to be okay, and that it was just only a matter of time (p. 73). |

FINDING	JETT (2010, 2011)	MARTIN (2006)	MCGEE & MARTIN (2011A, 2011B)
Learners developed identities based on values, which were affirmed by others with whom they interacted; these values were identity-affirming and supported perseverance in mathematics.	Roger: But I see right now that's not in God's plans for me to do. So at that point in time I was kind of frustrated, but right now I'm glad that it didn't go through (p. 1138).	Keith: I honestly feel that through my struggles and working and living as long as I have so far, that math is an essential foundation for everything (p. 221).	The majority of the students in this study admitted to gravitating toward mathematics and engineering to be perceived as smart. The respondents recognized that excelling in mathematics meant being the beneficiary of privileged status and having access to the educational opportunities they need to get ahead (p. 26).
Learners negotiated their own definitions of success; perseverance was anchored by meeting learners' new and evolving definitions of success across time.	A common internal characteristic among the chosen ones was that they were all spiritually grounded and their spirituality positively contributed to their mission to fulfill their academic goals (p. 330).	Raheem: That's why I decided to become a teacher, because I want to help too. . . . If I demonstrate to children that a Black person is intelligent and they know what they are talking about, that will help them have more confidence in themselves and their own people (p. 218).	Valerie: My ultimate career goal is to become a professor in engineering. . . . I'd rather be a role model, and show them like I said "you could achieve this, you could become a professor." I want to be a role model and help other younger people who are in engineering who need a face to put with that goal they are trying to achieve. That's my goal (p. 30).

Learners encountered issues of awareness and access along their experience pathways and persevered in order to overcome these issues.	Roger: To be honest with you, I really haven't dealt with racism, but I have. It was just that it wasn't, it was more behind the scenes instead of out in the open. They did things behind my back (p. 1137).	Raheem: I remember Ms. Berks at the end of the school year telling me that she made a mistake not putting me in the algebra class in the 8th grade. And I remember her telling me this and not realizing what algebra was and I was just, "Oh well, no big deal to me." . . . that's to me an example of the fact that Black children, even when you do well, your educational future is not planned out properly for you. . . . I was bored as hell in that class . . . by the time I got to algebra in 9th grade, I had kinda lost interest in math (pp. 210–11).	Tinesha: I came to realize, like, these people [teachers and her peers] don't expect too much of me in this class. . . . If you tell me that I can't do something, then I want to prove to you that I can. And so for the rest of the time in all my upper- level classes, that was my goal. . . . I took that attitude from that point on in all my math classes (p. 19).
At the intersection of academic and racialized images, learners negotiated ways to persevere in mathematics.	Antonio: These transformative, spiritually attentive approaches also helped to validate my own academic success in that they grounded me both spiritually and academically (p. 328).	Raheem: I didn't see Black people in positions of power, authority. . . . I can count on one, just about one hand the Black teachers that I had. I look back and reflect on the way I thought, in the way I perceived things. That had an impact on the way I felt about my own people. I saw people that were not Black as my teachers. So that made me self-consciously come on with the thought that Black people are just not that smart (pp. 209–10).	The pressure of stereotypes, his love of mathematics, and parental expectations drove Rob to develop a strong mathematics identity. Rob has long seen himself as an excellent mathematics student—according to him "one of the best" (p. 18).
Learners with a high sense of agency persevered with mathematics across time; they chose to pursue their own pathways to success sustained by the work ethic of practice and perseverance.	Roger mentioned that he did not think that he would achieve so much as it pertains to school. . . . He made reference to the fact that he was "lost" as it pertains to his educational goals. . . . He was going through the motions as a football player, not contemplating the ramifications of his own education for his life. He now, however, has a clear vision of his future in mathematics, one that includes attracting with more African American male students. the mathematics pipeline (p. 1140).	Amber: I knew it right away. They do that because they want to push them along and keep us back. A lot of minority students knew this but they accepted it. I hated it. Why should I accept this, just because I'm a Black person? This is not fair. You're advancing them and letting them advance. . . . So that's why I said forget it. "I hate this, I'm leaving." I checked out, getting a GED and went ahead and did what I needed to do (p. 216).	In order to preserve his racial self- esteem, he dropped out of Science Tech and moved back to the safe haven of his childhood neighborhood, taking an entire year off from school. . . . He has no regrets about leaving Science Tech because that year was critical to rebuilding his racial self-esteem. Rob eventually received three master's degrees . . . as well as his PhD in applied mathematics (p. 56).

FINDING	NOBLE (2011)	STINSON (2008)	THOMPSON & DAVIS (2013)	THOMPSON & LEWIS (2005)
Learners developed identities based on values, which were affirmed by others with whom they interacted; these values were identity- affirming and supported perseverance in mathematics.	Corey: I was recruited to participate with the math club due to my performance in class. As we competed against other schools, I stood out and began to form a real love for the subject. . . . It was the only subject that I didn't fall asleep through in school. . . . Math has always challenged me, and this is what keeps me drawn to it (p. 198).	Nathaniel: I got a sense [from my parents] that learning was something important, it was something that . . . put food on our plate, and eventually led us to moving up in social standing (p. 988).	Antonio: I mean every report card my teachers would say, "I don't expect no 85 or 89 total, I expect 100's. I don't even expect a 90." I'm like "okay, ya'll hold me to high expectation, well I'm going to hold myself to a high expectation, because if ya'll going to expect more from me, then that's what I'm going to expect from myself" (p. 508)	Malik's desire to be highly regarded as the best at whatever he does is a recurring theme throughout our interviews. It is his desire that drives him to seek admittance "to the best colleges," and to focus more on mathematics where he was "dominant" and "almost untouchable" as opposed to athletics (p. 13).
Learners negotiated their own definitions of success; perseverance was anchored by meeting learners' new and evolving definitions of success across time.	Alfred: I always scored a perfect score in the math Section. . . . I took this as a sign that I was a pretty good mathematician in my younger years. As the years progressed I took these scores plus my many A's that I got in my math classes as something to be proud of (p. 197).	No matter how participants conceptualized success, implicitly or explicitly stated throughout their conversations was the undisputed need for education, whether it was to pass knowledge on or to ensure that one could financially care for loved ones (p. 988).	Antonio: They [peers] influence me to do better, like all the smart students in this school. I think about them whenever I do something. I'm not here to just get a grade, I'm here to prove that I'm one of the smartest kids in the school and I wanna be at the top. I wanna show everybody that I can sit with the best and brightest at this school (p. 509)	The deep-seated goals that a career as a fighter pilot allow Malik to realize are: (a) to be highly regarded as the best at whatever he does; (b) to help people; and (c) to be physically active (p. 13).
Learners encountered issues of awareness and access along their experience pathways and persevered in order to overcome these issues.	Alfred: When I have friends who I know are good at math, then a lot of times we'll work together. And so they help me learn more and become better (p. 201).	Each of the participants had been tracked into honors programs early in his education, providing him with access to enriched schooling experiences and academic programs and access to the most credentialed and experienced teachers (p. 996).	Bruce: Man, me and Mr. Lee used to get along. He used to be my buddy. I used to stay after school with him and I would come early in the morning and we would sit there and have breakfast and lunch together. He would have tutoring sessions and all types of stuff and I would be right there. He was just cool. Math was pretty easy with Mr. Lee (p. 508).	Malik: I want to go to one of the best colleges. I want to be something. . . . I was looking at the required classes [for college] and I realized that where I stand right now as a junior, I don't have what it takes to succeed at that type of college. . . . I knew I had to try to find a way to better prepare myself. So I went to Mr. King and asked him if there's any way we could add more advanced math classes to the schedule (p. 11).

| At the intersection of academic and racialized images, learners negotiated ways to persevere in mathematics. | Dexter: I never really felt like somebody that's in the same class as me is smarter than me. I've never really felt that way. So, when they succeed, I feel like that shows me that I could have succeeded if I didn't succeed. I realize that I should have set the bar higher (p. 201). | Spencer: I make sure that I raise my hand to answer the questions early. . . . I try to prove my worth, show that I belong (p. 994). | Antonio: There ain't nobody out there for us, you know, no black males with math and all that in their heads. All we see is gang bangers on TV, rapping and sports (p. 510) | Malik: When you're at Garvey High School, the competition may not be as great as maybe some of the other schools . . . you're on this false sense of confidence. But once you start to compare yourself to kids nationwide, you're like oh, "I'm kinda weak compared to these guys" . . . so when I was going into my senior year I was like, "I gotta do something now" (p. 7). |
| Learners with a high sense of agency persevered with mathematics across time; they chose to pursue their own pathways to success sustained by the work ethic of practice and perseverance. | Elijah: I've taken more math courses than I've actually had to, which is something I don't mind doing. . . . I've taken some of the more difficult classes as electives, some of the classes that people generally try to stay away from (p. 199). | Ethan: I was always . . . willing to learn . . . what I needed to do to achieve, and if the core curriculum [which included mathematics] was what they needed me to do, I was willing to do it (p. 990). | Bruce: Well because I'm playing football, I plan to get recruited and get a scholarship. An athletic scholarship is what I want, but if I can't I'll definitely take an academic scholarship (p. 510). | Malik: I had always wanted to be part of the in crowd and do what was cool; and what was cool was to play sports. So I never really focused on the books. . . . When I got to high school, I started to make a change. Math class really changed everything for me because I started seeing myself putting the kind of effort into the classroom that I put into the field and I was dominant. . . . It made me realize that this is where I compete, this is my passion and it can be just as fun as sports. This is where I can make a difference (p. 6). |

■ **References**

Aguirre, J. M., Mayfield-Ingram, K., & Martin, D. B. (2013). *The impact of identity in K–8 mathematics learning and teaching: Rethinking equity-based practices.* Reston, VA: National Council of Teachers of Mathematics.

Berry, R. Q., III. (2005). Voices of success: Descriptive portraits of two successful African American male middle school mathematics students. *Journal of African American Studies 8*(4), 46–62.

———. (2008). Access to upper-level mathematics: The stories of successful African American middle school boys. *Journal for Research in Mathematics Education 39*(5), 464–88.

Berry, R. Q., III, & McClain, O. L. (2009). Voices, power, and multiple identities: African American boys and mathematics success. *New England Mathematics Journal 41*, 17–26.

Berry, R. Q., III, Pinter, H., & McClain, O. L. (2013). A critical review of American ĸ–12 mathematics education, 1954–present: Implications for the experiences and achievement of black children. In J. Leonard & D. B. Martin (eds.), *The brilliance of Black children in mathematics: Beyond the numbers and toward new discourse.* Charlotte, NC: Information Age Publishing.

Berry, R. Q., III, Thunder, K., & McClain, O. L. (2011). Counter narratives: Examining the mathematics and racial identities of black boys who are successful with school mathematics. *Journal of African American Males in Education 2*(1), 10–23.

Cornell, S. E., & Hartmann, D. (2007). *Ethnicity and race: Making identities in a changing world.* Thousand Oaks, CA: Pine Forge Press.

Côté, J. E., & Schwartz, S. J. (2002). Comparing psychological and sociological approaches to identity: Identity status, identity capital, and the individualization process. *Journal of Adolescence 25*(6), 571–86.

Dixon-Woods, M., Shaw, R. L., Agarwal, S., & Smith, J. A. (2004). The problem of appraising qualitative research. *Quality & Safety in Health Care 13*(3), 223–25.

Ellington, R. M., & Frederick, R. (2010). Black high achieving undergraduate mathematics majors discuss success and persistence in mathematics. *Negro Educational Review 61*(1–4), 61–84.

Ellis, M. W. (2008). Leaving no child behind yet allowing none too far ahead: Ensuring (in)equity in mathematics education through the science of measurement and instruction. *Teachers College Record 110*(6), 1330–56.

Erwin, E. J., Brotherson, M., & Summers, J. (2011). Understanding qualitative metasynthesis: Issues and opportunities in early childhood intervention research. *Journal of Early Intervention 33*(3), 186–200.

Finlayson, K., & Dixon, A. (2008). Qualitative meta-synthesis: A guide for the novice. *Nurse Researcher 15*(2), 59–71.

Gutiérrez, R. (2008). A "gap gazing" fetish in mathematics education? Problematizing research on the achievement gap. *Journal for Research in Mathematics Education 39*(4), 357–64.

Hattie, J. (2012). *Visible learning for teachers: Maximizing impact on learning.* New York: Routledge.

Jett, C. C. (2010). "Many are called, but few are chosen": The role of spirituality and religion in the educational outcome of "chosen" African American male mathematics majors. *Journal of Negro Education 79*(3), 324–34.

———. (2011). "I once was lost, but now am found": The mathematics journey of an African American male mathematics doctoral student. *Journal of Black Studies 42*(7), 1125–47.

Martin, D. B. (2006). Mathematics learning and participation as racialized forms of experience: African American parents speak on the struggle for mathematics literacy. *Mathematical Thinking and Learning 8*(3), 197–229.

———. (2007). Beyond missionaries or cannibals: Who should teach mathematics to African American children? *High School Journal 91*(1), 6–28.

———. (2008). E(race)ing race from a national conversation on mathematics teaching and learning:

The national mathematics advisory panel as White institutional space. *Montana Mathematics Enthusiast 5*(2–3), 387–98.

———. (2009). Researching race in mathematics education. *Teachers College Record 111*(2), 295–338.

McGee, E. O., & Martin, D. B. (2011a). "You would not believe what I have to go through to prove my intellectual value!": Stereotype management among academically successful Black mathematics and engineering students. *American Educational Research Journal 48*(6), 1347–89.

———. (2011b). From the hood to being hooded: A case study of a Black male Ph.D. *Journal of African American Males in Education 2*(1), 46–65.

Nasir, N. (2002). Identity, goals, and learning: Mathematics in cultural practice. *Mathematical Thinking and Learning 4*(2–3), 213–48.

National Council of Teachers of Mathematics. (2014). *Principles to actions: Ensuring mathematical success for all.* Reston, VA: National Council of Teachers of Mathematics.

National Science Board. (2012). Science and engineering indicators 2012. Arlington, VA: National Science Foundation.

Noble, R. (2011). Mathematics self-efficacy and African American male students: An examination of models of success. *Journal of African American Males in Education 2*(2), 188–213.

Noblit, G. W., & Hare, R. D. (1988). Meta-ethnography: Synthesizing qualitative studies. Newbury Park, CA: Sage.

Paterson, B. L., Thorne, S. E., Canam, C., & Jillings, C. (2001). *Meta-study of qualitative health research.* Thousand Oaks, CA: Sage.

Sandelowski, M., Docherty, S., & Emden, C. (1997). Qualitative meta-synthesis: Issues and techniques. *Research in Nursing and Health 20*, 365–71.

Scruggs, T. E., Mastropieri, M. A., & McDuffie, K. A. (2007). Co-teaching in inclusive classrooms: A metasynthesis of qualitative research. *Exceptional Children 73*(4), 392–416.

Smith, M. S., & Stein, M. K. (2011). *5 practices for orchestrating productive mathematics discussions.* Arlington, VA: National Council of Teachers of Mathematics.

Solomon, Y. (2009). *Mathematical literacy: Developing identities of inclusion.* New York: Routledge.

Sousa, D. A. & Tomlinson, C. A. (2010). *Differentiation and the brain: How neuroscience supports the learner-friendly classroom.* Bloomington, IN: Solution Tree Press.

Stinson, D. W. (2008). Negotiating sociocultural discourses: The counter-storytelling of academically (and mathematically) successful African American male students. *American Educational Research Journal 45*(4), 975–1010.

Snyder, T. D., & Dillow, S. A. (2012). *Digest of education statistics 2011.* Washington, DC: National Center for Education Statistics.

Strauss, A., & Corbin, J. (1997) *Grounded theory in practice.* Thousand Oaks, CA: Sage.

Thompson, L. R., & Davis, J. (2013). The meaning high-achieving African-American males in an urban high school ascribe to mathematics. *Urban Review 45*(4), 490–517.

Thompson, L. R., & Lewis, B. F. (2005). Shooting for the stars: A case study of the mathematics achievement and career attainment of an African American male high school student. *High School Journal 88*(4), 6–18.

We Real Cool

Toward a Theory of Black Masculine Literacies

David E. Kirkland and Austin Jackson

For the young men in the My Brother's Keeper (MBK), a program for at-risk black males, playing with language and style seemed central to literacy practice. Even their body was a tablet that rendered the self textually, allowing powerful forms of composing to be accomplished and shared. Regularly, we observed the young men of MBK—who, by school accounts, were thought to be barely literate in the narrow, print-based sense of the term—operate within multiple symbolic systems to define themselves and shape what they saw as "cool." They made literate decisions, indeed, scribing identity texts in unstable social situations, for example, in the events of dress and speech. The texts that defined these events—and we include here "cool" vernacular and apparel in addition to traditional print and other multimodal semiotic forms (Hull & Nelson, 2005), such as songs, films, and so on—were circulated, shared, and picked up by the young men in sophisticated ways. The texts they produced were also symbolic, offering a narrative of who these young men were and wanted to be.

As we sought to locate meaning in their texts, this study took shape around a particular set of literacy practices firmly rooted within black masculine and pop-cultural models. Although a growing body of literacy research on urban youth has seemed to harden literacy into a performance of race and gender, we have resisted this impulse. Instead, we present the constructs of race (blackness) and gender (masculinity) merely to present a telling case (Mitchell, 1984). What follows is an examination of literacy revealed through the language and style of eleven- to fourteen-year-old black boys.

The initial purpose of the study was to examine the critical literacy practices of the young men of MBK. As we became more familiar with the young men, we became more aware of the social ecology of the group. Important to us was understanding how the literacy practices of seven of its members, "the cool kids" (the phrase "the cool kids" is actual language taken from one of the students in the program), had lifted literacy off the page. As two young black men ourselves, the literacy practices of these young men were both unique and familiar. However, we experienced difficulty finding theories of literacy that acknowledged the particular ways in which these young men employed a variety of symbol systems to shape their lives (Jackson & Moore, 2006; Kirkland, 2006). As opposed to examining the ways in which young black men lacked literacy, we examined how literacy formed and functioned within the group, particularly among the cool kids. To prevent confusion, we would like to explicitly state that this is not a report of critical literacy. The research reported in this study deals in general with black male literate lives and in specific with the ways in which coolness, as cultural phenomenon, embodies and gives visible form to liminal (or in between) aspects of black male subjectivity as expressed through literacy. The texts produced by black males acting cool can, thus, be seen as giving visible form not only to coolness but also to the seemingly hidden (or underacknowledged) practices of black masculine literacies.

We argue here that the cool kids enacted blackness and masculinity through coolness. By association, they constructed coolness using identity texts and what Turner (1970) has called a "forest of symbols" (p. xiii). The symbols through which coolness is revealed link to our understanding of literacy as a symbolic ritual. For Turner (Deflem, 1991), symbols, as in literate forms, are representative of cultural phenomena. They produce meanings through associations, resemblances, and conventions. Quite simply, they communicate a range of messages—metaphorically and figuratively, allegorically and by implication. They are also shared locally and gain intelligibility in the common culture of a given group (Willis, 1990). When most effective, the symbol itself becomes the phenomenon.

It is in this way that we use Turner's (1970) concept of symbology, the study of symbol systems, as a way to make sense of what things like speech and style symbolized in the cultural practices/ritual performances of the cool kids. What is at issue, then, is an explication and articulation of a theory about the relationship between the coolness cultural model and the uniquely black masculine literacy practices associated with it. To this end, we explore how coolness evolved within the particular social situation of the cool kids to enhance the nature of what it means to be literate in our society. The theoretical framing of the study is presented in the next two sections.

Defining Literacy

In this article, we define literacy broadly, as a cultural practice that is embedded in social and cultural phenomena, such as coolness (Dyson, 2003; Freire & Macedo, 1987; Gee, 2001; Mahiri, 2004). Literacy, then, is capable of operating from a diversity of representational systems, particularly when combining written and oral forms with visual, gestural, and other kinds of symbols.

This definition of literacy is consistent with scholars who see literacy as a cultural practice that involves multiple sign-and-symbol systems (Hull & Nelson, 2005; New London Group, 1996). That is, individuals and groups communicate by using more than just words (Bean & Harper, 2008; Gallego & Hollingsworth, 2000; New London Group, 1996). Youth, in particular, practice literacy by weaving together identities and common worldviews. They use numerous symbolic tools, sometimes even clothes, to communicate values, produce meanings, and participate in desired social and cultural communities (Bakhtin, 1981, 1986; Dyson, 2001, 2003; Moje, 2004).

Building on these understandings of literacy, we see literacy as also involving critical cultural competencies, or the situated understanding of the consequences of symbolic tool use within a particular group (Cushman et al., 2001; Gutiérrez, 2008; Morrell, 2002). Scholars in this tradition contend that although one can have access to a variety of modes through which to represent things, one must also have an understanding of how these modes operate within a given social, cultural, and political context. These scholars see literacy as tied to multiple modes of expression. They also see literacy as tied to the individual potential for social and cultural critique, which involves a critical awareness of cultural competencies as they relate to issues of power and desire at their extremes. By critical, we mean an awareness of things, such as the symbol that is language and the social and ideological contexts that exist beyond it. By competency, we mean the ability to demonstrate awareness of this context (and its limits) within situational events in both appropriate and skilled (or competent) ways.

Defining Literacy

In this chapter, we define literacy broadly, as a cultural practice that is embedded in social and cultural phenomena, such as coolness (Dyson, 2003; Freire & Macedo, 1987; Gee, 2001; Mahiri, 2004). Literacy, then, is capable of operating from a diversity of representational systems, particularly when combining written and oral forms with visual, gestural, and other kinds of symbols.

This definition of literacy is consistent with scholars who see literacy as a cultural practice that involves multiple sign-and-symbol systems (Hull & Nelson, 2005; New London Group, 1996). That is, individuals and groups communicate by using more than just words (Bean & Harper, 2008; Gallego & Hollingsworth, 2000; New London Group, 1996). Youth, in particular, practice literacy by weaving together identities and common worldviews. They use numerous symbolic tools, sometimes even clothes, to communicate values, produce meanings, and participate in desired social and cultural communities (Bakhtin, 1981, 1986; Dyson, 2001, 2003; Moje, 2004).

Building on these understandings of literacy, we see literacy as also involving critical cultural competencies or the situated understanding of the consequences of symbolic tool use within a particular group (Cushman et al., 2001; Gutiérrez, 2008; Morrell, 2002). Scholars in this tradition contend that although one can have access to a variety of modes through which to represent things, one must also have an understanding of how these modes operate within a given social, cultural, and political context. These scholars see literacy as tied to multiple modes of expression. They also see literacy as tied to the individual potential for social and cultural critique, which involves a critical awareness of cultural competencies as they relate to issues of power and desire at their extremes. By critical, we mean an awareness of things, such as the symbol that is language and the social and ideological context (and its limits) within situational events in both appropriate and skilled (or competent) ways.

Further, by focusing on black male subjectivity (Walten, 2001), how young black men imagine themselves and their possibilities for acting, we see literacy as the practice of shaping identities and as a tool for participating in culturally valued experiences. The young men we studied, in fact, used items such as eyeglasses symbolically—not only to style but also to revise themselves as serious and studious members of a learning community. This symbolic practice struck us as insightful, particularly in the wake of dominant deficit discourses that too often define black males as deviant. For one of the young men, "My glasses make me look smart. Not nerdy, but serious like Malcolm X. It says to people who think we're dumb or only into bling and stuff like that, that we are deeper."

It is in this way that even eyeglasses can be used as tools to communicate larger points. Hence, fashion can be seen as literacy practice. To understand this practice involves merging ideas of literacy. By understanding literacy as critical cultural competence and literacy as multimodal social practice, we define literacy in this article as a complex system of symbological patterns and practices. These practices involve the skilled use and manipulation of tools taken from multiple symbol systems, including eyeglasses, that gain meaning and purchase in the common culture that youth create and sustain (Willis, 2003).

Framing Coolness

In recent years, two perspectives have tended to dominate the discourse on coolness and black males. These perspectives regard coolness as either negative or positive and black males as deviant or misunderstood. Majors and Billson (1993), attempting to understand the deeper psychology behind why black males fail, viewed coolness (or "cool pose") as a "ritualized" expression of masculinity that involves speech, style, and physical and emotional posturing. They suggested that many black males use these attributes to evoke distance from, contrast to, and superiority over outsiders. For Majors and Billson, coolness communicates a clear message of strength and control. However, they argued that it also shields young black men from intimacy, commitment, and caring relationships.

In line with Majors and Billson's (1993) psychological assessment of coolness, scholars from a range of disciplines have argued that the social numbing that being cool produces explains, in part, why many black males struggle in school. These scholars have argued that, for the most part, black males' lives are compromised deeply by the pursuit of coolness, as coolness corresponds with a set of negative behaviors that impair their ability to succeed academically (Cose, 2002; Davis, 2001; Marable, 1994; Ogbu, 2003). These scholars view many cool black males as marginal to the established social mores that influence appropriate social behavior.

In this line of thinking, Patterson (2006) has viewed coolness as a bleak and dangerous pursuit for black males, what he calls a "Dionysian trap" (paragraph 22). This Dionysian trap, what Patterson sees as the deadly illusion of acceptance, can seem appealing to young black men but in the end ensnares them in a process of self-sabotage and eventual destruction. For Patterson, the luster of this illusion is not disconnected from mainstream culture. Patterson insists that the illusion functions within it, supported by some of its most influential structures and ideals. Among them, hip-hop, professional sports, and "homeboy" fashions, viewed by many black males as cool, Patterson has argued, have become as mainstream as the Big Mac. He explained that although mainstream America is very much into these items, most Americans are not threatened by them. In particular, middle-class whites, who enjoy the cool and sometimes negative accoutrements of hip-hop and sports, have structures to filter through and safety nets to stave off their consequences. For Patterson, black males do not enjoy such luxuries because the same supports are not available to them.

Not all scholars agree with Patterson's bleak assessment of black male cool culture. Scholars such as Connor (1995) have viewed coolness as a general state of well-being, a transcendent calm, internal peace, and serenity. They have suggested that being cool might help black males cope with (or conceal) stress caused by social oppression, rejection, and racism. It may also furnish black males with a sense of control, strength, confidence, and stability that could help them handle the closed doors and negative messages pervading modern culture. Connor viewed coolness as being associated with black males' silent and knowing rejection of racist oppression, a self-dignified expression of masculinity developed by black males denied by mainstream expressions of manhood. She critiques mainstream perceptions of coolness for being narrow, distorted, and even racist.

So as not to be confined to a particular perspective, we use the term *coolness* here to mean a unique performative act, an attitude, comportment, or way of being characterized through verbal presentation and style. It is historically and cross-culturally rooted and has symbolically served as the disposition of rebels and underdogs, slaves, prisoners, bikers, political dissidents, and the like. It has also been the attitude widely adopted by individuals such as artists and intellectuals interested in pushing social, cultural, and political boundaries (Connor, 1995).

Although we find the torrential debate surrounding coolness alluring, the mere fact or claim as to whether or not coolness is bad or good is beside the point. Our point is that coolness as cultural phenomenon, as disposition toward life to connect with others, to push against social norms, maps onto language and literacy in unique ways. For instance, there is a poetics of self and of others housed in its symbolic construction, which intensifies with the expression of self that is made available when examining black male symbolic tool use (Gee, 1989). In the case of the young men of MBK, literacy was used as a tool for mediated participation in a world where the unwritten rules of coolness were represented.

The young men's constructions of themselves as cool coincided with their black masculine literacy practices. These practices mapped onto the popular cultures that Patterson (2006) laments—hip-hop and sports. Nonetheless, we conducted this study to build on the work of scholars, such as Dimitriadis (2001), who proclaimed, "We have only just begun to get a sense of how young people actually use these texts to construct their identities, their unique subjectivities, and the social networks in which they are embedded" (p. 29). In understanding coolness and its relationship to literacy practice among black males, we believe it is important to explain why adolescent black males act cool in the first place and begin to describe the kinds of meanings they accomplish through this cultural model.

Connor (1995) offered four reasons to explain why black males adopt postures of coolness:

1. As a strategy for navigating their world
2. As a system to establish their own manhood
3. As a source of resilience
4. As a form of aggression, strength, and power

For Connor, these reasons for acting cool have developed, partly, in a subculture of poverty and educational neglect and have, yet, emerged as an option for young black males with a desperate need for guidelines concerning maturity. This is perhaps why acts of coolness continue among adolescent black males, why they are absorbed by other groups, and why they appeared so prominently in the MBK program. But even if we accept these explanations, it is difficult to say whether or not they are the sole reasons why adolescent black males gravitate to coolness. There is more that needs to be understood.

How might we view coolness as a way of representing other things, such as the everyday values and viewpoints of particular black males? Specifically, how do cool black males use a range of symbolic materials to construct their values and views? For instance, what blends of sound and substance figure into the language of cool? How might this language be capable of lettering the world in a spoken and an unspoken vernacular? Although we do not go into it here, we can include other features to this vernacular, such as movements and gestures (Neal et al., 2003; Spivak, 1985). Our point is that coolness at MBK influenced the things the young men said and represented. It was embodied and expressed in multisymbolic forms that emanated from multisensual spaces. Such forms and spaces should be considered when reasoning why black males adopt cool postures.

Another reason why adolescent black males adopt postures of coolness, then, might deal with the specific symbols and symbol systems that many black males use to communicate meaning. Cool symbol systems were discernable in the MBK group, where symbols, themselves, acquired meaning and gained value within the specific contexts of the young men's lives. It is within this context that the "complex, emergent, and messy relationship" among coolness, young black men, and literacy becomes clearer (Dimitriadis, 2001, p. 29).

For us, this complex interrelationship serves as a telling case, a situation "in which the particular circumstances surrounding a case, serve to make previously obscure theoretical relationships suddenly apparent" (Mitchell, 1984, p. 239). According to Mitchell, a telling case is not representative of a population group but rather serves as an example of deeper phenomena and is, therefore, capable of illustrating theoretical issues not previously visible. This is to say, in-depth examination of cultural phenomena, such as coolness, can elucidate more general theoretical principles that underpin the social construction of literacy within a given group. This examination tends to focus attention on the critical cultural competencies needed to participate fully within a given literacy event, the cultural models that govern social relations among participants who practice literacy within the event, and the activities (i.e., what is done, said, performed, worn, etc.) that relate to textual production and social meanings around the event.

Using this approach, we have explored literacy within the particular situation of the cool kids to offer a telling case through which theoretical concepts and hypotheses about black males and literacy can be drawn. Our inquiry was guided by two questions:

1. How did coolness relate to literacy among the young men at MBK?
2. What symbolic patterns helped to shape these relations?

Methods

We explored our research as participant-researchers in MBK, an early intervention program for at-risk black males at Detroit's Malcolm X Academy (MXA). MXA, a k–8 public school, was established in response to community demands for an educational intervention into the crisis facing black males living in Detroit. According to Hopkins (1997), MXA emerged in Detroit during the severe economic recession and crack cocaine epidemic from the last quarter century. During this period in inner-city Detroit, one in three black men found themselves caught in a deadly cycle of school failure, drugs, violence, incarceration, and murder (Watson & Smitherman, 1997). From its inception, MXA, among the nation's first all-male public schools with an Afrocentric focus, boasted a culturally relevant curriculum that emphasized the contributions of people of African descent to traditional school disciplines, such as mathematics, the sciences, and the humanities.

At the time of this study, MBK serviced sixteen adolescent, black male mentees and operated over a thirty-week expanse, from September 2003 to June 2004. Two or three times a month during that period, MBK transported Michigan State University (MSU) undergraduate-student mentors (both women and men) to MXA to interact with mentees. Sessions occurred on Saturdays and lasted approximately three hours. Each session was typically structured around the following activities: welcome and pledges, community news / current events, one-on-one mentor-mentee sessions, and service-learning projects.

In addition to mentoring sessions at MXA, mentees participated in two weekend retreats on the campus of MSU (one in the fall and one in the spring) and attended a one-week workshop on career building and personal growth during the summer, also at MSU. During their visits to MSU, mentees learned details of collegiate life. They also visited dorms and classrooms, learned about college majors and careers, and were introduced to numerous university faculty, staff, and students who provided tips and pointers for making successful transitions to college and beyond.

Table 1. My Brother's Keeper Program Mentees

NAME	AGE	NAME	AGE	NAME	AGE	NAME	AGE
Derrick	12	George	12	Job	13	Lucious	12
Devin	12	Hakim	13	Justin	12	Mark	13
Ernest	13	Jacob	13	Keith	11	Reggie	12
Etherin	13	Jamal	12	Larry	14	Terrence	13

The Cool Kids

We focus on seven young men in the MBK program (see table 1). We purposefully selected these young men to be focal participants as they stood out from the rest of the group. Importantly, they considered themselves and were considered by their peers to be cool. Hence, the criteria for their selection was based on three factors: (1) their reputations among peers as cool, (2) their perceptions of themselves as cool, and (3) their willingness to participate in the study. Not all youth were willing to participate.

Larry was the eldest of the group at fourteen years of age. The group also included the following: Hakim, who seemed quiet; Terrence, Hakim's cousin; Etherin, the most expressive in the group; Lucious, the self-proclaimed "coolest"; Job, the "righteous one"; and Keith, the youngest at eleven years of age (all names are pseudonyms selected by the participants of this study). Although all sixteen of the young men in the program had in some way been labeled "at risk," the cool kids exemplified the tenuous aspirations of that label. They also placed a value on being confident, or as Etherin put it, "They don't think we know nothing . . . but our game on lock." Together, these seven young men comprised an interesting subcommunity in the program. As noted earlier, they called themselves the cool kids.

Data Collection

To collect data, we would do what Willis (1977) advised:

> Go to the cultural milieu . . . and . . . accept a certain autonomy of the processes at this level which both defeats any simple notion of mechanistic causation and gives the social agents involved some meaningful scope for viewing, inhabiting and constructing their own world in a way which is recognizably human and not theoretically reductive. (p. 172)

Understanding that the "cultural level is marked by contestation, resistance, and compromise" (MacLeod, 1995, p. 20), we sought to capture data at intimate levels of participation within the group, observing and listening to the cool kids in their personal settings, hoping to understand them through the consequences of their viewpoints, values, and voices.

Accordingly, our collection of data implied "the active, collective use and explorations of

Table 2. Ethnographic/Sociolinguistic Data Sources

SOURCE	QUANTITY	DESCRIPTION
Video records	10 (3 hrs/recording)	An unmonitored video recorder was set in a back corner of the field site to capture and document what students were wearing, to "eavesdrop" on their in-class conversations, and to get a better picture of classroom activities.
Field notes	10 (172 total pages)	Field notes were constructed by jotting down, in some detail, instances that revealed students' language and literacy practices (i.e., singing, bragging, rapping, talking about "gittin girls," and being cool, etc.).
Interview/transcripts	300 pages	Informal interviews were conducted to clarify information, ideas, and literacy practices. We also talked with students randomly to get a sense of how they made sense of their literacy practices and how these practices related to being cool.
Site artifacts	317	Site documents were collected to contribute to an overall understanding of coolness and its relationship to how the cool kids practiced literacy.

Note: Subjects and the practices that reveal them can be understood more clearly through a wide range of data sources (Erickson, 1986).

received symbolic . . . and cultural resources to explain, make sense of and positively respond to 'inherited' structural and material conditions" (Willis, 1983, p. 112). To receive the "symbolic . . . and cultural resources" of this group, we focused generatively on the young men's language and style, as each symbol system made such items visible. What was rendered for us was an elaborate portrait of consistencies and inconsistencies, finely etched in unanticipated brush-strokes of complexity (Willis, 2003).

We compiled four types of information that helped reveal this portrait to us. They included the following: video records, field notes, audio transcripts, and site artifacts. Video records were captured using a camcorder and tripod placed in the back of the MBK meeting space. Usually within an hour of leaving the field, we wrote field notes from scratch notes and initial jottings. Using video records, we transcribed significant segments of talk, detailing each episode in the form of a transcript. Finally, we collected site artifacts, including student writings and descriptions of the young men's clothing and style choices.

Altogether, we collected ten three-hour video records, multiple site artifacts, and close to three hundred pages of transcripts (see table 2). These data were immediately indexed and cataloged to correspond with one another.

Data Analysis

In our analysis, we set out to describe, interpret, and explain the relationships between coolness as a cultural phenomenon and the young men's literacy practices through their symbols of coolness. Specifically, our interpretation of data focused on identifying how coolness was produced through language and style. In doing so, our goal in analyzing data was to make sense of the ways in which the cool kids manufactured meaning and practiced literacy in the context of MBK through talk and dress. We further analyzed the cool kids within the complex activity system of the MBK program, which was itself enriched by a range of symbols that sanctioned a variety of possible meanings, routines, activities, and ways of being.

Themes and codes were developed based on relationships that emerged between the group's language and style. To understand these relationships, we identified patterns in spoken communication, what we labeled "cool talk." To understand cool talk, we created three organizing categories: pragmatic/functional, cultural, and geospatial. These categories emerged base on themes we identified in the data.

We also identified patterns in the young men's style choices, what they called "sportin phat gear." To make sense of the symbolic significance of "gear," we organized style data by type. Two predominant types emerged: hip-hop and athletics. The categories of cool talk and sportin phat gear allowed us to code data for patterns that would help us (*a*) determine how coolness related to literacy among the young men at MBK and (*b*) distinguish the symbolic patterns that helped to shape these relations. In sum, we used our understandings of how cool talk and phat gear functioned in the young men's construction of themselves to better understand the relationship among coolness, literacy, and black males.

Positionality of Researchers

We feel that it is important to point out our particular roles in this study. We served as mentors, program coordinators, and researchers in the program, one of us for several years. In this capacity, we saw ourselves as mirrors to the young men, especially the cool kids; however, neither of us considered ourselves very cool. Notwithstanding, as black males with keen interests in hip-hop and sports, we shared many common characteristics with the young men of MBK. One of us, along with several MBK participants, was born and raised in the city in which the study takes place. To these points, we acknowledge how our proximity to the study and our roles in shaping its results can be limiting.

Despite the similarities shared with the young men, we are also both academics and cultural cousins of the young men of MBK. Leaving neither of these identities behind, this study is shaped by who we are and where we exist in relation to them. Indeed, other researchers, positioned much differently from us, might arrive at different results. To limit the impact of our backgrounds on this work, we relied heavily upon our relationships with the young men of MBK, particularly the cool kids, to make sense of their experiences and to get their input on the data we collected from them. As we present our findings, we do our best to provide rich description over didacticism and the students' voices over our own.

Results

In the sections to follow, we present findings based on the themes and patterns that emerged in our data. Consistent with the practices of ethnographic research, results and discussion are integrated. Specific patterns that relate to the cool kids' use of symbols illustrate how they constructed coolness and identity. This identity, as we will note, can be traced beyond coolness through the aforementioned patterns in talk and style. In particular, the cool kids, who borrowed their talk and style from black masculine models in hip-hop and sports, constructed cool through a set of literacy practices, which were also part of a much larger black pop-cultural scene.

Larry, for example, opting against modesty, declared in permanent ink against the sides of his new sneakers, "I'm the man." This proclamation of masculinity was, for the group, a symbol of coolness, which splintered into a variety of spoken forms: (Terrence) "I'm da man"; (Hakim) "I gotta get my grown man on"; and (Lucious) "I'm the shit." These expressions point to the multiple ways in which cool could be pronounced in the group.

Asked why he wrote, "I'm the man" on his shoes, Larry shrugged his shoulders and replied, "I don't know. We be tryin to stand out." Although brief, Larry's admission is instructive. In an attempt to distinguish themselves from others, the cool kids were enacting black masculine selves in writing and in speech, in style and in appearance. However, there was a nuance in this discursive practice worth making note of. For them, the term *man* adopted relative meanings. The same young man who declared, "I'm the man," also railed against the Man on a number of occasions (e.g., "The Man is holdin us down"). In this use, the phrase "the Man" did not represent the exaggerated exploits of cool black men (see Smitherman's [1977] conversation of Stagger Lee for an example of black male models of exaggerated/performed linguistic exploits). Instead, it symbolized the Establishment as opposed to the Fringe, a symbol of the perversion of power, domination, and oppressive rule.

This semantic nuance in the group's talk reveals the complexity of the symbolic systems through which the cool kids' literacies operated. The young men's expressions/representations of things, whether written or spoken, were equally complex. For example, the young men would talk about the baggage or, as one of them put it, "slave mentality" associated with brand-name items. While this critique of brand name was tied specifically to Tommy Hilfiger fashions, it vanished in relation to hip-hop and athletic apparel items.

Regardless of how we make sense of them, the social transcripts—the language the cool kids used to critique or accommodate the world—functioned to demonstrate to others how cool they were. In this way, their sense of coolness, although complex and contradictory, did not yield to conventional wisdom. It had its own logic, which was articulated through a black masculine model of discourse—what Smitherman (1999, p. 219) called "braggadocio" and what Alim (2006, p. 13) referred to as that "sacred, streetified, slick-ass" black language.

The literacies that helped to construct them as cool were also about style, for example, the writing on shoes—which was much like tagging (MacGillivray & Curwen, 2007) or the inscription of "claimed" spaces. There literacy practices were about posturing, showing how cool they were—a kind of ritual performance that for decades has incubated in the posthumous underground of black male speech communities.

Larry's shoes, for all intents and purposes, were marked with the echoes of these communities and enriched by the linguistic "flava" of centuries-old black male conversations. Understanding these conversations, like any form of literacy, requires intimately understanding talk. And by understanding talk—cool talk in this case—we contend that researchers might get a glimpse at a particular kind of literacy that helps shape black male lives.

Cool Talk as Symbol System in the Construction of Cool Identities

By cool talk, we refer to the recognizable discourse patterns that governed language use and literacy practice among the cool kids. Indeed, the cool kids had their own language, which became an interior anchor that allowed them to straddle the scholastic margins of school and the social parameters of peers. As we alluded to earlier, this language possessed various elements: (*a*) a hybridized syntax borrowed from mainstream and black popular cultures, (*b*) semantic qualities that gave unique and complex meanings to familiar words, (*c*) a musical phonology that operated almost like poetry or rap, allowing words to slip rhythmically from the young men's lips, and (*d*) a style that transcended even their talk.

It is not entirely without a sense of irony and humor, however, that in attempting to gain insight into the cool talk of the young men that one of us would be barred from the young men's language practices. The cool kids saw the one of us charged with instructing them as not so cool. The unwanted albatross of an "adult" hanging around in an uncool turtleneck sweater, speaking in an uncouth dialect, made the young men suspicious. When asked for an explanation, several of the young men explained, "It's because he sound white." This explanation illustrates how the young men "raced" language. For them, cool talk was black talk. Importantly, they used language to express who they were. It is in this way that cool talk was pragmatic in the general sense of the term, where language, for the young men, was as much about relevance and utility as it was about anything else.

"They Gotta Rap about Something": The Functions of Cool Talk

For the cool kids, language was a pragmatic resource for participation in valued cultural contexts. For example, the language of the cool kids, cool talk, operated as a means of linking the young men to pop culture, which in their eyes was the essence of cool. Cool talk was also a utility for social distinctions and operated as a discourse of critique. This discourse of critique, which has roots in a larger black linguistic tradition (Smitherman, 1977), itself was a sort of pragmatic activity. An example of this activity can be observed in Terrence's assessment of "marketplace ideologies" (Collins, 1999) that influence hip-hop consumerism.

> Many people trying to be like rappers, like Baby, when they first came out wearing Burberry, everybody wearing Burberry. Like when Fifty Cent [started driving] a Hummer, then everybody wants a Hummer.

Terrence's critique of hip-hop's commercial influence on "many people" represents the group's rhetorical pragmatism. That is, Terrence's comment was contextualized in his social world, remade through his own sense of what was relevant to be said within the group. In a sense, it was cool to critique market dogma in hip-hop because hip-hop was a known and valued commodity. Terrence's criticism of hip-hop's commercial influences, therefore, was useful to the group as long as the critique was driven by the group's pragmatic impulse.

Pragmatic linguistic practices were used by the cool kids as a way to stand apart as well as a way to be pooled together. Cool talk, thus, operated based on a paradoxical dynamic—to help the cool kids distinguish themselves from others but also to align them with the cooler elements of their peer worlds.

The contradiction that shaped their pragmatic language was also the contradiction that shaped their thoughts. For example, misogynistic messages—as opposed to critique—were as prevalent in the young men's cool talk as they were in the hip-hop lyrics to which the young men listened. It was difficult during the course of this study to mediate between students' right to their own language (Kinloch, 2005) and challenge what we saw (even as members of the first hip-hop generation) as hip-hop culture's and the young men's irresponsibly materialist and inexcusably (at least in our view) misogynistic language.

In one session in particular, there appeared to be strong student resistance to criticizing rap lyrics that clearly demeaned women. As a prompt for a writing assignment in which they would critically examine rap lyrics and hip-hop culture, students were asked to read an article that argued against the popular rapper Jay-Z speaking at a high school in Detroit. As expected, the students' responses were complex and sometimes contradictory. Many students criticized the article as wrong for endorsing censorship of Jay-Z because of his lyrics. All sixteen of the young men in the program became quite animated and assertive when their idea of Jay-Z as a role model possessing something valuable to say to black youth (besides "Buy my new record") was complicated by the piece.

HAKIM: They gotta rap about something. I think it's exciting.
LARRY: Giving people what they want . . .
AUSTIN: What about crack?
HAKIM: I just like [Jay-Z's] clothes.
LARRY: I don't think nobody has nothing to say; he got money.
ETHERIN: He talk about whatever he needs to in order to sell records . . . some of the stuff he says is true.

Hakim's attempt to circumvent the issue completely drew attention to Jay-Z's appearance ("I just like his clothes"). Larry's and Etherin's argument reflected the pervasive capitalist, laissez-faire sentiments that the MBK program had as its goal of disrupting ("I don't think nobody has nothing to say, he got money," "He talk about whatever he needs to in order to sell records"). Their responses offered a view of cool talk as colliding with forms of communication or perspectives the young men perceived as irrelevant to their lives, as being antiblack or uncool. In this sense, even their discourses of accommodation to a sexist status quo were pragmatic.

In particular, the theme of relevance—either as a situational awareness of what language to use or as a social critique of "uncool" language—emerged significantly in the young men's responses. One could "talk about whatever," even voicing hatred toward women, as long as the reasons seemed practical. For them, using language in a way that helps one to make money practically makes one cool, which for them was the highest form of relevance.

What was most surprising about their responses was not necessarily the young men's defense of Jay-Z and his right to free speech but the various, shifting rationales used to support their positions. Their line of argumentation moved from moral relativism ("They gotta rap about something") to simple supply-and-demand economics ("giving the people what they want to hear") and from democracy ("They got the freedom to say what they want to say") to what appears to be open misogyny. For scholars such as Young (2007), these arguments are not always leveraged against dominant discourses; they are the dominant discourses. As far as misogyny is concerned, the pragmatism behind the young men's arguments seemed to subscribe to Western male dominance.

This does not mean that the cool kids lacked agency in cool talk. Rather, it speaks to a complexity concerning the pragmatics of cool talk. Cool talk, like other language systems, was hinged against the young men's internal and external worlds; it succumbed to both black cultural and American mainstream influences. This aspect of their talk was revealed in a conversation one of us had with Lucious.

> LUCIOUS: It's hard to hear him [Austin]. He sounds like a white dude.
> DAVID: Why is that?
> LUCIOUS: I mean . . . I understand what he saying about Jay-Z. I don't care for him anyway, but he misinterpreting us. I think he misinterpreting Jay-Z too. That's why I don't want to talk about stuff like that in here [school]. [School] takes what's ours and changes it. It makes it so not cool. . . . I like the way that we sound and what we have to say. We have our own thing. We be rappin, not just talking.

Lucious's thoughts about language, "rappin" in his words, is telling. For him, rapping was something that was created by and for the group. It served the purposes of the group, whatever those purposes were at the time. His assessment of language, then, must be seen as consistent with the assessments of scholars who describe a culturally and even racially relevant linguistics (Clark, 2003; Kinloch, 2007; Purcell-Gates, 2002; Richardson, 2003; Villanueva, 1993; Young, 2004). Indeed, other scholars share Lucious's observation that co-optation of language by authorities poses a threat to its relevance (Kirkland & Jackson, 2008; Richardson, 2006; Smitherman, 2006). It is no wonder, then, that the cool kids felt protective of their linguistic property.

Figure 1. Terrence's Drawing

"That's How We Be Talking": The Culture of Cool Talk

Cool talk also played on language in culturally specific ways (see Alim, 2006; Rickford & Rickford, 2000; and Smitherman, 2006) for a discussion of African American language play). Words like "dog," for example, were frequently used among the cool kids as terms of endearment. Such terms were also used as affirmations of coolness, reserved for those young black men who, according to the cool kids, were "down," a word they used to signify allegiance.

They appropriated their vocabulary from black culture (Alim, 2006). Moreover, the lexicon of African American language often spilled into the young men's forms of writing. Terrence, for example, drew two "cool"-looking figures (see figure 1), one dressed in Phat Farm saying to the other, "What up young pimp juice"—a phrase made popular by rapper Nelly. The other character in the figure, sporting a FUBU shirt, responds with an affirmative, "Forsheezee" (coded hip-hop lexicon for "for sure").

While these examples further demonstrate the pragmatic aspects of cool talk—that is, language use for practical/relevant reasons—an important link can be made between the lexicon of coolness and the lexicon of black people. Morgan (2005) has suggested that because of its perception as cool, many words and expressions from African American language have passed into the mainstream lexicon. This includes the contemporary term *cool* itself, which adopted new meaning on the black jazz scene. Instead of referring to something that is temperately cold, the jazz use of cool referred to the smooth demeanor and slick style of jazz artists. In this way, terms like *cool* have transcended time in black space. The term *cool*, as used by the cool kids, stretched through the black linguistic tradition, from jazz to hip-hop, from the talk of black athletes to the chilling rhythms of rap.

It is within this larger black pop-cultural backdrop that the cool kids used the term, defining *cool* as easygoing, smooth, skilled, or capable of extraordinary exploits. As an adjective, the

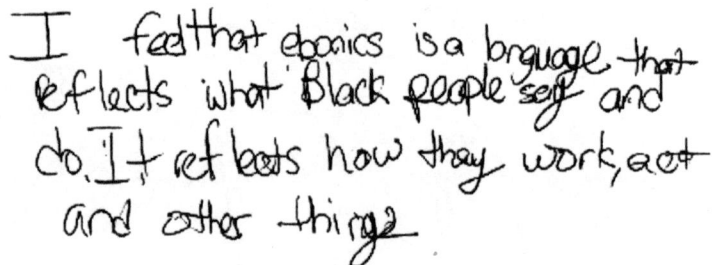

Figure 2. Hakim's Thoughts on African American Language

Figure 3. Etherin's Thoughts on African American Language

term was used to modify various aspects of the cool kids' lives, including their talk and style. For example, their use of expressions like "chill" characterized a Zen-like contentment. The use of the phrase "That's cold" characterized something they found appealing. Both of these utterances have origins in African American language, and both their meanings have been extended through the language of rap (Alim, 2006; Smitherman, 2000). Therefore, it was not surprising that during our analysis of the cool kids' talk, we found coolness to be marked by black pop culture and African American language. These markings were visible in the young men's writings.

Figures 2 and 3 illustrate how the young men understood African American language, or as they put it, Ebonics. For them, this cool language variety was tantamount to "what rappers do." Hence, at a cultural level, cool talk was a form of rappin—a cultural code that could help shape black male identities. This claim is further illustrated in figure 3, which depicts two supposed cool young men greeting each other using African American language in the black masculine pitch. In the figure, one of the young men asks, "What's up main [man]?" The other responds, "Nuthin much, cuz." Etherin, commenting on his characters, explained, "That's cool talk. That's how we [the cool kids] be talkin."

In this instance, African American language contributed not only to the oral but also the textual products of the cool kids. It functioned as what Halliday (1978) referred to as antilanguage—exclusive, coded speech created by a subgroup to signify a shared sense of identity and group membership. In the context of MBK, the cool kids employed this antilanguage to promote solidarity. For example, Keith, a seventh grader with family roots in Alabama, observed this strategy during a trip to his parents' home state. "I was down south," Keith explained. "People were shouting and stuff like that. I was with my mother. People were talking proper. They was talking *straight English*, but then they switched when white [people] were around . . . People do this to have their own little language."

Based on his comments, we can see that Keith observed a flexibility in language that allowed speakers— black or cool—to have "their own little language." This language could erect cultural fences to join groups together and yet help them to stand apart. For him, this rhetorical maneuvering amounted to a self-conscious rhetorical strategy used in the southern vernacular to "keep folk out yo bid'ness." Indeed, the cool kids inherited this linguistic trick. They could move in and out of cool-talk situations seamlessly. In fact, they used talk—as Keith would later inform us—to "protect their secrets."

While it was cool to code language to protect the group's secrets, it was perhaps cooler to play with language to extend its style and use. This point explains how a sort of hip-hop pig Latin, made popular by California "gangsta" rapper Snoop Dogg, emerged in the group. In a paper he wrote for the program, Keith used the phrase, "Off the hizzle fo' shizzle, my nizzle," which translates to "Off the hook, for sure, my nigga." Similar to how "heezy" or "hizzle" altered the surface appearance as a suffix in this last example, another student used z + nits as a suffix to accentuate the expression "the shit" (i.e., "shiznits" as in, "my pec[s] are the [shit]"). The use of this morphology comes between two cool interlocutors, writing in class, wearing dark shades, one with a "fly" Afro, the other with dreadlocks (see figure 4).

The drawing and its accompanying printed texts further demonstrate how the cool kids worked within and extended the black linguistic tradition and connected themselves to pop culture. Moreover, through pop culture, the young men extended their cultural connections to a common, more mainstream heritage (cf. Dimitriadis, 2001; Fisher, 2004), creating new words that fit within the apparent cultural model of cool (cf. Alim, 2006; Makoni et al., 2003). However, pop culture and African American tradition alone did not make their ways with words meaningful. Their uses of language resided in particular plots of social real estate, where rapping was viewed not only as cool but also as a spatially "appropriate" discourse.

"Ebonics Is Like Being Ghetto": The Location of Cool Talk

The cool kids saw language—whether linked generally to the larger black culture or specifically to hip-hop culture—as a tool for meaningful communication within specific situated contexts. In separate conversations, each of the young men shared with us his thoughts about Ebonics. For Lucious, Ebonics "shows how characters would act on the street." Larry explained the special rules that governed appropriate use this way: "Ebonics is like being ghetto . . . when

Figure 4. Example of (Hip-Hop) Cultural Influences on Cool Talk

you around your parents, you talk proper, but when you around your friends, you change roles and cuss and stuff. It's cool." This understanding of language beyond culture to location ("the street") is important. It suggests that coolness and cool language could be positioned in the group not only functionally and culturally but also geographically. This means that language gained meaning for the youth in the specific physical contexts of use. However, their public positioning of language did not include all spaces. For example, "It's . . . OK to use Ebonics when you around your boys and stuff," Hakim explains, "but when you get around people . . . you never know." Similarly, Keith suggests, "It's like, you know, you can actually like chill with your boys and stuff . . . but when you talking to adults and . . . you can't do that because you supposed to respect your elders." In this sense, context denoted more than physical place. It was also about audience and stage, or physical situation.

In this way, cool talk had geographic functions that were defined by their contextual parameters, in most cases the peer space. Whereas African American language was used in-group to establish and manage peer relationships, cool talk was contextually inappropriate for communicating outside the peer group with uncool people, such as parents and teachers, and in uncool places, such as official speech events. What strikes us as ironic about this sentiment is that, based on our understanding, language is learned in particular social environments (Filmer, 2003; Foster, 1992; Hymes, 1974; Isenbarger & Willis, 2006). If the cool kids acquired most of their language skills from home, then why did they feel that their language was inappropriate for talking with adults at home? The question is interesting, as most black parents have a home language policy for their children. They want their children to not only speak but master what Smitherman (1999) called "the Language of Wider Communication" (p. 38). Hence, they might correct their children's use of cool talk so that they could gain access to a "wider" world, or so the thinking goes. Based on their situational flexibility, however, it seems that these young men did not fully adopt their parents' mores.

We have not talked much about coolness and the linguistic making of blackness and masculinity. This, however, is not the point of this section. Our point here has been to examine the language of the cool kids—its functional, cultural, and contextual dimensions—to understand how coolness relates to the young men's practices of literacy. We argue that these dimensions of talk are rooted within the young men's beings. They spill into the young men's rendering of life. It is important— we believe—to also illustrate how cool talk helped the cool kids make sense of the world beyond themselves. How did their cool talk factor into the symbology of MBK? How did it play out in what we have come to see as a black masculine literacy practice? We attempt to address these questions next.

"Sportin Phat Gear": Style as Symbol System in the Construction of Cool Identities

The cool kids' clothing and personal appearance extended cool talk and indexed for them beliefs, behaviors, thoughts, and values. Since the cool kids could manipulate clothes like they could words, their unspoken forms of language expressed their own cool meanings that their talk did not. We call this dimension of their symbolic lives *style*—a term that, for us, serves multiple purposes.

By style, we mean the aesthetic values associated with the young men's composition of themselves (e.g., styles of [ad]dress). Style also refers to a particular form of practice, such as "cool style," that we use to index coolness and the symbolic techniques employed to construct it. We also use style here to refer more specifically to the modes of being that the cool kids manufactured as much with cloth and their dress as they did through language and their speech. Hence, their style along with their talk and other symbolic vestiges, including print, helped them construct and sometimes quite literally write coolness.

In this much larger view of literacy—literacy as a practice of symbolic construction—the young men were well aware of the politics and yet potential of style. For example, Etherin acknowledged this point when discussing Tupac Shakur, his hip-hop hero, who had branded "ThugLife" across his abdomen. For Etherin, this branding was not a criminal act or an act of hostility but rather a way "to stand out." We again highlight this point. As much as they wanted to connect, the cool kids wanted to simultaneously be set apart. For Etherin and his peers, Tupac's appearance, his dress as well as his skin, made a political statement that helped him stand apart. Specifically, Etherin acknowledged Tupac's inversion of the term *thug*, which was branded across his abdomen. For Etherin, "Tupac used 'thug' to acknowledge hardworking people. People who don't get talked about." We as authors understand Etherin's sentiments to be akin to Karl Marx's inversion of the term *proletariat* (as Marx used *proletariat* to describe the exploited working poor as opposed to the common outlaw, Tupac used *thug* to bring attention to the underdog as opposed to the common criminal) or black folks' inversion of terms like *bad* and *nigga*. Hence, understanding how texts can be manipulated calls attention to the relative degree of autonomy the young men perceived they held over symbolic forms like clothes, for if Tupac could do it, so could they. That is, they understood that clothes could be imbued with meanings, that they could be imprinted upon and be imprints themselves. According to Etherin,

> I like to wear clothes that got stuff written on them. Sometimes it's funny, but other times it's just real. . . . You like make a statement. Next thing you know, everybody be wearin [what you wore] because your statement is true. You like create a new way to dress, a new way to do things.

As Larry would explain, "what you wear says as much about who you are" as what you say. Hakim also believed that clothes communicate meaning; they "make you cool. . . . They say something to people about you." Standing squarely in the same tradition of meaning inversion (Smitherman, 1977) that describes how Tupac or Marx bent words to mean new things, Etherin's and Larry's statements speak to the power of style shifting to reshape the meaning of lives. This shifting involved the ability to play with, reclaim, and invert texts, where even clothes served as symbol for composing narrative and critique.

"Phat gear," their phrase for cool clothing, extended their cool vocabularies. In function, phat gear served to help the young men compose cool selves. In their dress and appearance, the cool kids also projected images they associated with coolness, such as the images of hip-hop artists or popular athletes. They fashioned selves in multimodal layers (i.e., clothing stained with letters and pictures) and expanded what these texts could mean.

Similar to their talk, in style, the cool kids frequently appropriated material from the pop cultures of hip-hop and sports. In expressing themselves on a tapestry of flesh, a cool, new literacy did emerge—a practice that entered the MBK program with profound frequency. This point is best illustrated in the following exchange:

> DAVID: Now Larry explained why clothes are so important. But help me understand. Does anything go?
> [LAUGHTER]
> LARRY: Naw man. It ain't like that . . . [interrupted]
> ETHERIN: There is just one rule: You can't expect to be cool and wear something wack.
> DAVID: What's wack?
> ETHERIN: You know. . . . Stuff that ain't saying nothing.

For Etherin, clothing could speak. Moreover, opportunities to "control the mic" or "hold the floor" should not be wasted. This wasting or misuse of opportunity was deemed by Etherin

**Figure 5. Example of Hip-Hop
Apparel in Young Men's Drawings**

and his peers as "wack." Indeed, the young men were always in a position to be judged and to judge others.

To avoid unfavorable judgment, the young men used their clothes as a subversive tool, which allowed them to declare "what they gotta say without sayin it." In this way, clothing helped them communicate their ideas on their terms despite being entrenched in a contested educational domain that is commonly hostile to black males. Nowhere else was this feature more evident than in the young men's appropriation of hip-hop style.

Hip-Hop Symbolism in the Cool Kids' Style

As figure 5 suggests, the young men read and wrote with their wardrobes. These texts usually involved hip-hop symbols and style and were uniquely influenced by the young men's impressions of what it meant to them to be cool black men. Hip-hop style, then, contributed greatly to the cool kids' writings. During one of the program meetings, the young men were asked to conduct a meta-analysis of African American language using both words and illustrations. In their writings, the cool kids wrote and illustrated characters wearing popular hip-hop apparel items, from Sean John and Phat Farm to RocaWear. Other students constructed characters adorned in clothing that was lettered in hip-hop vernacular (cf. Alim, 2006; Richardson, 2006). The next example illustrates how hip-hop offered the young men a style that figured significantly into their views of themselves and the world.

According to Keith, "We gotta wear stuff like FUBU and RocaWear. That's part of what make you cool . . . That's part of how people know you cool. You learn that in kindergarten, but you don't learn that in school." We use Keith's statement to illustrate the relationship between being cool and wearing it. That is, the cool kids understood that to communicate themselves as cool,

Figure 6. Example of Sports Apparel in Young Men's Drawings

they had to practice the literacy of cool dress. Moreover, the symbols of (ad)dress they used played on the symbols of hip-hop culture. It played on the symbols of sports culture as well.

Sports Symbolism in the Cool Kids' Style

The cool kids turned to sports culture for symbols to script cool. In their written responses, the young men created several characters wearing athletic apparel. We collected artifacts of characters drawn that were wearing basketball jerseys, baseball caps, and various other sports-related items. Figure 6 illustrates an example of how sports and sports symbols played a role in the young men's practice of literacy.

According to Lucious, "We wear jerseys and things of that nature because athletes are cool." Like Lucious, Keith believed that "sporting a baseball cap or a good jersey is hot. I mean girls like it. Dudes respect it. . . . We got our own little thing going on." Asked about what that "own little thing" was, Keith replied,

> We know what's up. It means something when you fresh to death. I mean people notice you. And for us, fresh don't mean . . . wearing suits unless it's Easter [laughing]. A suit ain't always cool. But if you wear something like this [pointing to his basketball jersey] then people gone notice you because it says something to people.

During a conversation with David, Larry expressed a similar sentiment.

LARRY: We all know what's hype to wear. . . . It's important to sport phat [interrupted]
DAVID: What's that?

LARRY: You know . . . clothes like . . . [Michael] Jordan's [shoes] or a Snoop Dogg's outfit. You can't be coming in here with just anything on. People gone think you not cool. So, we [like] under pressure to get it right. Most of us just wear what we see stars on TV wearing.

DAVID: Which stars?

LARRY: Rappers . . . basketball players . . . football . . . athletes. Most people think they cool. So a lot of us, we want to be like them. They make the freshest stuff [i.e., clothing apparel].

Larry's comments illustrate the ways that coolness, as expressed in the dress of rappers and athletes, influenced his own clothing choices. These clothing choices, which we argue connect directly to the black masculine cultural models communicated in hip-hop and sports, offered Larry and his peers a way to write selves, make sense of pop culture in their lives, and extend shared perspectives about what it meant to be a cool black man. The young men embodied and embraced (i.e., "sported") hip-hop and sports materials to articulate a particular version of themselves that was not only acceptable in their own performances of cool but also desirable in their greater peer contexts—the places in which these literacies made most sense (cf. Bakhtin, 1981; Ball & Freedman, 2004).

While our view of clothes as tools is important to understanding how these young men practiced literacy, we acknowledge that clothes are also tools of the marketplace. They promote consumerism, particularly among poor people. However, in spite of the consumerist impulse to place value on expensive gear and arbitrary items, the cool kids used clothes as language to express a desire—among other things—to be accepted and to stand apart (cf. Piacentini & Mailer, 2004). This does not dismiss the marketplace ideologies that bait kids into craving clothes. It simply suggests another way of looking at clothes. From the young men's perspective, clothing was also symbolic material that could be used to shape identities and define what it means to be cool. While the market forces attached to these items may have offered the young men a lot of help, these young men never fully succumbed to these forces but instead operated within a style system in multiple ways, manipulating through the use of style symbols (e.g., cloth) what it meant to be cool.

We find this latter point important, especially in thinking about the two questions that have guided this study: How did coolness relate to literacy among the cool kids, and what symbolic patterns helped to shape these relations? In practicing a black masculine literacy, the cool kids constructed coolness through symbols of speech and dress taken from pop-cultural locations. These larger symbol systems helped to shape complex relations—relationships between how the young men wanted to be cool and how they articulated this desire through literacy.

This relationship cannot be separated from the physical and social characteristics of the young men's identities. Rather, their constructions of coolness were as much about reading and writing, hence fully understanding coolness, as it was about being cool. This understanding too was a kind of identity text that, in large part, the young men appropriated from elsewhere even as they were producing it themselves. As they appropriated symbols from pop culture, they reaccentuated them to serve their very own purposes. Still, much of what it meant to be cool resided elsewhere, which was the complexity of their cool culture—being present in that contexts of peers yet being elsewhere in the contexts of pop black masculinity.

Implications: Toward a Theory of Black Masculine Literacies

It is likely that the cool kids practiced literacy as much to figure out new ways to exist in a world defined by a tapestry of traits, blacknesses, and masculinities as to decode and encode texts. Indeed, they carved lives out of letters, stained skin with social meanings, and embraced multiple symbol systems to manufacture meaningful existences. The symbols within these systems, moreover, shed light on a world where literacies are alive and expressed in ways that have been difficult for literacy researchers to see. Particularly, they shed light on what young black men do in the dark, the obscure grounds upon which black masculine literacies are taking shape.

In recent years, a research base for black masculine literacy practices has developed, which reports on the relationship among race, masculinity, and literacy (Brozo, 2002; Gilbert & Gilbert, 1998; Maynard, 2002; Newkirk, 2002; Rowan et al., 2001; Smith & Wilhelm, 2002; Tatum, 2005). These studies, along with ours, we feel, are outlining a new theory of literacy, of black masculine literacies, capable of helping literacy scholars explain the unique and dynamic forces influencing literacy in the lives of black males.

It is important to note that our study is not without its limitations. For example, some readers will regard adolescence unlike we do, as less an age range than a dimension of development. As a dimension of development, adolescence is difficult to pin down. Thus, we use the term *adolescent* to refer to the age range of the young men we studied, which given the variability in the term is itself limiting.

Additionally, as we noted earlier, much of what we found in this study is based on our ability to see things as black males. To this end, one must use caution in interpreting these results. In this case, we have not intended to generalize our findings to all black males. Rather, we use our findings to theorize black males into conversations on literacy. Moreover, our use of one group of students, although not a sufficient sample for generalizing to population, has in the ethnographic tradition proven helpful for generating theory about situated phenomena.

Indeed, a theory of black masculine literacies is timely as relatively little is currently known about what motivates black males to practice literacy. Therefore, it is essential to explore literacy in the lives of black males because black males are a unique and often stigmatized social group. To this point, Young (2004) has described black male uniqueness as characterized through a "difference between black boys and white boys." For him, "Black boys not only feel coerced to give up their masculinity if they do well in school, but they also feel forced to abandon their race" (p. 700). This pressure that young black men face to choose between a mainstream and fringe world, between race and educational rights, we argue, is the force motivating black masculine literacies—literacy as practiced by the cool kids.

In keeping with the findings of this study, we understand black masculine literacies in terms of the cool kids' literacy practices and processes. As practice, black masculine literacies exist in the nexus of the oxymoronic arrangement of tension, a kind of push-pull dynamic that characterizes a function of black masculine literacies as simultaneously inclusive and exclusive. As in the case of the cool kids, this arrangement shaped the cool kids' constructions of self and others and structured their language and style. A good example of this is in how the cool kids practiced literacy to pull themselves together, to fill in the black masculine space between them and black popular culture. To do so, they used a variety of symbolic forms: cloth, print, drawings, and so on. The young men also practiced literacy to push themselves apart, away from threatening and uncool individuals and groups. In so doing, the young men critiqued the world around them and at times the world they were writing, using varied symbolic forms to connect to it.

Even the functions of language in their black masculine literacy practices fitted within this dynamic. For example, the young men's language was pragmatic as opposed to flowery. This pragmatism was essential for performing male identities and constructing cool. It had cultural roots, which attached the young men to cool destinations, such as hip-hop and sports. Each of these locations enhanced the young men's talk and style so that they could unlock the hidden and protected vaults of their cool world. In sum, the language of black masculine literacies functions in a systematic way, as a means for helping young black men fit in and gain entry into cool cultures and contexts but also to distinguish them.

As a process, black masculine literacies imply the skilled use and manipulation of multiple systems, where even talk, in this case, symbolizes what's cool. It is in this way that we observed a particular pattern of literacy emerging from the specific and situated experiences of the cool kids. These experiences included what we consider to be positive attributes of coolness (e.g., rejection of racism, self-dignified expressions of masculinity, meaningful and socially relevant performance of identity)—attributes, to the cool kids, essential for being a black man.

They also include negative attributes, such as misogyny and benign prejudice toward effeminate male identities (cf. Young, 2004). Yet as a whole, these patterns reveal a process of symbolic play, where the tools of literacy harden into race-specific and gender-specific meaningful configurations. Although raced and gendered, these literacy processes cannot be essentialized into any fixed configuration. Even among the cool kids, literacy could be described as a practice that undergoes its own processes of constructions and ongoing and forever-changing configurations. For the cool kids, these configurations were characterized by how black males symbolically embrace and collapse multiple forms of black male identity through systems such as talk and style. These systems tend to be uniquely defined in black male social circles, particularly in the cultures of hip-hop and sports (Cooks, 2004; Dimitriadis, 2001; Johnson & Roberts, 1999; Morrell & Duncan-Andrade, 2002). We note here that these cultures too are everchanging (Taylor & Taylor, 2007).

There is another important point to be made with regard to theorizing black masculine literacies; that is, to insist upon black masculine literacies, one must first insist that black males are literate. Although we disagree with his rigid representations of masculinity and, sometimes, deficit constructions of blackness, we agree with Tatum's (2005) description of adolescent black males as multiply literate (hence the phrase "black masculine literacies"). For Tatum, the multiple literacies of black males have various dimensions: cultural, emotional, and social. By cultural literacy, Tatum is referring to a deliberate awareness that black males have of historical and current events. Such events, he maintains, help to shape a black male identity.

By emotional literacy, Tatum (2005) is referring to black males' abilities to manage their feelings and cope with their lived traumas. Tatum's concept of emotional literacy suggests that black males initiate a set of practices to work through their feelings and traumas to come to a sense of how to live with emotions that have too often taken troubling forms. Finally, by social literacy, Tatum is referring to black males' abilities to navigate a variety of settings to construct manageable meanings of a world where items like blackness, maleness, and even literacy are contested.

We build upon Tatum's typology by acknowledging the linguistic and stylistic dimensions of black masculine literacies. Beyond the cultural, emotional, and social dimensions about which Tatum writes, black masculine literacies share a common linguistic code, familiar among many black males. This code is not so much invented by black males as it is an artifact of black maleness that cool black men play on and revise. Nonetheless, the view of black males as multiply literate within the narrowed scope of language and style presents a striking deviation from the public perception that black men are barely literate.

Studies such as ours and Tatum's (2005) have begun to present a clearer picture of black masculine literacies. This picture illustrates a range of literacy practices, from bragging to rapping, from tagging to other forms of symbolic play. It also provides a glimpse of literate processes—how some adolescent black males read and write (Fashola, 2005; Kirkland, 2006; Tatum, 2006).

Although a clearer picture of black masculine literacies is emerging, more research is needed to determine the specific themes presented in texts produced and consumed by black males. Specifically, one wonders whether or not there is a relationship between the texts that young men write and the texts they read. We know from this particular study that the cool kids tended to write coolness as they read it from within the group and the pop-cultural world that enveloped the group.

These acts of scripting, reminiscent of the cool kids' writing with clothes, reveal significant ways in which personal narratives of literacy relate to how writing, reading, sharing, and creating multilayered understandings of self and others take on new meanings. But one also wonders, what exactly is the substance of black male writing? To this point, we have only been able to gather that the cool kids sometimes used their flesh as parchment to write about the deep things affecting and sometimes afflicting them. However, it remains unclear how and why particular black males use their bodies as texts, for example, to capture the range of meanings found in their lives.

Developing a clear picture of black masculine literacies will be complex, messy, and ongoing undertaking. It cannot be limited to a futile quest to simply explain what black males read and write. The work of theorizing black masculine literacies must go beyond simple explanations. It must inquire about the range of reasons why young black men practice literacy—even when we do not find those reasons real cool.

■ Note

We would like to thank all those who provided helpful comments and suggestions on earlier drafts of this article. Specifically, we thank Geneva Smitherman, Anne Haas Dyson, Fabienne Doucet, Gordon Pradl, Elaine Richardson, Maisha Fisher, Jhumki Basu, the editors of *RRQ,* and its referees for their invaluable feedback.

■ References

Alim, H. S. (2006). *Roc the mic right: The language of hip hop culture.* New York: Routledge.

Bakhtin, M. (1981). *The dialogic imagination: Four essays.* Ed. M. Holquist. Trans. C. Emerson & M. Holquist. Austin: University of Texas Press.

———. (1986). *Speech genres and other late essays.* Ed. C. Emerson & M. Holquist. Trans. V. McGee. Austin: University of Texas Press.

Ball, A., & Freedman, S. W. (eds.). (2004). *Bakhtinian perspectives on language, literacy, and learning.* Cambridge: Cambridge University Press.

Bean, T. W., & Harper, H. (2008). Literacy education in new times: In these times. *Journal of Adolescent & Adult Literacy 52*(1), 4–6. doi:10.1598/JAAL.52.1.1.

Brozo, W. G. (2002). *To be a boy, to be a reader: Engaging teen and preteen boys in active literacy.* Newark, DE: International Reading Association.

Clark, J. T. (2003). Abstract inquiry and the patrolling of black/white borders through linguistic stylization. In R. Harris & B. Rampton (eds.), *The language, ethnicity and race reader* (pp. 303–13). London: Routledge.

Collins, P. H. (1999). Reflections on the outsider within. *Journal of Career Development 26*(1), 84–88.

Connor, M. K. (1995). *What is cool? Understanding black manhood in America.* New York: Crown.

Cooks, J. A. (2004). Writing for something: Essays, raps, and writing preferences. *English Journal 94*(1), 72–76. doi:10.2307/4128851.

Cose, E. (2002). *The envy of the world: On being a black man in America.* New York: Washington Square.

Cushman, E., Kintgen, E. R., Kroll, B. M., & Rose, M. (2001). *Literacy: A critical sourcebook.* Boston: St. Martin's.

Davis, J. E. (2001). Black boys at school: Negotiating masculinities and race. In R. Majors (ed.), *Educating our black children: New directions and radical approaches* (pp. 169–82). London: RoutledgeFalmer.

Deflem, M. (1991). Ritual, anti-structure, and religion: A discussion of Victor Turner's processual symbolic analysis. *Journal for the Scientific Study of Religion 30*(1), 1–25. doi:10.2307/1387146.

Dimitriadis, G. (2001). "In the clique": Popular culture, constructions of place, and the everyday lives of urban youth. *Anthropology & Education Quarterly 32*(1), 29–51. doi:10.1525/aeq.2001.32.1.29.

Dyson, A. H. (2001). Donkey Kong in Little Bear country: A first grader's composing development in the media spotlight. *Elementary School Journal 101*(4), 417–33. doi:10.1086/499679.

———. (2003). Popular literacies and the "all" children: Rethinking literacy development for contemporary childhoods. *Language Arts 81*(2), 100–109.

Erickson, F. (1986). Qualitative methods in research on teaching. In M. C. Wittrock (ed.), *Handbook of research on teaching*, 3rd ed. (pp. 119–61). New York: Macmillan.

Fashola, O. S. (ed.). (2005). *Educating African American males: Voices from the field*. Thousand Oaks, CA: Corwin.

Filmer, A. A. (2003). African-American vernacular English: Ethics, ideology, and pedagogy in the conflict between identity and power. *World Englishes 22*(3), 253–70. doi:10.1111/1467- 971X.00295.

Fisher, M. T. (2004). "The song is unfinished": The new literate and literary and their institutions. *Written Communication 21*(3), 290– 312. doi:10.1177/0741088304265475.

Foster, M. (1992). Sociolinguistics and the African-American community: Implications for literacy. *Theory into Practice 31*(4), 303–11.

Freire, P., & Macedo, D. (1987). *Literacy: Reading the word and the world*. South Hadley, MA: Bergin & Garvey.

Gallego, M. A., & Hollingsworth, S. (2000). Introduction: The idea of multiple literacies. In M. A. Gallego & S. Hollingsworth (eds.), *What counts as literacy: Challenging the school standard* (pp. 1–23). New York: Teachers College Press.

Gee, J. P. (1989). What is literacy? *Journal of Education 171*(1), 18–25.

———. (2001). A sociocultural perspective on early literacy development. In S. B. Neuman & D. K. Dickinson (eds.), *Handbook of early literacy research* (pp. 30–42). New York: Guilford.

Gilbert, R., & Gilbert, P. (1998). *Masculinity goes to school*. New York: Routledge.

Gutiérrez, K. D. (2008). Developing a sociocritical literacy in the third space. *Reading Research Quarterly 43*(2), 148–64. doi:10.1598/ RRQ.43.2.3.

Halliday, M. A. K. (1978). *Language as social semiotic: The social interpretation of language and meaning*. Baltimore: Edward Arnold.

Hopkins, R. (1997). *Educating black males: Critical lessons in schooling, community, and power*. Albany: State University of New York Press.

Hull, G. A., & Nelson, M. E. (2005). Locating the semiotic power of multimodality. *Written Communication 22*(2), 224–61. doi:10.1177/0741088304274170.

Hymes, D. (1974). *Foundations in sociolinguistics: An ethnographic approach*. Philadelphia: University of Pennsylvania Press.

Isenbarger, L., & Willis, A. I. (2006). An intersection of theory and practice: Accepting the language a child brings into the classroom. *Language Arts 84*(2), 125–35.

Jackson, J. F. L., & Moore, J. L., III. (2006). African American males in education: Endangered or ignored? *Teachers College Record 108*(2), 201–5. doi:10.1111/j.1467–9620.2006.00647.x.

Johnson, N. G., & Roberts, M. C. (1999). Passage on the wild river of adolescence: Arriving safely. In N. G. Johnson, M. C. Roberts, & J. Worell (eds.), *Beyond appearance: A new look at adolescent girls* (pp. 3–18). Washington, DC: American Psychological Association.

Kinloch, V. F. (2005). Revisiting the promise of "students' right to their own language": Pedagogical strategies. *College Composition and Communication 57*(1), 83–113.

———. (2007). "The white-ification of the hood": Power, politics, and youth performing narratives of community. *Language Arts 85*(1), 61–68.

Kirkland, D. (2006). The boys in the hood: Exploring literacy in the lives of six urban adolescent black males. Doctoral dissertation, Michigan State University, East Lansing.

Kirkland, D., & Jackson, A. (2008). Beyond the silence: Instructional approaches and students' attitudes. In J. C. Scott, D. Y. Straker, & L. Katz (eds.), *Affirming students' right to their own language: Bridging language policies and pedagogical practices* (pp. 132–50). Urbana, IL: National Council of Teachers of English.

MacGillivray, L., & Curwen, M. S. (2007). Tagging as a social literacy practice. *Journal of Adolescent & Adult Literacy 50*(5), 354–69. doi:10.1598/JAAL.50.5.3.

MacLeod, J. (1995). *Ain't no makin' it.* Boulder, CO: Westview Press.

Mahiri, J. (2004). New literacies in a new century. In J. Mahiri (ed.), *What they don't learn in school: Literacy in the lives of urban youth* (pp. 1–17). New York: Peter Lang.

Majors, R., & Billson, J. M. (1993). *Cool pose: The dilemmas of black manhood in America.* New York: Simon & Schuster.

Makoni, S., Smitherman, G., Ball, A. F., & Spears A. K. (eds.). (2003). *Black linguistics: Language, society, and politics in Africa and the Americas.* New York: Routledge.

Marable, M. (1994). The black male: Searching beyond stereotypes. In R. Majors & J. U. Gordon (eds.), *The American black male: His present status and his future* (pp. 69–78). Chicago: Nelson-Hall.

Maynard, T. (2002). *Boys and literacy: Exploring the issues.* New York: Routledge.

Mitchell, J. C. (1984). Typicality and the case study. In R. F. Ellen (ed.), *Ethnographic research: A guide to general conduct* (pp. 238–41). New York: Academic.

Moje, E. B. (2004). Powerful spaces: Tracing the out-of-school literacy spaces of Latino/a youth. In K. M. Leander & M. Sheehy (eds.), *Spatializing literacy research and practice* (pp. 15–38). New York: Peter Lang.

Morgan, M. (2005). Hip-hop women shredding the veil: Race and class in popular feminist identity. *South Atlantic Quarterly 104*(3), 425–44. doi:10.1215/00382876-104-3-425.

Morrell, E. (2002). Toward a critical pedagogy of popular culture: Literacy development among urban youth. *Journal of Adolescent & Adult Literacy 46*(1), 72–77.

Morrell, E., & Duncan-Andrade, J. M. R. (2002). Promoting academic literacy with urban youth through engaging hip-hop culture. *English Journal 91*(6), 88–92. doi:10.2307/821822.

Neal, L. I., McCray, A. D., Webb-Johnson, G., & Bridgest, S. T. (2003). The effects of African American movement styles on teachers' perceptions and reactions. *Journal of Special Education 37*(1), 49–57. doi:10.1177/00224669030370010501.

New London Group. (1996). A pedagogy of multiliteracies: Designing social futures. *Harvard Educational Review 66*(1), 60–92.

Newkirk, T. (2002). *Misreading masculinity: Boys, literacy, and popular culture.* Portsmouth, NH: Heinemann.

Ogbu, J. (2003). *Black American students in an affluent suburb: A study of academic disengagement.* Mahwah, NJ: Erlbaum.

Patterson, O. (2006, March 26). A poverty of the mind. *New York Times.* query.nytimes.com/gst/fullpage.html?res=9C06EFD71730F935A15750C0A9609C8B63.

Piacentini, M., & Mailer, G. (2004). Symbolic consumption in teenagers' clothing choices. *Journal of Consumer Behaviour 3*(3), 251–62. doi:10.1002/cb.138.

Purcell-Gates, V. (2002). ". . . As soon as she opened her mouth!": Issues of language, literacy, and power. In L. Delpit & J. K. Dowdy (eds.), *The skin that we speak: Thoughts on language and culture in the classroom* (pp. 121–44). New York: New Press.

Richardson, E. B. (2003). *African American literacies.* New York: Routledge.

———. (2006). *Hiphop literacies.* London: Routledge.

Rickford, J. R., & Rickford, R. J. (2000). *Spoken soul: The story of black English.* New York: John Wiley & Sons.

Rowan, L., Knobel, M., Bigum, C., & Lankshear, C. (2001). *Boys, literacies and schooling: The dangerous territories of gender-based literacy reform.* Philadelphia: Open University Press.

Smith, M. W., & Wilhelm, J. D. (2002). *"Reading don't fix no Chevys": Literacy in the lives of young men.* Portsmouth, NH: Heinemann.

Smitherman, G. (1977). *Talkin and testifyin: The language of black America.* Detroit: Wayne State University Press.

———. (1999). *Talkin that talk: Language, culture and education in African America.* New York: Routledge.

———. (2000). *Black talk: Words and phrases from the hood to the amen corner.* Boston: Houghton Mifflin.

———. (2006). *Word from the mother: Language and African Americans.* New York: Routledge.

Spivak, G. (1985). Three women's texts and a critique of imperialism. *Cultural Inquiry 12*(1), 243–61.

Tatum, A. W. (2005). *Teaching reading to black adolescent males: Closing the achievement gap.* Portland, ME: Stenhouse.

———. (2006). Engaging African American males in reading. *Educational Leadership 63*(5), 44–49.

Taylor, C., & Taylor, V. (2007). Hip hop is now: An evolving youth culture. *Reclaiming Children and Youth 15*(4), 210–13.

Turner, V. W. (1970). *The forest of symbols: Aspects of Ndembu ritual.* Ithaca, NY: Cornell University Press.

Villanueva, V. (1993). *Bootstraps: From an American academic of color.* Urbana, IL: National Council of Teachers of English.

Walten, J. (2001). *Fair sex, savage dreams.* Durham, NC: Duke University Press.

Watson, C., & Smitherman, G. (1997). *Educating African American males: Detroit's Malcolm X Academy solution.* Chicago: Third World Press.

Willis, P. (1977). *Learning to labour: How working class kids get working class jobs.* Farnborough, England: Saxon House.

———. (1983). Cultural production and theories of reproduction. In L. Barton & S. Walker (eds.), *Race, class and education* (pp. 107–38). Kent, England: Croom Helm.

———. (1990). *Common culture: Symbolic work at play in the everyday cultures of the young.* Boulder, CO: Westview Press.

———. (2003). Foot soldiers of modernity: The dialectics of cultural consumption and the 21st-century school. *Harvard Educational Review 73*(3), 390–415.

Young, V. A. (2004). Your average nigga. *College Composition and Communication 55*(4), 693–715. doi:10.2307/4140667.

———. (2007). *Your average nigga: Performing race, literacy, and masculinity.* Detroit: Wayne State University Press.

Culturally Sustained Debaters

Understanding the Legacy Learning Literacies of Young Black Men

Raven Jones Stanbrough

I, too, sing America.

I am the darker brother.
They send me to eat in the kitchen
When company comes,
But I laugh,
And eat well,
And grow strong.

Tomorrow,
I'll be at the table
When company comes.

Nobody'll dare
Say to me,
"Eat in the kitchen,"
Then.

Besides,
They'll see how beautiful I am
And be ashamed—

I, too, am America

—Langston Hughes, "I, Too, Sing America"

In addition to the above assertion from Hughes (1926), in the song "Ultralight Beam" (2016) Chance the Rapper stated "When they come for you, I will shield your name / I will field their questions, I will feel your pain." Hughes and Chance the Rapper's thoughts are in dialogue with one another across decades and in artistic and intellectual in ways that are necessary for understanding the current climate of literacy and the lived experiences of young Black men. For Hughes, it is paramount that he is seen and understood as aware, beautiful, and visible—despite the snares and racist actions of his oppressors. In this way, he is using his oral and written literacies to forward his purpose of laughing and growing strong, although he is the "darker brother." For Chance the Rapper, a hip-hop artist, his use of creative and picturesque storytelling has garnered him many successes and platforms, in which his musical genius and talents have brought attention to issues that plague marginalized communities, including the ongoing gun violence in his hometown of Chicago. In 2014, Chance was named "Outstanding Youth of the Year" for his activism and promotion of ideas surrounding racial justice and civic engagement for young men of color. Because he has witnessed his friends dying and other losses, he understands what it means to "field their questions" and "feel your pain." The works of both Hughes and Chance the Rapper embody the challenges, complexities, and successes of young Black men that are often debated against, forgotten, or vilified by the dominant world. However, literacy educators and others should seek to affirm, support, and teach from the lived experiences and stories of young Black men in their classrooms today. After all, the beautiful literacies of young Black boys and men no longer call for them to be sent to "eat in the kitchen" as Hughes states, but to take their rightful places at the table, where their narratives matter.

In this chapter, I look to examine the literacies and lived experiences of Hawk, Macaw, Toucan, and Kingfisher—young Black men student-debaters and debate supporters that I call Legacy Learners, in order to highlight the varied ways in which young Black men encounter and engage with debate in multiple contexts, in an after-school debate program called ACTION Debate (AD), in which I was a former high school debater. I seek to understand how their participation with high school and college debate teams served as a vehicle for them to navigate through school, home, and their communities.

Theoretical Framework

In this chapter, I work from the lens of culturally sustaining pedagogy, CSP. The goal of CSP is to "perpetuate and foster—to sustain—linguistic, literate, and cultural pluralism as part of the democratic project of schooling" (Paris, 2012, p. 95). While desiring to examine how Black student-debaters and supporters participate in a debate community and employ teaching and literacy practices that are culturally engaging and sustaining to instruct and inform their debate choices, I decided to focus on asset-based pedagogy. Asset-based pedagogies have widely developed as a way to resist and challenge deficit approaches that have tried to offer suggestions for the academic achievements among students of color (Paris, 2012). In his underlining of deficit approaches, Paris (2012) states that "the goal of deficit approaches was to eradicate the linguistic, literate, and cultural practices many students of color brought from their homes and communities and replace them with what were viewed as superior practices" (p. 93). Deficit approaches, as described by Paris, suggest that students' of color ways of being, living, and knowing should be overshadowed by dominant ways of thinking.

Desiring to nuance CSP further, Paris & Alim (2014) offer a loving critique to problematize and push their thinking about CSP. While seeking to shift the terms, stance, and practices of asset-based pedagogies, Paris & Alim suggest that deficit approaches and ways of teaching have spanned many decades in the United States. When this happens, they denote that students of color and their cultural ways of being and literacy practices are seen as deficient. These same ideals were apparent in the AD community when Black student-debaters sometimes debated their white peers. Participants reported feelings of exclusion and isolation. To combat such feelings, they purposely engaged with hip-hop and other cultural practices to forward their arguments, cross-examinations, and rebuttals in debate rounds. In their own work and communities, Paris & Alim deemed it necessary to delineate a reflective stance to encompass the importance of being inclusive when teaching and learning with students of color. To draw this out more, they state:

> Here, we are primarily interested in creating generative spaces for asset pedagogies to support the practices of youth and communities of color while maintaining a critical lens vis-à-vis these practices. Providing the example of Hip Hop as a form of the cultural and community practice that pedagogies should sustain, we argue that, rather than avoiding problematic practices of keeping them hidden beyond White gaze, CSP must work with students to critique regressive practices (e.g., homophobia misogyny, racism) and raise critical awareness. (2014, p. 92)

Disrupting discriminatory acts within and outside of debate spaces is what the AD participants in this study revealed they had experiences with. Prior to the development of CSP, Ladson-Billings (1995) proposed culturally relevant pedagogy (CRP). She defines CRP as a pedagogy "that would propose to do three things—produce students who can achieve academically, produce students who demonstrate cultural competence, and develop students who can both understand and critique the existing social order" (Ladson-Billings, 1995, p. 474). In this vein, CRP requires that all "teachers attend to the students' academic needs, not merely make them 'feel good' in order to provide students the opportunity to choose academic excellence and success" (Ladson-Billings, 1995, p. 160). In keeping with this frame of thinking, but seeking to sustain these practices, Paris (2012) challenges us to consider whether practicing CRP is sustaining the languages and cultures of communities of color. Ultimately, in his view, Paris (2012) conceptualizes CSP as a pedagogy that extends and moves beyond being relevant or responsive to multiethnic and multilingual communities to "support young people in sustaining the cultural and linguistic competence of their communities while simultaneously offering access to dominant cultural competence" (p. 95). Similarly, Ladson-Billings (2014) revisits her development and thinking of CRP to suggest that the concept of CRP needed to be pushed further. She acknowledges Paris & Alim's (2014) work as an example of such a push.

> In developing this theory, culturally *sustaining* pedagogy (Paris, 2012), these authors use culturally relevant pedagogy as the place where "the beat drops" and then layer the multiple ways that this notion of pedagogy shifts, changes, adapts, recycles, and recreates instructional spaces to ensure that consistently marginalized students are repositioned into a place of normativity—that is, that they become subjects in the instructional process, not mere objects. (2014, p. 76)

In this regard, Ladson-Billings understands and works to honor the need for a "remix" of thinking, learning, and teaching through the lens of CSP. This is important to note, considering that today's educators and youth, like the ones in the AD community, deem it necessary to learn from various teaching approaches and not just a singular idea.

Next, I conceptualize *legacy learning* as the sharing of knowledge that occurs within the AD community. I also suggest that legacy learning can include "the everyday meanings and uses of literacy in specific cultural contexts and link directly to how we understand the work of literacy in educational contexts" (Street, 2005, p. 417). This also includes debate and knowledge spaces where individuals, such as debate coaches, peer student-debaters, debate supporters, and others who have had experience with debate can offer information and resources for debate success, which most times leads to the literacy learning and academic success for Black student-debaters. Oftentimes, in addition to high schools, debate communities and spaces are evidenced on the campuses of colleges and universities (Baker-Bell, Jones Stanbrough, & Everett, 2017). For young Black men student-debaters, the process of debating is also about storytelling—having the opportunity to reveal and share their experiences and stories with others. Issues of debate literacies, legacy learning, and storytelling guide the questions that the larger study poses, including

- How and in what ways is ACTION Debate (AD) a culturally sustaining space?
- How do students perceive and understand their participation in ACTION Debate as relating to debate, school, their communities, and college?
- Are there specific literacy and culturally sustaining practices that are employed by students, coaches, and debate supporters in the ACTION Debate program to prepare Black students to debate in racially welcoming or racially hostile environments?

Urban Debate Leagues

In 1985, Emory University's debate instructor, Melissa Maxcy Wade, created an urban outreach program in Atlanta, Georgia, through a grant from the National Forensic League and Phillips Petroleum. The grant increased the participation of inner-city, minority youths in high school over a three-year period. Starting with D. M. Therrell, a public high school in Atlanta, the Emory outreach program grew to serve and include numerous Atlanta inner-city schools (Reid-Brinkley, 2008). With a focus on bringing competitive policy debate to minority youth, the program's goals were to improve reading, research skills, speaking, and writing. To assist with this, Wade sent college students from her nationally ranked debate team to volunteer and coach in schools in Atlanta. Facilitating this allowed participating high school students and teachers to be connected to a local college and debate team. This is also a very critical and salient tenet of the AD program. The Atlanta model of the urban debate league (UDL) has since garnered a nationwide presence with programs in over twenty cities, including Chicago, Detroit, Kansas City, New York, San Francisco, and Washington, DC, to name a few (National Association for Urban Debate Leagues, 2016).

Currently, UDLs are largely funded through grant funding from the Open Society Institute of practice. Participants stemmed from lower socioeconomic backgrounds and the participants involved were mostly Black. Wolf's work enhances Fine's study in that it explores the debate participation of African American students, a group largely ignored by Fine.

Wolf's research gleaned that students and program volunteers communicated through three languages: the language of popular culture, the language of African American vernacular English, and the language of debate. Wolf describes urban debate as an access point rather than a means for students to be competitively successful in the larger debate community. These ideas are contradictory to the ones Fine notes, in which his attention to Black debaters is limited. However, over the past twenty years, inner-city Black communities have reclaimed a history of debate and activism. Policy debate as a space of dialogue has historically been perceived as an affluent, white, and predominantly male activity (Cridland-Hughes, 2011). However, with UDLs emerging in 1985 in the Atlanta Public School District, Black students and other students of color have been afforded opportunities to provide a facelift to the former world of debate through the establishment of UDLs.

Historic overviews of literacy trends in the United States tell a story of systemic denial of literacy to the Black community during enslavement. For much of the history of the United States, African Americans were not allowed to read or write. In the history of literacy in the United States, Graff (2001) noted that 36.1 percent of free Black men and 28.4 percent of free Black women were described as literate in 1870. By 1900, that number had increased to 44 percent. The percentages document the increasing numbers of Blacks acquiring literacy after emancipation and highlight the value placed on education and literacy as "literacy and schooling represented great promises of progress as well as symbols of liberation" (p. 226). A common theme of Black literacy acquisition has been the enduring role of nontraditional spaces. Out-of-school learning has occupied an important role in the acquisition of literacy for Blacks (Cridland-Hughes, 2011). Connected to this history, UDLs seek to push a relationship between reading and current events even farther, asking youth to consider how to incorporate new knowledge into the decisions they make about how to live their lives. Even with these goals in mind, there are not studies in existence that connect how Black coaches can engage in and utilize culturally sustaining and literacy practices when instructing and coaching Black debaters—in both supportive and sometimes hostile spaces, such as what occurs in UDLs.

Methods

When selecting the research methods for any study, it is essential that researchers choose methods carefully and implement these methods in order to appropriately explore the guiding questions (Mallette & Duke, 2004; National Research Council (U.S.); Shavelson, & Towne, 2002). In an effort to explore my research questions, I designed a single, qualitative case study. In this chapter, I examined the culturally sustaining and literacy practices of young Black male high school student-debaters within AD, an urban debate community, in which coaches and students participate in local, regional, and national debate competitions and tournaments.

(OSI), which is run by the Soros Foundation. Soros believes in the educational outcomes connected to debate, especially for disenfranchised populations. In 2002, the OSI formed a new national organization to take over the UDL. The organization, the National Urban Debate Initiative, was renamed the National Association for Urban Debate Leagues (NAUDL) in 2005. Reid-Brinkley explains that the NAUDL "provides a number of critical services in the maintenance and support of UDLs around the country. It promotes and advocates on behalf of all UDLs. It serves as a vital hub for all the UDLs providing an Urban Debate Network" (2008, p. 27).

With the growth and expansion of UDLs, the AD community has been able to forward its goals and mission of offering debate programs and participation to high school debaters. Through storytelling and countering of specific negative portrayals, the Black student-debaters in this study echo that AD allowed them a space to be themselves because their lives and experiences were and are centered in the debate spaces they occupy. For them, being centered, valued, and affirmed was more important sometimes than their growth with reading, writing, thinking critically, and researching. I argue that when Black student-debaters' stories and narratives are respected and valued, their academic and educational ways of being will follow. Speaking to this, UDLs and the AD program have received success through the improvement of grades, increased attendance and participation in other extracurricular activities, and increased matriculation to college (National Association for Urban Debate Leagues 2016). Similarly, UDL and AD supporters have argued that UDLs serve as hubs for empowerment for educationally disenfranchised students and provide them with opportunities to develop communication and academic success (Lee, 1998).

A Lens into Debate Literacies

Studies of debate participation and its role in education have examined ways to foster critical literacies among urban youth. Huber and Plantageonette (1993) make a case for supporting the expansion of debate in urban cities not for competitive purposes but for the sake and potential of individual and community transformation. They argue, "The debaters I've met care more about than just winning, they carry questions of 'should' beyond debate rounds, into homes, and hearts, and back to people who once believed they could make a difference in the world" (p. 35). Similarly, Edward Lee (1998) published a memoir examining the growth of debate access in urban public schools. He reflected on the importance of debate for developing his voice and a sense of his own power. Fine's book *Gifted Tongues* (2001) offers a comprehensive examination of debate as a community in which the worlds of education, adolescence, and talk intersect.

In his work Fine discusses the world in which students from elite backgrounds, predominantly white and affluent, prepared to debate with specific rules and structures. Student participants learned argumentation skills, presentation skills, and "the ability to understand multiple perspectives" (p. 226). Fine specifically notes the experiences of the elite high school debaters, but limits his descriptions of inner-city debaters and debate programs, such as ACTION Debate. However, Wolf (2008) analyzes a middle school urban debate program as a community

By examining young Black men high school student-debaters, I learned from the pedagogical moves Black students and supporters utilized in an effort to prepare Black student-debaters for both debate and non-debate spaces, such as college. I relied on data collected from interviews, field notes, observations, artifacts, and audio and video recordings.

Conducting a case study of my participants within the AD program allowed me to foreground the importance of culturally situated and sustaining experiences and literacies as practiced by the participants. Overall, my in-depth case study provided insights and knowledge about the Black student-debaters, supporters, the AD program, and the communities that the participants occupied. Findings illustrate how the teaching, learning, being, and doing can contribute to both in-school and out-of-school educational spaces that educators should work to sustain for young Black men who are student-debaters. Additionally, the findings from this study strengthen the existing body of urban debate studies by centering the counternarratives, experiences, stories, and voices of Black student-debaters and supporters. Connected to this, Kinloch and San Pedro (2014) state that recognizing the act of embodying performances around listening is a "literacy-rich practice that can foster what we refer to as Projects of Humanization" (p. 22). They further suggest that projects of humanization are related to theoretical contributions that highlight telling, retelling, and re-representing stories in nonlinear ways. This is important to note here because the complicated and rich narratives, stories, and counternarratives of participants in this study will serve as data and evidence.

In this way, I will forward the notion that "nonlinearity leads us to present stories in ways that appear messy, complicated, complex, and multi-voiced, which is why we rely on storying" (Kinloch & San Pedro, 2014, p. 22). The act of providing counternarratives or stories affirms and values the voices of the marginalized and disenfranchised. This chapter offers context and counternarratives that are specific to the lived debate experiences of the Black student-debaters and supporters, which speak to the importance of why and how they deem(ed) AD to be a culturally sustaining space that encouraged their literacy and literature practices, supported them in racially welcoming and unwelcoming spaces, and exposed them to legacy learning and college life.

Participants

Participants included young high school and college student-debaters and supporters who volunteered in the AD community, after school and at weekend debate tournaments. They were involved in AD in a variety of ways, including debating, peer-coaching, teaching, and judging. The larger study focused on eight AD members and supporters, including one young Black man high school student-debater, two college student-debaters, and one high school debate coach. All four AD members participated in after-school debate practices twice a week for two hours and compete and travel in regional and national debate tournaments. This chapter focuses on the four AD participants. Additionally, they all had participated in a weeklong AD summer debate institute. Three of the high school and college student-debaters also served as student-debate coaches at other summer debate institutes, which ranged from one week to seven weeks. All four of the participants were Black and born in the same southeastern city.

Data Collection and Analysis

When engaging in case-study research, it is important to gather data from multiple sources in an effort to build an accurate and rich case for what is being explored (Yin, 2009). As a participant-observer, I kept field notes at each site during AD after-school debate practices, during weekend tournaments, and at the summer institute. I also collected audio and video sessions, including warm-up activities and exercises, and sessions where the participants discussed and prepared for their debate competitions. Also, I collected copies of speeches, flows, and other jottings, which were all a part of their processing and preparation. I interviewed the AD participants, including the coach and director. Interviews were conducted at the debaters' schools and at debate tournaments at the convenience of each participant. Each interview was audio recorded and accompanied by detailed field notes.

Although I originally developed preliminary questions, I anticipated that other important points of discussion and topics might arise. Considering this, I remained flexible in adding additional questions, as they were relevant to the study. I also employed member-checking. The process of member-checking (Stake, 1995) is a technique for validating data collected through interviewing and observing. I organized data by themes (i.e., ideas that emerged from particular debate-related and legacy learning literacies and practices, definitions of debate related to cultural awareness and practices, and the functions of debate-related literacies and by site, e.g., school, classroom, lounge, hallway, community center, home, work) to capture "theoretically rich" debate practices and performances, where differences occurred between academic literacy and nonacademic literacy practices (Dyson & Genishi, 2005, p. 88). Once I established my initial codes, I engaged in more focused coding, which concerned "breaking down field notes even more finely into subcodes" to uncover nuances, "new themes and topics and new relationships" that existed within the discussion and conversation with the participants that might reveal definitive things about their engagements with literacy (Emerson, Fretz, & Shaw, 1995, p. 161).

I also organized data based on certain characteristics and perceptions. Subcategories included *successful students, struggling students, positive postings,* and so on. When a participant debated or asked questions of peers, I investigated what it meant to rely on peer teaching and learning, identified what the individual participant and the group thought of the explanations, and explored if these ideas served as motivations for debating in racially welcoming and racially hostile spaces. Finally, after arranging data by codes, I generated ideas regarding the relationships among debate, literacy, legacy learning, media portrayals, college-going, and Black youth. From these hypotheses, I rearranged data into two categories—confirming and disconfirming (Erickson, 1986). Learning from these categories offers evidence and reflective sharings regarding how participants viewed their experiences and understandings with debate and literacy.

Table 1. Coding Categories

CATEGORIES	CONFIRMING DEBATE IDENTITIES	DISCONFIRMING DEBATE IDENTITIES
Codes	College-going Counterstories for media correction	Media portrayals
Subcodes	Successful students Positive postings	Struggling students

Hypotheses based on satisfactory data were kept and hypotheses that were not supported were denied or used to categorize other sets of assertions. The goal of data interpretation for this study was to develop scholarship that is related to and advances the understandings of debate and literacy in the lives of Black student-debaters, coaches, and other debate supporters within a sustaining debate community.

After developing a set of claims that could be supported through data and grounded in evidence and testimonies, I used these claims, as illustrated in table 1, to answer my questions. The goal of data interpretation for this chapter was to develop scholarship that is related to and advances the understandings of debate and literacy in the lives of Black student-debaters, coaches, and other debate supporters within a sustaining debate community.

Researcher's Role

It is important that researchers remain conscious, thoughtful, and considerate of their positioning when engaging with research participants. My role as a former student-debater and coach within the AD program and community enriched me with loving and sustaining relationships that allowed me to return to the space as a researcher to better understand the experiences of the Black student-debaters, coaches, and other supporters. While at debate tournaments or in Kingfisher's classroom, I could be found assisting with registration, coffee and food preparation, debate drills, flowing debates, and other related tasks. In other words, I hardly ever sat still or idle and solely observed what was taking place in each setting. In this way, I was thoroughly connected to the work and ideas I was seeking to understand. Spradley (1980) identifies five types of participant-observers, ranging from a "non-participant" to a "complete participant." During weekend tournaments, afterschool practices, and at summer debate institutes, I was an "active participant" and often spoke about my own experiences with novice, junior varsity, and varsity debaters. Similarly, I offered support to coaches and students by sharing debate sites and resources, putting them into contact with my former students and coaches, and providing books and donations for books and debate materials to be purchased. My roles changed, depending on the needs of the program.

Legacy Learning and the High School to College Debate Pipeline Data

Debating in college is similar and different from when I debated in high school. I still have to practice a lot now, like I did then, but it's on an elevated level now. One aspect that's different from high school is that my college team is larger and we have more resources to use when we practice and when we travel to tournaments.

　　　　　　　　　　　　　　　　　　　　　　　　　　　　—Hawk, October 2015

Sometimes I feel like my experiences as a college debater are an extension from when I was in high school. Since I attend and debate at a Black college, I'm always feeling supported. My coach has my back and so do my teammates. And in return, I have theirs. Similar to UDLs, our team doesn't have a lot of resources, but we still make things happen.

　　　　　　　　　　　　　　　　　　　　　　　　　　　　—Toucan, October 2015

With the growth and expansion of UDLs across the country, there have been exponential efforts to increase high school debate participation. The actions and resources to forge high school debate participation with college access and coaching and mentoring by college debaters have also grown, as noted by Hawk and Toucan's sentiments above and high school and college experiences. During my debate tenure, as both a student and coach, the frequency with which I practiced, debated, coached, and learned on college campuses was regular and recurring. In many ways, my connection to debate is and will always be linked to my exposure to college students, colleges, and universities. In these same settings, I was also coached and mentored by Black students, coaches, parents of debaters, and other community members. The lessons learned in these spaces allowed me to appreciate the historical and contemporary meanings within the Black debate community. Connected to this, both Hawk and Toucan underscore the ways in which debate resources or a lack thereof can assist or stymie the progression of individuals or a team. While their high school debate contexts were similar—their college experiences differed in ways that allowed them to reflect on the importance of having access to debate resources. However, it is important to note that for Hawk and Toucan—even when resources may have been few, absent, or plentiful—having the support of their teammates and coaches played a pivotal role in their success as debaters.

I became a debate coach because I felt affirmed and supported as a debate student. I was afforded opportunities that granted me admission to high school and pre-college extracurricular and debate programs, including attending a seven-week debate institute prior to graduating high school. In these contexts, I embraced endless possibilities, which was an important factor in my being admitted to college. I am, have been, and continue to be sustained in these spaces as what I am characterizing and defining as a *legacy learner*, the sharing of knowledge that occurs within the AD community from debate coaches, peer student-debaters, debate supporters (i.e., family members, judges, school officials, policymakers, administrators) and others who have had experience with debate. Within the context of debate and this chapter, I highlight the voices and experiences of legacy learning with the AD participants—both in high school and in college, which took place at predominantly white institutions and at a histori-cally Black college. Considering AD participants occupied high school and college spaces, it is important to glean from their experiences as Black student-debaters within both contexts and how they engaged with debate, their peers, and in other communities where they felt sup-ported. Additionally, I illuminate the explicit and strategic ways in which debate supporters like Kingfisher created and supported learning and professional development opportunities for debate students and coaches.

(Re)defining Legacy Learning

In order to draw from legacy learning, it is imperative that Black student-debaters be situated in communities or spaces where individuals, such as debate coaches, peer student-debaters, debate supporters, and others who have had experience with debate can offer them resources for debate success, which most times leads to academic success. Oftentimes, in addition to high schools, debate communities and spaces are evidenced on the campuses of colleges and universities. Debate coach and activist Rose-Reid (2008) asserts that the college and university policy debate community has become increasingly interested in diversifying the racial repre-sentations at the collegiate level. Given that Black representation in postsecondary spaces has been low, debate organizations, such as the National Association for Urban Debate Leagues (NAUDL), have worked to address this gap. In doing so, the NAUDL—though largely concerned with increasing the participation and awareness of urban high school debaters—also supports the relationship from high school to college debate access.

Considering its long history and place in urban communities, UDLs, such as the AD, and other debate entities have been in existence for many years, the student-debaters have been sustained in these debate communities and spaces. Features of their sustaining were revealed through their cultural, social, and academic developments, from their positive racial identities, and from their belief in debate serving as a vehicle for high school to college with matriculation. Specific examples of this included AD participants debating on college campuses across the country, forwarding their positive racial identities as Black student-debaters in trying times when anti-Blackness was prevalent.

Additionally, as a legacy learner, having learned from individuals within the debate com-munity since the 1990s, I am positioning myself as a sustained legacy learner, alongside the young Black men participants in this study. Rogoff (2003) explains the importance of students, specifically students of color in community contexts, learning culturally in communities through active participation. My enthusiasm and motivation for creating and employing such a term as legacy learner stemmed from the multiple communities and spaces I learned with and from debate supporters who were an important factor in my being a successful debater and student in school. Likewise, it was crucial to position my thinking and learning in all debate spaces, but especially in ones that were racially hostile. Being associated with such communities and spaces posits what Yosso (2005) defines as *community cultural wealth*, "providing youth of color with stories and resources meant to inspire their academic success and create cultures of possibility" (p. 78). While analyzing the varied debate experiences of Macaw, Toucan, Hawk, and Kingfisher apart from and in connection to my own, I comprehended that for them as AD supporters, the ways in which they were legacy learners and engaging in legacy learning were also connected to their families being involved with their debate identities, who regularly supported them in their debate communities and spaces by attending tournaments, driving them (and sometimes their teammates) to and from debate practices and tournaments, serving as judges at tournaments, purchasing food for tournaments, and attending professional development workshops.

Similarly, when thinking of the word *legacy*, I am reminded of the African proverb "It takes a village to raise a child!" As a Black woman who believes in these words and their robust and powerful meaning, my village, which includes family members, friends, mentors, teachers, and others, is filled with loved ones from all walks of life, narratives, and counternarratives. Still, in this same village are members of the debate community who have taught me, cried with me, laughed with me, and driven me across the state of Michigan to attend debate tournaments. Further, the word legacy is used in diversified ways in Black communities. For example, when an individual is interested in pledging or joining a sorority or fraternity and has family members who already belong to sororities and fraternities, the person is considered a legacy in the Black Greek-letter community.

As family members of legacy Greek-lettered organizations, they are able to listen, learn, dialogue, and then decide if they, too, want to become a part of such a legacy. Although this example is in the context of sororities and fraternities, the type of legacy learning is also visible in debate communities and spaces. The forthcoming reflections and understandings from the AD community are linked to being supported and sustained by a village via legacy learning. As I investigated how the ADers and the AD program embodied validating practices of its student-debaters and coaches, I was able to understand why these oral, written, and performative literacies and practices in debate were important for them.

Legacy Learning in High School

In reflecting about the differing nature of communities and spaces that evoke legacy learning for Black debaters and debate supporters, it is necessary to examine how high schools achieve or do not achieve this. Throughout this chapter, I forge the idea of legacy learning when it is both absent and present in the AD community. Specifically, the voices and experiences of the participants in this chapter highlight how they perceived their engagement with debate across high school, college, and other debate space contexts. Hearing from Macaw, Toucan, Hawk, and Kingfisher through their interviews will provide further analysis from their views as high school debater, college debater, coach, and executive director.

Across each interview, I asked the AD participants to discuss their experiences with learning while in multiple debate settings and how their involvements with learning impacted their debate maturation. Macaw, a senior high school debater at Jefferson High, saw his school as a place of learning that supported his growth in debate.

> I originally did not want to attend this school. It has a reputation of being filled with bad students. So every time I tell someone where I go to school, they make mad assumptions about me. After being a student here for a while, I discovered that it wasn't that bad. Being a part of the debate team and practicing a few times a week after school gave me the room to grow and learn. I even studied the evidence when I went home and began to think that I could even be a college student. (October 2015)

Macaw's uncertainties about being a student at Jefferson High stemmed from the school's negative reputation. As someone who previously had behavior and academic issues at his previous schools, he was hesitant to attend Jefferson High. Instead of internalizing what he heard and already knew about Jefferson High, he decided to remain there to try to see it as a place and space in which he could thrive as a student. His decision to not leave Jefferson High led to his joining the debate team and learning from his peers and coaches. If Macaw had enrolled in another high school, he would not have been able to report positive involvements with legacy learning at Jefferson High.

Another component of Macaw's interview that stood out were how his learning continued beyond the school context. Specifically, he exclaimed, "I even studied the evidence when I went home." This is essential to evaluate, considering home for Macaw also was representative of his community, which speaks to his legacy learning literacy involvement. In a time where the narratives of young Black men students and debaters comprise inadequate and insufficient information, Macaw's pride with connecting his school to home life offered a counternarrative that enriches the positive experiences of Black men debaters. Macaw also expressed that he saw learning and debate as being synonymous. Since he and his partner often experienced success at local and regional tournaments, I asked him more about this in an October 2015 interview.

> JONES STANBROUGH: What makes you and your partner successful when debating?
> MACAW: It definitely starts with what we learn from Kingfisher and use while we're at school and at practice.
> JONES STANBROUGH: OK. Say more about that.
> MACAW: Because we practice more after school than we did when we first started, I think that plays a part [in] what information we get and how often we get it.
> JONES STANBROUGH: Is that important to you? If so, why?
> MACAW: If we didn't practice, we wouldn't be able to get better. Kingfisher is supportive of everything we do and is actually like a father to us. I want to go to college and I think I may want to debate in college, so what we're doing now in high school can impact what colleges we get into and other kinds of opportunities.

After asking Macaw if he had an example of something he used in practice that was important to him, he shared an image of a raised Black fist that Macaw and his debate partner use as flow paper when debating. They would write on this in debate rounds and have the template saved on their computers for debating and flowing purposes. Again, flowing is necessary in a debate round. When attempting to counter an opponent's arguments, debaters must take notes or flow what they say. As Black debaters, Macaw and his partner acquired the Black fist template from a Black college debater who coaches and mentors them at weekend tournaments. In this way, Macaw and his partner were operationalizing literacy in a way that centered legacy learning. During the same interview, when asked how he first engaged with it, Macaw stated:

> I use that fist for all of my speeches. I write them down and type them. I got it from our college-student coach who comes to our high school to assist Kingfisher. He's mad cool. I definitely plan to use it in college too.

The Black fist expressed his appreciation for debate in general, his coach, and his college-student debate coach. Doing so was imperative for him, since he was proud to be a young Black high school debater in the AD community. Similarly, he felt and communicated his gratitude for those in the AD community who contributed to the ways in which he was being sustained as a legacy learner. Moreover, Macaw's insertion of himself and how he learned from and with his peers and coach supports the importance of legacy learning and how it occurs in multiple contexts.

Another perspective that is important to highlight here is that of Kingfisher. As a Black man and high school debate coach, he is committed to AD, including teaching and coaching during and after school, securing funding sources for students, and assisting with weekend tournaments. Even beyond his own team, Kingfisher was well received by students, especially young Black men in AD. During observations, I noticed that Kingfisher was passionate about debate and often told students that he wished he debated when he was in high school and saw it as a vital part of communicating effectively and being a critical thinker. The absence of Kingfisher's role would mean that the young Black men who were Black high school debaters would not have many of the opportunities that they do. Weekly, he sends correspondences to students and parents to encourage them, to invite them to debate seminars and workshops, and to inform and remind them of upcoming tournaments. He expounds upon all of this more in a June 2015 interview.

> Serving in my role provides me with so much joy. I've been doing this for a little while now and I absolutely love it. I've seen young guys who could barely read or write get involved with debate and go on to win, to do well in school, at tournament, and in life. It's awe-inspiring to experience and witness. I also like how the students involved have access to colleges and getting outside of their comfort zones.

As previously mentioned, Kingfisher's identity and presence in the lives of the young Black men high school debaters is appreciated and serves as a way in which legacy learning is present in the AD community. In addition to his coaching, he is considered a father figure and mentor to Macaw and others. In this way, Kingfisher's being available and responsive to Macaw's interests and needs as a young Black man, debater, and aspiring college student was vital for his success in school and in life.

Legacy Learning at a Predominantly White Institution

The following section highlights legacy learning literacies and the realities of college debaters Hawk and Toucan. It also reveals deliberations shared with me from Kingfisher. Both Hawk and Toucan were high school debaters in AD before being accepted to college. Their trajectories have been both akin and dissimilar. They both expressed to me that within the college debate circuit they travel more; more traveling posed more challenges, which led to instances of their not feeling affirmed or valued in certain spaces. Hawk attends a university that has a lot of resources. While this is usually viewed as something positive, Hawk comprehended that money is not everything. As one of the only Black college debaters on his team, Hawk attends a nationally ranked college. Having won national debate tournaments, the college policy debaters at Evergreen College have certainly earned their bragging rights. However, Hawk's stories of being a Black debater at a predominantly white institution (PWI) is one that has been heard before. We explore some of his accounts in an October 2015 interview.

> JONES STANBROUGH: So, how do you like debating at Evergreen State? And how is it different or similar to debating with AD?
>
> HAWK: I travel more. When I was in AD, my school and team didn't have a lot of money or a large budget, so we pretty much only participated in local and regional tournaments.
>
> JONES STANBROUGH: Is that something you enjoy?
>
> HAWK: I like traveling and being able to be a coach for high school students in the summer. It also helps that I get free room and board when I coach at Rouge State.
>
> JONES STANBROUGH: OK. Cool. Basically, it's a good trade-off for you. I noticed that you're one of the only Black debaters here. Tell me why you think that is the case.
>
> HAWK: Well, to begin, there just aren't a lot of Black college policy debaters. It's really sad too. So not only do I not see many Blacks on my team, but even when I'm coaching high schoolers at Woodward University in the summers. Woodward is different from Rouge State in that way. I'm used to being around majority Black debaters at Rouge, but at Evergreen and Woodward that's not the case. So I pretty much have to get creative with how I debate and sometimes interact with my peers. I have even had to call some of my fellow Black debate peers to help me think through arguments and other ideas.

As Hawk shared his experiences, there were times we both shook our heads in despair, reflecting on the absence of Black bodies in collegiate debate spaces. He felt as if more efforts needed to be made to attract Black debaters beyond just engaging with debate in high school. However, he expressed his disdain for not being able to connect with other Black debaters, both at Evergreen College and at Woodward University. He revealed that each summer he looked forward to traveling back home to work with high school debaters in AD so that he could be surrounded by other Black debaters and to engage in conversations with them that would assist with his being able to participate within and outside of the AD community. Given he is a product of AD, he felt a responsibility to help sustain the positive nature of AD. Later in his interview, Hawk revealed the idea of legacy learning by stating, "It always feels good to go home and see my people. I'm not the only one who's in college but returns home to give back. There's a lot of us and we learn from each other." In this way, Hawk preferred to be around other debaters who looked like him, despite receiving free room and board at Woodward University in the summer. He considered legacy learning as the support that carried him through some of his experiences as one of the only Black college debaters at a PWI.

Although Hawk shared some concerns with the lack of Black presence on college campuses, he still demonstrated a critical awareness of the differences between his upbringing with debating in Aurora at Rouge State in comparison to his newer debate spaces at Evergreen College and Woodward University. Despite being one of the only Black debaters on his team, Hawk's love for debate kept him from desiring to quit. Although Hawk noticed and defined what a lack of Black debate bodies means, it is still important to complicate his points. I argue that Hawk was still participating in legacy learning, although he was not necessarily learning from other Black debaters and debate supporters when he was at Evergreen College and Woodward University. His comments, "So not only do I not see many Blacks on my team, but even when I'm coaching high schoolers at Woodward University," reveal that he thinks something is missing from his experience as a Black college debater when he is not around other young Black men debaters or supporters of debate.

Legacy Learning at a Historically Black College

Toucan, a college debater at a historically Black college, South College, previously introduced to us how he feels supported at his institution. He stated, "Similar to UDLs, our team doesn't have a lot of resources, but we still make things happen." When Toucan uttered this comment, there was so much pride in his voice. He showed a happiness that was void from the words that Hawk spoke. Although Hawk and Toucan both originated from the AD community, their college worlds are very different. However, even in such differences, both of their voices and experiences provide narratives of Black debate embodiment. In my October 2015 interview with Toucan, I asked whether he wished he attended another institution of learning.

> I can't see myself being anywhere else right now. Although it's hot as heck at South College, the camaraderie that I share with my teammates and coach make everything great and worth the challenges we do face. Since we don't have a lot of money, we don't travel as much as I did in AD.

I'm cool with that, though, because being on campus here encourages me to do my best. I see my peers and debate teammates all the time. We're all pretty much getting good grades. We study together, grocery shop together, and hang out. We do our work first though. I like it here. I can be myself here.

Listening to Toucan, I immediately noticed a few things. In addition to the pride that he wore on his face, I also took note of the bond with his college teammates and debate coach. Next, I heard him state that South College does not have a large debate budget. I ascertain this was not a new phenomenon to Toucan, given the AD community did not have a lot of money. He stated that he did not and does not worry about money. Lastly, he highlighted his academics and how his schoolwork takes precedence over shopping and other nonacademic events. Learning from his lived experience made me want to understand more about his narrative. As someone who originally desired to attend a Black college, I am often interested in the stories and experiences I hear people have at HBCUs.

For Toucan, he happily revealed that he enjoyed being a college student-debater at South College. Unlike Hawk, Toucan expressed how his college community affirmed him in ways that made him feel like he belonged there. It was not something he had to question. Unfortunately, this was not Hawk's reality. Although he did not explicitly say it, I think the ways in which Toucan felt good when he returned to Aurora and to teach at Rouge State were feelings that he was interested in feeling more often. For Toucan, his mere presence on his campus was a validating one. He did not reveal to me that he questioned his peers or wondered where people were that look like him.

Toucan's sharing assisted me with understanding and learning from him. Still, I desired to learn more. When I engaged him in dialogue about debate and his team, he said the following:

JONES STANBROUGH: Tell me more about what you mean when you say you can be yourself at South College.

TOUCAN: I can dress how I want to. I can talk like I want to and essentially just do me. I don't have to feel like I have to impress anyone.

JONES STANBROUGH: OK. That makes sense, but what do you mean by you can dress and talk like you want to?

TOUCAN: I don't wear a lot of name brand clothes. I never have. I don't need to spend money on that kinda stuff. I'm at a Black college, so I don't feel like I have to act white or be something I'm not.

JONES STANBROUGH: When have you ever felt like you had to be someone else?

TOUCAN: Mainly in high school. Even though I had a great coach and teammates, sometimes things just got ugly. Don't get me wrong, there are crazy people here too, but generally it's a community that shows love.

In his response, Toucan brought up a few significant points. Similar to Hawk, Toucan reiterated the importance of being able to learn and be successful in college as a Black student-debater.

When characterizing his stance on materialism, Toucan's dismissal of name brand clothing was connected to being self-aware and comfortable in his own skin. However, his statement "I'm at a Black college, so I don't feel like I have to act white" suggested that he is aware that in other spaces, he might feel like he has to try to assimilate to dominant white-normed practices in debate. The white norms of policy debate are linked to social performance and identity. This means that white, straight, economically advantaged males are the norm for successful debaters. In these same spaces, Blacks and other students of color and ethnically diverse individuals sometimes feel pressured to perform according to the white-centered norms of the debate community. Toucan was resisting this idea because he could dress and talk the way he wanted to. These varied ways in which he identifies and dresses are all a part of the legacy learning literacies that he has been able to enact since his high school debate days as a participant in ACTION Debate. Legacy learning is not only in operation with Toucan, but with each Black participant in this study. Their individual and collective stories and experiences are what needs to be sustained when it comes to the schooling and educational identities of young Black men and other youth of color.

Conclusion

One of the most important lessons that literacy educators and teacher educators can learn from ACTION Debate and the literacies and lived experiences of its participants is how their home, school, and community lives are intertwined. Debate participation is essential for a positive self-concept, critical thinking, and the academic success and for the possibility of going to college. Macaw's, Hawk's, Toucan's, and Kingfisher's awareness of their Blackness and how others perceive them means they have to consciously think about everything they do and say. The sometimes taxing and tiring practice of cultural self-reflection leads to racialized individuals having low self-esteem and low self-concepts, which at times encourage self-hate. It would be easy for me to deduce that Hawk would be quicker to question his worth and skills because he is surrounded by white people at a PWI and that Macaw and Toucan are in better situations because one is still in high school and is surrounded by Blacks and the other one attends an HBCU.

This chapter did not seek to state who was in a better situation, but to highlight that regardless of what school they attended, Macaw, Hawk, Toucan, and Kingfisher were still actively engaged in and representing legacy learning. In all contexts, each debater always had access to a peer who either debated with him in high school or college, or to other debate supporters. These working definitions and examples of legacy learning suggest why it is necessary within debate contexts. Each and every participant developed as a debater from his interactions with legacy learning debaters.

Their individual and collective stories about their debate experiences illustrate a need for more opportunities for students to engage in multiple forms of culturally sustaining literacies within school. The AD participants' debate literacy practices led to their seeing themselves as students of success. This study also has implications for teachers and teacher education. There must be a push for teachers and educators to be more culturally relevant and sustaining by drawing from what Paris and Alim (2014) define as asset-based pedagogies. It is imperative not only that teachers be aware that more affirming and validating teaching needs to occur in their classrooms, but that they intentionally work to teach in these ways. Ultimately, the time is now for thinking and moving toward legacy learning to occur in settings that support young Black men and other marginalized youth. As a legacy learner, I proudly share my narratives as a former high school debater and coach and gladly express how serving in both roles led to my sustained voice and participation in debate communities.

■ References

Baker-Bell, A., Jones Stanbrough, R., & Everett, S. (2017). The stories they tell: Mainstream media, pedagogies of healing, and critical media literacy. *English Education 49*(2), 116–29.

Chance the Rapper. (2016). "Ultralight Beam." From Kanye West's *Life of Pablo*. New York: GOOD Music.

Cridland-Hughes, S. (2011). African American community literacy and urban debate. *Reflections: Writing, Service-Learning, and Community Literacy 11*, 109–25.

Dyson, A. H. & Genishi, C. (2005). *On the case: Approaches to language and literacy research*. New York: Teachers College Press.

Emerson, R. M., Fretz, R. I., & Shaw, L. L. (1995). *Writing ethnographic fieldnotes*. Chicago: University of Chicago Press.

Erickson, F. (1986). Qualitative methods in research on teaching. In M. C. Wittrock (ed.), *Handbook of research on teaching* (pp. 119–61). New York: Macmillan.

Fine, G. A. (2001). *Gifted tongues: High school debate and adolescent culture*. Princeton, NJ: Princeton University Press.

Graff, H. (2001). The nineteenth century origins of our times. In Ellen Cushman, Eugene R. Kintgen, Barry M. Kroll & Mike Rose (eds.), *Literacy: A Critical Sourcebook*, 211–33. Bedford/St. Martin's: New York.

Huber, G., & Plantageonette, A. (1993). Speaking out: Tapping potential in urban public schools. *Cross Streets: Ideas for Cities and Citizens 1*(1), 29–36.

Hughes, L. (1994). *I, too: The collected poems of Langston Hughes*. New York: Vintage Books.

Kinloch, V., & San Pedro, T. (2014). The space between listening and storying: Foundations for projects of humanization. In D. Paris & M. T. Winn (eds.), *Humanizing research: Decolonizing qualitative inquiry with youth and communities* (pp. 21–42). Thousand Oaks, CA: Sage.

Ladson-Billings, G. (1995). But that's just good teaching! The case for culturally relevant pedagogy. *Theory into Practice 34*(3), 159–65.

———. (2014). Culturally relevant pedagogy 2.0: A.k.a. the remix. *Harvard Educational Review 84*(1), 74–84.

Lee, E. (1998). Memoir of a former urban debate league participant. *Contemporary Argumentation and Debate 19*, 93–93.

Mallette, M. H., & Duke, N. K. (2004). *Literacy research methodologies*. New York: Guilford Press.

Mulvey, E., & Schubert, C. (2012). Transfer of juveniles to adult court: Effects of a broad policy in one court. *Office of Juvenile Justice and Delinquency Prevention*. Https://www.ojjdp.gov/pubs/232932.pdf.

Paris, D. (2012). Culturally sustaining pedagogy: A needed change in stance, terminology, and practice. *Educational Researcher 41*(3), 93–97.

Paris, D. & Alim, H. S. (2014). What are we seeking to sustain through culturally sustaining pedagogy? A loving critique. *Harvard Educational Reviewer 84*(1), 85–100.

Rogoff, B. (2003). *The cultural nature of human development*. Oxford: Oxford University Press.

Rose-Reid, S. (2008). The harsh realities of "acting Black": How African-American policy debaters negotiate representation through racial performance. Doctoral dissertation, University of Georgia.

Shavelson, R. J., & Towne, L. (eds.). (2002). *Scientific research in education*. Washington, DC: National Research Council, National Academy Press.

Spradley, J. P. (1980). *Participant observation*. New York: Holt, Rinehart, and Winston.

Stake, R. E. (1995). *The art of case study*. Thousand Oaks, CA: Sage Publications.

The Notorious B.I.G. (1999). *Mo money mo problems*. New York: Bad Boy Records.

Wolf, I. (2008). Learning the language of debate: Literacy and community in the Computer Assisted Debate Project. Master's thesis, Emory University.

Yin, R. (2009). *Case study research: Design and methods*. 3rd ed. Thousand Oaks, CA: Sage.

Yosso, T. J. (2005). Whose culture has capital? A critical race theory discussion of community cultural wealth. *Race, Ethnicity and Education 8*(1), 69–91.

Perseverance Will Prevail

Three Young Black Males Whose Lives Matter

Stuart Rhoden

This chapter focuses on three young Black males who epitomize the transitioning of the discourse surrounding Black males and males of color from a deficit model to what Alber (2013) describes as an abundance model, which is a way to describe students through a strength-based lens rather than a deficit lens. Even though many young Black males must navigate a history of racial discrimination, challenges in family structure, low income, and, in many cases, extremely violent neighborhoods, communities, and schools, many experience positive academic and social supports. These strength-based supports help them maintain an optimistic mind-set that assists in increasing positive academic achievement. Persistence and resilience are central to being able to be productive academically and to achieve socially. However, persistence and resilience are mitigated without a certain level of trust. Thus, trust is an important reason students achieve.

To increase positive educational outcomes, it is critical to examine why some young Black males are able to build trust and achieve in the face of adversity, while many of their peers do not. Utilizing more strength-based approaches to examining students of color and their academic achievement is central to dismantling the pervasive deficit model of thinking. Specifically, examples of the stories and narratives of students of color in their own voices are tantamount to shifting the narrative. This chapter focuses on the accounts of three participants who exemplify the transition of Black male students from high school to college. These three participants were chosen to offer a glimpse of the diverse range of students who embody persistence and resilience in very different ways, and represent a high, middle, and challenged academic record.

Methodology

The work in this chapter includes a qualitative analysis of interviews with three graduates of a predominantly Black, all-male Du Bois Charter High School (a pseudonym) in the mid-Atlantic region of the country. Denzin and Lincoln (2011) highlight the importance of qualitative research as a methodology that helps the observer make sense of the world of the participant. All of these students attended college after high school and were interviewed during their second (sophomore) year. All names (school, students, teachers, administrators) are pseudonyms to protect confidentiality. Interviews focused on participants' familial and community background, high school experiences, and their experiences either currently or formerly attending college. Each of the individual participant interviews helped to create a landscape that began to highlight that trust was an important factor in their academic and social achievement. This methodology was able to assist in this finding because of the benefit of being able to delve more deeply into the narratives of the participants (Wolcott, 2008).

These three interviews took places on the college campuses of the individual participants, were conducted at several coffee shops located near each of the individual participant's residence, or at Du Bois Charter High School. The interviews lasted between approximately thirty minutes and one hour and fifteen minutes. Each of the participants was selected by Du Bois Charter High School to participate in the research, and each received a $25 gift card for their participation. The names of the participants have been changed, but the quotations expressed in this paper are their own. Levine and Nidiffer (1996) highlight that a smaller sample size for a qualitative study such as this emphasizes the depth of analysis rather than the breadth. Accordingly, while it is impossible to make significant uniform conclusions based on the small sample size, it is possible to identify and highlight themes that can contribute to a better understanding of the lived lives of the participants through their own narratives.

In addition to the participant interviews, a group interview with two key administrators, the CEO and the College Counselor at Du Bois Charter high school took place. These interviews provided contextual background information on the participants' high school experience.

Tyrone Breaux

Tyrone Breaux is a young, intelligent, twenty-year-old sophomore at a small liberal arts college in the Northeast. He is roughly six foot one, lanky, and fairly bookish in his appearance. When we met at a bookstore coffee shop for our interview, he was extremely polite and engaging. A part of the first graduating class at Du Bois Charter, he informed me that he was comfortable talking about anything, since he had been interviewed several times. As I mentioned in my field notes about my first impressions of him, "He was very forthcoming, self-reflective, and insightful, not to mention funny." He was very forthcoming about his upbringing, noting that his father, who had met his mother when they were in middle school, was in and out of his life, and that he primarily he grew up on the north side of a major mid-Atlantic city with just his mother and brother. He describes his mother being raised in a "broken home," but also speaks extremely highly of her skills in raising him and his brother virtually alone. Tyrone views his mother as one of his first mentors and an inspiration. Her message to him was that he is responsible for what he does.

> You are a young Black individual from age—whatever age . . . you have to keep your nose clean. You have to make sure you have a certain amount of education, or you're not going to make it in the world. Because everyone is going to judge you by that.

Tyrone is extremely comfortable in his own skin and is a self-described nerd. Before attending Du Bois Charter, he attended several Catholic grade schools, where he was often bullied and harassed for being "different." In our interview, he astutely highlighted the similarities between Catholic schools and public schools in regard to what he describes as "moral codes."

> Most people believe Catholic schools have certain moral codes and upstanding. Catholic schools are plagued with the same things as public schools; there are still bullying, there's fighting, still sex and drugs happening in Catholic schools, even in middle school and elementary, which is kind of disconcerting sometimes.

Precollegiate Academic Experiences

One of the major differences Tyrone speaks of regarding his precollegiate schooling is that Du Bois immediately felt like a "family." He describes the first-year experience in the trailers when the school building was being remodeled to house the high school as basis for forming a "brotherly love for each other" among the students at Du Bois. He was not the only student interviewed who expressed how their tight quarters and newness were a contributing factor for the closeness the Class of 2011 exhibits with one another. Tyrone seems to be a student who thrived in this type of school, where he was no longer seen as an outcast or, in the Freirian sense, "othered." Du Bois was founded in part to help Black boys succeed in becoming both college ready and an inspiration to their communities. It is likely that Tyrone would have succeeded in becoming a college attendee regardless, but Du Bois really helped him form a sense of identity and community.

> Even when something would happen, for instance, when someone would come and harass one of the students, people had their back. For instance, one of the kids was jumped right in front of the school and I had to like shoo away the people trying to fight him. And Mr. Simmons and Mr. Nate and others on the staff at Du Bois were so good about it. They would help the kid out. They would also make sure that there was action taken and not just like, oh, it's just boys being boys.

As he mentioned about his middle school years, he was ostracized from the time he was little. Some would claim that he was a victim of the "acting white" phenomenon articulated by many scholars (Allen, 2015; Fordham & Ogbu, 1986; Harper, 2007; Howard, Douglas, & Warren, 2016; Tyson, 2011). He believes that his peers in middle school felt that he was the "whitest Black that they'd ever known." He mentions his friend Malik, who has been integral in his maturation and, it seems, his positive transition into his teen years and early adulthood. Tyrone says that he "probably wouldn't be as successful" if he didn't have Malik in his life. Malik serves as a lifeline to Tyrone:

> I was almost about to give up and fall into the same things that a lot of other people, other people of my statistics fell into. . . . Everyone was against me. They were saying, oh you think you're so smart, you're so better than everyone else. I constantly, I'm thinking, I'm actually the dumbest kid in the class.

Malik served as a peer mentor to Tyrone who, as the literature articulates, helped Tyrone overcome some of the social obstacles so many teenagers face, particularly the tribulations faced by many Black boys growing up in urban environments where there is a nearly singular definition of what it means to be young and male (Steele & Aronson, 1995; Steele, 1997; Noguera, 2003). If you're Black and male, to be socially accepted you have to be hard, for the most part. This means you have to fight when provoked, not be too book smart, but street smart, be a fan of or participate in sports (namely football and basketball). Tyrone did not fit this mold. Until he went to Du Bois Charter, he seldom saw other Black boys who held similar academic and social interests.

One of the potential reasons for these stereotypes of Black males, Tyrone believes, falls at the feet of some of his teachers in middle school who did not create a safe environment for "others." I asked him why he thinks he was constantly bullied and ostracized, and he suggested that "it was due to bad teaching . . . it was just that my teacher wasn't the best . . . . I didn't learn anything, so I was pretty much behind." Unlike many who would have fallen prey to the temptations surrounding them, especially in the face of incessant physical and psychological abuse, Tyrone shows a great amount of resilience. Rather than succumbing to what the teachers thought of him, or sitting idly by and accepting not "learn[ing] anything," Tyrone says,

> As I grew, I had this drive. . . . One of the things that helped me get past the statistic was this fire inside me to want to learn, to not be the dumbest kid, because I would constantly see the honors awards, and there was first honors and second honors and I would know that I would never get those. And then there was that honorable mention. I would always covet this [laughter]. I may not be the smartest, might not be the second, but at least let me be mentioned. . . . I just kept working, kept confident because all wanted was that honorable mention. And got into middle school, I got that honorable mention. . . . I started keeping my grades up. Malik basically taught me how to socialize, how not to be that kid who everyone was going to pick on and even if they did, [Malik said,] I've got your back.

Peer Socialization and Schooling.

Although Tyrone, through the assistance of his friend Malik, less often fell prey to being bullied and ostracized, he still wasn't the "nicest kid around." He was antisocial for a long time. Malik followed him from the north side of town to Du Bois Charter and helped Tyrone to become "more of a social person." Another mentor who assisted Tyrone in his maturation and both social and, equally important, academic growth was the CEO of the school, Mr. Simmons.

> Mr. Simmons saw that, saw something in me, and from day one . . . even before we got into school, he invited me to a special lunch with a certain amount of people who he thought would eventually come to make something of themselves. And throughout that time, he constantly would be [saying], "Hey, Mr. Breaux, whatcha doin' here?" And he would constantly mentor me, telling me what I should be doing in order to get better.

Rather than having a single mentor, which is often mentioned as a contributing factor in a Black males' academic and social success (Noguera, 2008), Tyrone highlighted three unique individuals who helped shape him: his mother, Malik, and Mr. Simmons. More importantly, each of the three highlighted aspects of Tyrone's personality that helped him become both socially and academically prepared to leave his neighborhood and city and go away to college. Tyrone repeatedly mentioned in his interview that he "made it a point to myself to associate with people who I've learned can better help me." Tyrone identifies individuals who can help him as mentors and role models to help him improve "my skills and such." This ability to see individuals as helpers and mentors is not unique to Tyrone, but is rare in young people. As much of the literature highlights, the millennial generation Tyrone is a part of is constantly berated as being selfish, individualistic, and needy (Bourke & Mechler, 2010). Tyrone goes against the grain of many of his peers and sees opportunities to learn from people of all ages, including his mother, his friend Malik, and Mr. Simmons. Each of these individuals helped Tyrone succeed and achieve "first honors until the end of his high school career."

Influence of Du Bois Charter High School

Several other contributors to Tyrone's maturation and the development of that "fire inside" him include some of his teachers at Du Bois Charter. After being bullied and miseducated in middle school, Tyrone did not trust teachers

> until high school. . . . Du Bois' teaching is what made me regain trust in teachers because . . . the teachers actually cared. They made sure to give you their cell phone numbers. They would stay late to help you. Whenever I didn't understand something in math, they would sit there and help me and would go out of their way. And they weren't just like, "Sit down, shut [up], sit in this chair, here is this textbook, read it."

Tyrone also spoke highly of his teacher's ability to treat him with respect and how they took the time to learn about his family history so that "they could better teach you and come around. . . . Certain teachers would actually come visit you at home and stuff. . . . These teachers at Du Bois really cared about you, which helped me trust them a lot more." While Tyrone acknowledges explicitly that what he experienced at Du Bois Charter is not indicative of all teachers at all charter schools, especially the experiences of Black boys, he did allude to the idea that his teachers brought out something that was already inside him. The "fire inside" that Tyrone speaks of began with his mother's trying to provide a better educational opportunity for him by sending him to Catholic school, where he did not receive the type of education and socialization that she and Tyrone desired. Still searching for a positive educational opportunity for her son, she enrolled him in a brand-new charter school. Her mind-set was, "Let's try charter schools." Tyrone eloquently (and maturely beyond his years) describes his thought process on life as it pertains to his schooling.

> I do believe that life is hard. Life is hard, it ain't fair, it's a game. And you've got to play it a certain way. And when you get a certain card and it sets you back, you've got to play it, and then you've got to move past it. If you let it defeat you, you're going to be defeated and that's all you're going to be. I've been taught once you accept defeat . . . you can accept defeat. When you lose, it's not the failure that's the bad thing, it's sitting and dwelling in the failure.

Tyrone articulates a notion of resilience and grit that exceeds what many young Black males exhibit. Many speak of overcoming obstacles or fighting through challenges, but Tyrone has clearly considered the characteristics that have helped him get to college and be somewhat more successful academically than many of his peers. He puts his ability to face obstacles in context:

> See, throughout my life, I have always had that wall. And at certain times I've learned . . . I've learned in those times that there's always the fifth or fourth option to that, actually, that there—that wall in front of you, and you can climb up it. You can sit there and look at it. You can bust through it. Or you can go around it. It takes less effort. Busting through it, you've got to get a running start. Climbing over it, you've got to actually climb. Sitting there ain't gonna do you no good. Walk around it. Takes you less effort, and you still get where you need to go. So many people are constantly putting conflict in front of themselves and going, "This is one ginormous wall that I can't get past." And they don't look around to see how they can get around it. Sitting there crying about it isn't going to solve anything. Climbing over it might take you too long to get to where you need to be. You need to assess the situation and work around it. And that's where a lot of people lose that fire. Where they see this, they [say,] "I can't get a college degree, it's hard, it's gonna cost me too much money." They're not looking around to see that there is financial aid, there is people who will help get you where you need to go. You can take out a loan. And even if you get that loan, eventually you'll be able to pay it off if you get a good job. . . . And that's where people don't know . . . they need to look around and move toward their goal instead of just constantly wasting so much time and energy.

Tyrone's experiences epitomize the African proverb that it takes a village to raise a child. His mother has consistently put him in positions where she believed that he could succeed academically—and more importantly, constantly had faith in him and instilled in him that "fire inside." Malik, his best friend, gave him the social skills to not only be successful academically, but also have positive social outcomes outside of the classroom with his peers. Mr. Simmons and the teachers at Du Bois continued to build on the fire Tyrone's mother created; they helped augment and solidify those positive lessons learned in the home. All of these individuals combined helped to prepare Tyrone for his biggest obstacle in his young life, college.

College Ready

When asked who spoke to him about college first, Tyrone mentioned his mother. When asked when, he said it was before he was "even able to think about college. I was ten years old and she was like, 'Tyrone, you're going to college.' And I was like, 'What's college?'" Once he found out what it was and what getter there entailed, he felt that it was something that he wanted and could achieve. His mother played an integral role in his early exposure to college, and she instilled in him a belief that it was possible:

> She always made it seem like you could do anything, and she led by example even as a high school student. . . . She basically graduated with a high school degree and is making money that people are coming out of college with a bachelor's degree can't even make.

Financial incentives were not the only inspiration Tyrone had for attending college. He knew what his attending college would mean not only to his future, but to his family.

> I'm really the first one to go to college. My mother has taken community classes, but she wasn't able to stick with them. But I'm the first one to go away for college. So my mom was busy, wanted to keep the relationship that we had, which is me being close. But at the same time she wanted more and better for me, so she wanted me to go away.

Tyrone also knew the impact attending college would have on him socially and the impact that it would have on his future both socially and professionally. He talks about the increase in the "credentialing" of American society and his need to be on par with others competing in the professional arena.

> You also need that social aspect of school and what college, college teaches you so much. It's not just learning for your job, it's the social aspects. You get to learn about people, you get to learn about rapport that will help you find internships, that'll help you basically get along in life. People who don't go to college miss out on that aspect, along with actually getting a degree, which is beneficial

in all sorts of ways. Even at McDonald's they look. Do you have a degree? On every application, do you have a degree? If you have a degree, it puts you in a better standing in any job.

It appears that Tyrone was prepared socially for what to expect in college by his mother and his association with Malik. He is constantly "interested in anything that I can learn culturally that'll put me ahead." He also appears to not be easily swayed by the temptations of being away from home and the pitfalls many first-year, first-generation college students fall prey to. What was a bit disconcerting was his judgmental comments about his peers and their under-age behaviors, which traced their actions to their upbringing.

> You get to see where people came from, how they were raised and how that affected them. So you really get to see how much, how much your raising, how much your parents played a role in making you who you are. Because I've met friends who were pretty much raised by nannies, pretty much raised themselves. And you see it. You see it in their manners, you see it in . . . their moral compass and stuff like that. Because when you're raised by parents, it does have an effect. It might not have the biggest effect. It does. From studying psychology, parenting, early childhood development is something really big. You're pretty much a sponge, you're absorbing everything around you. You're constantly looking. Children are the most adaptive little things ever.

Tyrone sees the class and race distinctions drawn by the behaviors of his peers in college. His major, psychology, has perhaps given him the advantage of being able to draw distinctions about socialization that some of his peers are not able to perceive. He is also fortunate that he has learned from his mentors about what is and is not acceptable behavior. While Tyrone articulates his distaste for some of the social behaviors of his peers, academically he feels as if he is not on par with his classmates.

> I'm not on the level of . . . some of my peers in college, which is a very sad realization. . . . Even in [Du Bois] there were certain courses that you just weren't offered. Because it was a new school, they're trying to get those nice things that other schools have. But I've taken classes where people, and I've gone into my psychology classes and people have already taken intro to psychology, people have already taken German, people have already taken all of these . . . and I'll come in and I'm the guy who hasn't taken any of these and this is all a new world for me. And I'll start scribbling down notes. I've [been] so frustrated because I've taken an exam and get like a 70, and people who have taken this class already are like, "You just need to study harder . . ." I'm like, "Well, I haven't had all the opportunities as you." While I might not be on par with grades and things, I feel as though I work harder than them. I want it more than they do most of the time.

What Tyrone lacks academically, he makes up for in drive and resilience. His persistence in the face of understanding that he may not be as academically prepared for college as some of his peers, makes him more prepared, perhaps, than some who had academic advantages in high school. His ability to reach out and seek assistance, to learn from his peers, and to acknowledge his own shortcomings while at the same time pushing ahead unafraid of the challenges is exactly the type of resilience and grit educators need to instill in more students, Black boys in particular.

Tyrone attends a private coeducational small liberal arts college in a rural setting in the mid-Atlantic portion of the United States. The 110-acre main campus is home to over sixteen undergraduate students. According to the college's website, there are approximately 43 percent males and 57 percent females. According to Forbes.com, the racial makeup of the college is 79 percent white, 3.0 Latino, 2.0 percent Black, and 16 percent other. *US News and World Report* cites the 2012–13 tuition at over $35,000 and total cost at $47,000 per year. Academically, approximately 95 percent of its students graduate in four years, with an overall first-year student retention rate of 85 percent. The average high school GPA is 3.75. The SAT scores' range is 520–640 in critical reading, 540–650 in math, and 520–610 in writing. *US News and World Report* ranks this college a most selective liberal arts college.

My discussion with Tyrone came to what transpired on his first day at college. Unlike most students, who were trying to find the cafeteria, the bookstore, or the nearest party, Tyrone was in search of something else:

> We learned from high school that we need a certain group to help with certain things. That first day was finding that group to be able to help me with my plans for the year [laughter]. I know it sounds . . . See, in college, I've learned this. [At Du Bois Charter and] all my other schools, there is a structure. In high school and down, there's a structure. There's a teacher, there's a syllabus, this is what they're going to stick to.

Thus Tyrone was immediately in search of that village, that group of mentors who would help him succeed in college from day one, hour one. This is exceptional behavior for any young person entering college, much less for a first-generation, urban Black male entering a college two hundred miles away from home and his familiar surroundings.

Conclusions

It appears that Tyrone has the potential to achieve whatever he sets his mind to accomplish. Despite being the first in his family to attend college, he set a goal of trying to graduate in three years and planned on taking seven courses his first three semesters. Due to an unhelpful adviser and potential burnout, he was unable to keep that pace, but is still on track to graduate in four years. He concludes about his first year on campus:

> I didn't have the structure. I didn't have Mr. [Simmons] or people looking out for me. I didn't have an adult actually looking out for me. When I went into this, he basically said, "Here's your schedule." I was like, this looks adequate. First semester I took twelve credits. I was like, this is a good semester. This is going to let me move and get ahead. Came out with pretty much Bs across

the board. But then the second semester, I want to take this math class. I want to take all of these and he was like, "Go ahead! Maybe you should take this with that." And . . . I was like, this is a lot harder. The whole time I'm struggling to get work done. I'm like staying up all night. Caffeine has become my friend—tea, not coffee. It's a little better. . . . So staying up all night, staying up three days without sleep, just working through. And just putting paper after paper, test after test. And . . . I built up this anxiety because I was like, if I sleep, I won't be able to finish this paper. If I don't sleep, I'll be able to finish this paper and do this test, but I might not be able to do this guitar lesson. For like the whole two semesters I was able to do it. This last semester, the hardest semester I've ever taken. I took statistics, German, and a few other things. I was like, this is a bad idea. I realized—no actually I didn't realize it because I was so blinded by, I had those moments, when even I have too much pride . . . [laughter]. I'm like, I can do this, I'm gonna get it. . . . I'm looking at the progress I'm supposed to have, Student . . . Activities pretty much calls and tells me, "Hey, you're failing three classes." I'm like, oh. So I had to meet with the dean of students.

Even with his seeming inability to find the academic mentors at college he found in high school, he continued to push ahead until he physically and academically was unable to do so. While his goal of graduating in three years is lost, he will graduate with the rest of his entering class, and he has also gained a greater appreciation of his own resilience in the face of challenges. Further, Tyrone, in finding a new adviser in the dean of students, has found that necessary mentor to help guide him through his academics while in college. Socially, Tyrone has found his mentors and peers in college, and unlike his experiences in middle school and high school, seems to have settled into a social niche. About being a Black male on campus, Tyrone says,

I love it. . . . It one of those moments where there are two things that can either happen. You can either have a bad experience and let yourself have a bad experience of being a different minority. And that would ruin your whole college experience. Or you can learn to make it work for you. When you are a minority, there are different things that people won't do around you. Different things they *will* do around. Different things they'll ask you, which is nice because I've been asked, "Hey do you smoke weed?" Do you do this, do you have the connections? I'm like, "No, I don't." A lot of them I don't do. . . . A lot of people were like, "He's the Black guy." That they were freer to do different things around me, which allowed me to learn more about them. . . . It was a lot easier to make friends, it was a lot easier to talk to people. When I would go, "Oh, I'll play Dungeons & Dragons!" they were like, "The Black guy plays Dungeons & Dragons?" They were so interested. . . . It was almost, certain times it was disrespectful. It was like, "I want to learn about this Black culture I've heard so much about." Well, I'm like, "Well if you want to learn . . ." I always have that thing too where I want to learn. If we can learn about each other together, it's . . . it's better for ourselves. Throughout my college, I've learned how to make my minority work for me.

Antoine Wright

Antoine's interview took place at Du Bois Charter. He had arranged for a room that was off the main entrance and was somewhat private for us to converse in. Antoine was extremely polite, cordial, and friendly. When not in college, he volunteers around Du Bois, doing a bit of everything. Everyone around the school loves him still, even two years after he graduated.

His appearance was one of a very athletic-looking young man. He was dressed like a typical college student, jeans, T-shirt and headphones around his neck. He was rushed and in a hurry to finish the interview, but he wasn't rude. He had worked all day at Du Bois and was scheduled to meet a friend from college after work.

Background

Antoine was born into a family of seven children. He is the fifth of seven kids and the first in his family to go to college. He grew up with just his mother around and his father not in his life. One of his brother's is incarcerated, and he mentions that he prefers to not venture outside where there are negative distractions, but instead prefers to stay "in the house." It appears that his early schooling was fraught with discipline issues and lack of structure. He attended middle school in his neighborhood and had good grades but was "cutting school, disrespecting teachers, but still graduating on honor roll. Just As and Bs." When asked if that was an indictment of him or his school, he felt it was a combination of both. He did just enough to get by, and didn't feel academically exceptional. He repeatedly mentioned that he "didn't care" when it came to his schooling, which implies that he was being influenced more by his peers than by his teachers.

When he was in middle school he was "being bad for no reason." He had a Therapeutic Staff Support (TSS) record, so he felt that he had carte blanche to do anything he wanted. (A TSS is a paraprofessional that works in public schools to support students social and emotional needs.) Antoine goes on to say:

> I was actually being bad, knowing I cannot get kicked off trips, so I was just being bad for no reason. Other kids would get kicked off, so I was like I got special privileges. Maybe that was only because I had a TSS record, so it was, really, I couldn't get into trouble. It was like to my advantage. . . . Most of the teachers thought, . . . we can't take this trip away from him, so we're just going to let him be.

He knew he could work the system and be as bad as he wanted to be because he had the TSS record and felt that the teachers did not care or support him. When pressed about exactly what he did that was so bad, he wouldn't go into specific details about his middle school experiences. However, when he talked about the differences between his middle school and Du Bois Charter, he mentioned his mother as one who directed him toward Du Bois. A representative from the school called his house—ironically, on a day that he had been exceptionally bad in middle school—and his mother attended an information session about the school and suggested that he "should go . . . it's a good start, a new beginning." Antoine seemed hesitant to leave his old ways behind, and even though he mentioned the laptop all students received upon acceptance into Du Bois, he didn't seem ready to give up the "distractions" of girls and his peers. One of the turning points came during the summer intersession before school began.

> One day I disrespected . . . Mr. [Simmons], believe it or not. And it's like, bring your mom up the next day. My mom came up and she's like, "Please do not start this again." And I was like, "Mom, he was disrespecting me and I don't like the way he talked to me." And she's like, "You're going to have to deal with it . . . I believe she talked to Mr. Simmons, saying I came a long way. Which I did because I got sent away a couple times when I was younger, so it was like I came a long way and I'm ready for a new beginning. And he gave me another chance.

This experience with Mr. Simmons seems to have been an academic and life-changing turning point. Something clicked in Antoine, and he decided that he would take advantage of the opportunities afforded him. As the literature mentions, it only takes one mentor to change the life of a child (Noguera, 2008). However, if the individual is not receptive, then change does not come. Fortunately in this instance, the transformation from middle school Antoine into high school Antoine stuck. He felt for the first time that someone had given him a chance, had "vouched" for him.

> So after that day, me and Mr. Simmons have been very, like, good. He's been like a mentor to me throughout high school. . . . I think for him to give me a second chance [was] him seeing something in me. After him giving me a second chance, I was just like being on my P's and Q's.

In addition to Mr. Simmons, several of his other teachers helped him gain trust in both his academic abilities and in other students. He cited his English teacher as someone who taught him not to give up and to keep improving his writing.

> He was the one who gave me Cs on every paper and was like, "This is not good. This is not good. This is not good." I was like, "What am I doing wrong?" He said, you're going to college, they're just going to give you an F for that. He said, you're not ready. I just kept writing and writing and writing. I think my overall grade was a B. He was like, I see an improvement in your writing. And if you keep writing and writing over again and reading and things like that, your vocabulary will expand and things like that. So me just studying a lot and reading over my work, that's what got me prepared.

This perseverance helped Antoine not only at Du Bois, but also in his considering college an option. When he was in eighth grade, a teacher mentioned was a significant cost to college, and Antoine was confused. Antoine thought education was free:

And she's like, no, college is expensive. I said, well I won't be going to college then. And she was like, I guess you won't. And it didn't really mean anything . . . I just left it at that because it didn't really mean anything to me because I was like, college costs.

Like so many lower-income students, Antoine felt that even if he were smart enough to attend college, financial constraints would mean that it was not a viable option. However, once he arrived at Du Bois Charter School and entered a college preparatory atmosphere, his mother began to inquire about what it would entail for him to attend.

Academic and Social Preparation for College

Another influence in Antoine's life, outside of his mother and Mr. Simmons, was his experience with Upward Bound. He went on a three-week program to North Carolina while a sophomore in high school. He cites this experience as being influential in opening his eyes to the bigger world and in his gaining a more compassion outlook about others. One of the requirements of Du Bois Charter is that students must participate in extracurricular activities. So in addition to his Upward Bound experiences, Antoine was also one of the first members of the school's rowing team. The local newspaper and a YouTube video chronicled his experiences on the crew team. Antoine himself speaks of the experience:

We made history, being the first African American team on the water in over fifty years, I believe. We had to get up at 4:00 A.M. and get there on time. . . . I was determined to do it. And then after practice we come back to school from 8:00 A.M. to4:00 P.M.

In an interview with the major local newspaper, Antoine's principal said about the group,

Crew demands a lot of time, preparation, conditioning, teamwork, and when you plop that down into a rigorous high school program, it really forces students to be organized and efficient with their time in order to make it all work.

When pressed about why he didn't play other more typical sports (i.e., football or basketball), Antoine replied, "Crew was the only thing I did like to do." Antoine's activities outside of school seem to suggest the type of student Antoine was becoming—not in regard to his academic achievement, but rather his resilience and determination to face obstacles. He continuously challenged himself to not just spend the summers in the neighborhood with friends, but to go into a challenging, unfamiliar environment. During the school year, he challenged himself to not just play a typical sport, but to be an innovator and break down the stereotypes of what it means to be a Black male in an urban city environment. Not only did Antoine break down these stereotypes, his school encouraged him to do so. These types of expectations, to rise beyond the accepted to be exceptional, manifest themselves in Antoine's college journey.

College Acceptance and Attendance

Antoine's college application experience was typical of many first-generation college students, that is, difficult. Fortunately, unlike in many urban schools, he had a great counselor at Du Bois, Ms. Carter. On her own time, she took many members of the first graduating class at Du Bois to visit mid-Atlantic and East Coast colleges. The college he is attending was not his first choice, but he did an overnight at another institution and did not like it. As soon as he "set foot on the campus [where he is attending], I was like, I really like the environment here." When talking about his college, he mentions that one of the "downfalls" of the college is the cost. For decades, it has consistently ranked as one of the more expensive college in the country. However, Antoine has received significant financial assistance from Du Bois and from his employment. He seems to be as concerned with the financial aspects of college as much as, if not more so than, its academics or social aspects. He does not want to let anyone down and is pushing himself to succeed in spite of the financial burdens.

According to *US News and World Report*, the 2012–13 tuition for the school Antoine attends is $37,640. It is a small suburban liberal arts college in the Northeast and sits just outside a major city. It is home to approximately fourteen hundred students, of which 33 percent are male and 67 percent are female. The average SAT composite score is 1740. It is considered a selective college. The racial composition of the college is 54 percent white, 9 percent Black, 4 percent Latino, and 2 percent Asian. (The remaining 41 students were classified as bi-racial, native, and indigenous.)

Diversity was an issue when it came to Antoine's choosing a college. He wanted to go to a school that had some diversity but wasn't as monolithic as his high school. When he visited another college, he noticed the lack of Black students:

> The crazy part about it was that there were three Black people there and they were like, we need you to come, please come. And I'm like, I don't mind coming, but if I do come, I'll be miserable here.

Antoine felt the pressure of having to go to a college solely based on his racial identity and being one of the few to fit into a culture. At the college where he is attending, there is a significant Black culture, and he fits right into an already established group of peers and feels less pressure to be a sole representative of his culture. Goffman (1967) articulated the notion of onstage and backstage performances. Du Bois (1903) speaks of Blacks having a "double consciousness" when it comes to living in two worlds, one Black and one white. In this instance, Antoine not only feels pressure in college to perform his race, he feels internal pressure to succeed academically at a high level:

> As soon as I got into college, it was like a shovel because we were already behind. . . . I felt like we are on our own. Since this being a low-income [high] school, we already come from schools that were low-fund schools, so once we got into high school, some of us were behind, which I was one of them, and some of the things I couldn't do. I had to go to F-score programs to catch up. Some

people were high and some people were low. Once we got into college, most of the students I go to school with now been going to private school their whole life. Their speaking will be much different from mines, and their vocabulary will be different from mines. . . . So I'd be in class, like, I don't know, what did you just say? So please, not dumb it down but just like . . .

Unlike in high school, where the class of 2011 created camaraderie based on their proximity to one another in the trailers and the experience of being the first graduating class at a new high school, in college, Antoine knew that he had to create the type of climate that would be socially beneficial for him on his own. Prior to coming to campus in the fall of 2011, Antoine was proactive and contacted his future classmates via the Class of 2015 Facebook page. He was a prolific poster.

Everybody knew who I was and was like, oh my God, can you stop posting stuff. Then after that I met my friend, [who] is here today. Her name is LaRonda and I met her and we've been friends ever since. After that we started connecting with other people and then connecting with the basketball team. Because my CA [community assistant] was a basketball player . . . I got in touch with other basketball players because of him. I got into talking to the girls' basketball team and got to [know them] and talking to other people around. . . . And then I volunteered at public schools, because our school had our own program called Read-a-Story / Write-a-Story so we'd just go to inner-city schools and help students read and write. Things like that. I don't think it was hard for me meeting people because it came naturally to me.

Antoine's use of social media made his actual transition to college much easier. In addition, he created a community of people who have served as peers, mentors, and friends who helped ease the transition into a new environment—one in which he knew very little of what to expect and whether he'd fit in. Proactive in creating a social network, Antoine was very resilient and demonstrated that he had the ability to be independent and survive away from both Du Bois and home. Antoine also knew that he would have to reach out to his professors as well. He attended every class his first year and still felt he was academically behind. However, attending class every day and doing his best paid off.

I actually went to every single class, until I had a final presentation and I slept through it because I finished the project at seven o'clock in the morning. The class was at eight-thirty, and after I closed my eyes and went to sleep, I woke up and missed my presentation. So I actually ran to the class, pajamas and all, ran to the class and was like, I'm so sorry. And he let me go again only because I went to every single class. So your coming to every single class makes a difference.

Unfortunately, sometimes even attending every class does not result in a good grade. Antoine experienced some difficulties in his course work and fell behind in credits because he had to drop a course. He is still on the "right path to graduate on time" and is trying to raise his GPA. He is also reaching out to his professors in courses where he is having problems:

I would go to my teacher. I would go to her every day after class for an hour. I was like, I don't care, I have to know this material. She would actually stay with me the whole hour going over the material. She'd give me extra time on the exams and things like that. She actually emailed me over the summer, and we still keep in contact today even though she doesn't teach me, she's like another mentor in college.

Conclusions

Antoine is a very resilient and hardworking young man. He has come a long way from being a troubled youth on the path so many young Black boys travel—suspensions, expulsions, trouble with the law, and is well on his way to becoming his family's first college graduate. There was no magic event in Antoine's life that led him toward a more positive outcome, just a series of individuals who saw his potential, nurtured that potential, built trust and faith in him, and did not give up. Antoine now knows what a positive social and academic network looks like and has mirrored his experiences in high school on his college campus. Talking about his academic ability in relation to his peers, he says,

I feel like, and I'm not the only person, like a few people I still talk to this day from our class, we still struggle in our academics. Even though some of us might graduate with a 2.5 or some might graduate with over a 3.0, I felt like we're still coming out with our degree. We're putting in hard work, and right now, it doesn't matter about our GPA as long as we graduate. But I feel like we still are going through some kind of struggle in college with academics. I feel like it's still a struggle, because we weren't as prepared as we should be.

Antoine sees that he is not merely a statistic—either his SAT score, GPA or other quantifiable measure—but rather is a student who knows that graduation is the goal. While it may be challenging for him to enter into graduate school or qualify for certain careers, his social skills and resilience seems to be a strong indicator of his willingness to not give up, either on himself or his colleagues. He sees himself in the bigger picture as a role model and mentor to the next generation as well as his own generation.

I'm going to expand on the Black Student Union. Last year it was just all Black people in there. People look in there and think, there's a Black meeting in there and things like that we're against everybody. This year what we did was more like, it's not for Black people, it's for white people and all kinds of people. This year it's more diverse like we want it.

Andre Wallace

Andre was the first interview conducted on the campus where he is attending college. He was extremely cordial and had reserved a quiet room on campus for us to talk. His appearance was the antithesis of what a Du Bois student while in high school looks like. He had on a do rag, baggy hooded Temple University (not where he was attending) sweatshirt, and sweatpants. If he were not on a college campus, he would have looked to some like a stereotypical Black young man on the streets. I'm not sure if his dress was intended to provoke others on campus or if it was just Andre being Andre. He is a football player and is built like a lineman, except he is roughly five seven or so. Imposing, but not menacing.

Background

Andre was raised in a matriarchal home with both his mother and grandmother. He has a younger brother who is eleven years younger than he is and is currently in middle school. Prior to attending Du Bois Charter, he attended a small Roman Catholic grade school in his neighborhood. His middle school was pretty good academically compared to the neighborhood public school. Other Catholic and traditional public high schools both in the city and around the state heavily recruited him to play football. He was drawn to Du Bois Charter School by his mother, who asked him to "look at it and research it yourself." At an early age, he was given a choice—to attend a high school that had the potential to be academically beneficial, or to attend a traditional football powerhouse school where oftentimes academics comes second. Either way, it appears that Andre was on a trajectory of college. The question he was faced was whether would be academically prepared for the rigor of college.

> I looked at things that they [Du Bois] offered, and [in other schools] they don't really offer this to Black males or any males in inner city in general, so I was like, I might as well take this opportunity to go to Du Bois. . . . After doing my research on what Du Bois was about at the time, . . . they were telling me that Latin is the root of all languages and it will help me on the SAT. So I was like, yeah, I'm going to consider it.

High School Experiences

While at Du Bois, Andre established himself as more than just a football player. He was an avid member of the chess team, was on the stage crew for theatrical performances, was in the Latin Club, and participated in the weightlifting club. Upon graduation, Andre was very highly decorated academically and received an exceptional student award. In addition to his on-campus extracurricular activities, Andre volunteered at his church and participated as a volunteer at a prestigious golf tournament, where he was exposed to golf for the first time. He also understood the correlation between his extracurricular activities and his studies.

> I think it's great for Black males to come to [Du Bois] and go through experiences with those different extracurricular activities. . . . That was pretty fun, but I feel as though the things, the extracurricular activities that [Du Bois] offer are pretty decent for the boys . . . I think [it] gets you to sit down and concentrate and focus and strategize . . . especially if I'm being at [Du Bois] from eight in the morning to five at night. So you better be focused and be on your A game.

Academically, Andre felt prepared to attend college and was ready for the challenge after his four years at Du Bois. His only regret was that he did not learn African American history while in high school.

> I think having an African American history class could be one thing. Because I never would have gotten to this, to this place I'm at now in my life. I met my roommate and lived in the house that I love here on campus is an Africana Studies House . . . And there I've learned so much about what it means to be a Black man in the society today. And seeing the things that our youth are so blinded by and since they never were there back in the sixties to see what was happening around America, and so they don't know what was basically going on about what MLK and Malcolm X was fighting for. They don't even know the basics.

Andre has an acute awareness of his racial identity. Andre is the first student interviewed who articulated a profound understanding of race from his experiences in the neighborhood, while at Du Bois Charter, and while attending college. In high school, he experienced some backlash from the neighborhood for attending a charter school that had a dress code and for studying Latin and was perceived by neighborhood kids to be "better than" they were. Andre shielded himself from this backlash in several ways:

> [I] put myself around friends that have the same mind-set as myself and want to succeed and be successful and hopefully open their own businesses and do things with their lives. . . . I never really had a group a friends that were around my neighborhood, but I did know a few of the guys there. They knew who I was, but there always was some hostility to the [Du Bois Charter] students because we wore a shirt and a tie and a blazer.

Andre knew that in order to be "successful" he had to associate himself with successful peers who were on a different trajectory than some of his peers in the neighborhood. Rather than being upset by the hostility exhibited by some in the neighborhood, he seemed more perplexed. He articulates an excellent analysis of this issue:

> [I] always felt as though there was little hostile situations walking around our neighborhood. Oh, who is he, walking around with a suit and blazer on going to school and coming from school? I

think because they want the same opportunity as I have and they just can't get the same opportunity. I think that's one of my reasons and the other reason is that, you know how growing up back in the eighties and nineties the saying of, you're wearing a shirt and tie and everything, you're like a geek or you're basically looked down upon . . . because of the influence of the media and the portraying of Black culture. And seeing how they never had the opportunity to do things and once you see a Black person trying to do something with themselves, with their life, you always have that other person saying, "You're not going nowhere with your life. You don't need to be doing that." I think that's the reason why the guys were acting that certain way when I'd see them going to school and coming from school because they want that same opportunity, but they just can't get it at the time.

Thus to Andre, the media play a role in how some of his peers at other schools in the neighborhood respond to those who are on a different academic track. Possible explanations for their response include the "acting white" phenomenon, jealousy, fear, and ignorance. In response, when it came time for Andre to look at colleges, he wanted to leave the city and not be around an urban area. At the same time, he did want the diversity that is prevalent in urban areas. Andre applied to several colleges in a "four hours away" radius of his home. He finally selected a college he visited with Ms. Carter and a few of his peers. His first impressions of the college were that he'd fit in academically and also be able to play football.

College Acceptance and Attendance

Andre was eager to begin his college experience. Upon receiving all the awards and praise he earned at Du Bois, he felt he was prepared to start college with a strong footing. In addition, he noted,

> We had a 96 percent graduation rate, acceptance rate [N = 85]. So I was pretty thrilled and excited for that because we were going down to the school district and showing them we have a 96 percent acceptance rate. I was pretty fired up ever since then.

Andre felt that Du Bois did a good job preparing him for college both academically and socially. "I was ready to go, leave home, try to be out on my own. Towards the end of the [senior] year, I started going out and hanging out more with my friends."

Andre's school is a small liberal arts college in the suburbs of a major metropolitan city in the mid-Atlantic region. According to the school's website, there are 1,650 students from across the country and approximately 20 percent minority enrollment, of which 6 percent are Black. In addition the population consists of 47 percent males and 53 percent females. The college boasts on its website that it has a nationally renowned first-year program, which unfortunately does not bolster its graduation rate, which is 81 percent in six years, and 65 percent for Black students. The overall cost is an astronomical $55,000 per year. That accounts for why 98 percent of students are on some type of financial aid. The school is noted for its intersectional approach to the study of science and society.

Academically, Andre took on the challenge of being a science, technology, engineering, and math (STEM) major. Specifically, Andre is focusing his studies on exercise and sports science (ESS). Being a football player and a Black male, Andre has been challenged by these difficult courses. He is often one of the few Black students in a class. In addition, since he has been on the football team (he is considering not returning next season), he feels an additional burden or stereotype of being the "jock":

> People have told me that we can easily pick out who the football players are because of their size and their build and everything. And I've known a few people that said—they were pointing to me—that Black guy goes here because of football, that white goes here because of football. And I said, that's not true because I didn't join the football team until . . . my second semester of my freshman year. I wasn't here for football. . . . I always felt as though they had some feeling because I was Black and I'm playing football and oh that's the only thing he's really good for. . . . [The college he attends] is a pretty good school, so you have to have some type of knowledge to get in here.

His academic experiences with professors has been mixed. When asked why type of learner he is, he acknowledges that he is "more of a visual hands on" learner. Some of his course work has consisted of pure lectures, but other courses have included a mix of differentiated instruction. In addition, similar to many interviewed from Du Bois, Andre is not afraid to ask for assistance from his professors when the need arises. He feels that learning Latin in high school has helped him learn the terminology in ESS, but he still feels the need on occasion to go to his professors during office hours;

> The professors are just trying to get me to what they want me to be just like the rest of the students, they're teaching the same class. . . . They [professors] would just help me if I need help and I go to them. They'll come back to me and help me out . . . any day . . . and they'll answer your questions and everything.

At the same time he is astute and humbled enough to ask for assistance, he also feels pride:

> I walk around here with my head held high, like nobody can knock me off of my shoulders. So my head is straight up and just going about my goals of going to class.

When pressed as to how he built this type of drive, resilience, and grit, he feels that his experiences playing sports have helped him mentally prepare for the rigors of the classroom. He has grown into an outgoing, intelligent young man in part based on his experiences not only at Du Bois Charter High School, but also on the gridiron:

> It all started with football for me. Everything originated, that's the one thing about me, I was a shy person before I went to [Du Bois Charter]. Then as I spent my four years there I started breaking out of my shy shell, and then playing football also brought out that side of, oh, I can do this. I'm

going to dominate that. I always take that athlete's side to basically everything I do. . . . You have to be willing to give it your all to be successful.

Racial and Identity Challenges

One of the more interesting aspects of the interview were the questions posed to Andre surrounding race and identity. Whereas many twenty-year-old college sophomores are just beginning to formulate their own identities, Andre seems to have surrounded himself from the beginning of his collegiate experience with individuals who have helped him shape his views on race and his own positionality on campus. He begins by stating a commonly held belief by many in the Black community, that "being a Black man in America's society today is a challenge on its own." But rather than articulating the colloquial, stereotypical sentiments on this issue, he expresses a deep philosophical understanding of some of the differences between Black males and Black females on his campus:

> Black women are looked down upon today even though they're going to college more often than the Black males are. . . . I think it's more favorable to women than men here. Like being a Black man here is like, oh, you look like you're from the hood or something like that. I've gotten a lot of retaliation from people like that because they come to me and say, oh, then once I start talking to them, oh, you're not mean or anything like that. Because I'm a football player, they think, oh, I'm Black and I'm mean and strong, and so I'm going to do something to them. They're always like, I'm intimidating them or so, and that wasn't the case. It's like [Andre], you're just a nice guy.

Andre has taken the lessons taught from his mentors and has become an intellectual, thoughtful young Black man who is on a positive trajectory toward whatever goal he wishes to achieve. When discussing his high school experiences and the role they have played in both his college experiences and his maturation, in addition to Mr. Simmons, he mentions another role model who has helped him formulate his viewpoint;

> I tend to grab pieces of information from all the men that were around, in my life, to make who I am to this day. I'd like to thank Mr. Jordan, he works in the computer department at Du Bois. After and during school, during my lunch time I would go hang out with him because there I was the IT assistant during the summer, and when I worked for Du Bois during the time . . . he inspired me by him going to the military. Because every man in my family has been a part of the military, and I think I'm going to be the one that's going to break the chain.
>
> So, that's not the way I want to go, but from everything from what he's been telling me and the knowledge that he's been giving me, and he tells me to go research on this to see if he's right about it. And that's the one thing that he always tells me and my friend, that I'm going to give you this information, but I want to point your view in this certain way. I want you to come up with

your own view about it. I'm going to give you that information to look at, and when he did that, I thank him for that, and he's been one of my role models to this day.

Discussion

Each of these extraordinary young men demonstrated various types of resilience and perseverance in both graduating from high school and persisting through their third year of college. What is interesting to note is that although they all went to the same high school, they did not have the same prior schooling experiences before coming to Du Bois. Antoine, if he had gone to the local high school, may not have persisted through to high school graduation. He was helped by the trust that he built first with Mr. Simmons, who gave him a second chance when he failed to perform up to expectations, and then, perhaps most importantly, the trust he built within himself to acknowledge that he could succeed both academically and socially and become the first in his family to attend college. Tyrone, while socially awkward, had the intellectual capacity to be successful in college from a young age. However, his schooling trajectory might have been different if he had gone to a traditional school because he might have fallen victim to what some scholars controversially call the "acting white" phenomenon. He might have lashed out at his teachers and been ostracized by his peers if he had not had Malik and the safety of the trusting, intellectual community of Du Bois Charter. Finally, Andre was comfortable being in diverse environments at Du Bois, which really helped him build both trust and resilience, not just being a jock football player, but someone who was recognized for his intellectual prowess and academic ability. This environment affected his academic and socioemotional development such that he was able to bridge two worlds, both at Du Bois and at college. He was able to associate himself with those who were athletically inclined on his college campus as well as those who were aspiring to high achievement and academic success.

These young Black men exemplify what is imaginable when institutional trust manifests itself in positive individual achievement. It is possible that these three would have graduated from high school and attended college no matter where they went to high school, but it is probable that their trajectory to higher education would not have been as smooth. When institutions give individuals the tools to build trust in themselves, support for them to grow and learn from their mistakes, positive peers to support their academic and social development, and teachers and adult mentors to help guide them to an achievable goal—one that they may have thought about, but never knew the specific steps to attain—anything is possible. While these three narratives are by no means the totality of every young Black male's educational experience, they do demonstrate that it is possible to overcome social and academic shortfalls and contribute positively to society.

■ **References**

Allen, Q. (2015). "I'm trying to get my A": Black male achievers talk about race, school and achievement. *Urban Review 47*(1), 209–31.

Bourke, B., & Mechler, H. S. (2010). A new me generation? The increasing self-interest among millennial college students. *Journal of College and Character 11*(2), 1–9.

Denzin, N. K., & Lincoln, Y. S. (eds.). (2011). *The Sage Handbook of Qualitative Research.* Thousand Oaks, CA: Sage.

Fordham, S., & Ogbu, J. U. (1986). Black students' school success: Coping with the "burden of 'acting white.'" *Urban Review 18*(3), 176–206.

Goffman, E. (1967). On face-work. In *Interaction ritual: Essays on face-to-face behavior*, 5–45. New York: Anchor Books.

Harper, S. R. (2007). Peer support for African American male college achievement: Beyond internalized racism and the burden of "acting white." *Journal of Men's Studies 14*(3), 337–58.

Howard, T. C., Douglas, T. R., & Warren, C. A. (2016). "What works": Recommendations on improving academic experiences and outcomes for Black males. *Teachers College Record 118*(6), number 6.

Levine, A. & Nidiffer, J. (1996). *Beating the odds: How the poor get to college.* San Francisco Jossey-Bass.

Noguera, P. (2008). *The trouble with Black boys . . . and other reflections on race, equity, and the future of public education.* San Francisco: Jossey-Bass.

Steele, C. M. (1997). A threat in the air: How stereotypes shape intellectual identity and performance. *American Psychologist 52*(6), 613–29.

Steele, C. M., & Aronson, J. (1995). Stereotype threat and the intellectual test performance of African Americans. *Journal of Personality and Social Psychology 69*(5), 797–811.

Tyson, K. (ed.). (2011). *Integration interrupted: Tracking, Black students, and acting white after* Brown. New York: Oxford University Press.

Tools for teaching: Ditching the deficit model. (2013). *Edutopia*, http://www.edutopia.org/.

Wolcott, H. F. (2008). *Writing up qualitative research.* Thousand Oaks, CA: Sage.

Examining Campus Climate for African American Males at Predominantly White Institutions

James Bridgeforth

African American males are an endangered species in society today and the most threatened human beings in the United States (Knight, 2014). In recent years, African American males have been subject to senseless killings by the police that created a national outcry demanding an increase in sensitivity and support for African American males (Moore et al., 2016). America's Black Holocaust Museum (2016) suggests that the issues facing African American males are not new, as thousands of African American males have harassed, assaulted, and even murdered by Caucasians since the 1600s; therefore, African American males have been historically disenfranchised by the structural underpinnings of American culture. Indeed, the persistent assault on African American males can be characterized as a systematic attack against civil rights that has resulted in a national pandemic of fear that has crippled the social mobility of African American males in American society. The recent incidents around the murders of Trevon Martin, Michael Brown, Eric Garner, and so many other African American males created a great sense of apprehension and concern among African American men that has impacted their social, economic, and cultural capital. The apprehension centers on the simple question of worth and value for African American males and leads to fear and concern. African American males on college and university campuses are not exempt from these feelings; in fact, African American males at predominantly White institutions (PWIs) experience heightened levels of fear, isolation, tension, and psychological pressure. PWIs can be described as postsecondary institutions of higher learning, classified as universities in the United States where the overwhelming majority of undergraduate students enrolled identify as Caucasian (Bridgeforth, 2016). Research by Robertson and Mason (2008) suggests that African American males face greater challenges and barriers at PWIs than Caucasian males and females, and

441

these barriers contribute to higher levels of attrition among African American males. A study conducted by researchers Robertson and Chaney (2015) demonstrates that African American males have much higher levels of attrition in college than both Caucasian males and Caucasian females. Additionally, these high levels of attrition have long-term and lasting implications that negatively affect employment and contribute to a lowered economic status that can devastate the quality of life for African American males.

This chapter investigates whether the attitudes of African American male college students differ from Caucasian males and females regarding feelings of being targeted at a PWI. This chapter will review the White Racial Consciousness Model as a theoretical framework that may be used as a method for Caucasians to leverage their privilege to create equality on campus and break down barriers of institutionalized racism at PWIs. This study will also explore findings from a recent pilot study involving 159 college students that explores attitudes toward feeling targeted on campus. Targeting is described in this study as experiencing any or all of the following when engaging in the campus environment: feelings of being discriminated against, unfairly treated, isolated by others, being mistreated, profiled, and/or misunderstood by those in authority. This chapter will close with recommendations for PWIs to create a more nurturing and supportive environment for African American males.

Background

Challenges Facing African American Students at PWIs

Research suggests that African American students in general are more likely to experience stereotypes during college than any other racial or ethnic group, which often leads to attrition (Fries-Britt & Turner, 2001). Helms ([1990] 1993) proposes that African Americans are among the most misunderstood racial groups in the United States. Moreover, African American students generally report that Caucasian faculty avoid interactions with them outside of class, which negatively impacts the students' level of academic success. Tinto (2006–7) states that relationships with faculty are essential for the success of African American students, as these relationships are critically important because they can support retention. Additionally, African American students report great difficulty in establishing "good" relationships with Caucasian faculty (Jackson, 2013). Moreover, research (Green, 2016) indicates that institutionalized racism on college campuses creates an emotional barrier for African American students that also leads to attrition. The combination of being misunderstood on campus and marginalized by faculty makes it extremely difficult for African American students to engage and transition into the campus culture in the same way as Caucasian students (Steel, 1992).

Oftentimes racism causes African American students in college to suffer from "double consciousness," which forces students of color to live in two identities (Dubois, 1897; Green, 2016). A study released by the JED Foundation (2016) found that 75 percent of African American college students do not feel comfortable sharing their experiences about racism at PWIs. Simply stated, colleges and universities have not done a good job shielding students from racism and, at times, institutions have exacerbated and supported structural racism (Green, 2016). McGee and Stovall (2016) found that racial oppression on college campuses has a negative effect on the mental health of African American students that may increase attrition specifically at PWIs. All of these challenges are even more severe for African American males.

The US Census Bureau (2000) reports that African American males represent approximately 6 percent of the US population. Yet African American males only make up 4 percent of all college students, and only 36 percent of those who attend college earn a baccalaureate degree (Robertson & Mason, 2008). McClure (2006) submits that African American males have the highest attrition rate of any demographic in college. Nearly 70 percent of African American males that attend college never earn a baccalaureate degree (Anyaso, 2007). Research suggests that African American males are the most misunderstood and stigmatized of all racial and ethnic groups in the United States (Helms, [1990] 1993; Spurgeon & Meyers, 2010). Moreover, Robertson and Chaney (2015) suggest that African American males are among the most marginalized groups in the United States. This can be true for African American males on college campuses, as African American males enter college, specifically PWIs, with the sense that society, and perhaps the university community, expects negative outcomes from them (Robertson & Chaney, 2015). These researchers suggest that retention of African American male students can be improved by increasing relationships with faculty, developing a supportive classroom environment, and providing mentorship. As an example, African American males graduate from historically black colleges and universities (HBCUs) at a higher rate than at PWIs because the campus environment is more supportive and designed to nurture their growth (Edelin-Freeman, 2004).

College attrition among African American males is a serious, systematic problem in higher education today (Washington, 2013), as African American males are noticeably absent from college campuses throughout the United States. African American males represent less than 5 percent of all college students in the United States (Roach, 2001; Robertson & Mason, 2008). Not only is there great concern regarding the number of African American males going to college, but the attrition of these students has long-term debilitating effects on the African American community. In many cases, African American male attrition is related to issues of racism and structural institutionalized barriers at PWIs that fail to support African American males. Johnson (2013) suggests issues creating African American male attrition can be condensed into three major factors: lack of environmental support, poor social support, and psychological impairment. These three major factors can determine the success of African American males in college. Solorzaro, Ceja, and Yosso (2010) contend that out-of-class experiences play a significant role in African American male attrition.

Preston-Cunningham et al. (2016) indicate that African American males face numerous challenges while enrolled at PWIs that contribute to extreme levels of attrition. Their research suggests that African American males experience microaggressions from their peers outside of the classroom, leaving them feeling targeted, threatened, hopeless, psychologically tired, and emotionally discouraged. The burden to cope with these microaggressions and deal with covert racist tactics negatively affects African American males' ability to perform in the academy. Moreover, Brooks, Jones, and Burt (2012) indicate that African American males face greater challenges in college than Caucasian males and females, as they face cultural, societal, academic, and lifestyle differences that Caucasian students do not have to grapple with at PWIs. These challenges often require intentional support mechanisms for students of color and specifically African American males. Yet college executives, administrators, faculty, and staff at PWIs fail to acknowledge and understand these issues. Additionally, African American male undergraduates are more likely to be underprepared, face more financial hardships, and struggle to transition into the campus culture at PWIs than Caucasian students; this is said to lead to higher levels of attrition for African American males (Cuyjet, 2006).

Davis et al. (2017) reveal that students of color do not feel that PWIs are welcoming, hospitable, or nurturing environments. This study suggests that Caucasians on campus often engage students of color with negative stereotypes in mind, leaving African American males and other students of color feeling mistrusted, uncomfortable, and seemingly demoralized. Davis et al. (2004) suggest that the demonstrated behaviors at PWIs can create a hostile environment for all students of color; yet African American males are more susceptible to these behaviors and attitudes of the majority culture. Therefore, there is a need for more quantitative research to investigate the attitudes toward racism and being targeted at PWIs across race and gender to determine if African American males report higher levels of feeling targeted on campus than Caucasian males and Caucasian females.

Theoretical Framework

Racism is a major problem in American higher education today (Smith, Altbach, & Lomotey, 2002). Over the last year there has been a dramatic increase in racial incidents at predominantly White college campuses (Bridgeforth, 2016), and there seems to be little movement toward establishing solidarity, trust, and equality for students of color, specifically African American males. More profoundly, the attrition of African American males appears to be a major casualty of racism and racial targeting on college campuses. There is a need for a paradigmatic shift within the campus culture at PWIs that will create a more nurturing and supportive environment and improve retention for African American males on campus. There are several models that may be effective for establishing a caring and warm environment for African American males at PWIs; however, in light of the many recent incidents around racism nationally, the White Racial Consciousness Model, as outlined by Rowe, Bennett, and Atkinson (1994), may be best choice to acknowledge racism and explain how White privilege can be used to create equality at PWIs.

Rowe, Bennett, and Atkinson (1994) suggest that there is a particular privilege and power in being Caucasian that can impact institutions, organizations, and society. Their framework suggests that there are varying levels of consciousness that Caucasians can achieve to develop an awareness of their power, privilege, and access as well as the role that race and racism plays in society. Moreover, Rowe, Bennett, and Atkinson's (1994) model can be used to help Caucasians use their White privilege to change institutional culture to a more sensitive and supportive environment for African American males.

The White Racial Conscious Model indicates that Caucasians must move from an unachieved awareness (unconsciousness) to an achieved awareness (consciousness) that will allow them to become agents of change and reduce or eradicate racism, social injustice, and prejudice. This model proposes that unconsciousness is demonstrated by three major characteristics: avoidance, dependence, and dissonance. Avoidance is described as being unaware of the role race plays in society and avoiding difficult conversations about the realities of race and racism. Likewise, dependence is characterized as being aware of Whiteness as a racial status along with a demonstrated group commitment to those racial values and beliefs, even if it overshadows other minority cultures. Surpassing avoidance and dependence, dissonance is characterized as being deeply dedicated to one's White identity and rejecting information, beliefs, and events surrounding racism and social justice.

Rowe, Bennett, and Atkinson (1994) contend that conscious Caucasians can play a major role in creating equality. Their model suggests that an achieved White racial awareness creates a level of consciousness that is critical for social equality. For example, they suggest that there are four phases Caucasians can move through to achieve racial consciousness; these stages are dominant, reactive, active, and integrative.

The dominant stage is characterized by being aware of one's White identity and the privilege held by being White in institutions, organizations, or society in general; additionally, this is the first stage where Caucasians begin to believe there are stereotypes that do exist. The reactive stage is characterized as a higher level of consciousness where one understands White privilege as a Caucasian as well as the inequalities surrounding race and the emotional reality that there is indeed some kind of racism that does occur. Often the reactive stage triggers thoughts of activism at some level. This leads to the active stage, which is characterized by one's getting involved, using Whiteness to correct issues of racism and prejudice within the organization, institution, or community. Finally, the integrative stage is characterized by demonstrating a depth of knowledge and understanding regarding the intricacies of race and the powerful role that race plays in society.

The White Racial Consciousness Model is a powerful framework that outlines the manner in which Caucasians can understand race as well as how to become agents of change to improve a campus culture. For example, this framework can be applied by any faculty, staff member, administrator, or student to help that individual move from racial unconsciousness to racial consciousness. Consciousness can lead to a greater level of activism and advocacy as well as an established appreciation for diversity on campus. However, it is important to note that advocacy is not enough, as action is critical. For example, establishing a campus culture where Caucasians understand the power of racism will create a more hospitable and welcoming environment for African American males. This study suggests that African American males who attend PWIs experience racism and are targeted more often than their Caucasian peers.

Methodology

This pilot study examines whether African American male college students' attitudes differed from Caucasian males and females regarding their attitudes toward being targeted at a PWI. This section illustrates the design and analysis that was used for this study. It describes how the participants were selected, the instrument that was used to collect data from the participants, and the statistical tests used to analyze the data. The dependent variables in this study focus on four constructs that measure student attitudes toward their campus experience: attitudes toward being targeted by professors, attitudes toward being targeted by classmates, attitudes toward being targeted in their residence halls, and attitudes toward being targeted in class. The independent variables used in this study are race, gender, and the combination of race and gender, so as to understand whether African American males reported feelings of being targeted at the same level as Caucasian males and Caucasian females enrolled at PWIs.

Participants

This study was situated at a large, predominantly White, research-intensive, public university in the southeastern United States with an enrollment of more than thirteen thousand students. At the time of this study, 67 percent of the students enrolled identified as Caucasian students and 23 percent of the students enrolled identified as African American. Regarding the participants, 60 percent identified as female, 40 percent as male. One hundred and fifty-nine students participated in this study; 61 percent of the participants identified as Caucasian, 25 percent as African American, 6 percent identified as biracial, 5 percent as Asian or Asian American, 2 percent as American Indian or Native American, and 1 percent were unidentified. Ninety-eight percent of the participants were undergraduate students.

Instrumentation

The instrument was designed by the researcher to capture demographic data including information regarding race, gender, classification, and academic college enrolled in. This questionnaire, based on the review of current literature, comprises twenty-two items in an agreement scale designed to measure college students' attitudes toward the campus environment.

This instrument was pilot-tested to identify and clarify confusing items and followed up by Cronbach's alpha (α) to test internal consistency. An expert panel of graduate and undergraduate students piloted the instrument to ensure content validity. The data were collected via Class Climate Survey Software; the response rate is unknown as the instrument was sent electronically via email and there is not a method to determine the number of the participants who received the instrument. Cronbach's alpha indicated that the questionnaire produced reliable scores ($\alpha = 0.86$).

Procedure

The research project was approved by the Institutional Review Board at the participating university for the purpose of conducting this study. The instrument was administered live via the Class Climate Survey Software by the Office of Institutional Research and Assessment on the participating campus. The participants in this study were randomly selected; the research aimed to collect a represented sample of the student body. The Office of Institutional Research and Assessment sent emails to individual students enrolled at the university and invited them to participate in this study. However, it was not possible to determine which or how many of the emails were read. A follow-up email was sent to all participants two weeks after the initial questionnaires had been distributed. Prior to participating in this study, each participant was provided with a statement of informed consent, which was included in the questionnaire. The questionnaires were administered and maintained via the Class Climate Survey Software. All data collected were stored in an electronic, password-secured data warehouse.

Research Questions

1. RQ1: Do African American males report higher levels of feeling targeted by their professors than Caucasian students?
2. RQ2: Do African American males report higher levels of feeling targeted by their classmates than Caucasian students?
3. RQ3: Do African American males report higher levels of feeling targeted in their class than Caucasian students?
4. RQ4: Do African American males report higher levels of feeling targeted in residence halls than Caucasian students?

Research Design

This study examined whether African American males reported higher levels of being targeted when compared to Caucasian males and Caucasian females enrolled at PWIs across four factors: by professors, by classmates, in class, and in their residence hall. This study focused on the four specific research questions previously noted. Therefore the dependent variables are reported levels of targeting by professors, by classmates, in class, and in the residence hall; race, gender, and the combination of race and gender are the independent variables. These variables were collected only once through the electronic questionnaire. The data in this study were analyzed by descriptive statistics and through conducting a means (M) test to determine if scores or attitudes varied based on race and gender regarding the four research questions.

Results

This section will discuss the results and the analysis that was conducted. The purpose of this study was to examine if African American males report higher levels of being targeted at PWIs in comparison to their Caucasian peers. The population in this study consisted of undergraduate students enrolled in a large PWI in the southeastern United States.

Regarding Research Question 1, which examines reported levels of being targeted by professors across race and gender, the data reveal that African American males (M = 3.50, SD = 0.70) reported higher levels of being targeted by professors than Caucasian males (M = 2.16, SD = 0.75) and Caucasian females (M = 2.20, SD = 1.64). This data indicates that African American males seemingly indicate higher incidents of being targeted by professors. Based on the definition used in the study, this could mean that African American males are more likely to experience discrimination by faculty members than Caucasian students at PWIs. These data also reflect that Caucasian males (M = 2.16, SD = 0.75) and Caucasian females (M = 2.20, SD = 1.64) report similar levels of agreement when asked if they feel targeted by faculty at PWIs.

Regarding Research Question 2, which examines reported levels of being targeted by classmates across race and gender, the data indicates that African American males (M = 3.50, SD = 0.71) report higher levels of being or feeling targeted by classmates. Table 1 shows that African American males project that they are more likely to be or feel targeted by classmates than Caucasian males (M = 2.00, SD = 0.63) and Caucasian females (M = 1.80, SD = 0.84). Based on the definition of targeting in this study, the data suggest that African American males are more likely to feel isolated on campus than Caucasian students. Additionally, this indicates that African American males are also more likely to experience discrimination by classmates than Caucasian students.

Regarding Research Question 3, which examines reported levels of being targeted in class across race and gender, the data indicate that African American males (M = 3.50, SD = 0.71) report higher levels of being or feeling targeted in class. Table 2 shows that African American males are more likely to be targeted, or feel targeted while in class than Caucasian males (M = 2.16, SD = 0.75) and Caucasian females (M = 2.40, SD = 1.40). The data imply that African American males are more likely to associate feelings of unfair treatment with PWIs than Caucasian students. Table 2 outlines that African American males report a higher level of feeling targeted in class than their Caucasian peers, whose scores are similar.

Regarding Research Question 4, which examines reported levels of being targeted in the residence halls across race and gender, the data indicate that African American males (M = 3.50, SD = 0.71) report higher levels of being or feeling targeted in their residence halls. Table 3 shows that African American males are more likely to be targeted or feel targeted in their residential environment at PWIs than Caucasian males (M = 2.00, SD = 0.63) and Caucasian females (M = 2.00, SD = 0.71). The data imply that African American males may be more likely to experience feelings of being mistreated, profiled, and isolated while living in their residence hall at PWIs than their Caucasian peers. Table 3 outlines that African American males report a higher level of agreement than Caucasian males and females, whose scores are similar.

Table 1. Experienced Targeting by Classmates (*N* = 159)

ITEM	MEAN	STANDARD DEVIATION
African American males	3.50	0.71
Caucasian males	2.00	0.63
Caucasian females	1.80	0.84

1 = Strongly disagree, 2 = Disagree, 3 = Somewhat agree, 4 = Agree, 5 = Strongly agree.

Table 2. Experienced Targeting in Class (*N* = 159)

ITEM	MEAN	STANDARD DEVIATION
African American males	3.50	0.75
Caucasian females	2.40	1.40
Caucasian males	2.16	0.75

1 = Strongly disagree, 2 = Disagree, 3 = Somewhat agree, 4 = Agree, 5 = Strongly agree.

Table 3. Experienced Targeting in My Residence Hall (*N* = 159)

ITEM	MEAN	STANDARD DEVIATION
African American males	3.50	0.71
Caucasian males	2.00	0.63
Caucasian females	2.00	0.71

1 = Strongly disagree, 2 = Disagree, 3 = Somewhat agree, 4 = Agree, 5 = Strongly agree.

Summary

The data in this section suggest that African American males report experiencing higher levels of discrimination, isolation, being profiled, mistreated, and misunderstood than Caucasian students at a PWI. In fact, across every factor, African American males scored highest in regard to experiencing some level of discrimination and targeting. Moreover, across the factors studied, Caucasian males and female seem to report a similar level of being targeted. These data suggest that the PWI campus environment is more welcoming and supportive for Caucasian students than African American males. The data presented in this study support the literature regarding the consistent struggles that African American males face while attending PWIs; therefore, there is a strong assertion that these campus environments are indeed unwelcoming, uninviting, and insensitive to African American males.

Therefore, this study suggests that administrators, faculty, and staff reevaluate their campus environments to establish a more caring, considerate, and hospitable atmosphere aimed at engaging African American males. These data suggest that because PWIs are indeed unwelcoming, the current campus environment may contribute to the extreme levels of attrition for

African American males, meaning that, a more nurturing campus culture and environment may improve retention among African American males. This indicates that administrators at PWIs must change the campus culture at PWIs to better support African American males by creating a more comfortable environment. If campus administrators change culture to a more inclusive environment, it may result in greater retention among African American males at PWIs.

Discussion and Recommendations

The data in this study suggest that African American males enrolled at a PWI report experiencing racial targeting more often than Caucasian males and females. The literature (Solorzaro, Ceja, & Yosso, 2010) indicates that racial discrimination may negatively impact the academic persistence of African American males at PWIs. This study supports recent literature (Brooks, Jones, & Burt, 2012) indicating that African American males indeed experience racism more than Caucasian students at PWIs. Moreover, this study concludes that African American males report facing higher levels of targeting and racial oppression at PWIs than Caucasian students across the university spectrum (e.g., with regard to faculty, classmates, in class, and in residence halls). Unfortunately, these can be described as the four major pillars of students' engagement with the campus culture. Therefore, if students feel rejected across any of these four components, they are more likely to drop out. Hence, this study supports the claim (Cuyjet, 2006) that African American male attrition is greatly heightened because the campus environments at PWIs are simply not welcoming. This study recommends that campus leaders at PWIs implement a new theoretical model to improve institutional culture to become more nurturing, supportive, and inviting for African American males. Henceforward, there must be a new theoretical model introduced to help college and university executives to enhance and improve how African American males are engaged at PWIs.

Intercultural Model of Inclusion

The data presented in this study, along with the theoretical framework of the White Racial Consciousness Model previously discussed in this chapter, reveal that it is critical to implement a new theoretical model that may improve that academic landscape for African American males at PWIs. The Intercultural Model of Inclusion (IMI) is a model that may positively impact the African American male experience at PWIs. This model simply suggests that Caucasians use their racial privilege to create a more inviting, nurturing, and welcoming campus for African American males. The IMI introduces three major actions that campus leaders may apply that may revolutionize the how students of color perceive PWIs.

The Intercultural Model of Inclusion is derived from the data in this study, coupled with previous research conducted by Rowe, Bennett, and Atkinson (1994) that indicates that Caucasian students enrolled at PWIs experience little or no racism, while African American males report heightened levels of racial bias throughout the campus community. Moreover, research by Rowe, Bennett, and Atkinson (1994) also suggests that Caucasians have a deep-rooted privilege that transcends institutional culture. Thus, the Intercultural Model of Inclusion builds on their previous research and advances the findings of this study as it identifies three actions that campus executives and leaders can weave into the campus culture at PWI to improve inclusivity for African American males.

EMPATHIC TRANSCENDENCE

Empathic transcendence is the first major action that campus administrators must implement to improve diversity and inclusion for African American males at PWIs. This action requires that campus leaders create an interconnected system of programs, events, and opportunities for administrators, faculty, staff, and students to learn, understand, and appreciate the historical context of what it means for a someone to be African American and male in a predominantly White society. This includes a series of productions where Caucasians on campus experience a simulation of the challenges African American males face daily in society; this can be executed by programs similar to the "tunnel of oppression." The idea is that these simulations will allow Caucasians in the campus community to develop and display a sense of empathy and understanding in regard to the historical marginalization and discrimination that African American males face throughout America society. Empathic transcendence will ensure Caucasians reflect on their racial privilege and become motivated to create a more sensitive and supportive atmosphere on campus for African American males.

INTERCULTURAL MENTORING

Intercultural Mentoring is the second major action that will require campus executives to develop a formal mentoring program that focuses on strong cross-cultural relationships between professors and African American males. The intercultural mentoring action of IMI is the process of pairing all first-year African American males with a Caucasian faculty member who has experienced empathic transcendence. During the intercultural mentoring process, the faculty member will introduce the African American male to the various formal and informal nuances of institutional culture. The faculty member will serve as a key supporter and institutional compass for the African American male to navigate the various barriers and challenges at the institution; moreover, the faculty member must display a high degree of caring and become a champion and advocate for the African American male mentee. Finally, the faculty member will be expected to use his or her racial privilege to engage constituents on campus to establish a better and more welcoming environment for African American males. Intercultural mentoring will eliminate many barriers between academics and African American males and establish a high level of academic and social engagement between African American males and Caucasian faculty.

INTERCULTURAL DEPENDENCE

Intercultural dependence is the final step, which requires campus leaders to develop a robust, deeply diverse, interconnected campus culture that centers on a respect for multiculturalism as a priority. Intercultural dependence is characterized by the significance that social justice, as opposed to racism, plays within the campus community. It is during the intercultural dependence process that all students, specifically Caucasian students who have had little interaction with African American males, begin to understand and appreciate racial differences. It is at this point that Caucasian students are introduced to African American culture through campus-wide programs, events, and academics. For example, the campus may add required courses on racism into the curriculum, require programming that exposes students to African American history, or feature institutional dialogues on preventing racism. Additionally, the campus policy may require Caucasian students to become exposed to roommates, classmates, and peers who are African American males, which will create a sense of personal relationships for both students. This action will enhance Caucasian students' knowledge and awareness of African American males and break down issues of racism and targeting. In fact, this action will likely allow Caucasian students to develop a sense of advocacy for African American males in that when Caucasian students witness racial discrimination, they will be motivated to correct the issue. Additionally, intercultural dependence will create a campus culture where the institution will set a campus expectation that racism, bigotry, and racial bias will not be tolerated, meaning that the campus will display an institutional dependence on interculturalism. This action will allow the campus environment to become more inviting and inclusive for African American males at PWIs.

The IMI will allow for a greater sense of diversity and inclusivity on campus. Moreover, it will establish a transition where Caucasians will be empowered to use their racial privilege to remove issues of racism on campus. If implemented correctly, as an institutional process, the campus environment will dramatically improve for African American males at PWIs, which may improve their retention.

Limitations

This study has several limitations; however, the biggest challenge is that this is a pilot study with a relatively small sample size ($N = 159$). Additionally, another nuanced limitation related to a modest sample size of this study is that the numbers of African American males are disproportionately lower than Caucasian males and Caucasian females at PWIs nationally, but that is also the reason for conducting this study. Another limitation is the challenge of getting the students (participants) to return the instrument, as there is no way to require students to participate. While the overall percentages of racial minorities in this study were equal to or greater than the national population at PWIs, this study could be more impactful if a larger number of racial and ethnic minorities participated in this project. Additionally, it is important to note that having a larger sample size for each category may produce significantly different results. The data in this study were solely collected electronically, which may have limited the findings of this study. The researcher would like to expand the collection of data beyond electronic surveys to include focus groups and face-to-face interviews.

Recommendations for Future Research

While there is an abundance of literature and qualitative studies regarding attrition of African American males at PWIs, there appears to be limited quantitative data that seeks to support the existing qualitative reports. It would be appropriate to further investigate the topic to determine the nexus between racial discrimination and college attrition for African American males at PWIs as well as the cost of such attrition for institutions of higher learning. Given the political and budgetary challenges facing higher education today, there is much room for additional research in this area, as improving the college retention among African American males may improve the institution's financial bottom line.

The data in this study suggest African American males report higher levels of being targeted at PWIs than Caucasian males and females; this study does support current qualitative literature indicating that African American males face great barriers at PWIs. It may be important to break down the various specific racial/ethnic categories to determine if there is a relationship between a particular racial or ethnic gender in order to determine whether significant differences occur. To that end, studies involving larger samples from each demographic to include institutional type may produce more impactful findings in regard to better practices to improve diversity in the academy.

Conclusion

Racism and discrimination are a major problem in American higher education today. This chapter discussed the role that racial targeting plays at PWIs and how it may negatively impact African American males. Literature (Davis et al., 2004; Green, 2016; Jackson, 2013) suggests that the discrimination within a campus environment has adverse implications for African American male attrition. This chapter suggests that it is paramount for higher education administrators to become aware of these challenges and create a more appealing, welcoming, and supportive environment for African American males at PWIs. The chapter asserts that there is a need to introduce a new model for the improvement of diversity at PWIs; the Intercultural Model of Inclusion provides a process to reduce racism on campus as well as a systematic approach to providing support for African American males. While this chapter has provided insight into recent challenges facing African American males at PWIs, it is critical that current higher education leaders recognize their role and responsibility to implement changes that will transform their institutions to create a more hospitable campus for African American males. More importantly, campus administrators must take responsibility for the deplorable numbers of African American males enrolled at PWIs and work to improve their retention. This study recommends implementing the principles outlined by the White Racial Consciousness Model and the Intercultural Model of Inclusion in such a manner that PWIs can transform into vivacious, invigorated institutions where African American males are understood, appreciated, and celebrated as students who have overcome numerous societal barriers just to gain access to higher education. Such an environment will boost retention for African American males and create a more diverse and socially just America.

■ **References**

America's Black Holocaust Museum (2016). What is the Black holocaust? Http://abhmuseum.org/what-is-the-black-holocaust/.

Anyaso, H. (2007). Sobering statistics. *Diverse Issues in Higher Education 24*(15), 3.

Bridgeforth, J. S. (2016). Multicultural leadership in higher education. In R. Styron & J. Styron (eds.), *Comprehensive problem-solving and skill development for next-generation leaders* (pp. 139–64). Hersey, PA: IGI Global.

Brooks, M., Jones, C., & Burt, I. (2012). Are African American retention programs successful? An evaluation of undergraduate African American retention programs. *Journal of African American Studies 17*(2), 206–21. doi:10.1007/s12111-012-9233-2.

Cuyjet, M. J. (2006). *African American men in college.* San Francisco: Wiley.

Du Bois, W. E. B. (1897). Strivings of the Negro people. *The Atlantic.* Http://www.theatlantic.com/magazine/archive/1897/08/strivings-of-the-negro-people/305446/.

Edelin-Freeman, K. (2004). African American men and women in higher education: "Filling the glass" in the new millennium. In A. McDaniel & O. McDaniel (eds.), *21st century African American cultural issues: A reader* (pp. 123–37). Mason, OH: Thomson Publishing.

Fries-Britt, S. L., & Turner, B. (2001). Facing stereotypes: A case study of black students on a White campus. *Journal of College Student Development 42*(5), 420–29.

Green, A. (2016). The cost of balancing academia and racism. *The Atlantic.* Http://www.theatlantic.com/education/archive/2016/01/balancing-academia-racism/424887/.

Helms, J. E. ([1990] 1993). Toward a model of White racial identity development. In J. E. Helms (ed.), *Black and White racial identity* (pp. 49–66). New York: Greenwood/Praeger.

Jackson, L. (2013). The benefits of a comprehensive retention program for African American students at a predominantly White university. *Interdisciplinary Journal of Teaching and Learning 3*(1), 38–54.

JED Foundation. (2016). Http://jedfoundation.org/press-room/press-releases/Steve-Fund-JED-Announcement.

Johnson, R. (2013). Black and male on campus: An autoethnographic account. *Journal of African American Males 4*(2), 25–45.

Knight, D. J. (2014). Don't tell young black males that they are "endangered." *Washington Post.* Https://www.washingtonpost.com/opinions/young-black-males-trapped-by-rhetoric/2014/10/10/dcf95688-31e2-11e4-9e92-0899b306bbea_story.html?utm_term=.

McClure, S. (2006) Voluntary association membership: Black Greek men on a predominantly White campus. *Journal of Higher Education 77*(6), 1036–57. doi:10.1353/jhe.2006.0053.

McGee, E. O., & Stovall, D. (2015). Reimagining critical race theory in education: Mental health, healing, and the pathway to liberatory praxis. *Educational Theory 65*(5), 491–511. doi:10.1111/edth.12129.

Moore, S. E., Robinson, M. A., Adedoyin, A. C., Brooks, M., Harmon, D. K., & Boamah, D. (2016).

Hands up don't shoot: Police shooting of young black males: Implication for social work and human services. *Journal of Human Behavior in the Social Environment 26*(3–4), 254–66. doi:10.1080/10911359. 2015.1125202.

Preston-Cunningham, T., Boyd. B. L., Elbert, C. D., Dooley, K. E., & Peck-Parrot, K. (2016).What's up with this leadership thing? Voices of African American male college undergraduates. *Journal of Leadership Education 15*(3), 54–74. doi:1012806/v15/i3/r1.

Solorzaro, D. G., Ceja, M., & Yosso, T. J. (2010). Critical race theory, racial microaggressions, and campus racial identity: A reconceptualization of African American racial identity. *Personality and Social Psychological Review 2*(1), 18–39.

Roach, R. (2001). Where are the black men on campus? *Black Issues in Higher Education 18*(6), 18–21.

Robertson, R. V. & Chaney, C. (2015). The influence of stereotype threat on the response of Black males at a predominantly White college in the south. *Journal of Pan African Studies 7*(8), 20–42.

Robertson, R. V., & Mason, D. (2008). What works? A qualitative examination of the factors related to the academic success of African American males at predominantly White colleges in the South. *Challenge: A Journal of Research on African American Men 14*(2), 67–89.

Rowe, W., Bennett, S. K., & Atkinson, D. R. (1994). White racial identity models: A critique and alternative proposal. *Counseling Psychologist 22*(1), 129–46. doi:10.1177/0011000094221009.

Smith, W. A., Altbach, P. G., & Lomotey, K. (eds.). (2002). *The racial crisis in American higher education: Continuing challenges for the twenty-first century*. Albany: State University of New York Press.

Steel, C. M. (1992). Race and the schooling of black Americans. *The Atlantic.* Http://www.theatlantic. com/magazine/archive/1992/04/race-and-the-schooling-of-black-americans/306073/.

Tinto, V. (2006–7). Research and practice of student retention: What next? *Journal of College Student Retention: Research, Theory & Practice 8*(1), 1–19. doi:10.2190/c0c4-eft9-eg7w-pwp4.

Washington, M. (2013). Is the Black male college graduate becoming an endangered species? A multi-case analysis of attrition of Black males in higher education. *LUX: A Journal of Transdisciplinary Writing and Research from Claremont Graduate University 3*(1), 1–19. doi:10.5642/lux.201303.20.

No Positive Role Models

Growing Up in Prison

Louis Napoleon

Incarcerating Black juvenile males in adult prisons is counterproductive and threatens to create a permanent underclass of young Black males who are ineligible to vote, unlikely to be employable, and will remain unproductive members of society. Black male identity is still forming in adolescence, and spending time with adults in prison has the potential to embody negative influences. Black juveniles who are prosecuted and imprisoned with adults will likely adopt and internalize the behaviors that are the norm in the prison environment. These adverse effects become almost impossible to reverse after incarceration. Growing up in prison means there are less opportunities to be exposed to positive role models.

This chapter will explore the inequalities in rates of minority incarceration due to systemic racism and a history of harsh treatment of juveniles. Following is a discussion of how the adult prison environment is ineffective and harmful to youth offenders, contributing to recidivism. Another section acknowledges how American politics and culture have contributed to both the problem and the solution to the imprisonment of juveniles with adults, which eliminates chances of rehabilitation through skill-building opportunities and interaction with adults who are positive influencers.

Analysis

In the documentary *They Call Us Monsters*, released in January 2017, three teens growing up in an adult prison system tell their stories. The film highlights questions that the justice system struggles to answer: Are young criminals dangerous monsters, or wayward youth who need programs involving social skills training? Can juvenile incarceration be solved with social skills training and better education? By placing juveniles in prisons where they are forced to interact with hardcore, seasoned criminals, society is assuming the former, that juvenile delinquents are "dangerous," and exacerbating the problem. Though many people would like to think they can wash their hands of these teens once they're behind bars, the tough-on-crime impact of imprisonment will have detrimental effects on society for decades to come (Mulvey & Schubert, 2012; Redding, 2005).

Juveniles face not only a punishment that is ill-fitting for their age and level of development and maturity, but also an environment that is destructive to their future. The purpose of prison is to punish the offender for crimes committed. The hope is that prisoners will repent and that, if they are fortunate enough to return to society, they will lead new, better lives. But in the majority of cases, statistics show that prisons fail to rehabilitate offenders. As a result of mass incarceration and disproportionate minority confinement, African American and Hispanic juvenile males know this failure all too well, as adult relatives and family friends recycle in and out of prisons, halfway houses, and treatment centers. Many minority juvenile males actually expect to serve prison time at some point in their life, and they are, in fact, entering the adult prison system in alarming numbers, incarcerated at a rate of six times that of whites (NAACP, 2017). The inequality of minority incarceration is not a new phenomenon. Researchers and prisoner rights advocates, like the Sentencing Project, have characterized the criminal justice system as having a "cascade of disparities," including policing tactics that increase the odds that minority males will be stopped, frisked, and taken to jail. The juvenile justice system has been throwing African American kids to the wolves for a long time, dishing out unimaginable punishments. Black males are arrested at a higher rate, often due to a greater police presence in their communities; are prosecuted at a higher rate; serve more time incarcerated than other ethnic groups; and are sentenced to death at higher rates than white counterparts (Reisig et al., 2007).

As history reveals, change is possible in the prison system. Throughout the late eighteenth century, children as young as seven years old stood trial in criminal court for crimes committed and were sentenced to prison or death. The nineteenth century saw a move toward more humane treatment of juvenile offenders and the understanding that they were not miniature adults but rather immature adolescents still developing, devoid of full cognitive capabilities. Around 1825, the Society for the Prevention of Juvenile Delinquency advocated the separation of juvenile and adult offenders. This policy picked up momentum, and facilities for juvenile offenders were opened in major cities throughout America. The mission to rehabilitate was stated clearly in the laws that established juvenile courts, and this yielded fundamental and procedural standards, separating juvenile and criminal justice systems. For many years the focus was on the juvenile offender, not the offense, on rehabilitation, not punishment, but the social justice pendulum began to swing toward punishment and retribution in the 1980s. The public wanted "just us" and a "crackdown on crack" in urban cities. States removed certain classes of offenders from the juvenile justice system, expanded eligibility for criminal court, and created punitive sentencing laws, and the boys in blue operated with impunity. Sentencing juveniles to an adult prison was seen as unethical during the eighteenth century, so why is it acceptable now?

Systemic racism is the number one reason so many African American juvenile males are growing up in adult prisons and, when released, are unprepared to face astronomical reentry barriers. The design and calculation of this system is inarguable, the history long and destructive. The Scottsboro Boys are classic examples: nine teenagers, thirteen to nineteen years old, were falsely accused of raping two white women in Alabama in 1931. The Scottsboro Boys were convicted and sentenced to death by an all-white jury, despite medical evidence that they were innocent and that one of the alleged victims recanted her accusations. The prosecution, aware of their innocence, told the jury, "If you don't give these men death sentences, the electric chair might as well be abolished." Found guilty initially, the Scottsboro Boys were later exonerated, but their time served in maximum security prisons, including on death row, shattered their innocence and their futures dramatically (US Supreme Court, 1932). Because African American male youths were being tried as adults, the death penalty was a legal option for their punishment, setting a tone for how juveniles could be treated despite their age, a mind-set that remains in how juveniles are imprisoned with adults today.

Even though the US Supreme Court eventually illegalized the death penalty in all states for defendants under the age of eighteen at the time of their crime in *Roper v. Simmons* (2005), it did not benefit George Stinney, a fourteen-year-old African American, the youngest person executed in America. Charged with first-degree murder, he was convicted by an all-white jury in less than ten minutes and sentenced to death with no mandatory appeal, as is the procedure with capital cases. He died in South Carolina's electric chair on June 16, 1944. On December 17, 2014, his conviction was posthumously vacated, seventy years after his execution; the circuit court judge ruled that the prosecution and trial were fundamentally flawed, that he had not received a fair trial, that his defense was ineffective, and that the confession was likely coerced and thus inadmissible. The court also found the execution of a fourteen-year-old constituted "cruel and unusual punishment" (Mullen, 2014).

The legal treatment of youths as adults has been astounding; although the law currently protects juveniles from the death penalty, Black male juveniles still experience discriminatory and unjust sentences. In addition to facing the death penalty, young Black males have experienced dangerous and brutal prison environments for decades due to exposure to older career criminals after being sentenced as adults. For example, O. C. Harry, an eleven-year-old African American, was taken from his classroom at school, arrested on a misdemeanor charge, and ushered into a county jail cell block with adult male pedophiles. A deputy returned a half hour later, just in time to prevent a gang sexual assault. Harry was moved to the women's section of the jail, where he remained for a week (1959, Madison County Jail, Edwardsville, Illinois). Unfortunately, in both past and present, youths have been placed in prison systems that are potentially and significantly more harmful than incarceration with their peers.

What populations of juveniles are tried as adults? Minors prosecuted as adults in New Jersey are almost 90 percent Black and Hispanic, selected for adult prosecution based on where they live—and their race. On October 12, 2016, New York Public Radio broadcast a series called

Kids in Prison, which explores what it was like for a juvenile in an adult prison. They accessed data from the New Jersey Administrative Office of the Court, for July 2011 through May 2016. Of the 1,251 petitions to the court by prosecutors to try juveniles as adults, 87.6 percent were Black or Hispanic and 692 were granted (WNYC, 2016).

Research has shown that incarceration of juveniles in adult prisons reduces criminal activity less than time served in juvenile facilities where adequate rehabilitative services, that is, school, appropriate counseling, and life skills activities, are more likely to be available (Aizer & Doyle, 2013). Adult prisons are punitive, designed and built to punish, and the necessary programs that can contribute to young Black males' rehabilitation are rarely available. Prisons and correctional facilities are often built and located in rural areas, requiring six or seven hours of travel for urban parents seeking to visit their children who are incarcerated. In these remote areas of the state, the number of minority guards and support staff tend to be minimal, which further limits the personal contact minority youth have with adult, noncriminal males. The only adults of color with whom a juvenile in prison might bond are likely to be drug dealers, robbers, burglars, pimps, con men, and veteran convicts who themselves are in need of positive Black male interaction. Consequently, communication between incarcerated adults and teenagers promotes the influence of seemingly grandiose "gangsta" lifestyles, dominating and negatively affecting young minds. Two or three years, or even less, into a sentence, any chance of juvenile offenders gravitating toward careers as engineers, scientists, or doctors is dubious at best. The harsh, day-to-day reality of dog-eat-dog, no-compromise, stand-your-ground-no-matter-what, get-your-money, you-against-the-world indoctrination can wipe out any sense of right and wrong. Right becomes anything that enhances one's "hustle." Wrong is only contemplated when the former convict is arrested again. A young offender's lifestyle has been shaped by the prison environment. What else could he become but a career criminal, mimicking his prison mentors and peers?

Take James Lewis, for instance, an inmate in the Wisconsin State Reformatory, captivated by the exciting and glamorous crime escapades narrated by older, respected Black prisoners; he was arrested just eight hours after his release, attempting to apply burglary "techniques" his prison mentor taught him and other young offenders (parole release, 1965). Undaunted, he pursued a career as a criminal that spanned more than thirty-five years, returning to prison seven more times before "retiring" in 1993. In order to prevent repeat offenses and provide a better and more effective consequence for juveniles, separation from adult criminals is vital.

More recently, the government has taken steps to address these significant problems with incarceration and rehabilitation. The Obama administration initiated bipartisan legislation to address overcriminalization and mass incarceration. The Sentencing Reform and Corrections Act of 2015 reduced mandatory minimum prison terms of nonviolent drug offenders, and the Fair Chance to Compete for Jobs Act of 2015 prohibited federal agencies and federal contractors from requesting criminal history information before the applicant has received a job offer, thus giving previously incarcerated job seekers a chance to obtain employment based on job skills and qualifications alone (Congress.gov, 2016). The former president commuted 1,715 sentences and pardoned 148 prisoners. These are steps in the right direction, but may not find much support in the Trump administration. Trump's white-right cabinet and political appointees speak volumes and suggest a bleak future for minorities during his presidency. Michael Collins of the Drug Policy Alliance said in reference to Barack Obama, "He is to be applauded for his actions . . . but we know that the next occupant of the White House is unsympathetic to the cause of mass incarceration, and to the plight of those serving unjust sentences in federal prison." A recent Pew Research Study pointed out that 76 percent of white Republicans believe police officers generally treat African American arrestees fairly, that police violence and discrimination are exaggerated: "About three-quarters of Republicans say that police around the country are doing an excellent or good job when it comes to treating racial and ethnic groups equally, using the right amount of force for each situation and holding officers accountable when misconduct occurs" (Pew Research Center, 2017). The views of both the current administration and its supporters may create further barriers for more just treatment of juvenile offenders, specifically those who are minorities.

Unbiased researchers can clearly see that the US criminal justice system is fraught with racism and, by design or not, is tantamount to twenty-first-century slave labor for corporate tycoons who have invested in the prison industrial complex. The police, prosecutors, courts, and Wall Street investors have a synergetic, efficiently run ATM machine that recruits and recycles African American and Hispanic prisoners. The corporate bigwigs lobby state legislatures and courts for longer sentences, "truth in sentencing," and three-strikes-you're-out laws to keep prisons operating at capacity and the contracts coming. Corrections Corporation of America, the largest private prison company, has worked with legislators to draft model legislation impacting sentencing policy, prison privatization, and tough-on-crime proposals. It has contributed funds to sit on issue task forces and sponsor events hosting legislators. Whether crime rises or falls, for-profit prisons need to keep cells occupied to ensure that an able-bodied, healthy workforce is readily available.

Corporations who invest in prisons lose money if prisoners reform, get out, and stay out. They have vested economic interest and the political influence to maintain the world's largest penal system. As long as reducing incarceration is tied to fiscal pressures, little attention will be paid to the root causes: racism and poverty. It is unlikely that the powers-that-be will allow the recidivism rate to be significantly reduced without a fight. At least thirty-seven states have legalized the contracting of prison labor by private corporations (deVuono-powell et al., 2015). Some of the companies that have used prison labor are McDonald's, Victoria's Secret, Starbucks, and Boeing. So has the US military. As seen from these perspectives, many hurdles exist in the way of eliminating juvenile sentencing to adult prisons and the disproportionate incarceration of minorities. Corrections Corporation of America said in its 2010 annual report, filed with the Securities and Exchange Commission, "The demand for our facilities and services could be adversely affected by . . . leniency in conviction or parole standards and sentencing practices" (ACLU, 2011a).

Conclusion

The practice of sentencing juveniles to adult prisons should be terminated, "except for extraordinary exceptions," for example, the South Carolina church murders and the Sandy Hook Elementary School massacre. Any time spent in an adult prison has an indelible negative effect on a juvenile offender. Once juvenile offenders arrive in an adult prison, radical changes must be contemplated, reconciled, and implemented to establish their identity as either predator or prey. There is little chance for offenders to avoid this violent culture. If a young African American male is going to be imprisoned for any length of time, as a matter of self-preservation, he will gravitate to the etched-in-stone prison code—"kill or be killed," "the strong survive"—which means he will harden his heart, cultivate secret survival skills, and feel compelled to collaborate with peers in various activities that may or may not conform to his personal value system. This abnormal environment will not allow a youth to be or become normal, wholesome, and well-meaning for long.

Juveniles in adult prisons are unserved, underserved, or inappropriately served because they can be preyed on by adults, as seen in the case of O. C. Harry, or because they are simply not provided the resources for learning academic and social skills. While it is possible to convert a prison experience into an opportunity for future success, astronomical odds and real-time realities stand in one's way, and that is a great deal of territory for most juvenile minds to absorb and navigate effectively. If rehabilitation is the expectation of criminal justice professionals, the environment must be less stressful, less violent, and conducive to education, growth, and empowerment so young offenders can gain insight into their behavior that recognizes alternatives and opportunities for positive transformation. Effective intervention programs must target the culture of being male, African American, and adolescent, as well as the contextual factor of having lived in high-risk, inner-city neighborhoods. Reaching "street savvy" juvenile offenders requires a bit of "hustler insight," specific street knowledge, and life experience they can "feel," spoken in a language they understand that is socially and culturally acceptable to them. If properly engaged, young offenders will learn how to avoid the typical pitfalls of post-prison life. They will find regular work, avoid drugs, and stay free of new crimes. Prerelease and postrelease training are necessary to leave a life of crime behind.

This chapter examined the history of the treatment of youth offenders as adults leading up to modern practices, as well as the failures of the government in policymaking and the dangerous influence of adult criminals on youth offenders, to oppose the incarceration of juvenile Black males in adult prisons and point out systemic racism in criminal justice administration. Incarcerated lives matter!

■ **References**

ACLU. (2011a). Banking on Bondage: Private Prisons, Labor and Mass Incarceration. *American Civil Liberties Union.* Https://www.aclu.org/banking-bondage-private-prisons-and-mass-incarceration.

ACLU. (2011b). The 2010 Annual Report filed with the Securities and Exchange Commission by Corrections Corporation of America. Https://www.aclu.org/ banking-bondage-private-prisons-and-mass-incarceration.

Aizer, A., and Doyle, Jr. J. (2013). Juvenile incarceration, human capital and future crime: Evidence from randomly-assigned judges. *NBER Working Paper* No. 19102.

Ashkar, J. P., & Kenny, T. D. (2008). Views from the inside: Young offenders' subjective experiences of incarceration. *International Journal of Offender Therapy and Comparative Criminology 52*(5), 584–97.

Congress.gov. (2016). S.2021—Fair Chance Act. Https://www.congress.gov/bill/114th-congress/ senate-bill/2021.

deVuono-powell, S., Schweidler, C., Walters, A., & Zohrabi, A. (2011s). *Who Pays? The True Cost of Incarceration on Families.* Oakland, CA: Ella Baker Center. Https://ellabakercenter.org/sites/ default/files/downloads/who-pays.pdf.

Fagan, J. 2008. Juvenile crime and criminal justice: Resolving border disputes. *Future of Children 18*(2):81–118.

Mullen, C. T. (2014). *State of South Carolina v. George Stinney, Jr.* State of South Carolina: The Circuit Court of the Fourteenth Judicial Circuit. Https://s3.amazonaws.com/s3.documentcloud.org/ documents/1382796/stinney-ruling.pdf.

NAACP. (2017). Criminal justice fact sheet. Http://www.naacp.org/criminal-justice-fact-sheet.

Pew Research Center. (2017). Fact tank: News in the numbers. Http://www.pewresearch.org/fact-tank.

Redding (2005). Office of Juvenile Justice and Delinquency Prevention: Juvenile Transfer Laws: An Effective Deterrent to A Message From OJJDP.

Reisig, M. D., Bales, W. D., Hay, C., & Wang, X. (2007). The effect of racial inequality on black male recidivism. *Justice Quarterly 24*(3), 408–34.

Roper v. Simmons. (2005). Https://deathpenaltyinfo.org/execution-juveniles-us-and-other-Countries.

The Sentencing Project. (2016). *The sentencing project.* Http://www.sentencingproject.org.

US Supreme Court. (1932). *Powell v. Alabama,* 287 U.S. 45. *Justia: US Supreme Court.* Https://supreme. justia.com/cases/federal/us/287/45/case.html

US Supreme Court. (1967). *In re Gault,* 387 U.S. 1. *Justia: US Supreme Court.* Https://supreme.justia.com/ cases/federal/us/387/1/case.html.

WNYC. (2016). Kids in prison: racial disparities, longer sentences and a better way. New York Public Radio. Http://www.wnyc.org/series/kids-prison.

⧉ VIGNETTE

Today Ronnie works in higher education and has a graduate-level degree. Even though he is well educated, he does not receive the same respect or get the same opportunities as others in his workplace. He is constantly passed up for job advancements for which he is qualified, oftentimes in favor of people who are less qualified and have less seniority. He sees a continuous pattern of disrespect and eventually gives up. He becomes less engaged in work socially, but still gets the bare minimum job done. His coworkers and supervisor see his change in demeanor and question him. He doesn't give them the answers they seek. A colleague in another unit sees this and begins to engage with him. Eventually, an opportunity in that department opens and Ronnie applies. He is granted the position and acquires a renewed sense of hope that all individuals are not entrapped by their own biases. Ronnie has since thrived in his field and continues to get great opportunities passed to him.

PART 5

Criminal and Social Justice

INTRODUCTION

Steven Randolph Cureton

Theodore Ransaw, C. P. Gause, and Richard Majors, the editors of this volume, have embraced a huge undertaking in crafting a handbook about black males. This book attempts to provide an effective assessment of the multifaceted phenomena of the black male. I was recruited to be a part editor, charged with the duty of assembling four contributors who could provide insight concerning black men's experiences with social justice. I am proud of this part. The contributors offer insight concerning masculine performances that lead to self-harm, intraracial gendered victimization, and legal agent discretionary practices.

America at its worst has demonstrated that it harbors an aversion to embracing the humanity of blackness. America has demonstrated an indifference toward the sufferings of blacks under the pretense that blacks have successfully assimilated, continue to be progressive, and have a socially mobile and robust middle class. Hence, blacks who face various types of misfortunes are most likely to blame for their fate. For those who fall in this camp, the belief is that oppression has subsided. Just as important is the reality that an expansive permanent underclass is disenfranchised, and racial casting is still pervasive, signaling that blacks are still subject to traditional stereotypes that socially construct blackness as having character deficits and underlying depravity. The legacy of blackness includes colonization, exploitation, cultural imposition, co-optation, racial ranking, and intentional personhood negation. The essence of blackness is forever altered from its authentic African energy.

The black male experience is beset by social injustice, starting with adverse cultural narratives that have become cultural codes effecting a moral panic over the black male's potential to cause social harm. Racial fears concerning his criminality are heightened by misleading conversations about being disproportionately criminal, violent, homicidal, arrested, and incarcerated. These conversations are partly misleading because the raw numbers of black males that comprise all of these categories is less than the instances of black males that are law-abiding citizens. Still, concentrations on proportions or percentage representations of criminogenic populations work to confirm long-standing stereotypes. More than that, these perceptions, while perhaps definitive of a minority group of men within the black male population, continue to be so pervasive as to reflect a caste system. In this caste system, mainstream society is seemingly comfortable with discretionary justice, abuses, brutality, and black males being subjected to lethal force by police officers, individuals acting on behalf of law enforcement, or ordinary citizens. Fear is the popular word used to convey one universal meaning, and that is that the black male acted in ways or displayed mannerisms significant enough to warrant his being shot to death.

Fundamentally, the life course of black males is not independent of their social biography, inclusive of long-standing, adverse public opinions. The contributions in this part, when read separately, highlight black masculinity as combustible and black femininity as vulnerable to victimization when defined by black masculinity. When considering the sum of the individual contributions, the takeaway is that black masculinity is troublesome enough to cause black men to victimize like-circumstanced individuals, engage in a self-destructive agenda, or be victimized by law enforcement agents.

LaWanda Simpkins is appropriately the lead-off author in this part because of the implications of black masculinity for black femininity, relationship troubles, and gender-norming conflicts. Simpkins's "Victimized Victim: The Consciousness of Black Femininity in the Image of Masculinity" explores the nature of black femininity when exposed to the black masculine gaze and more profoundly when other black women use masculine performances to manage black woman-to-woman relationships. Simpkins's offering is uniquely embedded in black feminist ideology as an appropriate framework for deciphering problematic discourse and exchanges between black males and black females. Simpkins contends that poisonous cultural codes infiltrate intraracial and intragender exchanges. The result is a social injustice because a master narrative has operated to hinder positive affirmations and security and has created social rifts that socially damages the institution of black families and black social networks.

Kimya Dennis's "Black Male Suicide: Inward-Expressed Frustration and Aggression" investigates economic, employment, political, social, and cultural factors related to black male suicide. It turns out that a stream of violence that can be either homicidal or suicidal has connections to perceptions of social injustice. More specifically, awareness of black empowerment, employment status, political activity, and deprivation has a significant impact on homicide and suicide. While the black community seems to brush black male suicide aside in favor of concentrating on homicide, inward violence plagues the black community. What's more, as the black community ignores suicide, instead thinking that exposure to religion is enough to counter suicidal contemplations, definitions of masculinity that suggest manhood is exemplified by controlling one's own fate are strong enough to persuade some black men to transcend helplessness by terminating their life.

Armondo Collins's "The Media Assault on the Black Male: Echoes of Public Lynching and Killing the Modern Terror of Jack Johnson" details the intentional character assassination of a gifted athlete by media outlets. Collins offers a thematic discourse whereby the media are exposed for engaging in campaigns to destroy black men for the purpose of promoting solidarity among whites by uniting them with the creation of a common enemy. Collins's work opines on the nature of media-infused public opinion that is less about social facts than about perceived challenges to white privilege, security, and the sanctity of white women. Evidently, it is a falsehood to think that sports entitle athletes to wholesale integration, inclusive of pursuing the affection of white women. Partial assimilation needs to be tempered by measured access to a version of the American dream that does not encroach upon white privilege and security. Whenever black males challenge this notion by attempting to fully integrate, their actions are viewed as infiltration by an unwanted and unwelcome guest. Such men are seen as trespassing and deserving of social and physical lynchings. For these black male evildoers, there is no such thing as injustice.

Jack Monell's "A Preliminary Examination of Hegemonic Masculinity: Definitional Transference of Black Masculinity Effecting Lethal Tactics against Black Males," while just a research note, is hard hitting because transcripts of two high-profile shootings are examined. Content analysis of transcripts of shooters who have used a firearm to cause the death of an unarmed black male is rare. Monell examines Zimmerman's and Wilson's personal accounts about the lethal force used against Trayvon Martin and Michael Brown, respectively. Analysis reveals that the killings of these two unarmed black male teenagers happened because an individual acting on behalf of the law and a sworn police officer were prompted to use lethal force by fear, suspicion, and perceptions of threat more than by actual behavior. Moreover, the killings of Martin and Brown were most likely action-oriented cultural codes that demonized and cast these two black males as enemies of civility.

An even more powerful affirming takeaway from this part is that Simpkins, Dennis, Collins, and Monell were not aware of the contents of one another's contributions, and yet the cumulative product speaks to long-standing cultural narratives and cultural codes that have transcended time to negatively impact the social welfare of blacks. The social injustice present in all four contributions is that the humanity of blackness is long suffering and currently under attack, as evidenced by victimization and death. These chapters identify value differentiation between blacks and whites, media campaigns that extend negative cultural narratives, and black masculinity as a troublesome social hazard for inter- and intraracial interaction. The reverence for black lives is the matter of concern. However, after one reads this part, it is no wonder how the modus operandi of demonizing blacks and openly killing them can continue with impunity.

Steven Cureton's "Hoovers and Night Crawlers: When Outside In Becomes Inside Out," emphasizes the importance of black researchers engaging in ethnographic research on black populations. There is a pertinent need for authentic narratives regarding the nuances of assimilation and integration for black people. The contributions of Simpkins, Dennis, Collins, and Monell taken together also indicate that media outlets cannot be trusted to promote positive social biographies of blacks and are complicit in creating detrimental outcomes. Therefore, black researchers have an obligation to conduct risky research when focusing on deviant, criminal and violent populations. This obligation is paramount because these are the black people who are the likely recipients of social injustice at the hands of the criminal justice machine.

Victimized Victim

The Consciousness of Black Femininity in the Image of Masculinity

LaWanda M. Simpkins

> To be changed by ideas was pure pleasure. But to learn ideas that ran counter to values and beliefs learned at home was to place oneself at risk, to enter the danger zone.
>
> —bell hooks, 1994

Since the inception of America, there has been a cultural war declared on the humanity of blackness. Black men and women have been subjected to unthinkable brutality for the benefit of white manifest destiny and white privilege. This oppression hasn't lessened over time. The hierarchy of race, created by and for the benefit of white people, has been detrimental to the collective identity of the black race. It has presupposed a level of inferiority among many and has caused a level of intraracial racism and intraracial sexism that can only be found within minority communities. The level of distrust that comes from loving a country that does not love you back, evidenced by both past and present events, has sparked an internal loathing that will take just as many centuries to dissolve as it did to create. Within communities of color at the height of the distrust is the internal and oftentimes unspoken competition that takes place between feminine charisma and masculine mystique.

Favorable status is critical to existing with equity, and quite frankly, nobody wants to be at the bottom of the socially constructed hierarchy. Unfortunately, with race and gender combined, the black woman finds herself located at the bottom. In 1982 three black women, Gloria Hull, Patricia Bell-Scott, and Barbara Smith introduced a groundbreaking text for black women's studies that underscores this very idea. This edited text single-handedly speaks to the isolated nature that black women feel. Appropriately titled *All the Women Are White, All the Blacks Are Men, but Some of Us Are Brave*, this book speaks to the history of black women's oppression.

More unfortunate than being placed at the bottom of the social hierarchy is accepting that place by reenacting roles assigned by others. Black femininity is fluid and important to understand, but it can also be understood through the lens of black masculinity. Although a black woman can have an independent existence, her existential reality often gets confined to the contextual realities of black manhood. This existence goes far beyond any genetic or biological basis to encounter the ways in which femininity is juxtaposed to masculinity.

For the purpose of this discussion, femininity can be understood as general characteristics and traits that are assigned to cisgender females. Some of this gendered behavior can be classified as being sensitive, kind, and gentle. Also, nurturing, emotional, loving, and dedicated are attributes assigned to women. The quintessential woman would be one who is both a wife and a mother, leaving her womanhood last on her list of priorities. She is the absolute to a man but never the absolute to herself. Very loosely, heteronormative masculinity can be defined as being strong, confident, dominant, and decisive. According to patriarchal master narratives, a man should be able to lead and provide for a family.

Alternatively, with respect to race there is a historical pretense where black men were socially castrated by a continuum of macro- and micro-level oppressions, creating a condition where many black women help black men embrace manhood (Collins, 2000, 2005).

This chapter offers discourse on three ways in which black female identity has been constructed through the lens of masculinity. These influences are our elders and traditional and contemporary social media. The male gaze is never far removed from a woman. Heteronormative ideals appeal to the majority of black women; therefore, black womanhood is definitively linked to black manhood. Moreover, the social construction of black femininity is also influenced by social forces and cultural shifts over time, which can impose gender role expectations to the point of actually silencing black women or relegating them to voiceless performers (Carby, 1987).

Female Solidarity and My Subjectively

The term *we* will be used to describe black women as a whole throughout this work. This idea is underscored by Collins (2000), who suggests that although changes have occurred in the United States, being a black woman offers unique experiences that makes black femininity an exclusive category. Therefore, black female are primary agents to provide insight about black femininity. I am an autoethnographer. This form of qualitative inquiry is both personal and invasive, but for the reader it can be very informative. Research suggests that the most authentic stories come from investigators who have close connections to or are themselves part of a society, culture, community, or social distinction they are trying to explain (Hobbs, 2001).

Who better to tell a story about black women than a black woman?

> Out of race must come its own thinkers and writers. Authors belonging to the white race have written good books, for which I am deeply grateful, but it seems to be almost impossible for a

white man to put himself completely in our place. No man can feel the iron which enters another man's soul. (Carby, 1987, p. 62)

I acknowledge that my voice cannot speak for everyone but presume that this work will resonate on some levels. I am especially honored and yet pressured in writing a narrative that exposes layers of black femininity that may oftentimes be untouched. This has everything to do with the nature of the conversation and nothing to do with the profoundly intelligent black women who have come before me. I take strength in telling a story that may be accepted as relatively universal. The fact that I am able to do so within a part on black masculinity surrenders my soul to all the foremothers who came before me who fought for a voice at the table. In this way, my subjectivity is my strength. To be subjective implies that one is able to acknowledge her thoughts and perhaps even her biases about a subject matter (Peshkin, 1988). Therefore, my insider's perspective, while surely influenced by my gender and racial ascriptions, will serve as an asset toward contributing a chapter in a part that is focused on black masculinity.

What Our Elders Taught Us: Wo/men Please Do, Please Don't

I have offered a fluid definition of what it means to be a cis female. For the remainder of this chapter I would like to narrow this understanding to what it means to be a cis African American woman. More specifically, I would like to offer three ways by which black womanhood is assumed, all while linking this understanding to black masculinity.

For the majority of my life I have been socialized in black educational environments, and my academic discipline was heavily influenced by black women, from the early days of elementary school to earning my master's degree.

It is because of this that much of what I subscribe to as codes of appearance and conduct is influenced by the *do's and don'ts* of black femininity. Please *do* act like a lady at all times, which means stand up straight, wear clothes that will not distract the opposite sex (especially in church), and be strong but not too strong as to not *let* a man be a man. *Do* handle your *business* because the only thing that a black woman gets to be is strong. Weak is not in our DNA. *Please don't* give in to male influences, especially at an early age. *Don't* speak about your insecurities in the company of the dominant race or gender. *Don't* take shortcuts because *we* must always work harder, and whatever you do, *don't* ever portray yourself as an angry black woman.

Maturity, coupled with dating and mate selection, adds to the list of heteronormative do's and don'ts, especially if you are affiliated with a church. At times it is difficult to decipher personal standards and expectations that are not tied to gender and intraracial normative expectations. Personal identification and even images of self are further confounded by cultural imposition and co-optation from the dominant mainstream culture (Benedict, 1934; Cleaver, 1968; Dyson, 1996; West, 2001).

Black female maturity coincides with upholding a fundamental standard of strength. It is presumed that this role was constructed as a defense mechanism or to equip women with the fortitude to ward off being passive or a willing accomplice to situational circumstances intended to humiliate or victimize. Moreover, it takes a measure of strength to successfully navigate being a matriarch or sole provider in female-headed household.

The ingredients of being strong are dominance, confidence, independence, innovation, and pride, which can become detrimental characteristics that hinder traditionally masculine performances within a relationship (Collins, 1989; hooks, 2004; Morgan & Bennett, 2006; Richardson, 2007). In fact, a black man who has difficulty measuring up to the strength that a black woman possesses may conclude that she is not a worthy mate because she is noncompliant, bitchy, a male hater, overbearing, cunning, and resilient enough to negotiate success without a significant other. Part of this perception may be due to what black men have been taught over the years. In the same way that black women are given a dos and don'ts list, it is likely that black men are negotiating masculinity using some culturally relevant set of normative expectations (Morgan & Bennett, 2006; Wallace, 2007).

For black men, the checklist resembles some of the following normative expectations as performance indicators of solid masculinity. *Do* make sure that you take care of the women in your life, especially in the absence of an older man in the household. *Do* position yourself as strong and dominant at all times. *Don't* ever show signs of weakness. Doing so could get you hurt, depending on your social circle. *Don't* show vulnerabilities among your peers; doing so will lead to status decline in respective peer circles. Competition among black male peer groups is fierce as they attempt to negotiate and maintain respect by demonstrating an ability to control situations and people within their immediate environment, suppress credible challenges to their reputation, and sex numerous women without commitment to monogamy or fatherhood (should that situation arise) (Anderson, 1990, 1999; Cureton & Wilson, 2012).

The most prominent functional masculinity performance is to successfully assimilate for purposes of social mobility, improving life chances and life course outcomes to ensure a stable future and ultimately to take care of family obligations. I find this role to be most intriguing because it is the same dichotomous situation that black women also find themselves in. Both are taught to be resilient when faced with discrimination. In fact, both receive racial socialization that incorporates personal accountability and resistance as a coping strategy for overcoming racial barriers. Thus, in terms of racial resiliency, black masculinity and black femininity have the same cultural code for handling adverse institutional barriers to success (Bell, 1992; Carter, 2008; Delgado & Stefancic 2001; Solomon, 1992).

In instances where competition for resources gets reduced to racial alliances and strategies that are inherently the result of white privilege, black males and females have to adjust the tenacity of their attitudes in order to promote comfort or notions of being a team player or good colleague. Failure to do so may result in reprisals and even reversals of good fortune (Rothenberg, 2002; Woods et al., 2012). The thought of weakening their unmerited power and superiority causes many whites to retaliate against black masculinity. This retaliation is done in so many ways and is exhibited differently depending on social hierarchy and potential for social mobility. Unfortunately, black masculine and black feminine performances may have to incorporate a measure of code switching, whereby both are left feeling weakened and perhaps frustrated to the point of releasing unintended harmful emotional fumes on one another in relationships.

Black men feeling particularly suppressed throughout the workday can take solace in knowing that their masculinity power codes are supposed to be naturally dominant in households and relationships, effecting suppression of black femininity codes of power (Ford, 2006; Morgan & Bennett, 2006). This is yet another impediment for relationship negotiations between black men and black women. For the strength that black women embody clashes with black men who are taught to have the same strength, and one side usually ends up perceiving these clashes as belittling (hooks, 2004). An essay written by a black man shares his reaction to his ex-girlfriend speaking back to him. He reflects:

> I felt fragile, as fragile as a bird with clipped wings, that day my ex-girlfriend stepped up her game and spoke back to men. Nothing in my world, nothing in my self-definition, prepared me for dealing with a woman as an equal. My world said women were inferior. . . . Since the racist sexist white world sees black women as angry bitches who must be kept in check, it turns away from relational violence in black life. (qtd. in hooks, 2004, pp. 56–57)

Instead of celebrating the strength black women uphold, society, and sometimes our own men, entangle many years of fear and myths about black femininity. This combination further perpetuates the myth of the strong black woman, or some would say the angry black woman. She is demoralized for possessing many of the characteristics that a black man would be praised for possessing and using to successfully negotiate his masculinity (Griffith & Cornish, 2018).

Synopsis up to This Point

So far this chapter has laid out a checklist of sorts that reflects normative expectations and cultural codes of conduct for how black masculinity and black femininity are processed and negotiated, effecting a troubled tradition for relationships between black men and black women.

The feminist lens used here is appropriate given black femininity is impacted by black masculinity in terms of the masculine gaze and interactional exchanges. Acknowledging personal subjectivity at the onset was for the benefit of transparency and to operate as a checking system for me as I attempt to journey through this maze of intraracial and gendered relationships. The top portion of this chapter also is appropriate for introducing a conversation about racial resiliency as a coping strategy to combat racial injustice, opportunity blockages, and reprisals that stagnate life course chances at upward mobility. The social injustice incurred is that as macro-level institutions process the ingredients of black masculinity, focusing only on that which appears to be threatening, the impact is not an affirmation of his inability to succeed but a social injustice to his existential being. What follows is micro-level repercussions aimed at black women who are contending with macro-level institutional impediments of her own. Hence, both are entering into exchanges already conditioned by severe headwinds, whereby the simplicity of a relationship becomes another proving ground for both black males and females. What follows then is a gravitation toward interpersonal victimization. Accordingly, the second half of this chapter will incorporate personal disclosures with respect to social facts, which is the duty of an autoethnographer.

The cycle of authority has been such that black men must claim their space in the presence of white men and white women must also claim their space in the presence of white men. Black women must claim their space in presence of white men, white women, and black men (Collins, 2000; Jean & Feagin, 1998; Staples, 1973). This fight for social capital oftentimes leaves black women positioning themselves to play by the rules that men do, which can be very exhausting at times.

The very hand that in many ways oppresses women is often the same hand that is researched in order to get a seat at the table, albeit true black women are careful to not dishonor black men, as this is one of the very first *dont's* that we are socialized to believe. Even as I write this chapter, I am questioning how much I should reveal, which further validates the title, the victimized *victim*.

What Does He See in Her?

Black men and women stand face to face in a reflection of our most troubled past in America. The strength of each other is realized through voluntary exchanges and entering into meaningful relationships. It is in this space that many of the *do's* that both genders are taught are manifested. Black masculinity in its most pure form can best be understood through family and love. Historically, black men have been the ones to choose with whom and when they are ready to be committed. This falls in direct alignment with one of the first do's, protect the women in your life. With so many women (of all races) vying for their attention, men are tempted to prolong settling choices while engaging in sexual conquest. The sex ratio equation that favors men (too many women and not enough men) affects the perceived importance of a monogamous relationship with black women. The perspective of not being bound by calls of racial solidarity in mate selection provides an opportunity for racial and ethnic variance in the mate selection pool (Baars, 2009). Even though black manhood can be investigated with respect to intraracial relationships with black women, relationships are not always homogenously black. Arguably this may not seem like an issue. It certainly does not appear to be an issue for black men; however, the legacy of value estimations placed on black femininity is hurtful.

No matter the rational for selecting mates who are not black, the end result is black women being at the bottom of the social hierarchy when it comes to mate selection (Kaba, 2012; Perry, 2015). This begs the question, are black women black men's least desirables, and if so, is it because of employment, income, education, and other social mobility issues, preferential appearance factors, or because of being socialized to be opponents? The answers to these questions are embedded in social justice issues because any time there is a blocked opportunity to improve life course outcomes or well-being and social mobility are adversely impacted by stratification and family dynamics, then there is an inherent social justice problem.

Social Circles, Social Media, and Race/Gender Norming

Our elders are perhaps eclipsed by our immediate social circles when it comes to race and gender conditioning. When offering commentary on perceptions of strength, women hold an adverse view (myself included) of other black women who seem predisposed to acting helplessly weak. Black women are not allowed the freedom of appearing to be damsels in distress. Our race and gender legacy rebuffs this reality in every way. Although many black women understand that we can't be superhuman, there is no rush to prove that we lack the strength necessary to overcome adversity, independently of men.

There was a point in time where the influence of a woman went as far as her elders, her family, and her social circle but with media, more specifically social media, the never-ending cycle to attract the male gaze has increased by leaps and bounds. No longer do women have a filter by which to be influenced. Social media have exploited the black woman in ways unseen before.

Media portrayal of black women has always been dangerous, but the access that people have now has taken this danger to unprecedented heights regarding personal value assessments, appearance, and desirability (Perloff, 2014).

Facebook was launched in 2004, forever changing the dynamics of social networking. Prior to Facebook, Black Planet and Myspace seemed to be viable social media outlets geared toward cyber social networking among interested groups. Facebook currently reigns as the supreme social network connection engine because it continues to provide ways to disseminate information and connect with desired people or groups in ways that are both personal and discrete. Sign up for any social media site and you get immediate confirmation concerning the degree of social acceptance a subject matter has because social media are interactive (Eveland, 2003; Joinson & Paine, 2007; Sundar & Limperos, 2013).

Social media are used to create and sustain communities that share common interests. For purposes of this chapter, I will focus on the desire for social recognition and approval. It appears that a noticeable number of black women are offering intimate details about personal attributes, body traits, and emotional disclosures that may not necessarily be beneficial for social development but do garner support from people who desire to be titillated. In the age of social media, offering ingredients that seem embedded in temptation is a popular way to gain notoriety. It's a thirst trap of sorts, which involves the sexual alluring of the opposite gender (in some cases the same gender) to one's page.

The presentation of self for reason of endorsement of men can be degrading and demoralizing, especially when such displays objectifies black women, lending confirmation to the various typologies that will be discussed later (Hesse-Biber, 2007).

Unfortunately, when women display black femininity in ways that negatively impact value estimates that may already be low (when comparing it to nonblack females), it reinforces and perhaps packages messages that lead to victimization. As ladies, we stand to lose traction in the fight for equity and equality when we portray ourselves in this manner. We victimize ourselves by seeking the approval of men to confirm beauty. The social fact that beauty is on the forefront of our conversations stands to be problematic because beauty can be an arbitrary point of view but still affect the objectification of black women by black men.

Shades and Boss Chics

One of the more damaging intraracial preferences that have led to prejudiced behaviors is related to skin tone. Social media have underscored the reality that skin tone is bantered as if it were a fashion statement. Too often black women become victims of the ideal standard of beauty set forth by mainstream society. Regrettably, many black men perpetuate this narrative by favoring lighter-hued women over darker-skinned women. This is problematic on many levels. Skin tone variation resonates because of the co-opted image construction and culturally imposed standards of beauty reflective of a social value system steeped in racism. One of the countless realities of bigotry is certainly internalized racism (Lebron et al., 2015; West, 2001). Certainly the days of overt claims of inferiority have regressed, but such times have been replaced by a color code stratification system that affirms that nearness to white is better than distance from white.

It's in one respect a social justice issue because it directly dismisses the content of one's character, and casts derogatory value assessments based solely on skin tone. The cultural conditioning of attaching negative views to darker skin and affording positive halo-like qualities to those with lighter skin is so pervasive that black men voluntarily adjust their behaviors based on notions that skin tone is predictive of what is relatively acceptable behavior. The social damage that is done is evidenced by using skin tone as an appearance appraisal, leading to self-esteem and self-efficacy issues that are detrimental to the social development of black women who seek beauty affirmations (Hunter, 2005; Jackson, 2006; Lawrence, 1999; Russell-Cole, Wilson, & Hall, 2013).

Skin tone appraisals are perpetuated through social media but so too is the idea of masculinity through femininity. In some ways I agree that gender may be a social construction. I am not an elitist or a totalitarian when it comes to gender, but I subscribe to notions that there are significant differences in men and women. I am sure that this is because of my upbringing and my religious beliefs. Like most people, I am able to better identify myself and others by their perceived gender (it is important to note that their assigned gender may be different). The gender that one identifies with is important, just as negotiating gender is important.

Boss chics (fiercely, strong unstoppable, independent black females) have become popular portrayals on social media. A boss chic negotiates social mobility on her own terms, professes control of her immediate environment and people, and in so doing, seizes an aura of empowerment and confidence that rivals her male counterparts'.

Being a boss chic does not take on the exact characteristics of manhood, but instead offers a version of feminine hardness or refusal to be sentimental (By, 1991; Fleetwood, 2012). This type of black woman is the antithesis of what most black men are attracted to. In fact, "Most black males are not looking for a woman who is a peer; they want a woman who is traditionally feminine as defined by sexist thinking, who subordinates her will to his, who lives to please him" (hooks, 2004, p. 120).

Social media are the newest vessel for portrayal for black women and perhaps the most dangerous because they follow a twenty-four-hour cycle, and the content is impossible to filter in terms of the social damage it can cause. It is a performance stage consisting of actors who engage, anonymously or not, to promote some agenda that oftentimes can be more self-serving than altruistic. The media realm, whether it be traditional hard copy, television, or radio, has not been kind toward the image construction of black women, as these outlets seem to protect the sanctity of white women (Carby 1987; Carter-Punyanunt, 2008; Cleaver, 1968; Collins, 2005; Kulaszewicz, 2015; West, 2001).

Then there is reality television, which seems to contribute very little to positive value appraisals with respect to black femininity. Over the course of time, reality television has become increasingly popular. Gone are the days when writers and producers had to create fictitious characters to play the stereotypical roles of black women. It seems black women are in the business of a self-promotion that ironically matches traditional stereotypes even when there are degrees of freedom for creative expression. The overly dramatic black women who are about money, fortune, and fame are the ones being casted, gloried, and praised on television.

As soon as one show is canceled, another one quickly arises just long enough to continue to destroy the image of black womanhood.

Media Have Strong Socialization Agency

Throughout the years, black women have been typecast as mammy, sapphire, and jezebel. Traditionally the character of a mammy has been used as a controlling figure to depict black women. It is one of the most pervasive images originating during slavery. Through the years the mammy has been portrayed as a large, dark-skinned woman whose sole purpose in life was to take care of her master's needs (West, 1995). The most pervasive image during early times was that of the mammy, with the sapphire running a close second. The sapphire, also known as the angry black woman, or the superbitch, originated from a character on the radio show *Amos 'n Andy*. Sapphire Stevens frequently berated her husband on the program. The sassiness that is associated with being a sapphire has almost become synonymous with being a black woman (Bogle, 2001; Collins, 2005; Ladson-Billings, 2009; West, 1995), as if to say that if you are black and you have some type of attitude, then you must be angry. A black woman can be labeled this even without having an attitude. First Lady Michelle Obama endured the angry black woman label for eight years. Of the three portrayals, this is the one that most black women fiercely try to distance themselves from because it invites false assumptions that to control an angry black woman, one must be overly aggressive, which could lead to victimization (Anderson, 1990; Cureton & Wilson, 2012).

The final depiction of black women in mass media is that of jezebels. The image of the jezebel has been in movies for almost a century. The first woman to play this role was Nina Mae McKinney in the film *Hallelujah* in 1929. In this role she was described as a sexy, seductive chic. It is important to note that Ms. McKinney was of lighter hue and, therefore, was deemed most attractive during this era (Howard, 1996).

In attempting to understand these roles it is important to first note that none of them were created or would exist outside of masculinity. Women have been portrayed as objects solely for the physical, emotional, and aesthetic pleasure of men (Baldwin, 1999; Ladson-Billings, 2009). Cultural narratives have flooded the American psyche and for that matter have forced an identity crisis for black women by casting their femininity as subordinate in the form of mammies, contemptuous in the form of sapphires, and hypersexed in the form of jezebels. None of these speak to the intestinal fortitude of black women, nor do any of these stereotypes embody the complexities of negotiating womanhood in a racially oppressive society. Finally, given that these three typologies render black femininity as servitude to men, they are detrimental to pursuits of equity and social justice for black women in that they negate the humanity and dignity of black womanhood and block opportunities to experience the full weight of the promise of the American dream. Patriarchal processing has proven unequitable in the pursuit of happiness. Therefore, it is mandatory that images of black women be challenged using a logical framework where women are primary agents of information and knowledge construction (Collins, 2000).

Autoethnography Takes Center Stage: Revelations of Masculinity in Victimization

The primary point of contention here is that by standing in the way of social justice intraracially and in gendered ways, we are indeed imposing self-inflicted social injustice. The most dangerous way that black women have been victimized by masculinity is that black women socially cannibalize one another. I recently attended a conference that was spearheaded by women for women. In one of the sessions I heard a black female facilitator state that her mentor (a male) told her not to trust any woman that cried on the job. She discussed her personal experiences with one woman who had cried to her and how awful she was for being emotionally driven to tears in a professional setting. Even with the constant comments from the audience about not holding women to masculine standards, the facilitator remained vigilant with respect to tears as symbolic of something negative. The irony of the presentation was evident from the beginning when the facilitator disclosed that she had experienced adversity with, in fact she had been wronged by, black women. The irony is that this occurred in academia, among women who seemed set on sabotaging careers over the matter of perceived jealousy about appearance, fitness for the job, and knowledge gatekeeping. These are areas where masculinity seems to have a primary focus: matters of appearance, judgments about capable abilities, and assuming omnipotence with respect to intellectual currency.

Professional success for a woman is not independent of a masculine gaze, starting with the assumption that emotional connections with other women are not ideal for a workplace setting because they may effect a competitive disadvantage.

If you are fortunate enough, you may find a workplace where other women are noncompetitive, but chances are if you have been working for any length of time you have encountered the type of woman that I am about to describe.

During my tenure at a historically black university (HBCU) I was keenly aware of the masculine influence on the competitive culture within the department. The most reckless behavior I ever experienced came at the hand of another black woman who acted in verbally abusive ways, reminiscent of some men. Her image of me seemed embedded in male standards with respect to her prejudgments about my physical appearance. The clothes I wore, the language I used, and even my interaction with male students were constantly scrutinized by her. She once stated that she was an advocate for black women. Perhaps this may have been the case with respect to scholarship production, but it certainly did not appear to be reflective of her behavior toward me. I am not suggesting that she was a fraud, but perhaps she was more of an advocate for black women who fit the ideals or standards that she believed to be most like her. This begs two questions. First, how many of us get the same *do's and don'ts* list, and second, perhaps in addition to not tearing down black men, we should be taught to not tear down another black woman in public or in private. Her personal attacks left me feeling victimized. There were a few times that I began to question myself, which is a primary indicator of manufacturing a vulnerability. Unfortunately, this is not all that uncommon for intrarace or intragender professional relationships, which can be attributed to that fact that there are simply not enough seats at the table for capable women. Even when moving beyond my personal feelings, I suspect that the woman I encountered envisioned other black women as threats and not allies.

Her inability to move beyond her professional and perhaps even personal insecurities created a hostile work environment. Professionally, perhaps she felt challenged by an equally disciplined scholar and teacher. Personally, perhaps she couldn't help but react to the complexities of using her female gaze to assume what a masculine gaze would see in me and therefore, came away with the need to compete for male attention. Let me be clear: I was there for reasons of scholarly, teaching, and research growth, the areas that warrant successful tenure track candidacy. The last thing on my mind was how I would look in the presence of male colleagues. This black woman, who in many ways is similarly circumstanced in regard to being black, female, and feminine in a masculine-dominated department, was a bully, and I became the victim. As in a playground setting, where noncombatants are voyeurs, other academicians stood in silence. I suspect they were attempting to remain neutral; however, that silence seemed to represent an endorsement symbolizing the need for social cannibalism between black women. Moreover, her behavior affirmed the legitimacy of masculinity as primary.

Now comes the part that I initially questioned myself about, concerning how much I should disclose. Part of me hates to move forward, for it may come across as character assassination; however, if it were that, I would disclose the school and department and identify this woman. I move on for the sake of autoethnography, as this is information is reflective of how aggressive tactics (primarily an ingredient of masculine socialization) became a source of victimization and infected the atmosphere of education such that grade assignment was less about in-class performance than about professor-to-student alliances.

A devastating casualty of this woman's performance package was her lack of professionalism in failing to withhold personal feelings for the benefit of promoting a positive educational environment for the students. I witnessed academic integrity violations in the form of her turning students against me in exchange for favorable grades. A lesser person would have sought revenge. When you are in the cycle of oppression oftentimes you plot and scheme on how to oppress the person who is adamantly opposing you. Another *do* that is learned over the years and is only taught based on the path in life you take is to always take the higher road. The opportunity to relocate to an environment designed to promote a positive experience for me, with excellent growth potential, and that will prove beneficial to an academic career came my way. I enthusiastically applied and was hired. I am now working at a collegial predominantly white institution where my blackness may illicit different meanings but so far has not collided with my femininity in a way that it had at an HBCU. My HBCU experience taught me that gendered relations influenced by gender norming inherently yield intrasexism that is damaging.

This rather personal workplace disclosure was not an easy contribution. For the experience was extremely disappointing in that it happened at an HBCU, in a department that is supposed to be nurturing, with a black female, supposedly an ally, who actually bullied me while others stood by and did absolutely nothing. The aftermath is simple for me. I got out! Consequently, I am careful not to dismantle the realities of other black women and careful not become a bullying agent, victimizing another black woman or anybody else for that matter for purposes of manufactured personal security.

Discussion: The Call for Black Femininity May Be Similar to Black Masculinity

A black woman should be strong and not be moved by emotion, especially in professional environments. A black woman should separate herself from all other aspects of her life to be successful and only mention them when they can be used as a social or political positive. Avoid the appearance of being moved to anger, except in defense of loved ones. Given she holds a central focus as being a sexual object, which further objectifies her femininity, her social life should be a negotiation combining characteristics of jezebel and mammy. The street vernacular identifies this call to black femininity as a lady in the streets but a freak between the sheets. Her femininity should not be strong enough to rival black masculinity (Jean & Feagin, 1998).

Media are one of the largest influences of our cultural expectations. Adding social media to the equation has further elevated that influence. If media were used as simple entertainment, then the portrayal of black women would not be an issue. Unfortunately, what people see as fantasy becomes reality. During the eight years of the Obama presidency, the media were infatuated if not obsessed with the body image and facial expressions of First Lady Michelle Obama. This type of microscopic examination of black women is not unusual. In the beginning of the Obama's term many described her as robust. This narrative softened over time to a degree. Without asking (whoever really asks a black woman who she is or wants to be), she was assigned two primary labels: sapphire and the angry black woman. It was not anything that First Lady Obama could have done to avoid this title because race and gender norming has such predictive power and cultural transcendence that it can be defined as a legacy.

Additionally, the rise of reality television has fueled negative narratives of black women. The routine activities of our lives seem contingent upon cultural narratives that have morphed into codes of conduct. I am thoroughly embarrassed every time I watch any show where similarly circumstanced blacks are combatants. They are constantly aiming to dismantle the security of one another without awareness of the patriarchal cultural regalia that has contextualized our social battles. Black masculinity and black femininity are at odds, causing troublesome relationship dynamics; black femininity, when using a black masculine lens, ensures female-to-female victimization.

Generally speaking, blacks benefit from generational advice from our elders. It could very well be that generational gender roles are entrenched in traditional expectations where emphasis is placed on stability and strength for men and relative submission for women. Still, out of the three major influences on masculine and feminine narratives, I am less concerned about what is passed down from our elders, given they have our best interests at heart. Life is best understood and taught through experience; therefore, I gravitate toward the wisdom of elders. As for me, I will be inclined to teach that negotiating desired success should be guided by a respect for interpersonal freedoms and a moral compass that breeds integrity. Additionally, I will proudly offer advice that encourages disowning expectations, and decline to obey rules that impede personal growth. Instead, we should engage in transformative behaviors that produce successful life course outcomes.

Black women have a unique legacy, and all of that legacy reflects my intimate reality. This chapter has been a mixture of straightforward reporting of social facts and personal disclosures.

All the while, I am reflecting and abiding in a spiritually harmonious love affair that comes with motherhood. I sit here blessed with the condition of being pregnant with a daughter! I am slightly troubled with filtering my academic thoughts with my social ones. Do I raise her to be a postmodern, strong black woman or do I raise her to be gentle and submissive, which is a reflection of the gender norming that I received? I do not yet know the answer because postmodern strength, gentleness, and submission may not be mutually exclusive but rather fluidly inclusive of one another. I do know that I will instill in my daughter a definitive identity, one that speaks to her interpersonal growth and her intimate energy. I am aware of the vestiges related to black femininity, and I believe I possess the appropriate skill set and love necessary to deliver these honorable messages to my daughter.

Conclusion: The Aftermath

I have learned that people are okay with you as long as you are faithful to the place they prescribe. I believe that it is the duty of blacks to dismantle the master narrative that subjugates, complicates, and fosters relationship troubles among black males and females. Repositioning ourselves requires political, economic, educational, social, cultural, and spiritual solidarity that includes a strong oppositional gaze and counterdeclaration that is advantageous for image reconstruction and cultural codes (Coleman, 2011; Collins, 2014; Cooper, 2014). It is a social fact that personhood narratives develop social biographies; therefore, blacks are thoroughly positioned to rebuff cultural codes that negates dignity and humanity. Stated another way, blacks have the power to decline assimilation and numerical integration in favor of forcing full integration. Only full integration confirms equitable value.

Affirming equitable value bridges the divide between black masculinity and black femininity in a manner that promotes progressive social justice. Unification between black males and females is fundamental to social justice.

This chapter is woven into my personal social fabric. It's the result of an insider's perspective. I am black, I am a woman, I am an expecting mother, I am an academic and a feminist who exists in a complex world principled by patriarchal norms and rules of engagement. I believe that writing with an autoethnographic edge, like journaling, is a form of liberation (Grayson, 2005). The difficult disclosures revealing personal victimization at the hands of a black woman in an HBCU environment could have been avoided, and yet the researcher in me was able to frame these personal experiences as important social facts about the pitfalls of femininity when masculinity is the primary gaze and when masculinity is performed by black women. Black masculinity is not a virus, it's not an infection or a social hazard, but it is an essentially strong core set of traits that must be understood as vulnerable to exploitation and corruption. This exploitation and corruption have to be rooted out or at least treated before they become an ingredient of black femininity. The critique of femininity in the light of masculinity could theoretically be problematic, especially for a self-proclaimed black feminist. Still this contribution is relevant for understanding the historical wholeness of black women.

■ References

Anderson, E. (1990). *Streetwise: Race, class, and change in an urban community*. Chicago: University of Chicago Press.

———. (1999). *Code of the street*. New York: Norton.

Baars, M. (2009). Marriage in black and white: Women's support for law against interracial marriage, 1972–2000. *Intersections 10*(1), 219–38.

Baldwin, D. L. (1999). Black empires, white desires: The spatial politics of identity in the age of hip hop. *Black Renaissance 2*(2), 138.

Bell, D. (1992). *Faces at the bottom of the well: The permanence of racism*. New York: Basic Books.

Benedict, R. (1934). *Patterns of culture.* New York: First Mariner Books.

Bogle, D. (2001). *Toms, coons, mulattoes, mammies & bucks: An interpretive history of blacks in American films.* New York: Continuum.

By, M. C. (1991). Female rappers sing of smut and spice and nothing nice—they make it in men's world by being rude and nasty especially to each other. *Wall Street Journal*, April 11.

Carby, H. (1987). *Reconstructing womanhood: The emergence of the Afro-American woman novelist.* New York: Oxford University Press.

Carter, D. (2008). Achievement as resistance: The development of a critical race achievement ideology among black achievers. *Harvard Educational Review 78*(3), 466–569.

Carter-Punyanunt, N. (2008). The perceived realism of African-American portrayals in television. *Howard Journal of Communications 19*, 241–57.

Cleaver, E. (1968). *Soul on ice.* New York: Random House.

Coleman, R. (2011). "Roll up your sleeves!" Black women, black feminism in feminist media studies. *Feminist Media Studies 11*(1) doi:10.1080/14680777.2011.53723.

Collins, P. H. (1989). The social construction of black feminist thought. *Signs 14*(4): 745–73.

———. (2000). *Black feminist thought: Knowledge, consciousness, and the politics of empowerment.* 2nd ed. New York: Routledge.

———. (2005). *Black sexual politics: African Americans, gender, and the new racism.* New York: Routledge.

Cooper, B. (2014). Does anyone care about black women? *Meridians 12*(2), 153–55, 225.

Cureton, S., & Wilson, C. T. (2012). The deceptive black knight campaign: Clique loyalty and sexual conquest. *Journal of Black Masculinity 2*(3), 1–24.

Delgado, R., & Stefancic, J. (2001). *Critical race theory: An introduction.* New York: New York University Press.

Dyson, M. E. (1996). *Race rules: Navigating the color line.* New York: Vintage Books.

Eveland, W. P. (2003). A mix of attributes approach to the study of media effects and new communication technologies. *Journal of Communication 53*, 395–410.

Fleetwood, N. R. (2012). The case of Rihanna: Erotic violence and black female desire. *African American Review 45*(3), 419–35.

Ford, K. A. (2006). *Masculinity, femininity, appearance ideals, and the black body: Developing a positive raced and gendered bodily sense of self.* Doctoral dissertation, University of Michigan.

Griffith, D. M., & Cornish, E. K. (2018). "What defines a man?": Perspectives of African American men on the components and consequences of manhood. *Psychology of Men & Masculinity 19*(1), 78–88. http://dx.doi.org/10.1037/men0000083.

Hesse-Biber, S. N. (2007). Exploring the interconnections of epistemology, methodology, and method. In S. N. Hesse-Biber (ed.), *Handbook of feminist research theory and practice* (pp. 1–26). Thousand Oaks, CA: Sage.

Hobbs, D. (2001). Ethnography and the study of deviance. In P. Atkinson, A. Coffey, D. Delamont, J. Lofland, & L. Lofland (eds.), *Handbook of ethnography* (pp. 204–19). Thousand Oaks, CA: Sage.

hooks, b. (1994). *Teaching to transgress: Education as the practice of freedom.* New York: Routledge.

———. (2004). *We real cool: Black men and masculinity.* New York: Routledge.

Howard, J. (1996). *Hallelujah!* Transformation in film. *African American Review 30*(3), 441–51.

Hull, G., Bell-Scott, P., & Smith, B. (1982). *All the women are white, all the men are black, but some of us are brave: Black women's studies.* New York: Feminist Press at the City University of New York.

Hunter, M. (2005). *Race, gender, and the politics of skin tone.* New York: Routledge

Jean, Y., & Feagin, J. (1998). *Double burden: Black women and everyday racism.* Armonk, NY: M.E. Sharpe.

Joinson, A. N., & Paine, C. B. (2007). Self-disclosure, privacy and the Internet. In A. Joinson, K. McKenna, T. Postmes, & U.-D. Reips (eds.), *The Oxford Handbook of Internet psychology* (pp. 237–52). New York: Oxford University Press.

Kaba, A. J. (2012). Black Americans and inter-racial marriage: A focus on black women. *Sociological Mind 2*(4), 407–27.

Kulaszewicz, K. (2015). Racism and the media: A textual analysis. Masters of Social Work Clinical Research Papers. St. Catherine University and University of St. Thomas.

Ladson-Billings, G. (2009). "Who you callin' nappy-headed?": A critical race theory look at the construction of black women. *Race, Ethnicity and Education 12*(1), 87–99. doi:10.1080/13613320802651012.

Lawrence, G. (1999). *Our kind of people.* New York: HarperCollins.

Lebron, D., Morrison, L., Ferris, D., Alcantara, A., Cummings, D., Parker, G., & McKay M. (2015). *Facts matter! Black lives matter! The trauma of racism.* New York: McSliver Institute for Poverty Policy and Research.

Morgan, M., & Bennett, D. (2006). Getting off of black women's backs: Love her or leave her alone. *Du Bois Review: Social Science Research on Race 3*(2), 485–502.

Perloff, R. (2014). Social media effects on young women's body image concerns: Theoretical perspectives and an agenda for research, *Sex Roles 71*(11–12), 363–77. doi:10.1007/s11199-014-0384-6.

Perry, T. (2015). Race, marriage, markets, choice, and some reflections on *Is Marriage for White People?*. *Duke Journal of Gender Law and Policy 23*, 99–120.

Peshkin, A. (1988). In search of subjectivity—one's own. *Educational Researcher 17*(7), 17–21. doi:10.3102/0013189x017007017.

Richardson, R. (2007). *Black masculinity and the U.S. South: From Uncle Tom to gangsta.* Athens: University of Georgia Press.

Rothenberg, P. (2002). *White privilege: Essential readings on the other side of racism:* New York: Worth Publishers.

Russell-Cole, K., Wilson, M., & Hall, R. (2013). *The color complex: The politics of skin color in a new millennium.* Rev. ed. New York: Random House.

Solomon, R. P. (1992). *Black resistance in high school: Forging a separatist culture.* Albany: State University of New York Press.

St. Jean, Y., & Feagin, J. R. (1998). *Double burden: Black women and everyday racism: Black women and everyday racism.* New York: Routledge.

Staples, R. (1973). *The black woman in America.* Chicago: Nelson-Hall.

Sundar, S. S., & Limperos, A. M. (2013). Uses and grats 2.0: New gratification for new media. *Journal of Broadcasting Electronic Media 57*, 504–25.

Wallace, M. (2007). It's a M-A-N thang: Black male gender role socialization and the performance of masculinity in love relationships. *Journal of Pan African Studies 1*(7), 11–22.

West, C. (2001). *Race matters*. New York: Vintage Books.

West, C. (1995). Mammy, sapphire and jezebel: Historical images of black women and their implications for psychotherapy. *Psychotherapy 32*(3), 458–86.

Woods, V. D., King, N., Hanna, S. M., & Murray, C. (2012). *We ain't crazy! Just coping with a crazy system: Pathways into the black population for eliminating mental health disparities.* California: The California Reducing Disparities Project, African-American Strategic Planning Workgroup.

Black Male Suicide

Inward-Expressed Frustration and Aggression

Kimya N. Dennis

Death by suicide, homicide, or soul murder is still just death, not the winning of a cause but a way to bow out. When black males are unable to move past reactive rage they get caught in the violence, colluding with their own psychic slaughter as well as with the very real deaths that occur when individuals see no alternatives.

Creative alternative ways to live, be, and act will come into being only when there is mass education for critical consciousness—an awakening to the awareness that collectively black male survival requires that they learn to challenge patriarchal notions of manhood, that they claim nonviolence as the only progressive stance to take in a world where all life is threatened by patriarchal imperialist war.

—bell hooks, *We Real Cool: Black Men and Masculinity*

Residency in permanent underclass communities presents a host of challenges that work to impede the progress of far too many black males. Permanent underclass communities beset by social disorganization, social decline, economic challenges, opportunity blockages, resource strain, social regulation, abuses and brutality by the legal agents of social control, and dysfunctional family dynamics yield alternative social adaptations that prove troublesome for status-seeking black males. The dominant narrative concerning black males seeking status, respect, and some level of success is that they will more often than not invest in criminogenic opportunities and a subculture of violence to transcend or offset institutional rejection and failures. While conversations about black males' criminality seem to take center stage, especially when dealing with homicide and gangsterism, there is an apparent degree of silence about black males who die by suicide. The author is in agreement with researchers who contend that black males engaging in outward or inward violence are just as much a private problem as a community trouble (Anderson, 1990, 1999; Dyson, 1996; Pyke, 2010; Stewart, Schreck & Simons, 2006; Tucker, 1968; West, 2001; Wilson, 1987; Hunter, 1994; Wilson, 1996, 2009). Suicide may be a taboo subject for black communities; however, suicide is occurring frequently enough to warrant serious examination. Hence, this research attempts to shed some insight about the macro- and micro-level factors that influence decisions to engage in self-harm.

This chapter is an important contribution to this Handbook because we already understand suicide to be correlated with mental challenges, developmental issues, and all things deemed innately problematic; however, what if suicide, specifically black male suicide, has just as much to do with perceptions of social injustice? Would it not be prudent to understand how institutions function to pose hardships on black males, causing them to carry out suicide?

Black Masculinity: The Outward Display of Violence versus Engaging in Kill-Self Mode

While definitions and variations in manhood and masculinity can be debated, both are often established through mainstream culture. Black masculinity influences, and is influenced by, self-identity, social interactions, and social expectations. Black boys and black men are taught to be strong, assertive, and unemotional across most experiences and circumstances, even in instances where they are subjected to negative life experiences. Men across races and ethnicities, cultures, and languages are similarly socialized to be economic providers, have a dominant presence in social and cultural institutions, and most certainly be head of their respective households. All of this is contingent upon one's ability to seize and maintain the necessary resources and status to make such expectations a reality. In other words, successful assimilation into the mainstream, seizing opportunities to improve life chances and life course outcomes, is a definitive measure of manhood (Black Mental Health Alliance, 2014; Calloway, 2006; Smith, Allen, & Danley, 2007; Suicide Prevention Resource Center, 2013).

Black boys and black men are expected to conform to these dominant, mainstream power ideologies, definitions, and expressions of masculinity, and failure to do so becomes a declaration of deviance. Negotiating manhood is made easy when there is access to socially acceptable resources and means; however, masculine performances may be altered when the environment is ravaged by social disorganization, social decline, deprivation and depravity, criminogenic vices, a subculture of violence, gangsterism, and lethal predation. Residency in permanent underclass enclaves breeds a different assessment of access to the American dream.

In fact, black males turn away from attempts to gain entry into a system that seems to reject them and instead pursue street respect, which is the primary social currency that governs lifestyle success in permanent underclass areas. Street respect mandates an aura of invincibility and a willingness to engage in violence to resolve conflicts. Street respect requires that black males subscribe to aggressive tendencies and even lethal violence as ways to suppress personal challenges and validate their manhood (Anderson, 1990, 1999; Stewart, Schreck, & Simons,

2006). Respect is often gained (particularly for lower-income black males) by proving they do not have fear engaging in predatory behavior, even if such behavior has lethal outcomes (Anderson, 1999; hooks, 2004; Richardson & St. Vil, 2015; Wilchins & Gilmer, 2016).

Traditionally narrow definitions of masculinity that emphasize self-reliance can impact the mental health of men across race and ethnicity (Wong et al., 2016). They can have an even bigger impact on black males whose self-identity, self-respect, and proving of themselves is highlighted in low-income, at-risk environments with fewer health resources—which provide fewer resources for black males' need for survival and for emotional processing (Richardson & St. Vil, 2015). They can also affect overall mental-emotional health and, potentially, mental illness (Griffith, Gunter, & Watkins, 2012; Wade & Rochlen, 2013). Not only does this illustrate outward-expressed frustration and aggression, in the form of violence toward other people, it can also be an illustration of suicidal and self-harming behaviors in which black males intentionally place themselves at risk of dying. Intentionally placing oneself in deadly circumstances is potentially an example of homicidal tendencies *and* suicidal tendencies, as black males might have a reduced sense of choice in social outcomes and a reduced will to survive, which can be expressed in forms of violence (hooks, 2004).

Stream-of-Violence Theory: The Black Male's Burden

Generally, men have a higher rate of completed suicides than women, whereas women have a higher rate of attempted suicides than men. Black men have a higher rate of death by suicide and homicide than black women (Black Mental Health Alliance, 2014). One central reason for this variance is men are likely to use firearms (over 60 percent), while women are likely to use less lethal methods such as pills. Researchers argue that suicide rates for the fifteen to thirty-four age group may be higher in areas with greater levels of economic and social frustration and weakened social integrative and protective factors (Hamermesh & Soss, 1974; Kowalski, Faupel, & Starr, 1987). Interest in economic and social correlates of black suicide were generated from the reported rise in black suicide rates, which from 1980 to 1993 increased 64 percent (from 12.3 to 20.1 per 100,000) for black males ages fifteen to twenty-four (Burr, Hartman, & Matteson, 1999; Fitzpatrick, Piko, & Miller, 2008). Generally speaking, blacks have lower suicide rates than whites; however, when blacks are under increased stress and tensions due to socioeconomic circumstances, the result is outward displays of aggression or self-harm (Henry & Short, 1954; Whitt, 1994). Younger generations of blacks are more exposed than their predecessors to environments that adversely impact mental and emotional health. Coping with developmental issues, while simultaneously contending with a lack of community nurturing, contributes to psychological distress and, perhaps, contemplating suicide (Joe, 2006; Hamermesh, 1974).

A fundamental tenet of the stream-of-violence theory is that suicide and homicide are different manifestations of the same causal process (Henry & Short, 1954; Unnithan et al., 1994; He et al., 2003; Wu, 2003). Various social forces, particularly economic and status deprivation, can generate frustration, anger, aggression, and impulses toward violence that can be expressed outwardly or inwardly depending on whether individuals can identify an external source for discomfort and problems. People who can identify an external oppressor have a tendency to express outward violence, usually in the form of homicide. The stream-of-violence argument does not assume externally directed violent impulses will automatically be directed toward identifiable oppressors. External oppressors that are powerful or threatening may be inaccessible, and able to respond or retaliate (Bernard, 1990). For this reason, people who are aggrieved will choose more visible and accessible targets for which there should be fewer repercussions. Based on social interactions and social routines, members of one's own social and racial and ethnic group are more likely to be the victim of such external violence.

It logically follows that black males should have lower suicides in counties with few black political officeholders or where few blacks occupy high-status positions. That is because in such counties young black males can identify an external, oppressive source, such as racial discrimination, and to attribute to these sources their economic problems. In such instances, any emerging violent impulses generated by economic deprivation will tend to be externally directed, in which case death might be linked to homicide rather than suicide.

For example, civil rights legislation was successful in increasing opportunities to generate an upwardly mobile black middle class (South, 1984; Wilson, 1987). A significant portion of blacks positioned to seize upon opportunities to improve their life chances prompted many to move to the suburbs (Krivo & Peterson, 1996; Peterson & Krivo, 1993; Sampson, 1987).

Black flight contributed to social isolation and a sense of abandonment for blacks left behind (Fernquist, 2004; Joe, 2006; Rockett, Samora, & Coben, 2006). Abandoned blacks stuck in unsettled communities probably experienced increased homicide due to a combination of an inability to lash out against an imagined discriminatory agent, concentrated misery, and proximity of like-circumstanced individuals. Discussion about homicide is offered to satisfy the logical extension of the stream-of-violence theory; however, exploring the predictive value of this theory with respect to homicide as an outward masculine performance is beyond the scope of this research.

The Problem to Be Explored: A Research Note on Correlates of Suicide

This research concerns suicide as an inward form of masculine self-harm. Suicide rates for blacks could be affected when blacks cannot identify an external oppressor, and allow the nihilistic quality of self-hate and personal blame to consume their personal outlook. This project explores the assumption derived from the stream-of-violence theory that macro-level forces related to empowerment, employment visibility, and socioeconomic status will impact black suicide rates.

For purposes of this research black elected officials and blacks in professional and managerial occupations are measures of black empowerment and socioeconomic status. The assertion in this study is that in counties with low percentages of black elected officials and blacks in professional and managerial occupations, black males will more often find external sources and reasons to explain their economic deprivation and will not blame themselves for their plight. Hence, there will be lower levels of suicide among young black males.

The perceived absence of black elected officials and the apparent low visibility of blacks in professional and managerial positions perhaps fosters impressions that mainstream institutions are biased against blacks in general, thereby negating self-harming behaviors. In other words, the evidence of lacking political empowerment coupled with the absence of perceived tangible employment that improves socioeconomic status removes personal blame from personal failures. The hypothesis under investigation is the following: Black empowerment increases instances of black male suicide in counties with high levels of deprivation.

Data and Methods

Data are extracted from the National Vital Statistics Center for Disease Control Mortality Statistics, the Joint Center for Political and Economic Research, and the US Census Bureau Population and Housing Statistics and Census of Government for all U.S. counties with at least 5 percent black residents in 1999, 2000, 2001, and 2002. Complete data are available for 1,134 US counties. This research examines counties with populations greater than 100,000 (>100K; $N = 314$).

In addition to controlling for population bases for the age-, sex-, and race-specific models, suicide data (dependent variable) were retrieved from the National Vital Statistics Center for Disease Control Mortality Statistics. Despite increases in suicide, suicide is a relatively rare event (Center for Disease Control and Prevention, 2014). Hence, using four-year totals increases the suicide counts of sparsely populated counties and increases the counties in the analyses for which nonzero suicide data are available. The summed suicide instances for counties is represented by (Σ BM suicides for ages fifteen to thirty-four from 1999 to 2002).

There are 314 counties with populations greater than 100,000. The highest number of young black male suicides is 130, with an average of 9 suicides among these larger counties from 1999 to 2002.

Black Empowerment and Black Socioeconomic Status Attainment

Black empowerment and black socioeconomic status attainment are measured in this study using (1) the percentage of black elected municipal, judicial, and law enforcement officials, derived from Joint Center for Political and Economic Research 2000 Black Elected Officials (BEO) data; and (2) the percentage of blacks in managerial and professional occupations (Krivo & Peterson, 1996) derived from 2000 US census. Percentage of black elected officials is used rather than the count of black elected officials to standardize for the size of the black population in each county. The percentage of elected county municipal, judicial, and law enforcement officials who are black is an improvement upon previous measures of black empowerment, which has usually been simply whether the mayor of the city or chief executive officer for a unit is black (Bobo & Gilliam, 1990; Headley, 1995; Emig, Hesse & Fisher, 1996). In the present study, larger counties have an average percentage of blacks in professional and managerial occupations of approximately 14 percent; however, the average percentage of black elected officials is about 7 percent for counties included in this research. It is important to note that there are counties with zero black elected officials, and the minimum percentage of blacks in professional and managerial occupations is 4.2. The maximum value of black elected officials is 170 (an average of 7 per county) and the maximum value of the percentage of blacks in professional and managerial occupations is 36 percent (an average value of 14 per county).

Modeling the Variables

Henry and Short (1954) explained variations in suicide rates relative to homicide rates among low-status and high-status groups. They found suicide and homicide are inversely related and both respond to frustration, as measured by unemployment rates. Unnithan and colleagues (1994) revised the attribution theory and incorporated the social psychology of perceived control over one's circumstances and internal or external attribution of causality. Their findings indicated an inverse relationship between suicide and homicide, a positive relationship between homicide and income inequality, and a positive relationship between suicide and economic development. Many studies suggest that both deprivation and inequality lead the disadvantaged victims to search for sources to attribute causality for their circumstances and often identify those in power (Whitt, 1994).

Therefore, it seems logical to consider deprivation. The Black Deprivation index was measured by: (1) black family median income for persons fifteen years and older with income ($10,000); (2) percentage of black residents twenty-five years and older without a high school diploma (26 percent); (3) percentage of blacks below the federal poverty line (24 percent); and (4) the 2000 Gini coefficient for income inequality (0.439).

Size of black population is positively correlated with black suicide rates in urban counties. Urban counties with higher percentages of residents who are black have been found to exhibit greater structural disadvantage for blacks, as well as greater disparity between blacks and whites (Kowalsk, Faupel & Starr, 1987; Stack, 1980; Wu, 2003, 2004). The average black population for the 314 counties in this research is 82,426, with black males between the ages of fifteen and thirty-four representing an average just above 57,000 across counties.

The measure of southern-born residents is derived from the 2000 US census on the birthplace of county residents. The southern region is controlled because blacks' community ties and strongly held social and religious beliefs are often considered to be protective factors that are more pronounced in the South than in the North (Warshauer & Monk, 1978; Willis, 2003; Wingate et al., 2005).

A measure for suicide by firearms (approximately 55 percent) was included because evidence suggests that suicides with a firearm are a proxy for firearm availability (Joey, 2006; Kaplan &

Geling, 1998; Kleck, 2004; Krug, Powell, & Dahlberg, 1998). Data for this variable were derived from the National Vital Statistics for 1999–2002, based on the total county population.

One significant social artifact associated with using county data is that there is no clearly defined measure for how people self-identify with respect to gender other than predetermined gender ascriptions. Hence, this analysis does not contain measures of masculinity, manhood, and overall gender self-identity. Instead, this is a presumed component of gender identity and self-identity for the sample of black males.

Results

The data supports the general social fact that a larger population of black males between the ages of fifteen and thirty-four (that average across 314 counties is approximately 57,000) contributes to more instances of suicides. In other words, counties nearing the average population of 57,000 black males fifteen to thirty-four were responsible for higher numbers of suicide. An objective of the present study is to examine the extent to which the effect of deprivation on suicide varies by black political representation and black occupational status attainment. Eight OLS regression models were estimated separately for suicide counts for black males ages fifteen to thirty-four.

Each set of models was estimated for counties with less than or equal to 100,000 population (≤100K, where the number is 787 counties); however this research focuses on counties with greater than 100,000 population (>100K, $N = 314$). Of the eight models, the results of this study focus on the complete model, Model 8, and are illustrated in the table 1.

Model 8, where all of the variables have been entered, explains approximately 88 percent of the variance in young black male suicide. The explained variance in this full model is lower than previous models and greater than the baseline Model 1 (0.873) by less than 1 percent. Thus, all of the variables added in the models beyond the population base add little to the predictive power of the analysis. Moreover, in Model 5c there is evidence that the percentage of black elected officials has a reduced effect (–0.010*) on young black male suicide with higher percentages of blacks in professional and managerial occupations in a county. However, that effect disappears in the other models. Again, this is only small support for the stream-of-violence theory as partially investigated by the hypothesis *Black empowerment increases instances of black male suicide in counties with high levels of deprivation.*

Still, the data indicate consistent significant predictability across models, particularly for Black Elected Officials from Model 4 through Model 8. There is a steady increase in predictive value across all models. Black Elected Officials ranges from predicting 6.9 percent to 9.6 percent of variance in black male suicide in Model 4 through Model 6. The predictive value of Black Elected Officials increases in Model 7 and Model 8. Black Elected Officials predicts 12.3 percent of black male suicide when Total Southern is controlled in Model 7, and decreases to predicting 11.6 percent of black male suicide when Suicide with Firearm is controlled in Model 8.

This can also be substantively significant as blacks in elected offices can have decision-making

Table 1. Unstandardized (and Standardized) Regression Coefficients for Black Males Ages 15 to 34 Suicide Counts for Counties with Populations Greater than 100,000 (>100K) (N = 314)

	MODEL 1	MODEL 2	MODEL 3	MODEL 4	MODEL 5A	MODEL 5B	MODEL 5C	MODEL 5D	MODEL 6	MODEL 7	MODEL 8
Constant	8.197	8.197	8.197	8.197	8.069	8.174	8.188	8.084	8.089	7.991	8.010
Demographic Control Black males 15–34	0.153*	0.152*	0.153*	0.148*	0.148*	0.148*	0.148*	0.148*	0.148*	0.129*[a1]	0.129*[a2]
Production and Direction	(0.934)	(0.925)	(0.934)	(0.901)	(0.901)	(0.902)	(0.904)	(0.903)	(0.900)	(0.783)	(0.785)
Black Deprivation		0.946*	0.608	0.215	0.152	0.224	0.126	0.113	−0.124	−0.236	−0.171
		(0.041)	(0.027)	(0.009)	(0.007)	(0.010)	(0.006)	(0.005)	(−0.005)	(−0.011)	(−0.008)
Black Occupation			−0.071	−0.068	−0.072	−0.076	−0.085**	−0.083	−0.056	−0.098	−0.074
			(−0.036)	(−0.035)	(−0.037)	(−0.038)	(−0.043)	(−0.042)	(−0.028)	(−0.051)	(−0.038)
Black Elected Officials				0.093*	0.069*	0.093*	0.096*	0.076*	0.079*	0.123*	0.116*
Interaction Effects				(0,081)	(0.061)	(0.081)	(0.084)	(0.066)	(0.069)	(0.110)	(0.103)
Black depriv.*BEO					0.112*			0.090	0.089	0.114*	0.112*
					(0.054)			(0.043)	(0.042)	(0.056)	(0.055)
Black depriv.*Blackoccup deprivation*Blackoccup						−0.030		−0.007	−0.002	−0.083	−0.058
						(−0.007)		(−0.002)	(0.000)	(−0.021)	(−0.015)
Blackoccup*BEO							−0.010*	−0.006	−0.006	−0.001	−0.001
Economic and Cultural Controls							(−0.041)	(−0.025)	(0.024)	(−0.006)	(−0.005)
Black Unemployment									0.099	0.071	0.087
									(0.031)	(0.023)	(0.028)
Total Southern										0.004*[a1]	0.004*[a2]
										(0.127)	(0.127)
Suicide with Firearm											0.016
											(0.021)
AdjR2	0.873	0.874	0.875	0.879	0.881	0.879	0.880	0.881	0.881	0.879	0.878

[a1] Variance inflations for Black male 15–34 population and southern born 4,762 and 4,136, respectively.
[a2] Variance inflations for Black male 15–34 population and southern born 4,789 and 4,136, respectively.
*p < 0.05, **p < 0.10.

power, which can serve as a sign that there is an opportunity for black male liberation and empowerment. At least this can be a reasonable working narrative that impacts behavioral outcomes, even if there is no proven effect on opportunities for black males and black socio-economic status.

It is important to note that the interaction is also statistically significant in Model 5a (as the first interaction controlling for demographics and measures of production and direction) and Model 7 (with all interaction effects and two of the economic and cultural measures). This is not substantively different from the value of the interaction in the full model with the addition of Suicide by Firearm. The interaction explains 11.2 percent variance in black male suicide in Model 5a, 11.4 percent in Model 7, and 11.2 percent in Model 8. This interaction does not substantially increase in explaining variance in black male suicide when additional interactions and economic and cultural measures are added to the models.

Discussion

The present study examines whether black male suicide is an inwardly aggressive adaptation when contending with deprivation in locales where blacks have relative political and occupational status. Black males are hypothesized to respond to black deprivation through suicide and suicidal self-harm when black occupational prestige and black political representation make black males less likely to be able to attribute failures to social inequities. Unable to place the blame of personal failures on outside social forces, black males may internalize their frustrations, misery, and despair, leading to suicide. Stream-of-violence theory provided a sound theoretical lens to examine the impact of sociocultural factors on black male suicide.

It is perhaps the case that black males desire to control their destinies, and when there are obvious blockages where hopelessness gains traction, the result could be suicide. Whether black males blame themselves or blame social injustice for their life conditions, black males in counties with black deprivation might conclude that black elected officials represent a symbol of increased social justice. However, if black elected officials are not found to reduce black deprivation in their respective counties, some black males may respond with aggression and violence to force a personalized version of social justice. This is a definitive and transcending way to express masculinity and manhood, and to establish individual control over deprived environments.

According to Bonilla-Silva and Dietrich (2011), some black elected officials and some blacks with sociopolitical power do not initially (or ever) view themselves as being at the forefront of addressing racial and ethnic socioeconomic inequalities.

Blacks living in counties with greater representation of blacks in positions of political and socioeconomic status might become silenced, less able to articulate and combat complex inequalities. Blacks in positions of power may be a false proxy for social mobility, but still function to suppress voices of racial discontent (Bonilla-Silva & Ray, 2009). The absence of a significant effect on black male suicide can be explained by the overwhelming influence of deprivation and inequality on black males. Such an overwhelming influence can supersede the impact of blacks in political and occupational realms (Fernquist & Cai, 2000). The political visibility of blacks may indeed have a low impact on the socioeconomic conditions of blacks and whites (Bobo & Gilliam, 1990; Headley, 1985; Bositis, 2000; & Conley & Yeung, 2005). For instance, while some evidence suggests that black political representation can positively shape the perceptions of race and the voting practices of some whites, other whites may choose to ignore local politics in areas with high black political representation. Blacks, too, can choose not to pay attention to local politics and be unresponsive to the prevalence of black elected officials (Hajnal, 2001). Furthermore, evidence suggests that black occupational status attainment may be met with greater discriminatory and exclusionary responses from whites, thereby enhancing the influence of deprivation and inequality (Cole & Omari, 2003; Gibbs & Martin, 1964). This may, ironically, increase black empowerment and socioeconomic status attainment but not reduce blacks' identification of external sources as key to their oppression. Moreover, conditions of deprivation and inequality may be attributed to ineffective elected officials, even if those elected officials are black, therefore avoiding the self-attribution that might lead to increased suicide among blacks (Hajnal, 2001; Harris, Sinclair-Chapman, & McKenzie, 2005; Wadsworth & Kubrin, 2004).

It is therefore reasonable to conclude that black political representation and black occupational status do not automatically signal universal awareness of black empowerment. These are somewhat generic assumptions that need exploration, which was the goal of this research.

Generally speaking, there may be conditions unique to urban county residency that are consistent with the suicide component of the stream-of-violence theory. There is an impact of having black elected officials, which was statistically significant across models (refer to table 1, where there is evidence of the highest value in Model 7 and a slight decrease in value in Model 8). The percentage of black elected officials has a conditioning effect on the relationship between deprivation and black male suicides in larger counties; and suicide appears to increase in high-deprivation counties where black elected officials have a presence. However, the interaction between deprivation and blacks in higher-ranking occupations was not significant (refer to table 1, black depriv*blackoccup Models, 5b, 5d, 6, 7, and 8). This is contrary to the hypothesis and indicates that the relationship between deprivation and black male suicide is not moderated by, and does not vary based on, the percentage of blacks in professional and managerial occupations in larger counties. It appears that *either* black elected officials *or* blacks in professional and managerial occupations have a conditioning effect on the deprivation-suicide relationship for most of the analyses, but not *both* black elected officials *and* blacks in professional and managerial occupations.

There are a number of factors related to suicide and alternative explanations for black male suicide. Black males in low-income areas may be more vulnerable to stressors and more susceptible to a number of factors related to suicide and suicidal self-harm. The lethal violence process is complex, and scholars have examined a number of potential explanations for suicide, such as mental health, psychological stress, and racial microaggression (Nadal et al., 2014; Wing et al., 2007); social status and social integration; and a number of economic correlates

(Fitzpatrick, Piko, & Miller, 2008; Spann et al., 2006). Moreover, blacks are potentially at a disadvantage regarding access to medical resources (Fitzpatrick, Piko, & Miller, 2008; Kaslow et al., 2005; Spann et al., 2006). The lack of access to defense tactics and protective factors during times of mounting stressors and frustrations may explain an increase in suicide among black males regardless of black empowerment (Wingate et al., 2005).

A Note on Manliness: Processing and Negotiating Masculinity and Manhood

One limitation of this study is that there were no direct measures of masculinity and manhood; instead they were presumed more than measured as a self-proclamation identity variable. As covered in previous research, manhood and masculinity are more often than not restricted to status attainment. Restricting manhood and masculinity to negotiating status in a stratified society will ultimately yield achievement gaps, resulting in anger and frustration. Whenever there are no credible avenues to counter failure, then frustrations become vulnerabilities to criminogenic opportunities and participation in subcultures, which can lead to self-harm and deviant, criminal, and violent behaviors.

Perhaps the reason why the black community has a tendency to be dismissive of suicide is related to having to process the intricacies of mental health. Psychodynamic complexities and emotional difficulties that can lead to negative mental-emotional health conditions include apprehension, anxiety, fear, frustration, and anger (Griffith, Gunter, & Watkins 2012; Wade & Rochlen 2013; Wilchins & Gilmer, 2016).

Underlying mental disturbances and processing conflicts can manifest as harmful behaviors, particularly in occupational, educational, family, and social network environments where blacks feel isolated, invalidated, judged, ignored, or rejected (Jacobs et al., 2006; Nadal et al., 2014; Torres-Harding, Andrade, & Romero-Diaz, 2012; Torres-Harding & Turner, 2015).

A counter to the emotional stress associated with failed attempts at status attainment or successful participation in mainstream institutions is to begin socializing young black males using a broader definition of manliness, masculinity, and manhood (hooks, 2004; Griffith, Gunter, & Watkins, 2012; Hunter & Davis, 1994; Schrock & Schwalbe, 2009; Wilchins & Gilmer, 2016). Black males need stronger cultural messages clarifying manhood as a rite of passage, manliness as functional adaptations to the situational-circumstances at hand, and masculinity as performance based but inclusive of reflective individual efforts that are flexible in seeking mental-health assistance as a primary coping strategy (Day, 2006; Jacobs et al., 2006; Nadal et al., 2014; Torres-Harding, Andrade, & Romero-Diaz, 2012; Torres-Harding & Turner, 2015).

Perhaps a renewed investment in mental health care that de-emphasizes the power of personal control and highlights accepting various forms of counseling geared toward mental stability would yield healthy responses to mistreatment and inequality that do not result in microaggression, fatigue, anger, and aggression in the form of violence expressed toward oneself and toward other people (Fox & Swatt, 2008, Wade & Rochlen, 2013; Wilchins & Gilmer, 2016; Willis et al., 2002; & Wong et al., 2016).

Conclusions: Protective Factors against Suicide as a Masculine Performance

This project is at best a research note to generate increased attention on black suicide, which seems to be downplayed in lieu of homicide, and dismissed partly due to assumptions made on the basis of race and gender. Within the black community there is an informal belief that suicide and suicidal self-harm only happens to people other than blacks. Religiosity and spirituality play a big role in this notion. While research finds the role of religion and religiosity as protection against negative emotionality and suicide, the issue is unresolved because forms of self-control and religiosity have been studied and discovered to have weak to moderate predictive value for conformity (Gearing & Lizardi, 2009; Welch, Tittle, & Grasmick, 2006). Still other research has found that self-control has an effect on behavior, support, and social integration (Welch et al., 2008). For this reason, a protective measure against suicide can be religiosity and spirituality because black men can be quite traditionalist and religious, particularly in cases where strong bonds have been established (Mattis et al., 2000).

The general disadvantaged position of blacks and the socioeconomic disparity between blacks and whites have persisted despite civil rights legislation (Wilson, 1987; Massey & Denton, 1993; MacLeod, 1995; Joe, 2006). Many suggest that these disadvantages and increased inequality inevitably forced blacks to develop and maintain tight-knit family and community bonds. This enclave mentality affects the potential for suicide in two ways. First, tight-knit social institutions often provide social support for individuals (Burr, Hurtman, & Matteson, 1999; Sampson, 1987; South, 1984; Welch et al., 2008).

Second, the communal component, where black communities are concerned with the general welfare and well-being of its residents, does encourage black males to not yield to the stress and trauma of failed achievements experienced in mainstream society but to focus on measures of success within the context of one's immediate reality (Breed, 1966; MacLeod, 1995). Crediting low suicide rates to reflective rationalized success is consistent with Durkheim's proposition that within resource-strained communities, stronger social integration reduces anomie and perhaps suicide (Burr, Hartman & Matteson, 1999; Durkheim, [1897] 1951).

Finally, for as much as there has been negative attention for those black men who seem to adopt a cool pose, there are some beneficial psychological effects that mediate the negative life experiences of black men. Oftentimes, adopting a cool pose is viewed as negative because it becomes linked to accepting failure with a nonchalant attitude (Majors & Billson, 1992).

However, there is something to be said about adopting a cool pose as a coping strategy for black males who continue to process their reality and attempt to improve their life chances by taking advantage of the resources and opportunities set before them. For social advocates looking to decrease suicide among black men, perhaps there is a need to embrace some level of awareness that black masculinity is about securing status and taking control of one's life. Such awareness should prompt efforts to provide immediate and realistic access to legitimate opportunities to achieve success in a manner that effectively counters reasons to participate in criminogenic enterprises.

Suicide is an emotional choice and certainly leaves speculation among those who never saw it coming. Control and respect are valuable to black males whose manhood and masculinity are grounded in overcoming life-stagnating limits. In conceding the power of personal control over life's circumstances, the one thing a black male can do is control how he dies. To this end, this research offers the possibility that suicide is not necessarily a cop-out but ultimately a last-ditch, fatal attempt to prove manliness.

■ References

Anderson, E. (1990). *Streetwise: Race, class, and change in an urban community.* Chicago: University Press of Chicago.

———. (1999). *Code of the street: Decency, violence and the moral life of the inner city.* New York: Norton.

Bernard, T. (1990). Angry aggression among the "truly disadvantaged." *Criminology 28,* 73–96.

Black Mental Health Alliance. (2014). Souls of black men: African American men discuss mental health. *CommunityVoices.org.*

Bobo, L., & Gilliam, F., Jr. (1990). Race, sociopolitical participation, and black empowerment. *American Political Science Review 84,* 377–93.

Bonilla-Silva, E., & Dietrich, D. (2011). The sweet enchantment of color-blind racism in Obamerica. *Annals of the American Academy of Political and Social Science 634,* 190.

Bonilla-Silva, E., & Ray, V. (2009). When whites love a black leader: Race matters in Obamerica. *Journal of African American Studies 13,* 176–83.

Bositis, D. A. (2000). *Black elected officials: A statistical summary.* Joint Center for Political and Economic Research.

Breed, W. (1966). Suicide, migration, and race: A study of cases in New Orleans. *Journal of Social Issues 22,* 30–43.

Burr, J., Hartman, J. T., & Matteson, D. W. (1999). Black suicide in U.S. metropolitan areas: An examination of the racial inequality and social integration-regulation hypotheses. *Social Forces 77,* 1049–81.

Calloway, N. C. (2006). The mental health of black men: A problem of perception. *Challenge Journal: A Journal of Research on African-American Men, the Journal of the Morehouse Research Institute 12*(1), 55.

———. (2011). *Leading Causes of Death by Age Group, Black Males in the United States.*

———. (2014). Ten leading causes of death. National Vital Statistics System, National Center for Health Statistics.

Cole, E., & Omari, S. (2003). Race, class, and the dilemmas of upward mobility for African Americans. *Journal of Social Issues 59,* 785–802.

Conley, D., & Yeung, W. J. J. (2005). Black-white differences in occupational prestige: Their impact on child development. *American Behavioral Scientist 48,* 1229–49.

Day, K. (2006). Being feared: Masculinity and race in public space. *Environment and Planning A 38,* 569–86.

Durkheim, E. ([1897] 1951). *Suicide*. Trans. J. A. Spaulding & G. Simpson. New York: Free Press.

Dyson, Michael. (1996). *Race rules: Navigating the color line*. New York: Vintage Books.

Emig, A., Hesse, M. B., & Fisher, S. H., III. (1996). Black-white difference in political efficacy, trust, and sociopolitical participation: A critique of the empowerment hypothesis. *Urban Affairs Review 32*, 264–76.

Fernquist, R. M. (2004). Educational attainment and the payoff of education: Black male suicide in the United States, 1947–1998. *Current Research in Social Psychology 9*, 184–93.

Fernquist, R. M., & Cai, J. (2000). African American and white suicide in Kansas City, Missouri, 1995–1997: Individual and aggregate circumstances. *Missouri Electronic Journal of Sociology 1*, 1–13.

Fitzpatrick, K. M, Piko, B. F., & Miller, E. (2008). Suicide ideation and attempts among low-income African American adolescents. *Suicide and Life Threatening Behavior 38*, 552–63.

Fox, J. A., & Swatt, M. L. (2008). The recent surge in homicides involving young black males and guns: Time to reinvest in prevention and crime control. Law and Justice Statistics Program of the American Statistical Association and the Bureau of Justice Statistics.

Gearing, R. E., & Lizardi, D. (2009). Religion and suicide. *Journal of Religion and Health 48*(3), 332–41.

Gibbs, J., & Martin, W. T. (1964). *Status integration and suicide: A sociological study*. Eugene: University of Oregon Books.

Griffith, D. M., Gunter, K., & Watkins, D. C. (2012). Measuring masculinity in research on men of color: Findings and future directions. *American Journal of Public Health 102* (Supp. 2), S187–S194.

Hajnal, Z. (2001). White residents, black incumbents, and a declining racial divide. *American Political Science Review 95*, 603–17.

Hamermesh, D. S. (1974). The economics of black suicide. *Southern Economic Journal 41*(2), 188–99.

Hamermesh, D. S., & Soss, N. M. (1974). An economic theory of suicide. *Journal of Political Economy 82*, 83–98.

Harris, F. C., Sinclair-Chapman, V., & McKenzie, B. D. (2005). Macrodynamics of black political participation in the post-civil rights era. *Journal of Politics 67*, 1143–63.

He, N., Cao, L., Wells, W., & Maguire, E. R. (2003). Forces of production and direction: A test of an expanded model of suicide and homicide. *Homicide Studies 7*, 36–57.

Headley, B. D. (1985). Black political empowerment and urban crime. *Phylon 46*, 193–204.

Henry, A. F., & Short, J. F. (1954). *Suicide and homicide*. New York: Free Press.

hooks, b. (2004). *We real cool: Black men and masculinity*. New York: Routledge.

Hunter, A. G., & Davis, J. E. (1994). Hidden voices of black men: The meaning, structure, and complexity of manhood. *Journal of Black Studies 25*(1), 20–40.

Jacobs, E. A., Rolle, I., Ferrans, C. E., Whitaker, E. E., & Warnecke, R. B. (2006). Understanding African Americans' views of the trustworthiness of physicians. *Journal of General Internal Medicine 21*, 642–47.

Joe, S. (2006). Explaining changes in the patterns of black suicide in the United States from 1981–2002: An age, cohort, and period analysis. *Journal of Black Psychology 32*, 262–84.

Kaplan, M. S., & Geling, O. (1998). Firearm suicides and homicides in the United States: Regional variations and patterns of gun ownership. *Social Science and Medicine 46*, 1227–33.

Kaslow, N., Sherry, A., Bethea, K., Wyckoff, S., Compton, M., Grall Bender, M., Scholl, L., Price Webb, A.,

Kellermann, A., Thompson, N., & Parker, R. (2005). Social risk and protective factors for suicide attempts in low income African American men and women. *Suicide and Life Threatening Behavior 35*, 400–412.

Kleck, G. (2004). Measures of gun ownership levels for macro-level crime and violence research. *Journal of Research in Crime and Delinquency 41*, 3–36.

Kowalski, G. S, Faupel, C. A., & Starr, P. D. (1987). Urbanism and suicide: A study of American counties. *Social Forces 66*, 85–101.

Krivo, L., & Peterson, R. (1996). Extremely disadvantaged neighborhoods and urban crime. *Social Forces 75*, 619–50.

Krug, E. G., Powell, K., & Dahlberg, L. (1998). Firearm-related deaths in the United States and 35 other high and upper middle income countries. *International Epidemiological Association 27*, 214–21.

MacLeod, J. (1995). *Ain't no makin' it: Aspirations and attainment in a low-income neighborhood.* Boulder, CO: Westview Press.

Majors, R., & Billson, J. M. (1992). Cool Pose: *The dilemmas of black manhood in America.* New York: Lexington Books.

Massey, D., & Denton, N. (1993). *American apartheid: Segregation and the making of the underclass.* Cambridge, MA: Harvard University Press.

Mattis, J. S., Jagers, R. J., Hatcher, C. A., Lawhon, G. D, Murphy, E. J., & Murray, Y. F. (2000). Religiosity, volunteerism, and community involvement among African American men: An exploratory analysis. *Journal of Community Psychology 28*(4), 391– 406.

Nadal, K. L., Griffin, K. E., Wong, Y., Hamit, S., & Rasmus, M. (2014). The impact of racial microaggressions on mental health: Counseling implications for clients of color. *Journal of Counseling & Development 92*, 57–66.

Peterson, R., & Krivo, L. (1993). Racial segregation and black urban homicide. *Social Forces 71*, 1001–26.

Pyke, K. (2010). What is internalized racial oppression and why don't we study it? Acknowledging racism's hidden injuries. *Sociological Perspective 53*(4), 551–72.

Richardson, J., & St. Vil, C. (2015). Putting in work: Black male youth joblessness, violence, crime, and the code of the street. *Spectrum 3*(2), 71–98.

Rockett, I. R. H., Samora, J. B., & Coben, J. H. (2006). The black-white suicide paradox: Possible effects of misclassification. *Social Science and Medicine 63*, 2165–75.

Sampson, R. J. (1987). Urban black violence: The effect of male joblessness and family disruption. *American Journal of Sociology 93*, 348–82.

Schrock, D., & Schwalbe, M. (2009). Men, masculinity, and manhood acts. *Annual Review of Sociology 35*, 277–95.

Smith, W. A., Allen, W. R., & Danley, L. L. (2007). "Assume the position . . . you fit the description": Psychosocial experiences and racial battle fatigue among African American male college students. *American Behavioral Scientist 51*(4), 551–78.

South, S. J. (1984). Racial differences in suicide: The effect of economic convergence. *Journal of Social Science Quarterly 65*, 172–80.

Spann, M., Molock, S. D., Barksdale, C., Matlin, S., & Puri, R. (2006). Suicide and African American teenagers: Risk factors and coping mechanisms. *Journal of Suicide and Life Threatening Behavior*

36, 553–68.

Stack, S. (1980). The effects of interstate migration on suicide. *International Journal of Social Psychiatry 26*, 17–26.

Stewart, E., Schreck, C., & Simons, R. (2006). "I ain't gonna let no one disrespect me": Does the code of the street reduce or increase violent victimization among African-American adolescents? *Journal of Research in Crime and Delinquency 43*(4), 427–58.

Suicide Prevention Resource Center. (2013). Suicide among racial/ethnic populations in the U.S.: Blacks. Waltham, MA: Education Development Center.

Torres-Harding, S. R., Andrade, A. L., & Romero Diaz, C. E. (2012). The racial microaggressions scale (RMAS): A new scale to measure experiences of racial microaggressions in people of color. *Cultural Diversity and Ethnic Minority Psychology 18*(2), 153–64.

Torres-Harding, S. R., & Turner, T. (2015). Assessing racial microaggression distress in a diverse sample. *Evaluation and the Health Professions 38*(4), 464–90.

Tucker, S. (1968). *Beyond the burning. Life and death of the ghetto.* New York: Association Press.

Unnithan, N. P., Whitt, H. P., Huff-Corzine, L., & Corzine, J. (1994). Charting the currents of lethal violence. In N. Prabha Unnithan et al. (eds.), *The currents of lethal violence: An integrated model of suicide and homicide* (pp. 161–70). Albany: State University of New York Press.

Wade, J. C., & Rochlen, A. B. (2013). Introduction: Masculinity, identity, and the health and well-being of African American men. *Psychology of Men & Masculinity 14*(1), 1–6.

Wadsworth, T., & Kubrin, C. E. (2004). Structural factors and black interracial homicide: A new examination of the causal process. *Criminology 42*, 647–72.

Warshauer, M. E., & Monk, M. (1978). Problems in suicide statistics for whites and blacks. *American Journal of Public Health 68*, 383–88.

Welch, M. R., Tittle, C. R., & Grasmick, H. G. (2006). Christian religiosity, self-control and social conformity. *Social Forces 84*(3), 1605–23.

Welch, M. R., Tittle, C. R., Yonkoski, J., Meidinger, N., & Grasmick, H. G. (2008). Social integration, self-control, and conformity. *Journal of Quantitative Criminology 24*(1), 73–92.

West, C. (2001). *Race matters.* New York: Vintage Books.

Whitt, H. P. (1994). Old wine in a new wineskin. In N. Prabha Unnithan et al. (eds.), *The currents of lethal violence: An integrated model of suicide and homicide* (pp. 35–51). Albany: State University of New York Press.

Wilchins, R., & Gilmer, M. (2016). Addressing masculine norms to improve life outcomes for young black men: Why we still can't wait. *truechild.org.*

Willis, L. A. (2003). Uncovering the mystery: Factors of African American suicide. *Journal of Suicide and Life Threatening Behavior 33*, 412–29.

Willis, L. A., Coombs, D. W., Cockerham, W. C., & Frison, S. L. (2002). Ready to die: A postmodern interpretation of the increase of African American adolescent male suicide. *Social Science and Medicine 55*, 907–20.

Wilson, W. (1987). *The truly disadvantaged: The inner city, the underclass, and public policy.* Chicago: University of Chicago Press.

———. (1996). *When work disappears: The world of the new urban poor.* New York: Knopf.

————. (2009). *More than just race: Being black and poor in the inner city*. New York: Norton.

Wing, S. D., Capodilupo, C. M., Torino, G. C., Bucceri, J. M., Holder, A. M., Nadal, K. L., & Esquilin, M. (2007). Racial microaggressions in everyday life: Implications for clinical practice. *American Psychologist 62*(4), 271–86.

Wingate, L., Bobadilla, L., Burns, A., Cukrowicz, K., Hernandez, A., Ketterman, R., Minnix, J., Petty, S., Richey, J. A., Sachs-Ericsson, N., Stanley, S., Williams, F., & Joiner, T., (2005). Suicidality in African American men: The roles of southern residence, religiosity, and social support. *Journal of Suicide and Life Threatening Behavior* 35, 615–29.

Wong, Y. J., Ho, M.-H. R., Wang, S.-Y., & Miller, I. S. K. (2016). Meta-analyses of the relationship between conformity to masculine norms and mental health-related outcomes. *Journal of Counseling Psychology, 64*(1), 80–93.

Wu, B. (2003). Testing the stream analogy for lethal violence: A macro study of suicide and homicide. *Western Criminology Review 4*, 215–25.

————. (2004). Testing three competing hypotheses for explaining lethal violence. *Violence and Victims 19*, 399–411.

The Media Assault on the Black Male

Echoes of Public Lynching and Killing the Modern Terror of Jack Johnson

Armondo R. Collins

> The media is a source of titillation, more than information . . . the mission of the media is to produce comfort and primarily sell. The media paints false pictures of the nation and the world. Pictures designed to serve corporate masters, and to make America look good. This "feel good: media approach serves the American delusion of white supremacy.
>
> —Rass Kass, "TV Guide"

A study of Jack Johnson, America's first black heavyweight boxing champion, reveals that mainstream media's dissemination of information and social construction of manhood was historically detrimental to the social health of black masculinity. The past election cycle, where the Electoral College provided President Donald Trump with a decisive victory over Hillary Clinton, was engulfed in a cultural war over the use of the term *superpredator* when describing criminogenic black males. Long before the superpredator became a political talking point, there was the social construction of Jack Johnson, and more importantly a seemingly wholesale consumption of his being a depraved savage intent on inflicting social damage to the sanctity of white womanhood. Jack Johnson was cast as an example of black males' underlying desire to enter into a relationship of some kind with white women. Moreover, Johnson's public image was used by the media to solidify a narrative of black male marginality and criminality.

Johnson's life is a canvas that aids in better understanding the black male human drama as it exists in the midst of systemic oppression—including dismissal of the profound meanings fueling the slaughter of black males by law enforcement agents. This chapter investigates Johnson's exemplary accomplishment in the sport arena and his contribution to revealing this country's adverse stance on black males prior to the civil rights movement. The discourse then moves to investigate whether the negative social constructions about black masculinity can be classified as a race legacy variable impacting modern-day interracial and social injustices. Stated another way, this chapter is seeking an answer to the question, has the social construction of the black male evolved in such a way as to promote equitable humanity, or are black men modern-day Jack Johnson terrors experiencing socially oppressive modern-day lynchings?

On December 26, 1908, Jack Johnson became the first African American man to win the world's heavyweight championship boxing title, defeating champ Tommy Burns. Overnight, he was thrust into the position of a crossover success in the fight business. Like so many other black male superstars after him, Johnson was socially constructed as a larger-than-life, superhuman representative of his entire race. His personal attributes were racially codified and made to stand as authentically true about all black men. Immediately after the fight, he was forced into the media spotlight and turned into a celebrity. If it is the case that the media, as an institutional machine designed for purposes of information sharing and cultural constructions, did deliberately engage in a program to manufacture moral panic and force mass conformity by using Johnson as a vessel to align mainstream society's collective conscience along a continuum of social aversion, then it is a worthy research endeavor to investigate whether Johnson's legacy does serves as a critical framework to engage negative constructions of black masculinity.

In other words, Jack Johnson is an important figure in the history of white America's cultural war against blacks because the white media used his masculinity to indict all African Americans in a manner that arguably has transcended time, effecting a postmodern racial narrative with adverse inter- and intraracial life course outcomes for black males.

For many, Johnson's win proved to blacks and whites alike that he could physically compete on the highest levels of the boxing world. To many, his win also symbolized the potential ability of blacks to successfully compete in arenas where there is a concentrated level of attention, affecting assimilation, social attachments, and encroachments on relationship taboos. The dominating social framework, prior to the civil rights movement, was invested in segregation, or a sense of separate societies with race-specific privileges afforded to whites, the most fundamental of which is security from competition that would cause whites to lose out on life improvement resources, opportunities, and home and public territorial spaces that negated interracial mingling. The last crust of security is violated when there is the perception that family dynamics can be altered because of competition for the attention and affection of women that would be wives and mothers. In short, Jack Johnson's win brought with it unconventional interracial choices that challenged the fundamental tenet (security) of whiteness in America (Alexander, 2010; Rothenberg, 2002; Morgan, 1998; Marable, 1991). It is almost a foregone conclusion that aggressive black masculinity is acceptable when used in competition for purposes of entertainment, and yet Johnson's high-profile sporting victory morphed into strong racial declarations (Alexander, 2010; Rhoden, 2006; West, 2001; Morgan, 1998; Dyson, 1996).

Jack Johnson's Heavyweight Reign, 1908–1915

War has causes and consequences long after wars are over; therefore, during the early 1900s, white America was still recovering from social and cultural divisions that were remnants of the American Civil War (Blattman & Miguel, 2010). To save the fractured union between northern whites and southern whites, our country's media used black men like Jack Johnson to promote white solidarity by identifying a common enemy. Another cornerstone of white fear (the most fundamental one being access to white women) was enhanced by the media's portrayal of blacks as antithetical to white privilege, and economic, employment, educational, cultural, public and housing entitlements. Whites at the top of the information hierarchy (news media executives, writers, etc.) saw it as part of their public duty to paint a picture of blacks as white America's public enemy. With this logic, Jack Johnson was elevated by the news media to superstar status, just to be destroyed. Johnson was a symbolic pawn that represented proof that other black men possessed the same kind of caged fury, and antagonistic behaviors should be suppressed by any means necessary. Johnson's media assassination is arguably similar to contemporary media outlets' ceremonial character assassinations of prominent black public figures, entertainers, and sports' stars (Rhoden, 2006).

Jack Johnson's story offers a very good starting point for investigating the public demise of a talented athlete spearheaded by a segregationist ideology. Johnson's triumphs and disasters were covered by newspapers that not only presented social facts about Johnson's experience, but also opined about his lifestyle decisions in a manner that made Johnson out to be an un-welcome countercultural intruder. Johnson's story shows the direct link between the media rhetoric, information consumption, and responsive group behavior.

This turn of events demonstrates at least two things: (1) that Johnson's public image was engineered and ruined by media members who appeared to be in alignment with ideas pro-moting the superiority of whiteness and the inferiority of blackness, and (2) that the media's assault on Johnson's public image had detrimental effects on black men.

Johnson's brash disrupting of America's racial status quo in certain ways made it necessary to encapsulate his image into a digestible package for whites. It also made it all the easier to label him a villain and use his image as a tool to oppress other blacks (Gilmore, 1973; Fleischer, 1949). Hence, at every turn of Johnson's meteoric rise and fall in the public eye, there is evidence that adverse coverage of Johnson effected a prejudice toward blacks. It logically follows, then, that black masculinity played a part in the reproduction of white racist discourse in that the public construction of black masculinity represented a hauntingly dark silhouette conjuring fear for whites and nonwhites alike (Allen, 1994).

Crime, violence, and sexual misconduct arrest mainstream society's collective conscience, restricting it to blacks' perceived elevated criminality and sexual immorality. This identity is, in part, a construct of the media's representation of black masculine performances as viewed through a white cultural lens whereby Johnson and men like him are a threat to the survival of whiteness. Perhaps the media was culpable because even in some of its most innocuous liberal formats, it still represented an ideological arm of white supremacy in America (Ward, 2004; Dijk, 1991).

Media Spin: Media Bias and Killing Jack Johnson

The public image of black males suffers by way of the common message that blacks are dispro-portionately represented in the criminal justice system. Media infuses the reality that blackness is a proxy for increased criminality and therefore, deserving of heavy-handed social regula-tion. In other words, it seems when media outlets attempt to construct black masculinity, the narrative does not provide enough distance from notions that wrongfully emphasize moral depravity and troublesome behaviors, which fueled Jim Crow ideology and perpetuates a racist public image of black masculinity as monolithic and criminal (Alexander 2010; Wilson, 2009; Welch, 2007; West, 2001; Wilson 1987).

Jack Johnson's heavyweight championship reign was volatile for the black community, which was both attracted and repulsed by his social selectivity. Moreover, members of the black community no doubt were victims of white backlash, manifested by lynching and eco-nomic, employment, cultural and social reprisals. The ultimate problem for race relations is that Jack Johnson's character and black masculinity were allowed to survive as a threat to the sanctity of white safety; therefore, Johnson and black men like him don't have the requisite equitable humanity that would exempt them from harsh and even lethal policing tactics (Al-exander, 2010; Morgan, 1998). The contribution made by American media (inclusive of news and entertainment outlets) was that they did confirm the mood of the country with respect to black males being prone to crime, more than they advanced the idea that crime is reflective of social forces, social conditions, resource opportunities, and community troubles over innate predispositions (Carter & Villaverde, 2014; Keith, 2014).

Johnson's rise and fall have been used as the American media's model for manufacturing a destructive public image of black masculinity (Farr, 1964; Johnson, 1927). Today, this type of manufactured destruction may be partly responsible for black men ending up on the wrong side of the American justice system. This type of forced distancing from humanity seems to impact the apparent disregard for the alarming number of black men shot in the streets by police and vigilantes. The parallels between Johnson's public life and the media's treatment of many of today's black superstars offer clear evidence. It has become a formula. A talented black man is lifted from obscurity to superstardom. The praises for his individual talent are sung throughout the world via American media outlets. As his individual public fame increases, so too does the public's interest in his personal life. Just as it seems to the masses that this black person has escaped the oppression of stereotyped black American life, an information agent appears on the scene with actions made into a scandal that eventually makes that person a vil-lain. Worst of all, the implication of that individual's less than ideal situational circumstances is usually attributed in some way to racial character flaws and depravity. Inevitably, the onetime hero is disgraced as a villain (usually criminal), and taken into consideration by the public in various ways as a prime example of malevolent black masculinity. The implicit nightmare of the American dream is that the self-assertive successful black man is a controversial figure. Jack Johnson's public image was created to show that black men, and black masculinity, appear to be consistently derailed by their investing in lifestyle choices that are reserved for whites (Opportunity Agenda, 2011; Ward, 2004; Farr, 1964).

A common pattern seems to emerge with respect to labeling black men. As the country adjusts to the shifting realities of the information age, it is clear black men are still an expendable antithesis to the democratic money market system (West, 2001; Dyson, 1996). As a result of blacks' shifting position in the nation's economy, employment, and political sectors, as well as black men's incarceration rates and the ever present optics of police shootings aired on public television on a routine basis, it is critically important to investigate the relative negation of black men's equitable humanity, or white indifference concerning the sufferings of black men (Hall et al., 2016; Alexander, 2010; Ali, 2008; Carlson, 2005; Holbert, 2004; Allen, 1994).

Class and Caste in a Post-Civil Rights Society

The post-civil rights era expanded the black middle class, marked by achievements in education, employment, entrepreneurship, and improved access to housing and public accommodations. Additionally, the post-civil rights era empowered blacks' political and religious voice. Alternatively, this very same era produced a permanent underclass of blacks reflective of marginality, high male unemployment, community physical and social decline, homelessness, dysfunctional family dynamics, black-on-black crime and victimization, arrests, and mass incarceration (Alexander, 2010; Wilson, 1987, 2009).

The legacy of black masculinity reveals that it has consistently had to contend with labeling, societal reaction, and the channeling of opportunities consistent with the social consciousness of mainstream society. Certainly, the imagery of black manhood is responsible for black males' lived experiences. When looking at the life course performances of ordinary black men and those who would go on to become prominent challengers to institutional systems of oppression, attempts to cast them as positive agents of change took a back seat to a deliberate assassination campaign (Newton, 2005; Messner, 1997; Marable, 1991, 1995).

Antebellum-era images of docility were countered by racial fears of Nat Turner; the competitive excellence of early athletes was countered by the angst of Jack Johnson; the nonviolence component of the civil rights movement that was symbolized by Dr. Martin Luther King Jr. was countered by black consciousness, black power, and the Nation of Islam's revolutionary stance, symbolized by groups like the Deacons for Self-Defense, the Black Panther Party for Self-Defense, and Malcolm X. With the possible exception of the Deacons, those who endeavored to challenge the oppressive system faced character assassinations, which set the stage for a public opinion campaign resulting in demise and ultimately a public killing (Blackmon, 2008; Hilliard et al., 2006; Hilliard & Weise, 2002; Magida, 1996; Ture & Hamilton, 1992; Lincoln, 1961). The majority of ordinary black men are functional citizens, successful in their pursuit of the American dream, in no way linked to the criminal justice machine, and still fear prevails along with concentrations on the happenstances of permanent underclass black males. Black men regardless of class are portrayed in a manner that reduces them to parasitical and predatory citizens reflective of the perceived disproportionate participation in countercultures that contradict mainstream society. This framework has its roots in the early twentieth-century media (Opportunity Agenda, 2011; Jackson, 2006; Messner, 1997).

Hutchinson (1994) identified the mood of this country's current culture when reflecting on the destruction of the black male image by the American media system (modern American books, newspapers, TV, radio, public speeches, and legislation). Hutchinson (1994) contends that media outlets have engaged in a propaganda war against black males because of interracial interactions and exchanges that for all intents and purposes were contemptuous and unsettling.

The media's seemingly unrelenting attack on the moral character of black men stokes fears and paranoia and functions as a method of social-psychological control leading to social indifference relative to the oppressive, brutal, and even lethal social regulation practices of law enforcement.

Hutchinson's work is very insightful; however, it fails to provide a historical background that explains the long-standing social campaign designed to devalue masculinity. Without this, the scope of black male image bashing is easily written off as an accident of history, or an example of inherent deficiencies within black men. Essentially, attempts to cast black manhood have evolved over time to be inclusive of lived successes, evidenced by successful assimilation and actions to uplift the black race; however, it remains a social fact that narratives remained focused on the black man's troublesome potential, relegating him to the role of society's perpetual problem from the 1920s through the 1980s (Hernandez, 2014; Jackson, 2006; Newton, 2005; Ture & Hamilton, 1992; Killian, 1972; Killian & Smith, 1972).

Johnson's Terrorizing Image Foreshadowed Today's Niggaz

Johnson's story personalizes the start, and echoes the anticipated continuation, of black male image bashing in the United States through its media systems. It also vividly displays the dangers that beset black men trying to reach the heights of the American dream. Boyd (1997) posits that the black male experience after the 1980s produced three categories of black men: (1) race men whose endeavors were for the benefit of uplifting the black race by successfully seizing upon the American dream; (2) new black aesthetics, who were primary beneficiaries of the civil rights movement and therefore assimilated to elite employment institutions and white ivory tower schools, resulting in intellectual and social currency that improved interracial social networks and perhaps the social capital of black men; and (3) niggaz, who were so labeled because of their boastful proclamations of being empowered to overcome the pitfalls of being subject to mainstream society's institutional methods of oppression. This last category is complex, given that it is one that many athletes and rap artists invest in because it has an authentically black component associated with being from a neighborhood that holds street respect as an omnipotent ingredient of manhood. This last category also comprises black male residents trapped in the permanent underclass who invest in subcultures of deviance, crime, and violence as a lifestyle to achieve some bastardized version of the American dream. Unfortunately, although this last category of so-called niggaz residing in permanent underclass communities represents a small proportion with respect to black men's success in this country, they are receiving the lion's share of current media attention. The media seem to overconcentrate on this specific class of niggaz who present a problem of terror because they are viewed as personally responsible, more than are institutional structure and social factors, for their less than ideal social circumstances. Stated another way, the presence of niggaz has been exploited and exaggerated by way of an overflow of messages about urban poverty, social decline, criminal participation, homicides, arrests, and incarceration. The court of public opinion succumbs to the onslaught of black males as something negative because of the presentation of them as inferior, and hopelessly unrestrained in their criminal and sexual preoccupations (Kulaszewicz, 2015; Gause, 2014; Opportunity Agenda, 2011; Carter-Punyanunt, 2008). Therefore, it should be no surprise that black males (a minority of this country's general population) are twice as likely as white males to have lethal force used on them by police officers (Smith, 2014; Wines, 2014). Estimates are that in the twelve months prior to October 2016, 194 black people, the majority males, were killed by police officers (Craven, 2016).

Police shootings are real life-and-death consequences that stem from social prescriptions resulting from an overconcentration on long-standing negative cultural narratives. These narratives have become affirmation codes of police conduct by affecting definitions of situations involving black men as representing a risk.

Discussion

In order to secure the safety of black men who face a heightened risk of being lethally shot by police officers, there are three proposed strategies. I offer these as a corrective, and as a suggestion for surviving within the framework of America's inherently racist media environment. First, critical thinking is necessary and should be used to engage all forms of information outlets with respect to black males. As evidenced through Johnson's story, the culture being produced in our society is strained through a history of violent racial inequality that seeks to mask its presence at every turn. Media consumers must understand how to ferret out racism's presence and discern for themselves the truth and validity of the information being presented. The American media's history of identity constructions demonstrates that what many view as normal is a part of the larger racialized history that came before it, and isn't readily asking to be done away with. A major component of critical engagement is disengagement. There is substantial evidence that media outlets are racially skewed in a manner that does not positively underscore the equitable humanity of blackness. Therefore, stop watching, reading, and listening to mainstream genres of American media uncritically.

The second strategy is to resist investing in negative constructions of black men. Black masculinity is varied, complex, and differently negotiated with respect to class and culture stratification. Despite characterizations that suggest otherwise, black men experience masculinity differently based on any number of individual differences.

The third and final strategy is to increase awareness of social media. Today's participatory web media offers access to intercultural communication, and identity affirmations impossible to imagine during Jack Johnson's lifetime. A great example of this is occurring on Facebook. The hashtag campaign #FatherhoodFridays has been going on for two years and serves as a significant indicator of black men actively taking control of their public image. The campaign involves black men posting pictures of themselves with their children, using the hashtag to counter the myth that black men are absentee fathers.

The preceding strategies are suggestive, not prescriptive. It is up to individual media consumers to make their own choices on what to tune into and what to believe. The point of this chapter is to create awareness that black men endured a legacy of stigmas that do nothing to promote their general well-being and security. Jack Johnson's chances at survival and self-gratification were drastically limited by his public assassination via the American media system because of his race. The phenomenon still happens today, but it doesn't have to continue into perpetuity. The strategies suggested above were given with the aim of ending the phenomenon of black male media lynching. Johnson's public image was used to fabricate a stereotype of black men as threatening to public safety, but black men are too vital to the functioning of this nation and world to continue to let falsehoods go unchecked.

The perceived threat of black masculinity has indeed transcended time to be considered a race legacy variable that infects cultural narratives and cultural codes of conduct affecting public panic, mass incarceration, and fatal policing tactics. Johnson's tragic story of personal rebellion shows that he was used as a public pawn to create civil terror that resulted in the deaths of African Americans around the country. Unchecked media bias transforms every black man into a modern-day Jack Johnson.

Conclusion

An original inquiry of this chapter is whether the social construction of the black male evolved in such a way as to promote equitable humanity, or are black men modern-day Jack Johnson terrors experiencing socially oppressive modern-day lynchings? In extreme cases of media abuse like Johnson's, negative imagery can lead to the unnecessary death of innocent people. In 1908, whites turned Jack Johnson's genius into a black terror campaign. Today, that same black terror is a regrettable social ascription attached to black males. If there is no sincere attempt to address those perceptions that incite fear and loathing, then that is an endorsement for killing unarmed black males with impunity.

■ References

Alexander, M. (2010). *The new Jim Crow: Mass incarceration in the age of colorblindness.* New York: New Press.

Ali, O. H., (2008). *In the balance of power: Independent black politics and third-party movements in the United States.* Athens: Ohio University Press.

Allen, T. (1994). *The invention of the white race.* London: Verso.

Blackmon, D. (2008). *Slavery by another name: The re-enslavement of black people in America from the Civil War to World War II.* New York: Doubleday.

Blattman, C., & Miguel, E. (2010). Civil war. *Journal of Economic Literature 48*(1), 3–57.

Boyd, T. (1997). *Am I black enough for you? Popular culture from the hood and beyond.* Bloomington: Indiana University Press.

Burke, K. (1974). *The philosophy of literary form: Studies in symbolic action.* Berkeley: University of California Press.

Carlson, D. (2005). *When cultures clash: Strategies for strengthening police community relations.* Englewood Cliffs, NJ: Pearson Prentice Hall.

Carter-Punyanunt, N. (2008). The perceived realism of African-American portrayals in television. *Howard Journal of Communications 19,* 241–57.

Carter, R., & Villaverde, L. (2014). The inherent social contradiction in the angry but mystical Negro: Hollywood is making us crazy. In C. P. Gause (ed.), *Black masculinity in America: Can I get a witness* (pp. 35–48). Bradenton, FL: Book Locker.

Craven, J. (2016). Here's how many black people have been killed by police this year. *Huffington Post,* October 13.

Dyson, M. E. (1996). *Race rules: Navigating the color line.* New York: Vintage Books.

Farr, F. (1964). *Black champion: The life and times of Jack Johnson* London: Macmillan.

Fleischer, N. (1949). *The heavyweight championship: An informal history of heavyweight boxing from 1719 to the present.* New York: G.P. Putnam & Sons.

Gause, C. P. (2014). Transgressive black masculinities: Can I get a witness. In C. P. Gause (ed.), *Black masculinity in America: Can I get a witness* (pp. 1–8). Bradenton, FL: Book Locker.

Gilmore, A.-T. (1973). Jack Johnson and white women: The national impact. *Journal of Negro History 58*(1), 18–38.

Hall, A. V., Hall, E. V., & Perry, J. L. (2016). Black and blue: Exploring racial bias and law enforcement in the killings of unarmed black male civilians. *American Psychologist 71*(3), 175–86. doi:10.1037/a0040109.

Hernandez, K-A. (2014). Advancing research on religious/spiritual affiliation and constructions of black masculinity. In C. P. Gause (ed.), *Black masculinity in America: Can I get a witness* (pp. 9–34). Bradenton, FL: Book Locker.

Hilliard, D., Zimmerman, K., & Zimmerman, K. (2006). *Huey: Spirit of the panther.* New York: Thunder's Mouth Press.

Hilliard, D., & Weise, D. (2002). *The Huey P. Newton reader.* New York: Seven Stories Press.

Holbert, S., & Rose, L. (2004). *The color of guilt & innocence: Racial profiling and police practices in*

America. San Ramon, CA: Page Marque Press.

Hutchinson, E. O. (1994). *The assassination of the back male image*. Los Angeles: Middle Passage Press.

Jackson, R. (2006). *Scripting the black masculine body: Identity discourse and racial politics in popular media*. Albany: State University of New York Press.

Johnson, J. (1927). *Jack Johnson: In the ring and out*. Chicago: National Sports Publishing.

Keith, A. (2014). Reframing black male homo-sociality as critical spaces to explore black masculinity. In C. P. Gause (ed.), *Black masculinity in America: Can I get a witness* (pp. 65–81). Bradenton, FL: Book Locker.

Killian, L. (1972). The significance of extremism in the black revolution. *Social Problems 20*(1), 41–49.

Killian, L., & Smith, C. (1972). Negro protest leaders in a southern community. *Social Forces 38*, 253–57.

Kulaszewicz, K. (2015). Racism and the media: A textual analysis. Masters of Social Work Clinical Research Papers. St. Catherine University and University of St. Thomas.

Lincoln, E. (1961). *The black Muslims in America*. Boston: Beacon Press.

Magida, A. (1996). *The prophet of rage: A life of Louis Farrakhan and his Nation*. New York: Basic Books.

Marable, M. (1995). *Beyond black and white: Transforming African-American politics*. New York: Verso.

Marable, M. (1991). *Race, reform, and rebellion: The second reconstruction in black America*. Jackson: University of Mississippi Press.

Messner, M. A. (1997). *Politics of masculinities: Men in movements*. Thousand Oaks: CA: Sage.

Morgan, D. (1998). Jack Johnson: Reluctant hero of the black community. *Akron Law Review 32*, 3–26.

Newton, J. (2005). *From Panthers to Promise Keepers: Rethinking the men's movement*. Maryland: Rowan and Littlefield.

Opportunity Agenda. (2011). *Social science review: Media representations and impact on the lives of black men and boys*. October. Tides Center.

Rhoden, W. (2006). *Forty million dollar slaves: The rise, fall, and redemption of the black athlete*. New York: Three Rivers Press.

Rothenberg, P. (2002). *White privilege: Essential readings on the other side of racism*. New York: Worth Publishers.

Smith, W. (2014). How often white officers shoot black men. *Chronicle*, September 3, 2014.

Ture, K., & Hamilton, C. (1992). *Black power: The politics of liberation*. New York: Vintage Books.

Van Dijk, T. (1991). *Racism and the press: Critical studies in racism and migration*. New York: Routledge.

Ward, G. C. (2004). *Unforgivable blackness: The rise and fall of Jack Johnson*. New York: A. A. Knopf.

Welch, K. (2007). Black criminal stereotypes and racial profiling. *Journal of Contemporary Criminal Justice 23*(3), 276–88.

West, C. (2001). *Race matters*. New York: Vintage Books.

Wilson, W. (1987). *The truly disadvantaged: The inner city, the underclass, and public policy*. Chicago: University of Chicago Press.

———. (2009). *More than just race: Being black and poor in the inner city*. New York: Norton.

Wines, M. (2014). Are police bigoted? *New York Times*, August 30, 2014.

A Preliminary Examination of Hegemonic Masculinity

Definitional Transference of Black Masculinity Affecting Lethal Tactics against Black Males

Jack S. Monell

Since precolonialism, African American males have perceived and categorized by Europeans, not for their level of intelligence, but for their physical appearances and abilities. This was quite evident in the transatlantic slave trade and how African male slaves were marketed and sold to their captors. Deeply ingrained in cultural belief systems, we see this presently in how African American males are viewed in athletics, music, and even Hollywood. These early identifications continued throughout history in reference to gender socialization, stereotypes, and media perceptions of African American males. Expanded into modern-day society, such stereotypes have been detrimental in how African American males are perceived by other racial and ethnic groups, and specifically law enforcement.

African American males were historically socialized, forcefully through slavery to be submissive, obedient, and enduring, particularly for the purposes of the intense labor needed for their daily work in the fields and on the plantations. The stronger the appearance of the slave (mesomorph), the more appealing he was for purposes of working. This process of submission and obedience continued well into postslavery, with postmodern realities. Quite paradoxically, the same attributes and characteristics used to ensure that African slaves were suited for fieldwork are presently used to praise their athletic prowess, and also used to convey fear, bias, and negative stereotyping.

Black masculinity and its impact on modern-day perceptions are deeply rooted in not only slavery, but in how capitalism impacts society. Matlon (2016) argues because of slavery, modern-day gendering was related to capitalistic profit. "Colonialism was a project of racial capitalism" and contributed to emasculating African slaves for the purposes of mass production of goods (Matlon, 2016, p. 1014).

Although masculinity and gender-specific roles are not unique to one ethnic group, none-theless, their impact on African American males surpasses the stereotypical adaptations exhibited in the media and embraced by popular culture. In fact, Jeffries (1995) argues "one of the greatest inventions of the twentieth century is the African American male—invented because black masculinity represents an amalgam of fears and projects in the American psyche" (p. 56). Such ideological beliefs reinforce how people (1) adore African American males in reference to athletics and entertainment but then (2) fear them in every other aspect of the societal stratum.

Johns (2007) expands on this quite poignantly:

> The concept of black masculine identity was fashioned during and codified after the formal collapse of the American institution of slavery. Thus, black masculine identity is a product of American history. It has been socially constructed from narrowly defined understandings of white male-ness. Black masculine identity is heavily imbued with pernicious stereotypes introduced to strip enslaved Africans of humanity. These stereotypes are still prevalent in contemporary U.S. society and this prevalence is at least one factor contributing to the cycle of black male disengagement, alienation and misrepresentation. (p. 1)

DuBois (1903) further provided context to the problem of being both gendered and raced in a society wherein each construct exists as separately marked. For the existence of African American males in America, he underscores their significance because of the continuous shifts in the narrative to their contributions. In looking at generational poverty and class stratification, DuBois (1903) articulated how through institutional and systemic barriers, African Americans found it difficult to progress. These barriers, once overt in brash racist and discriminatory practices, have become more subtle, and masked with educational and prison reform, and poli-cies driven to suppress voter turnout. To date, despite the advancements during the twentieth century, the African American male is marveled at for his athletic prowess and entertainment abilities, but intellectualism is often downplayed or characterized as an anomaly.

Looking at masculinity from Connell's theory of hegemonic masculinity (2005), masculin-ity is heavily idealized as white Christian males, while demonizing African American males outside of entertainment purposes. Hegemonic masculinity is a concept that legitimizes white men's dominant position in society, justifies the subordination of women, and marginalizes alternate presentations of manhood by their appearance, mannerisms, dispositions, or at-tempts to seize upon life course opportunities.

As white superiority and masculinity dominated society from precolonial times, its effect on African slaves, then African American men, socialized them into adopting gender-specific practices and ideologies toward themselves and women. Consequently, as it pertains to African American males or other marginalized men, their identification in hegemonic masculinity is more about going along rather than total acceptance. Hence, because of their status in society, particularly as a lower group or class, hegemonic masculinity affirms con-trol and power, neither of which is representative for African American males (Connell and Messerschmidt, 2005).

Statement of the Problem

Although police brutality is not exclusive to African American males, nor violence of any sort, there continues to be a nationwide epidemic in the amount of shooting deaths of unarmed African American males. This is not a new phenomenon and yet there has been no standardized theory-driven assessment of shooters who perceive themselves to be defenders of the law of the land. Hence, this research examined first-person accounts of two high-profile shooting transcripts. Content analysis was employed to examine Darren Wilson's postoperational narrative in the shooting death of Michael Brown and George Zimmerman's verbal expressions prior to his use of lethal force in the shooting of Trayvon Martin. The problem under investigation is a definition of the situation involving decisions to use lethal force against black males. The research focus then is to determine if hegemonic affirmations of masculinity with respect to interracial control and power results in lethal force when perceived challenges or confrontations occur on the streets.

Macro-Level Institutions of Labeling and Micro-Level Adaptations

While the nineteenth and part of the twentieth century viewed African American males from a sociopolitical perspective of servitude, submissiveness, and deviancy, the latter part of the twentieth century appears to have shifted with respect to how black males were viewed in relation to social stratification. These vantage points varied while still maintaining strong stereotypical references to what masculinity was, and how black males were perceived (Morrow & Torres, 1995).

Despite the intellectual contributions of DuBois, Baldwin, Woodson, and other black twentieth-century philosophical thinkers, African American males were idolized for their athletic prowess or entertainment abilities in theater and music, while simultaneously being relegated to deviant, criminal, rebellious, or violent typologies. Black authenticity, a twentieth-century marketing formula used to promote black stereotypes through the media and popular culture, was instrumental in reinforcing such perceptions in communities nationwide, and unfortunately was embraced by segments of the black community (Jeffries, 2011). Portrayals of black culture were skewed in the direction of residency in poverty-stricken areas beset by social decline, criminogenic vices, dysfunctional family dynamics, and misogynistic males. As these narratives became more robust, sources with the biggest influence on visual and conceptual images reinforced these negative stereotypes (West, 2001; Dyson, 1997; Jeffries, 1995).

Black males in cinema are glorified for their villainous roles more than positive portrayals. Actor Denzel Washington is a great example. Among his many roles spanning twenty years, roles that received fame or Oscar honors, were those depicting him as a relatively submissive soldier in the movie *Glory* and a rogue vice detective in the movie *Training Day*. Sexton (2009) argues that despite valiant efforts from filmmakers like Spike Lee, who worked to portray the black community in positive terms throughout the 1980s, Hollywood's acknowledgment of a legitimate or respectable black presence was not preferred. The Blaxploitation[1] films of the 1970s reinforced negative stereotypes of both black men and women. Despite some of the prominent actors of the time like Sydney Poitier and Bill Cosby, black males were viewed as America's criminal element. Directors like Spike Lee, the Hudlin brothers, and Antoine Fuqua attempted to strike some balance between casting blacks in negative roles and presenting black males in roles that countered negative Eurocentric stereotypes.

Seemingly, media outlets have been responsible for a steady presentation of social narratives promoting character flaws and depravity among permanent underclass black males. The impact has been subcultural constructions and behavioral adaptations by that very same demographic (Anderson, 1990, 1999). Film typologies and music preferential influence has been a problem often discussed by African American actors, artists, and musicians. Where each decade has had a shift in the social commentary of the African American struggle, record executives have resisted musical genres that convey positive imagery or messages for addressing systemic, institutional, and racial barriers within the societal construct (Dyson, 1997). Transitioning from socially conscious music during the 1980s to early 1990s, rap music quickly adopted a street vice, criminogenic persona whereby black males seemed boastful about deviant, criminal, and violent predation. More specifically, gangster rap is notorious for promoting dangerous personas embedded in one's ability to exploit others at the expense of victimizing them (Jeffries, 2011; Jeffries, 1995).

This observation has been consistent throughout the industry, particularly from producers like Ivan "Doc" Rodriguez (Boogie Down Productions, KRS-One fame), who once stated that "you see record labels treating artists like puppets, promoting whatever they wish to sell records" (Monell, 2012, p. 66; Monell, 2010).

Industries that offer narratives of black men, be they sport, media, or music, have powerful socialization agency, leading to cultural definitions that become adopted as cultural codes of conduct. These cultural codes of conduct inform interactions, resulting in a perceived reasonable measure of social regulation and control (Jeffries, 2011; Johns, 2007). It is beyond the scope of this research to search for a legacy continuum of negative assertions of black males that prove significant enough to infuse mainstream society's collective conscience, and ultimately interactional behavioral outcomes with respect to policing suppression tactics. However, it is a reasonable contention that slave-era and Jim Crow-era negative perceptions about black males transcended time and continue to impact their postmodern life chances and life course outcomes.

In spite of a barrage of negative images and character assassination of African American males, there is evidence to suggest that subcultures with accompanying modes of adaptations that emphasize garnering street respect have become a mainstay in permanent underclass communities (Wilson, 2009; West, 2001; Anderson, 1999). Alternatively, on the positive end of the spectrum there is evidence that successful participation in the employment industry, educational institutions, and exposure to positive religious philosophies improves self-esteem and self-efficacy of African American males (Mincey et al., 2014; Franklin, 1994; Hunter & Davis, 1992).

Essentially, an overview of entertainment outlets presents a concern that accepting the potentially troublesome predisposition of black males leads to inter- and intraracial internalization and subsequent adverse behavioral outcomes. Police charged with the duty to protect and serve may often encounter people who are less inclined to be conformists, which can work to promote notions that there are enough nonconforming minorities to be classified as social health hazards. Specifically, embracing social facts that seem to highlight black males as more criminal than any other comparable racial category elevates perceptions of their potential for harm and criminality, thereby manufacturing reasonable fears resulting in lethal social regulation methods (Welch, 2007).

Methods: Sample Selection and Content Analysis

The universal acceptance of blacks' prevalence in crime and disproportionate representation in prison (population percentage compared to criminogenic representation) continues to fuel the perception that blacks are predisposed to be criminal (Welch, 2007).

> In the law enforcement community culture can be described as an invisible style or a way of doing business that in many ways is more powerful than the rules and regulations of a police department . . . it is an unwritten guide. . . . The police culture provides meaning and direction to officers and has the effect of shaping, driving, and sustaining the group's choices and actions. . . . It is a force field of energy with an existence and life all to its own and often it is entirely separate from the organization's mission. . . . Ultimately, it is the force that controls members' behaviors and attitudes in the workplace. (Carlson, 2005, p. 29)

Police departments are inheritors of a social history inclusive of overt social control that has been perceived as combative, suppressive, and unjustified. It could very well be that policing is related to informal cultural codes that define black males as having a predisposition toward violence. It logically follows that policing decisions are influenced by perceptions of immediate danger to the officer and the community.

In two scenarios, the presumption is that a black male waives his right to personal security and life when (1) he provides clues by making gestures that present immediate dangers and enhance fears that not to act could mean personal harm to the officer; and (2) a fleeing black suspect is taken to be more than an attempt to evade an officer, it is a significant threat to the life of citizens (Carlson, 2005).

Connell's theory of hegemonic masculinity appears to provide a prediction that threatening encounters come in the form of perceived challenges by minority groups toward authority figures. For purposes of this research the authority figures are a sworn police officer and a participant in a neighborhood security watch, and two teenage black males. Connell contends that confirmation of power and control over subordinates could take the form of oppressive regulation when challenges are perceived to be threatening enough to conclude that lethal force is necessary (Connell and Messerschmidt, 2005).

This chapter is a research note that initially examines two shooting cases involving a white and a Hispanic shooter that resulted in the deaths of two unarmed black male teenagers. Content analysis (sometimes referred to as document analysis) is employed to explore whether there was evidence of bias relative to the potential to cause trouble on two separate occasions where a black male teenager encountered a police officer and a person acting in a law enforcement capacity (Manser and Mitchell, 2012; Bowen, 2009).

Two transcripts were selected to show various patterns and themes in reference to perceptions related to African American males. The first transcript was the grand jury trial interview of Ferguson police officer Darren Wilson, who shot and killed unarmed eighteen-year-old Michael Brown in Ferguson, Missouri, in 2014.

This shooting began a nationwide wave of protesting to address police brutality and the continued violence toward unarmed African American males and females. In this case, Officer Wilson reported that Michael Brown attacked him after a verbal confrontation, and because he feared for his life, he was forced to use his weapon to fatally shoot Brown. On November 24, 2014, a grand jury decided not to indict Wilson.

The second source was the 911 transcript of George Zimmerman (civilian acting in a law enforcement capacity as a neighborhood watch security personnel) who fatally shot seventeen-year-old, unarmed Trayvon Martin in 2012, in Sanford, Florida. George Zimmerman was charged with second-degree murder and was acquitted on July 13, 2013. In this case, Zimmerman had called 911 to report a suspicious individual (Martin) walking in his neighborhood. Martin, whose father lived in the community, was returning from a trip to the store. Zimmerman was working as a neighborhood watch volunteer at the time of the tragic incident. After repeatedly being asked not to follow Martin by the 911 operator, he continued to do so, which caused a confrontation. After the two engaged in an apparent argument, there was a scuffle, which resulted in Martin being shot and killed.

Analyzing first-person accounts of a shooting provides an opportunity to scrub language that serves as authentic indicators of cultural codes. This research involved constructing measures that represent logical indicators of primary concepts related to Connell's hegemonic masculinity theory. The qualitative data analysis tool used for this research was NVivo 11, which allowed for a systematic construction of nodes (categories) and a logical count (code) that could be classified as an observation for a thematic node.

Following the contention that hegemonic masculinity yields differences in interactions between powerful and minority groups, and that perceived challenges form minority groups could generate negative definitions of the situation (Connell & Messerschmidt, 2005). Two transcripts were evaluated to determine if there was evidence of language that reflects estimations of personal threat and fear (Node 1), observed behaviors categorized as suspicious (Node 2), and negative appearance appraisals (Node 3). Codes or units of observation were identified as commentary or phrases that were indicative of the three nodes identified above. Words and phrases that logically appeared to be evidence for Node 1 were assigned a code of 1, Node 2 was assigned a code of 2, and Node 3 was assigned a code of 3. The frequency of code counts that appeared to represent the nodes can be described as themes,

Table 1. Themes, Definitions and Supporting Commentary

THEME	DEFINITION	EXAMPLES OF SUPPORTING COMMENTARY
Node 1: Fearing for one's life	Words and phrases that indicated some aspect of fear by the respondents (white fear)	Something's wrong with him. Yup, he's coming to check me out, he's got something in his hands, I don't know what his deal is.
Node 2: Acting suspicious/ troublesome behavior	Words and phrases that indicated some level of suspicion (criminality) was perceived by respondents	This guy looks like he's up to no good, or he's on drugs or something. It's raining and he's just walking around, looking about.
Node 3: Appearance appraisals	Words and phrases that indicated some level of association with looking like a criminal	Yeah. A dark hoodie, like a gray hoodie, and either jeans or sweatpants and white tennis shoes. He's unintelligible; he was just staring.

Note: Alphabet increases with frequency counts, so transcripts were coded 1a, 1b, 1c for Node 1; 2a, 2b, 2c for Node 2; and 3a, 3b, 3c for Node 3.

and of course the higher the frequencies (counted phrases or commentary), the stronger the thematic pattern.

Results

In the analysis of the data from the transcripts, several themes emerged that covered areas of interest in relation to the problem statement (see table 1). Recall that the problem statement or research focus was to determine if hegemonic affirmations of masculinity, with respect to interracial control and power to suppress, result in lethal force when perceived challenges or confrontations occur on the streets. Nodes 1, 2, and 3 had responses and similarities in language from Wilson and Zimmerman about Brown and Martin, respectively.

Officer Darren Wilson's Use of Lethal Force on Michael Brown

The social artifact of this project is that Darren Wilson's transcript is not littered with hegemonic indicators, which is a fundamental problem given it represents a void in capturing the culture of conflict that is implicit in how actors define a situation before engaging in a behavior.

> DW: My thought is, I was still dealing with a threat at my car. You know, we're trained not to run away from a threat, to deal with a threat and that is what I was doing. That never entered my mind to flee[2] (supporting commentary for Node 1; 1a).
> DW: He was a really big one. His hand was really big; I felt like a four year old in Hulk Hogan's arms and that's how big and strong he was (supporting commentary for Node 3; Code 3a).
> DW: And then after he did that, he looked up at me and had the most intense aggressive face. The only way I can describe it, it looks like a demon, that's how angry he looked (supporting commentary for Node 3; Code 3b).

Unfortunately, there is a small sample of testimony that may be representative of patterns of thought resulting in a theme. However, one can reasonably argue that these remarks may have a severe enough effect on lethal force. In the case of Darren Wilson, appearance appraisals occurred two times (Node 3), and fear for one's life was mentioned once (Node 1), while there were no instances of perceptions that Brown was acting in a suspicious manner (Node 3). The scarce data permit a cautionary summary statement that appearance appraisals more than fear or suspicious behaviors resonated with Darren Wilson. This content analysis does not provide a method that would determine strength of association, so we can only speculate that Wilson's verbal disclosures about Brown were definitive enough to prompt a shooting causing Brown's death.

Neighborhood Watch Associate George Zimmerman's Use of Lethal Force on Trayvon Martin

The combination of the 911 call and the jury trial provided evidence that George Zimmerman perceived he was acting lawfully because he was acting as an agent for the state, with both the power to suppress troublesome behavior and protect his personal right to life, in the event he was threatened. Even though the case of Trayvon Martin was not directly related to a police shooting, Zimmerman (identifying as a Hispanic) seemed to demonize black males resulting in another death of an unarmed black male teenager. The powerful takeaway here is that George Zimmerman is a part of a minority group, but when prompted to act on behalf of a law enforcement institution did offer adverse estimations about Trayvon Martin, resulting in Trayvon being killed.

George Zimmerman's transcripts revealed consistent references to Trayvon's being black, and even when the 911 operator attempted to ascertain other information, Zimmerman would go back to his visual description. The fact that Zimmerman mentioned race several times during the 911 call could indicate preconceived notion about black males.

ZIMMERMAN: Yeah, now he's coming towards me.
DISPATCHER: OK. Zimmerman: He's got his hand in his waistband. And he's a black male.
DISPATCHER: How old would you say he looks?
ZIMMERMAN: He's got button on his shirt, late teens.
DISPATCHER: Late teens ok (supporting commentary for Node 2; Code 2a).
ZIMMERMAN: Somethings wrong with him. Yup, he's coming to check me out, he's got something in his hands, I don't know what his deal is (supporting commentary for Node 2; Code 2b).
DISPATCHER: Just let me know if he does anything ok.
ZIMMERMAN: How long until you get an officer over here (supporting commentary for Node 1; Code 1a)?
ZIMMERMAN: Okay. These assholes they always get away. When you come to the clubhouse

you come straight in and make a left. Actually you would go past the clubhouse[3] (supporting commentary for Node 3; Code 3a).

ZIMMERMAN: This guy looks like he's up to no good, or he's on drugs or something. It's raining and he's just walking around, looking about (supporting commentary for Node 3; Code 3b).

The results for George Zimmerman indicate that suspicion (Node 2) and appearance appraisals (Node 3), more than fear (Node 1), prompted him to engage an unarmed black teenager. Interactions between people of color and police officers or citizens acting in a legal agent capacity turn out to be far more negative than positive. Certainly, the optics of deadly force has pushed law enforcement discretionary behaviors to the forefront, and yet there is still the issue of social justice relative to legal agent-to-minority citizen contact hours that don't result in deadly force.

Revelations from Wilson and Zimmerman

Evaluation of transcript responses for Darren Wilson and George Zimmerman made it apparent that in both confrontations fear was mentioned (Node 1, on two occasions). It seems that people are born with a fear potential, an emotion that is learned through various degrees of socialization. Similarly to racial and discriminatory views, many of these beliefs are generationally passed down and taught in ethnocentric beliefs (Lane et al., 2014). More importantly, the node, white fear, shows how preconceived notions about a certain group or person can contribute to a behavioral outcome not because of training, but because of a misplaced sense of being scared.

Moreover, with respect to the fear node, and how whites view African American males, there has been some debate that police officers are more hesitant to shoot because of perceived or implicit bias. According to Fachner & Carter (2016) threat perception failures revealed that police officers were more to likely discharge their weapons on African American males as opposed to other races for what they deemed perceived threats. These are defined as mistake-of-fact shootings where officers believe a person is armed when he is not. In their research of the Philadelphia Police department, it was determined that threat perception failures were more prevalent for African American males. Unfortunately, research continues to confirm shooter bias exhibited by police officers who use their weapons to suppress unarmed African American males (James et al., 2016).

Theme 2 explored how the transcripts conveyed how both confrontations began. For Darren Wilson, his initial interaction stemmed from asking two teens to refrain from walking in the middle of the street and to move to the sidewalk. From there, he and Michael Brown began a heated exchange.

Officer's Wilson transcript did not reveal that the black males were acting suspiciously; the confrontation began when Officer Wilson delivered a command. Arguably, a person walking in the middle of the street was not doing anything odd or criminal but in the mind of Officer Wilson, it was enough to engage. With respect to Trayvon Martin, he was allegedly looking "suspicious," as deemed by George Zimmerman, who was not a trained police officer (Node 2, Zimmerman accounted for the total two instances when looking at his and Wilson's transcript). Suspicion (Node 2) provides more context in how African American males are viewed from a societal perspective because suspicion is often linked to higher criminality (Welch, 2007). In these cases, we have a trained law enforcement officer and a civilian posing as one who both felt that the two teenagers they came in contact with were walking suspiciously enough to warrant an encounter.

Appearance appraisals reflecting negative stigmas emerged as the leading Node for both Wilson and Zimmerman (Node 3, code for an appearance appraisal). Much of the literature in reference to stereotypes and perceptions, especially to African American and Latino males, shows a disproportionate amount of police interaction, particularly in the stop-and-frisk policy in New York City (Rios, 2011).

Discussion

The post–civil rights era reveals that "discrimination based on racial cues is a primary cause of the disproportionate number of minority suspects being shot by the police" (James et al., 2016, p. 458). In the case of Michael Brown, and more importantly the St. Louis Police department, there has been documented systemic and institutional bias against the majority of African Americans residing in that city, so much so that the US Justice Department intervened and noted serious policing indiscretions and culturally adverse perspectives that fed police bias and abuse of force (Hall et al., 2016). Examining the cases of Michael Brown and Trayvon Martin, as well as those of Renisha McBride, Jordan Davis, Walter Scott, and far too many others, reveals that although they were not in possession of a deadly force instrument, their deaths were perhaps related to affiliation with a minority group, which was enough to elevate perceptions of troublesome potential and perceived threat to the responding officer, civilian, and community at large.

The language used by Darren Wilson and George Zimmerman seemed to convey that the presence of a black male elevates threat levels, independent of concrete evidence of wrongdoing. Arguably, the view that black males have character flaws, heightened criminality, and moral deficiencies that classify them as a risky social hazard has not diminished enough to have established community trust in policing tactics (Carson, 2009). The findings from this research are limited to two occurrences where lethal force was used against unarmed black teenage males on two separate occasions, also separated by approximately two years (Brown in 2014 and Martin in 2012), and two different locales (Brown in Ferguson, Missouri, and Martin in Sanford, Florida); therefore, there is a desperate need for content analysis of transcripts where there was a shooting involving persons acting in a legal capacity and/or citizens who feel the right to defend their right to life no matter what conditions initiated the deadly encounter.

Conclusion

Functionalism[4] provides some context for understanding police-to-civilian interactions. From a policing perspective, behaviors matter more than racial identity or group affiliation because policing is about fulfilling a duty to intervene whenever societal norms of conformity are challenged in a manner that disrupts the continuity of citizens' social welfare and well-being when there is evidence of legal code violations. The primary objective of police officers is to protect and serve the community in a functional capacity. This would also encompass having an appreciation for the diverse nature of the communities being served by law enforcement.

Connell's theory of hegemonic masculinity posits that variation in power promotes oppressive social regulation because of differenced appraisals of masculinity. The content analysis of scarce testimonies offered by Wilson and Zimmerman lends support to Connell's general assumption. Unfortunately, a postmodern America still harbors racially oppressive frameworks that have extended far beyond the criminal justice system and overzealous officers. America is still a country that apparently continues to be indifferent enough in its failed convictions of those who use deadly force against blacks, resulting in an eroding of community trust. The social fact is that more police shootings are on the horizon. Additionally, the internalization of stigmas stemming from macro-level institutions (e.g. sport, entertainment, media outlets, and information systems that detail crime trends, arrests, and incarceration rates) will no doubt contribute to increased personal definitions of a situation where civilians feel empowered to use lethal force on blacks with the sole justification that their lives were at risk of being terminated if they did not respond (Gabbidon & Greene, 2009; Correll et al., 2007). Exonerations across the land have hinged on exhaustive definitions of "stand your ground" laws[5] or the right to be secure in your own person, which works to further embolden civilians to use deadly force based on a set of racially charged inferences more than evidence of actual harm. In other words, long-standing negative stereotypes about black males work to the detriment of their survival because shootings may continue to be pervasive regardless of the fact that black males are unarmed (Hall et al., 2016; Lane et al., 2014; Holbert, 2004; Hagan, 2010).

The inequitable treatment of African American males is far more than an imagined phenomenon. Living in an information age society with twenty-four-hour news cycles, and social media outlets that are not limited to major networks, has resulted in the broadcasting of black bodies being slaughtered without regard for the victim's family, friendship ties, and social networks. Broadcasting lethal force used against unarmed black males, coupled with a not so transparent judicial process that typically results in a failure to indict, fuels protests that have a frail balance between civil disobedience and volatile confrontations aimed at persons and property.

If anything was evident in what Darren Wilson or George Zimmerman did, it was that despite two different circumstances, an unarmed teenage black male is dead. In closing, further content analysis of first-person shooter narratives needs to be explored to provide more insight into whether bias and stereotype can be implicated as significant contributions toward the use to lethal force. The right to life is at stake as it has always been, and social ecological shifts with evolving societal dynamics mandate changes that must be met with equitable conditions that promote life, not eliminate life.

■ **Notes**

1. Blaxploitation, an ethnic subgenre of the exploitation film, emerged in the United States during the early 1970s. Blaxploitation films were originally made specifically for an urban black audience, but the genre's audience appeal soon broadened across racial and ethnic lines.
2. Darren Wilson Transcript—Gore Perry Reporting & Video, St. Louis, Missouri.
3. George Zimmerman 911 Transcript—transcripts.cnn.com.
4. Theory that stresses the interdependence of the patterns and institutions of a society and their interaction in maintaining cultural and social unity.
5. "Stand your ground" is a justification in a criminal case, whereby a defendants use otherwise unlawful force without retreating, in order to protect and defend themselves or others against threats or perceived threats.

■ **References**

Anderson, E. (1990). *STREETWISE: Race class and change in an urban community.* Chicago: University of Chicago Press.

———. (1999). *Code of the street: Decency, violence and the moral life of the inner city.* New York: Norton.

Bowen, G. (2009). Document analysis as a qualitative research method. *Qualitative Research Journal* 9(2), 27–40.

Carlson, D. (2005). *When cultures clash: Strategies for strengthening police community relations.* Upper Saddle River, NJ: Pearson Prentice Hall.

Correll, J., Park, B., Judd, C., Wittenbrink, B, Sadler, M., & Keese, T. (2007). Across the thin blue line: Police officers and racial bias in the decision to shoot. *Journal of Personality and Social Psychology* 92, 1006–23.

Connell, R. W. (2005). *Masculinities.* 2nd ed. Crow's Nest, NSW, Australia: Allen & Unwin.

Connell, R. W., & Messerschmidt, J. (2005). Hegemonic masculinity: Rethinking the concept. *Gender & Society 19*, 829–59.

DuBois, W. E. B. (1903). *The souls of black folk.* Chicago: A.C. McClurg.

Dyson, M. E. (1997). *Between God and gangsta rap: Bearing witness to black culture.* New York: Oxford University Press.

Fachner, G., & Carter, S. (2015). Collaborative reform initiative. *An assessment of deadly force in the Philadelphia police department.* Community Oriented Policing Services, US Department of Justice.

Franklin, C. W. (1994). Men's studies, the men's movement, and the study of black masculinities:

Further demystification of masculinities in America. In R. G. Majors & J. U. Gordon (eds.), *The American Black male: His present status and his future* (pp. 3–19). Chicago: Nelson-Hall.

Gabbidon, S., & Greene, H. (2009). *Race and crime.* 2nd ed. Washington, DC: Sage.

Hagan, J. (2010). *Who are the criminals? The politics of crime policy from the age of Roosevelt to the age of Reagan.* Princeton, NJ: Princeton University Press.

Hall, A. V., Hall, E. V., and Perry, J. L. (2016). Black and blue: Exploring racial bias and law enforcement in the killings of unarmed black male civilians. *American Psychologist 71*(3), 175–86. doi:10.1037/a0040109.

Holbert, S., & Rose, L. (2004). *The color of guilt and innocence: Racial profiling and police practices in America.* San Ramon, CA: Page Marque Press.

Hunter, A. G., & Davis, J. E. (1992). An exploration of Afro-American men's conceptualization of manhood. *Gender & Society 6*(3), 464–79. doi:10.1177/089124392006003007.

James, L., James, S. M., & Vila, B. J. (2016). The reverse racism effect. *Criminology & Public Policy 15*(2), 457–79. doi:10.1111/1745-9133.12187.

Jeffries, D. (1995). "They're poisoning our kids": Is gangsta rap all a white conspiracy? *Independent,* July 31, p. 2.

Jeffries, M. (2011). *Thug life: Race, gender, and the meaning of hip-hop.* Chicago: University of Chicago Press.

Johns, D. (2007). Re-imagining black masculine identity: An investigation of the "problem" surrounding the construction of black masculinity in America. In *The State of Black America.* New York: National Urban League.

Lane, J., Rader, N. E., Henson, B., Fisher, B., & May, D. C. (2014). *Fear of crime in the United States: Causes, consequences, and contradictions.* Durham, NC: Carolina Academic Press.

Manser, T., & Mitchell, L. (2012). Strengths and weaknesses of specific interview methods and qualitative data analysis strategies in identifying team performance requirements. *Proceedings of the Human Factors and Ergonomics Society 56th Annual Meeting 56*(1), 840–44.

Matlon, J. (2016). Racial capitalism and the crisis of black masculinity. *American Sociological Review 81*(5), 1014–38. doi:10.1177/0003122416658294.

Mincey, K. D., Alfonso, M., Hackney, A., & Luque, J. (2014). Being a black man: Development of the masculinity inventory scale (MIS) for black men. *Journal of Men's Studies 22*(3), 167–79. doi:10.3149/jms.2203.167.

Monell, J. (2012). *Delinquency, pop culture & generation why.* Create Space. Original work published, CPCC Press, 2010.

Morrow, R., & Torres, C. (1995). *Social theory and education. A critique of theories and social and cultural reproduction.* New York: SUNY Press.

Rios, V. (2011). *Policing the lives of black and Latino boys.* New York: New York University Press.

Sexton, J. (2009). The ruse of engagement: Black masculinity and the cinema of policing. *American Quarterly 61*(1), 36–93.

Welch, K. (2007). Black criminal stereotypes and racial profiling. *Journal of Contemporary Criminal Justice 23*(3), 276–88.

West, C. (2001). *Race matters.* New York: Vintage Books.

Wilson, W. (1987). *The truly disadvantaged: The inner city, The underclass, and public policy*. Chicago: University of Chicago Press.

——. (2009). *More than just race: Being black and poor in the inner city*. New York: Norton.

Hoovers and Night Crawlers

When Outside In Becomes Inside Out

Steven Randolph Cureton

W hen it comes to race, crime, and victimization, the consistent social narrative about African Americans' higher percentage of incarceration (approximately 47 percent) in comparison to general population representation (approximately 12.9 percent), and intraracial person-to-person crimes nearing 90 percent certainly contributes to heightened fear about African Americans' criminality. Mainstream society's collective conscience seems in agreement that African American adults and juveniles are more likely than any other race to be involved in behaviors that warrant legal sanctions. Specifically, federal, state, and local prisons and jails house close to one million African American adult males and females, and the juvenile justice system detains an additional one million males and females under eighteen years old.

In spite of the reality that approximately forty million African Americans (inclusive of males and females in every age category) represent functional citizenship, the prevailing theme is that African Americans are disproportionately criminal predators. Black males are perceived as perpetrators of heinous crimes, and inclined to engage in inter and intraracial crimes for reasons of economic, social, and cultural deprivation, social development deficits and depravity, social control and containment issues, and adopting code of the street ethics that promote full-scale participation in deviant, criminal and violent subcultures (Cureton, 2011a; Alexander, 2010; Wilson, 2009; Welch 2007; Anderson, 1990, 1999; Mauer, 1999; Kennedy, 1997; Dyson, 1996).

Currently, politicians, lawmakers, and legal agents are scrambling to understand black-on-black lethal street violence in places like South Los Angeles, Chicago, Houston, Miami, New Jersey, New York, Philadelphia, Washington, DC, and even smaller locals with higher concentrations of underclass blacks. There has been a noticeable decline of ethnographic research on violent subcultures, so much so that social scientific knowledge concerning blacks' participation in crime more often than not is derived from quantitative methods analyzing secondary data sets, police narratives, and content analysis of autobiographies. More and more, qualitative approaches examining the contextual realities of blacks' subculture of violence involve focus groups with community leaders, interviews with street corner groups (usually in safe locations, miles away from their natural environment), and captive audience interviews from prisoners. These quantitative and qualitative approaches are instrumental in providing some logical correlation and causation facts about the routine activities of blacks' participation in crime (Hunter, 2010; Cureton, 2008; Brunt, 2001).

However, the evolving nature of the subculture of violence demands a renewed interest in field research in order to provide a fresh perspective concerning black males' masculine behaviors in deviant, criminogenic, and violent environments. Moreover, there continues to be a desperate need to explore troublesome black masculine performances in order to arrive at logical answers that could demystify arguments offering pathology and depravity as more appropriate than modes of adaptation to less than ideal life course circumstances.

One assumption related to this research is that participation in person-to-person violent crimes is a strategy for impression management and negotiating manhood, while simultaneously attempting to avoid shame and humiliation. However, these are underestimated pursuits because there is a lack of authentic understanding relative to blacks' investment in respectful street credibility (Cureton, 2011b; Grazian, 2007; Williams, 2004; West, 2001; Anderson, 1990, 1999; Gilligan, 1997; Shakur, 1993). The second assumption related to this research is that ganglands and nightclubs represent prime performance stages for impression management, and negotiating manhood. Ethnographic research on black gangs in a post-civil rights era is rare. Additionally, there is limited research that has an insider's perspective on the subculture of violence that occurs in black nightclubs (Hunter, 2010; Cureton, 2008; Grazian, 2007; Monaghan, 2002; Hutchinson, 1999).

There are two fundamental problems related to ethnographic research on African American gangs and nightclub violence. First, community isolation breeds suspicion of outsiders, forcing residents, particularly gang members, to assume an alien disposition. In other words, outsiders are often greeted by the perception that researchers are there to investigate crimes and not to gain insight into gangsterism.

Second, the subculture of violence related to gangsterism and going to clubs that attract gangsters, hustlers, and drug dealers may be so hostile and unpredictably violent that it negates genuine interest in conducting participant observation research on gangsterism and club nightlife (Cureton, 2008, 2011b; Wilson, 2009; Welch, 2007; Williams, 2004; Monaghan, 2002; Sawyer, 1973).

Participant Observation: Hoover Gangland and Greensboro's Nightclub Scene

South Central Los Angeles is a gangland where hesitation is rewarded by death and gangster achievements often lead to long-term incarceration. South Central is a gangland were boys become men in territories with fixed informal boundaries divided by civil war histories spanning back to the early 1920s. It's territorial turfs where gangs are the number one socialization agent, trumping school, church, law enforcement, and family institutions, particularly those families beset by broken homes, single-female-headed households, and sibling gang involvement (Cureton, 2008, 2009; Wilson, 2009; Williams, 2004; Shakur, 1993). Currently, South Central Los Angeles remains the gang capital of America with an estimated 200 to 225 Crip and Blood sets. It is with respect to these social facts that I continue to refer to South Central Los Angeles as South Central, and not the officially approved renaming to South Los Angeles in April 2003. Moreover, the core of my field research began before the name change in 1999, and has not officially ended because of the ongoing relationships, return visits, and consistent communication with Hoover gang members.

The third largest African American gang in South Central is Hoover. Generations of Hoovers have claimed territory spanning nine branches of Hoover streets from 43rd, 52nd, 59th, 74th, 83rd, 92nd, 94th, 107th, and 112th. Hoover intersects with Florence and Normandie, which are considered ground zero for the infamous 1992 riots (Cureton, 2008).

This project partly reflects on my experiences while investigating the Hoover gang during the summers of 1999 and 2000 when gang wars were ongoing. More specifically, the field component covering 170 interview and observation hours provides evidence to discuss race as a form of social capital that effected an all-access pass through Hoover with the company of well-respected General Level Original Gangsters. Because Hoover continues to extend an open invitation to me (my most recent visit being March 2014), I have been fortunate enough to meet newer generations of Hoovers. I continue to talk to Hoovers once a week whose information keeps me updated; therefore, it is difficult to buy into the fact that my research on Hoover has officially ended.

Greensboro, North Carolina, was the primary city for my nightclub research. As early as the 1930s Greensboro was cast as a progressive business and educated New South town, advantaged by constitutionally aware lawyers who were sophisticated enough to provide a fair and impartial application of the law, and as having the community fabric that was racially tolerant of its diverse class of black citizens. Greensboro appeared to embody racial tolerance that was perhaps relatively inconsistent with the day-to-day practices and treatment of minority populations. The negative modes of inter- and intraracial interaction were affected by context, class, and caste systems, and still Greensboro was placed on a morally, progressive pedestal. Greensboro like many other places had to embrace blacks' awareness of dignified personhood, deservedness, and rights to transcend the limits of existential absurdity. There was simply no dodging the protest era that pursued all of the freedoms associated with American citizenship.

Fundamentally, the civil pursuits of Greensboro's black residents forced nonviolent protests, reactionary violent protests, and grassroots clashes in the streets that illuminated the shadows of inconsistency between life course chances and standard-of-living results between blacks and whites. Greensboro's claim of being progressive is related to success in medical professionalism, industry, banking, and transport, and home to North Carolina Agricultural and Technical State University (an HBCU), Bennett College (predominantly black female student population), Greensboro College (small private institution), Guilford College (several branches of community colleges), and the University of North Carolina at Greensboro (predominantly white institution). Greensboro's population is approximately 280,000, and 33 percent of that population is black with noticeable economic inequality issues that continue to affect racial segregation. Hence, it should be no surprise that Greensboro is home to working-class and permanently underclass populations who contribute to Greensboro's crime problem, illegitimate economy, and underbelly hedonistic behaviors that are acted out in nightclubs (Brown et al., 2006; Chafe, 1980).

In 2001, I began researching Greensboro's nightlife, particularly those nightclubs that were frequented by gangsters, drug dealers, and hustlers. Very little is known about the risks associated with club security (e.g., bouncers) (Hunter, 2010; Grazian, 2007; Monaghan, 2002; Hutchinson, 1999). I decided to fully participate by way of becoming a bouncer for clubs that offer limited restraints on hedonistic pursuits related to sexual exploits, drinking, and drug use (specifically marijuana and cocaine), and aggressive behaviors aimed at partygoers who decide to become physical combatants.

The purpose of observing Hoovers in South Central and becoming a bouncer for several violent club locales was to decode behaviors related to gangsterism and the subculture of violence and to identify value systems and gangster and street code ethics that black males endorse as evidence of masculinity. It's been seventeen years (dating back to 1999) of ethnographic research. The participant observant balance has led to interesting self-discovery. Whether I was observing Hoovers or participating in regulating violence at nightclubs, my reservations approached concern about the possibility that this method of research could eventually lead to personal injury and even a casualty of lethal violence. I managed to repress my concern by trusting what I thought was a calling to understand black masculinity, violence, and gangs. As far as being a member of a club security team, concern was countered by embracing whatever challenges I was forced to endure within the subculture of violence with the necessary suppression tactics to emerge healthy enough to return home.

Observation versus Participation: In Too Deep Means No Escape

Even though I am over twenty-four hundred miles away from the Hoover gangland, it remains difficult to completely divest from the gangsters. At one point in time, I felt I was somehow cheating the gangsters (who took the time to reveal their social world) every time I left South Central to return to North Carolina. It was a strange feeling then that continues to resonate, and one I couldn't understand as rational at the time. However, experiencing extended relationships with certain gang members over a period of seventeen years enhanced a brotherhood of defined meanings related to unique lifestyle stressors, social identity issues, and social value assessments shared by black males in this country. Moreover, I suspect I am emotionally branded by observing violence and witnessing the aftermath of death.

My reflections rest with a degree of emotional trauma and heartache for those who suffered the misery of lethal violence. Essentially, the field research on gangsterism, while initially keeping me at a suspicious distance until the right dominos of acceptance fell in place, evolved into some level of mutual understanding because of shared situation of circumstance related to being black.

With respect to Greensboro's nightclub research (2001–2016), "Gunz for Hire!," an organized group of personal bodyguards and club bouncers, represented my entry point as a club bouncer. For the past fifteen years I have been thoroughly embedded in the local nightclub scene by way of being a bouncer/bodyguard. The methodology for the nightclub research included a heavy dose of participation. In retrospect I believe that the more I became involved in keeping the peace, specifically breaking up fights or trying to resolve conflicts, the more overall surveillance of the club scene was lost. Therefore, my field notes reflect a panoramic assessment of the scene at the beginning of most nights but often narrowed to focus on those patrons that were engaging in behaviors that warranted hands on attention. Too many vivid images of violence, and combatant encounters requiring self-defense, have forced a realization that my actions were dictated by moment of circumstance related to doing club security. My roles as husband, father, and professor failed to significantly enter the equation quickly enough to be counteracting forces that should have curtailed the depth of reactionary social regulation that was used to suppress combatant challenges. What's more may be the desire to make it home safely created a sense of urgency that proved more dominant, affecting security decisions. Honestly, when both of these explanations are stripped away, the raw fact was that I wanted to demonstrate enough aggressive masculinity to earn respect from other bouncers and definitely from the deviant crews that frequented the nightclubs.

The unfortunate reality for the nightlife scene is that the combatants involved with club security could not care less about any attempts to stop doing security or end the ethnographic research project. For them, if they felt disrespected (more than a few have felt this way), their memories of that encounter and quest for revenge is timeless. For this reason alone, I may never have a clear path away from the subculture of deviance, crime, and violence.

Ganglands and Criminogenic Subcultures: Ruled by Similar Street Codes

My early upbringing included residency in low-income, government housing projects; therefore, my exposure to violence within the context of a community and even a dysfunctional household was commonplace. It seems fitting that I have a vested research interest in black-on-black crime and victimization because it was seeded during my early life experiences. Attending graduate school at Washington State University provided direct contact with black male college athletes who were from South Central. My interactions with them served to intensify my interest in gangs.

Apparently, intraracial person-to-person crimes are the result of community physical and social declination, isolation, and marginalization, effecting the emergence of black enclaves where gangs and street code politics dominate the socialization and life course outcomes of its residents. No matter the group type, gang or clique, collective violence is a community trouble (Cureton, 2017). The violence acted out on streets travels to clubs, in likeness to a virus with negative health and sometimes fatal consequences for persons unfortunate enough to be in the company or in close proximity to individuals who harbor gangster or thug mentalities (Wilson, 2009; Williams, 2004; Anderson, 1990, 1999; Dyson, 1996; Shakur, 1993; Katz, 1988; Wilson, 1987).

It appears that South Central's gangland streets and Greensboro's nightlife clubs represent important performance stages where social audiences witness gangsters' and thugs' behavioral solutions to negotiating masculinity and suppressing challenges to respect. Social audiences also become gossip networks creating or adding to narratives that inform others about behavioral outcomes, which in turn translate into positive or negative social capital (depending on who gained the upper hand in combative situations). Social capital becomes the social currency that informs community residents about the measure of respect an individual has earned. It seems logical to assume that black males are on a quest to acquire and maintain respectable manhood that is consistent with their residential status.

Research Blueprints: Ethnography, Theoretical Themes, and Concepts

Ethnography attempts to arrive at authentic truisms pertaining to routine activities within the context of environments, culture, and social networks. Given that ethnography requires some degree of immersion and/or observational contact, ethnography represents an appropriate method to decode intrinsic value systems, meanings, and behavioral expectations specific to various social settings (Brunt, 2001; Agar, 1983; Emerson, 1983; Frake, 1983). The research on the Hoover gang and nightclub violence was more than just window shopping without perspective. In fact, the research was a social-scientific effort anchored by appropriate theoretical themes, and conceptual assumptions. It is impossible to observe everything in the field; however, having some type of theoretical perspective allows for routine adjustments based on reflective thinking and critical assessments. The benefit is that researchers may be flexible enough to not turn a blind eye to unanticipated information the field is presenting (Ocejo, 2013; Lovat, 1995; Emerson, 1983; Frake, 1983).

Although my research on the Hoover gang and the subculture of violence taking place in nightclubs did not directly test any specific theory, observations and interviews with Hoovers were guided by themes and concepts consistent with Jack Katz's (1988) street elite perspective, and the observations in nightclubs were influenced by Elijah Anderson's (1999) code-of-the-street perspective.

Katz's (1988) street elite perspective implies that males seek the gang as a way of transcending the negative emotions they experience as a result of perceived societal rejection. Katz contends that educational, employment, and other institutions designed to improve the welfare and well-being of males fail to offer reasonable opportunities (in terms of what these males have the ability to seize upon). Males having experienced some degree of failure to gain societal acceptance interpret their failure as society's unwillingness to intervene and acknowledge their state of deprivation with any sense of urgency. Existing in a state of deprivation for a period of time translates into humiliation, a perceived inability to seize opportunities of mainstream success, which leads males to seek the company of like-circumstanced males. This collective misery manifests as a local culture of control, ruled by participation in an illegitimate economy. At this point, life becomes a hustle, and earning respect requires predatory violence. Essentially, a local culture of control functions to provide an avenue of success for males turned away by mainstream society. The local culture of control provides opportunities for rejected males to overcome insecurities related to failing by replacing insecurity with some measure of control at the expense of victimizing others (Katz, 1988).

The local culture of control is a deviant, violent, and criminogenic subculture that contradicts the importance of mainstream social approval and legitimacy as the only avenue for success.

It's not enough to be an active participant in the local culture of control. According to Katz, potential gang members endorse a hostile, volatile, and alien disposition as they engage in bad-ass behaviors laced by a nonchalant attitude directed at mainstream employment and educational and governmental institutions and agencies. Unfortunately, the ways of the bad ass manifest as predatory behaviors against residents from other communities who are similarly circumstanced (Katz, 1988). Ultimately, these behaviors represent health hazards, community threats, prison, and fatal outcomes. In spite of the evidence that participation in local cultures of control and engaging in bad-ass behavior represent dead-end pursuits, males continue to gravitate toward the only organization (the gang) that appears to be in a position to empower them to become street elites (Katz, 1988).

Anderson's (1999) code-of-the-street perspective posits that urban residents or locales dominated by street hustlers abide by subcultural rules that govern interpersonal behavior, including a rationale for violence. These rules are established and endorsed mainly by those who are thoroughly invested in the illegitimate money market economy (drugs, guns, gambling, prostitution, and any other hustle that has utilitarian outcomes). However, these very same rules are powerful enough to dictate behavioral expectations for an entire community, even for those families that attempt to live a socially legitimate lifestyle but are confined by residency. Thus, decent families may be opposed to street code ethics but often find that they have to socialize their children to become familiar with street code ethics as means to avoid victimization. The following passage highlights the importance of understanding the code of the street as a defense mechanism that is critical in navigating the routine activities related to status attainment.

> The inclination to violence springs from the circumstance of life among the ghetto poor—the
> lack of jobs that pay a living wage, limited basic public services (police response in emergencies,

building maintenance, trash pick-up, lighting, and other services that middle class neighborhoods take for granted), the stigma of race, the fallout from rampant drug use and drug trafficking, and the resulting alienation and absence of hope for the future. Simply living in such an environment places young people at special risk of falling victim to aggressive behavior. Although there are often forces in the community that can counteract the negative influences—by far the most powerful is a strong, loving, decent (as inner city residents put it) family that is committed to middle-class values—the despair is pervasive enough to have spawned an oppositional culture, that of "the street," whose norms are often consciously opposed to those of mainstream society. These two orientations—decent and street—organize the community socially, and the way they coexist and interact has important consequences for its residents, particularly for children growing up in the inner city. (Anderson, 1999, p. 3)

Anderson's (1999) code-of-the-street perspective offers a valuable assessment concerning the importance of respect and how it is pursued through aggression, troublesome behavior, fighting, and lethal violence. More specifically, for those communities that have suffered enough economic stress, resource strain, isolation, and marginalization, the code of the street has emerged as the dominant value system governing the behaviors of young males (between the ages of nine and twenty-four) who are actively campaigning for respect. Hence, the code of the street is the germ for thuggish and collective deviance, crime, and violence.

At the heart of the code is the issue of respect—loosely defined as being treated "right" or being granted one's "props" (or proper due) or the deference one deserves. However, in the troublesome public environment of the inner city as people increasingly feel buffeted by forces beyond their control, what one deserves in the way of respect becomes ever more problematic and uncertain. This situation in turn further opens up the issue of respect to sometimes intense interpersonal negotiation, at times resulting in altercations. In the street culture, especially among young people, respect is viewed as almost an external entity, one that is hard-won but easily lost—and so must constantly be guarded. The rules of the code in fact provide a framework for negotiating respect. With the right amount of respect, individuals can avoid being bothered in public. This security is important, for if they *are* bothered, not only may they face physical danger, but they will have been disgraced or "dissed" (disrespected). . . . The hard reality of the world of the street can be traced to the profound sense of alienation from mainstream society and its institutions felt by many poor inner-city black people, particularly the young. The code of the street is actually a cultural adaptation to a profound lack of faith in the police and the judicial system. (Anderson, 1999, pp. 33–34)

Katz's street-elite and Anderson's code-of-the-street perspectives seem to be logical sociological frameworks with which to examine a subcultural value system with a different meaning of manhood for those black males who are willing to embrace deviance, crime, and violence as a way to affirm masculinity. The evidence concerning black masculinity for males trapped in socially disorganized areas is difficult to ignore. The reality is that mainstream rejection, isolation, and marginalization leads to powerlessness, which makes males susceptible to sub-culturally specific status attainment endeavors at the expense of exploiting and harming others.

Methodology: Stepping Out There and Taking What You Get

Voisin and Guilamo-Ramos's (2008) community violence exposure perspective suggests that witnessing or being a victim of abuse, including violence, increases the risk of engaging in troublesome behaviors that either lead to self-harm or harm others. The community violence exposure perspective focuses specifically on self-destructive behaviors among adolescent African American males. Voisin and Guilamo-Ramos's community violence exposure perspective can be stretched to account for my research interest in violence because I grew up in various government-subsidized housing areas, witnessed domestic abuse, experienced parent-to-child physical abuse and neglect, and was an active participant in peer group delinquency. It makes sense that my academic journey would include sociology, criminology, and the family.

The research that framed my experience started during my seven-year graduate school experience at Washington State University in Pullman, beginning in 1990. Pullman is a college town where black males were a minority, and most were there to play football or basketball. I experienced a natural gravitation toward these athletes and also found a shared identity with the Omega Psi Phi fraternity. I suspect that our unique presence as black males on a predominantly white campus influenced a desire to want to be in the company of one another.

They were interested in my southern ways (coming from North Carolina) and my experiences as an undergraduate at North Carolina Agricultural and Technical State University (a historically black college). I was equally interested in the communities they came from, which happened to be South Central Los Angeles.

My first trip to California during a spring break was an eye-opening experience, and I was astonished by California's daytime beauty and its nighttime gangsterism. For the first time, I was exposed to the dominance of traditional Crip and Blood gangs. The more I was exposed to those athletes recruited out of South Central, the more I developed a curiosity for gangster rap, particularly the sounds of Death Row records, Tupac Shakur, Dr. Dre, Snoop Dog, Ice T, Ice Cube, and the West Side Connection. I can only speculate that the lyrics detailed story lines that strangely resonated with me. Then there was Hollywood's cinematic productions of gangsterism. Movies like *Boyz in the Hood* (1991), *South Central* (1992), and *Menace to Society* (1993) provided opportunities to conduct a content analysis of black masculinity in a gangland. Eventually, my sociological interests ignited a desire to separate truth from fiction. The social network of black male athletes allowed me to ask community, social, cultural, family, and friendship affiliation questions and I received astonishing answers. I had met good friends in and became a member of the Omega Psi Phi fraternity in 1991, but we all would go our separate ways in 1997. Fortunately, these very same friendships and membership in Omega Psi Phi produced an opportunity to examine the Hoover community. In 1999, I started ethnographic research on gangs, and my entry point was made possible because of my fraternity brother

Chris, who had so connections as a result of being a lifetime resident of California. Chris grew up in Inglewood, so he understood the necessary street protocol to garner support from gang members for my field research.

Chris introduced me to Mann, a Five Deuce Hoover. Mann and I had immediate rapport because he too is a member of the Omega Psi Phi fraternity. Thus, the initial setup involved Omegas, and from that point a domino effect took over as I was introduced to one of the most respected Hoover gangsters, Duck, an Eleven Deuce Hoover. Duck, while initially suspicious of me began to let his guard down because our initial conversations were not recorded, and I answered every question he asked. The strongest ingredient working in my favor, leading to a deeper progression into Hoover, was that Duck felt a need to look out for me. Perhaps Duck felt this way because he had lost a sibling named Steve. The interviews and field observations were planned and executed by Hoover, which quickly erased my grand plan to also research Bloods. Hoovers felt their story was the most important and no other gang mattered. This is an example of taking what the field offers, and adjusting the scope so as not to offend the first gang that stepped forward.

Jack Katz's (1988) street elite perspective provided an overall blueprint for observations and open-ended interview questions (e.g., societal rejection, humiliation, humility, personal outlooks on opportunities, bad-ass behaviors, and joining the gang); however, the friendships that were forged while a graduate student at Washington State became primary points of observation while in the field. The impact of race, research caveats, findings, and researcher reflections about my research on the Hoover gang will focus on the twenty-four days of field observations, interviews, and interactions taking place over two summers (fourteen days in May 1999 and ten days in August 2000). I was able to log 170 interview, observation, and interaction hours, journaling responses of twelve original gangsters, observing, interacting and video recording an additional seventy-five young male and female gang bangers, gang members, and gang affiliates. An additional ten nonmember residents were interviewed, and there were an additional ten hours of video footage capturing the routine activities happening in the Hoover community (Cureton, 2008).

Energized by the field research on Hoover gangsterism, I wanted to explore the subculture of violence in North Carolina. Although I had absolutely no direct connections or knowledge of gang activity occurring in Greensboro, North Carolina, I decided on Greensboro because it was home base, which meant I could conduct field research for an extended period of time (2001–2016). I turned to Mr. Deans (my cousin), who had been a Greensboro police officer for over fifteen years. I participated in the police-citizen ride-along program a few times with Mr. Deans in order to gauge the extent and nature of crimes occurring in Greensboro. Mr. Deans suggested that I become a bouncer because clubs represent places where all the action comes to you. Mr. Deans introduced me to Roc, who had assembled a group of bouncers/bodyguards known as Gunz for Hire. Thus, in similar fashion to my entry portal to Hoover, becoming immersed in the nightclub scene was the result of familiar relationships resulting in a domino effect landing me a position as a doorman and bouncer at the Klick, a club off of Highway 29, the south side of Greensboro. My club security and bodyguard duties required total immersion; only Mr. Deans and Roc were aware that I was researching the subculture of violence as a participant and observant from 2001 through 2016.

Methodology

My notes were often written in the aftermath of the experiences that took place during a shift that lasted from 9:00 P.M., until approximately 3:00 A.M., Thursday through Sunday; on weekends adult entertainment venues opened up from 2:00 A.M. to 6:00 A.M. Data-gathering techniques included voice recorders, and journaling in small pocket-size notepads. Initially, my small voice recorder, pocket size notepad, and pen were often kept on me, but this soon became a bad idea as these items were destroyed or lost, or my pen would end up being stuck in my leg as a result of breaking up fights or throwing patrons out of the club.

In the beginning of my fifteen years as a bouncer/bodyguard, I could take small fifteen-minute breaks and go to the car to do some journaling. However, as my leadership role increased, the demands made it necessary that I not take any breaks, especially if it meant walking outside the club. Although I worked clubs that attracted older, more sophisticated people (e.g., The Comedy Zone, Churchills, and George K.), my focus will be on those clubs that were routinely visited by individuals who subscribed to code of the street ethics to resolve conflicts (e.g., Atlantis, Greensboro Ballroom, the Rib Shack, Club Ménage, Green Street, and Suga Bears). Partygoers from different cities, towns, rural areas, neighborhoods, projects, and colleges with different social biographies (i.e., drug dealers, block hustlers, and thugs prepared to settle conflicts through violent means, college students, and young professionals focused on hedonistic behaviors linked to alcohol, drugs, and sex) frequented these clubs weekly, Thursday through Sunday.

Caveats and Researcher Accountability

The field participant observation method afforded opportunities to personally witness and actively engage with black males who seemed to be consumed by impression management by pursuing and seizing respect in a gangland and the nighttime clubs scene. There were two significant caveats related to interviewing and observing the Hoover gang and one caveat related to participant observation of certain clubs in Greensboro. The first caveat related to Hoovers was that Mann (a Five Deuce Hoover) and Duck (an Eleven Deuce Hoover) were in complete control of how Hoover was presented, as they controlled when and where I traveled and even which gangsters (young and older, male and female) I could interview. Therefore, it's reasonable to suggest that a truthful presentation of Hoover could have been impacted by their subjective vision of what and who was important for gathering information about Hoover.

One reasonable counter to this caveat was that using Katz's perspective on street elites provided researcher reflection, which allowed for field observation adjustments and requests to pursue relevant issues that I captured and wanted to further explore. The second caveat was that Hoover's version of authentic gangsterism depended on honest disclosures. This caveat was countered by walking a fine line between rapport and professionalism, realizing that too much rapport could lead to a lopsided, positive offering of gang activity (Cureton, 2008).

The most significant caveat related to participant observation via being a club bouncer is that I could not consistently provide a timely and panoramic assessment of deviant, criminal, and violent occurrences. Reflections on the subculture of violence are limited to those activities that clubgoers openly displayed in a way that I was able to notice. The logistical counter was to stay informed about street gossip, pay attention to the warnings of club management and promotors, and stay in tune with the criminal reports offered by local news stations. Additionally, profiling was a tactic used based on the evidence that groups of males routinely announced (by their actions) that they required the attention of bouncers (by way of interceding in fights or removing them for violating club rules).

Results: Revelations about Hoover

The Hoover gang represents a predominantly black gang that covers territory spanning from 43rd to 112th street, which is nine street branches of the Hoover gang. The evidence reveals South Central is a gangland ruled by street gangs with wholesale claims of being the strongest social force governing the street socialization of black males. Hoover is just one out of an estimated 200 to 225 Crip and Blood gang sets. After 170 interview and observation hours in the Hoover neighborhood, several key findings emerged.

One takeaway was that the gang is a product of social, political, economic, structural, cultural, and spiritual shifts in the black community. Evidence indicates that gang membership both causes criminal behavior and attracts males who are already doing crime. Observations suggest that gangs recruit already delinquent individuals who, once a member, are affiliated with a group that encourages further criminogenic behaviors. Ghetto-confined males act on an agenda to become ghetto superstars in the hood (Cureton, 2008). Becoming a ghetto superstar requires pursuing a gangster lifestyle with an understanding that the definitive measure of respect is linked to a willingness to meet challenges with lethal violence. It seems that gang recruitment is no longer relevant because young black boys' pursuit of respectable manhood and ghetto success forces a natural gravitation toward the gang (Cureton, 2008).

Even though this project was focused on masculinity in the Hoover gang, issues concerning perceptions of female gang members did come up. The normative expectation that female gang members are excused from participating in all aspects of gang banging, including murder, or that females should not be targeted for murder does not apply to Hoover. In other words, female gang members are expected to do the same things as male gang members.

Another significant observation is that in a seemingly chaotic environment, ghetto passes (informal control mechanisms that govern safety and afford protection for designated individuals) imply that intergang relations are governed by street protocol. Hoover does have compassion and, at times, demonstrates true friendship and civility. Hoovers have a sense of civic responsibility and recognize what it takes to be successful in mainstream society.

Moreover, upon recognizing an individual's positive potential to be successful in mainstream society (e.g., education and sports), the gang will work to make sure that individual makes it out of the hood by negotiating ghetto passes or trying to keep them separate from gang activity (Cureton, 2008). In an abstract sense, there is evidence to support Katz's street elite perspective. Observing Hoover leads to logical conclusions about the existence of gangster politics in a gangland that could be an example of a local culture of control. Also for Hoover, it does seem that black males embrace and endorse bad-assing as a way to reach ghetto superstardom or become a gangster street elite (Cureton, 2008; Katz, 1988). However, it's just as reasonable to conclude that Shakur (1993) provided the most accurate ad hoc explanation about gangster activity for males in a gangland when he described the three steps toward becoming an Original Gangster:

1. You must build the reputation of your name as an individual.
2. You must build your name in association with your particular set, so that when your name is spoken your set is also spoken in the same breath for it's synonymous.
3. ou must establish yourself as a promotor of Crip or Blood, depending, of course, on which side of the color bar you live. (Shakur, 1993, p. 5)

The ugly reality is that Hoover is beset by lethal violence to the point that gang wars have been a dominant theme, resulting in gang injunctions being instituted to suppress gang activity (Klein, 2007; Klein & Maxson, 2006). The narrative that gangsterism continues to be fueled by criminogenic opportunities associated with guns and the drug underground economy was substantiated. At worst the Hoover gang turned out to be a mostly uncivil predatory group programmed to inflict social and physical devastation.

Results: Revelations about Greensboro's Nightclub Scene

Reflecting on my experiences as a bouncer/bodyguard, what stands out is that I started as a doorman, and eventually became the leader of a twenty-five-man security team. Violence was a routine occurrence, and I was expected to meet that violence with necessary force that suppressed combatants. There was no room for indecision, hesitation, or reluctance to get involved in conflicts, as these were taken as signs of weakness from the security team and the clubs' patrons.

The most profound finding in regard to being a bouncer is that responding to violence as a group served to strengthen our commitment toward one another. Our goal was to make sure we all made it home safely, and looking back the only way we were successful in accomplishing that goal was to be just a violent as the situation required. The security team in many respects became a band of brothers or an institutionalized gang because of our employment status with the clubs we were hired to protect. During the most violent times, I waited until I returned home to write in my journal because sitting in the parking lot after a night filled with violence potentially put me at risk to become a target for angry partiers who were out for revenge. At the end of each night, distance from the club would bring about peace, and I routinely glanced at the passenger's seat to see my version of nigh time passengers (a copy of the Holy Bible and my .45 caliber firearm). When I got home, I thanked my God, reflected for ten minutes, and then began journaling about the night's events. This was my routine from Thursday through Sunday for the better part of fifteen years.

Unfortunately, not one weekend passed that did not involve social conflicts causing injuries that required first aid from club personnel, an ambulance for more severe injuries, or police involvement due to a homicide on club property.

The club provided the perfect stage for impression management given that (1) club locales were in areas known for higher concentrations of crime; (2) clubs were not immune to drugs and gun trafficking, prostitution, and gambling; (3) clubs attracted residents of local neighborhoods who frequently brought and acted upon rival neighborhood and intraneighborhood conflicts, in addition to ganging up on college students and club attendants from surrounding cities; and (4) clubs provided a volatile mix of intoxicated attention-seekers looking to impress women and settle disputes with violence. Greensboro's nightclub scene revealed irrational, often dangerous hedonistic pursuits, and a willingness to engage in a subculture of deviance, crime, and violence. In other words, a criminogenic subculture emphasizing violence encouraged males to engage in troublesome behavior.

A group of black males from the south and east side areas of Greensboro exploded on the scene (in 2006) as the Blood Gang. Newly initiated males (called Goonies) who subscribed to a "Be Bloody Code" of (hustling, thugging, bullying, and suppressing any peer group resistance through fighting) began to dominate the club scene. The potential victims of Bloods who frequented the club were rival Crip gang members, drug dealers, hustlers, and street corner thugs who also adopted the philosophy that street success meant confronting and quickly suppressing personal challenges through violent means. The prevailing doctrine appeared to reflect a street version of respect, which implies that male residents must be physically and emotionally tough and actively engage in enough deviant, criminal, and violent behavior (putting in work) to be respected as men. In other words, street code ethics seemed to be a dominant theme for the black males that came through the doors of the clubs I worked. Black males seemed intent on demonstrating that they were men because they had money, understood how to survive, and were willing to be combative as a first response to any challenge.

Challenges warranting a violent response could be as trivial as bumping into someone without apologizing, invading personal space, stepping on someone's shoe, spilling a drink, starring too long, or interacting with females that have a prior relationship with someone else. Instances involving lethal violence seemed to be related to drug deals, robbery, and snitching. Essentially, the most significant ingredient for club violence appeared to be the perception that someone was challenging another's masculinity in the presence of his peer group, and that failure to retaliate would be perceived as a sign of weakness. The clubs were staging arenas for impression management, where black males staked their claim to respectful manhood by overtly engaging in aggressive behaviors and violence as solutions to conflicts. It seems that Anderson's (1999) code-of-the-street perspective has explanatory power because earning and maintaining respect is critical to reputation, social currency, and ultimately social capital (Cureton, 2011b; Anderson, 1999; Anderson 1990).

Discussion: Going in as I am

I agree with Staples (1973) that there is a critical need for black sociologists to return to the field for a front-line analysis of blacks' participation in deviant, criminal, and violent subcultures. However, there are some critical issues that black sociologists researching deviant communities and black ganglands must contend with. Three critical issues black researchers conducting field research on deviant communities contend with are (1) maintaining an appropriate distance in order to be objective; (2) contemplating withholding social facts out of fear that information could further stigmatize, or demonstrate racial depravity; and (3) assuming that racial allegiance endows the researcher with racial expertise (Ocejo, 2013; Wax, 1983; Sawyer, 1973).

These-race specific issues were countered by maintaining a social scientific lens grounded by two logical perspectives, street elites and code of the street, respectively (Anderson, 1999; Katz, 1988). Moreover, the hesitancy to withhold social facts was eased by an obligation to remain as objective as possible while also being sensitive to the reality that racial life course outcomes are significantly related to institutional opportunity access, economic, social, cultural, residential, and spiritual variables (Wilson, 1987, 2009; West, 2001; Dyson, 1996).

Conclusion: Views from the Field

Permanent underclass communities with higher concentrations of blacks (e.g., ghettos, hoods, low-income areas, and government housing projects) continue to be adversely impacted by black-on-black crime and victimization. Unfortunately, a subculture of violence emphasizing gangsterism, street code ethics, and person-to-person predatory violence as a primary means to resolve social conflicts dominates the routine activities of black males who seemingly embrace this reality as a rite of passage to manhood (Cureton & Wilson, 2012; Cureton, 2009, 2010; Wilson, 1987, 2009; Williams, 2004; West, 2001; Anderson, 1990, 1999; Dyson, 1996; Shakur, 1993; Tucker 1968).

With the exception of Goffman (2014) and Venkatesh (2008), two high-profile ethnographies where an outsider was embraced by participants in criminogenic subcultures in Philadelphia and Chicago, respectively, updated field research on permanent underclass communities and social settings is lacking. Post–civil rights ethnographic research on permanent underclass black communities and violent spaces and places is rare because residents are suspicious of outsiders and therefore are not receptive to being subjects of ethnographic research.

Also, these environments seem to be chaotic and unpredictably violent, resulting in the perception that participant observation is risky. Unfortunately, the narrative about these communities have been taken over by political journalism, stoking public fears about black males. The solution may be that more black academics become involved in ethnographic research. The contention is that understanding of a particular phenomenon is enhanced by the characteristics, attributes, and perceptions of the researcher conducting ethnography (Feldman and Aldrich, 2005; Finkelstein, 2005; Sawyer, 1973).

In both instances of participant observation with the Hoover gang and club security, being a black male with an athletic physique represented race and social capital that symbolized racial allegiance. Operating with the basic premise that respect is a linchpin for black manhood enhanced my ability to negotiate troublesome and sometimes dangerous situations, which led to acceptance from gang members and other bouncers. Being embraced positively affected immersion, which improved the research experience, data collection access points, and ultimately authentic truisms about gangsterism and nightclub violence.

Conclusion: The Call for Black Sociology and Black Sociologists

Black America continues to be plagued by devalued humanity, explanations of criminal behavior as depraved and pathological, and narratives criminalizing civil groups who dare to protest threats to existential rights. Even with President Barack Obama as the face of America, the body of blackness was slaughtered by intraracial violence and fatalistic policing with impunity. Permanent underclass black communities in Chicago are beset by lethal predation so much so that a violent subculture has emerged infamously known as Chiraq (Cureton, 2017). Unfortunately, there have been limited explanations incorporating inter- and intraracial gangsterism and *omertà* policing in impoverished communities as contributors to homicide rates in Chicago (Hagedorn, 2009).

A Black Lives Matter movement with focal concerns similar to the Black Panther Party for Self-Defense has emerged and has immediately encountered narratives attempting to stigmatize the movement as collective chaotic discontent led by radicals who race-bait, violate the law, inspire terrorism within their own communities, and endorse killing police officers. The intellectual conversation about Chiraq and Black Lives Matter has been overshadowed by social panic and manufactured fears of black hostility, criminality, and protest riots. Essentially, Chiraq's subculture, which could be reactionary to misery, is branded pathological, and the valuable Black Lives Matter movement has been criminalized. Additionally, witnessed postmodern racial proxies aimed at character assassinations with respect to former president Barack Obama. There is no shortage of political maneuverings and narratives attempting to negate Obama's policy legacy and label his presidency as the worst in history. The election resulting in President Donald Trump was a political racial realignment steeped in a cultural war.

Teaching curriculums are being overhauled to focus on preferential universal Americanism at the expense of sacrificing race legacy social facts. Generations of blacks are being reindoctrinated with whitewashed history, further severing them from authentic truisms about Africans who became black in America. Black America's discontent has seemingly been successfully cast as meritless protest, and embraced as problematic by mainstream as well as black traditional and neoconservative opinion-makers. The call for a renewed investigation of blackness and black masculinity is necessary because blacks are again contending with value assessments that have adverse implications for the black body. The result is insensitivity and indifference with respect to their humanity.

There is a need for research that is cutting edge and at the forefront of the ongoing cultural processing of blacks. *The Handbook of Research on Black Males* is a significant corrective measure and should be read as such.

■ References

Agar, M. (1983). Ethnography and cognition. In R. Emerson (ed.), *Contemporary field research: A collection of readings* (pp. 69–77). Long Grove, IL: Waveland Press.

Alexander, M. (2010). *The new Jim Crow: Mass incarceration in the age of colorblindness.* New York: New Press.

Anderson, E. (1999). *Code of the street: Decency violence and the moral life of the inner city.* New York: Norton.

———. (1990). *STREETWISE: Race, class and change in an urban community.* Chicago: University of Chicago Press.

Brown, C., Clark, P., Jost, M., Lawrence, A., & Peters, R. (2006). *Greensboro truth and reconciliation commission report.* Greensboro, NC: Executive Report.

Brunt, L. (2001). Into the community. In P. Atkinson, A. Coffey, S. Delamont, J. Lofland, & L. Lofland (eds.), *Handbook of ethnography* (pp.80–91). Thousand Oaks, CA: Sage.

Chafe, W. (1980). *Civilities and civil rights: Greensboro, North Carolina, and the black struggle for freedom.* New York: Oxford University Press.

Cureton, S. (2008). *Hoover Crips: When Cripin' becomes a way of life.* Lanham, MD: University Press of America.

———. (2009). Something wicked this way comes: A historical account of black gangsterism offers wisdom and warning for African-American leadership. *Journal of Black Studies 40*(2), 347–61.

———. (2010). Lost souls of society become hypnotized by gangsterism. *Journal of Gang Research 18*(1), 39–52.

———. (2011a). *Black vanguards and black gangsters: From seeds of discontent to a declaration of war.* Lanham, MD: University Press of America.

———. (2011b). Night-crawlers: The potential health risks associated with criminogenic masculinity and clubbing. *Journal of Black Masculinity 2*(1), 135–51.

———. (2017). Chiraq: Oppression, homicide, concentrated misery, and gangsterism in Chicago. *Journal of Gang Research 25*, 1–18.

Cureton, S., & Wilson, C. (2012). The deceptive Black Knight campaign: Clique loyalty and sexual conquest. *Journal of Black Masculinity* 2(3), 1–24.

Dyson, M. (1996). *Race rules: Navigating the color line.* New York: Vintage Books.

Emerson, R. (ed.) (1983). *Contemporary field research: A collection of readings.* Long Grove, IL: Waveland Press.

Feldman, H., & Aldrich, M. (2005). The role of ethnography in substance abuse research and public policy. In W. Palacios (ed.). *Cocktails and dreams: Perspectives on drug and alcohol use* (pp. 14–28). Upper Saddle River, NJ: Pearson Prentice Hall.

Finkelstein, M. (2005). *With no direction: Homeless youth on the road and in the streets.* Belmont, CA: Thomson Wadsworth.

Frake, C. (1983). Ethnography. In R. Emerson (ed.), *Contemporary field research: A collection of readings* (pp. 60–67). Long Grove, IL: Waveland Press.

Grazian, D. (2007). The girl hunt: Urban nightlife and the performance of masculinity as collective activity. *Symbolic Interaction 30*(2), 221–43.

Gilligan, J. (1997). *Violence.* New York: Vintage Books.

Goffman, A. (2014). *On the run: Fugitive life in an American city.* Chicago: University of Chicago Press.

Hagedorn, J. (2009). A genealogy of gangs in Chicago: Bringing the state back into gang research. Presented at the Global Gangs Conference, Geneva, Switzerland, May 2009.

Hutchinson, J. (1999). The hip hop generation: African-American male-female relationships in a nightclub setting. *Journal of Black Studies* 30(1), 62–84.

Hunter, M. (2010). The nightly round: Space, social capital and urban black nightlife. *City and Community* 9(2), 165–86.

Katz, J. (1988). *Seductions of crime: Moral and sensual attractions in doing evil.* New York: Basic Books.

Kennedy, R. (1997). *Race, crime and the law.* New York: Vintage.

Klein, M. (2007). *Chasing after street gangs: A forty-year journey.* Upper Saddle River, NJ: Pearson Prentice Hall.

Klein, M., & Maxson, L. (2006). *Street gang patterns and policies.* New York: Oxford University Press.

Lovat, T. (1995). *Teaching and learning religion: A phenomenological approach.* Wentworth Falls, NSW, Australia: Social Science Press.

Mauer, M. (1999). *Race to incarcerate.* New York: New Press.

Monaghan, L. (2002). Regulating "unruly" bodies: Work tasks, conflict and violence in Britain's night-time economy. *British Journal of Sociology 53*(3), 403–29.

Ocejo, R. (2013). *Ethnography and the city: Readings on doing urban field work.* New York: Routledge.

Sawyer, E. (1973). Methodological problems in studying so-called deviant communities. In J. Ladner (ed.), *The death of white sociology* (pp. 361–80). New York: Vintage Books.

Shakur, S. (1993). *Monster: The autobiography of an L.A. gang member.* New York: Penguin.

Staples, R. (1973). What is black sociology? Toward a sociology of black liberation. In J. Ladner (ed.), *The death of white sociology* (pp. 161–72). New York: Vintage Books.

Tucker, S. (1968). *Beyond the burning. Life and death of the ghetto.* New York: Association Press.

Venkatesh, S. (2008). *Gang leader for a day: A rogue sociologist takes to the streets.* New York: Penguin.

Voisin, D., & Guilamo-Ramos, V. (2008). A commentary on community violence exposure and HIV risk behaviors among African-American adolescents. *African-American Research Perspectives 12*(1),

83–100.

Wax, R. (1983). The ambiguities of field work. In R. Emerson (ed.), *Contemporary field research: A collection of readings* (pp. 191–202). Long Grove, IL: Waveland Press.

Welch, K. (2007). Black criminal stereotypes and racial profiling. *Journal of Contemporary Criminal Justice 23*(3), 276–88.

West, C. (2001). *Race matters*. New York: Vintage Books.

Williams, S. (2004). *Blue rage, black redemption*. Pleasant Hill, CA: Damamli Publishing.

Wilson, W. (1987). *The truly disadvantaged: The inner city, the underclass, and public policy*. Chicago: University of Chicago Press.

Wilson, W. (2009). *More than just race: Being black and poor in the inner city*. New York: Norton.

 VIGNETTE

Ronnie was a high school student with an outstanding GPA and no criminal record. He didn't bother anyone. However, each day after leaving school, Ronnie would get followed by security, pulled over by police, and harassed for how he looked. He was consistently stereotyped as a product of his environment, being the son of a drug dealer, and was treated as such even though he'd never been in a run-in with the law. He was perceived as a criminal just because of his ethnicity and background. At a student dance, Ronnie was introduced to a teacher at his school who had had similar experiences. He went on to take classes from him and decided on a different major when he enrolled in college. Because of this individual's influence, Ronnie pushed through the adversity and graduated earlier than expected. Ronnie has since gone on all the way to graduate school and has started a career in higher education. He continues to challenge adversity and helps others do so as well.

PART 6

Hip-Hop

INTRODUCTION

Toby S. Jenkins

> I reminisce for a spell, or shall I say think back
> 22 years ago to keep it on track
> The birth of a child on the 8th of October
> A toast but my granddaddy came sober
> Countin' all the fingers and the toes
> Now I suppose, you hope the little black boy grows . . .
>   —Pete Rock & CL Smooth, "They Reminisce over You (T.R.O.Y.)"

The emotions felt at the birth of a child are indescribable. It is a special and miraculous experience. But in the current racial outlook in the United States, the birth of a black son is serious business. Black men live complicated lives in the United States, and parents often find themselves being hopeful, happy, concerned, and scared all at the same time. This is what makes the lyrics shared above a vivid representation of black life. A child is born, which is cause for a family toast and celebration. But grandpa comes sober and serious, counting fingers and toes, knowing that they have work to do in order for this little black boy to grow and live a healthy, safe, and fruitful life. This song, "They Reminisce over You (T.R.O.Y)" is about remembering the life of a black man. Troy Dixon, also known as Trouble T-Roy, was a dancer who died in the 1990s while on tour with the rapper Heavy D. He was a son, a brother, and of course a friend. And so his boys, Pete Rock & CL Smooth, penned a song about the act of remembrance in his honor. "They Reminisce over You" defines the acronym that mirrors his name (T.R.O.Y). It is often the spirits that have passed through this life who encourage us to sit and reflect—to reminisce and remember. And we have been doing a lot of this lately.

In 2016, we lost several black men who were music icons. We lost the Prince of pop music. We lost Maurice White, one of the elements of Earth, Wind & Fire. And in the world of hip-hop we lost our native son, Phife Dawg. While the world shook from utter shock and devastation with the death of Prince, a music genius who, in many ways, was untouchable and magical, our mourning of Phife was a bit more intimate. You see, hip-hop artists feel like friends, cousins, our boys, our girls, our peeps. For the hip-hop community, remembering Phife's life pushes us to wrestle with issues of physical and mental health, friendship, ambition, success, and culture. These are the issues of black life. These are the issues of hip-hop. So, as educators search for better ways to understand and to serve young black men, we must engage in the necessary practice of reminiscing over the critical issues of black life. This is what hip-hop culture has always done so well—uncover the complicated layers of our cultural experience. In this part, we examine hip-hop culture as a conduit to explore critical issues facing black men, including concepts of masculinity, mental health, and educational participation. Through the lens of hip-hop, the authors reminisce on the black male as a person, not just as a student—who black men are, what black men experience, and what black men are feeling.

In our critical reflection and exploration of hip-hop culture and black male life, we seek to honor and remember, not analyze and dissect. Black men have been placed under the social radar and microscope for centuries in an attempt to better define what it is, means, or feels like to be a black man. Everything from genetic makeup to mental psyche has been examined. The views have changed as much as the experiences that our men have faced. From enslavement to imprisonment, from no education to miseducation, from predatory practices leading to lynching to police profiling leading to the systemic loss of life—black men have most definitely faced an ever-changing experience in America. Even hip-hop culture refuses to be stagnant and is constantly changing. The element of music that is such a critical part of the culture is not without its own complicated contradictions and problems. The commodification of the music and culture has often played into extremely negative stereotypes of black men (from misogyny to hypermasculinity; from corporate co-opting to unguided self-distribution). Those of us who truly love both black men and hip-hop know that they are much more than their flaws. In her book *We Real Cool* (2004), bell hooks shares her beautiful reflections on and memories of her grandfather:

> "His smells fill my nostrils with the scent of happiness. With him the broken bits and pieces of my heart come together again." These visions of black men as healers, able to nurture life, are the representations of black masculinity that "keep it real" for they offer the vision of what is possible, a hint of the spirit that is alive and well in the black male collective being, ready to be reborn. They take our minds and hearts away from images of black males who have known soul murder and speak to us of resurrection, of a world in the making where all is well with black men's souls, where they are free and made whole. (p. 125)

These are the type of memories of black men that I knew growing up. My father was the most warm and sensitive spirit in our home. He was a hard worker who loved his family. My cousin Pedro, who grew up more like my brother than cousin, was sweet, quiet, and different. He liked different music. He thought differently. He was incredibly imaginable. He still is. And when it came to the brothers of the block, I can remember when our community sweated not the hard and thug nature of men, but rather the socially defiant and culturally original talent of the men that embraced hip-hop culture. We hung on their every word, bobbed our heads to every beat, and kept our eyes glued to every spin of the break dance.

And those that weren't artists still captured our hearts and personified the culture. It might have been the way a man walked, the language he used, the confidence he exuded, or his style of dress. It's that part of one's personality that makes those in New Orleans love being black down south or those in New York love being black up top. But let's be clear, the image of a "strong black man" is an image of goodness—intelligent, kind, hardworking, cool, and approachable. Cousins. Neighbors. Beautiful black sons. This is the "hip-hop" that I know and love.

For many Gen Xers, hip-hop is both how we got over and how we got through life in America. It helped form our friendships and connected us to other kindred spirits (ciphers); it motivated us to get through our homework and was the soundtrack to our extracurricular sports involvement (headphones); it woke us up culturally and moved us to consider activism ("conscious rap"); it gave us confidence, uniqueness, and swag (style); it provided us with the permission to be ourselves. And hip-hop is still incredibly compelling to young people. Hip-hop still greatly influences who young people want to be and how they want to behave. It still gives them a sense of freedom. Ultimately, an educational praxis that respects and embraces difference, that values the unique traits of the individual, that allows space for new ways of knowing, being, and learning also gives students permission to be themselves.

What makes hip-hop such an approachable form of art are the ways in which it was born and is still based in the community experience. For years, graffiti art gave young, talented canvas artists a platform to share their art with the world when galleries did not welcome them and when society saw them as criminal. As an art form, graffiti is another example of place making and claiming. Artists paint themselves onto the bricks and mortar of their community. Today, graffiti art has been embraced and included in many community arts programs, providing a structured way for young people to develop themselves as artists. These programs are also examples of how communities have transformed their opinions of graffiti and now see it as a valuable tool to help beautify communities through murals. This provides important social and political agency for young people. It allows them to assist their communities in their own unique way. Hip-hop as a culture has always provided a physical space that brought marginalized communities into the center. This is what makes the visual image of the "cipher" so compelling.

A cipher is a circle of energy created by members of the community standing shoulder to shoulder, forming a circle and giving each person in the circle an opportunity to "spit" or rhyme. What originally motivated my inquiry into understanding the value that hip-hop culture has within educational settings was my witnessing a cipher in the parking lot of a grocery store. As I approached my car, I glanced at a group of black youth. They were all black boys and they had formed a cipher in the middle of the parking lot. One kid was in the center of the circle, spitting a rhyme. The others were so intensely listening that they were physically bent over leaning in to ensure they didn't miss a word. The visual was striking and I thought that many teachers would love to have young black boys listen that intensely in class. As I continued to observe the group, it occurred to me for the first time the level of self-confidence engineered within hip-hop culture. When the kid in the center finished, he was immediately applauded. He felt great. He felt listened to. He felt that his thoughts mattered. That is something else the educational arena can learn from hip-hop—cultivating a sense of mattering.

The last compelling visual from that day was when the next kid entered the cipher. There was a clear sense of healthy competition. He genuinely applauded the boy before him, but he was determined to be better. Hip-hop culture shows us how to create genuine communities of excellence and a healthy competitive spirit rooted in kinship. Again these boys were free to simply be themselves—bright, playful, smart youth who aspired to be great at something. Participation in hip-hop cultural activities gives young people guts. The guts to take a chance. The guts to be vulnerable. And most importantly the guts to engage in important forms of truth telling.

Hip-hop is a cultural space that welcomes the authentic rage, frustration, and critique that young people might have about the world in which they live. They don't have to edit their words, quiet their voice, or comply. Hip-hop and performance poetry are cultural spaces where individuals who have been kicked out of schools, locked out of opportunity, and imprisoned in oppression have created a space where they can shine, excel, and be great. And generating a sense of greatness is important when you have lived a life on the margins of society. In their creative work, hip-hop artists have always talked about their greatness, their skill, and their aim to be the best. At its core, hip-hop is about truth, nonconformity, excellence, and love.

Hip-hop culture shows educators what real love looks like. Love is action—it is something that you do, not a simple expression that you say. It is easy to say, "I love kids. I love my students." But how do you love them? You see folks that love hip-hop, *love* it. They wear it on their bodies, tattoo it on their skin. They sing it, rap it, and memorize it because it matters so much to them. They dance to it on a dance floor, bob their heads to it in an elevator, and party to it in the club. They draw it on walls, design it on clothes, sketch it into the concrete. They write about it, read about it, teach it, and lecture on it. They blog on it, create magazines about it, and launch podcasts discussing it. They create community organizations grounded in it and build enterprises that sell it. They develop documentaries and movies about it and create television series that pay homage to it. They build their life on the foundation of hip-hop. For folks who truly love hip-hop, it is everywhere and everything. So I ask again, how do you love kids? Is at least a part of your professional foundation built on genuinely loving black boys who need you? The music of hip-hop embodies the lives of youth—loves them even with all of their flaws. The culture of hip-hop embraces the experiences of youth and gives them a sense of knowing that they are not alone and that their life matters. In her 2004 book, *Stand & Deliver: Political Activism, Leadership, and Hip-Hop Culture*, Yvonne Bynoe explains:

> Rap music and hip-hop culture factored heavily in the shaping of the United States. In the late twentieth century this dynamic music and subculture bubbled up in the early 1970's and gave

voice to Black [and Latino] Americans who had previously existed on the periphery of the nation's consciousness. . . . The music not only highlighted their struggles, but also shed light on
their aspirations. (p. 54)

Bynoe (2004) goes on to call for a continued political evolution of hip-hop culture, stating,
"True revolutionaries will demand a new thing, rap music that not only tells stories, but also
speaks truth to power and encourages folks to image new realities" (p. 55). When they are at
their best, the lyrics penned by young hip-hop artists and the poems written by spoken word
artists are a valuable form of nontraditional knowledge and social critique of the American
experience. It is important to state explicitly that cultural production in communities of color
is more than just a cultural convenience—a form of entertainment. There is intellectual and
educational merit in culture, art, and community folkways. A community often uses culture
(cultural production, engagement, education) as a politic of social survival—as a life raft for
those drowning in oppression. In her critical work *Black Feminist Thought*, Patricia Hill Collins suggests that wrestling with the ways in which nontraditional knowledge has been used to
educate, create self-awareness, raise self-efficacy, and steward social change among communities
of color offers important insight into the complex relationship between culture and education
in America. In his work, Paulo Freire (2008) stressed how important raising critical consciousness is among the oppressed. Resistant education helps traditionally oppressed communities to
grow critical literacy and form their own strategies to resist oppressive systems and structures.
Carter G. Woodson stressed this same ethic in his classic text, *The Mis-education of the Negro*.
Rarely do institutions built on frameworks of oppression do the necessary work of educating
for freedom. And so communities use every means necessary to educate our people—porches,
stoops, kitchen tables, churches, and cultural production. I learned from hip-hop things that
I never learned in school. Growing up in South Carolina, we rarely learned about any other
social experience beyond South Carolina. The South was all that mattered. So, I learned about
the critical experiences that my racial and cultural peers were experiencing in northern cities through hip-hop. I was exposed to international culture through the music that mixed in
West Indian culture. Many folks make the argument that the days of a KRS-One, Chuck D, or
Grandmaster Flash are gone. There is no longer a message in hip-hop. But one of the main
tenets of my scholarship is to understand and appreciate the contemporary manifestations
of culture—to believe and show that young people still care and our cultural ethics of survival
are still very much alive.

A contemporary hip-hop artist that personifies the concept of art as educator and social
commentator is Kendrick Lamar. In his work, Lamar has specifically and directly called out the
system that creates chaos in the lives of black men like himself. In his song "Institutionalized"
he raps: "I'm trapped inside the ghetto and I ain't proud to admit it . . . Institutionalized, I keep
runnin' back for a visit." Cultures of oppression are often institutionalized. The psychological
trauma of life becomes routine and normal. Lamar is a reflective artist who allows us to enter
his life and understand the ways in which society has a role of responsibility in the flaws of
youth. Bettina Love (2016) explains:

In his music, Lamar complicated the contemporary everyday narratives and realities of urban youth who endure the social, economic, physiological, and psychological trauma of coping with the racial injustices of "post-racial" America by indicting the system. Specifically, in *Good Kid, M.A.A.D City*, Lamar does not hide from his flaws, but instead confronts them by recognizing that many are the result of a system that was built and thrives on racism, exploitation, entangled hierarchies, and eviscerating Black leadership in already fragile communities of color. In short, Lamar seemingly acknowledges that no matter how good he is, the system is not set up for him to survive. Jeffrey St. Clair (2005) has argued that the system has not failed; it is doing exactly what it is supposed to do in a nation built on racism, state violence, and domestic terrorism. (p. 1)

In many ways, schools are no different. In fact, they are central to affirming and continuing this very structure. So discussing how to better serve black males in the educational system is a discussion about invention—making something out of nothing. A healthy and loving educational system designed to help young black men become their full, brilliant, and talented selves does not exist. Programs exist that are accomplishing this. Organizations exist that are doing this. Individual educators are going against the grain and making inroads. But there is not a national educational system built to lovingly educate black boys.

In this part of the handbook, Mazi Mutafa offers a community-based educator's perspective on hip-hop and youth engagement. As the executive director of a hip-hop nonprofit that does incredible work with youth both in Washington, DC, and in global partner cities abroad, he helps us to understand the special position and experience of both educators and students who create and participate in educational programs grounded in hip-hop culture. Crystal Endsley then explores the performance of masculinity through spoken word poetry. In "Discussing Suicide without being Crucified," Edward Smith discusses the ways that black men confront critical issues of mental health through a lyrical and critical analysis of hip-hop music. We then end this part with a discussion on love. In "Mama, Am I Hip-Hop?" Chelda Smith Kondo discusses issues of intersectionality related to culture, gender, and race from the lens of mothering a black boy.

Ultimately, educators who imagine ways to educate and serve young black men through a hip-hop praxis are engaging in one of essential rooted practices of hip-hop. Creating something out of nothing. We must create something out of nothing like the young folks who birthed hip-hop did in the impoverished boroughs of New York City. Unlike the broader history of education in the United States, there is not a history of more than three hundred years demonstrating how to effectively utilize hip-hop to guide educational practice. There is simply a deep love and authentic respect for the culture that drives this work. So this is what we must do. We must love and respect the cultures that black and brown youth create. We must create and build something new and creative because our children's lives depend on it.

■ **References**

Bynoe, Y. (2004). *Stand and deliver: Political activism, leadership, and hip-hop culture.* New York: Soft Skull Press.

Freire, P. (2008). *Pedagogy of the oppressed.* Trans. M. B. Ramos. New York: Continuum.

hooks, b. (2004). *We real cool: Black men and masculinity.* New York: Routledge.

Love, B. (2016). Good kids, mad cities: Kendrick Lamar and finding inner resistance in response to Ferguson USA. *Cultural Studies 16*(3), 320–23. doi:1-.1177/1532708616634837.

Morrell, E. & Duncan-Andrade, J. (2002). Promoting academic literacy with urban youth through engaging hip-hop culture. *English Journal 91*(6), 88–92.

Rock, P., & CL Smooth. (1991) They reminisce over you (T.R.O.Y). *Mecca and the Soul Brother.* Elektra Records, New York.

Words, Beats, and My Life

Mazi A. E. Mutafa

After fifteen years of leading a hip-hop nonprofit organization whose work is in service to youth and young adults, I have learned so much about strategies to promoting individual and community transformation. Our organization, Words, Beats & Life started as a project by a university student group. An idea created by young people. The fact the we began Words, Beats & Life as a conference at the University of Maryland (UMD) that was hosted by multiple student groups is important because those college years shaped much of what I believed was possible and necessary in the larger world as I graduated. We chose to build an organization rooted in hip-hop for a range of reasons, including the fact that hip-hop was the reason I went to college—not because I am an MC or even consider myself to be an artist (except for the occasional love poem). Hip-hop put important aspects of my life story at the center of the discussion and has done the same for multiple generations, ethnic communities, and nationalities. To be clear, when I say *hip-hop* I mean the five foundational elements as defined by the Universal Zulu Nation, hip-hop's first organization: DJ'ing, graffiti, MC'ing, B-boying/B-birling, and knowledge of self.

When I was enrolled at Arrowhead Elementary School, the principal created detention just for me. Every day I was sent to the principal's office. The principal once told me it was for my own protection, because my homeroom teacher, Mr. Waters, was concerned that he might put me through a wall if I continued to come to his class. So this was my first experience of receiving special treatment. I had a desk in the principal's office. Eventually, he decided that I needed a room all to myself, so he created in-school detention in what was an empty classroom. Once I was in this room, the school decided this would be a great place to send other problem students.

I continued to find myself in administrative offices in Kettering Middle School and then in Largo High School. I was socially promoted out of elementary school, diagnosed with a learning disability in the final year of middle school, and stuck in remedial classes for the first two years of high school. I was special. I am sure this is why I love "special" children so much. When I visit schools, I almost exclusively talk to the students in the back row. And even as an adult, I still sit in the back row myself.

Recently, I have come to see this special educational experience of isolation as one of the greatest blessings of my life. The institutions where I was sent for my education failed me. Rather than create a system that would actually encourage my success and the success of other mostly black boys, instead they chose to warehouse us in their walls with detention or in-school suspension. We were not allowed to attend class, but we were still expected to do the work, so we had to teach ourselves, which honestly was fine with me. I was always my favorite teacher and that has continued to this day.

School administrations decided early on that they would not fulfill their responsibility. They rarely challenged us to tap into our collective brilliance, so I had to challenge myself. Most of us had no aspirations beyond some future where we would be out of school—a position in life where adults would have no say about what we did or thought, how long we could play, or what we had to eat. I remember the greatest goal many of my peers had was to be done with school. Not to be educated or knowledgeable. For what? Why would we want the approval of people who had such clear disdain for us? Sadly, this has not changed. Black boys often get suspended, expelled, or put in remedial classes or receive individual education plans, and the expectations for our lives are always just a little better than survival.

It's interesting that I did not have this experience in the inner city of one of America's cities. All this happened in Prince Georges County, the richest majority-black county in the United States of America. Looking back, it's clear that the only reason I actually graduated from high school was due to sports. I found a way to train my body, build my community, and develop a different kind of intellectual dexterity. Like most black or brown boys, my talent was celebrated in games.

I was fortunate enough to have had a coach who had gone to college. As I think back, he was one of maybe two or three adults employed by the school that talked to us about college. But a more central influence was a peer who was applying to college, and when she asked where I was going, I had to figure it out. Fortunately, to play sports, I had to maintain a 2.5 GPA, which basically made it so I qualified for all the schools to which I applied. Yep, I was a solid C student-athlete in a majority-black county in a majority-black school.

I was a graduating senior from Largo High School and received my acceptance letter to one of the four schools to which I applied. I was rejected from Bowie State, Howard University, and Morgan State due to incomplete applications. Yet somehow that same application got me into the flagship university of the state, the University of Maryland. But by the time I received the final acceptance, I had decided that college was not for me, mostly because I never felt like school was a place for me. I cut school all the time beginning in elementary school. I left early, was in detention, or was suspended for most of my fourth-grade to tenth-grade education. I had some good teachers, but I was always more interested in what was going on outside than what was happening at the front of the classroom. I still remember my Spanish teacher in Largo High School who told me I would never be somebody, and that she thought less of the University of Maryland for enrolling me.

How could she understand what mattered the most to my education were never the topics of discussion in the classroom? For me, school was a twelve-year experience of adults telling me what should be important to me, but never actually asking me. I still remember the first day I got excited about learning in a school-based setting. It was about four months after I graduated from high school sitting in an African American studies class at the University of Maryland titled Blacks and Popular Culture.

The teacher was a woman named Eva George, and the topic of discussion for the day was assigned reading from Dr. Tricia Rose's first book, *Black Noise*. This book was about hip-hop, but mostly about how music from a particular era incorporated the soundscape of New York City into the music. The topic was especially relevant for me because I spent my summers in New York with my mother's side of the family, the Puerto Ricans and the Venezuelans. Having grown up listening to way more Luther Vandross than LL Cool J, I found this discussion of place and hip-hop culture extremely interesting and one with which I could understand through personal memory. Her lecture was the first time my life experience was at the center of the dialogue. This was a signpost moment. In some parts of the ancient world, travelers would find signs that offered direction to the next city. Those signposts were pivotal in guiding folks along their journey. I like to think of signpost moments as points in time I can point back to and show how it changed the direction of my life.

This was the beginning of what would be a truly transformative six-year college experience making my way through multiple majors and ending up as an English and African American studies major. One of the first things I did in college was get involved with student life on campus. I worked at the university's Black Cultural Center, cofounded four students organizations, wrote for the black student newspaper, and ran to be (losing twice and finally winning) president of the largest black student group, the Black Student Union. The following year, I became a brother of a majority-black Greek-letter organization Phi Beta Sigma. All of these experiences were signpost moments. In their own way, each colored the way I would think about education, community transformation, and the role of culture in transforming individual lives and whole communities.

The People: Keepers of Culture

The people who were my mentors were all keepers of culture. Jihad Aziz, Saafir Raab, Toby Jenkins, and Clayton Walton were the most important teachers I had in college, and I never took a class with any of them. They were all my mentors, and in their own way they each helped me to add context to what I was learning in class and trying to do as a student leader. This is the role that all of our master artists play in the lives of our students. They are people adding on to the educational experience by helping to add a context, make connections, and fill in gaps missing in our students' educational experience. These relationships are at the center of our approach to creating transformational learning experiences.

I share all this to provide a context, to locate myself as a leader and creative actor. It's important to know that the people who do this work are usually the adult version of the young people who need this work the most. In the formation of Words, Beats & Life, we understood that culture is about passing down history, tradition, and identity. For many Americans regardless of racial identity, culture is something discussed primarily during cultural heritage months, holidays, and family gatherings. Often, culture is not taught using school-based methods of education. It is handed down through experience, from elders, parents, and community members through music, food, dress, and language. Hip-hop becomes the perfect vehicle to hand down traditions related to technology, politics, culture, and tradition in America and around the world.

It is important to acknowledge that black boys are often learning about themselves through life experiences while participating in a traditional educational experience that asks them to leave that knowledge out of their engagement with history, literature, math, and science. Culture matters, and participating in an educational experience that centers your experience, as a human being, is vital. Good teachers know this in traditional and community-based alternative classrooms. This is why they often work to make cultural heritage months meaningful for students to learn about themselves and other. Hip-hop allows us to teach the full spectrum of human history 365 days a year through music, visual art, textile designs, dance, and knowledge of self—the fifth element of hip-hop.

However, traditional school-based approaches to identity are almost exclusively rooted in understanding the past, but rarely about helping students to understand the current moment as they prepare for their futures. The freedom to create transformational educational experiences in nontraditional classrooms has been central to the approach of Words, Beats & Life. Because we are not a school, we have a different kind of freedom— not simply to create classrooms, but to create communities. Our community breaks geographic boundaries by having all sites open to anyone who can get there, age boundaries by having such a large cross section of ages of students, and we also have multiple classes taught in the same space so students can float from class to class and engage in ways that make sense for them.

We know the value of assessment, evaluations, and experiential learning opportunities. We evaluate multiple forms of learning, including belonging, school engagement, community service hours, skill set mastery, and promotion within the program based on skills mastered, knowledge, and performance. We have built a culture of celebration and collaboration among students and among teachers. This works especially well because our work is rooted in hip-hop.

The Academy: Nontraditional Classrooms

Hip-hop is a community survival strategy created as a response to attacks upon the creativity, health, and well-being of NYC public school children and families. We chose hip-hop exactly

Figure 1. The Academy, taken from the Word Beats & Life website.

for this reason. It was a survival strategy created by young people for young people. We have built our program around the idea that hip-hop today is really rooted in three principles: remixing, sampling, and the central role of technology in art making and education. This was done intentionally for a few reasons. First, our nontraditional (community based) classrooms allow us to create learning communities of young people ages fourteen to twenty-three. This means a class can literally have a middle school student and a college senior both learning from a master teacher and in a position to learn from each other. Breaking down the artificial barriers that are reinforced by school is critical to building community. Your age, your address, or how much money your parents make has no relevance in our classroom. A willingness to learn, teach, and share determines if you are in community with us. This approach is especially important when engaging boys of color—breaking down who their community is and where it is. The place they come from is not the only community of which they are a part. Hip-hop opens their entire city up to them, and for that matter the entire world.

Our pedagogy is rooted in a practice called "the dynamic classroom." A student's skill level determines who he learns with and what kind of access to opportunity he has in the WLB Academy. We make a multiyear investment in the education of our apprentices from the first day they enroll in our program. We celebrate their brilliance and interest in the things we teach. We also make room for each student to bring his individual knowledge and interest to the classroom, as an expert in his own experience. The idea that our students are apprentices being taught by master artists (who make a living as artists and also teach) is an important fact. The master artists instantaneously have a level of credibility with the students that many traditional classroom teachers don't. The teaching and learning process is not adversarial. It is not about power. It is collaborative from the very first day.

On their first day, all apprentice students receive a copy of the WBL Academy handbook. One of the most important things about the handbook is it functions as a kind of contract with students about what they can expect to learn, receive, and be encouraged to do, and at what rates they can be compensated for their performances. We ask our younger students to memorize our apprentice oath. It is posted in all our sites for our high school and college-aged students to see and so be reminded of why our program exists. The "Apprentice Oath," by Bomani Armah, represents how and what we want our students to think about themselves and their responsibilities as keepers and teachers of culture.

THE HOT 16 (APPRENTICE OATH)

I'm an artist, I'm a leader

I'm a scientist, I'm a reader

I'm a self-confident over-achiever

I'm a believer

Cause I'm Words Beats & Life

I can complete any task

I strive to be the best in my class

I'm the link between the future and the past

What I build will last

Cause of Words Beats & Life

I'll make the most of opportunity

I promise work for my community

And use hip-hop to build peace and unity

Success isn't new to me

Cause I'm Words Beats & Life

This world needs more positivity

I take on this responsibility

And promise to use my abilities

I'm full of possibilities

Cause I'm Words Beats & Life

A young person who works to live this oath is a person on a journey to self-mastery. For WBL, self-mastery is a combination of two ideas. The first idea is "knowledge of self," which is the fifth element of hip-hop culture after DJ'ing, graffiti, MC'ing, and B-boying/B-girling. The second concept is "mastery and future," which is a youth development principle. We remixed these ideas to create "self-mastery." Mastery of self is the journey we ask every apprentice student to take with our master teachers. It is a journey of lifelong learning working to discover the connections and relationships between multiple forms of knowledge. We ask young people questions to learn their answers. You might be surprised how infrequently young people are asked questions for which the right answer is whatever they say. You might also be surprised how infrequently those questions come from men that look like them in a classroom.

Beginning-level apprentices learn in classes with lots of direction and support from the master artists in terms of instruction. The beginning apprentice is really focused on skill set mastery. Intermediate students still receive instruction, but to a much more limited degree. Their primary focus is project-based learning using their techniques and methods they received during formal instruction to create their own art. That artwork and its progression are tracked in the form of a digital portfolio maintained by Academy interns.

Intermediate students qualify for performances for pay as a way for us to promote employability and entrepreneurship. Our approach is not education just for its own sake. It's education for community, art production, and the ability to provide for yourself with your skills and talent. Intermediate apprentices are also assigned a college material coach to take them through a three- to six-month college prep, application, and enrollment process in our effort to promote the pursuit of a postsecondary education.

Advanced apprentice students also qualify for paid performances; they have access to open studio time to create works of art using our supplies and equipment without supervision. They also engage local working artists, arts managers, and activists during our various speaker series and alternative spring break and alternative winter break experiences. Their engagement with WBL is centered on independent learning, art making, and marketing. We are working now to create a new curriculum that centers on theoretical aspects of each of the art forms we teach, encouraging students to create using techniques of their own, those that they have observed, and those that they have been taught.

Our approach is as much about art as it is driven by the art we create. "In 5 Seconds" is a poem we commissioned that reflects the way we think about our students. It's critical to us that our apprentice students understand we love them. That we believe in them. That we have high expectations of them rooted in what we have seen them do, what we have taught them, and most importantly what they have taught us.

In 5 seconds a teacher will begin to speak
This is for the kids who
wither away in classroom boxes and
cicada themselves out windows when the teacher begins
leaving empty shells behind
whose voices whine "What's geometry for?"
"I'm never gonna use it"
Colossal kids who shrink under spotlight
expecting to hear, "FREEZE! Stop!"
but instead, they hear, "Go. Move . . . Now's your time"
always loosen up first / deep breath everybody
inhale to uprock / pause to think
exhale to emcee / stare & don't blink

Don't ever let them tell you that you need
laser cartridges or high priced anything
all you need is your voice—your hands—comfortable shoes
an empty space—a landscape—And The Will
but you want geometry, so . . .
. . . are all beats quadrilateral?
Depending on the location of the center of rotation

Figure 2. The Jam, taken from the Word Beats & Life website.

can you tell the diameter of this Cameo record?
Is there any symmetry to this picture?
What is the radius of a 5th graders windmill?
How much area will 3 cans of spray paint cover?
Yes, the metaphors are three-dimensional, cuz
we've been rockin' this since Converse
We are WBL
helping teens discover their mutant powers since 2002
—like making canvas chromatically explode
—Freezing entire crowds in awe
—or reaching thru milk crate portals bringing historic singers
back to life just to play with musicians of today
It aint easy, though
some days the floor will feel indifferent
trains will break down like cracked albums
and friends will morph into shadows
But then what??
There's a long hard walk back to your seat unless you
Show and Prove—who got the props?
Ante Up & Ace that contest!

Grab that diploma.

Don't just get a job—Create One

THAT's what we're giving

That extra Bop in your step as you stride into any office

cipher

art gallery or

across any stage

to speak with conviction and with rhythm

to find layers and colors still unseen

this is our mission—we are WBL

& we don't want you to just rock a crowd . . .

We expect you to rock the entire world.

(By Black Picasso, https://www.reverbnation.com/poemcees)

It is our responsibility as culture keepers and educators not simply to encourage our students but more importantly to build the scaffolding to make their dreams and aspirations attainable. I have always understood it to be our responsibility to open doors, knock down walls, and build bridges that members of our community can cross. This includes adult artists in our community who also need support and who are willing to work in collaboration with us.

The Jam: Celebrations of Excellence

It is important to know that community, much like success, cannot just happen in a vacuum. It is not something that just happens in a classroom. Community has to happen in the world. Some organizations create complex rites of passage programs rooted in traditional African rituals, but hip-hop has its own way of handing down tradition and recognizing the transitions of members of the community. To that end, we organize events for our students to showcase their talent through the performance of songs, routines, and gallery shows. We also bring them into community by having them participate in paint battles where people create murals as part of a competition, dance battles where students in some instances compete against their teachers, and slam poetry or MC battles. It is critical that opportunities be created to demonstrate skill set mastery in a community.

We invite communities to review portfolios as part of showcases, but invite pioneers and legends from the hip-hop community to witness, challenge, and support our students in their efforts as young artists. It is vital that they know that they are part of a long tradition of practitioners, and that they are part of a larger community of local young artists of all ages. Their challenge is to excel and create work that makes them memorable. Peace, love, unity, and having fun are as important to hip-hop as any of the art forms, or knowledge of self. It is essential that every student understand and experience that the nature of their community is a participatory one. They cannot artists whom nobody knows or has seen.

We host graffiti street art and fine art paint jams for between fifty and seventy-five artists every year, of which ten to fifteen are our apprentice students. Our students compete in every dance battle we host in an effort to showcase their skills and their innovation on the dance floor and to be in community with a larger dance community. We convene both of these communities to keep them rich, strong, and connected. We do this in order to remind our students that they are being brought into community that makes real their oath, "This world needs more positivity / I take on this responsibility / And promise to use my abilities / I'm full of possibilities." They have a responsibility to continue to create, innovate, and take their place in the larger community as artists, scholars, and eventually leaders. They belong at the center of any cipher. They belong at the front of any boardroom. They are self-confident overachievers who take advantage of every opportunity to learn and showcase their creative brilliance. It is this very spirit we work to cultivate within the larger community by building what we call ciphers.

The Cipher: Building a Movement

The concept of a cipher in hip-hop comes from the Arabic word *sifrs*, which is the number zero. It's a circle in which competition usually takes place between either dancers or MCs. We have worked to redefine this concept as a sacred circle of interconnectedness, where what happens in the circle of observers is just as important as the observers themselves. The observers are the community responsible for protecting the participant in the circle. For Words, Beats & Life, the cipher, as a program, was a way to build bridges among other nonprofits, for-profits, teaching artists, artists, and activists and to think about our work to transform communities in collaboration. This program has been important to the organization, but also important as we demonstrate that we do not need to be in competition to do good. We can be in cooperation.

One of the most important books I read in college was *The Crisis of the Negro Intellectual: A Historical Analysis of the Failure of Black Leadership* by Harold Cruz. The crux of the book was that the greatest challenge to black leadership especially during the civil rights movement was a perpetual fight for resources from benefactors and attention from the media. As a college student, this profoundly changed how I understood my responsibility when I became the president of the Black Student Union, and even how I thought about the creation of the Words, Beats & Life Hip-Hop Conference. Though most people would describe hip-hop as black culture, I understood that its roots were both black and Latino, but its fans and participants looked like the whole human family. It was important that the host committee look like the human family and that the panels and workshops be appealing to students at UMD that were Latino/a, Asian American, Jewish, Muslim, African, Caribbean, and so on. That experience of creating a conference for all students by a black student organization made history at UMD. That experience informed the way we built the nonprofit and its programs and established partnerships with organizations that were supposed to be our competitors. They were our community. Our effort has been to learn from the mistakes of previous generations by always celebrating the success of our peers, lifting up the work of others, finding opportunities for

Figure 3. The Cipher, taken from the Word Beats & Life website.

collaboration, and securing the funding to support our collaboration. We are all working to do good or, as we call it, "doing good better," so why not work together to do it.

To that end we publish the world's first peer-reviewed academic journal of hip-hop, in which we publish the essays, scholarship, poetry, and academic articles of scholars, artists, and activists from all over the world. In the thirteen-year history of the publication, we have never published the work of anyone affiliated with WBL. We host a quarterly consortium in Washington, DC, of museums, after-school programs, university courses, and funders to create collaborative projects, develop a legislative agenda, and build a hip-hop history month calendar. For the last nine years, we have hosted and curated an annual teach-in and awards ceremony called the Remix Awards. All of these efforts are outward facing and never about the work of WBL, but rather about our peers. It is critical that our students know that they are a part of a community that is larger than WBL, and that artists can and should be advocates for the transformation of the institutions that directly impact our lives, families, and communities. It is in the apprentice oath, "I promise work for my community / And use hip-hop to build peace and unity / Success isn't new to me." It is vital that even as an organization they see us doing what we ask them to work toward.

The importance of this approach cannot be overstated. It is a reflection of how we teach, and what we have seen work. At the heart of every decision we make are the following four questions. Why doesn't this exist? If it did exist, how would the world be different? If we were successful, how would we sustain it? Who can be our partner? Nothing is ever for its own sake.

We teach to transform the way young artists think about themselves and their power to make a difference in the world.

Being an organization based in the nation's capital also means that we are able to engage artists from all over the world through federal institutions like the Smithsonian and the State Department. As an international city, we are able to host artists from all over the world that the State Department brings to America, and often their first stop in America is in Washington, DC. Six years ago, one of those artists invited us to visit his home country of Uganda. We were able to secure funds from the DC government through its Sister City Program to take a delegation of four people, three artists and one arts administrator.

The Embassy of Hip-Hop: Cultural Ambassadors

Over the last five years we have been able to share our learning to engage young people in Africa (Senegal, Uganda, and South Africa), Asia (Lebanon, Saudi Arabia, Pakistan, and South Korea), Europe (Brussels, England, France), and South America (Brazil). In all of these places we found organizations just like WBL, serving little boys and girls of color. We were often invited to provide master teachers, or host capacity building trainings. We are now working to develop a public arts strategy in Pakistan, introducing new contemporary American dance forms in Korea, and developing commercial ties with the organizations with whom we work. We believe that economic development has to be at the heart of our organization-to-organization collaborations. It is not enough to just teach; we have to invest in the work we believe in, and create two-way exchanges.

It is for this reason that we have created a new approach that outlines a four- to five-year commitment to working in each country. In the first year of working in a country, we send teaching artists for master classes. They lead master classes in community spaces, universities, and art schools. This allows us to connect through culture and create shared experiences and opportunities for peer-to-peer learning.

In the second year, WBL hosts a retreat for teaching artists, arts managers, and creatives to build their capacity to make/raise money, evaluate their programming, scale up their programming, and develop partnerships. As part of the retreat we provide seed funding for a project and in year three we will invite the leaders of that project to come to Washington, DC, to present their learning's at the John F. Kennedy Center for the Performing Arts as part of the Words, Beats & Life Festival. We have done this with organizations from Morocco, Uganda, and Brussels.

In year three we commission the creation of a new WBL apparel inspired by textiles in that country. It is also in year three that the work of selected artists is added to the WBL shop for WBL staff to sell in America. We will buy their products in bulk and be their American distributer for one year. Our apprentice students are employed to fulfill those orders. The first two countries we have partnered with for this step are Pakistan and Uganda.

In the fourth year, we take advanced WBL apprentice students to perform in the country, offering an opportunity for our students to collaborate with international artists while

Figure 4. The Embassy, taken from the Word Beats & Life website.

abroad and perform abroad in the process. This opportunity is available for currently enrolled students and alumni. The first two countries to partner for this step were Korea and Brussels. This step in the process is important because for the first three years of the partnership our students have been learning about the organizations and communities we engage with around the world. They know that their community is not just their block, and why we expect them "to rock the entire world."

We have already completed the first three steps in Uganda. We expect to complete the fourth step in 2017–2018 by taking apprentice students abroad. We know how transformative these travel experiences have been for the master artists we have been able to take abroad. We anticipate that taking apprentice students will be even more impactful, because it will be a student-to-student exchange.

The Hustle: The Creative Core

For the last two years, the Creative Core has operated as a workforce development initiative in the Words, Beats & Life Academy. The Core was created as a way to engage our most advanced arts students in paid performance opportunities in the District and beyond. Moving into this, the third year of the Creative Core, we are expanding who can join the Core, to include nonartists interested in working in creative businesses.

Figure 5. The Hustle, taken from the Word Beats & Life website.

According to the office of planning, the creative sector is the second largest employment sector in Washington, DC, after the federal government. We believe it is critical that young people throughout the District all have a pathway to those employment opportunities. To that end, a year ago we hired a Creative Core coordinator whose job has been to book performances for our students. The year prior to her hire, our students had nine performances over the course of a year. In our most recent fiscal year she scheduled fifty-two performances, and participated in the creation of fifteen murals around the District. Through this work, we engaged a number of young people who want to work in the creative sector but who are not artists. This expanded purpose of the Core allows us to engage those young people as well.

We have thirty creative businesses, throughout the District, that have agreed to receive a WBL Creative Core intern in 2017–2018. These interns will be young people that have completed our three-month long workforce development training to prepare them to work in a creative business as part of a paid internship. In 2015, we began employing students from the Words, Beats & Life Academy to perform through the District of Columbia as part of special events and festival. We submitted a pilot program to train and place Department of Youth Rehabilitation Services court-involved youth at thirty creative businesses throughout the District as a gateway into the creative economy. This was a game changer because it was the result of a policy recommendation we developed, to create gateway employment in the creative sector for the most difficult-to-employ youth in the District of Columbia, the court-involved.

Again, in 2017 we expect to have secured letters of agreement from hip-hop-based nonprofits throughout the United States and around the world to accept the placement of university students as paid interns. This will allow us to announce the launch of our national and international internship placement program with Columbia College in Chicago. The future is looking bright for our organization, but most importantly for our students.

Coming Full Circle

In the end, all this work brings me back to where I started, working to build community among people that the larger society seeks to divide along class, race, and economic standing, working through hip-hop to build bridges and community. I know the value of creating intentionally for other people what I have always believed happened to me by chance. Pivotal to my own progress was the realization of how much I have to learn, and the awareness of how many people are in my life to be my teachers. Anyone working to create transformational educational experiences for black boys needs to do it by building a community. You should not look for people with whom you agree. You need people with whom you can agree enough to work together. Share passion. You also need ideas that are big enough that when some people leave, others will work with you because they see themselves in the ideas. We are facing big challenges. Our black boys are facing big challenges. Don't be afraid to dream and to create. Educating black boys in our contemporary society means building consensus around big and bold ideas.

Dopeboys and Mic Fiends

Spoken Word Poetry as a Performance of Black Masculinity

Crystal Leigh Endsley

The MC plays a critical role as a foundational element of hip-hop culture and an equally critical role for Black men. Where else but in hip-hop culture can young Black men narrate their own stories in their own words, and quite literally at their own pace or rhythm, for a listening audience hanging on every word? When a young Black man holds a microphone and steps onto a stage to perform as an artist, he instantly gains access to a global platform to creatively express himself. There is no other space that can make the same offer. The role of the MC is special because it also signifies power—a quality not typically ascribed to young Black men—and authority as tale-bearer and mouthpiece for a community. This chapter shifts the role of the MC to the center of an analysis that combines the elements from hip-hop shared by spoken word poetry: the mic and the performance. If "hip-hop occupies a crossroads between the literary and music," then spoken word poetry and performance link up with them on the same corner (Perry, 2004, p. 33). This crossroads of performances, literary, identity based, and musical in nature, is the construction site for this chapter. There are significant intersections between hip-hop, spoken word poetry performance, and the performance of identity for Black men. These components of hip-hop are examined for their efficacy when practiced by Black men from a framework seeking social transformation composed by Dr. Martin Luther King Jr. Dr. King provides a blueprint for this intersection, complete with instructions on how to confront fear. When applied as a historic and analytical framework for the rich and varied performances of Black masculinity within hip-hop and spoken word poetry, Dr. King's (1963) sermon entitled "Antidotes for Fear" offers us a classic position from which to learn from the performance of Black male artists.

Although referencing Dr. King's core list of ways to confront fear may seem dated at first glance, when applied to contemporary lyrics and Black male spoken word artists in these crushing and desperate political times, they provide critical insights for the ways that creative works can address fear when performed by Black men. Indeed, the present day seems not so far from the echo of King's words: "In these days of catastrophic change and calamitous uncertainty, is there any man who does not experience the depression and bewilderment of crippling fear, which, like a nagging hound of hell pursues our every footstep?" (p. 115). King goes on to unpack the ways that fear manifests itself and outlines four remedies for the impact of fear in daily life. Dr. King provides a plan steeped in spiritual practice for the benefit of his congregation, and while many hip-hop heads would never set foot in a traditional church, there is yet a remarkable overlap between the embodied tools of expression and performance that are intangible and these spiritual practices that thread through Dr. King's design for responding to fear.

Indeed, many MCs confide in their microphones, transforming the stage and their own musical performances into acts of penance, and crowded concert venues become intimate confessionals. For Black men who are MCs, the act of performance creates an unusual opportunity to express emotion and to share secrets or private personal experiences that might otherwise be too emotional for them to publicly display. One of the clearest examples of this unique confessional performance is Jay-Z's 2001 *MTV Unplugged* acoustic performance, which was taped live with full instrumentation provided by the Roots. Jay-Z performed "Song Cry," which describes several instances of regret and deeply emotional and traumatic autobiographical experiences from his life. Yet, as he reminds in the chorus, "I can't see it coming down my eye / so I gotta make this song cry" (2001), and in front of that incredibly small audience in an exceptionally personal venue, the tears indeed almost came down his face.

Jay-Z's scaled-down performance primes the audience and other artists to dig deeper and listen closer when Black men perform multiple versions of their masculinity through artistic expressions. I want to shift the spotlight from mainstream hip-hop artists like Jay to the more reachable Black men: those we know and love, those who love hip-hop but don't consider themselves "rappers." They still find sanctuary through the mic and stage, just not as a hip-hop artist. Instead, these artists find the spoken word poetry scene combines the appeal for a performance-based energy that hip-hop demands, but removes the necessary or expected accessories of a musical backdrop. The focus for the spoken word poet is the words and the words alone. Open mics provide a venue for young Black men who are ready to share their lyrics publicly without the addition of the other elements of hip-hop. For many hip-hop heads who don't rhyme, the practice of a hip-hop lifestyle is appealing because in addition to a mode of expression and activism, it provides an ethos. This ethos governs a sense of direction and way to determine right and wrong similar to the way that Dr. King's words once offered his congregations and constituents guidance for the choices they had to make. Hip-hop provides a code to live by, one that will guide decisions and choices for the traditional MC. Much like those who mobilized under Dr. King, those who used to gather to listen to him drop knowledge on a Sunday night, I find that the open mic night is often a sanctuary, providing shelter and confidence enough for confession and ultimately the redemption of the spoken word poet.

As such, Dr. King's remedy overlaps in interesting ways with the contemporary issues facing young Black men and how they address those through the vehicle of spoken word poetry. Spoken word poetry and performance can provide this specific group of artists with several entrances to engage with the four areas Dr. King lists: facing fears, courage, faith, and love. Dr. King's list of core values drives this reflection on how the hip-hop MC and spoken word poet can understand his identity and cultural context. A consideration of the core four values will also better equip the MC and poet to build a foundation of content on which to develop his artistic skill. These core values are the cement, the foundation, of Dr. King's blueprint, and I argue that themes of confronting fear, exhibiting courage, enduring by faith, and manifesting love are already resonating within the performance poetry of young Black men. King's list shapes the analysis of lyrics and artists highlighted in these pages, and offers a working template for how Black male poets take up the following questions: How does spoken word equip Black men with tools to adequately identify and confront the fear and depression that target their dreams? How does a spoken word performance create a transfer of power and vulnerability for Black men, sustaining them with the courage to imagine new ways of being in the world? Why is participating as a community member with other like-minded artists critical to constructing the faith it takes to challenge fear? By exploring the poetic work of several Black men, I will demonstrate how the shift between the limited subjectivities permitted for Black men occurs through performance of spoken word poetry. Dopeboys are perceived as those who make a profit off of transactions that aren't legal. They might sling drugs, they might move in other shady dealings for income, but one thing they undoubtedly aim to do is survive. A dopeboy is a man who is willing to do whatever is necessary to provide, and he does so with style and with traditionally masculine swagger. When dopeboys who are strategically armed with the approaches outlined by Dr. King must engage with fear, they are introduced to a deepening complexity of Black masculinity as performed through spoken word. Mic fiends are hustlers who move in the commodity of words, of lyrics, of performance. Mic fiends demand a place to perform and then do so ruthlessly; they weaponize the microphone with their lyrics and take no hostages in the open mic night crowds. They are the MCs and poets who must feed their addictions to perform. The stage is their drug of choice and the only way to satisfy that jones is to write and perform spoken word poetry at an open mic. Dopeboys and mic fiends might share many commonalities—a street code of ethics, onstage bravado, and relentless wordplay—but the strongest link between the two is their politic of survival. When dopeboys transform into mic fiends, they are able to pursue life beyond survival. The same skill sets necessary to hustle as a dopeboy can be applied to spoken word poetry and the position of a mic fiend. However, mic fiends develop an appreciation for the performance and composition of poetry, and by using the art of spoken word to master fear, these Black male poets utilize the mic as a weapon to do just that.

Behind the Curtain: Spoken Word as Praxis for Young Black Men

One of the fastest ways to change a person's perspective is to move him, to literally put his body or at least his thoughts in motion. Perspective is of critical importance to the artist and to the performer as he creates and then shares what he simply could not keep to himself. Once a poem is written, memorized, and then spoken aloud by a poet, even to himself, that poem transforms. When the same poem is performed in public for an audience, it is the audience and the artist who transform. These steps of transformation, first of the poem itself and then of the people who are part of the performance event, are critical to changing perspectives through shifts of focus. Through performance, a poem shifts attention from the individual occurrence being recounted to the structures that allow such occurrences. Focus is transferred toward the systems that are in place that create the conditions of the experience and pulled from the individual artist, or the audience's need for some Truth about their life. The first step of this transformation alters the state of being for the poem. Words harden and solidify intangible emotions. The artist commits the poem to a form, making the invisible visible and creating matter out of an idea. The poem, the words then become matter or flesh as soon as the artist speaks them aloud. The state of the words is converted. The poem becomes mobilized.

The second step emboldens poets and autonomizes the choices they make on stage at an open mic performance event. They decide which poem to share, whether or not to provide other context, and which physical cues and clues they will give their audience via performance. The second transformation also involves the audience who witnesses the performance of a poem; they are converted to actors who coconstruct the meaning of a performance based on their own point of view and experience (Boal, 1979). Through these two steps of transformation, the poem and the performance work in tandem to adjust the positions and thus the points of view of the audience and artist (Endsley, 2016). In this way, spoken word poetry and performance have the unique power to convert mind into matter, so to speak. Ideas and experiences are infused with energy that moves an audience member and the artist, amending their perspective. Once a person's perspective shifts, his day-to-day patterns and interactions are also shifted; in other words, his relationships after the experience of an open mic performance are altered in a subtle way. This creates social transformation.

The first step that Dr. King suggests as a way to reign over fear requires that we "face our fears and honestly ask ourselves why we are afraid" (p. 117). He continues to suggest that this confrontation will empower us because it causes us to identify how the imagination is misused to amplify what we are afraid of. For the spoken word poet, raising consciousness about fear by asking and answering the question "Why am I afraid?" usually occurs on the stage at an open mic. Dr. King is right about the power of the imagination, and if that power is harnessed and put to use via performance, the Black male poet has acknowledged fear and demonstrated how to master it.

James Baldwin (1962) writes of the creative process of the artist and states that "the war of the artist is that of the lover, to make the beloved known to himself" (p. 3) and to do this requires that the artist "must be willing to tell the truth about us and the truth is always at variance with what we wish to be" (p. 2). Truth and honesty are the first two practices that Dr. King insists on if fear is to be conquered. Baldwin extends the practice of truth-telling from an internal reflection of the artist on himself to beyond and suggests the artist is doubly reflective—a two-way mirror—beginning with himself and then, in turn, reflecting and revealing society through his artworks. Considered together, the double reflection is the poet's epistemology and honors both ancestral and everyday knowledge alongside that formal learning process produced in institutions of education (Richardson, 2006). When the Black male poet composes a new piece, he is reflexive and working through internal struggles, and composing poetry is typically done privately in solitude. When he performs the poem, he reveals aspects of his audience they could not previously see, reflecting how his individual experience is really a microcosm of their larger relationship and oftentimes exposing a truth and producing new knowledge about them that is likely at odds with how they "see" themselves. There is risk involved for the artist who discloses unpleasant truths by highlighting the complexities of Black manhood. So the artist poses a danger and a threat to the stabilized normative caricatures that are passed off as Black men, which present them only as hypermasculine and hypersexualized predators.

Enter poet and advocate Tony Keith, who embodies the role of an agent of social change. Employing his skills as a poetic story teller, Tony works within the community that raised him in a multitude of ways but primarily as a social justice educator. Tony's poem entitled "Black Man's Call to Action" responds directly to these caricatures by first calling them up and then dismantling them. An excerpt of his powerful poem begins this way:

> . . . I DECLARE YOU FREE
>
> No longer property
>
> No longer a weapon for society to continue to arm you with massive missiles of misguided percep-
> tions of manhood into your looking glasses
>
> So F*CK sitting in the back writing R.I.P. to your friends on that dirty desk now you're in the front
> teaching classes
>
> So F*CK being afraid to use slang; I'm granting you the right to use the language of your people
> to move the masses
>
> So F*CK waiting in the back of the line to get to the front; I'm giving you a lifetime supply of free
> VIP backstage passes
>
> And if someone says you didn't pay your way, say F*CK you it's already being deducted from my
> taxes. (Keith as in Endsley, 2016, p. 18)

Within this short excerpt Tony's praxis of spoken word poetry synthesizes his lived experience with this social issue and undergirds the aspects everyday life he highlights above with the disrupting theories of critical Black feminist theory and performance ethnography that center art as activism (see Boal, 1979; Collins, 2006; Denzin, 2003; Freire, 1972; hooks, 1994). Tony faces down multiple nagging fears that threaten social mobility and progress in these few lines. First he invokes the imagery of the uneducated Black boy, who "acts up" in school and gets pushed out of the public education system and into a life of criminalization and prison or death. Tony hints that the student in the class is already familiar with, and therefore unafraid of, death since he is writing RIP to his friend on a desk that is dirty—one that likely is in an overcrowded classroom. This student is one that becomes a statistic, one who meets the societal expectations that does not strive for anything higher than what he sees around him. Tony calls the student out for being a rule-breaker (he is defacing school property) and for not paying attention in class. Tony quite literally flips the script as he positions this same student as teacher. In a sudden switch of roles, the former student, uninterested, exposed to violence (inflicted by the state? By his community? We don't find out), who is disinterested or too distracted by trauma and grief to engage with a class that doesn't care about him anyway, finds himself empowered with enough knowledge to lead that same class as the teacher. Tony's positioning of the student flips the classroom from traditional "banking methods" of teaching and learning to a critical pedagogical practice of education that situates students as valid producers of knowledge. In this poem, young Black men who are in public schools wishing to disappear in the back of the class are recognized by Tony and suddenly thrust to the forefront as leaders and valid meaning makers. Tony takes internal reflection of his own fears and transforms his audience's perspective via the performance of his identity and imagination. Tony was that kid and now he's pursuing his doctorate degree.

Tony continues by informing Black men that they no longer have to be content with "waiting at the back of the line," which calls up images of the social violence that was normative during civil rights and Jim Crow America. Instead, he encourages himself with a blatant refusal to wait any longer for what belongs to him. Tony takes it a step further by insisting on not just moving through the line like everyone else, but receiving preferential treatment because he enjoys "VIP" status. This flagrant disregard for social rules—wait your turn, don't make any noise, keep your head down—positions Tony as a troublemaker. He is walking a dangerous line now, challenging the status quo perceptions about Black men. As an appropriate response to the respectability politics and the power struggle of language, Tony uses profanity and the middle finger to ensure that there is no misunderstanding of this, his unapologetic and deeply committing artwork. Tony's lover's war is with himself and his audience and he is not sorry about going into battle. He is nonchalant about consequences and refuses to give negative possibilities any space within his poem. Coming face to face with his fear stirs up a desire to practice new subjectivities and social positions that aren't otherwise readily available for Tony. Resistant to the flatness of a caricature drawing, these are subjectivities that slip and turn, swell and bulge, and sit in silence in front of a two-way mirror.

In his own powerful words, Tony Keith has modeled the reflexivity of the two-way mirror that Baldwin and Dr. King seemed to wish for; Tony summons his fears, inspects them, and then shoves them back onto the audience, demanding that they be made accountable for creating and colluding in the birth and manipulation of the fears. Indeed Tony will use his spoken word and performance, "no longer a weapon for society to continue to arm you with massive missiles of misguided perceptions of manhood," and instead a praxis to shatter the mirror, offering fragments of a Black man's identity that he will mosaic together as he so chooses (Endsley, 2016, p. 18).

Shape Shifters: Power and Vulnerability

Hamza "the Seventh Sun" Taylor is a spoken word artist hailing from Norfolk, Virginia. Well known for his unapologetic performances, this poet is one who has defied the social odds that were stacked high and thick against him. Hamza's background is varied: a former gang member, rapper with a contract, recording artist, and now husband, father, and author of several fiction books, to name a few of his roles. His lived experiences, shaped at various times in his life by equal parts environment, influence, and consciousness have combined to formulate his perspective, which he shares powerfully in his live performances. This dopeboy turned mic fiend has shifted the same hustling mentality to his pen that substantiated his reputation as a gangster, establishing Hamza the Seventh Sun as one of the most well-respected poets both on and off the stage. This same reputation, saturated with a willingness to become vulnerable about his mistakes, sufferings, and where he finds glory, has Hamza featured on Atlanta-based rapper T.I.'s album *Us or Else Letter to the System* (2016) on a track entitled "Pain." Hamza's voice is heard at the start of the track, warning his listeners "human nature of this society / will flat-line your reality / when you fail to realize that pain is a part of the game" and T.I. elaborates for the rest of the track on the theme of his chorus: "Pain is just weakness leaving the body."

Hamza's introduction is an excerpt of a poem drawn from the landscape of his life, and he uses his experiences to educate and protect listeners about the dangers of being unaware. Pain, and ultimately "flat-lining" or death, is the outcome if the listener refuses to accept and even welcome pain as a part of "the game" of life. Unfortunately, it strikes us as unremarkable that a Black boy who grew up in the hood experiences pain—what *is* worth noting is that Hamza uses the access created through a song recorded with a platinum-selling artist as a platform to make himself vulnerable by admitting that he has experienced pain.

Black men face a particular onset of challenges when it comes to performing other than the societal role, revealing weaknesses or sharing about internal pain and often; when they are brave enough to share, they are subjected to even worse ridicule for making their vulnerability public. Consider the episodes that occurred as early as 2013 involving producer and MC Kid Cudi to turn the spotlight on his private struggles with mental illness. Fast-forward to a few years later in 2016, when Kid Cudi checked himself into a rehab center for having suicidal tendencies and a dependency on prescription drugs. This incident was widely publicized and the subject of several of Kid Cudi's songs, which later supplied fellow megastar Drake with ammunition to diss Kid Cudi using his earlier confession about mental illness and addiction to attack him for a personal beef (Pearce, 2016). Journalist Rahiel Tesfamariam (2013) writes, "We must acknowledge those times when hip-hop breaks its silence and depicts black men struggling to confront their pain, fear and anger rather than trying to mask or escape it" (para. 5). We are reminded that although the performing arts has a history of creating what is practically the only space for Black men to verbalize the sort of internal pain experienced by Kid Cudi and verbalized by Hamza, it is not necessarily a safe zone. The discourse surrounding mental health perpetuates embedded stigma about Black masculinity and shaming Black men who seek help remains a persistent normative response. Attacks like the ones lobbied at Kid

Cudi's struggle are not uncommon, even in those artistic professions where leniencies around the performance of masculine identity are typically more flexible.

Participating in a reconstruction of the political discourse that shapes their manhood, young Black men who are also spoken word poets take up their positions as performers in ways that interface with structures of power while challenging them (Endsley, 2012). The spoken word poet is required to dig into the darkness that he experiences and translate the grime and precious minerals he finds through the vehicle of his body for the benefit of an audience. The willingness to tangle with themes like emotional hurt, trauma, shortcomings, and pain on a public platform during a live performance is exactly the sort of expressions of courage that Dr. King suggests might assist us in mastering fear. King (1963) defines courage as "an inner resolution to go forward in spite of obstacles and frightening situations . . . courage breeds creative self-affirmation" (p. 119). If we understand the practice of spoken word poetry as a framework to analyze how identity is performed and thus reconstructed by and for young Black male poets, then spoken word performance can be an effective method of shifting power. Allowing their own pain to come alive on stage, the poets are creating an adjustment, however slight, to their own identities. Once pain has been performed, it cannot be erased from the audience's mind. The body of the performer creates a new memory of a painful event of their past in order to educate, warn, and survive. The creation of this new memory is one aspect of the shift toward a more agentic representation of an oppressive history. These poets are using their "body-spirit," a term employed by performance studies scholar Richard Schechner (2002) to reference the site of the body when it becomes the space for "playing out many of the conflicts troubling American society, especially those about race, ethnicity, and neighborhood" (p. 206). They literally embody the conflicts they are encountering and translate them for others, in Hamza's case, encounters that often encompass both pain and yet the triumph of survival at the same time. When young Black men perform their original spoken word poetry, they are honoring their individual experiences while at the same time undeniably implicating the systemic operations of inequity that work to puppeteer and profit off their oppression. This courageous "inner resolution" translates into an outer action through spoken word performance. Performance provides a rehearsal for the poets to modify their typical course of decision-making offstage and instead creates an alternative choice the next time pain or "frightening situations" are encountered. The act of rewriting and sharing defies reality without denying the material consequences and veracious hurting inflicted on Black men by injustice. When a poet identifies what causes fear and then speaks up and out loud against those things that work to intimidate him, it constitutes an authentic means of practicing resistance that is unique to spoken word poetry. Duplicitous spaces are opened up for Black men to both be afraid and be feared, to employ the experience of conflict and to refuse the confrontation through performances. Spoken word and performance make ambiguities inhabitable and prove that subversion is always possible and powerful. The obsessive focus on seeking dominance through power is a part of the "human nature of society" that Hamza refers to in his lyrics, and the spoken word poet has the opportunity to use pain caused by the enactment of society's power, as propulsion.

Dr. King adamantly clarifies that the creative self-affirmation he refers to is not selfishness, "for self-affirmation includes both a proper self-love and a properly propositioned love of others" (p. 119). The type of true love of self that is interdependent on courage relies on the ability of the artist to love others, and therefore serve them, and to then assess fear and yet face the reality that trouble does occur. There are menacing political forces at play and terrifying historical legacies that shape the types of trouble facing Black men, especially the troubles that will "flat-line you" unless the game is recognized. This is more than a metaphor for young Black men; this is a critical and ever-present threat. Can the creative self-affirmation King writes of take shape in the form of spoken word poetry and be enough? Will this gird and protect Black men's hearts and flesh? Is Kendrick Lamar's (2014) anthem "i" enough, whose chorus shouts "I love myself"? Is Kendrick's reminder that "life is more than suicide" potent enough to undermine Kid Cudi's self-harm and to halt Drake's shaming of his asking for help? When dopeboys turn into mic fiends, they both wield and yield enormous power to self-determine and yet are only able to do so at the high price of complete vulnerability.

We Gon' Be Alright: Between the Poet and the Community

Dr. King's third core value identified faith as an integral component of resisting fear. The faith he writes of is of course a spiritual one, rooted in the institution of the church and deep-seated belief in Christianity. While at times this belief system is problematic, it's important to consider the context during which Dr. King wrote and to consider his audience, similar to the ways in which an artist must consider his. Dr. King's character and choices during his lifetime reflect his humanity and also his vision. His was a life centered on service to others, and because of his consistency of character around this leadership style, I believe it is possible to explore and challenge the problematic areas of his belief system while also finding usefulness in them. Ultimately, when it comes to mastering fear, the faith Dr. King refers to is often located in the life of the spoken word poet, especially when he is in community with other artists. Dr. King (1963) writes that faith "does not offer an illusion that we shall be exempt from pain and suffering ... rather it instills in us an inner equilibrium needed to face strains, burdens, and fears that inevitably come, and assures us that the universe is trustworthy and God is concerned" (p. 123). The inner equilibrium, the core strength that gets demonstrated through balance, is only made manifest through relationship with others. Consistency in our reaction and response to circumstances is often a sign of faith. How does the Black male poet put faith into his artistic practice? How does he know it's working? The two-way mirror of Baldwin reflects something else entirely when it is operationalized by a fellow artist instead of the poet to himself or his audience. Community with other artists provides the poet with protection and sustenance to construct a faith that masters fear.

Carlos, Jonathan, and Tony Keith all participated in a yearlong cultural immersion experience to develop as emerging student artists. They also identify as Black men and are poets and singers. One of their tasks during this experience was to develop a "group piece" to perform together, combining their skills. Their piece entitled "Fly Away" includes the following lines:

> CARLOS: "One of ya'll got my lyrics, I said one of ya'll got my lyrics
>   So why doesn't anyone speak to me
>   Nothing speaks to me anymore so neither do I
>   I look for sound waves to change my brain waves
>   To help me see light waves to help light the way
> JONATHAN: Lately my mind is wrapped up in deep contemplation
>   Is this a dream or is this my imagination
>   I'm using maps for words that lead to no location
>   Struggling inside my mind to find articulation
>   Trying to find my voice, when all I can hear is yours
>   Who I really am is lost inside of your discourse
>   Is it you or is it me who's really in control?
> TONY: I will find my way
>   Nothing more that you can say
>   I'm writing my own words now, grabbing ownership of my own lyrics now
>   Piecing words to melodies just so my soul can hear it now.

(as in Endsley, 2016, p. 54)

Dr. King elaborates that faith "produces a sense of worth, belonging, and at-homeness in the universe" (p. 125). Artistic collaboration like the example above creates a space for Black male poets to lucidly express their thoughts and make relatable connections with one another, or, on the other hand, examine the differences in their individual pockets of experience. Carlos's first line opens up by asserting in fact that "one of ya'll got my lyrics," which we can interpret to mean his words, and as Jonathan later states, even his voice is lost, drowned out by the overwhelming echoes of dominant discourse. Communal artistic practice provides a peer group that encourages and uplifts while also consistently telling the truth. Community demands accountability, and for Black male poets, that relationship is not readily available. The pressures of American life conspire in particular ways to silence, mute, shush, and disregard the very lives of Black youth. Carlos verifies this by admitting that "nothing speaks to me anymore so neither do I," showing his listeners that he has been effectively ignored, and in turn, he remains quiet. Carlos's silence means that the broader audience and his community undergo another deduction from their already shrinking human resources—his voice might have been raised to sound an alarm, ring out a battle cry, or mobilize the people. Police brutality, state violence, school push-out, abuse, neglect, and respectability politics conspire to, at most, end their lives and at least train their voice to regurgitate colonial and capitalistic rhetoric.

We know that Carlos is heavily impacted by the disconnection he is forced to endure because he states, "I look for sound waves to change my brain waves" in the present tense; his search is ongoing, presently taking place, and his desire for relationship is so raw that he is looking for what he knows isn't actually tangible—sound waves. Carlos wants his mind and thoughts to be changed, redirected from the course they are on. Carlos is listening hard for someone who "has [his] lyrics," someone who will speak to him and thus transform his thoughts and his words into light "that will light the way." The hazardous path Carlos, Jonathan, and Tony trod is monitored by a system whose top priority is to maintain an environment of isolation, convincing the Black male poet that he has lost all connection to others. The methodical process of this maintenance is what cultural scholar Ngũgĩ wa Thiong'o (1986) defines as a "cultural bomb" when he writes

> The effect of a cultural bomb is to annihilate a people's belief in their names, in their languages, in their environment, in their heritage of struggle, in their unity, in their capacities and ultimately in themselves . . . economic and political control can never be complete or effective without mental control. To control a people's culture is to control their tools of self-definition in relationship to others. (p. 16)

Faith, then, as defined by Dr. King is a core component necessary to dismantle this bomb. The faith that is "full of purpose" and our only "eternal fallout shelter" can resist the mental control tactics by re-establishing and shoring up the tools of self-definition, identity, and ultimately strengthening relationships between and among Black male poets (p. 124). The Black male poet can put this faith into practice by acknowledging his need for it, as Carlos, Jonathan, and Tony do so bravely, and then performing their struggle and support on stage. As Tony continues in the poem, "I'm writing my own words now, grabbing ownership of my own lyrics now / piecing words to melodies just so my soul can hear it now" (as in Endsley, 2016, p. 52). Exercising ownership of his feelings, loneliness, and words allows Tony to shift these three poets away from a state of fear and victimization toward an embrace of their autonomy and sovereignty through spoken word poetry performance. Tony pushes the isolation articulated by Carlos's search for lyrics and sound waves forward when he responds with "piecing words to melodies just so my soul can hear it now." Tony doesn't conduct this activity for the benefit of an audience; instead his focus is on his immediate crew. He fulfills Carlos's hunt for camaraderie by reassuring him that assembling melodies for the sake of his own soul is more than enough. Together, they compose and perform this piece to define themselves for themselves, thus repositioning their social location through performance. Their collaborative work is undertaken with the expectation of an outcome that operates "in service to and for the benefit of the communities in which they were created" (Brown, 2013, p. 112). The relationship between artist and community remains the richest site of cultural production and empowerment in part because it is the most difficult to negotiate. Ever shifting and never consistent, this relationship requires stamina. As such, mastering fear through spoken word performance requires endurance and faith that "we gon' be alright."

Love Jones: Final Thoughts

The final ingredient in Dr. King's core values list is love, and he insists that "perfect love casteth out fear. Not arms, but love, understanding and organized good will cast out fear" (p. 121). He goes on to list the ways that fear often manifests itself: envy, jealousy, inferiority, "fear of the superiority of other people, of failure, of the scorn or disapproval of those whose opinions we value" are examples (p. 122). For the Black male poet this list is useful as he works through the continuous process of identity and dismantling ingrained social pressures and lessons that life imprints us with. The praxis of spoken word poetry and performance offer up methodologies to creatively implement "organized good will." When spoken word and performance are taken up in the work of confronting dream killers, the transformation and transference of power and (re)connection with the audience and one another, then change occurs in meaningful and not always predictable ways. The template laid out by Dr. King illuminates these possibilities for the life and practice of a young Black male poet who is about the work of mastering fear.

■ **References**

Baldwin, J. (1962). The creative process. In John F. Kennedy et al., *Creative America*, pp. 17–21. New York: Ridge Press.

Boal, A. (1979). *The theater of the oppressed.* New York: Urizen Books.

Brown, R. N. (2013). *Hear our truths: The creative potential of Black girlhood.* Urbana: University of Illinois Press.

Collins, P. H. (2006). *From Black power to hip hop: Racism, nationalism, and feminism.* Philadelphia: Temple University Press.

Denzin, N. K. (2003). *Performance ethnography: Critical pedagogy and the politics of culture.* Thousand Oaks, CA: Sage.

Endsley, C. L. (2012). "This is the re-mix: President Obama, racial ambiguity, and hip hop." *Journal of Black Masculinity* 2(2): 39–52.

———. (2016). *The fifth element: Social justice pedagogy through spoken word poetry.* New York: SUNY Press.

Freire, P. (1972). *Pedagogy of the oppressed.* New York: Herder and Herder.

hooks, b. (1994). *Teaching to transgress: Education as the practice of freedom.* New York: Routledge.

Jay-Z. (2001). *Jay-Z: MTV unplugged.* Roc-A-Fella Records.

King, M. L. (1963). *Strength to love.* Philadelphia: Fortress Press.

Lamar, K. (2014). *To pimp a butterfly.* Interscope Records.

Ngũgĩ w. T. (1986). *Decolonising the mind: The politics of language in African literature.* Woodbridge, UK: Boydell and Brewer.

Pearce, S. (2016, November 1). Is Drake's Kid Cudi depression diss a step too far? Https://www.theguardian.com/music/2016/nov/01/drake-kid-cudi-diss-track-depression.

Perry, I. (2004). *Prophets of the hood: Politics and poetics in hip hop.* Durham, NC: Duke University Press.

Richardson, E. (2006). *Hip hop literacies.* New York: Routledge.

Schechner, R. (2012). *Performance studies: An introduction.* 2nd ed. New York: Routledge.

T. I. & Jae. (2016). Pain. *Us or else a letter to the system.* Roc Nation Records.

Tesfamariam, R. (2013, January 17). Breaking hip hop's silence: Kid Cudi speaks on mental health. Https://www.washingtonpost.com/blogs/therootdc/post/breaking-hip-hops-silence-kid-cudi-speaks-on-mental-health/2013/01/17/257828fe-60b0-11e2-9940-6fc488f3fecd_blog.html?utm_term=.99986c89a104.

Discussing Suicide without Being Crucified

The New Renaissance of Mental Health in Hip-Hop

Edward J. Smith

Tacoma Savage was my idol. His locks were long and luscious, dressed in a colorful headscarf, or unleashed, similar to the mane of Bob Marley. His skin was rich and smooth, the stunning shade of coffee brown, donned with several tattoos as if to illustrate the story of his life. His raspy, charred voice (which he never, ever raised) sounded like the crispness of rainfall in the summer. To me as a child in the late 1980s, it felt like he would glide into a room, in a soft fog, bringing calmness and patience to the people he met.

In addition to these attributes that aroused my imagination of him, he had a distinct smell. I would drown in his intoxicating aroma of marijuana, tobacco, and dark liquor. What is more, his bangles, rings, and chains would clank together as mood music during conversations. Over the course of the decade, he played keyboard and bass guitar in my uncle's new wave rock band. As if he descended from the lineage of Miles Davis, John Coltrane, and Prince, he always seemed collected, reserved, and generally "together." He was the epitome of cool, and I wanted to grow into his presentation of manhood. Little did I know the degree of inner turmoil his battle with depression and anxiety would harbor.

He emerged from the 1980s without the support of most of his bandmates. After a run of nine years, the group disbanded, in large part because of crevices caused by Tacoma's substance abuse. He would often arrive at shows several hours late or miss them entirely. He would have frequent, unprovoked vocal outbursts with bandmates, family, and friends. He often took solace under the mixture of weed, alcohol, and pills. As he transitioned into his forties, only my uncle remained in his corner. No amount of prayers or sermons, or tough love quotes like "Snap out of it" or "Get yourself together" could pull him from his daily battles. In fact, they only drove him deeper into isolation.

He evolved into a songwriter and rhythm-and-blues instrumentalist in the early 1990s, experiencing a rebirth when groups like SWV, Soul for Real, and Jodeci took notice of his ability to compose love ballads. After a few years working in studios, he was back on his feet, performing at jazz clubs across the United States, touring internationally, and writing songs and composing music for a number of high-profile recording artists. Soon thereafter, he became manic—working around the clock with no sleep, frequently forgetting to eat, and drifting ever so deeply into paranoia. He told my uncle that he "never wanted to experience life without music, even if it meant a life without love and self-care." His face became withered and withdrawn; the same raspy voice I enjoyed hearing became a cacophony of jumbled words and sounds. He would tell people, "I just have to push through this. I'm good." But the pushing eventually broke him.

I later understood that neither what he was saying nor my boyhood imagination of him was real. And the more he tried to deny his struggles, the more he unraveled into despondency. He was hospitalized on the fifteenth anniversary of his wife's death; I did not find that fact ironic. For years, he withheld the grief of losing the only person he truly loved. Years of drug abuse helped him retreat further and further from a reality that would eventually deal with the loss. Upon evaluation, he was rendered a diagnosis of major depressive disorder with psychotic features. He committed suicide within one year after rejecting the diagnosis. All these years, I was unaware that he was using drugs to deal with—and recover from—his inner turmoil and grief.

When I hear of and read about artists such as Kanye West, DMX, and others who publicly experience the struggle to achieve sound mental health and wellness, I think of Tacoma Savage. And when I hear artists like Kid Cudi, Kendrick Lamar, and Pharoahe Monch courageously recount their tales of trauma, self-diagnose their depression, and use their lyrics as a way to bring about healing and self-preservation, I ponder the painful lesson Tacoma's life taught me; I do not have to tell people I am "good" all the time—especially when I feel otherwise.

This chapter illustrates a new renaissance in hip-hop coinciding with evolving cultural and communal norms among Black men as it pertains to mental health and wellness. While violence, death, and suicidal ideation have been long-standing themes in rap music, more recent offerings in hip-hop include narratives of mental and emotional vulnerability, and artists more readily evoke help-seeking—a virtue seemingly unfamiliar in those that align more with the prevailing themes of escapism, self-control, and hypermasculinity (Kitwana, 2002). The chapter concludes with implications for the recursive effect of promoting mental health and wellness through rap music (such as the potential to evoke the critical nature of therapy, healing, and self-preservation among Black boys and men) and the potential of hip-hop therapy and hip-hop psychology to bring about a sense of radical healing among traumatized young people (Ginwright, 2010).

Mental Health and Wellness in the United States: A Review of Data

The United States is experiencing a duality of consciousness with regard to mental health and wellness.[1] While there remains a societal stigma around the challenges experienced by those with mental illnesses, there is an emerging recognition (among those in the health care community, as well as policymakers, researchers, and the public) of the importance of access to consistent, culturally relevant, and socially practical mental health supports. Approximately one in five adults (over 40 million Americans) have a mental health condition (Mental Health America [MHA], n.d.; American Psychological Association [APA], n.d.). Additionally, more than 22 million people have a substance abuse disorder resulting from a mental illness (APA, n.d.).

A closer examination reveals that the status of youth mental health and wellness is evolving. Either society is increasing the frequency, rigor, and thoroughness with which it evaluates the mental health of young people or their mental health conditions are deteriorating.[2] For example, rates of youth depression increased from 8.5 percent in 2011 to 11.1 percent in 2014 (MHA, n.d.). This is an increase from 6.4 percent in 2005 (APA, n.d.). Even with severe depression, 80 percent of youth are left with no or insufficient treatment for the condition (MHA, n.d.). The share volume of mental health challenges as well as the increasing severity of illnesses experienced by young people elevates the importance of access to sound mental health supports.

Mental Health and Wellness in the Black Community

The history of Black life in America has foregrounded the contemporary mental health challenges within the community. Centuries of systematic oppression (e.g., slavery, Black codes, Jim and Jane Crow,[3] inferior education, residential segregation, extra-judicial killings at the hands of law enforcement), institutionalized racism, and frequent microaggressions (Sue, 2010) have levied blatant physical, emotional, and mental assaults on the minds and spirits of Black people in America. Indeed, Black people are in need of healing from various forms of trauma.

Chronic fear of these experiences may lead to constant vigilance or even paranoia, which over time may result in traumatization or contribute to post-traumatic stress disorder (PTSD) when a more stressful event occurs later (Carter, 2007; Williams, 2015). Of little surprise to many social scientists, data from a recent study by the US Department of Health and Human Services' Office of Minority Mental Health (2016) suggest that Black adults in the U.S. are 20 percent more likely to report serious psychological distress than White adults. Similarly, while depression is one of the most common disorders in the United States (affecting over 17 million lives per year), Black adults, in particular, are 20 percent more likely than Whites to contend with serious depression and anxiety in their lifetime (APA, n.d.). Even more, findings from national studies indicate that, while African Americans[4] have lower risk for many anxiety disorders, they have a 9.1 percent prevalence rate for PTSD, compared with 6.8 percent among Whites (Himle et al., 2009). A recent study by Malcoun, Williams, and Bahojb-Nouri

(2015) found that depression and PTSD affected almost 50 percent of Black men and women being treated for trauma exposure, ranging from car accidents to deaths in the family, to physical and sexual assault. Lastly, Black people are twice as likely as Whites to be diagnosed with schizophrenia (APA, n.d.).

Several cross-sections of the Black community remain in deep need of mental health care and service. For example, Black people living below the poverty line are three times more likely to report serious psychological distress than their same-race peers living above the poverty line (Office of Minority Mental Health, 2016). Additionally, while Blacks are less likely than White people to die from suicide as teenagers, Black teenagers are more likely to attempt suicide than are White teenagers (8.3 percent vs. 6.2 percent). Suicide among African American preteens ages ten to fourteen increased 233 percent over the period 2005 to 2014 (MHA, n.d.). Lastly, research finds that Blacks are more likely to be victims and witnesses of a serious violent crime than any other racial group in the United States (Office of Minority Mental Health, 2016). Thus, Blacks are more likely to meet the psychological criteria for PTSD (Carter, 2007; Himle et al., 2009).

Black Men and Mental Health and Wellness

The research on the mental health and wellness of Black men in America is scant. Yet many mental health professionals, scholars, activists, parents, and educators agree that the ways in which Black men address mental illness (particularly depression and suicide) is in sore need of transformation. For instance, scholars find that there are consistent gender differences in the prevalence and treatment of major depressive disorders within the Black community (Hankerson et al., 2015). Men, regardless of race and ethnicity, tend to experience lower rates of mental health service utilization than women (Hankerson et al., 2015); Black women are four times more likely to use mental health services than Black men (Himle et al., 2009). The impacts of underutilization can be devastating. Suicide among African American men is four times more likely to occur than it is for African American women (Hankerson et al., 2015).

Similar disparities exist when comparing Black men with their same-gendered peers. For example, despite evidence that rates of conditions like bipolar disorder and depression and anxiety are experienced equitably across races and ethnicities, Black men are statistically much less likely than White, Latino, and Asian American and Pacific Islander men to seek treatment or even publicly acknowledge mental health challenges (Chao, Asnaani, & Hofmann, 2012; Hankerson et al., 2015). Similarly, Hammond's study (2012) concluded that depressed Black men are significantly less likely to seek help compared with depressed White men. An examination by Woodward, Taylor, and Chatters (2011) of national treatment rates of men with a lifetime of mood, anxiety, or substance disorders indicates that just 14 percent of Black men received care from professional mental health services, compared with 29 percent of men in their entire sample.

Disparities in Accessing and Help-Seeking Explained

In the groundbreaking comprehensive report on the mental health status of racial and ethnic minorities in America, former US surgeon general David Satcher reported that

> minorities in the U.S. suffer a disproportionate burden of mental illness because they have less access to services than other Americans; receive lower quality care, often from services that are fragmented, costly, and inadequate; and are less likely to seek help when they are in distress, in part because the considerable stigma attached to mental illness in many cultures. (DHHS, 2001, p. 108)

Satcher's observations captured a historical analysis, as much as they foregrounded future trends, as disparities in access to care and treatment for mental illness have also persisted over time. In 2011, 54.3 percent of African Americans with a major depressive episode received treatment, compared with 73.1 percent of White adults (Agency for Healthcare Research and Quality, 2013). Similarly, compared to 45.3 percent of White Americans, 40.6 percent of African Americans age twelve and over were treated for substance abuse and completed their treatment course (Agency for Healthcare Research and Quality, 2013).

There are a host of complex and enduring reasons for race- and gender-based disparities in the usage of mental health care and support. For example, many Black men worry that some mental health care professionals are not culturally competent enough to treat their specific issues (Ward et al., 2013) and further contend that cultural insensitivity and bias can cloud the relationship they can develop with mental health professionals (National Alliance on Mental Illness, n.d.). Further to the observation of cultural misalignment, only 2 percent of American Psychological Association members are Black (APA, 2014). Moreover, the issue of cultural misalignment is compounded by the fact that some Black patients have reported experiencing an onslaught of racial microaggressions and bigotry from therapists (Williams, 2013). Newhill and Harris (2007) found that Black consumers of mental health services voiced concerns of cultural insensitivity and the propensity to miscommunicate with providers as major obstacle to seeking services and engaging in treatment.

Cultural misalignment and cultural insensitivity often fester, developing into mistrust of health professionals, based in part on historically higher-than-average institutionalization of African Americans with mental illness; and on previous mistreatments, like such tragic events as the Tuskegee syphilis study (Hankerson et al., 2015). It bears repeating: the weight of systemic oppression, institutional racism, and microaggressions ostensibly moderates access to mental health and wellness services for African Americans.

On the other hand, a recent study by Ward and associates (2013) revealed that African Americans tend to hold stigmas related to psychological openness and help-seeking, which in turn affects their coping behaviors. Generally, the participants in this study were not particularly open to acknowledging psychological problems. Not surprisingly, only 30 percent of participants who reported having a mental illness reported receiving treatment or underwent therapy (Ward et al., 2013). Consistent with previous research (see Agency for

Healthcare Research and Quality, 2013; Himle et al., 2009), the authors found Black men to be particularly concerned about the stigma (i.e., appearing weak, vulnerable, and unable to self-identify solutions to their problems). While the men appeared to be apprehensive about seeking professional help for mental health issues, the men in the study seemed willing to pursue other forms of help, such as talking to romantic partners, spouses, or mentors (Ward et al., 2013). Unfortunately, most individuals with a diagnosable mental illness, regardless of race or ethnicity, do not receive appropriate treatment. Yet still, Black men are least likely to receive such treatment (DHHS, 2001).

Taken together with misdiagnoses, inadequate treatment, a lack of cultural understanding, gendered stigmatization, as well as the gendered disposition to "toughing it out," access to sound mental health care and treatment can be tenuous for Black men. This oftentimes leads to unwillingness to confront challenges, eventually leading those who experience these challenges to suffer in isolation (Newhill & Harris, 2007). It would seem that traditional gendered norms around the aversion to help-seeking and "toughing out" problems as long as possible are doing Black men more harm than good. As Newhill and Harris (2007) observe, if left untreated, mental illness exacts a heavy toll not only on the ill individual, but also his or her family, community, and society as a whole.

Hip-Hop and Mental Health

Jeff Chang (2005) chronicled the extent to which New York City's economic decline during the 1970s gave rise to hip-hop culture. Advancing Chang's recollection, noted legal scholar Akilah Folami (2007) explains:

> Historically, Hip-hop arose out of the ruins of a post-industrial and ravaged South Bronx, as a form of expression of urban Black and Latino youth, who politicians and the dominant public and political discourse had written off, and for all intent and purposes, abandoned. (p. 244)

Hip-hop scholars and historians accurately draw connections between the critical nature of the art form and the rawness that grew out of adverse economic, social, and political conditions. During the 1970s and 1980s, New York would suffer immense job losses coupled with decreased local and federal funding for social services (Folami, 2007). The South Bronx alone would lose 600,000 manufacturing jobs (40 percent of the sector) (Chang, 2005). By the mid-1970s, average per capita income in the South Bronx dropped to half of the New York City average and 40 percent of the nationwide mean (Chang, 2005). The youth unemployment rate on record climbed to 60 percent (up from 40 percent a decade before) (Chang, 2005). Such conditions would leave "30 percent of New York's Latino households, and 25 percent of Black households at or below the poverty line" (Chang, 2005, p. 46). Youth in many of America's urban centers were alienated from decent, life-affirming employment opportunities and confined to underfunded schools and community programs (Rose, 1994).

Based on his analysis, political prisoner and former Black Panther Mumia Abu-Jamal posits that hip-hop was born from a culture of young people who felt "that they are at best, tolerated in schools, feared on the streets, and almost inevitably destined for the hell holes of prison" (Abu-Jamal communicated to Immortal Technique, 2003). Abu-Jamal continues, "They grew up hungry, hated, and unloved. And this is the psychic fuel that seems to generate the pain and anger that seems endemic in much of the music and the poetry."[5]

The response Abu-Jamal spoke of came in the form break-dance clubs, DJ crews, and block parties, all of which engaged youth from neighborhoods that once fought each other to come together and compete and collaborate through dancing, rapping, and creating music. Hip-hop increasingly became a pivotal tool for helping deconstruct forms of systematic oppression, while fostering a sense of self-worth, community, and cultural vibrancy. With the emergence of Afrika Bambataa, the pulse of hip-hop was turned to Black Nationalism, positive creativity, vision, and healing (Henderson, 1996). Some of the positive creativity, vision, and especially healing that Henderson interprets (1996) did not take root until 1981, when Melle Mel coauthored "The Message," "the first nationally recognized 'progressive' rap statement on the condition of Black people in urban America" (Henderson, 1996, p. 311).

Despite this emergence of a significantly positive grounding in the music, artists embraced conversations about environmental elements they experienced in their communities and the impacts their environments had on them. Artists often discussed pain and hurt, still reeling from the aforementioned societal and communal conditions. It is common for depression to emerge as a major theme for musicians; of no surprise, depression and suicidal ideation remain central themes in hip-hop.

Rap Therapy and Hip-Hop Psychology

Hip-hop has always been a personal, spiritual, and social vessel (KRS ONE, 2009). Therefore, it is not difficult to see the therapeutic properties contained in the art form. The emergence of rap therapy (Alvarez, 2011) as well as hip-hop psychology (Roychoudhury & Garder, 2012) offers two conceptual and practical frameworks to both encourage and understand how and why artists vocalize depression and thoughts of suicide. Given the previously described obstructions such as perceived or realized cultural insensitivity, as well as the associated stigma of utilizing supports, mental health professionals and the public are unlikely to find another therapeutic resource more utilized by Black men than rap music.

One theory behind why rap music has been effective (in ways that traditional modes of therapy have not) includes the purposeful integration of the original four elements of hip-hop culture (i.e., MC'ing, DJ'ing, break dancing, and graffiti art) in a therapeutic setting to achieve catharsis and facilitate psychosocial development (Alvarez, 2011). Numerous empirical studies have found rap therapy to be highly effective in improving therapeutic experience and mental health outcomes, particularly among young people living in urban settings (Alvarez, 2006, 2011; DeCarlo & Hockman, 2003; Tillie-Allen, 2005; Tyson, 2002). Alvarez (2011) provides a strong summary of the form of therapy and how it can be adapted to different educational contexts (e.g., elementary schools, high schools, schools in a criminal justice system, postsecondary institutions).

Psychologists Edgar Tyson (2002) and Don Elligan (2004) were the first to publish research about the use of hip-hop music in therapy. Hip-hop psychology is often utilized to engage clients in treatment by helping establish a working relationship with the client (Elligan, 2004; Tyson, 2002). Music and vocal performances can also help clients identify emotions, reframe cognition and traumatic experiences, and facilitate sense-making (or processing). In many cases of hip-hop therapy, clients are encouraged to compose their own rap verses. It has become a creative, yet effective way to address the cultural and intellectual needs of Black teens (Robinson, 2014).

Psychologist Janie Ward (2000) argues that parents who successfully instill health psychological resistance in their children help them express and cope with, rather than repress, anger and frustration. Therefore, outlets such as hip-hop provide an essential forum to building psychological health among African Americans (Ginwright, 2010). Rap music offers the potential for a culturally specific intervention that can help psychologists and other mental health professionals connect with and help Black youth (Kitwana, 2002).

An Analysis of the Framing of Trauma and Mental Health in Rap Music

This chapter spotlights the transition from the more traditional framing of trauma and mental health challenges in rap music to the renaissance of the vulnerable, yet increasingly healthy, offerings by more recent artists. I analyzed a sample of fourteen songs by hip-hop recording artists from the 1980s through the present day (see appendix), selecting songs that focus specifically on depression, anxiety, and suicide. I read through each song's lyrics to discern how and why the artist discussed these themes and scrutinized the content to see if any reflections or diagnoses on mental illness challenges emerged as a factor that rationalized the focus on these themes. The following summary includes a select sample of passages from six artists that highlight the argument.

Several examples of depression, suicidal ideation, and threat to harm emerge from songs both pre-2010 and post-2010 eras. However, the first period of music from the sample produces rappers who establish a certain degree of distance with the environmental conditions, pain, or activities causing them trauma. The artist is more likely to state desires attain relief and to evade or end the trauma, as opposed to seeking help to materially address the trauma. Moreover, most of these artists maintain the perception of control over their circumstances; treating their trauma rarely emerges as a prominent feature of the song. For example, 1982's "The Message" performed by pioneering rap group Grandmaster Flash and the Furious Five, provides a sample of the enormous influence the aforementioned material conditions of the Bronx have on Black youth, as well as the output of hip-hop (Chang, 2005; Henderson, 1996). Many scholars and hip-hop historians acknowledge the record for its critique of the political economy (Henderson, 1996) and for lucidly illuminating the politics (and tactics) for survival in the South Bronx. Although not the first song to provide social commentary or "socially conscious" lyrics about structural inequality, abject poverty, and substance abuse (see the early music of Kurtis Blow, Brother D, and Tanya "Sweet Tee" Winley), "The Message" would provide the first mainstream, commercially successful record to speak seriously about these issues (Henderson, 1996; Rose, 1994).

Yet Melle Mel (the lead vocalist) provides insight into the anxiety of a young Black man struggling to reconcile the conditions he's experiencing with a desire to evade these conditions. Indeed, he discloses an inner turmoil, reminiscent of someone feeling physically, as well as emotionally, trapped. He shares the faint desire to evade, or eventually leave, these conditions, even after stating how these conditions frustrate him:

> Broken glass, everywhere
> People pissing on the stairs, you know they just don't care
> I can't take the smell, I can't take the noise
> Got no money to move out, I guess I got no choice
> Rats in the front room, roaches in the back
> Junkies in the alley with a baseball bat
> I tried to get away, but I couldn't get far
> Cause the man with the tow-truck repossessed my car.
>
> (Fletcher et al., 1982)

Another example of a song that uses suicide as an escape mechanism is provided by the Geto Boys. Specifically, in a song widely acknowledged to be about psychosis (Ellis-Petersen, 2016), Scarface vividly discusses his paranoia and suicidal ideation after describing a plea for repentance and while traveling through the darkness of depression and paranoia. These reflections eventually lead him to feelings of suicide, where he, like Melle Mel, seeks relief and escape from current conditions. Scarface uses the term "worry free" to evoke the feeling of ultimate relief, in of the same way many patients dealing with depression and suicidal ideation evoke.

> Praying for forgiveness
> and trying to find an exit out the business
> I know the Lord is looking at me
> and yet it's still hard for me to feel happy
> I often drift while I drive
> I'm having fatal thoughts about suicide
> Bang and get it over with
> and then I'm worry free, but that's bullshit.
>
> (Jordan, King, & Dennis, 1991)

A song like The Notorious B.I.G.'s "Suicidal Thoughts" (1994), rooted in depression and built around the idea that regret, self-doubt, and worthlessness eventually lead Biggie to discuss suicidal ideation, is a prime example of both elements that capture this era of depression-themed rap. While Biggie, too, seeks relief and escape, as Pearce (2015) finds, Biggie writes from a position of perceived control. After stating a list of actions that may infringe on the happiness of others, he turns inward and ponders ways to evade judgment—not address it, make amends, or heal from these activities. Notwithstanding Biggie's honesty and introspection, his lyrics emerge from a position of perceived control, foreclosing any real opportunity for a diagnosis, treatment, or acknowledgment of the feelings that undergird his conclusions.

> My baby mother's eight months, her little sister's two
> Who's to blame for both of them (puffy: nah nigga, not you?)
> I swear to God I just want to slit my wrist and end this bullshit
> Throw the magnum to my head, threaten to pull shit
> and squeeze, until the bed's, completely red
> I'm glad I'm dead, a worthless fuckin Buddha-head
> The stress is building up, I can't, I can't believe
> Suicide's on my fucking mind, I wanna leave
> I swear God it feel like death is fucking calling me
> nah you wouldn't understand (puffy: nigga talk to me, please!)
>
> (Wallace & Hall, 1994)

Biggie and Scarface share feelings of despondency as a result of their environment, as well as acts they have committed themselves. Living in the hood can be stressful—sometimes the life of a hustler can be even more stressful.

Another hip-hop icon, Tupac Shakur, espouses similar desires for relief in "So Many Tears" (1995). In the spiritual monologue, Pac shares:

> And fuck the world cuz I'm cursed
> I'm having visions of leaving here in a hearse (God can you feel me)
> Take me away from all the pressure and the pain
> Show me happiness again

Pac continues, evoking elements of paranoia and anxiety:

> and though my soul is deleted, I couldn't see it
> I had a mind full of demons trying to break free
> they planted seeds and they hatched, sparking the flame
> inside my brain like a match, such a dirty game
> no memories just the misery,
> painting a picture of my enemies killing me, in my sleep
> will I survive till the morning, see the sun
> please Lord forgive me for my sins, cuz here I come
>
> (Shakur et al., 1995)

Perhaps to acknowledge and name *depression* is to project vulnerability onto these lyrics. But to appear in control, yet vocalize the desire for relief and freedom from anxiety while avoiding depression, is to disassociate oneself with the image of an archetypical hip-hop star.

Stic.man of rap duo dead prez painfully professes the emotional trauma he experiences as he watched his older brother develop a drug addiction. Rather than blame the individual, Stic. man addresses the larger socioeconomic forces that influence and often dictate the choices of the urban poor. Moreover, Stic.man discusses how he experiences the trauma and pain secondhand, and how witnessing this struggle influences his motivation to persist. In asking, "How did Black life, my life, end up so hard?" (dead prez, 2003), Stic.man states:

> The same conditions that first created the drug problems still exist
> And on days off, we blow off them crumbs like nothing
> Getting high, cause a nigga gotta get into something
> But we get trapped in a cycle of pain and addiction
> And lose the motivation to change the condition
>
> (Ibomu & Olugbala, 2003)

It is possible that Stic.man is interpreting his brother's drug use as a coping mechanism for the conditions under which he lives. Like Tacoma and many others, drug use is a way to escape a reality that could be extremely adverse and harmful to bear. Hence, Stic.man captures another evasion device and contextualizes the dual meaning of losing "the motivation to change the condition," both personal, as well as structural (Ibomu & Olugbala, 2003).

The Beginning of a Renaissance

The conversation around mental health in the music industry has evolved over the period between 2010 and 2016, particularly with a new cadre of rappers, and some veterans, harnessing the courage not only to chronicle their pain and anxiety, but to take themselves and their listeners to a vulnerable place through music. In addition to wrestling with depression, anxiety, and suicidal ideation in their lyrics or positioning these issues as central to the composition of songs and albums, artists have been discussing these issues in the media.

Veteran emcee Pharoahe Monch has been outspoken about his battle with depression, which he has stated has been induced by a combination of medications he was taking following his hospitalization for his asthma (Harris-Perry, 2014). As foregrounded by his 2014 album title, *PTSD*, Monch includes frank, vulnerable lyrics about his struggles to stabilize his mental health and wellness, as well as candid discussion about the stigma of depression within the Black community. In "Losing My Mind" (2014), Pharoahe Monch raps, "My family customs were not accustomed to dealing with mental health / It was more or less an issue for White families with wealth." He continues, "Void, I defected, employed self-annoyed / Went independent, enjoyed stealth / Now doctors prescribed sedatives and Prozac." In an interview with Melissa Harris-Perry (2014), Monch elaborated on the first passage, "Coming up, you couldn't talk about [mental health] out in the open. People would isolate you for many reasons. Your career might not last."

Elaborating on the second passage, Monch in several media outlets discussed the "cocktail of drugs" that drew him into depression. His revelation speaks to the concerns that many Black families have about the devastating implications of misdiagnoses and overprescriptions. Moreover, the first passage describes hesitancy to uncover some of these issues because, as many Black men share, his parents were "strong and hardworking," as if to make the point that his problems may pale in comparison to those experienced by previous generations of Black people in America. Both concerns are elevated in the literature; I saw both as salient features of Tacoma's trials. Yet, how is it that Monch finally finds the courage and artistic freedom to discuss mental health and wellness in a way that, as he implies, would have isolated him in the past?

Rapper and actor Kid Cudi told his fans and Twitter followers in the fall of 2016 that he had checked into a rehabilitation center to treat his ongoing battle with mental health illnesses. He wrote about his struggles in a long and forthright Facebook post:

> It's been difficult for me to find the words to what I'm about to share with you because I feel ashamed. Ashamed to be a leader and hero to so many while admitting I've been living a lie. . . . Yesterday I checked myself into rehab for depression and suicidal urges. I am not at peace.

In discussing rehabilitation, Cudi shares:

> If I didn't come [to rehabilitation], I would've done something to myself. I simply am a damaged human swimming in a pool of emotions everyday of my life. Theres a ragin violent storm inside of my heart at all times. Idk what peace feels like. Idk how to relax. My anxiety and depression have ruled my life for as long as I can remember and I never leave the house because of it. I cant make new friends because of it. I don't trust anyone because of it and Im tired of being held back in my life. I deserve to have peace. I deserve to be happy and smiling.

This post was emotionally raw and unexpectedly vulnerable, and although he apologizes to his fans for "letting them down," he acknowledges that he is indeed "scared" and that he is "sad."

Cudi's forthright Facebook post prompted several hundred responses, sparked a trending conversation on Twitter, and provoked a slew of opinion editorials, blogs, and essays on the status of Black men's mental health and wellness. Outgrowth from the social media firestorm included the hashtag #Yougoodman and #OKtonotbeOK, with tagged tweets including narratives, reflections, and advice from Black men who struggle with mental health challenges.

The overwhelming consensus was that Cudi's post was brave, touching, and necessary given the severity of mental health challenges experienced by Black men, as well as the implications of untreated illnesses. Yet Cudi has made a career of self-disclosure and vulnerability. It is possible that he has been at the forefront of this renaissance—and that he has adjusted the norms (or reflecting the changing norms) among Black men with respect to self-disclosure and help-seeking.

Cudi has a relatively short, but influential, history concerning vulnerability and has spoken publicly in many mediums about his mental health. For example, a spring 2016 interview with *Billboard* included reflections about the pressure of wanting to appear fine while he was using drugs to address his depression. Cudi states, "I thought about how much of a struggle it has been the past eight years, to be in the news and pretend to be happy when, really, I was living a nightmare" (2016). Moreover, the following passage is offered from the song "Soundtrack 2 My Life" from his first album, *Man on the Moon: The End of Day* (2009): "I've got some issues that nobody can see / And all of these emotions are pouring out me . . . my heart is an open wound that I hope heals soon."

A proclaimed advocate for suicidal prevention, Cudi explained the following in an interview with late-night talk show host Arsenio Hall (2014):

> My mission statement since day one has been to help kids not feel alone, and to stop kids from committing suicide. That's something that has affected me for the last five years. There wasn't a week or day that didn't go by where I said, "You know, I want to check out." I know what that feels like and I know it comes from loneliness not having self-worth, not loving yourself.

Cudi has not only spent the better part of seven years using his music has a therapeutic instrument, but he has intentionally encouraged others to identify their own challenges, unveiling a relatively dark mood in hip-hop, but a rather healthy one.

In a song widely recognized about depression and anxiety, California's Kendrick Lamar offers the gut-wrenching song "u" off of his second solo album, *To Pimp a Butterfly* (2015). In brutal honesty, he describes the life of someone slipping into bipolar episodes with manic features. Interestingly, the language Lamar uses is a bit more vivid and consistent with a formal diagnosis:

> I know your secrets, nigga
> Mood swings is frequent, nigga,
> I know depression is restin' on your heart for two reasons, nigga

Lamar continues, discussing the ways in which his anxiety and depression affect his loved ones:

> You the reason why Momma and them leavin'
> No, you ain't shit, you say you love them, I know you don't mean it
> I know you're irresponsible, selfish, in denial, can't help it
> Your trials and tribulations a burden, everyone felt it . . .
>
> You shoulda felt that black revolver blast a long time ago
> And if those mirrors could talk it would say "you gotta go"
> And if I told your secrets
> The world'll know money can't stop a suicidal weakness

(Duckworth, Arnold, & Brown, 2015)

Lamar raps as a character who appears to be drowning in his sorrows. The track is enhanced by the sound effects of clinking bottles and features Lamar rapping on- and off-beat, his cadence speeding up and slowing down without an apparent trigger, and his voice goes from smooth to deeply raspy. Lamar recounts the triumphs of a successful recording artist who finds himself alone in a hotel room, intoxicated with alcohol, and talking to himself in the mirror. He might be suffering with clinical depression, which would be evidenced by the language and key symptoms demonstrated in the lyrics (e.g., low self-confidence, self-worth, hopelessness) as well as suicidal ideation: "The world don't need you . . . I know depression is restin' on your heart" (Duckworth, Arnold, & Brown, 2015).

Several samples of the interconnectivity between drugs and mental health issues come from rapper Lil Wayne. Of particular note is the following passage from the song "I Feel Like Dying" off of his mixtape *The Drought Is Over 2 (The Carter 3 Sessions)* (2007):

> I am a prisoner, locked up behind Xanax bars
> I have just boarded a plane without a pilot
> And violets are blue, roses are red
> Daisies are yellow
> The flowers are dead
> I wish I could give you this feelin'
> I feel like buying
> And if my dealer don't have no more, then I feel like dying.

(Carter & Jonsin, 2007)

Finally, Chicago rapper Vic Mensa follows up on the theme of drugs and mental health issues, with the title track to his *There's Alot Going On* extended play (2016) sharing: "The violence and the lies slipped suicide into my mental health / I did acid in the studio one day and almost killed myself" (Mensah et al., 2016).

Two main reasons make it easy to overlook and underestimate the importance of the apparent shift in social and gendered norms and language either brought about or reflected by these artists. First, the language is clear and vivid and illustrates a tale of yearning, much richer and more vulnerable that past cohorts of emcees. It is clear that these artists are not immunized from depression or suicidal ideation by money or outward signs of success. And they do not run from vulnerability or self-help, either. Oftentimes, society fails to empathize with entertainers and celebrities, generally, who open up about their struggles to achieve sound mental health. It is often the case that society reinscribes the misguided notion that "successful" people should not be depressed, feel anxiety, or develop or espouse threats to harm themselves. Essentially, it may cause them to continue to spiral deeper into isolation, shame, and further impede them from seeking help.

Second, mental illness is oftentimes confused with pathology and violence (Alvarez, 2011; DHHS, 2001; Hadley & Yancy, 2012). Hence, when someone is struggling with mental illness (particularly a Black man in hip-hop culture), self-advocacy can sometimes be dismissed. Even still, rappers become active agents in their own recovery and treatment rather than passive receivers of treatment, or "clients." This is ownership and partnership with the listener—and hopefully this provides a therapeutic outlet to the listener. This therapeutic process is perhaps the longest-standing and durable outlet that acknowledges the ways in which systematic oppression and a history of joblessness, poverty, violence, and poor education have been toxic to Black men and Black communities in general.

Discussion, Implications, and Conclusion

Indeed, hip-hop is in dire need of a mental illness healing call. News of Kanye West's hospitalization in the fall of 2016, which landed him in the psychiatric ward of the University of California at Los Angeles, reportedly for stress and exhaustion, was jarring, but unsurprising to many (Ellis-Petersen, 2016). Following a week of erratic behavior on stage during his concerts that rocked fans and the public alike, several observers and mental health professionals predicted hospitalization and intense treatment would be the likely outcome of such behavior. The final straw, perhaps, was the report that West suffered a mental breakdown at his personal trainer's house (Ellis-Petersen, 2016); West abruptly cancelled twenty-one dates of his Saint Pablo tour. Reports claim, among other things, he has been struggling with paranoia and mental exhaustion from nonstop touring, the work on his fashion and sneaker lines, plus the ninth anniversary of the death of his mother, Dr. Donda West (Ellis-Petersen, 2016). These features of Kanye West's story are eerily similar to the decades-long battle with depression Tacoma Savage experienced.

In 2011, rapper DMX admitted in several interviews that many of his struggles with addiction and crime were related to his bipolar disorder (Pearce, 2015). In 2014, Chris Brown was diagnosed with bipolar disorder and PTSD (Pearce, 2015). Harlem's Charles Hamilton, who emerged to prominence in hip-hop culture from New York City's battle rap scene in the late 2000s, experienced a public unraveling years later with a similar tale of public outbursts and evasive behavior. He returned to rap in 2016 to admit in several interviews and media outlets that he lived with bipolar disorder. Hamilton spoke candidly about his hesitance about and financial challenges in accessing therapy and securing culturally responsive treatment. Chicago's Vic Mensa has extended the vulnerability listeners hear in his music, releasing several statements and interviews about his own suppressed mental health challenges. Mensa claims, "I just didn't trust anybody. I didn't leave my house, I just made music all the time. I was fighting depression, I shut myself in. I wanted to commit career suicide, physical suicide, spiritual suicide, I didn't care anymore" (Ellis-Petersen, 2016).

In light of the recent public, yet candid, discussions and activism around mental health illness, hip-hop still reels from a wave of suicides. Pro Era's Capital Steez committed suicide at the end of 2011, claiming to "end it all" and relieve himself from "suffering" (Ellis-Petersen, 2016). Former Def Jam executive Shakir Stewart and longtime talent manager Chris Lighty reportedly committed suicide, in 2008 and 2012, respectively. Stewart led one of hip-hop's most durable record labels and helped facilitate the careers of some of hip-hop's most successful acts, including Young Jeezy and Rick Ross. Lighty was a mainstay in the culture and represented some of hip-hop pillars like Q-tip, Busta Rhymes, Missy Elliot, 50 Cent, and LL Cool J. Indeed, whether a person is relatively obscure or at the top of the culture, mental health and wellness are an important aspect of the culture.

As hip-hop scholar and former Green Party vice president candidate Rosa Clemente asserts:

> Hip-hop and the larger community of Black and Brown, progressive, radical, social justice activists [need to] figure out a way to begin a dialogue, to not just break the silence around depression, but to stop the shamming of those who suffer from this disease. (Clemente, 2012)

One way to achieve such a dialogue may include integrating mental health services with general medical care. It would also be appreciated if medical insurance covered mental illness as well as physical ills, a recommendation proposed by the DHHS and several other organizations (DHHS, 2001; Newhill & Harris, 2007). Another viable option may include using rap therapy to expand discussions around treatment and recovery. Newhill and Harris (2007) suggest that many of the young Black men in their study would respond best to talking with other young Black men who have been "successfully treated for mental health problems themselves" (p. 115), adding that "such individuals would be viewed as credible role models for seeking treatment" (Newhill & Harris, 2007, p. 115). Indeed, some of the artists mentioned have helped operation-alize rap therapy. For many, rap music reflects a mirror on urban life in America and provides insight into the minds of a heterogeneous swath of Black men.

If mental health and wellness remains a taboo subject for Black men, hip-hop is bound to have unproductive conversations about it. And as social norms change—or, as in many cases, hip-hop itself changes social norms—Black folks and Black youth in particular will employ more positive, productive conversations on mental health and wellness. Many times, as in therapy, those conversations start with feelings, emotions, rawness, recollections of trauma, and possible feelings of suicide. As discussed in this chapter, these features are salient, yet durable, in rap music. Only then can Black men and hip-hop culture, at large, begin to heal and continue to evolve. It is my argument that although dark and uncomfortable to hear at times, the new renaissance of mental health conversations in hip-hop represents the best of what hip-hop has to offer society: a powerful and challenging critique of systematic and institutional oppression that I hope inspires collective action and healing instead of individual escapism.

Appendix. Songs Analyzed

SONG TITLE	PERFORMER(S)	YEAR	WRITER(S)
"The Message"	Grandmaster Flash and the Furious Five	1982	Clifton Chase, Edward Fletcher, Melvin Glover, and Sylvia Robinson
"Mind Playing Tricks on Me"	Geto Boys	1991	Brad Jordan, Doug King, and William Dennis
"Suicidal Thoughts"	Notorious B.I.G.	1995	Christopher Wallace and Robert Hall

"So Many Tears"	2Pac	1995	Tupac Shakur, Gregory Jacobs, Randy Walker, Eric Baker, and Stevie Wonder
"Slippin"	DMX	1998	Earl Simmons
"Window to My Soul"	dead prez	2003	Khnum Muata Ibomu and Mutulu Olugbala
"Whatever It Takes"	Joe Budden	2003	Joe Budden, Clinton Sparks, and Carolyn Franklyn
"I Feel Like Dying"	L'il Wayne	2007	Dwayne Carter
"Losing My Mind"	Pharoahe Monch	2014	Troy Jamerson and Jesse West
"u"	Kendrick Lamar	2015	Kendrick Duckworth, Terrace Martin, and Michael Brown
"Only Human"	Joe Budden	2015	Joe Budden, Emanny Salgado, and Karon Graham
"Soundtrack 2 My Life"	Kid Cudi	2016	Scott Mescudi and Haynie
"There's A lot Going On"	Vic Mensa	2016	Victor Mensah, Alex Baez, Darian Garcia, Kevin Rhomberg, Carter Lang, and Peter Cottontale
"Mad"	Solange featuring L'il Wayne	2016	Solange Knowles, Dwayne Carter, Dave Longstreth, Raphael Saadiq, and Sir Dylan

■ Notes

1. For the purposes of this chapter, mental health includes a person's emotional, psychological, and social well-being. The concept helps determine how people handle stress, relate to others, and make choices about their lives. For more information, see the US Department of Health and Human Service's web page, www.mentalhealth.gov, and the National Institute of Mental Health, www.nimh.gov.

2. For the purpose of this chapter, youth are defined as persons under the age of eighteen.

3. Jane Crow, in this context, describes the specific practices, laws, and customs that constrict the lives of US women of African descent. Additional interpretations of Jane Crow have been applied to capture the practices, laws, and customs that discriminate against women and alienate them from the Equal Protection Clause of the Fourteenth Amendment of the US Constitution. For more information, see the work of Rosalind Rosenberg (2017), *Jane Crow: The life of Pauli Murray.*

4. It is important to note that mental health research has used the term "Black" to describe individuals from various ethnicities of the African diaspora (e.g., African American, Caribbean, and others). The terms *Black* and *African American* are used interchangeably in this chapter to reflect the use of both terms in the relevant literature.

5. Immortal Technique (2003). Homeland and hip hop. *Revolutionary Vol. 2.* New York: Viper Records.

■ References

Agency for Healthcare Research and Quality, US Department of Health and Human Services. (2013). *National healthcare disparities report.* Washington, DC: Author. Https://www.ahrq.gov/research/findings/nhqrdr/nhdr13/chap2-txt.html#fig231.

Alvarez, T. T., III. (2011). Beats, rhymes, and life: Rap therapy in an urban setting. In S. Hadley & G.

Yancey (eds.), *Therapeutic uses of rap music* (pp. 117–28). New York: Routledge.

———. (2006). *Beats, rhymes, and life: Exploring the use of rap therapy with urban adolescents.* Unpublished master's thesis, Smith College School for Social Work, Northampton, MA.

American Psychological Association. (2014). Demographic characteristics of APA members by membership characteristics. Washington, D.C.: The Author. Http://www.apa.org/workforce/publications/14-member/table-1.pdf.

———. (n.d.). African Americans have limited access to mental and behavioral health care. Http://www.apa.org/about/gr/issues/minority/access.aspx.

Carter, D. M., & Jonsin, J. (2007). I feel like dying. *The Drought is Over 2 (The Carter 3 Sessions).* Cash Money/Universal Records.

Carter, R. T. (2007). Racism and psychological and emotional injury: Recognizing and assessing race-based traumatic stress. *Counseling Psychologist 35*(1), 13–105.

Clemente, R. (2012). Not ready to die, but wanting to die: Depression, hip hop, and the death of Chris Lighty. *Chronicles of a Black Puerto Rican Hip Hop Feminist Scholar Activist.* Http://rosaaliciaclemente.blogspot.co.uk/.

Chang, M. (2005). *Can't stop, won't stop.* New York: St. Martin's Press.

Chao, T., Asnaani, A., & Hofmann, S. G. (2012). Perception of racial discrimination and psychopathology across three U.S. ethnic minority groups. *Cultural Diversity and Ethnic Minority Psychology 18*(1), 74–81.

DeCarlo, A., & Hockman, E. (2003). Rap Therapy: A group work intervention method for urban adolescents. *Social Work with Groups, 26,* 45–59.

Duckworth, K. L., Arnold, T., & Brown, M. (2015). *To Pimp a Butterfly.* Top Dawg/Aftermath/Interscope.

Elligan, D. (2004). *Rap therapy: A practical guide for communicating with youth and young adults through Rap music.* New York: Kensington Books.

Ellis-Petersen, H. (2016). Kanye West's travails help hip-hop open up on mental health. *The Guardian,* November 25. Https://www.theguardian.com/society/2016/nov/25/kanye-wests-travails-help-hip-hop-open-up-on-mental-health.

Fletcher, E., Grandmaster Flash, Melle Mel, Robinson, S., & Chase, C. (1982). The Message. *The Message.* Sugar Hill.

Folami, A. N. (2007, June). From Habermas to "Get Rich or Die Trying": Hip Hop, the Telecommunications Act of 1996, and the Black public sphere. *Michigan Journal of Race and Law 12,* 240–54.

Ginwright, S. A. (2010). Peace out to revolution! Activism among African American youth. *Young: Nordic Journal of Youth Research 18*(1), 77–96.

Hadley, S., & Yancy, G. (2012). *Therapeutic uses of rap and hip hop.* New York: Routledge.

Hammond, W. P. (2012). Taking it like a man: Masculine role norms as moderators of the racial discrimination-depressive symptoms association among African American men. *American Journal of Public Health 102*(2), 232–41.

Hankerson, S., Suite, D., & Bailey, R. K. (2015). Treatment disparities among African American men with depression: Implications for clinical practice. *Journal of Health Care for Poor and Underserved, 26*(1), 21–34.

Harris-Perry, M. (2014). *The Melissa Harris-Perry Show*, April 14. MSNBC.

Hall, A. (2014). *The Arsenio Hall Show*, March 26. Fox Studios.

Himle, J. A., Baser, R. E., Taylor, R. J., Campbell, R. D., & Jackson, J. S. (2009). Anxiety disorders among African Americans, Blacks of Caribbean descent, and non-Hispanic Whites in the United States. *Journal of Anxiety Disorders 23*, 578–90.

Henderson, E. A. (1996). Black nationalism and rap music. *Journal of Black Studies 26*(3), 308–39.

Ibomu, K. M., & Olugbala, M. (2003). Window to my soul. *Turn Off the Radio: The mixtape, Vol. 2. Get free or die trying'*. Landscape.

Jordan, B., King, D., & Dennis, W. (1991). Mind playing tricks on me. *We Can't Be Stopped*. Rap-A-Lot/ Priority.

Kitwana, B. (2002). *The hip hop generation: Young Blacks and the crisis in African American culture*. New York: Basic Civitas Books.

KRS ONE (2009). *The gospel of hip hop: First instrument*. Brooklyn, NY: powerHouse Books.

Malcoun, E., Williams, M. T., & Bahojb-Nouri, L. V. (2015). Assessment of post-traumatic stress disorder in African Americans. In L. T. Benuto & B. D. Leany (eds.), *Guide to Psychological Assessment with African Americans* (pp. 163–82). New York: Springer.

Mental Health America. (n.d.). Black & African American communities and mental health. Http:// www.mentalhealthamerica.net/african-american-mental-health.

Mensah, V. K., Baez, P., Garcia, B., Rhomberg, K., Lang, K. F., & Cottontale, P. (2016). There's Alot Going On. *There's Alot Going On*. Roc Nation/Def Jam.

Mescudi, S. R. S., & Haynie, E. (2009). Soundtrack 2 My Life. *Man on the Moon: The End of Day*. Motown/ Universal Records.

Newhill, C. E., & Harris, D. (2007). African American consumers' perceptions of racial disparities in mental health services. *Social Work in Public Health 23*(3), 107–24.

Pearce, S. (2015). How Kendrick Lamar, Earl Sweatshirt, Heems, and Future are destigmatizing mental illness. *Consequence of Sound*. Http://consequenceofsound.net/2015/05/ stranded-in-a-mob-depression-and-rap-in-2015/.

Robinson, C. (2014). Dreams & nightmares: What hip-hop can teach us about Black youth. *In the Public Interest Newsletter*. Washington, D.C.: American Psychological Association.

Rose, T. (1994). *Black noise: Rap music and Black culture in contemporary America*. Middletown, CT: Wesleyan University Press.

Roychoudhury, D., & Garder, L. M. (2012). Taking back our minds: Hip-hop psychology's (HHP) call for a renaissance, action, and liberatory use of psychology in education. In M. Viola & Porfilio (eds.) *Hip-Hop(e): The cultural practice and critical pedagogy of international hip-hop* (pp. 220–234). New York: Peter Lang.

Shakur, T., Jacobs, G., Walker, R., Baker, E., & Wonder, S. (1995). So Many Tears. *Me Against the World*. Interscope/Death Row.

Sue, D. W. (2010). *Microaggressions in everyday life: Race, gender, and sexual orientation*. Hoboken, NJ: John Wiley & Sons.

Tillie-Allen, N. M. (2005). Exploring hip hop therapy with at risk youth. *Praxis, 5*, 30–36.

Tyson, E. H. (2002). Hip hop therapy: An exploratory study of rap music intervention with at-risk and delinquent youth. *Journal of Poetry Therapy 15*(3), 131–44.

United States Department of Health and Human Services Office of Minority Mental Health (2016). Mental Health and African Americans. Https://minorityhealth.hhs.gov/omh/browse.aspx?lvl=4&lvlid=24.

United States Department of Health and Human Services (2001). *Mental health: Culture, Race, and Ethnicity.* A Supplement to *Mental Health: A report of the Surgeon General.* Rockville, MD: U.S. Department of Health and Human Services, Substance Abuse and Mental Health Services Administration, Center for Mental Health Services. Https://www.ncbi.nlm.nih.gov/books/NBK44243/.

Wallace, C., & Hall, L. (1994). Suicidal thoughts. *Ready to Die.* Bad Boy Records.

Ward, E. C., Wiltshire, J. C., Detry, M. A., & Brown, R. L. (2013). African American men and women's attitude toward mental illness, perceptions of stigma, and preferred coping behaviors. *Nursing Research 62*(3), 185–94.

Ward, J. V. (2000). *The skin we're in: Teaching our teens to be emotionally strong, socially smart, and spiritually connected.* New York: Free Press.

Woodward, A. T., Taylor, R. J., & Chatters, L. M. (2011). Use of professional and informal support by Black men with mental disorders. *Research on Social Work Practice, 21*(3), 327–36.

Williams, M. T. (2013). How therapists drive away minority clients. *Psychology Today,* June 13. Https://www.psychologytoday.com/blog/culturally-speaking/201306/how-therapists-drive-away-minority-clients.

———. (2015). The link between racism and PTSD. *Psychology Today.* Https://www.psychologytoday.com/blog/culturally-speaking/201509/the-link-between-racism-and-ptsd.

Mama, Am I Hip-Hop?

Unpacking the Intersections of Race, Culture, and Gender with a Young Black Boy

Chelda Smith Kondo

"Mama, am I hip-hop?"

"Well. . . . I'm not sure, baby, but let me try to explain."

Dear Black Son, this essay is framed by an interest to make sense of insider/outsider discourse surrounding cultural membership in the hip-hop community. You, our African American son existing in predominantly white spaces, have the burden of a Haitian mother and Togolese father—a burden because your father and I never had to unpack this question as youth and certainly don't have a neat response as adults. To the best of our abilities, we curate a life for you that is steeped in diasporic aesthetics and experiences that affirm black pride. Willfully devoid of deficit constructions of black males, this improvisational curriculum fails us. Every time a microaggression challenges your humanity, you are reminded of your typecasting. Resolved, we press forward and now must explicitly grapple with the double consciousness required to unpack the prevailing narratives that inform your identity development—the black gaze and the white gaze. Recognizing tensions between the black community, dominant communities, and your household, individuality may seem elusive. It doesn't have to be.

What's the Black Community?

Although I said, "the black community," black people are not monolithic. We are a diaspora, a people originating from Africa who were spread throughout this world. In the United States, prior to the Civil Rights Act of 1964, black and white people were racially segregated. Under those circumstances, there was a macro black community. Although there existed cultural, economic, and social diversity among us, external perceptions limited us to stereotypes. Based on the degree of melanin present in one's physical appearance, standardization of macro community labels such as "colored people" or "the black community" was established. The involuntary nature of immigration relegated people with black skin to enslavement. Propaganda grounded in eugenics normalized white supremacy and consequently the inferiority of people of African descent. The false authority of eugenics resulted in mass self-classifications into racial categories (communities) that often went unquestioned. Generally, everybody knew where he or she belonged. We went from enslaved coloreds and Negroes to African Americans and blacks—from niggers to niggas, all while pursuing self-actualization and self-determination.

Since 1790, the US government, by way of a national census, has been officially classifying its citizens into racial categories. Initially, there were European (white), African (black), and Indian (Native American) people. Every decennial, the context and content of the document has experienced amendments (ranging from slight to radical) as a response to the sociopolitical transformations of the era. For example, in 1977, the census coded humans in four primary racial groups: Asian or Pacific Islander, American Indian or Alaskan Native, black, and white. The most recent 2010 census, listed fifteen racial categories, as well as a place to write in specific races not listed on the survey. Over time, some of the most sophisticated modifications included the addition of ethnicity, multiple race selections, and the "some other race" option. Most notable are the changes from third-party observatory classification to self-reporting forms. That particular change aligns with progressive notions of individual autonomy over racial identification. The radical revisions suggest a desire on the part of the US government to seek accuracy when coding the US population and by way of globalization, the world as a whole. However, the "check all that apply" approach has ignited a conceptual debate over the meaning and usefulness of racial categories. This begs the question, does not the option to self-identify as any race allow for people to opt in or out of the black community? Membership in the black community was historically discernible by enslavement, indentured servitude, imposed segregation limits, and then denial of civil rights. But in the age of integration, is the black community still race-based?

Thandeka (1999) theorizes that original racial divisions were a capitalist tactic orchestrated by white elitists to prevent or postpone an uprising by the lower class, which comprised both black and white indentured servants. She contends that racial kindred facilitated false alignment between those in power and the working poor, which fed the poor's ego while neglecting their stomachs. The distraction created a visible division between poor whites and blacks who once experienced similar persecution and domination. Thus race, according to Thandeka (1999), is a social construct that is used to manipulate society albeit lacking biological significance. Race, in spite of its potent economic, social, and psychological repercussions, is a human concept based on pseudoscientific taxonomy (Jackson & Weidman, 2004). Blumer (1958) hypothesizes that "fundamentally racial feelings point to and depend on a positional arrangement of the racial groups" (p. 4). In other words, races only exist in relation to or opposition of other groups. He explains racialization as a "collective process" (Blumer, 1958). Interestingly, Li (2010) conceptualizes race as "bound to a certain historical and social context. Consequently, race is evident in action, not expressions of color" (p. 341). Otherwise stated, blackness is most relevant in context. When you are alone, you don't have to be racialized.

What Is Racialization?

The United States purports a post-colonial and post-civil rights identity, a claim solidified by its election of a black president, twice. Although "post-racial" discourses thrive, racial stratification is ubiquitously experienced. Essentially, as whites position themselves as both the standard and normal, people of color function as the "necessary Other" (Hall, 1985, p. 106). In an Australian study of racial classification between classes 'white' was revealed as an unstable, not a biologically determined trait, but instead a "shifting set of social practices" (Dolby, 2000, p. 49). Extrapolating, it can be understood that just as whiteness is action-based, so too is blackness. Racialization occurs when cultural knowledge, values, practices and experiences are imposed upon a person based on the color of his or her skin. It is irrelevant whether that individual identifies with said group; one is racialized based on what others think of people who look like them. As DuBois's (1989) theory of double consciousness explains,

> It is a peculiar sensation, this double-consciousness, this sense of always looking at one's self through the eyes of others, of measuring one's soul by the tape of a world that looks on in amused contempt and pity. One ever feels his twoness—an American, a negro: two souls, two thoughts, two unreconciled strivings; two warring ideals in one dark body, whose dogged strength alone keeps it from being torn asunder. (p. 3)

The black community, in these respects, therefore is inevitably racially classified. America's obsession with colorization, as evidenced by the census's racial categories, demands double consciousness as people of color grapple with how they are read and how they read themselves. "Twoness" references one's fluidity of membership based on one's social context. The oppressive circumstances that once forced a collective linger while equity eludes the masses. Black people, alongside other marginalized groups, are still fighting for civil justice. As long as those inequities exist and disproportionately plague melanin-rich communities, the black community will exist. Institutionalized racism, coupled with individual racism, makes race relevant, thereby lumping people into race-based communities. Being racialized as black means contending with the effects of a hegemonic white gaze (Fanon, 1986; Yancy, 2008), but also a surveying black gaze (Canham & Williams, 2017; Moore, 2008; Rollock et al., 2013). These gazes put forth measures that mediate access, status, and quality of existence in their respective communities. These standards manifest into leveraged capital: "the sum of the resources, actual or virtual, that accrue to an individual or a group by virtue of possessing a durable network of more or less institutionalized relationships of mutual acquaintance and recognition" (Bourdieu & Wacquant 1992, p. 119).

We each have capital, unequally distributed of course, but nonetheless with a degree of agency. Actualizing one's double consciousness is an empowering form of social capital (Bourdieu, 1986). The ability to code-switch is a linguistic capital that often yields economic and social status returns. Credentials, such as academic and professional qualifications, are versions of institutionalized capital. Skin pigment and bodily aesthetic features (i.e., blond hair or blue eyes) are embodied capital. Social capital grants inequitable yields like group membership, border-crosser eligibility, and systemic privileges (Bourdieu, 1986). Capital rates are often relative. Institutional capital may have high exchange rates in white communities, but their possession in the hands of people of African descent can be ostracizing in the black community. Both black and white gazes racialize you, but you also have capital, and agency (Hewson, 2010). Your agency, complete with power, intentionality, and rationality, will guide your self-determination.

How Am I Racialized?

Baby, the white gaze is a diabolical force that must be resisted. It "draws on a homogeneous, undifferentiated, negative [mobilization] of blackness that implicates all black people and allows little room for individual expression of creativity and potential" (Canham & Williams, 2017, pp. 32–33). Their gaze relegates black people to stereotypes of being unintelligent, indolent, dependent, and hypersexual. Unfortunately, black people who position themselves as membership-police find association within these precincts and at times maintain these standards through a black gaze. Ergo, "The primary function of this gaze is to solidify markers of blackness so as to demarcate the boundary signifying who is really black and who is an imposter" (Canham & Williams, 2017, p. 36). Baby, irrespective of identities others attempt to impose, you can *never* be an imposter. Your blackness is solidified by the imminent threat you face living with your skin color and gender expression.

Wielding social capital under both black and white gazes is the burden you must carry. Black Lives Matter exists because no amount of social or institutional capital can eradicate your biological liability. Eric Garner (New York), Miriam Carey (DC), Michael Brown (Missouri), Laquan McDonald (Illinois), Natasha McKenna (Virginia), Tamir Rice (Ohio), Rekia Boyd (Illinois), Kathryn Johnston (Georgia), Walter Scott (South Carolina), Freddie Gray (Maryland), Sandra Bland (Texas), Alton Sterling (Louisiana) and Patrick Harmon (Utah) were some of the many unarmed black people murdered by law enforcement in recent years. Law enforcement, at disproportionately high rates, kill people with black skin, whether women or men, children or seniors. Black Lives Matter is a movement fighting for the recognition of your human life while resisting your racialization. Contrary to national efforts to dispel the existence of racism or the relevance of race, this ongoing atrocity affirms the collective black identity. Son, you are black. As a black boy, there are additional burdens. Your gender carries with it performative standards that are maintained within and across racial boundaries. As Creese (2015) explains, "Gendered representations of blackness are embedded in American popular culture through films, television, music and news, and shaping interactions with others in the broader society" (pp. 202–3). These media characterize black men as innately angry and violent. You are not inherently violent, but justifiably angry. Regardless, nothing about your blackness is inherent. Remember, blackness, like maleness, is a social construction (Creese, 2015; Dowd, 2016). Your blackness does not have to be defined; nevertheless "definitions" endure.

Perhaps one the most controversial decisions you'll face is your relationship to the term "nigga." By now, you've heard it used both to demoralize and to uplift. The white gaze uses "nigger" as a linguistic weapon to dehumanize your being. Meanwhile, the black gaze employs "nigga" as a term of endearment and recognition of brotherhood. Forsaking your stance, you will inevitably be recognized as a nig**. I am as certain of this as I am of your eventual encounters with law enforcement. The intersection of your skin and gender produces a degree of affliction unique to only to black males.

Canham and Williams (2017) note, "The distressing psychological, affective and embodied consequences of dealing with, or repressing, responses provoked by oppressive whiteness demand energy. This detracts from living freely and destabilizes blackness" (p. 33). Obsessing over external gazes suspends your self-actualization; however, denying their power can be fatal. Son, recognize their influence without holding their weight. There is hope because resistance takes many forms. #BlackBoyJoy exists as inspiration for you to thrive in your humanity. Defying racialization, black men are embracing a childlike insouciance they've historically been denied. They smile, dance, play—they hope. Discussing the quandary of black masculinity, Young (2016) explains, "Throughout history, our boys have been denied their childhood. When we learn about the stolen youth of Emmett Till, we're reminded that young black boys are seen as men by society or, worse, as a threat. #BlackBoyJoy presents a teachable moment to social media that allows us to reclaim the innocence of black boyhood." Beyond social media, #BlackBoyJoy serves as a living rupture that can distance you from both black and white gazes. From hip-hop artists to athletes, activists and politicians, black men self-actualize through resistance.

What Is Hip-Hop?

Hip-hop started as a resistance effort. From the constraints of racialization and socioeconomic oppression, graffiti art, break dancing, DJ'ing, and rapping banded to craft hip-hop culture. Far from its sociopolitical foundations of the 1970s, contemporary approaches to hip-hop are on a conceptualizing spectrum. One extreme centers its historical underpinnings of political analysis and community elevation while rejecting modern ahistorical iterations that abandon lyricism. The other extreme regards hip-hop as youth culture, externally shifting according to youth interests. Along this spectrum, there are those who embrace misogyny, bigotry, and homophobia, while others oppose them by emphasizing ethnic pride, empowerment, and critical consciousness.

Jenkins (2011) argues, "Hip-hop is a cultural space where individuals who have been kicked out of schools, locked out of opportunity, and imprisoned in oppression have created a space where they can shine, excel, and be great" (p. 1247). Similarly, cultural critic Rivas (2014) notes "hip-hop's ability to survive, to teach survival, to unite people, to give an expression for oppressed people, that it can be used as a culture of challenging oppression while raising consciousness." In spite of the hostile corporate invasion of hip-hop, and its global appropriation beneath the white gaze, hip-hop maintains its potential to liberate marginalized populations.

So . . . Am I Hip-Hop?

Globally, youth consume and produce iterations of hip-hop. Whether through art, consciousness, rapping, aesthetics, affiliation, or varied expressions, hip-hop culture is perpetuated. The choice to engage is yours. A perceived brotherhood with rappers and hip-hop artists, and the systematic injustice toward black males within the American educational system, typically draws in those on the margins (Oware, 2010). Your racialization may lead you to hip-hop, but it can equally deter you. The black gaze might perceive aversion to hip-hop as a motive to revoke your "black card." The black card is yet another social capital standard monitored by the black gaze. Much like the figurative Underground Railroad, the black card can be a passport to liberation. But unlike the railroad, its pursuit should never comprise your authentic self.

The anxiety of double consciousness cultivates a desire for fraternal energy. Hip-hop culture purports a sense of brotherhood among young black males and rappers. Analogous to the American dream, a corporate motif found in hip-hop is the perennial story of the underdog rising from obscurity and oppression to immeasurable fame and success. Pathologized black males in challenging situations identify with those who claim to have clawed their way out of financial destitution, racialization, and oppression. In doing so, hip-hop artists become standards of imitation. Take, for instance, the lyrics from "Hip Hop Saved My Life" by Lupe Fiasco:

> His man called, said: "your time might be now
> They played your freestyle over 'Wipe Me Down'
> They played it 2 times, say it might be crowned
> As the best thing out the H-town in a while"
> He picked up his son with a great big smile
> Rapped every single word to the newborn child
> Then he put him down and went back to the kitchen
> And put on another beat and got back to the mission of
> Get his momma out the hood, put her somewhere in the woods
> Keep his lady looking good, have her rolling like she should
> Show his homies there's a way other than that flippin' yay
> Bail his homie out of jail, put a lawyer on his case
> Throw a concert for the school, show the shorties that it's cool

Throw some candy on the Caddy, chuck the deuce and act a fool

Man it feels good, when it happens like that

Two days from going back to selling crack, yessir.

(Jaco, Jean, & Lopez, 2007)

These provocative and inspirational lyrics narrate the individual's successful rise above his circumstances; hip-hop provides an avenue to resist the stereotyping white and black gazes of an impoverished black man being forced to sell drugs to support his family. His lyrics will allow self-determination. Providing for his family, community, friends positions him as a hero able to escape imposed identities designed to limit his potential. This imagery is particularly arresting to young black men who may feel trapped by their double consciousness. Every individual wants to be able to say, in the immortal words of Drake, "Started from the bottom, now we're here" (Graham, 2013).

Son, black males and hip-hop can only be considered synonymous inasmuch as the word "hip-hop" instantly conjures images of a young black male. As a matter of origin, hip-hop is not the first musical genre or cultural movement to emerge from black communities. From heavy metal, rock 'n' roll, blues, gospel, rhythm and blues, country, soul, and jazz, people of African descent pioneered nearly all Western popular music (Tomlinson, 2016). Each genre began as a countercultural expression that lost its proverbial black soul through mainstreaming. Tomlinson (2016) explains, "History has shown while black musical genres were initially seen as culturally inferior and marginalized in mainstream popular culture, they later emerged as staples of a capitalist driven market that works hand-in-hand with white supremacy." Through mass appropriation, hip-hop is undergoing its whitening process. Certainly, hip-hop and blackness are in relation, but hip-hop and black maleness are freestanding. The black community, whether a symbolic cooperative or a biological network that links all people of the African diaspora, exists. Membership is fluid and agency is individually taken up and collectively granted. Between the white gaze and the black gaze, you are charged to negotiate and innovate your identity. Bhabha (1994) explains, "It is only when we understand that all cultural statements and systems are constructed in this contradictory and ambivalent space of enunciation, that we begin to understand why hierarchal claims to the inherent originality or 'purity' of cultures are untenable, even before we resort to empirical historical instances that demonstrate their hybridity" (p. 36). The difference between the aforementioned cultural movements and hip-hop is its intersection with your youth. If you're hip-hop, you are also heavy metal, rock 'n' roll, blues, gospel, rhythm and blues, country, soul, and jazz.

■ **References**

Bhabha, H. K. (1994). *The location of culture*. London: Routledge.

Blumer, H. (1958). Race prejudice as a sense of group position. *Pacific Sociological Review 1*(1), 3–7.

Bourdieu, P. (1986). The forms of capital. In J. G. Richardson (ed.), *Handbook of theory and research for the sociology of education* (pp. 15–29). New York: Greenwood.

Bourdieu, P., & Wacquant, L. J. (1992). *An invitation to reflexive sociology.* Chicago: University of Chicago Press.

Canham, H., & Williams, R. (2017). Being black, middle class and the object of two gazes. *Ethnicities 17*(1), 23.

Creese, G. (2015). Growing up where "no one looked like me": Gender, race, hip hop and identity in Vancouver. *Gender Issues 32*(3), 201–19.

Dolby, N., 2000. Race, National, state: Multiculturalism in Australia. *Arena Magazine 45,* 48–51.

Dowd, N. E. (2016). Black boys matter: Developmental equality. *Hofstra Law Review 45*(1), 47–116.

DuBois, W. E. B. (1994). *The souls of black folk.* New York: Dover Publications.

Fanon, F. (1986). *Black skin, white masks.* New York: Grove Press.

Hall, S. (1985). Signification, representation, ideology: Althusser and the post-structuralist debates. *Critical Studies in Mass Communication 2*(2), 91–114.

Hewson, M. (2010). Agency. In A. J. Mills, G. Durepos, & E. Wiebe (eds.). *Encyclopedia of case study research,* vol. 2 (pp. 12–17). Los Angeles: Sage.

Jaco, A., Jean, N., & Lopez, R. (2007). Hip-hop saved my life. Recorded by Lupe Fiasco and Nikki Jean on *Lupe Fiasco's The Cool.* 1st & 15th. Atlantic.

Jenkins, T. (2011). A beautiful mind: Black male intellectual identity and hip-hop culture. *Journal of Black Studies 42*(8), 1231–51.

Li, S. (2010). Performing intimacy using "race-specific, race-free language": Black private letters in the public sphere. *South Atlantic Quarterly 109*(2), 339–56.

Moore, K. S. (2008). Class formations: Competing forms of black middle-class identity. *Ethnicities 8*(4): 492–517.

Oware, M. (2010). Brotherly love: Homosociality and black masculinity in gangsta rap music. *Journal of African American Studies15*(1), 22–39.

Rivas, L. (2014, April 2). Hip-hop is resistance against the inequalities in society. *The Sundial.* Http://sundial.csun.edu/2014/04/hip-hop-is-resistance-against-the-inequalities-in-society/.

Rollock, N., Vincent, C., Gillborn, D., & Ball, S. (2013). "Middle class by profession": Class status and identification amongst the Black middle classes. *Ethnicities 13*(3), 253–75.

Thandeka. (1999). *Learning to be white: Money, race, and God in America.* New York: Continuum.

Tomlinson, L. (2016, Jan. 8). The ongoing economic exploitation of black music. *Huffington Post.* Http://www.huffingtonpost.ca/dr-lisa-tomlinson/black-music-exploitation_b_8934870.html.

Yancy, G. (2008). Colonial gazing: The production of the body as "other." *Western Journal of Black Studies 32*(1): 1–15.

Young, D. (2016, September 1). On reclaiming "boy" and giving young black men something to celebrate. *The Root.* Http://www.theroot.com/on-reclaiming-boy-and-giving-young-black-men-somethin-1790856576.

 VIGNETTE

Ronnie was a product of his environment. He grew up in a neighborhood where education wasn't important, and what set you were with was more important than getting good grades in school. Ronnie knew he wanted to get an education even in elementary school, but found solace in hip-hop. Hip-hop culture accepted him, and he focused on school and his artistic passions. From writing music to becoming more involved in dance, Ronnie found relief from his surroundings in hip-hop. Many said that he would get stuck in his environment and wouldn't amount to more than a common thug. Today, Ronnie still embraces the unique culture of hip-hop and educates others through his Afro-American studies course on the greatness of hip-hop. He has achieved in many ways, and has graduated from college.

PART 7

Programs and Initiatives

INTRODUCTION

Spencer Platt and Theodore S. Ransaw

Second star to the right and straight on 'til morning
—J. M. Barrie, *Peter Pan*

This section of the Handbook covers emerging trends of programs and initiatives that support Black males. As the previous parts have established, Black males are disenfranchised while simultaneously showing great resolve and promise. The North Star mentioned in the quote above serves as an allegory of the modern Black male as well as his ancestors, who both have sought to escape oppression by emerging from imposed shadows of despair by looking up toward a shining light of promise that leads us to a new direction. The Programs and Initiatives part leads to a different direction that includes methodologies and research that support Black males.

Our first point of departure is the chapter "All Eyes on Me: Culturally Responsive Approaches to Engaging Revenue-Playing Black Male Student-Athletes Who Attend PWIs," by Ronald W. Whitaker II and Adriel A. Hilton. Addressing Black male innovation cannot be done without first understanding the *mise en place* of culturally responsive pedagogies. Establishing a protocol that addresses valuing cultural differences as well as thinking critically about others puts education on the right heading to eliminate hidden biases and prejudices. For example, one of the numerous stereotypes that Black males are faced with is that they are perceived as either athletes or thugs, never scholars. However, Black male college athletes are still students while they attend postsecondary institutions. Addressing services that best serve Black male athletes achieve full academic persistence is one way to help eliminate negative stereotypes of Black masculinity.

623

Devin L. Randolph describes a course that far too many Black males follow. Randolph looks at how Black male students visualize what they say to help them make them effectively persist in school with his chapter, African American Male Students' Perceptions of Factors That Contribute to Their Academic Success." Randolph's novelty is not only that he makes a case that Black males can indeed achieve in school, but that he proves his point by using the experiences of African American males who dropped/stopped out of school before obtaining a high-school diploma, and their reasons for returning

Some assume that Black males can easily find their bearings when they get to college. Others think that Black males and their problems simply disappear when they simply set foot on the campus of post-secondary institutions. However, as resilient as they are, Black males need guidance to successfully navigate academe. "Holla If You Hear Me? Supporting African American Males at a Predominantly White Institution in the Midwest—a Tale from Southern River University," by C. P. Gause, goes into detail about the collegiate experience of far too many Black males: being one of the few Black males on a college campus.

"The Effects of Racial Exclusionary Disciplinary Practices on African American Male Students: Alternatives to Suspensions and Expulsions" by Tyree Robinson explores solutions to punitive practices that perpetuate the cycle that starts the school-to-prison pipeline. Firmly guiding students away from the turbulent waters of zero tolerance and low expectations toward bright seas of opportunity as well as fulfillment, is not only desirable but achievable in Robinson's chapter.

Finally, the last chapter, "Black Males in Higher Education: A Multiple Case Study Approach to Success and Retention at the University of Texas at Austin" by authors Gregory J. Vincent, Ryan M. Sutton, Jessica M. Khalaf, and, Kevin Almasy chronicles a journey of a program that increased the sense of belongingness for Black male students at the University of Texas at Austin. The research was compiled with data from the African American Male Research Initiative. AAMRI is a faculty-led academic initiative that focuses on both the professional and personal development of African American males. Utilizing evidence-based practices, AAMRI informs public policy experts, practitioners, and concerned citizens on how best to create and maintain a culture of Black male excellence in K–16 settings. Their overall goal is to increase the four-year graduation rate for African American males at the University of Texas and to increase the number of Black males attending four-year colleges and universities across the state of Texas.

The authors of this section, Ronald W. Whitaker, II, Adriel A. Hilton, Devin L. Randolph, C. P. Gause, Tyree Robinson, Gregory J. Vincent, Ryan M. Sutton, Jessica M. Khalaf, and, Kevin Almas are pathfinders. They have provided a wealth of information about the exploitation of Black male athletes, what makes Black males students have a successful schooling experience, strategies that improve persistence for Black males at majority White institutions, as well as illuminating practices that contribute to Black males being pushed out of schools. However, they have taken their individual perspectives on the barriers that impede the progress of Black males one step further. All of the authors have provided either methodologies or examples of initiatives and programs that help improve and sustain Black males. The hard work of the authors in this section prove that Black males have the potential to successfully travel toward bright futures touched by the heavenly stars.

All Eyes on Me

Culturally Responsive Approaches to Engaging Revenue-Playing
Black Male Student-Athletes Who Attend PWIs

Ronald W. Whitaker II and Adriel A. Hilton

T his chapter examines the impact of racism and projected negative stereotypes on the academic and social experiences of African American male student-athletes at predominantly White institutions (PWIs). Through our research, we have meticulously tried to understand the aforementioned. Although we are concerned with the plight of the entire African American male student-athlete population, this chapter will solely focus on those individuals who participate in the top revenue-producing sports, which are basketball and football. Like Melendez (2008), we also agree that African American male basketball and football players have higher visibility on campus (and society), which seems to justify a more exhaustive focus on this population.

African American male student-athletes still have to contend with negative beliefs about their intellectual abilities (Burke, 1993). Further, there is a common belief that Black male college students do not care about education (Benson, 2000). Our interactions with Black male college student-athletes dispel that myth, and are also consistent with Harper and Davis's (2012) conclusions:

> Black men do care about education. Despite their recognition of how schools, postsecondary institutions, and policies unfairly disadvantage them and others in their families and communities the undergraduates upon whom this article is based maintained a firm belief in the liberating potential of education. This is obviously inconsistent with Fordham and Ogbu's (1986) claims that those who forecast inequitable returns on educational investments are likely to resist schooling. (Harper & Davis, 2012, p. 116)

As a mean to highlight the fact that negative stereotyping of Black male student-athletes has always existed, the next section of the chapter explores the literature on the experiences of this population from the 1940s to the present. We then give an overview of our study, and provide narratives of Black male student-athletes who participated and highlight our key findings. Before concluding, in the "Discussion" section of this chapter, we give an example of culturally responsive programming that athletics and university leaders might consider for African American male student-athletes. Theoretically, this work is explored through the lens of "stereotype threat" and "recast theory."

Review of Literature

Black males began participating in collegiate athletics at PWIs in the 1940s (Govan, 1971). Oftentimes, these athletes were welcomed on the field and court, but scorned within their campus milieu (Edwards, 1969; McPherson, 1971; Olsen, 1968). The dual relationship with Black male student-athletes can be attributed to the fact that few people viewed them as scholars; rather, they were perceived as "dumb jocks" with superior athletic talent (Adler & Adler, 1985; Harrison, 2001; Miller, 1998; Wiggins, 1988). The aforementioned issue is raised by Edwards:

> For the black athlete in the predominately [sic] white school was and is first foremost, and sometimes only, an athletic commodity. He is constantly reminded of this one fact, sometimes subtly and informally, at other times harshly and overtly, but at all times unequivocally. The black athlete is expected to "sleep, eat, and drink" athletics. His basketball, football, or baseball (depending upon the season) is to be his closest companion, his best friend, and in a very real sense, the symbol and object of his religious concern. (1969, p. 9)

The vicious legacy of racism and Jim Crow laws played a major role in the stereotyping of Black male student-athletes and the debasement of this population at PWIs (Brooks & Althouse, 2000; Sailes, 1991; Singer, 2005). Specifically, racism for Blacks in employment, housing, and voting rights was also recapitulated in the realm of collegiate athletics. To further this point, Green et al. (1974) concluded:

> The most glaring fallacy about intercollegiate athletic competition in the United States is the assumption that fairness is inherent. Indeed ... college sports is not the haven of fair play and equal opportunity that we have been led to believe. To black athletes, coaches and officials, fairness and equal opportunity are myths. The patterns of racial discrimination, both overt and covert, institutional and individual, found in the larger society are reflected in and perpetuated by athletics in the United States. (p. 12)

Racism in collegiate athletics had profound effects on early Black male student-athletes who attended PWIs, given the fact that they were devoid of a "safe place" on campus. This is a problem that Olsen (1968) raised: "Recruited into a society for which he [or she] has no cultural or educational preparation, and isolated by its unwritten codes, the typical Negro athlete discovers an immense gap between himself [or herself] and the college community" (p.26).

The point is, from the moment Black male student-athletes began participating in collegiate athletics at PWIs to the present, this population has been plagued with racial stereotypes (Edwards, 1984; Hughes, Satterfield, & Giles, 2007, Oseguera, 2010), and the failure of collegiate administrative and athletic leaders to engage in substantive conversations about racial stereotypes negates "improvement" efforts for this population (Harper et al., 2013, p. 19).

Theoretical Framework(s)

Two theories serve as a framework for this chapter. They are (1) stereotype threat (Steele & Aronson, 1995), and (2) recast theory. Stereotype threat will be employed to understand social psychological factors that impact African American male student-athletes' social comfortability and academic performance at PWIs. Recast theory provides a lens to explore a racial coping mechanism that can reduce stress caused by racial conflict and racial stereotypes (Stevenson, 2014).

Steele and Aronson (1995) define stereotype threat as the risk of conforming, as self-characteristic, to a negative characteristic about one's group. Although Steele's original work focused strictly on the standardized test performance of African American students at prestigious universities, he also asserts: "It [stereotype threat] happens whenever these students are in the domain where the stereotype is applicable. So with any kind of intellectual performance or interacting with professors or teaching assistants or other students in a classroom, this stereotype is relevant and constitutes a pressure on those behaviors" (C. Steele, personal communication, 2006). Further, in utilizing stereotype threat as a lens to explore the experiences of Black male student-athletes who attend PWIs, we presume that "identity contingencies" exist because of one's social identity (Steele, 2010). Specifically, stereotype threat helps us to understand the contingencies that exist at PWIs for Black male student-athletes because they are (1) Black males, and (2) athletes (Steele, 2010).

Recast theory provides the framework for the interventions that we offer in the "Discussion" section of this chapter. Stevenson (2014) suggests that recast theory "borrows from the literatures on stress and coping, stereotype threat, physiological reactions to racial conflict, critical race theory, culturally relevant pedagogy, and the psychology of family systems" (p. 114). For half a century it has been well documented that Black athletes have had to contend with racial stereotypes, racism, and the vicious legacy of White supremacy at PWIs (Olsen, 1968; Edwards, 1969; Harper, 2015). Given the historical prevalence of racism at higher educational institutions, we suppose that the aforementioned will continue (Chesler, Lewis, & Crowfoot, 2005). Therefore, we argue that Black male student-athletes need to learn coping strategies to minimize racial stress.

The Study

Through our research study, we were able to gather narratives from Black male student-athletes at institutions in the Northeast, Southeast, and Midwest of the United States. We worked with athletic departments and support staff personnel to identify study participants. The findings rendered in this chapter are from a single institution (Seahawk University, a pseudonym), which is located in the Northeast region of the country. The university is located in a suburban area of the state, and recruits student-athletes to compete in one of the top mid-major conferences of the NCAA. This chapter will solely provide the narratives of Black male football players who competed at the aforementioned institution.

The purpose of the qualitative study was to explore how African American male student-athletes who compete in revenue sports (i.e., basketball and football) at PWIs (Division I classification) experience and perceive the climate on their campus and team. We sought to better understand how revenue-playing African American male student-athletes experience life at PWIs, where their "blackness" is often magnified. Further, we also hoped that this study would provide a better understanding about issues that impact African American male student-athletes who attend PWIs.

Critical case sampling, which is a technique of purposeful sampling, was used for this study. According to Patton (2002), critical case sampling can be decisive in explaining the phenomenon of interest. The study participants were current and former African American male student-athletes. Patton (2002) further suggests that within qualitative inquiry, rules for sample size do not exist. A total of eleven participants provided information that formed the basis of this chapter. Focus group interviews and individual interviews were employed; both were audio recorded and then transcribed. A series of ten to fifteen questions were employed for this research. We checked (proofread) all transcriptions against the audiotape and revised the transcript file accordingly. All transcripts were audited for accuracy, and study participants had a chance to review transcripts for accuracy and to indicate any needed revisions. All conversations in the focus group and individual interviews were kept confidential, and pseudonyms were used to protect their identity.

Key Findings from Seahawk University

Through our study, the following themes were identified: (1) Participants were cognizant of racial stereotypes, (2) participants felt unwanted on campus, and (3) participants knew that they could be treated through the lens of a negative racial stereotype. The findings are briefly discussed in this section. The participants that we interacted with through interviews and focus group sessions have been given pseudonyms to protect confidentiality; however, to illuminate the importance of each theme, verbatim quotes are utilized.

Cognizant of Racial Stereotypes

Steele argues that individuals are cognizant of the stereotypes other individuals in their society might hold against a certain group (Steele, 2010). "NJ" and "Dreads" would certainly agree with that claim. In an empowerment support group session, NJ shared the following:

> Ya'll remember when Coach L said that a Black quarterback will never play for him. These coaches treat us like we're stupid. They say stuff on the low, then they act like they joking. Then Coach N—I can't stand him. I'm still mad how he tried to play me in front of the team, saying that I can't read or play football.

Dreads, a twenty-one-year-old running back for the team, is also aware of the stereotypes that exist on campus against Black male student-athletes. In a focus group session, Dreads talked about racial stereotypes that are prevalent:

> I thought racism was dead, but when I got up here, oh boy. These cops harass us for no reason. They know we football players, so they're looking for a reason to mess with us. Then some of the White girls on campus are scared of us. They think we're eye-raping them.

Both NJ and Dreads highlight critical issues pertaining to the anxiety caused by negative stereotypes. In the case of NJ, he shares the "distress" caused by being verbally abused by a coach who is entrusted with his overall well-being (Etzel, 2009). NJ was adamant that he would never confide in his coaches about anything of importance, because he feared they would either misuse the information or make a joke out of it. Further, NJ said that he often "second-guesses" himself because of his coach's constant verbal abuse.

Feeling Unwanted on Campus

The theme of feeling unwanted in the classroom and community was shared by many of the student-athletes who we interviewed, but best articulated by "Badnews." Badnews is a nineteen-year-old running back from a mid-Atlantic state. If there ever was a poster child for the perceived "young Black thug," Badnews would be it. Short in stature, dark skinned, muscular, and known for his serious facial expressions, Badnews has been told that his persona is reminiscent of the character O-Dog from the movie *Menace II Society*. Apparently Badnews is also cognizant of how he is viewed by his peers and others. Recalling a time when an Asian student (whom he did not know) asked him for a car ride back to campus, Badnews said, "I didn't think anybody would ask me for a ride. That was crazy!"

Badnews ended the interview by sharing, "I hate this place. You can't do shit, you can't trust nobody. I don't expect White people to change, it's a culture here." Not only did Badnews express anger toward his coaches and the White community at Seahawk University, but he also was mad at the "regular" African American students (the good Black kids, as we called them), because he felt they wanted to disassociate themselves from the Black male student-athletes, out of their fear of being labeled as less serious students.

The statements of Badnews shed light on the fact that PWIs continue to be hostile spaces for Black people. The views of Badnews also compliment the following claim by Parham (2009):

> Student-athletes of African descent struggle with a set of challenges that often go beyond the ex-periences of both their Anglo student-athletes peers and their non-athlete student peers. Whether covert or overt, racism represents the most significant challenge facing today's athletes of African descent. Irrespective of sport, division, or student demographic profile of the institution they attend, overt daily "micro aggressions are common (p.220).

Treated through the Lens of a Negative Racial Stereotype

The title of Steele's (2010) book, *Whistling Vivaldi*, was inspired by the narrative of *New York Times* columnist Brent Staples. When Brent Staples was a graduate student at the University of Chicago, he realized some "individuals" appeared scared of his presence in Chicago's Hyde Park neighborhood. Recognizing that he was being negatively stereotyped (i.e., as a young African American thug) by residents in that community, Staples decided to whistle popular tunes to ease the tension. That intervention caused Staples to be viewed as a polished African American male instead of a violence-prone criminal.

"Mr. Polished" a twenty-year-old transfer student from the New England area, is also skilled at using interventions to counteract negative stereotypes associated with young Black males. Raised by two professional parents, Mr. Polished attended private schools and was socialized to show deference to authority figures. His parents also prohibited Mr. Polished from wearing fashionable trends associated with young African American males. During the focus group sessions, most of the participants had harsh feelings toward the police because of their constant harassment of Black male student-athletes. Mr. Polished took a different ap-proach. Not only did he defer to police authorities, but he also told the group that they need to stop looking like "targets." During one of the sessions, things became contentious between Mr. Polished and "Pitbull":

> PITBULL: So you telling me I need to change my image to stop being harassed by the cops?
> MR. POLISHED: Yes, look at you. Pitbull, you walk around here with wifebeaters on, you have tattoos, and you always blast your music. You make yourself stand out. That's your fault.
> PITBULL: Man, forget that! I'm a man just like them; I can do what I want to do.
> MR. POLISHED: Then do what you want to do and see what happens. You're stupid! If you want to keep putting yourself out there, then do that. That's why you keep having the same problems.

Although many of the participants agreed with most of what Mr. Polished was saying, he still was viewed as a "sellout" by teammates who had more "street credibility" than he. Ironically, during our final focus group sessions, Mr. Polished privately revealed to the group that as a result of lingering injuries and homesickness he was seeing a psychologist for depression (Etzel, 2009).

Summary of Findings

The narratives provided in this section of the chapter underscore that the Black male is still a threat in White spaces. Whether through initial racial acts or microaggressions, the participants in our study expressed mental, emotional, and psychological turmoil as a result of the conditions at Seahawk University. Lastly, the narratives of the participants also suggest that individuals targeted (whether intentionally or unintentionally) by a negative stereotype are affected by the label (Steele & Aronson, 1995; Steele, 1997). Specifically, the participants experienced "identity contingencies." They were cognizant that there were unique situations that they had to endure at Seahawk University because of their social identities of being Black, male, and student-athletes (Steele, 2010).

Discussion

"So Much Trouble in the World, N*%GGA, Can't Nobody Feel Your Pain"

—Tupac Shakur, "All Eyez on Me"

The above lyrical excerpt from the late rapper Tupac Shakur's classic song "All Eyez on Me" compliments the focus of this chapter. Specifically, we argue that vicious racial stereotypes continue to cause trouble for Black male student-athletes at PWIs. Sadly, on too many campuses, institutional leaders do little to address the inequalities and racial stereotypes that Black male student-athletes experience (Harper, 2015). We also argue that the inability of institutional leaders to address the "elephant in the room" causes pain for Black male student-athletes. Therefore, in this section, we attempt to provide strategies that campus professionals can employ in both their interactions with Black male student-athletes and their advocacy for Black male student-athletes.

Recast Theory as an Intervention

Recast theory compliments our psychoeducational approach regarding the racial and ethnic socialization of Black male student-athletes. It is our belief that we need to take a "both/and" approach to improving the conditions for Black male student-athletes. Professionals need to be challenged about the way they see, think about, and interact with Black male student-athletes, but they also need to employ culturally relevant interventions to help this population manage stressful racial/ethnic encounters that they experience at PWIs.

Stevenson (2014) states, "Recast theory proposes that through practice and application in social interactions, racial socialization can minimize the negative influence of racial stress on racial coping by bolstering racial self-efficacy" (p. 115). He offers the culturally relevant interventions of *affection, protection*, and *correction* as a way to reframe stressful racial encounters. Below is an example of how to employ those interventions when working with African American male student-athletes who attend PWIs:

1. Affection ("Stickin' to")
   - Physical nurturance: giving a handshake, hug, or other forms of "respectful" physical affection, as a means to reiterate that their presence matters
   - Emotional nurturance: letting them know that it is OK to hurt, be angry, or scared
   - Cultural nurturance: informing them about programs and/or centers on campus (e.g., Black Student Union) where they can feel "safe" and validated
2. Protection ("Watchin' Over")
   - Physical monitoring: talking about the importance of taking care of one's physical self, and not feeling bad for doing it
   - Emotional monitoring: having courageous conversations about the threat involved with arguing with authority figures (i.e., coaches, cops, professors)
   - Cultural monitoring: affirming them that their Black face is not a "curse," despite how others might view them
3. Correction ("Gettin With")
   - Physical accountability: Teaching Black male athletes to have their IDs with them at all times on campus.
   - Emotional accountability: teaching that "code switching" does not mean that you are "selling out"
   - Cultural accountability: teaching that they have to commit to being their "brother's keeper" on the field and also on campus

The aforementioned interventions provide suggestions for counteracting negative racial stereotypes that Black male student-athletes might experience at PWIs.

It is our belief that recast theory is culturally and contextually applicable to Black male student-athletes who attend PWIs. As Bimper, Harrison, and Clark (2013) argue, culturally relevant approaches "may better serve the needs of Black student athletes" (p. 19). Therefore, it is ignorant to continue to engage Black male student-athletes in a manner that negates their cultural and historical perspectives (Jonassen & Land, 2012). Recast theory imbeds those tenets into practice. We argue that the holistic educational experiences for Black male student-athletes will begin to improve once this population starts to conceptualize who they are, and institutional professionals start to engage (and respect) them in that manner.

Conclusion

Harper (2013) was precise when he asserted that improvement cannot happen for Black male student-athletes who attend PWIs without challenging the ways in which they are viewed, in addition to the low expectations set for them. To embellish the aforementioned claim, improvement is when this population feels safe and validated in their uniform on the football field and basketball court, but more importantly, also in their Black skin in the classroom and campus community. It is our belief that if institutional leaders can develop plans to construct premier athletic facilities to entice prime recruits to join their "program," then they certainly can also develop plans to improve their campus collegiate experiences once they commit. Improvement cannot be trite rhetoric that comes out of the mouth of leaders in times of crisis (e.g., during an embarrassing racial incident on campus), but rather, institutional leaders should persistently utilize data to improve the campus experience for "all students."

Although this chapter explored both the historical and contemporary plight of Black male student-athletes who attend PWIs, the core of this work is really about Black male identity and the threat that the Black male poses in society. From the nineteenth century to the present, Black male athletes have been negatively depicted. From the 1960s to the current day, scholars, educators, and activists have advocated for improvement for Black male student-athletes who attend PWIs (Edwards, 1969). Unfortunately, the moral of this work is that even in the twenty-first century, Black males are cognizant that race still matters, and as a result, this population continues to deal with the residue of White supremacy and vicious racial stereotypes that are still prevalent in both society and PWIs.

■ References

Adler, P., & Adler, A. A. (1985). From idealism to pragmatic detachment: The academic performance of college athletes. *Sociology of Education, 58*, 241–50.

Benson, K. F. (2000). "Constructing academic inadequacy: African-American athletes' stories." *Journal of Higher Education 26*(2), 171–82.

Bimper, A., Harrison, L., & Clark, L. (2013). Diamonds in the rough: Examining a case of successful Black male student athletes in college sports. *Journal of Black Psychology, 29*(2), 107–30.

Brooks, D., & Althouse, R. (2000). *Racism in college athletics.* Morgantown, WV: Fitness Information Technology.

Burke, K. (1993). Negative stereotypes of student-athletes. In W. D. Kirk & S. V. Kirk (eds.), *Student-athletes: Shattering the myths and sharing the realities* (pp. 93–98). Alexandria, VA: American Counseling Association.

Chesler, M., Lewis, A., & Crowfoot, J. E. (2005). *Challenging racism in higher education: Promoting justice.* Lanham, MD: Rowman & Littlefield.

Edwards, H. (1969). *The revolt of the black athlete.* New York: Free Press.

———. (1984). "The black dumb jock": An American sports tragedy. *College Board Review 131*, 8–13.

Etzel, E. (ed.). (2009). *Counseling and psychological services for college student-athletes*. Morgantown, WV: Fitness Information Technology.

Govan, M. (1971). The emergence of the black athlete in America. *The Black Scholar, 3*, 16–28.

Green, R. L., Smith, G. S., Gunnings, T. S., & McMillan, J. H. (1974). Black athletes: Educational, economic, and political considerations. *Journal of Multicultural Counseling and Development, 3*(1), 6–27.

————. (2009). Race, interest convergence, and transfer outcomes for Black male student-athletes. *New Directions for Community Colleges 147*, 29–37.

Harper, S.R., & Davis III, C.H.F. (2012). They (don't) care about education: A counternarrative on Black male students' responses to inequitable schooling. *Educational Foundations, 26*(1), 103–20.

Harrison, L. (2001). Understanding the influence of stereotypes: Implications for the African American in sport and physical activity. National Association for Physical Education in Higher Education, 53, 97–114.

Hughes, R. L., Satterfield, J. W., & Giles, M. S. (2007). Athletising black male student athletes: The social construction of race, sports, myths, and realities. *National Association of Student Affairs Professionals Journal, 10*(1), 112–27.

Jonassen, D. H, & Land, S. (2012). *Theoretical Foundations of Learning Environments*. New York, NY: Taylor & Francis.

McPherson, B. D. (1971). Sport and the black athlete. In *Conference on Sport and Social Deviancy*. Brockport: State University of New York College at Brockport.

Melendez, M. C. (2008). Black football players on a predominantly white college campus: Psychosocial and emotional realities of the black college athlete experience. *Journal of Black Psychology 34*(4), 423–51.

Miller, P.B. (1998). The anatomy of scientific racism. Racialist responses to black athletic achievement. *Journal of Sport History, 25*(1), 119–51.

Olsen, J. (1968). "The Black athlete: A shameful story. *Sports Illustrated*, July, 31.

Oseguera, L. (2010). Success despite the image: How African American male student-athletes endure their academic journey amidst negative characterizations. *Journal for the Study of Sports and Athletes in Education 4*(3), 297–324.

Parham, W. D. (2009). African-descendent collegiate athletes: An invitation to respond to their visibility. In E. Etzel (ed.). *Counseling and psychological services for college student-athletes*. Morgantown, WV: Fitness Information Technology

Patton, M. Q. (2002). Qualitative evaluation and research methods, 3rd ed. Thousand Oaks, CA: Sage Publications, Inc.

Sailes, G. A. (1993). An investigation into campus stereotypes: The myth of black athletic superiority and the dumb jock stereotype. *Sociology of Sport Journal, 10*, 88–97.

Singer, J. N. (2005). Understanding racism through the eyes of African American male student-athletes. *Race, Ethnicity & Education, 8*(4), 365–86.

Steele, C. M. (1997). A threat in the air: How stereotypes shape intellectual identity and performance. *American Psychologist 52*, 613–29.

————. (2010). *Whistling Vivaldi: And other clues to how stereotypes affect us*. New York: Norton.

Steele, P. C., & Aronson. J. (1995). Stereotype threat and the intellectual test performance of African Americans. *Journal of Personality and Social Psychology* 69(5), 797–811.

Stevenson, H. C., & Arrington, E. G. (2009). Racial-ethnic socialization mediates perceived racism and the racial identity of African American adolescents. *Cultural Diversity and Ethnic Minority Psychology* 15(2), 125–136.

———. (2014). *Promoting racial literacy in schools*. New York: Teachers College Press.

Watt, S., & Moore, J. (2001). Who are student athletes? In M. Howard-Hamilton & S. Watt (eds.), *New Directions for Student Services* (pp. 65–80). San Francisco: Jossey-Bass.

Wiggins, W. H. (1988). Boxing's Sambo twins: Racial stereotyping in Jack Johnson and Joe Louis newspaper cartoons, 1908–1938. *Journal of Sports History* 15(3), 242–54.

African American Male Students' Perceptions of Factors That Contribute to Their Academic Success

Devin L. Randolph

I nitially my purpose for selecting this project was to gain more understanding about the concept of schooling and its experiences and the role of academic achievement by African American males. I wanted to better understand how these experiences shaped their aspirations.

> Experiences grow out of other experiences, and experiences lead to further experiences. Wherever one positions oneself in that continuum—the imagined now, some imagined past, or some imagined future—each point has a past experiential base and leads to an experiential future. (Clandinin & Connelly, 2000, p. 2)

Each experience is important, and storied lives of people often have various narratives that can inform the researcher. This is important, as the conceptual approach to research should be relational across time, places, and relationships.

This project was designed to understand African American high school males' perception of factors contributing to academic success. Past literature has often used a deficit-informed framework to answer this question, portraying Black male students as incapable, unintelligent, disadvantaged, and at-risk to fail at best (Fries-Britt, 1997; Harper, 2009; Jenkins, 2006).

Contrary to the discourse that highlights "deficiency" as an explanatory and natural outcome for academic achievement among African American males, I discovered a common theme in the literature of success and interviews for this project is the *resiliency* of this group in trying to succeed academically, despite challenging circumstances. Researchers Bryan (2005) and Wang, Haertel, and Walberg (1997) refer to this form of resiliency as "educational resiliency," which is the ability of students to succeed academically despite difficult and challenging life circumstances and risk factors.

Moreover, participants leverage peers, family members, mentors, and spirituality along their journey to success (Bridges, 2010; Harper, 2006, 2009, 2012; Hébert, 2002; Herndon, 2003; Moore, Madison-Colomore, & Smith, 2003; Museus, 2011; Strayhom, 2008; Williamson, 2010). This project initially had five participants. However, as a result of external factors, only three completed their interviews. Each participant was asked nine questions to determine his perceptions on factors contributing to academic success and what solutions and challenges he perceived to be necessary for African American males to achieve academic success. Subsequently, additional questions followed to gain a deeper understanding of participants' background.

Questions were formulated to understand the discourse among race, class, and gender. The intent of this project was to provide a more heuristic framework that may guide future research on experiences of the academic achievement of African American males.

Background and Context

Despite holding high aspirations to attend college, Black men comprised less than 6 percent of the entire US undergraduate population in 2010 (US Department of Education, 2012). Efforts to improve ineffective schools and raise academic achievement are rising.

However, there is a well-documented, lingering achievement gap between affluent and poor students, as well as between white and Black students (Grissmer & Flanagan, 2001; Jencks & Phillips, 1998). This project was an important undertaking. There is a large body of literature that provides a deficit framework. Many academic indices highlight recent gains from a number of students in US schools. However, Black students rank at or near the bottom on nearly every quantifiable measure of scholastic achievement in grade school, high school, and college (Feagin & Sikes, 1995; Jencks & Phillips, 1998; Tierney, 1999; Porter, 2006; Harris, 2006; Cuyjet, 2006). All of these aforementioned consequences are drivers to long-term outcomes for African American males, including lower lifetime earnings and increased risk of imprisonment.

Many studies on Black male students in schools have analyzed school achievement and failure, resistance, accommodation, and reform (Dhondy, 1974; Fine, 1991; Fordham, 1988, 1996; Fordham & Ogbu, 1986; MacLeod, 1987; Noguera, 2008; Ogbu, 1974, 1978; Solomon, 1992). From these and other studies outcomes, student success among this group is influence largely by four factors: (1) supportive parents, (2) caring teachers and positive school environment, (3) peer support, and (4) community initiatives. Several scholars have also argued about the value of race-based epistemologies and methodological approaches for educational research (Delgado, 1999; Delgado & Stefancic, 2001, Solorzano & Yosso, 2002; Parker & Lynn, 2002). Despite the conclusive evidence supporting claims on both sides of the school achievement continuum, it is important to understand epistemological approaches, particularly as assertions are made not only in the literature on scholarships, but also in the literature on pedagogy.

Race-based epistemological approaches are important analytic lenses, particularly within qualitative research, because they offer the opportunity to challenge dominant ideology, provide transdisciplinary modes of inquiry, and suggest a space for insider accounts of their experiences (Solorzano & Yosso, 2002). Equally important is that theoretical approaches such as critical race theory that seek to illuminate the voices of individuals that have been historically silenced in educational research, thus providing a counter script to mainstream accounts of their realities (Tillman, 2002). More importantly, detangling voices of participants on the landscape of institutional and cultural discourses among race, class, and gender is vital to epistemological and ontological approaches to narrative inquiry. Conversely, counterstorytelling is an important methodological tool that reveals how participants understand their schooling experiences. These experiences are important, and storied lives of people often have various narratives that inform the researcher.

Methodology

Participants were asked to fill out a brief survey on demographic and descriptive information. Participants represented various schools from the South Carolina School District (pseudonym). The Evening High School program is geared toward students fifteen to twenty years of age interested in a nontraditional educational setting. Students can earn initial credits or recover credits. The program is not an alternative academic setting for students with chronic discipline problems. This program offers a unique learning environment that allows students access to online courses with support from certified instructors. Credits earned by successful completion of these courses count toward fulfilling requirements to obtain a South Carolina high school diploma.

The study explores the experiences of African American high school males' perception of factors contributing to academic success through individual interviews using a semistructured protocol. In all cases, permission was granted by the parents of participants. Interviews were audiorecorded, transcribed verbatim, coded, and analyzed. Individual interviews took between thirty and forty-five minutes each. Interview topics included experiences with schooling, sources of support, and high school culture. All of the participants in this study were African American males who were enrolled and in good standing with the Evening High School program. Participants were asked the following questions:

1. What was school like growing up (elementary, middle, and high school)?
2. How would you describe yourself (in school, with friends, and with family)?
3. Describe your academic performance in school.
4. Explain what role your parents play in your education.
5. What can the community do to help African American students achieve academic success?

The degree of participation between the researcher and participants in the qualitative research process is important. The objective of this study is move beyond the deficit paradigm as it relates to African American males' schooling experiences and coconstruct knowledge "with," instead of on, participants. I wanted this process to be as organic and fluid as possible; therefore, I discussed the overall project with the group. As interests increased, the participants and I would learn and understand the central phenomenon. I developed great rapport with the director of the program and some of the participants as a result of my visits. The outcome of this project was decided mutually by the participants and the researcher. This means that power was shared between participant and the researcher. In the context of schooling, this approach debunks the negative institutional dynamics and provides opportunities for participants and the researcher to express their lived experience, emotion, and knowledge construction. Freire (1970) argued that when participants express their embodied, emotional as well as intellectual knowledge, they are engaging in tradition of critical pedagogy and development of critical consciousness, the capacity to critically examine the world in order to transform it.

Conceptual Framework

The researcher's stance for this project is critical race theory. Critical race theory starts with addressing racial inequality, color blindness, and meritocracy. This approach challenges the liberal ideology that maintains white hegemony. Joe Feagin (2000) writes in *Racist America: Roots, Current Realities, and Future Reparations* of the unjust enrichment of whites. He explains:

> Unjustly gained wealth and privilege for whites is linked directly to undeserved immiseration for black Americans. This was true for many past generations, and it remains true for today's generations.... The average black person lives about six years less than the average white person. An average black family earns about 60 percent of the income of an average white family—and has only 10 percent of the economic wealth of an average white family.... Acts of oppression are not just immediately harmful; they often have systematic effects. (p. 27)

Critical race theory makes a compelling case for the importance of linking counternarratives and articulation of lived experience. In the context of mass incarceration, CRT engages and rejects many mainstream theoretical frameworks. In his article, *"Talk the Talk, Walk the Walk: Defining Critical Race Theory in Research,"* researcher Kevin Hilton posits that

> a CRT methodology can be identified by its attempt to include decolonised counter-narratives that question the nature of ideas whilst contributing to their development. CRT has a history, albeit recent, of presenting new voices to those more established ones as a way to counterbalance traditional perspectives and positions. (see Smith, 2006a).

In framing the Maori struggle for decolonization, Smith (2006b) describes five conditions of their struggle that could inform a CRT methodology: a critical consciousness; reimagining the world and our position within it; intersectionality; challenge to the status quo; and struggle against imperialist structures. Smith's approach to the Maori struggle in New Zealand offers support to an established CRT standpoint and therefore CRT methodology.

However, it is,

> also clear in this case that Maori history and reality has been deemed by Maori and other indigenous people to have been generally ignored forcing them to "prove our own history and to prove the worth of our language and values." (Smith 2006b, p. 155)

Lastly, a CRT approach

> allows us to understand everyday realities and challenges the value neutral, apolitical positivism that is de rigeur in many research circles. . . . the challenge for those writing culture is not to limit their moral perspectives to their own generic and neutral principles, but to engage the same moral space as the people they study . . . research strategies are not assessed . . . in terms of "experimental robustness" but . . . "vitality and vigour in illuminating how we can create human flourishing."(Christian 2007, p. 57)

"We live in a system that espouses merit, equality, and a level playing field, but exalts those with wealth, power, and celebrity, however gained" (Bell, 2002). In his noted work *Ethical Ambition: Living a Life of Meaning and Worth*, legal scholar Derrick Bell poses a central question: How to maintain integrity in the face of high levels of disenfranchisement and the pressure to succeed at any price? Bell's work is mentioned here to use as a backdrop to acknowledge the voices of individuals that have been historically silenced in educational research. Scholars in the critical race theory field have produced a significant body of literature relevant to education, equality, and social justice. This framework recognizes that experiential knowledge is legitimate, appropriate, and critical to understanding, analyzing, and drawing on lived experiences (Bell, 1987, 1992, 1996).

Disclosure of Personal Interest-Positionality

There was a time in my life, though, when not through ignorance, but misguided intellect, I rebelled and sought to destroy the very essence of what I value more—education. My story was not so different from the participants, and this was a commonality I observed when I conducted interviews. I had many of the same interactions with schooling that the participants expressed. At that time, I did not have enough confidence in "the system." My perception of teachers and administrators was largely negative, and I received multiple referrals. I was suspended and eventually expelled from school.

However, the interviews with participants provided a different lens that helped to broader my understanding. Of the three participants, two came from a single-parent household. All indicated they had negative relationships with the school environment and expressed the need for community support and after-school programs. Additional conversations with teachers and support staff revealed that each participant is performing well academically, in the Evening High School program.

Participants

The study explores the experiences of three African American high school males' perception of factors contributing to academic success. This section will give a brief introduction to each participant. I believe the decision to use critical race theory as a theoretical approach not only delivered a unique counternarrative for me, but allowed me to process the narratives from a broader field of storytelling. Equally important is that critical race theory "provides a suitable framework because it not only centers race at the core of it analysis, but it also recognizes other forms of oppression, namely class and gender, which have important implications for African American males as well" (Parker, 1998, p. 46).

Derrick

My first participant, Derrick, was a fifteen-year-old, tall, and slender male. Our meeting was in a small conference room surrounded by various affirming messages on bulletin boards, and above the conference room door. I explained to Derrick the rationale for my project and asked him to complete the demographic profile sheet. As the interview unfolded, it was evident Derrick's unique past had shaped his understanding of schooling, expectations, and identity.

Derrick was born in South Carolina and traveled a lot of places. He mentioned his upbringing was a challenge as a result of growing up in South Carolina and living in a "bad neighborhood" surrounded by shootings and frequent fighting. He mentioned that he liked living in South Carolina. He had aspirations of becoming a basketball player and going to college. He grew up in a single-parent household and that his sister attended college and his older brother was behind bars. Derrick did well enough in school and appeared to be concerned with being a good athlete. He was first to admit he was not the best student academically, but thought his grades "were good."

Derrick had a genuine distrust of schooling and moved from different schools before he ended up in the evening program as a result of being expelled for fighting. As I interviewed Derrick, I was preoccupied with how his experience and upbringing might have been different if his neighborhood conditions were not marked by frequent fighting and gun violence. In the interview, I was also curious how Derrick navigated schooling. Accordingly, Derrick stated that growing up in elementary, middle, and high school was all right:

> I had a lot of friends but now, not that much. It was fun. First, I attended Sweetwater Elementary
> for four years and then I went to Endicott. I was living with my mom at that time and then we
> moved to live with my dad and I attended Brooknight Elementary.

It appeared Derrick's experience with Sweetwater and Endicott was similar and that moving seemed to be a natural process for him. Each transition he had was in an environment that he was familiar with. Later, the interview revealed Derrick's feelings regarding the transitional moments in his life: "It was not a lot of fights at Sweetwater. It was all right. It was peaceful. But when I attended Brooknight it was a lot of loud-talking kids and people just arguing all the time." After reviewing Derrick's interview and hearing how he responded to the questions, I had a better understanding of "his" reality. Objectively, he uncovered layers to his experiences and used them to adapt to whatever environment he was in. He desired to be connected to people and seek to reimage his experiences. As stated by Derrick:

> My father and Ms. Appleton from the school district office encouraged me to go back. I also decided that it was important to me and I did not want to be a failure. So I was like, I rather do online classes instead of just being at home looking stupid. I don't have time to be messing around anymore. I don't get a lot of As or Bs. I would say I get some Bs, Cs, and Ds. I am a laid back and outgoing. When I am done with all of my work, I am laid back. My friends would say that I am cool and my family would say I am the same way with them.

Anthony

Anthony, like Derrick, was born in South Carolina. Initially, Anthony canceled our interview, but after speaking with his mother he decided to continue the project. At the time of the interview, Anthony had already missed a substantial amount of days from the Evening High School program. Before my meeting with him, his counselor wanted to speak with me regarding how I might be able to establish a relationship with Anthony and consider being a mentor. I immediately thought about how this conversation could change the nature of my research and about potential ethical implications. Working within "fidelity of relationships" (Noddings, 1986), the ethical considerations in narrative inquiries are commonly thought of as responsibilities negotiated by participants and narrative inquires at all phases of the inquiry (Clandinin & Connelly, 1998, 2000). I stated to the counselor that after the interview I would extend my contact information to Anthony. Our meeting was in a small conference room. I explained to Anthony the rationale for my project and asked him to complete the demographic profile sheet.

Anthony had traveled to a lot of places. He also mentioned that his upbringing was a challenge, as he had made a lot of bad choices, which ultimately had a negative consequence on his academic pursuits. He was regretful and understood what he needed to do to be successful. He enjoyed living in South Carolina and had aspirations of attending college. At the time of the interview, he was nineteen, the oldest among the participants. Anthony understood the concept of pursing his education. However, he would at times be resistant:

> I love South Carolina. The environment I grew up in was challenging and I made a lot of bad choices. I really did not know my father, and my mother was always around. I moved a couple of times to try to attend other schools but ended up back where I started. I did not understand this

before but now I realize that I am in charge of my own destiny. I can control my life and make choices that are positive and help me become a better person.

Like Derrick, Anthony conforms to the environment he is in. However, he struggles with excelling in his academics and oftentimes blames others.

> Sometimes I feel like when I am doing my work, things are okay. However, when I cannot figure it out, I get really frustrated. I like to try to do things myself, and I get mad when I do the assignment. When I do, I just give up and say I don't want to attend this program anymore. When I feel this way, I remind myself of the goal at hand.

Although this statement was reassuring, Anthony's counselor struggled to get him to complete his online coursework. Despite his aspirations to attend college, Anthony lacks consistent application:

> I had calm down a lot. I had a different outlook. When I started my twelfth-grade year, I was all the way calm down until one administrator triggered me. I was doing what I needed to do to maintain, but it seemed like people always remember your past and cannot see beyond this. Because of this, I got into a disagreement with that administrator. That was my last straw, and I got sent over to this program. When I first started the program, I realized I was the oldest student in the class. I did not want to be here with the young kids. I thought about this long and hard and change my perspective. I was determined to get a diploma because I want to go to college. I really want to go to college.

After the interview, Anthony's mother wanted to speak with me. She expressed that he does not have the support of his father, but believes Anthony is a brilliant person. He is the youngest of three siblings and each attends college. According to his mother, Anthony would get bored easily and would not complete important tasks that could move him farther along in the evening program. It was clear that she is the driving force behind Anthony: "My mother will do everything in her power for me to get my education. My father would give me a speech, but my mother is going to take action and make it happen."

DeAnthony

DeAnthony's father left when he was three. He is a native of Orangeburg, South Carolina. He currently lives with his stepfather. He has a great relationship with his mother. He describes his family experiences:

> It is good and sometimes it is bad. I grew up having my mother and sisters around. My dad left me at three months. I live with my stepfather. I tried to play sports to stay out of trouble. I just follow

Table 1. Descriptions of Respondents

	DERRICK	ANTHONY	DEANTHONY
Clubs/organizations	None	None	None
Athletics	Basketball	Wrestling	Basketball, football, track
Adults living with	Mother	Mother	stepfather
Reason for expulsion from high school	Fighting	Excessive truancy	Fighting
College aspirations	Yes	Yes	Yes

the wrong crowd. I like playing football. When I don't play sports, I end up following the wrong crowd. I was sent here for fighting. I did not mean to fight the person; we were best friends. I just had a bad day.

DeAnthony's narrative provides a context for school disciplinary practices. The glaring racial discrepancies in discipline measures as a result of zero-tolerance policies have direct links to the academic achievement of minority students in the classroom and potential larger societal context. The disproportionate number of written referrals, in-school detentions, suspensions, and expulsions imposed on this group of students fails to properly consider the likelihood of disengagement and dropout. The desire to continue these policies has led administrators and teachers to be increasingly dependent on exclusionary and zero-tolerance practices instead of education. Disciplinary representation is largely disproportionate, and African American males are dealt with what Monroe (2006) calls an *uneven hand*, implying that African American males are oftentimes "targeted for disciplinary action in the greatest numbers" (Monroe, 2005, p. 46; see also Children's Defense Fund, 1975; Gonzalez & Szecsy, 2004; Skiba et al., 2000; Skiba & Peterson, 1999; Ferguson, 2000; Skiba & Rausch, 2006). While schools must have some structure governing safety, and mechanisms to promote learning and stability, proactive strategies are needed to determine the most appropriate consequence for the offense in question. To this aim, the goal should be to consider the individual instead of applying a "one size fits all" approach.

DeAnthony's narrative highlighted the need for supportive institutional culture. He talked about some of the challenges in high school before he transitioned to the evening program:

They do not take actions when a kid tells them something. Say that some kids tell an administrator something, he or she would just tell them to stop playing around, but the kids continue to do the same thing and eventually the issue get bigger. If the administrator would just sit down and try to resolve the problem, then things could be better. The older students were always picking on the younger students. They do not do anything. Some care and when you take problems to them they listen. Some administrators are cool. They do their jobs and what is expected of them. They listen to you. They take action. I ended up in this program because I was having issues and people bothering me. When I told this information to the administrator . . . he did not do anything.

DeAnthony wants to get his diploma and desires to play professional football. He finds comfort in playing sports and being a leader for his younger sister. Unfortunately, the evening program does not provide opportunities for DeAnthony (or others) to participate in sports or prosocial activities. He has been excelling in his coursework and his counselor speaks highly of him as a student and leader. His narrative revealed past regrets that landed him in his current predicament. He described his placement as a quagmire.

Findings

Over the past three decades, scholars have investigated the schooling experiences of African American students, particularly African American male students in the area of school discipline (Skiba & Knesting, 2001; Townsend, 2000). These scholarly investigations have focused on the common phenomenon of the "discipline gap" that often occurs in many K–12 educational environments, particularly in urban school settings (Lewis et al., 2008; Skiba, Peterson, & Williams, 1997; Skiba, 2002). Each participant talked about missed opportunities for understanding and issues leading up his expulsion from his former school.

Research tends to express a general misunderstanding of the Black male experience. Hughes & Bonner (2006) discuss the need to confront the commonly held myths about Black males in school: "Transformation must begin with a radical attack on the myths that shape the thoughts and perceptions of individuals responsible for our educational systems; these individuals are ultimately responsible for enacting policies and procedures that are anabolic for black males" (p. 78). This line of argument is evidenced by each narrative as participants expressed anti-establishment behaviors toward school administration, schooling, and their engagement with learning.

Hidden Curriculum

Participants discussed challenges with understanding curriculum content. Socialization can, at times, challenge the cultural foundations prevalent among people of color, specifically African Americans and Latinos (Gonzalez, 2006). Students of color typically find their experiences not represented in a curriculum or merely presented from a deficit perspective. The central aim of curriculum and instruction is to expose students to knowledge construction and lifelong learning. Arguably, diversity should always exist in learning, along with various methods of instruction. As posited by Lisa Delpit (1995), "If we know the intellectual legacies of our students, we will gain insight into how to teach them" (p. 173). When there is a mismatch between the students' culture and the school's culture, teachers can easily misread students' aptitudes, intent, or abilities as a result of the difference in styles of language use and interactional patterns. This gives rise to teachers and administrators utilizing styles of instruction or discipline that are at odds with community norms.

The most salient issue in curricular content and instruction is the absence of culturally relevant pedagogy and, in many cases culturally relevant professional development (Gay, 2001). Classroom instruction should be multimodal and cooperative in nature. Adopting multimodal approaches would account for differences in knowledge representation and meaning-making. According to Freire (1970), the oppressed have a clearer vision of reality through their experiences. These experiences are valuable because they challenge traditional interpretations of African American implicit and explicit bias against schooling. Another observation from the participants was their relationships with learning. Learning is experiential and the purpose should be to "promote the growth of students as healthy, competent, moral people" (Noddings, 1992, p. 10). The challenge for teachers, administrators, students, and community is to acknowledge that learning is a transformative process and that "the school[,] like the family, is a multipurpose institution" (Noddings, 2005, p. 42). The system of education is not a perfect, but it is the right of every individual to attain.

Mentorship and Community Involvement

Mentorship is an important concept, and two of the three participants indicated the need for after-school programs and individuals to give back. This would supplement the evening program and local district as they look to enhance learning and create meaningful educational outcomes. The evening program is a success partly because it provides wraparound support. The path that students are on foretells of great success and goal attainment. The literature on mentoring and student resilience suggests community organizations and churches are effective in supporting the academic achievement of African American through after-school programs, social support, and positive role models (Noguera, 2003, p. 433).

Initiatives that are targeted and work collaboratively with districts are promising. Similarly, mentoring initiatives have been largely successful because of their ability to build long-term partnerships and networks. Also important is leveraging financial resources across sectors. The structure and culture of school plays a major role in reinforcing and maintaining racial categories and the stereotypes associated with them. As schools sort children by perceived measures of their ability and as they single out certain children for discipline, implicit and explicit messages about racial and gender identities are conveyed (Noguera, 1995). Deepening understanding of how these individuals interpret their "lived realties" and the intersectionality with gender, sexuality, and other identities could assist educators and administrators. During the interview process, participants frequently discussed not being fully engaged with schooling and learning as a result of home life. One side of this inquiry revealed unique challenges that some African American males face as they are navigating, and in most cases making, real-time decisions, challenges emerging from inherited responsibilities or home life. The other side assigns additional responsibilities to educators and administrators. This is a quagmire and a familiar scenario that often happens in schools.

Conclusion: The Need for Further Research and Programmatic Engagement

A goal of my analysis was to centralize participants' narratives while mapping onto the larger discourse around counternarratives. Ruston explains,

> Lived experiences can be translated into rich narrative stories useful for both teaching and research. More importantly, these experiences provide value and should serve as a "pedagogical tool to empower individuals who live and experience very different lives into spaces where they understand themselves, the other, and themselves in relation to the other. (Qtd. in Milner & Howard, 2013, p. 62)

The small sample of this project provided helpful information. It provided firsthand, detailed accounts from African American males about their roles and goals. A future project could benefit from a larger representative sampling. From this study, I concluded that student success among this group is influenced largely by four factors: (1) supportive parents, (2) caring teachers and positive school environment, (3) peer support, and (4) community initiatives.

National efforts have increased to improve the quality of education. However, African American males are not enrolled in effective schools that nurture and support them while simultaneously providing high-quality instruction. The High School Evening program provides positive support for these participants because of the nontraditional educational settings. Participants can earn initial credits or recover credits. The program is not an alternative academic setting for students with chronic discipline problems. This program offered a unique learning environment that allowed students access to online courses with support from certified instructors. Credits earned by successful completion of these courses count toward fulfilling requirements to obtain a South Carolina high school diploma. This project was designed to understand African American high school males' perception of factors contributing to academic success. Further research is needed to understand the evening program.

The "lived experiences" of participants suggest improvements are needed in institutional and schooling environments. Each participant's propensity for learning appears to be enhanced by the evening program. This has made all the difference, and this model should be studied to incorporate similar projects to help improved low graduation rates and disciplinary infractions. There are long-standing traditions within many Jewish and Asian communities to provide children with religious and cultural instruction outside of school. In several communities throughout the United States, Black parents are turning to churches and community organizations as one possible source of such support (McPartland & Nettles, 1991). Organizations that offer community-based mentoring programs provide African American males with academic support and adult mentors outside of school (Watson & Smitherman, 1996). They affirm the identities of Black males by providing them with knowledge and information about African and African American history and culture, and by instilling a sense of social responsibility toward their families and communities (Ampim, 1993; Myers, 1988). This observation is based on the research on African American males and schooling, as well as interviews with participants.

Education is a human right, and policies should embrace this concept by supporting effective intervention programs that promote learning, especially for African American males and other disenfranchised peoples. This approach is fundamental and addresses the holistic learner. Fostering African American males as an educated citizenry must be the main goal of schooling. The purpose of education and the most appropriate and effective type of program remains critical to policy recommendations for African American males. Public perception is important to this conversation, but should only serve in tandem with best practices from local and global perspectives. Given the socioeconomic discourses and varying views of schooling and African American males, the Evening High School's framework can certainly provide substantive implications for school discipline practices and provide a step in the right direction. A critical race theory framework supports gathering feedback from participants about their own perceptions of what their needs are and firsthand accounts of barriers to success. A critical race theory framework works only with established relationships between participants, educators, administrators, community supports, and allied agencies.

■ References

Ampim, M. (1993). *Towards an understanding of Black community development*. Oakland, CA: Advancing the Research.

Bell, D. (2002). *Ethical ambition: Living a life of meaning and worth*. Vancouver: Raincoast Books.

Bell, D. (1987). *And we will not be saved: The elusive quest for racial justice*. New York: Basic Books.

———. (1992). *Faces at the bottom of the well: The permanence of racism*. New York: Basic Books.

———. (1996). *Gospel choirs: Psalms of survival for an alien land called home*. New York: Basic Books.

Bridges, E. (2010). Racial identity development and psychological coping strategies of African American males at a predominantly white university. *Annals of the American Psychotherapy Association 13*, 14–26.

Bryan, J. (2005). Fostering educational resilience and achievement in urban schools through school-family-community partnerships. *Professional School Counseling 8*, 219–27.

Christian, C. (2007). Neutral science and the ethics of resistance. In N. Denzin & M. Giardina (eds.), *Ethical futures in qualitative research: Decolonizing the politics of knowledge*. Walnut Creek, CA: Left Coast Press.

Clandinin, D. J., & Connelly, F. M. (1998). Stories to live by: Narrative understandings of school reform. *Curriculum Inquiry 28*(2), 149–64.

Clandinin, D. J., & Huber, J. (2002). Narrative inquiry: Toward understanding life's artistry. *Curriculum Inquiry 32*(2), 161–70.

Cuyjet, M. J. (2006). *African American men in college*. San Francisco: Jossey-Bass.

Dhondy, F. (1974, February). The Black explosion in British schools. *Race Today*, 44–47.

Feagin, J. R. (2000). *Racist America: Roots, current realities, and future reparations*. New York: Routledge.

Feagin, J. R., & Sikes, M. P. (1995). How Black students cope with racism on white campuses. *Journal of*

Blacks in Higher Education 8, 91–97.

Fine, M. (1991). *Framing dropouts: Notes on the politics of an urban public high school.* Albany: State University of New York Press.

Fordham, S. (1988). Racelessness as a factor in Black students' school success: Pragmatic strategy or pyrrhic victory? *Harvard Educational Review 58*(1), 54–84.

———. (1996). *Blacked out: Dilemmas of race, identity, and success at Capital High.* Chicago: University of Chicago Press.

Fordham, S., & Ogbu, J. (1986). Black students' school success: Coping with the burden of acting white. *Urban Review 18*(3), 176–206.

Fries-Britt, S. L. (1997). Identifying and supporting gifted African American men. *New Directions for Student Services 80*, 65–78.

Gay, G. (2001). Educational equality for students of color. In J. A. Banks & C. A. M. Banks (eds.), *Multicultural education: Issues and perspectives*, 4th ed. (pp. 197–224). Boston: Allyn & Bacon.

Gonzalez, J. C. (2006). Academic socialization experiences of Latina doctoral students: A qualitative understanding of support systems that aid and challenges that hinder the process. *Journal of Hispanic Higher Education 5*(4), 347–65.

Grissmer, D., & Flanagan, A. (2001). *The role of federal resources in closing the achievement gaps of minority and disadvantaged students.* Santa Monica, CA: Rand.

Harper, S. R. (2006). Peer support for African American male college achievement: Beyond internalized racism and the burden of "acting white." *Journal of Men's Studies 14*, 337– 58.

———. (2009). Niggers no more: A critical race counternarrative on Black male student achievement at predominantly white colleges and universities. *International Journal of Qualitative Studies in Education 22*, 697–712.

———. (2012). *Black male student success in higher education: A report from the national Black male college achievement study.* Philadelphia: University of Pennsylvania, Center for the Study of Race and Equity in Education.

Harris, A. L. (2006). I (don't) hate school: Revisiting oppositional culture theory of Black resistance to schooling. *Social Forces 85*(2), 797–834.

Hébert, T. P. (2002). Gifted Black males in a predominantly white university: Portraits of high achievement. *Journal for the Education of the Gifted 26*, 25–64.

Herndon, M. K. (2003). Expressions of spirituality among African-American college males. *Journal of Men's Studies 12*, 75–84.

Hughes, R. & Bonner, F. A. II. (2006). Leaving Black males behind: Debunking the myths of meritocratic education. Journal of Race and Policy, 2(1), 76-87.

Jencks, C., & Phillips, M. (1998). *The Black-white test score gap.* Washington, DC: Brookings Institution.

Jenkins, T. S. (2006). Mr. nigger: The challenges of educating Black males within American society. *Journal of Black Studies 37*, 127–55.

Lewis, C., Hancock, S., James, M., & Larke, P. (2008). African American students and No Child Left Behind legislation: Progression or digression in educational attainment. *Multicultural Learning & Teaching 3*(2), 9–29.

MacLeod, J. (1987). *Ain't no makin' it: Aspirations and attainment in a low-income neighborhood.*

Boulder, CO: Westview Press.

McPartland, J. M., & Nettles, S. M. (1991) Using community adults as advocates or mentors for at-risk middle school students: A two-year evaluation of project RAISE. *American Journal of Education 99*, 568–86.

Milner, R., & Howard, C. (2013). Counter-narratives as method: Race, policy and research for teacher education *Race Ethnicity and Education 16*(4), 536–61. DOI: 10.1080/13613324.2013.817772.

Monroe, C. (2005a). Misbehavior or misinterpretation? Closing the discipline gap through cultural synchronization. *Kappa Delta Pi Record 42*(4), 161–65.

———. (2005b). Why are bad boys always Black? Causes of disproportionality in school discipline and recommendations for change. *Clearing House 79*(1), 45–50.

———. (2006). African American boys and the discipline gap: Balancing educators' uneven hand. *Educational Horizons 84*(2), 102–11.

Moore, J. L., II., Madison-Colomore, O., & Smith, D. M. (2003). The prove-them wrong syndrome: Voices from unheard African-American males in engineering disciplines. *Journal of Men's Studies 12*, 61–73.

Museus, S. D. (2011). Generating ethnic minority student success (GEMS): A qualitative analysis of high-performing institutions. *Journal of Diversity in Higher Education 4*, 147–62.

Myers, L. J. (1988). *Understanding an Afrocentric worldview: Introduction to an optimal psychology.* Dubuque, IA: Kendall/Hunt.

Noddings, N. (1992). *The challenge to care in schools: An alternative approach to education.* New York: Teachers College Press.

———. (2005). The challenge to care in schools. In C. Kridel (ed.), *Classic edition sources: Education,* 5th ed. (pp. 42–47). New York: McGraw-Hill.

Noguera, P. A. (1995). Preventing and producing violence: A critical analysis of responses to school violence. *Harvard Educational Review 65*(2), 189–212.

———. (2003). The trouble with Black boys: The role and influence of environmental and cultural factors on the academic performance of African American males. *Urban Education 38*(4), 431–59.

Ogbu, J. (1974). *The next generation: An ethnography of education in an urban neighborhood.* New York: Academic Press.

———. (1978). *Minority education and caste: The American system in a cross-cultural perspective.* New York: Academic Press.

Parker, L. (1998). *Race is . . . race ain't: An exploration of the utility of critical race theory in qualitative studies in education.* Boulder, CO: Westview Press.

Porter, J. R. (2006). State flagship universities do poorly in enrolling and graduating Black men, report says. *Chronicle of Higher Education 53*(8), 1.

Rushton, S. P. 2004. Using narrative inquiry to understand a student-teacher's practical knowledge while teaching in an inner-city school. *Urban Review 36*(1), 61–79.

Skiba, R. (2002). Special education and school discipline: A precarious balance. *Behavioral Disorders 27*(2), 81–97.

Skiba, R. J., & Knesting, K. (2001). Zero tolerance, zero evidence: An analysis of school disciplinary practice. In R. J. Skiba & G. G. Noam (eds.), *New directions for youth development* (pp. 17–43). San

Francisco: Jossey-Bass.

Skiba, R., Michael, R., Nardo, A., & Peterson, R. (2002). The color of discipline: Sources of racial and gender disproportionality in school punishment. *Urban Review 34*(4), 317–42.

Skiba, R., Peterson, R., & Williams, T. (1997). Office referrals and suspension: Disciplinary intervention and middle schools. *Education and Treatment of Children 20*(3), 295–315.

Skiba, R., & Rausch, M. K. (2006). Zero tolerance, suspension, and expulsion: Questions of equity and effectiveness. In C. M. Evertson & C. S. Weinstein (eds.), *Handbook of classroom management: Research, practice, and contemporary issues* (pp. 1063–92). Mahwah, NJ: Lawrence Erlbaum.

Smith, L. T. (2006a). Choosing the margins: The role of research in indigenous struggles for social justice. In N. K. Denzin & M. D. Giardina (eds.) *Qualitative inquiry and the conservative challenge.* New York: Routledge.

———. (2006b). *Decolonizing methodologies: Research and indigenous peoples.* London: Zed Books.

Solomon, R. P. (1992). *Black resistance in high school: Forging a separatist culture.* Albany: State University of New York Press.

Strayhorn, T. L. (2008). Fittin' in: Do diverse interactions with peers affect sense of belonging for Black men at predominantly white institutions? *NASPA Journal 45*, 501–27.

Tierney, W. G. (1999, Winter). Models of minority college-going and retention: Cultural integrity versus cultural suicide. *Journal of Negro Education 68*(1), 80–91.

Townsend, B. L. (2000). The disproportionate discipline of African American learners: Reducing school suspensions and expulsions. *Exceptional Children 66*(3), 381–91.

US Department of Education, National Center for Education Statistics. (2012). *The condition of education 2012.* NCES 2012-045. Washington, DC: Author.

Wang, M. C., Haertel, G. D., & Walberg, H. J. (1997). Toward a knowledge base for school learning. *Review of Educational Research 63*, 249–94.

Watson, C., & Smitherman, G. (1996). *Educating African American males: Detroit's Malcolm X Academy solution.* Chicago: Third World Press.

Williamson, S. Y. (2010). Within-group ethnic differences of Black male STEM majors and factors affecting their persistence in college. *Journal of International & Global Studies 1*, 45–73.

Holla If You Hear Me?

Supporting African American Males at a Predominantly White Institution
in the Midwest—a Tale from Southeast Missouri State University

C. P. Gause

T he educational discourse chronicling the experiences of African American educators has become more prevalent over the past twenty years. African American scholars are conducting research and producing significant amounts of scholarship in the social sciences. In reviewing the literature I have found the typical representation of African American educators to be negative. Educational literature in regard to African American educators since my birth year, 1966, has evolved, from how African American educators maintain the status quo and the dominant middle-class values of society are reproduced through dominant pedagogy, to forms of protest and anti-oppressive practices. However, scholars who seek to be successful in achieving promotion and tenure find themselves still balancing the acceptable "norms" of scholarship production based on Eurocentric values.

This is the duality in which some African Americans scholars must struggle. And because of the absence of the marginalized and silenced "other" within the literature, very few first-person narratives, which articulate the issues African American educators experience in educating today's youth, are in existence. This has created a "state of uncertainty" for me at times. This state of uncertainty is predicated upon the various conservative, liberal, and progressive politics that frame the writings of these academicians, as well as the range of discourses. The discourses of curricula, educational leadership, culture, teacher preparation, and language are also informed by the researcher's position regarding the intersections of race, class, and gender. This is my dilemma.

Functioning as an African American male educator, researcher, teacher, and social activist, I have experienced poverty and privilege, "white flight," and black masculine anxiety (Harper, 1996). It is with these lived experiences that I seek to impact all students; however, I am deeply concerned with our black male students who attend predominantly white institutions. I received my undergraduate and graduate education from predominantly white institutions, and I understand the challenges of attending those institutions, especially when you are not an athlete. All of my academic employments have been at predominantly white institutions.

My parents believed in the benefits of integration and sought to raise their children in that environment. As one of the direct beneficiaries of the civil rights movement, I was taught to be the best that I could be and to be able to compete at any level with anyone—this was coded language in our community to mean that nothing is going to be given to you—you have to be the best to just get your foot in the door. It is my desire that every student I encounter is presented with as many opportunities as possible to experience success, and if you are a black male student in the United States postsecondary education is still one of the best opportunities to experience economic success. This is why I am concerned for the black male, especially those at predominantly white institutions. I have met many who drop out or who are pushed out. I have met many who came to campus on an athletic scholarship and left without a degree. I have met many who do not take full advantage of the opportunities because of several issues. What is the institutions role in providing opportunities for African American male students to be successful? What is my role in supporting African American male students at SEMO? These are my guiding questions for this chapter.

State of Black Males on College Campuses

College affordability, dismal graduation rates, and appalling retention rates have renewed a call for American colleges to (re)evaluate their goods and services. Many parents and students alike are evaluating whether obtaining a college degree, once considered the gateway to the middle class, will create more employment opportunities or more economic hardship. For students of color, obtaining a college degree is still considered a viable way to overcoming poverty. According to the American Council on Education (2011), between 1998 and 2008 the number of African Americans in college increased by 55.2 percent. However this population's retention and graduation percentages are far lower than those of their white counterparts (Harper, 2006).

Two-thirds of African American men who begin their first year of college do not return the following year (Harper & Quaye, 2007). This represents the largest attrition rate among any gender, race, or ethnic group in higher education (Harper, 2006). Past research has focused on several methods for increasing the retention of African American males (Davis et al., 2004), but not all areas have been fully explored. First-year African American males enter college with several pre-entry characteristics that put them at risk for attrition. These risk factors include low high school GPA and class rank, lower socioeconomic status, being a first-generation student, and poor academic preparation (Astin, 1997; Cambridge-Williams et al., 2013; Davis et al., 2004; Tinto, Love, & Russo, 1994).

Research has also noted that, once African American males are on campus, their social integration and identity development play an important role in their persistence (Davis et al.,

2004; Guiffrida, 2003; Harper & Harris, 2006; Harper & Quaye, 2007; Palmer & Young, 2008; Tinto, 1993). However, many authors suggest predominantly white university campuses do not present an atmosphere that is welcoming, hospitable, and inclusive for minority students. Because of the Eurocentric educational offerings on these campuses, students who are "different" often feel unappreciated or come to devalue their own cultural group (Sue et al., 1999). Students of color; particularly black males, have indicated most faculty at predominantly white institutions are operating out of negative stereotypes in the classroom, consciously or unconsciously. Another aspect of campus climate is the comfort of African American students with white students. Many African American students are not used to being in classes with large numbers of white students. This is definitely a concern with black males. All of these factors can be mitigated with institutional support and faculty involvement. After spending twelve years at the University of North Carolina–Greensboro teaching and serving in various capacities, I was afforded the opportunity to come to Southeast Missouri State University for my current employer. Upon my arrival, I discovered very few African American faculty members were in the academic ranks. There were very few African American male faculty members. There were a small cadre of African American male staff members and no African American person at the executive staff level.

The Setting

Southeast Missouri State University or SEMO, as it is affectionately called by both students and alumni, is located near the Mississippi in the southeastern part of a Midwestern state. SEMO enrolls approximately 11,200 undergraduate and graduate students. It is in a small regional center that has a population of 38,000, so the city is considered a "town and gown" community. Ninety percent of the city residents are white, 8 percent are African Americans, and 2 percent are considered "other." The student headcount based on race and ethnicity consists of the following: 8,551 white students; 1,030 African American students; 1,139 nonresident alien students; 120 Asian students; 200 Hispanic students; and 988 not reporting any race or identity. Approximately 68 percent of the student body identify as female. There are several civic, religious, and community organizations in the town in which SEMO is located. Most the churches are United Methodist, Lutheran, Baptist, Catholic, and Presbyterian. There is an Islamic Center, or mosque, located in the city with a very active Islamic community. SEMO does not keep an actual count of students based on religious beliefs; however, it is noted that many of the international students who attend SEMO identify as Muslim, Hindu, or Buddhist. The Islamic Center is located approximately five blocks from the administrative building of the university. It serves as a gathering place for all Muslims in the community and region. Although SEMO is located in a small town and approximately 110 miles south of an urban city center, it is not immune to the elements of popular culture and influence of social media.

Black Males and Society

The statistics show a clear disadvantage to being born black and male in America: Black males have higher rates than white males of mental disorders, unemployment, poverty, injuries, accidents, infant mortality, morbidity, AIDS, homicide and suicide, drug and alcohol abuse, imprisonment, and criminality. African American males have poorer incomes, life expectancy, access to health care, and education (Allen, 1999; Watkins, 1993; Harper, 1996).

One irony of our present moment is that just as young black men are murdered, maimed, and imprisoned in record numbers, their styles have become disproportionately influential in shaping popular culture (Carbado, 1999; Weatherspoon, 1998; West, 1993). For most young black men, power is acquired by stylizing their bodies over space and time in such a way those bodies reflect their uniqueness and provoke fear in others. To be "bad" is good not simply because it subverts the language of the dominant white culture, but also because it imposes a unique kind of order for young black men on their own distinctive chaos and solicits an attention that makes others pull back with some trepidation. This is evident at SEMO.

We have African American males who engage in behaviors that are not deemed appropriate. For instance, the University Center (UC) is a gathering space for students to eat their meals and socialize. On several occasions during meetings that I was attending I could hear a group of students utilizing disrespectful and offensive language in the area. I went out to speak to the group. There were five African American men playing cards at a table. I informed them we were having a meeting and we could hear their interaction. I asked them to lower their voices. Then I asked them what time they were going to class and all of them responded that they were skipping class because they did not like the teacher and they did not prepare for the lecture. I gave each of them a business card and asked them to email me. I only teach graduate students, so I was not familiar with them at all; however, I often do special projects with undergraduate students and I wanted to get to know them, so I saw this as an opportunity.

The Personal Is Political

As a creative educational leader who embodies education as a praxis of freedom (hooks, 1994), my perspective on democracy is evidenced in my practice. I strive to cocreate learning environments where all member voices are given the opportunity to be heard, shared, and awakened. The dialogic encounter is central to (de)constructing and (re)constructing spaces for knowledge acquisition and development. Gause in Gause, Reitzug, and Villaverde (2007) asserts,

> Because the personal is political and because I view my role as a teacher/activist within a framework that my perspective of democracy cannot be de-linked from what I do as a teacher/activist in the academic space; I envision democracy as the interconnections that lie within the quest of knowledge; the faith that our humanity exercises as we navigate the manifestations of our destinies. (p. 221)

Knowing the challenges students face, particularly African American males at SEMO, I strive to make a difference by critiquing the current curriculum, the lack of diversity in all of its forms, and the policies and practices that are rooted in Eurocentric constructs. The associate dean of students who also facilitates Educational Access Programs for the university is an African American male and understands the culture of SEMO. He is a graduate and employee of SEMO. He provides various opportunities for African American males on this campus and seeks to employ them as well. He understands the importance of the dialogic encounter. We have shared many opportunities along with members of his staff to brainstorm and put into actions "focus groups" and mentoring sessions for African American males on this campus. In fact all of the African American faculty and staff on this campus understand that the personal is political and that we need to move this university away from the mind-set of just recruiting African American students, particularly black males for athletics and not academics.

According to Cooper and Gause (2007),

> The paradox of teaching for social justice in higher education—which comprises revered institutions grounded in patriarchal, Anglo-centric norms—challenges any faculty member striving to use critical, liberatory pedagogies. Faculty members of color doing this work, however, must confront a second paradox: that of being disproportionately oppressed, devalued, and scrutinized by the same structures, institutions, and social norms that we work within, critique, resist, and encourage others to defy. (p. 201)

Students of color report these experiences as well. As we note the rise of protests across college campuses in America and the rise of Black Live Matter, college students, particularly students of color, now realize their power and influence. The negative pathological labels utilized to identify these students, such as "permanent underclass," "at risk," "culturally deficient," continues to marginalize and banish them to the borders of the schooling process; however, many of them are fighting back. We have witnessed at SEMO the power of protest and uplifted voices in the name of social solidarity. Students of color are finding their voices and utilizing them to call attention to policies and practices that they deem problematic.

The SEMO queer student population has grown significantly; however, there are very few openly gay and out African American male students or lesbians. I advocate for a campus that is inclusive and that celebrates full gender-expressions. I am often reminded by colleagues that this is a conservative town with lots of churches, and my response is always that it is a conservative town with lots of churches and closeted lesbians and gays, as well. I mentor one African American male who is openly gay, and he often discusses the problems he experiences with closeted African American males on this campus. They are "down-low," closeted and homophobic, which I find interesting given the dynamics. An unequivocally strong argument for men to critique patriarchy and involve themselves in shaping the feminist movement and addressing male liberation is provided by bell hooks in her 2004 book, *We Real Cool: Black Men and Masculinity*. She expresses a hope that "Black men who care about the plight of Black males and who are themselves advocates of feminist thinking would do more to reach out to

Black males as a group" (p. xvi). Black men must negotiate their love for each other in a society that not only demonizes and hates them, but stigmatizes black gay and bisexual men. She (2004) states, "Black men are not loved by White men, White women, Black women, or girls and boys. And that especially most black men do not love themselves" (p. xi). As Bayard Rustin (1943) states, "If we desire a society in which men are brothers, then we must act towards one another with brotherhood. If we can build such a society, then we would have achieved the ultimate goal of human freedom" (p. 366). Dismissing racism, sexism, classism and all other isms does not grant deniability. In order to transform our communities we must engage in anti-oppressive practices, create inclusive educational environments, and support a radical democracy that fosters collaborative activism and social movements for change. This is why I engage this work. I believe we must stand against racism, sexism, classism, and all the other isms in their various forms. I desire a society in which men are brothers, and we must not demonize one another.

Black Males at SEMO

African American males comprise 4 percent of SEMO's total student population. That's approximately 448 graduate and undergraduate students combined. A review of the programs and organizations dedicated to African American male students, on campus, includes two Greek organizations, Alpha Phi Alpha and Omega Psi Phi. The following services or organizations serve all students, as well as the African American male student: Black Student Union, African Association, Association of Black Collegians, National Association of Black Journalists, and the Office of Academic Support Services (Educational Access Program, Learning Assistance Program, McNair Scholar Program). The only other opportunities for African American males to experience a type of social networking is through athletics on SEMO's campus. This in itself is problematic. Why? Because it continues to perpetuate the stereotype of the black male as athlete, a stereotype in which SEMO appears to be complicit. It heavily recruits African American males for the basketball, football, and track and field programs. As one black male graduate student poignantly reminded me during a discussion on the needs of black males at SEMO,

> My viewpoint of being a black student here on campus is that there is a deficiency in a lot of areas that are key to the growth and maturation of a black man, a lack of groups and organizations geared specifically towards them, lack of faculty and staff that can be an example to them, and a lack of overall attention from the university.

We need to establish programs specifically for black males at SEMO. There are several nationally recognized rites-of-passage programs, as well as living and learning communities (LLCs). An LLC is a program whereby students pursue a curricular or cocurricular theme by attending classes together, and also live together in a reserved section of a residence hall (Inkelas et al.,

2007). LLCs could be a powerful tool for increasing retention rates and time-to-graduation rates for African American males at SEMO.

SEMO and Diversity

During the 2014 calendar year, SEMO experienced five student-led protests on its campus. These protests were met with racist comments on anonymous social media sites. A President's Task Force on Diversity Education was established in November 2014, after the initial student protest. During this time many high-profile shootings of unharmed black men by white police officers occurred nationally. These incidents sparked protests across college campuses to include students in Missouri who had been advocating for improved race relations on their campuses for several years. Southeast's task force focused mainly on race relations; however, they began to realize there were deeper issues on campus. The task force provided recommendations for the pursuit of a just and inclusive community that embraces all members regardless of ethnicity, race, sexual orientation, age, gender identity, national origin, religion, disability, veteran status, and genetic information. The task force also recommended the need for diverse representation among faculty, staff, and students, as well as engaged alumni.

The task force presented their recommendations and final report in December 2015. There has been some movement on the recommendations; however, many are concerned that due to the state's budget cuts to higher education, there will be very little movement with regard to the recommendations of the task force. Through this process, two employee resource groups have been established, the Black Faculty/Staff Alliance (BFSA) and the lesbian, gay, bisexual, transgender, and queer (LGBTQ) employee resource group. A director of institutional equity and diversity for the university was hired and there has been an increase in food, festival, and cultural activities. Some of these are steps in the right direction; however, most of the Southeast faculty and staff community do not want to engage in deep reflective practices. The Center for Scholarship and Teaching held faculty trainings and presentations on creating curriculum for diverse learners, as well as how to engage in critical conversations with students around difference. Students on this campus often indicate the biggest problems they have are with faculty, and that's because the majority of the faculty are old white men and old white women. According to Roseboro and Gause (2009), this requires a greater sense of responsibility and accountability for predominantly white institutions:

> Creating professional learning communities that attract qualified faculty members, regardless of race, should be the goal of any institution of higher education. For predominantly White institutions that are committed to creating racially inclusive professional learning communities the constructing of communities that sustain faculty of color requires an identification of what the culture of the institution is as well as the ways the institution might exclude (whether explicitly or implicitly). And, it requires recognition of the roles faculty of color might be asked to fulfill. Most important, it demands a "truth telling" process in which White faculty hear their colleagues of

color, faculty of color hear their White colleagues, and both groups engage in dialogue about the institutional culture and how faculty members, administrators, staff and students might create sustainable, inclusive democratic learning communities. (p. 139)

Ultimately, increasing the number of faculty of color, ethnic-linguistic minority faculty, and queer faculty benefits the entire university community. Transforming SEMO into an inclusive and affirming institution for the twenty-first century requires equity, diversity, and inclusiveness in all communities present within the university structure to include faculty, staff, and student body. This will also involve an in-depth review of policies and practices that maybe hegemonic in construction.

In Conclusion: Supporting African American Males

The stigmatization of African American males has been embraced not only by European Americans, but by African Americans as well. The dominant culture continues to perpetuate negative imagery of African American males through media, film, and music. National broadcasts of African American males being apprehended by law enforcement locally and regionally are a daily ritual. This imagery further perpetuates the demise of the African American male. Damen (1987) presents to us that "culture is learned and shared human patterns or models for living; day-to-day living patterns; those models and patterns pervade all aspects of human social interaction; and culture is mankind's primary adaptive mechanism" (p. 367).

Based on this definition of culture, what the media reports constructs a framework of stigmatization of the black male through the culture. Media representations of black masculinity operate within the cultural politics of blackness on yet another important (and for some) oppositional front. This figure of black masculinity marks the racial and cultural boundaries of a counterhegemonic blackness, which stands for the black nation, the black family, and the authentic black (male) self. We must eradicate negative (re)presentations of black males with anti-stereotypical images that showcase the positive role models and individuals that are present in the African American community. Not all black men in America are committed to a life of criminality. Not all African American males are experiencing failure in their educational endeavors. For every negative image, there are many positive images of who we are and the lives we live. The challenges are rooted in our own self-image. Yes, there are systemic issues and systems of oppression that must be overcome; we must be up to the challenge.

In order to meet this challenge, I implore you to engage in the following seven principles of transformation:

- Use your voice to speak truth to power.
- Engage in intellectual enterprise as a mean to bring your ideas to fruition.
- Be an individual of integrity and have a sound work ethic.
- Be committed to your own self-development.

- Delay immediate gratification and invest in lifelong learning.
- Renew your faith daily and engage in a spiritual practice.
- Develop a mission and vision for your life and be committed to making it happen.

For those who work with African American males, I have previously (2008) provided twenty powerful strategies.

1. Embrace the multiple identities black males perform.
2. Respect their feeling, thoughts, and ideologies.
3. Do not be dismissive about who they believe themselves to be.
4. Maintain high expectation and often express them consistently.
5. Provide ongoing timelines for tasks to be completed, particularly in relation to classroom instruction.
6. Deconstruct your biases and be open and honest about your own perspective.
7. Be equitable in your decisions about consequences and enforcing policies.
8. Seek to be "just," not fair.
9. Build authentic relationships and maintain open communication.
10. Listen to their voices to discover what they are saying and most importantly what they are not saying.
11. Do not judge their life, community, relationships, or identity.
12. If you do not know the answer to the question, be honest in communicating this and seek their input.
13. Function in the role of student to gain an intimate understanding of the struggles in which black males engage.
14. Value their lived experiences.
15. Allow your engagement to be fluid and do not force your values, beliefs, and ideologies upon them.
16. Make sure your actions are in line with your statements by being a living epistle and role model.
17. View black males not as monolithic beings but as individuals who bring multiple perspectives to the worlds they inhabit.
18. Mentor black males beyond the occasional lunches and social outings to engage them intellectually, socially, spiritually, and emotionally.
19. Provide them multiple environments to interface with so that they can broaden their own worldview.
20. Build unguarded bridges across the multiple landscape we inhabit so that black males will feel open to crossing those bridges without fear and retribution. (pp. 174–75).

Southeast Missouri State University must fully support and value an inclusive community where there is visible and meaningful representation of the diversity present in the wider community at all university levels. If we are lacking in those representations, then we fail to increase them at our own peril. We understand that diversity is the combination of characteristics, experiences, and competencies that make each person unique, and that it increases the value of our community. We need to strive to maintain a climate of equity and respect, where we protect the rights of all to ensure that every member feels empowered, valued, and respected for his or her contributions to the mission of the university. Southeast Missouri State is committed to providing all staff, faculty, and students equitable access to services, benefits, and opportunities. By doing so, we will support all of our students, to include the African American male. Southeast Missouri State also needs to develop a Black Male Initiative that encompasses meeting the academic and social needs of black male students, and their mental, emotional, physical, and spiritual needs as well. Southeast also should develop a living and learning community (LLC) for this population in order to build academic stability. Ultimately, graduation and giving back to the community is our measure of success for black males, and this would be a step in the right direction.

■ **References**

Allen, W. R. (1999). Missing in action: Race, gender, and black students' educational opportunities. In D. Carbado (ed.), *Black men on race, gender, and sexuality* (pp. 194–211). New York: New York University Press.

American Council on Education. (2011). *Minorities in higher education: Twenty-fourth status report. 2011 supplement.* Washington, DC: American Council on Education. Http://www.acenet.edu/ news-room/Documents/Minorities-in-Higher-Education-Twenty-Fourth-Status-Report-2011-Supplement.pdf.

Astin, A. W. (1997). How good is your institution's retention rate? *Research in Higher Education 38*(6), 647–58. doi:10.1023/A:1024903702810.

Cambridge-Williams, T., Winsler, A., Kitsantas, A., & Bernard, E. (2013). University 100 orientation courses and living-learning communities boost academic retention and graduation via enhanced self-efficacy and self-regulated learning. *Journal of College Student Retention 15*(2), 243–68. doi:10.1007/s11162-005-8884-4.

Carbado, D. (ed.). (1999). *Black men on race, gender, and sexuality.* New York: New York University Press.

Damen, L. (1987). *Culture learning: The fifth dimension on the language classroom.* Reading, MA: Addison-Wesley.

Davis, M., Dias-Bowie, Y., Greenberg, K., Klukken, G., Pollio, H. R., Thomas, S. P., & Thomas, C. L. (2004). A fly in the buttermilk: Descriptions of university life by successful black undergraduate students at a predominantly white southeastern university. *Journal of Higher Education 75*(4), 420–45. Http://www.jstor.org/stable/3838741.

Gause, C. P. (2008). *Integration matters: Navigating identity, culture and resistance.* New York: Peter Lang.

Gause, C. P., Reitzug, U. C., & Villaverde, L. E. (2007). Beyond generic democracy: Holding our students accountable for democratic leadership and practice. In D. Carlson & C. P. Gause (eds.), *Keeping the promise: Essays on leadership, democracy and education* (pp. 217–31). New York: Peter Lang.

Guiffrida, D. A. (2003). African American student organizations as agents of social integration. *Journal of College Student Development 44*(3), 304–19. doi:10.1353/csd.2003.0024.

hooks, b. (2004). *We real cool: Black men and masculinity*. New York: Routledge.

Harper, P. B. (1996). Are we not men: Masculine anxiety and the problem of African-American identity. New York: Oxford University Press.

Harper, S. R. (2006). Enhancing African American male student outcomes through leadership and involvement. In M. J. Cuyjet (ed.), *African American men in college* (pp. 128–53). San Francisco: Jossey-Bass.

Harper, S. R., & Quaye, S. J. (2007). Student organizations as venues for black identity expression and development among African American male students. *Journal of College Student Development 48*(2), 127–44. doi:10.1353/csd.2007.0012.

Inkelas, K. K., Daver, Z. E., Vogt, K. E., & Leonard, J. B. (2007). Living-learning programs and first-generation college students' academic and social transition to college. *Research in Higher Education 48*(4), 403–34. doi:10.1007/s11162-006-9031-6.

Palmer, R. T., & Young, E. M. (2008). Determined to succeed: Salient factors that foster academic success for academically underprepared black males at a black college. *Journal of College Student Retention 10*(4), 465–82. doi:10.2190/CS.10.4.d.

Rustin, B. (1943). Bayard Rustin in his own words: I must resist. In M. G. Long (ed.), *I must resist: Bayard Rustin's life in letters* (pp. 340–66). San Francisco: City Lights Books.

Stake, R. E. (2005). Qualitative case study. In N. Denzin & Y. Lincoln (eds.), *Handbook of qualitative research* (pp. 443–66). New York: Sage.

Sue, D. W., Bingham, R. P., Porche-Burke, L., & Vasquez, M. (1999). The diversification of psychology: A multicultural revolution. *American Psychologist 54*, 1061–69.

Tierney, W. G. (1992). An anthropological analysis of student participation in college. *Journal of Higher Education 63*(6), 603–18. Http://search.proquest.com/docview/205332187?accountid=14604.

Tinto, V. (1975). Dropout from higher education: A theoretical synthesis of recent research. *Review of Educational Research 45*(1), 89–125. doi:10.3102/00346543045001089.

———. (1993). *Leaving college: Rethinking the causes and cures of student attrition/* 2nd ed. Chicago: University of Chicago Press.

Tinto, V., Love, A. G., & Russo, P. (1994). *Building learning communities for new college students: A summary of research findings of the collaborative learning project*. National Center for Postsecondary Teaching, Learning, and Assessment. Http://www.evergreen.edu/washingtoncenter/docs/buildinglcsfornew.pdf.

Roseboro, D., & Gause, C. P. (2009). Faculty of color constructing communities at predominantly white institutions. In C. A. Mullen (ed.), *Handbook of leadership and professional learning communities*. (pp. 139–50). New York: Palgrave Macmillan.

Watkins, W. H. (1993). Black curriculum orientations: A preliminary inquiry. *Harvard Educational Review 6*(3), 321–38.

Watson, L. W. (2006). The role of spirituality and religion in the experiences of African American male college students. In M. J. Cuyjet (ed.), *African American men in college* (pp. 112–27). San Francisco: Jossey-Bass.

Weis, L. (1988). *Class, race, and gender in American education*. Albany: State University of New York Press.

West, C. (1993). *Race matters*. New York: Vintage.

The Effects of Racial Exclusionary Disciplinary Practices on African American Male Students

Alternatives to Suspensions and Expulsions

Tyree Robinson

Inner-city African American males endure harsh punishment at school for a myriad of reasons, and they are suspended at higher rates than their Caucasian counterparts. According to a school discipline report created and released by the US Department of Education Office for Civil Rights (2012), "Black students are suspended and expelled at a rate three times greater than white students" (p. 1). Studies have verified that these out-of-school suspensions (and other punitive punishments) of African American males greatly increase their likelihood of future suspensions, which also increases the likelihood of their falling behind in their academic coursework. Such punitive punishment can ultimately discourage them from continuing school with the hope of successfully graduating high school. A report issued by the American Civil Liberties Union of Michigan (2009) suggests that suspensions and other exclusionary punishments can also increase the probability that African American males who reside in urban areas will resort to participating in the illegal activities of their environments, therefore increasing the possibility of their being subject to juvenile and adult incarceration (Dupper, 2010).

There are alternatives to suspensions that are integral to keeping these young men in school, academically learning, yet also learning how to effectively express their negative emotions and inner turmoil constructively, making amends and restitution for their mistakes and negative behaviors through restorative justice and practices. It is essential that urban public schools throughout the United States incorporate the practices that will be discussed throughout this chapter. If they fail to do so, it will be to the detriment of African American males in the public education system and in other facets of life; of those who care about them; of the probability of their success in academia and society; and of the odds of their avoiding criminal behaviors, increased incarceration within the prison system, or, worse, untimely violent death.

Review of Literature

Studies have confirmed that obvious racial disparities exist within the public education system nationwide in regard to zero-tolerance policies, punishments, and higher rates of suspensions for African American male students in comparison to their Caucasian counterparts. According to the US Department of Education Office for Civil Rights (2004) Civil Rights Data Collection: Data Snapshot: School Discipline confirmed in its 2011–2012 report that "Black students are suspended and expelled at a rate three times greater than white students. On average, 5 percent of white students are suspended, compared to 16 percent of black students. . . . Twenty percent (20 percent) of black boys . . . receive an out-of-school suspension" (pp. 1, 3). These percentages may appear to be relatively minute, yet these results are inclusive of 47,280,000 students of different races throughout the United States schools (p. 3). These figures are concrete evidence that large detrimental systemic policies such as racism and discrimination are in place to ensure the failure of African American boys to become educated. This review of literature is categorized by themes, which include the following in sequential order:

1. Punitive punishments
2. School-to-prison pipeline
3. Racial inequities in urban schools
4. Interventions and corrective measures

Punitive Punishment of African American Male Students, Grades P–12: Suspensions of Preschoolers

There should be no argument whatsoever about the fact that African American male students are punished, suspended, and isolated at a disproportionate rate than Caucasian males; the figures speak for themselves. Yet what should be of great concern is that suspensions of African American males begin as young as preschool. What could a preschooler possibly do to deserve suspension or, even worse, expulsion? According to Samuels (2014),

> The Civil Rights Data Collection for the 2011–12 school year shows that more than 8,000 public preschoolers were suspended at least once, with black children and boys bearing the brunt of the discipline. Black youngsters made up about a fifth of all preschool pupils but close to half the children suspended more than once. (p. 6)

There are other reasons besides systemic racism that cause African American preschool children to suffer consequences of zero-tolerance policies, including punitive punishments. According to Samuels (2008), "Research has proposed a number of potential explanations, including teacher bias, classrooms with high numbers of children per teacher, and a higher likelihood of children in poverty showing aggressive or impulsive behavior" (p. 6). Khadaroo (2014) states,

> Troubling behaviors in preschool—everything from hitting to throwing toys to being inattentive—often stem from adverse experiences, even trauma, research has shown. Children often don't know how to identify and cope with emotions when they've been separated from a parent or faced abuse, homelessness, or violence in their neighborhoods, for instance. (p. 2)

These reasons are not enough to justify out-of-school suspensions for preschool African American boys.

It appears that the systemic discipline policies are intentionally in place to sabotage the social and educational experience and advancement of these young boys that teachers deem problematic and incorrigible enough to suspend and expel. Suspended, isolated, and expelled preschool students cannot learn how to not exhibit the aforementioned behaviors if they are not in school to be taught.

The Cradle-to-Prison Pipeline: Where Are Our Priorities?

There is an urgent need to address the cradle-to-prison pipeline, for African American males are being incarcerated, tried as adults, and sent to adult prisons with lengthy sentences at extremely young ages. Edelman (2009) addresses the horrific treatment children (which are mostly minority) as well as adults receive while imprisoned. She boldly states with a sense of desperate urgency that "the failure to act now will reverse the hard-earned racial and social progress for which Dr. Martin Luther King Jr. and so many others sacrificed and died" (p. 67). Edelman continues by stating, "Inequitable drug-sentencing policies including mandatory minimums have greatly escalated the incarceration rate of minority adults and youths" (p. 67).

Several factors are to blame: racism and bias in charging an African American with greater charges than their Caucasian counterparts for the same amount of drugs in their possession and the same crimes; another issue is financial, for African Americans oftentimes cannot afford legal representation as their Caucasian counterparts can. Edelman implies that the United States has taken the focus off investing in children from birth to adulthood, and affirmed how turbulent that journey is by quoting Frederick Douglass: "It is easier to build strong children than to repair broken men" (Edelman, p. 67). She addresses the issues of racial disparities in services meant to help all children; poverty leads to a lack of physical and mental health care. The costs of these services would be much lower if we focused on meeting the needs of children, which cost a lot less than incarceration (p. 68). Her passion and advocacy are to see the day when poverty-stricken, uneducated, and underserved children will be the priority of not only a government that focuses on meeting their needs in an equitable fashion, but also the clergy, which must make it their focus to advocate for meeting the equitable needs of children as well.

RACIAL INEQUALITIES WITHIN SCHOOLS AND THEIR RELATIONSHIP
TO THE IMPRISONMENT OF BLACK MALES

Within urban public school systems, the inequitable execution of punishments places African American male students in the school-to-prison pipeline; these punishments, which include exclusion, suspensions, and classification as requiring special education, lead to discouragement and taunting of African American males and to their dropping out of school. Different cities are acknowledging and addressing this epidemic in an effort to obliterate these practices and keep African American males in school. In New York City, former state chief judge Judith Kaye organized a conference with the purpose of confronting the issues of suspension and expulsion, but also to eliminate the school-to-prison pipeline. In attendance of this event were approximately three hundred judges, school administrators, attorneys, and juvenile advocates from throughout the United States. Judge Kaye and other keynote speakers agreed that suspensions and expulsions could direct students right into the criminal justice system (Barker, 2012).

There is now collaboration between the Departments of Justice and Education on the Supportive School Discipline Initiative, which addresses the systemic discipline policies and practices that more often than not kick students out of school and in the direction of prison. Confronting the issues of safety and support within public schools is necessary amid the rising rates of detrimental systematic discipline policies (www.ocrdata.ed.gov). It's necessary that close monitoring and accountability practice be in place to ensure equality among the students within the schools that are blanketed under the initiative.

Racial Inequities in Urban Schools: Punishment Equality
and Zero Tolerance toward At-Risk Youths

There is a massive controversy as to whether the crimes that African American males are accused of committing in school are justly punished, and if the punishments match those handed out to their Caucasian counterparts for the same infractions. Congress passed the Gun-Free Schools Act in 1994, which "mandated that each state pass legislation that requires a one-year expulsion for any student who brings a firearm to school for schools to be eligible to receive certain federal education funding" (Dupper, 2010, p. 67). These appear to be reasonable consequence for breaking the law in such a manner, for safety of the students and staff is the number one priority in education. Yet implementation of this zero-tolerance policy affected African American youth the most, resulting in suspension rates of three times higher than those of their Caucasian counterparts. These zero-tolerance policies were not clear and concrete across the board, and punitive punishments such as suspensions and incarcerations of young African Americans for frivolous infractions became commonplace.

In categorizing these zero-tolerance policies, the term "catchall categories" include both major and minor infractions, yet what constitutes, and the consequences of, these infractions such as insubordination are too broad and inconsistent (Dupper, 2010). Many teachers and principals have suspended and expelled students out of personal dislike, and to make a point of who has the highest authority, while other students receive no punishments for the same violations. The minority students are being suspended at higher rates than their Caucasian counterparts.

Local, state, and federal governments need to hold school districts and the individual schools with high rates of African American suspensions accountable, and to provide intense training for staff on how to handle issues with students who are behaving poorly. There must be strong collaborative efforts of advocacy from families, communities, schools, governing bodies, and students themselves to ensure equitable discipline among all students.

RACIAL DISPARITIES AND PUNITIVE PUNISHMENTS IN EDUCATION

The fact that African American young men are punitively punished at higher rates than their Caucasian counterparts is evident, yet many in the education field are debating whether these punishments are race related. The aforementioned report that was published by the Department of Education confirmed that African American students, regardless of socioeconomic status, are more than three times more likely to be given out-of-school suspensions than Caucasians within the US school system (Jonsson, 2012).

Jonsson (2012), suggests that the counterargument is that there are other reasons besides race that differentiates punishment of black and white students, according to teachers and parent groups; they question the accuracy of the Department of Education Office of Civil Rights data collection, and suggest possible reasons for the racial disparities. However, if unequal punishments are disproportionately issued for the same or lesser offenses, with the Caucasian boys receiving lighter punishments and African American boys given punitive punishments such as suspensions, this counterargument does not hold up (Jonsson, 2012).

African American boys have been given negative labels because of other systemic factors beyond their control, such as coming from poor, single-parent families and living in impoverished areas; they are the ones who receive the higher suspension and expulsion rates. They are labeled as being troubled, and the schools have expectations of defiant behaviors from them versus their Caucasian students, yet there is little evidence that African American students exhibit greater rates of deviant acts than Caucasian children, which clearly shows that the teachers and school administration have overt prejudices against African American boys, which is clearly educational systemic racism (Jonsson, 2012, p. 2). As more evidence of racism and biases against African American boys emerges, it is beyond time to discontinue engaging in pointless arguments that defends racist beliefs and finding other reasons for the way that they are punished. It is now time to work on solutions of equity and access to opportunities to educate all schoolchildren, and with urgency.

TRANSPARENT REFLECTIONS OF RACIAL DISCIPLINE

Far too many young African American males are not waiting for opportunities to be suspended or expelled; they hate the experience of the daily stereotyping, labeling, and blatant discrimination they have endured. Such was the case of the high school brother of an educator. Laura (2011), herself an educator, shares the personal educational experiences of her younger brother, who experienced bad grades, behavioral issues, labeling, and finally a diagnosis of being learning disabled. Such a label comes along with discouragement, racial disparities, isolation, suspensions, and expulsions; Laura's brother hated school so much that he was looking for an escape; his plan became a reality when he was accepted to the Job Corps (p. 88). She describes the courses that she teaches to future teachers, and says her students haven't wanted to address the issues of students who attend urban schools and come with a myriad of traumatic issues; they only wanted to focus on "good" students. Laura provides statistics in regard to dropout rates among African American male students:

> The problem is particularly acute for African-Americans, who represent about 15 percent of those below the age eighteen but make up 14 percent of all school dropouts, 26 percent of all youths arrested, 46 percent of those detained in juvenile jails, and 58 percent of all juveniles sent to adult prisons. The school to prison pipeline is not an ideological claim; the numbers speak for themselves. (p. 89)

The aforementioned rates are not happenstance, but are part of the systemic plan of government, school administration, and other entities to ensure the educational failure and incarceration of African American males to fill the ever-privatizing prison system, in which these young men can be labeled as institutionalized, aggressive, and incorrigible, while prisons and the government reap financial benefits at the expense of ruining lives, and increasing tax rates to pay for the ever-increasing incarceration rates. Laura addresses the processes of incarceration and the school-to-prison pipeline:

> My teacher education students typically sat up a little straighter when I told them about my brother's schooling experiences. Eyebrows raised when I pointed to the published material about the ways in which contemporary educational policies and practices, such as school punishment and the application of special education categories, work together to move young people like him from schools to jails. (p. 89)

She gives the grim reality about African American boys' graduation rates: "Nearly half of all black adolescent males in the United States quit high school before earning a diploma" (p. 89). It is no secret that African American males are monitored at a very young age with measuring tools such as grades, school behaviors, familial and home life, environment, et cetera, to choose which ones are likely to complete school and go on to college versus those who will quit school and end up incarcerated. Laura (2011) states,

> Finally, black boys who have been sorted, contained, and then pushed out of schools become black men—men whose patterns of hardship are pronounced and deeply entrenched—men who comprise nearly 50 percent of the adult males in prison—men who have been well primed neither for college, career, nor full participation in our democracy, but instead for punitive in-stitutionalization. (p. 94)

Her passion is to see African American males succeed, and not follow in the same path as her brother, prompted her to share such a painful experience, hoping it would touch the hearts and minds of the government, educators, society, and the prison system, so that they may see clearly their own bigotry and hate toward children of color. Hopefully, many young African American boys will not suffer the same fate as her younger brother, which was incarceration at the age of eighteen.

Interventions and Corrective Measures: How to Create Safe Urban Schools for At-Risk Students?

So much attention is oftentimes focused on the supposedly dangerous students at schools that it's easy to overlook the plight of the "at risk" students, who also need a safety environment that is conducive to learning. Smith (2011) suggests at-risk students are often in urban school systems, where they endure a myriad of problems, including detrimental systemic discipline policies, which, as has been said throughout this review of literature, are rules and laws put into place to ensure the failure of African American and other young men of color. They may express a lack of interest in school and have poor grades and attendance and low standardized test scores, which are biased exams. Many are often poverty-stricken and reside within urban environments. The most frightening issue is that the at-risk student is not prepared to function and survive in contemporary society (Smith, 2011, p. 124). Many of the students considered at risk distrust the schools they attend, for they feel as if they're not understood by the teachers and staff, and face alienation because of this misrecognition (p. 124).

Although the outlook looks bleak for at-risk students, there is hope of creating a safer environment for them that provides an effective learning environment. One method to create safer learning environments is an institutional programming tool called *positive behavioral intervention and support*, which "is a decision-making framework that guides the selection, integration, and implementation of the best evidence-based academic and behavioral practices for improving important academic and behavior outcomes" (Smith, 2011, p. 125). This is a three-tier system that offers support to students ranging from small group support to one-on-one counseling. Another option offered is that of alternative schools, which keeps the students in school and not suspended, which perpetuates greater potential for students to get into trouble (p. 125). A collaborative effort by families, communities, churches, and schools is integral to the success of such intervention programs.

It would be interesting to know how many school administrators have considered how safe environments are created for at-risk students in urban schools, or have even successfully attempted to do so. It appears the focus has been more on the students who pose minimal threats to the safety of others, so much so, that there has been little focus on those who are at risk of engaging in violence, gang activity, drug sales and purchases, and carrying weapons, and making sure that they are able to learn in an environment conducive to their learning and safety. Smith suggests that there must be a collaborative effort among the stakeholders to ensure protection and success of all students; this collaboration must include staff, parents, students, and the community to ensure success (2011, pp. 123–24).

Who are the "at risk" students? They are students who have educational issues such as low test scores and low rates of attendance, and express a lack of interest in school. They're often poor, homeless, and minority. There are many more assumptions about "at risk" students, such as their being aggressive because of the environment and community in which they live. Because of such assumptions, teachers and students oftentimes fail to get along because the school culture does not understand the culture in which "at risk" students live, which are often-times violent, drug-infested, broken homes, with absent parents, hunger, fear, and emotional and mental distress. If the teachers themselves have never experienced any of these realities, then they are less likely to understand what urban students endure, and they are less likely to be trusted by students.

POTENTIAL SOLUTIONS

One remedy to making urban schools more safe and conducive places for learning is an instructional program called positive behavioral intervention and support (PBIS), which "is a decision-making framework that guides the selection, integration, and implementation of the best evidence-based academic and behavioral practices for improving important academic and behavior outcomes" (Smith, 2011, p. 125). There are four elements to PBIS: data, outcomes, practices, and systems. There are three tiers to this intervention system. In tier 1, everyone receives support; if students don't respond well to tier 1, they're moved to tier 2, which offers additional support through small-group settings. Tier 3 is more one-on-one and individualized support for the student. For PBIS to be successful, all stakeholders must participate (p. 125).

Another option to help keep students from suspensions and isolation, which perpetuates greater potential for greater trouble, is alternative schools. There are many alternative schools throughout the nation, and the benefit is that they keep the students in school and off the streets, and not involved in illegal activities. Yet many of these schools "babysit" instead of teaching our students; stakeholders must be committed to the success of the students. This chapter offers ten recommendations that foster safe learning environments; they are realistic, but will take time. It will take a tireless effort to turn our urban schools into safe places of learning, and it begins with self-evaluation.

COLLABORATIONS OF THE FEDERAL GOVERNMENT AND SCHOOLS' EQUITABLE DISCIPLINE POLICIES: CAN THEY BE TRUSTED?

There is a guarded desire to dismantle the detrimental systemic policies that currently plague African American males within the educational system by placing them in an environment that perpetuates their failure. Yet there is a glimmer of hope, granted that schools and the federal government do what they have promised. An article entitled "Federal Government Issues Guidance for Discipline Policies in Public Schools" (2014) affirms a collaborative effort with the Department of Education and the US Department of Justice, in which guidelines have been issued to assist public schools with developing student discipline policies with the hope of eliminating disparities based on race, color, and national origin (p. 42). It also acknowledges that there still exist racially discriminatory acts in regard to fair discipline of students ; ultimately, children of color are the ones who are disproportionately suspended.

After much research conducted by the federal Department of Education, three principles have been put into place that addresses school conduct, and how misbehavior will be addressed in an equitable manner for all students. The first principle, "Climate and Prevention," creates a positive learning environment for all students by supporting the students who are considered "at risk." The second principle, "Expectations and Consequences," requires disciplinary policies, codes of conduct, and other expectations to be clearly stated and enforced with the intent to improve behaviors, student engagement, and achievement. The third principle, "Equity and Continuous Improvement," is about building the capacities of staff and the consistent monitoring of schools' discipline policies and practices, ensuring equity and promotion for all students (p. 42).

The Department of Justice article is interesting, and guarded trust is appropriate. There must be much monitoring and accountability of both of the Department of Education and Justice to ensure that what they have put into place is equitable for all students, and lowers the suspension rates of African American males. With racism and discrimination rampant within the public school systems in the United States, it will be interesting to see the outcomes of these implemented principles, and to see if these principles are successful for the African American male student.

A MORE EFFECTIVE WAY TO DISCIPLINE: RESTORATIVELY

There is a gradual shift taking place from zero-tolerance policies to restorative justice practices in schools. It cannot be expressed enough that zero-tolerance policies have and always will be a leading contributor for the school-to-prison pipeline (Teasley, 2014). Research conducted by the American Psychological Association determined that suspensions, expulsions, and other policies of exclusion did nothing to improve the safety of students in schools; in fact, a study conducted by the Public Policy Research Institute at Texas A&M University found that the mandatory suspension guidelines did nothing to improve students' behaviors after serving their exclusionary punishments for various infractions. Zero-tolerance policies have actually had the opposite effect, and have increased the likelihood of future disciplinary problems of the students. "Punitive school discipline problems not only deprive youths of education opportunities, but also, according to the evidence, increase the likelihood of future disciplinary problems and, ultimately, youth contact with the criminal justice system" (Teasley, 2014). Punitive punishment is systematic for isolation and failure of students, with the intent of exclusion.

Restorative justice means restoring and developing students to accept responsibility and make restitution for their actions; it is practice of relationship building as well. Restorative justice must be implemented systematically, and it begins with training for educators and school personnel so that they may understand what restorative practices are; they must also get an understanding of community culture, norms, and values. Collaboration is necessary as well, in which parents, students, teachers, and community organizations and leaders come together in meetings to ensure the success of the transition (Teasley, 2014, p. 132). Transitioning from zero-tolerance policies and practices to restorative justice practices in schools is a daunting challenge for many. The process is extremely difficult for teachers and school administrators who believe in the practices of exclusion punishment; however, the hard work it takes to implement the positive changes of implementing restorative justice practices in schools will bring hope to African American males that they will be treated in an equitable fashion.

RESTORATIVE JUSTICE: REDUCING DROPOUT RATES AMONG BLACK MALES

There are schools and programs that practice restorative justice in cities throughout the United States that focus on reducing suspensions and dropout rates among African American male students. According to Aarons (2010), schools in Baltimore take extreme measures to ensure that black males within the city's school district remain in school and graduate. "The 82,000-student district's on-time graduation rate for black males increased from 51 percent in the 2006–07 school year to 57.3 percent in the 2009–10 school year—a 12.4 percent increase, district data show" (p. 2). Not only has the graduation rate increased for black males, so have standardized test scores (e.g., SAT, ACT). These standardized tests are also part of the systemic policies to ensure that African American males perform so poorly that the chance of their graduating from high school and proceeding on to college becomes remote.

So how has this great change come about? There has been a great focus on alternatives to suspensions.

> Schools in the city also have been held responsible for creating alternatives to suspension and building youth-development programs that give students opportunities to learn leadership skills. … District suspensions decreased from 16,000 three years ago to 9,721 last school year. Baltimore's schools have high success rates due in part to its "Great Kids Come Back" movement, in which for the young males who drop out of school, there are teachers, other school staff, and volunteers that will reach out to students via social media, and actually [go] knocking on their doors to encourage them to return. (Aarons, 2010, p. 3)

Such measures can be extremely risky; yet these extreme measures prove how passionate these educators are about the success of these young black males.

According to research, community-based organizations' involvement is contributing to retaining and graduating these young men, particularly in high-poverty areas, where many of the organizations' workers and facilitators have had similar experiences and were reared in similar poverty-stricken areas, so they are better able to reach the most combative and disruptive students; others who have not had similar familial, cultural, and environmental experiences might not be as successful at reaching them and getting their commitment to remain in school (Aarons, 2010).

SCHOOL SOCIAL WORKERS: PRACTICAL INSTRUMENTS OF REDUCING SUSPENSIONS

Another aspect of the collaborative effort in reducing out-of-school suspensions requires the school social workers. Dupper, Theriot, and Craun (2009) describe the roles and responsibilities of school social workers in reducing out-of-school suspensions, particularly for the disenfranchised African American males. It is imperative for the school social workers to be very knowledgeable and be able to relate to the experiences and needs of different cultures (p. 6).

The social worker should be the liaison between the students, teachers, and school administrators, and the advocate for young students who are suffering inequities. In-house suspensions are recommended by Dupper, Theriot, and Craun, yet I personally am not convinced that they are effective ways to provide young men with the necessary skills to interact and express their emotions in healthy ways, for in many cases they are isolated from their peers.

Different nationwide programs have been implemented to teach educators how to build stronger relationships with their students, as well as collaborative efforts to effect positive actions and reactions among teachers, principals, students, parents, and their communities. The National Education Association's CARE (Culture, Abilities, Resilience, and Effort) program, for example, has a curriculum to help educators reflect on the causes of racial disparities in student achievement and become aware of cultural sensitivity that can reduce teacher-student conflicts and result in fewer out-of-school suspensions (Dupper, Theriot, & Craun, 2009, pp. 9–10).

MADE SOME MISTAKES: YOU'RE STILL REMAINING IN A LEARNING ENVIRONMENT

An article entitled "Suspended—but Still Learning—in School" (Shah, 2012) is about another public high school in Baltimore that is strictly for frequent offenders who are unable to attend traditional public schools, for example, drug dealers or violent offenders; most of the students are African American. This school focuses on keeping the students in school, helping them to see the errors of their ways and to learn how to acknowledge and make healthy restitutions for their mistakes and detrimental behaviors, also known as "school-based discipline" (p. 17). Mental health professionals are available to help address deeply emotional issues, and to help students develop healthy social and communication skills.

High academic standards and behavioral management are required portions of the Success Academy's curriculum, with the goal of preparing students to transition back to more traditional high schools ready to meet the challenges that accompany such a journey (Shah, 2012, p. 18). Although there are many alternative schools throughout the country that serve as punitive punishment centers, where the students are labeled as criminals, unteachable, unable to learn, incorrigible, lost, and hopeless, Success Academy highlights a more holistic approach, helping students become well-rounded people who are better prepared to engage properly within society, their communities, their families, and other facets of life.

THE HEALING AND RESPECT OF RESTORATIVE JUSTICE

Indeed, there is a difference between punishment and discipline, and not all bad situations necessitate punishment; in fact, punishment should be a last resort after every other method of rectification has been attempted to make restitution for a wrong committed, including discipline and teaching right from wrong. Davis's (2014) article recounts a story about an aggressive fourteen-year-old student who was in the midst of a heated and threatening confrontation with his teacher, in Oakland, California. As he cursed at her in the presence of the principal and attempted to punch the school coordinator for Restorative Justice for Oakland Youth, the underlying cause of the confrontation was discovered, which consequently prevented this young man from being suspended, but restored and helped in many ways.

When the young student's teacher in Oakland yelled at him, instructing him to sit up straight, he became agitated, and so did the teacher. However, the teacher was unaware that this young man had not seen his mother in three days, for she had left her drug rehabilitation program and had relapsed. He had been taking care of his two younger siblings, and staying up late worrying about his mother. Later it was discovered that the teacher herself had been confronted before and had become afraid and was now seriously contemplating resigning from teaching. The student's mother was located and went back into rehabilitation. In the end, apologies and restitutions were made, and, fortunately, the teacher remained and the young man did not get suspended. At this school, a restorative justice approach was implemented instead of suspension. During the initial talk between the restorative justice coordinator and the young man, the student cautiously and out of frustration stated what he had been going through at home with his family; when it was reported to the principal, who had verbalized that the young man would be suspended, he changed his mind, and the restorative justice process continued.

A meeting was held with the student, his mother, the teacher, the principal, and the restorative justice coordinator. As they sat in a circle, they agreed that each person would express himself or herself in a verbally respectful manner without interruption, and that the listeners would have an open mind and heart. After each person had a turn to talk, the young man not only apologized, but offered to make restitution by assisting with after-school chores with the teacher. She agreed to be more compassionate and understanding when she saw a student with his head on the desk.

Davis's article is extremely helpful, for it expresses the hallmark of restorative justice, which is "intentionally bringing together people with seemingly diametrically opposed viewpoints—particularly people who have harmed people who have been harmed—in a carefully prepared face-to-face encounter where everyone listens and speaks with respect and from the heart no matter their differences" (Davis, 2014, p. 39). Punitive punishment, such as suspension, would have only made this young man more susceptible to seeking acceptance in dangerous ways and places, which would potentially get him expelled from school and arrested, and increase the likelihood of incarceration. As a result of this restorative practice within Oakland schools, the school board resolved to adopt the restorative justice system for all of their schools in lieu of punitive punishments and zero-tolerance policies for minute infractions. As a result, suspensions have decreased, and graduation rates and standardized test scores have increased (Davis, 2014, p. 41). Restorative justice has proven to be a method of collaboration, healing, restitution, and discipline, and of decreasing the school-to-prison pipeline for African American male students.

Summary

The purpose of this review of literature was to identify the issues within public school systems throughout the United States regarding disciplinary actions for African American male students, and the detrimental effects of zero tolerance and punitive punishment laws, policies, and enforcements that exclude boys of this race at much higher rates than their Caucasian counterparts. The literature presented focused on racial disparities when it comes to punishing Caucasian and African American boys, the African American boys receiving more severe punishments, oftentimes for the same offenses. Such exclusionary practices of punishments have increased the probabilities of African American boys being incarcerated, by taking them off the educational route to college and putting them in the school-to-prison pipeline. Alternatives to zero tolerance and punitive punishments have been established in different states, different school districts, and with positive outcomes; restorative justice policies and practices that have replaced the aforementioned exclusionary practices help keep African American male students in school while holding them responsible for their negative actions, and encouraging them to make restitutions for their wrong choices, therefore teaching them good decision-making skills, effective communication, and socialization skills. It is of utmost importance that more research be conducted within public schools to identify the differences between zero-tolerance policies and restorative justice practices, and to implement restorative justice policies and practices in all schools throughout this country.

Research Design

This study was conducted utilizing the qualitative research method. According to J. Creswell (2011), qualitative research "is an inquiry approach useful for exploring and understanding a central phenomenon. To learn about this phenomenon, the inquirer asks participants broad, general questions, collects the detailed views of participants in the form of words or images, and analyzes the information for description and themes. From this data, the researcher interprets the meaning of the information, drawing on personal reflections and past research. The final structure of the final report is flexible, and it displays the researcher's biases and thoughts" (p. 626).

In qualitative research, there are major phases:

- Exploring a problem and developing a detailed understanding of a central phenomenon
- Having the literature review play a minor role but justify the problem
- Stating the purpose and research questions in a general and broad way so as to accommodate the participants' experiences
- Collecting data based on words from a small number of individuals so that the participants' views are obtained
- Analyzing the data for description and themes using text analysis and interpreting the larger meaning of the findings

- Writing the report using flexible, emerging structures and evaluative criteria, and including the researcher's subjective reflexivity and bias (Sheldon et al., 2012, p. 16).

Qualitative research was chosen as the only method of study to analyze the thought patterns and subsequent behaviors of those being studied, educators and administrators within the San Francisco Unified School District, where restorative justice policies and practices are being incorporated.

In the present study, the researcher has designed three research questions. The qualitative method of research used in this study is interviewing. Qualitative interviewing is gathering information by asking questions; the conventional method is via a conversation between people in person. Interviews can also happen via telephone, online, and email. There are different types of interviews, so the method used for this study was structured interviews, which seek consistency by using questions from which the interviewer does not deviate.

Research Setting

Although the interviews took place with educators and school administrators within the San Francisco Unified School District (SFUSD), they are not the main focus of the study. This study focuses on how zero-tolerance and punitive punishments have adversely affected African American male students nationwide, and what has been successfully incorporated into policies and practices at the government level, as well as within public school systems, to ensure that these students remain in school, where they learn how to address and make restitution for wrong behaviors, learn how to positively resolve conflicts, and continue to progress academically.

Population

Three employees of the SFUSD agreed to be interviewed for this study. One of the interviewees, Annalisa (a pseudonym), is a former fourth- and fifth-grade teacher of seven years, and now currently serves as the instructional reform facilitator at an elementary school that is 75 percent African American and 63 percent male. The instructional reform facilitator's job is to improve classroom instruction by structuring teacher collaboration, facilitating and planning professional development, providing instructional coaching, and using school-wide data to inform class instruction. Other responsibilities include student discipline and the scheduling of all consultants or special assistance for teachers, such as dance, art, music, physical education, field trips, assemblies, et cetera.

Another interviewee, Natalie (a pseudonym) has worked for the SFUSD for the past nine years as a teacher, her pseudo-name is Natalie she is an assistant principal at an elementary school in one of the most poverty stricken and dangerous districts of San Francisco: Bayview /

Hunter's Point. The demographics of the student population are 85 percent African American; the remaining 15 percent are Pacific Islander and Latino.

The final interviewee has worked for the SFUSD since 2011; his pseudonym is Michael. He was hired first as a security guard; however, after school administrators observed his positive presence and the influence he had when talking with children of color, he was given the job of restorative practice site leader, in which his duties include mentorship, conflict resolution, and the liaison of communication between the school administration and the students' families. His school is 14 percent African American, 59 percent Latino; the remaining students are a combination of difference races.

Instrumentation

As aforementioned, the researcher designed three research questions, which are enumerated in the following list, and created and subcategorized interview questions that correlated with the research questions. Listed below are the interview questions for public school educators, administrators, and staff regarding zero-tolerance and punitive punishment policies within public schools, racial disparities in punishments, and restorative justice policies and practices as an alternative to punitive punishments. These questions were emailed to three SFUSD educators, two vice principals at underserved schools (where the student population are majority African American), and a restorative justice coordinator, also serving at a similar school. Their written responses were received in February 2015.

1. How has the enforcement of punitive punishments in schools contributed to placing African American male students in the school-to-prison pipeline?
    • Would you be so kind as to tell me a little about your background in California's education system? (How many years serving as an educator/administrator/principal.)
    • What is the demographic of students presently in your school? (i.e., racial and socioeconomic—as this may have a bearing on the educator's perspective regarding the students).
    • What is your perspective on the school-to-prison pipeline?
    • Is there a dominant ethnic group that has a higher rate of disciplinary action in the school-to-prison pipeline?
2. What practices and policies are available to eliminate punitive punishment and zero-tolerance policies within the public school system for African American male students?
    • What are the rates of suspension/expulsion for each group of boys?
    • Do you see, or have seen in the past, racial disparities as it relates to exclusionary punishments towards African American male students; if so, what can be done to eliminate such inequities?
    • Under what circumstances, if any, should punitive punishments i.e. suspensions and expulsions be enforced?

- Are there strategies and/or plans in place to work in concert with parent(s), teachers, and school administrators to address the issue of students who have had numerous disciplinary problems to correct perceived negative behaviors?
3. How have restorative justice policies and laws been incorporated into and practiced in schools as an alternative to punitive punishments?
   - Does this school practice restorative justice principles? When were they implemented, and by who?
   - What does or did the process of incorporating restorative justice entail in this school?
   - Was any type of training offered to your teachers before the implementation of the restorative justice policy?
   - How have teachers embraced or rejected the policies and practices of restorative justice in their classrooms?
   - Have zero-tolerance policies changes as well; if so, in what ways?
   - How successful have the practices of restorative justice been in decreasing zero-tolerance and punitive punishment rates of African American male students?
   - Are there specific goals and measurable outcomes that are to be achieved as a result of the implementation of the restorative justice policy at your school?
   - How is this school monitored to ensure restorative justice policies and practices are being followed?
   - What instruments and methods are used to measure the effects of restorative justice practices?
   - What are the consequences for schools that are out of compliance with restorative justice and policies?
   - Is there a grievance policy as it relates to your school's restorative justice policy or other disciplinary policies?

Results

The three interviewees all answered the same three research questions, followed by several subquestions. Their experiences, as revealed in their answers, were extremely similar at their particular schools. The responses from the three interviewees were quite consistent; however, there were some differences in experiences and opinions.

Findings

Research question 1: How has the enforcement of punitive punishments in schools contributed to placing African American male students in the school-to-prison pipeline? There were differences in their experiences and tenure: Annalisa and Natalie have eight and nine years of experience, respectively, working directly with students in the classrooms, as well as administratively at their school sites within the SFUSD; Michael has worked three and a half years, in comparison, with no classroom teaching experience. Michael works with students once they have expressed troubled behaviors or the propensity to do so, whereas Annalisa and Natalie have had the opportunities to work with them academically as well as socially.

Another difference is that Annalisa and Natalie have consistently worked in schools that have a majority of African American students, 75 percent and 85 percent, respectively, and are underrepresented (schools that are usually in poor communities that lack the educational technologies, and up to date educational materials and services in comparison to suburban and private schools) and underserved schools. Conversely, at Michael's school, the African American population is the minority, being only 15 percent of the overall student population. When asked about their perspectives on the school-to-prison pipeline, Annalisa and Natalie agreed that systematic inequities and other unfair practices are currently practiced within the SFUSD to ensure the academic failure of African American male students. Michael disagreed and stated that the unfair treatment of African American male students

> is not a system thing, but more of an individual thing, and because the school that I work with has a staff that is less than 5 percent African American; there aren't many adults that can understand and advocate for African American students.

Michael believes that personal feelings and the lack of cultural understanding that teachers have of African American students are the main reasons that punitive punishments exist. He also feels that another big reason African American male students are placed in the school-to-prison pipeline is familial and social issues, such as abuse, neglect, hunger, homelessness, and the mental health issues and substance abuse of parents and other adults in their lives. As a result of living in such dire environments on a daily basis, Black students are more likely to misbehave in school, making them more likely targets for punitive punishments.

Despite a drastic difference in the racial demographics of the student bodies at these schools, there still seems to be agreement among the three interviewees regarding the systematic policies and practices of punitive punishments that contribute greatly to placing African American boys in the school-to-prison pipeline. Annalisa provided very explicit examples to support her belief that there is a correlation between systematic inequalities and the placement of African American male students in the pipeline:

> The structure of the school system is set up in a way that perpetuates inequality for students of color. There are several things that happen at my school that would never happen at a school that had middle-class white families. One example of this is that our fifth-grade classroom was without a teacher for three months.

Such inequities, which are prevalent at schools with high populations of African American male students, appear to be a systematic conspiracy to exclude them, making them at greater risk of being placed in the school-to-prison pipeline.

When questioned about the ethnic group that has the higher rate of disciplinary action in the school-to-prison pipeline, Annalisa, Natalie, and Michael were in agreement that African American male students were the dominant group. All three interviewees were in agreement that punitive punishments and zero-tolerance practices, for example, suspensions and expulsions, should only be enforced when safety of students and faculty are at risk. Annalisa stated,

> In my school we have had three suspensions this year. Two of them were for the same first-grade African American student. . . . The other suspension this year was a fifth-grade African American male that receives special education services.

Research question 2: What practices and policies are available to eliminate punitive punishment and zero-tolerance policies within the public school system for African American male students? Natalie states that "expulsions should only be used on rare occasions when there is a major safety threat to others and problems cannot be resolved."

When asked if they had observed (in the past or currently) racial disparities and exclusionary practices toward African American male students, Annalisa replied,

> There is a first-grade Caucasian male student [at] my current school site who has done similar things as the students who were suspended had done, such as being violent with his teacher and other students, and he has not been formally suspended.

When asked if there were strategies in place to work with parents, teachers, and school administrators to assist with addressing the issues of students who have had repetitive disciplinary problems in an attempt to help correct the negative behaviors, Michael stated, "Our district Pupil Services Department is working with the NAACP on ways to strategize how to better work with students and their families that have numerous discipline problems." Natalie answers the question by mentioning that "the School Success Team (SST) meets with the family to create a behavior plan and provide interventions. . . . The Pupil Services Department can provide additional support to students, families, and staff when needed."

Annalisa speaks of her school having many social and emotional programs in place that the principal has tried to implement to assist students with their social, behavioral, and emotional skills, yet there is a lack of consistency in finding the right program and using it regularly. She states, "As a school that is part of the Response to Intervention cohort, we are supposed to be using RTI and setting up proactive classroom management strategies." All of the aforementioned programs, collaborations, and strategies are part of the SFUSD's incorporation of restorative justice policies and practices into every school within the district. Restorative justice policies and practices are currently being incorporated into all schools within the SFUSD; some schools are currently practicing them, while others are in the process of transitioning into practices that are still relatively new to the district.

Research question 3: How have restorative justice policies and laws been incorporated into and practiced in schools as an alternative to punitive punishments? Out of the three schools represented by the interviewees, two are currently using restorative justice practices. When asked about the practices, implementation, and faculty training processes of restorative justice, Michael said that in the school in which he works, the restorative justice program was directed by the school's social worker and counselor, and that training opportunities are available to all staff members throughout the year.

Natalie's school was part of "the first cohort of schools that started implementation" of restorative justice practices, approximately three years ago; therefore, she had more information to provide in regard to restorative justice policies and practices at her school. Many certified teachers have undergone restorative justice training; interestingly, other staff members who are not certified teachers are not trained in restorative justice. When she was asked the process by which restorative justice was incorporated in her school, she explained that district and on-site professional development trainings, coaching support, many meetings, and presentations that assist in the school's willingness to cooperate and accept restorative justice practices were necessary. She continued by stating,

> There have been ongoing trainings since then. The Behavioral Response to Intervention (BRTI) team receives trainings, then brings back information and trains the rest of the staff. We do have some access to district staff that focus on restorative practices that can work with individual staff members, if needed. It is an ongoing process. . . . Implementation across the school has been mixed. Personal belief systems and mindsets also play a role in how much a teacher embraces the ideas.

When asked how successful restorative justice practices have been in decreasing zero tolerance and punitive punishment of African American males, Natalie's response was, "I believe that the awareness of Restorative Justice Practices has made it possible for students to have more of a voice when conflict situations arise. All parties are given time to explain the situation and their perspectives."

When she was asked to discuss the specific goals, measurable outcomes, and other methods of monitoring to ensure that restorative justice policies and practices were being followed, Natalie stated,

> As a school we have been focused on implementing systems that track student data, then as a team use that data to make informed decisions about interventions and their effectiveness. We look at referral, suspension data, and academic data; this year we have been working directly with Pupil Services.

In regard to the potential consequences for schools that are out of compliance with restorative justice and policies, she stated,

> Different schools around the district are at different areas of BRTI implementation. For some schools, they have just started developing their understanding of restorative justice and their schools. There is currently no district wide enforcement of this. However, we do have various areas of BRTI that do come [to] our site to support. There is a new school quality index that will

be looking at how a school is doing in the social-emotional arena. Currently the schools that are lower performing are piloting how this will be measured. Eventually all schools will have the social-emotional piece factored into school accountability. Schools and the district look at suspensions and expulsions data; schools do feel pressure to lower those numbers, especially among African American males.

Annalisa's school has not yet incorporated restorative justice policies and practices. When questioned as to what is delaying the process, she stated,

> We are not yet implementing restorative justice. Our principal told me last week that she wanted to add this, but I told her that there are too many mandates for teachers happening right now; there is no way that teachers will be receptive to this. Although I believe that restorative justice principles can be beneficial, we need to have a clear vision at our school site before thinking a program can fix the issues we have.

From the tone of the answers, it appears that this school site already has many other programs in place to correct the issues plaguing the school, and nothing is working as of yet, and to add another practice would only contribute to the already existing confusion.

Annalisa shared that although her school site has not yet implemented restorative justice practices, if and when it does happen, she will present a workshop for the teachers, at the request of the principal, on restorative justice practices, and the teachers will be expected to immediately implement it. Currently there are professional development trainings via the school district that the teachers can participate in at their leisure. However, Annalisa is completely uncomfortable with the current method that the principal has in mind in regard to training and implementation of restorative justice practices; she feels it would be unfair to the teachers not to receive formal training through the district prior to implementing the practices at their school.

Summary

It is obvious that the San Francisco Unified School District is still in the process of implementing restorative justice practices throughout public schools; as the interviews suggests, there are different demographics of race populations, as well as differences in schools' acceptance and implementation of restorative justice policies and practices. There is yet more work to be done in regard to enforcement of restorative justice practices and measuring its effectiveness, and in regard to accountability and consequences for enforcement and positive outcomes within the schools.

Discussion and Conclusions

The purpose of this study was to identify how the enforcement of punitive punishments has contributed to the placing of African American male students in the school-to-prison pipeline, as well as racial disparities within the US educational system in regard to enforcing zero-tolerance practices when minor behavioral infractions occur. The study identified practices and policies that assist with incorporating restorative justice policies and practices in public schools throughout the United States, to bring about equity within them.

The purpose of interviewing the three educators as a part of this study was to obtain their perspectives and experiences as employees within the SFUSD, working at underserved and underrepresented schools (where two of the school's majority populations were African American males); and to learn how African American male students were disciplined for behavioral infractions in comparison to their Caucasian counterparts, as well as the transitioning processes of incorporating restorative justice practice within the schools in which they serve.

Since the SFUSD's restorative justice program is relatively new and a transition is under way from zero-tolerance and punitive punishments within the district, these interviews were extremely informative of the different perspectives of each interviewee. The study also confirmed that African American male students are the demographic within US schools that most often receives punitive punishments, oftentimes for infractions that are minute compared to those committed by their Caucasian counterparts; these punishments begin as early as preschool.

Having zero-tolerance and punitive punishment policies and practices in place, and suspending and expelling preschoolers from the schools where their foundational growth of socialization and academia begins, is completely asinine. That such practices are enforced clearly suggests that there is a systemic hierarchy within the government, school districts, educational administrators, and even teachers with an awareness of the school-to-prison pipeline, coupled with a great disdain for African American male students; instead of desiring and working hard to help them succeed, these persons would rather ensure their academic failure and transition into the criminal justice system.

The unfortunate and detrimental reality for the African American male student is that urban schools are losing funding that supports current academic needs such as textbooks, technology, arts, and extracurricular activities, and ultimately many of these schools close. However, the government and the privatizing prison system are in collaborative relationships with each other to make sure that as urban schools close, with the excuse of lack of funds, new youth detention facilities and adult prisons are being built. Both entities are aware that if detrimental punishment happens, African American male students are likely to become discouraged about being transferred to a different school, where the transition process may be quite difficult and violence and turf wars may be prevalent, and they stop attending school altogether and resort to criminal behaviors, which will put these young men into the criminal justice system.

Every time an African American male student receives a referral to the counselor, dean, or principal, it is not due to major infractions that require punishments such as suspensions or expulsions. Every time a referral is written, detention is given, a student is excluded from peers for a prolonged period of time, or a recommendation for special education, suspension, or expulsion takes place, it puts them more at risk for heading in the direction of the prison system. Many of the schools listed within the review of literature have curriculums, trainings, and enforcement policies and procedures for restorative justice policies and practices, with the goal of eliminating exclusionary practices that have been enforced upon African American male students.

What practices and policies are available to eliminate punitive punishment and zero-tolerance policies within public school systems? The adjustments required to incorporate restorative justice into schools and simultaneously phase out zero-tolerance and punitive punishments policies and practices are not simplistic; however, they are achievable, and as research has proved in the literature review, these changes have been successful in helping African American male students to learn how to positively resolve conflicts, be retained in school, continue to grow socially and academically, and graduate from school. These transitions to restorative justice practices have begun with the lowest-performing African American students, particularly males, in schools with high punitive punishment enforcement rates.

The research conducted suggests that many schools now have restorative justice coordinators, who are called upon to intervene in behavioral infractions that do not jeopardize the safety and well-being of students or faculty. For students who have become discouraged to the point of dropping out of school, restorative justice schools have been built to assist them with academics, socializations, anger management, and self-esteem building; the students are taught to be accountable for their actions and make appropriate restitution for their choices, and to consider how to respond should another confrontational situation arise, how it might be handled differently such that the outcome will be more positive.

Restorative justice practices are more effective when there are collaborations between the lawmakers, boards of education, individual schools, families, students, and the communities in which they live. There needs to be clarity in zero-tolerance policies as well as consequences for violating rules and regulations, consistently, and for all students, regardless of race. Where there is little communication, confusion and discord become the prevalent practices, and across-the-board equity and consistency become virtually nonexistent.

How have restorative justice policies and laws been practiced in schools as an alternative to punitive punishments? According to Natalie, the SFUSD now has several techniques, programs, and trainings to assist teachers with restorative justice practices:

> Social-Emotional Curriculum (SEL), Trauma Sensitive Training for staff, Behavioral Response to Intervention (B-RtI), Culturally Responsive Trainings, Social Justice focused trainings and De-escalation trainings. . . . Creation of systems such as CARE teams, School Climate Committees, B-RtI teams, Crisis Response Teams, and SPED teams can work toward implementing policies. More schools are now receiving school social workers as addition to support staff.

Restorative justice practices within the San Francisco Unified School District are a relatively new phenomenon that is still being developed within all district schools; many educators are buying into its principles, but many are not; many teachers and school administrators feel there are many programs in place without clear direction, that adding restorative justice policies and practices at this point would only contribute to their confusion.

No new educational technique has worked perfectly during its first application; so it is with restorative justice practices. The different trainings and teams need to be in place to ensure that restorative justice policies and practices are properly implemented; although schools have different demographics and needs, all urban public schools can benefit from having them available.

Within the SFUSD, systems of accountability to ensure equity in utilizing restorative justice practices are still being created and implemented, as well as data collection and analysis procedures to measure the effectiveness of restorative justice policies and practices. Other states that have had restorative justice policies and practices in place for quite some time now have reported positive outcomes for all stakeholders. The literature cited throughout this study has shown a decrease in violent altercations in school, and an increase in trusting relationships between families and school faculty members, in familial participation within the schools, and in African American male student retention and graduation rates from high school.

Another important aspect of restorative justice is building mutual, trusting relationships between parents, families, and the schools. It requires educators to involve parents in decision-making processes regarding their children, as well as open and reciprocal dialogue between the two parties. Teachers should not feel they better than any parent due to their position as educators, and potentially having more education than the parents. It also requires that parents and families not hold their children's teachers responsible for their own past horrific educational experiences, where they too may have faced prejudices and inequities, or maybe feelings of inferiority because they may not have completed school. From the adult perspective, restorative justice includes collaboration to work for the well-being of the children.

Conclusions

The information acquired during the course of this study includes that zero-tolerance policies and enforcements of punitive punishments among African American male students are systematic conspiracies of the government, school districts throughout the United States, and the prison systems to ensure the academic and social failures of these students, which often lead to lack of formal education and lengthy prison sentences. The study also concludes that there are obvious racial disparities within the educational system, in which African American male students are subject to harsher exclusionary practices than their Caucasian counterparts.

Slowly, throughout the United States, schools are implementing restorative justice practices (which focuses on keeping the student in school, hearing all parties involved in a respectful manner, and making necessary restitutions), in lieu of exclusionary practices that have not improved the safety or the quality of education of students. Within the last five years in the United States, approximately twelve states have implemented restorative justice practices in their schools (Teasley, 2014).

Prior to conducting this research, I had already come to the conclusion within myself that the African American male student within underrepresented and underserved urban schools t lacked access, equity, and opportunities to learn, progress, graduate, and go onto college or be prepared vocationally for the workplace. As I began to research the effects that punitive punishments and zero-tolerance policies and practices have on African American male students, the first piece of literature that I saw talked about preschoolers being suspended and expelled. As I delved deeper into the available scholarly literature, I was saddened by the fact that in 2015, many schools across the United States were separate and unequal, based on race, socioeconomic status, and location (urban versus suburban), and I felt as though the US Supreme Court ruling in 1954 was somewhat pointless and that much had not changed.

As I visited urban schools during my research and saw the inequities, such as hazardous infrastructure, outdated books and classroom materials, lack of technology, an increase in suspensions and expulsions, as well as referrals to special education, I did not see the fruit of those who labored tirelessly for equality within the educational system. When I went to my weekly group with incarcerated young boys and observed that the majority of the detainees were African American males, I knew this was the correct study for me; I had to learn what has been done, what is currently being done, and what will be done in the future to get young African American males out of the prison pipeline and back into an educational environment, prior to their committing crimes out of desperation. Exclusionary practices have forced them out of school and into a life of crime, ultimately resulting in untimely deaths or prison. Restorative justice appears to have the most promising effect on helping African American male students remain in school, if teachers buy into it, implement its practices, and are held accountable for doing so. Teaching Black males how to acknowledge their mistakes, make restitution for them, and stay in school is so critical for their success.

Observing, interviewing, and reading was quite difficult for me, for I was once where many of the African American males that I have referenced throughout this study are, and the process forced me to emotionally revisit those painful places. I am one of those young African American boys who grew up in an urban area of a beautiful city, and attended an urban school; I was punitively punished, accused, made fun of, was told I was not "college material," and that I should learn a vocational trade. Some teachers even encouraged me to leave traditional high school for Job Corps or a vocational school, where I could learn a trade that would make me more marketable for employment opportunities. Out of despair, rejection, and pain, I made a bad decision that landed me in Juvenile Hall (thankfully for just one night). Although I was discouraged, I had to make up my mind that I could not believe these school administrators and teachers; for if I had believed them and taken their advice, I would not be the living testament of one that overcomes obstacles in academia and society. If I can overcome the detrimental systematic policies set in place to destroy me in every way, then there is yet hope for African American males everywhere to be overcomers as well. I have a responsibility to learn more about restorative justice policies, and to teach them to at-risk young people everywhere, for these practices can literally save their lives; not just their physical lives, but their educational, emotional, financial, future vocational, and social lives. There is yet hope.

■ **References**

Aarons, D. I. (2010). City's black males stay in school. *Education Week 30*(10), 1–18.

American Civil Liberties Union. (2008). What is the school-to-prison-pipeline? Http://www.aclu.org.

Barker, C. (2012, March 15). Race, school and prisons probed. *New York Amsterdam News*, pp. 1–37.

Creswell, J. W. (2011). *Educational research: Planning, conducting, and evaluating quantitative and qualitative research*. 4th ed. Harlow, Essex: Pearson.

Davis, F. (2014). Discipline with dignity: Oakland classrooms try healing instead of punishment. *Reclaiming Children & Youth 23*(1), 38–41.

Dupper, D. R. (2010, April). Does the punishment fit the crime? The impact of zero tolerance discipline on at-risk youths. *Children & Schools*, pp. 67–69.

Dupper, D. R., Theriot, M. T., & Craun, S. W. (2009). Reducing out-of-school suspensions: Practice guidelines for school social workers. *Children & Schools 31*(1), 6–14.

Edelman, M. (2009). The cradle to prison pipeline: America's new apartheid. *Harvard Journal of African American Public Policy 15*, 67–68.

Federal government issues guidance for discipline policies in public schools. (2014). *American School & University 86*(5), 42.

Jonsson, P. (2012, March 6). Minority students are punished more than whites, US reports. Is it racism? *Christian Science Monitor*, n.p.

Khadaroo, S. (2014, March 21). Racial gap in discipline found in preschool, US data show. *Christian Science Monitor*, n.p.

Laura, C. T. (2011). Reflections on the racial web of discipline. *Monthly Review 63*(3), 87–95.

Samuels, C. A. (2014). Pre-K suspension data shines spotlight on interventions. *Education Week 33*(27), 6.

Sheldon, D., L., Angell, M., E., Stoner, J., B., & Roseland, B., D. (2012). The process of conducting research using quantitative and qualitative approaches. In J. W. Creswell (Ed.), *Planning, conducting, and evaluating quantitative and qualitative research,* 4th ed. (pp. vii–55). Boston: Pearson.

Shah, N. (2012). Suspended—But Still Learning—in School. *Education Week, 32*(11), 1–18.

Smith, S. M. (2011). Creating safe learning environments for at-risk students in urban schools. *Clearing House 84*(4), 123–26. doi:10. 1080/00098655.2011.564970.

Teasley, M. L. (2014, July). Shifting from zero tolerance to restorative justice in schools. *Children & Schools*, pp. 131–33. doi:10.1093/cs/cdu016.

US Department of Education Office for Civil Rights (2014, March 21). Civil rights data collection data snapshot: School discipline. www.ocrdata.ed.gov.

Black Males in Higher Education

A Multiple Case Study Approach to Success and Retention at the University of Texas at Austin

Gregory J. Vincent, Ryan M. Sutton, Jessica M. Khalaf, and Kevin Almasy

Higher education attainment for Black males has been modestly gaining: undergraduate degree attainment rose from 13 percent in 1990 to 22 percent in 2014; while graduate degree attainment rose from 2 percent in 1995 to 4 percent in 2014 (US Department of Education, 2015). Even though these numbers show slight increases, graduation rates point to a more inclusive picture of how Black males fare in higher education. Six-year graduation rates for Black males vary based on an institution's selectivity rate, but, overall, Black males had a graduation rate of 34.7 percent in 2013, the lowest rate for any group of male students (US Department of Education, 2014). What is leading Black males to not persist in their pursuit of higher education? And what are higher education institutions doing to address the low graduation rates?

The University of Texas at Austin (UT) is focusing on persistence issues for Black males through a variety of initiatives housed within its Division of Diversity and Community Engagement (DDCE). At UT, the six-year graduation rate for Black males was 65 percent in 2014 (UT, n.d.); nationally, at similarly selective institutions, the rate is only 38.8 percent (US Department of Education, 2014). This chapter examines the African American Male Research Initiative and the Thematic Graduate Student Initiative and their effect on persistence and attainment of Black male students at the University of Texas at Austin. The chapter also highlights the extensive work that UT has done as a public research university with the Sigma Pi Phi Fraternity, also known as the Boulé, with the My Brother's Keeper initiative, and with a national partnership with the White House.

Through a research-driven and evidence-based practice framework, these initiatives have provided Black male students with holistic opportunities throughout their undergraduate and graduate careers. Using both quantitative and qualitative data, this chapter provides a case study of the initiatives, analyzes their effects, and provides implications for UT and beyond. Creating educational improvements and recognizing the prevalence of intragroup diversity within the Black male student population are important facets of the work being done by faculty and staff in the Division of Diversity and Community Engagement at UT.

The University of Texas at Austin and Historical Factors of Black Student Admissions

In the sixty years since the *Brown v. Board* decision integrated UT, the percentage of Black students has increased at a slow pace. While a number of factors can be indicative of why Black student enrollment at the university is low, looking back at the history of the university and its role in state-sponsored segregation, integration, and finally affirmative action provides an important context as to why UT needs to continue to focus on the student success indicators of their students of color.

When the university was first established, it was racially segregated through policy and social mores. According to Lavergne (2011), "Texas constitutions from the days of the Republic to the time of Heman Sweatt were the products of a southern-leaning white policies class" (p. 66). As a result of *Plessy v. Ferguson* (1896) and its edict of separate but equal, the university continued to practice segregation for more than sixty years (Lavergne, 2011). It was not until 1946 that attempts to repeal segregation began at the university, when Heman Marion Sweatt applied to the UT Law School (Lavergne, 2011). Mr. Sweatt, a Black postal worker from Houston, Texas, was denied admission because of his race even though he met all the academic qualifications; as a result, Mr. Sweatt challenged the decision (Lavergne, 2011). Given the moderate racial climate of Texas, compared to its Deep South neighbors, the National Association for the Advancement of Colored People (NAACP) chose Mr. Sweatt's denial of admission to fight the doctrine of separate but equal (Goldstone, 2006). Whereas Texas may have been considered more open to integration than southern neighbors, an overwhelming majority of Texans (85 percent) still opposed the integration of the university at that time (Lavergne, 2011). The tumultuous case reached the Supreme Court in *Sweatt v. Painter* (1950). Given the numerated differences between UT Law School and the law school established for African Americans, especially the intangible qualifiers such as prestige, the Supreme Court sided with Mr. Sweatt (Goldstone, 2006). Thus, *Sweatt* was first in successfully challenging the idea of separate but equal at the judicial level (Lavergne, 2011).

Because of the victory for Mr. Sweatt, UT was required to allow Black students to apply and enroll in graduate and professional programs (Battle, 2010). However, if a program was offered at Prairie View A&M University or Texas Southern University, the two public historically black colleges and universities (HBCUs) nearby, then Black students could not attend UT for that same program (Battle, 2010). In the fall of 1950, seventeen Black students enrolled in graduate programs at the university (Goldstone, 2006).

While *Sweatt* desegregated some of the graduate education at the university, another Supreme Court case, *Brown v. Board of Education of Topeka* (1954), overruled separate but equal across the nation's public education systems (Lavergne, 2011). On July 8, 1955, the UT's board of regents announced the admittance of qualified students, regardless of race (Goldstone, 2006). Although Texas was the first in the South to integrate all of its higher-education institutions, UT attempted to restrict enrollment through a policy that required aptitude and subject tests as well as a formula "by which prospective students would be required to reach certain standards" (Goldstone, 2006, p. 41).

Two Supreme Court cases involving the University of Michigan also affected how the use of race in admissions would affect UT: *Gratz v. Bollinger* (2003) and *Grutter v. Bollinger* (2003). Because of the *Grutter* decision, which ruled that there was a compelling interest in promoting class diversity, UT was once again able to use race in its admission practices through a holistic approach that did not favor race as a lone indicator. Most recently, the Supreme Court case of *Fisher v. University of Texas* (2013 & 2016) on admission policy presented another challenge for UT. However, the Court opined in UT's favor, confirming that the use of race was narrowly tailored and therefore constitutional—that is, UT can continue to use race as a factor in admissions.

The University of Texas at Austin and Student Populations

UT's total student population has experienced, for the most part, incremental growth. Using data from the UT statistical handbooks from 1975—which includes data that dates back to 1967—to the most recent publications, the following section shows the changes in student populations based on race (UT, 2016b).

As stated above, the population as a whole has been increasing, but broken down by race and ethnicity, the student population shows some notable trends. Figure 1 presents the student population by ethnic and/or racial background. While there have been some slight rises in the White student population, the number of White students at UT has been decreasing since 1980. Given that the overall population is increasing, this is a strong indicator that underserved populations are becoming more represented at the university. In looking at the trends for Latinos, Asian Americans, and foreign students, while their numbers increased throughout the time frame of 1973 to 2016, it is only in 2016 that Latino students surpassed the 10,000-student mark (10,265). Native American students are the smallest in number and percentage of the total student population at UT; in 2016, only seventy-seven students identified as Native American.

Looking at Black student enrollment at the university shows a more significant trend. Figure 2 separates the Black student numbers to better show the trends from 1973 using UT statistical data. The noticeable dip began in 1997, one year after the *Hopwood* case. In 1996, 1,911 students identified as Black; in 1997, the number was 1,720; and in 1998, it was 1,616. The Top Ten Percent Rule was an attempt by the Texas Legislature to allow for diversity in higher education by allowing students ranked in the top ten percent of their class to be automatically admitted to a public university in Texas. Even though Top Ten passed in 1997, the number of

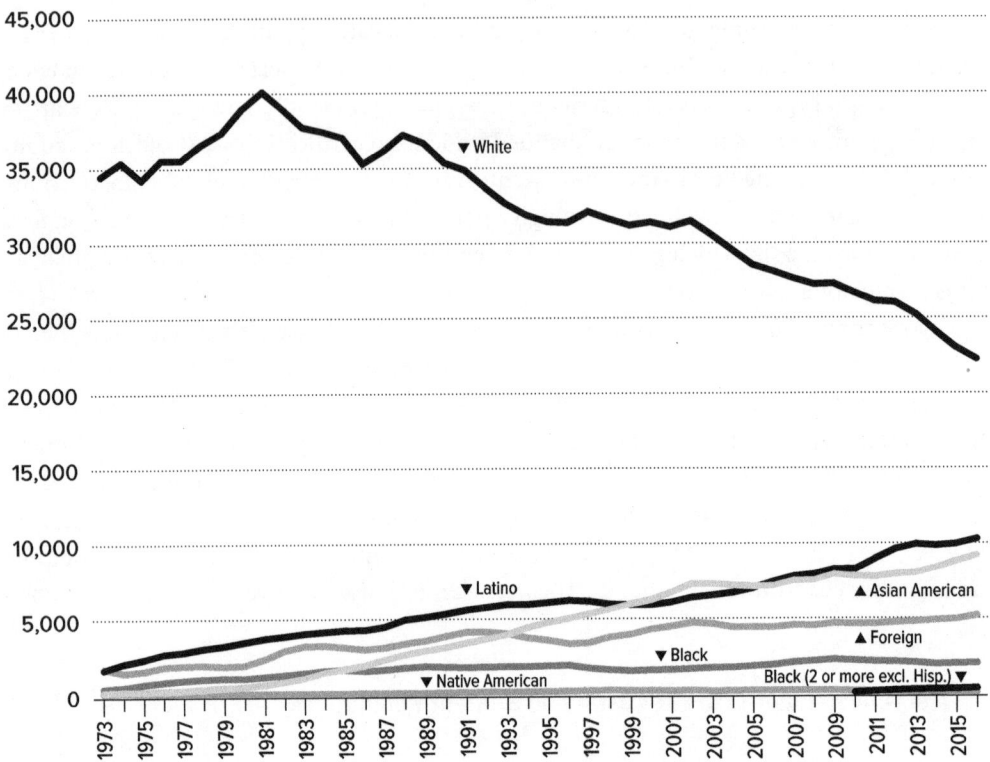

Figure 1. UT student population by ethnicity and/or race. This figure shows the student population broken down by ethnicity/race from 1973 to 2016.

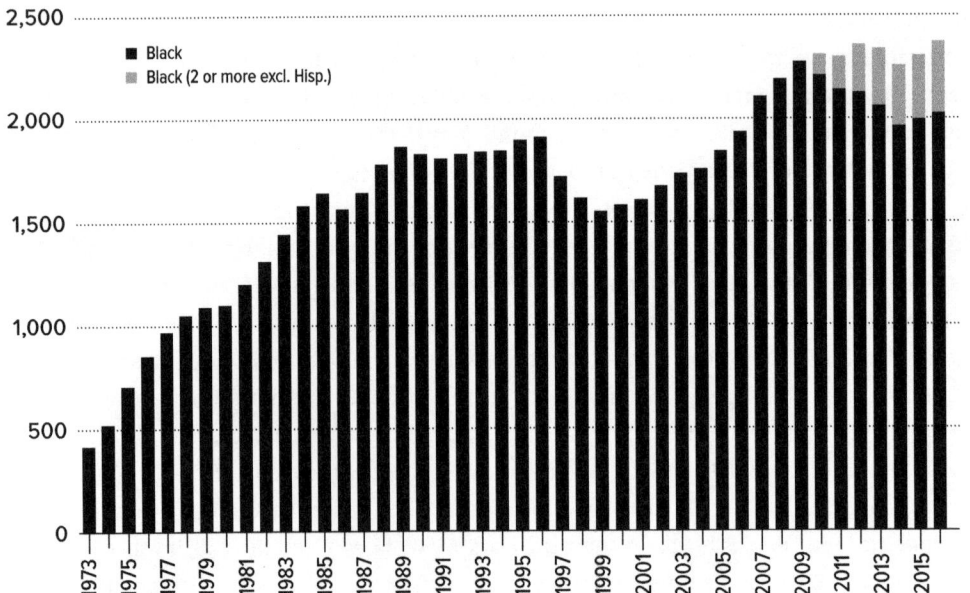

Figure 2. UT Black student population. This figure represents the Black student numbers at the University of Texas at Austin from 1973 to 2016.

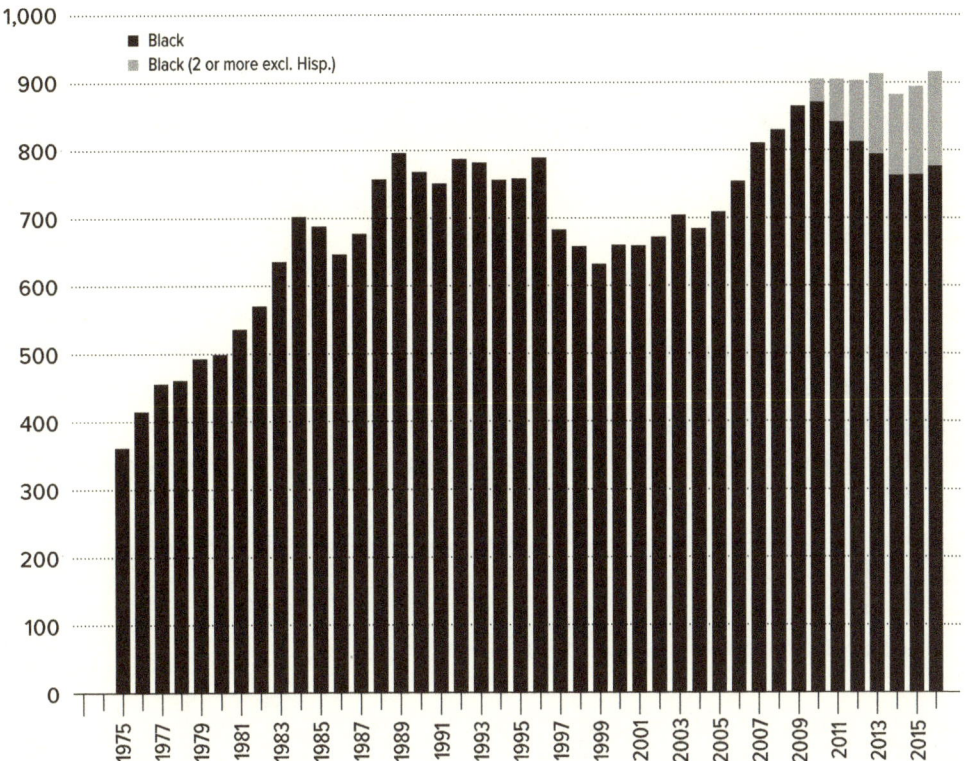

Figure 3. Black Male Student Population at UT. This figure represents the Black male student numbers from 1975 to 2016.

Black students at the university decreased by almost 200 students, or nearly 10 percent. The decreased enrollment accounts for 3.8 percent of the total UT student population. In comparison, the highest percentage of Black students occurred in 2009 with 4.5 percent.

In 2010, UT began expanding its racial and ethnic classification for students to self-identify with more than one race. Students who identified as Black with another racial identity, excluding Hispanic, represent an increasing population at the institution. In 2010, 99 students identified as being Black and another identity; in 2016, this number increased to 346.

The Black male population shows similar trends to the overall Black population. Figure 3 presents the population trends from 1975 to the present with the additional racial identity of Black with another identity, which the university started to record in 2010. Black male students suffered a setback after *Hopwood*, as did the overall Black population. Taking into consideration the greater racial identities of the students, then the number of male students who identify as Black or Black with another identity is currently 916.

However, looking at the data shows that overall the Black male population is currently greater than it has been in the university's history, taking into account the two identities shown. At the same time, the numbers seem to have plateaued since 2009, with the population hovering around 900.

DDCE and Programmatic Initiatives

Under President Williams Powers Jr., UT made diversity one of its strategic priorities. This led to the creation of the Division of Diversity and Community Engagement (DDCE) in 2006. Currently the DDCE comprises over four hundred employees, fifty units, and a budget of $50 million (DDCE, 2016a). The mission of the DDCE is to "advance socially just learning and working environments that foster a culture of excellence through diverse people, ideas, and perspectives. Those in the division engage in dynamic community-university partnerships designed to transform our lives" (DDCE, 2016b). Through four strategic pillars of campus culture, community engagement, education pipeline, and research, the DDCE creates initiatives, develops partnerships on and off campus, and implements research-based projects. Two notable initiatives are the African American Male Research Initiative (AAMRI) and the Thematic Graduate Student Initiative; they both directly work to ensure the success and persistence of Black male students at UT. A commitment to diversity and community engagement continues under President Gregory Fenves, who assumed office in the summer of 2015.

African American Male Research Initiative

AAMRI is a faculty and staff-led program geared to increasing the enrollment of Black male students in four-year higher educational institutions, specifically at UT. Additionally, AAMRI is dedicated to increasing the four-year graduation rate of Black male students at the university. Through the use of research and empirical proven strategies, AAMRI provides programming for the personal, academic, and professional development of Black male students. As entering freshman, Black males are invited to participate in the services and programming of AAMRI through a formal letter, as well as follow-up emails. Their participation is voluntary and subjective based on each student's schedule. These programs consist of, but are not limited to, pipeline programming, tutoring, academic coaching and advising, monthly workshops, hosting campus visits, student-athlete programming, study abroad, and leadership retreats.

AAMRI has seven graduate students who are responsible for mentoring, tutoring, programming, and research. These graduate students are part of the Thematic Graduate Initiative discussed in the next section. Graduate hires work closely with a faculty researcher who aids in the development of the graduate students' research agenda, as well as serves as a mentor for the graduate student. Faculty, staff, and thematic graduate hires meet on a weekly basis to discuss their research, mentoring relationships, and programming.

Through partnerships with national and local organizations, AAMRI also exposes students to Black male professionals within the community. The interactions between the professionals and AAMRI students increase access to opportunities, including mentorship, internships, and career exposure. As students are mentored and developed, they have the opportunity to mentor Black high school males through recruiting visits and mentoring programs in local area high schools.

In addition, graduate students serve as student leaders and mentors on study-abroad trips. Organized by AAMRI, these study-abroad experiences occur each summer in Beijing, China, and Cape Town, South Africa, on alternate years. These trips are staffed by faculty, staff, and thematic graduate hires. During the four-week period in which the students are abroad, they are required to engage in a service learning project that increases their familiarity with the community abroad, gain a greater understanding of community needs, and critically examine how they may partner with a community agency to create solution-focused strategies. Additionally, students attend a daily seminar on social capital and explore the country, learning the cultural, historical, and environmental aspects of society.

Thematic Graduate Initiative

Through thematic initiatives, DDCE has transformed learning, teaching, research, and service in an effort to support an inclusive and diverse environment at UT. The thematic initiatives incorporate a three-tiered approach to prepare, recruit, and retain faculty. The first approach entails supporting diverse students as they advance through graduate school and prepare for future academic careers; this is the Thematic Graduate Initiative. The DDCE hires graduate research assistants who are mentored within the division's many units and exposed to the value of working in an academic environment committed to diversity and inclusion. Second, in collaboration with colleges and schools across campus, DDCE recruits intellectually and culturally diverse faculty members, providing lines of partial or full funding for these hires; this is the Thematic Faculty Initiative. And third, through the Faculty Fellows Initiative, the division provides fellowships to faculty members across the university whose research, teaching, or special projects focus on diversity and community engagement issues. The DDCE has helped cultivate the professional careers of nearly sixty graduate students, many of whom have gone on to tenure track positions at various institutions across the nation as well as policymaking positions in numerous fields. The graduate student initiative inculcates the importance and role of community engagement in development.

Partnerships

In addition to these internal initiatives, the DDCE has over four hundred community partnerships, many of which directly and indirectly benefit Black male students in higher education, as well as in the entire educational pipeline from pre-K to PhD. Through a number of these partnerships, mentoring opportunities for Black male students at UT are created to help the students not only persist throughout their higher education career but also engage with successful Black males in various fields. Two such notable partnerships are those with Sigma Pi Phi Fraternity, the Boulé, and those through the My Brother's Keeper initiative, which includes a national partnership with the White House. The Boulé is the oldest Black professional fraternity in the United States (Sigma Pi Phi, 2016). Social action is an important element for the fraternity, as it provides an opportunity for Boulé members, also known as Archons, to better serve their community, especially young Black males in reaching their potential. Through its partnerships with UT, mentorship opportunities for both undergraduate and graduate students allow the students to interact with successful Black men and be a proactive part of their community, on and off campus. The Boulé uses both constellation and cascading mentoring to impact Black youth. Cascade mentoring is a tiered model that connects a senior mentor with a mentee, who then mentors a junior person. Through this connection, lessons and skills learned can be passed from one mentor to another. Constellation mentoring is another approach to mentoring. This method involves a network of supportive members who provide access to social and cultural capital, rather than the traditional one-to-one mentoring model. According to Reddick and Heilig (2013), "The responsibilities of mentorship are distributed across several mentors, and the mentee reaps the benefit of having multiple perspectives to solicit and follow" (p. 19).

The My Brother's Keeper initiative is a national call to action by initiated by former president Barack Obama to ensure the success and well-being of young men of color. UT has been a key player in bringing together various entities throughout the greater Austin area to form the Greater Austin Area My Brother's Keeper (GAAMBK) (GAAMBK, n.d.). For Black male students at UT, the GAAMBK has provided opportunities to engage with Black male students throughout the educational pipeline as mentors while also being mentored by older Black males in the community who serve in leadership positions within the GAAMBK. Through the DDCE's partnership with the Boulé, a national partnership with the White House has also ensured that the resources and purpose of the My Brother's Keeper initiative positively impact young Black men at UT.

From these initiatives, UT, through DDCE, is working to ensure the persistence of Black male students throughout the educational pipeline. While these initiatives are not the panacea for what Black male students face in higher education, they are providing outlets and opportunities to ensure that these students are succeeding inside and outside the classroom.

Literature Review

Higher education institutions must do more to combat the challenges faced by Black males. This is true for both undergraduate and graduate Black male students. This literature review focuses on the following areas for Black male students: belongingness and its effect on student engagement; the role of mentoring; and student programming geared toward persistence and support.

Belongingness and Engagement

Belongingness and satisfaction in the college experience are important characteristics that help with persistence for Black male students (Steele, 1997; Strayhorn, 2008a). Harper (2009), however, explains that Black males students are less likely to be engaged inside and outside the classroom during their college careers. Black male students are also more likely to suffer the effects of stereotype threat, racial fatigue, and oppression at higher education institutions, especially predominantly White institutions (Dancy, 2012; Steele, 1997; Smith, Allen, & Danley, 2007; Harper, 2007). Yet the advantages of being engaged has been well established for the benefit of all students (Astin, 1984; Harper, 2012; Kuh, 2003; Pascarella & Terenzini, 2005; Tinto, 2006). As a result, interventions of sorts that increase the sense of belonging can enhance engagement levels among Black male students. Walton and Cohen (2007) found that through such mechanisms, Black students' perception of fit at their institutions increased, which in turned increased their belief in their academic potential. Having a strong peer group of the same race is also indicative of academic success (Harper, 2010). Given the connection between belongingness and academic success for Black males, forming relationships with faculty and staff at the university and engaging in activities on campus and through specific initiatives can increase both the sense of fit and academic success at their institution (Harper, 2007; Strayhorn 2014).

Mentorship

For this study, mentors, both formal and informal, provide another conduit toward academic success. Accordingly, having a mentor during the college career of Black males, either through a direct mentoring program or through an organic process, provides benefits to the students' persisting and to postbaccalaureate goals (Dancy, 2012; Harper, 2012; LaVant, Anderson, & Tiggs, 1997). Strayhorn (2008b) found that supportive relationships with faculty, staff, and peers were helpful in ensuring academic success for Black male students, as have other researchers (Kuh & Hu, 2001; Pascarella & Terenzini, 1978). The benefits of a mentoring relationship for graduate students of color is just as significant (Brown, Davis, & McClendon, 1999).

Support Services

Providing a welcoming space for Black male students is another component to academic success. Through such an environment, Black male students' aspirations and successes can be enhanced and validated (Cuyjet, 1997). Student support services provide a mechanism through which this can be achieved. A number of theories have been developed to accentuate the need for involvement by students as well as faculty and administrators, as ways to ensure that students are retained through graduation (Astin, 1984; Tinto, 1997). Thomas (2002) found that having connections with staff and faculty through institutional programming and initiatives allowed students to feel confident and comfortable to interact with faculty and staff through a less structured association. In addition to providing such services, it is also important for Black students to feel ownership of initiatives that might be geared specifically toward them (Harper & Kuykendall, 2012).

Research Design and Methodology

The authors used mixed methods of archival record review and multiple single-unit case designs to highlight the successes that DDCE has had with the Black males on the UT campus. The single-unit case designs were achieved through a combination of observation, archival record review, and interviews. After expounding on the academic differences between Black males engaged with the AAMRI and those who are not, the authors utilize illustrative case studies in three areas of programming that contributes to these students' success: study-abroad programming, thematic graduate student hires, and community partnerships. Information-oriented sampling (Yin, 2009) was used to select the cases for the study based upon the information content provided by each case.

Grade point average (GPA) was used as the measurement of academic success for the purposes of this study. Using the archival record review process, researchers examined the GPAs of Black males who engaged in AAMRI programming and compared that to the overall GPA of Black males at UT. The data were further disaggregated according to the frequency of students' participation in AAMRI programs, in order to understand whether or not GPAs rose as program participation increased. Additionally, archival record reviews were also performed to understand the career placements of former DDCE thematic graduate hires.

In an effort to understand the impact that this programming has on the Black male population at UT, the authors selected three components of the initiative that influenced the academic achievement and persistence discussed in the record review. The first case study is a comprehensive description of AAMRI students' study-abroad experience. The students were interviewed using a semistructured set of questions through an informal interview process that was composed by the researchers (Creswell, 2013). The questions were designed to understand the student's collegiate experience prior to his engagement with the program compared to his experience afterward. Of the thirteen students asked to be interviewed, seven students agreed to the interview. Quotes from the interviews highlight the impact of this experience on the academic and personal development of the student.

The second case study is on DDCE thematic graduate hires, particularly within AAMRI, and the success the graduate students acquire after graduation. For this study, six Black male students, of the nine students identified as potential interviewees, who have a current or previous positions as graduate research assistants within the DDCE were interviewed. The questions were geared at exploring their experiences as thematic graduate hires. The researchers drew from the experiences of former and current thematic graduate hires to understand how the program has contributed to their current achievements. By using a mix of observational and interview techniques, this chapter highlights recurrent themes as significant indicators of success.

The third case study focuses upon the community partnerships shared between the DDCE and Sigma Pi Phi Fraternity (the Boulé), including the connections with the My Brother's Keeper initiative and the national partnership with the White House. Various aspects of the partnerships are emphasized as models contributing to successful student matriculation and

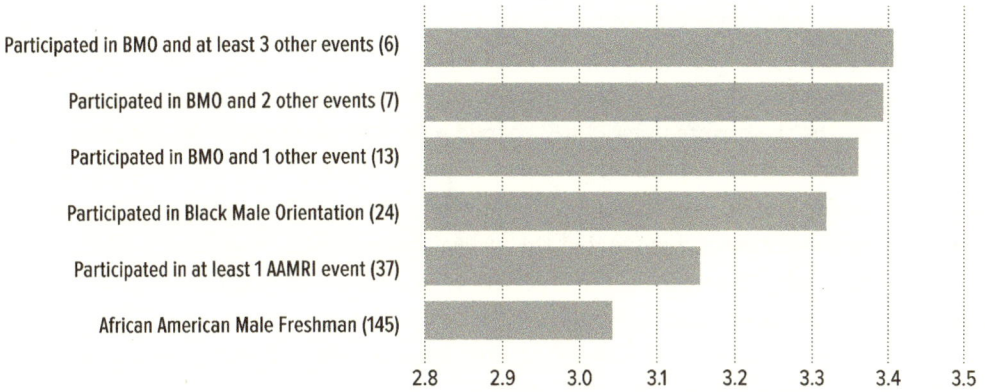

Figure 4. AAMRI Student Participation Levels and Accompanying GPAs from Fall 2014.

increased exposure to opportunity. Through observational methods, the researchers describe the programming through the relationship between both organizations.

The authors analyzed and extracted themes within the case studies that were identified as contributing factors to student success. These themes and patterns were detected in the comments of students or in the programming of the initiative. However, due to the nature of case studies, the results may not be generalizable to all Black male programming. Inasmuch as the themes are applicable to another initiative, the actual programming may need to vary.

Results and Discussion

Below are the common themes and trends found within the three case studies that Black male students have participated in at UT. Some limitations to this study include the small sample size and only including the perspective of the students within the data. Although these results may not be generalizable to other institutions of higher education, they do, however, provide some transferability as to how certain programs provide a conduit through which Black male engagement and potential persistence can be attained.

GPA and AAMRI Students

Currently, AAMRI has around 150 students engaged in various activities through the academic year, including study-abroad programs during mini-mesters—the few weeks between the end of one semester and start of the next. For AAMRI-affiliated students, their GPAs are as described in figure 4, which separates Black student population based on participation in AAMRI events.

As can be seen from the GPA data, students with higher GPAs also participated in more AAMRI activities within the 2014 school year. The baseline data start when any Black male enters the university and is invited to take part in AAMRI. The freshman data for 145 such students indicate a 3.042 average GPA. As Black male students participated in AAMRI activities, they were moved into the corresponding categories of participation and engagement. The first level past the freshmen baseline is participation in the Black Male Student Orientation (BMSO). Among the 24 students who participated in 2014, the average GPA was 3.319. According to the data, greater participation, beyond the BMSO, is associated with higher GPAs. Although one cannot assume that the increase in GPA numbers was a direct result of participation in AAMRI initiatives, the experiences offered through AAMRI are contributing factors in academic performance, as indicated through past empirical studies. Previous studies, as well as student development theory, demonstrate that higher engagement is related to higher academic achievement.

Study Abroad

Despite nationwide efforts to diversify study-abroad programs, these programs continue to lack the involvement of students of color (Salisbury, Paulsen, & Pascarella, 2011; Shih, 2009). Although study-abroad participation has increased over the years, there remains a discrepancy in participation in study abroad by race. The National Association of Foreign Student Advisors (2016) reported that White students comprised 58.3 percent of postsecondary enrollment during the 2013–2014 academic year, compared to 14.5 percent of Black student enrollment; however, White students represented 72.9 percent of study-abroad participants in 2015, while Black students were underrepresented at 5.6 percent.

Several studies show the immediate and long-term benefits of study-abroad experiences on the development of students. A few of these benefits are a more informed understanding of global matters (Douglas & Jones-Rikkers, 2001), increased career marketability and opportunity (Cocchiara & Studdard, 2008), and positive psychological adjustment and belongingness (Savicki & Cooley, 2011). These benefits were identified within the narrative of AAMRI students' study-abroad experiences.

INTERNATIONAL EXPERIENCE

The majority of AAMRI students who engaged in study abroad did not have prior experience traveling outside of the United States. Students perceived international experience as a strength in their development and preparation for their career paths, thus serving as motivation to engage in this experience. The notion of accumulating firsthand knowledge of international affairs and foreign cultures bolsters a sense of competence for students. A senior in the McCombs School of Business who was beginning job interviews indicated that he would "soon be graduating and had never traveled outside the [United States]. To be competitive in the business world, I felt I needed to gain international experience." The expanded worldview and firsthand knowledge of other cultures contributed to a perceived increase in competitive edge, professionally. This firsthand experience allows students to form their own understanding about various cultures, outside the dominant narrative of the United States. A junior liberal arts major who traveled to Cape Town, South Africa, stated that he "had never been out the country before and [had] let the media form his opinions of different cultures." Through the study-abroad experience, this student cultivated his own perceptions of international affairs, which translated into richer dialogue with job interviewers and more informed class engagement.

Students who participated in the study-abroad program indicated that they participated in more international traveling after this experience to expand their cultural horizons. Two students, an English major and a psychology major, spoke about their continued interest in traveling due to the relationships that were established during their study-abroad experience. One student indicated that since traveling abroad with AAMRI, he has felt comfortable enough to have "traveled to 11 different countries and plans to travel abroad at least once a year. I feel a certain level of responsibility outside my own country." The psychology major described this sense of responsibility in regard to the relationships that were forged while abroad. Referring to his experience in Cape Town, he stated that he "went again to South Africa to work with one of the same organizations who [he] now sees as family."

By traveling abroad, these students were able to foster relationships with local families and organizations that increased their sense of belongingness and connection to the communities in which they served. In turn, this sense of connection has increased their desire and perceived responsibility in engaging solution-focused strategies to improve international communities, thus furthering their international experience and cultural connectedness.

INCREASED OPPORTUNITY

AAMRI students who participated in the study-abroad program found that their willingness to step outside their comfort zones was expanded. Some students indicated the opportunity to try something new was their motivation to sign up for the program. One individual stated that "the possibility of stepping out of my comfort zone and experiencing something a lot of people do not experience was a major catalyst to studying abroad. This is something I continue to practice." Through the study-abroad experience, this student engaged with more campus and community resources than he did prior to studying abroad, which increased his academic performance and overall collegiate experience.

An AAMRI graduate student in higher education and cultural studies indicated that access to more opportunities stretched beyond the academic realm and further impacted his professional and social life. He reported that

> since returning from Beijing I have found that I am more willing to seize opportunities that I would have shied away from originally. This includes academic, professional, and social opportunities. I find that I even seek friendships with individuals I would not previously [have] had.

The social capital that was built through the study-abroad experience further enhanced his social support and network infrastructure.

An enhanced self-image contributed to the opportunity seeking behavior that many students experience once returning from abroad. An undergraduate liberal arts major, who studied in Beijing reported he has "been more open to taking opportunity, such as traveling more and going to graduate school. Things I never thought I would be doing before I went abroad." Although he previously did not consider graduate school an option, the international experience broadened his own self-concept and expanded his perception of the opportunities that were available to him.

INCREASED GLOBAL WORLDVIEW

Although students expressed a desire to enhance their worldview through firsthand experience, many actualized this desire when working alongside the community to which they traveled. Some students gained a broader understanding of the country they were in and the people they interacted with, while others realized they had an increased awareness of the diversity of Black experience through the diaspora. A student majoring in African and African diaspora witnessed "a connection to the people of Cape Town, South Africa through the perseverance and strength that is demonstrated by Black men in America and the Black people in South Africa." In discovering the similarities between his own experience in the United States and the lived experiences of Black people in South Africa, this student was able to highlight the daily resiliency he witnesses. This realization improved his racial identity and pride, while also expanding his sense of self and developing his connection to other cultures.

In experiencing a connection with individuals who may have formerly been seen as different, students increase their empathetic thinking abilities. Students mentioned being able to see things from a different perspective and appreciate the perspective of others, better enabling them to interact with a diversity of people. One student stated:

> The experience made me grateful for the luxuries that we take for granted, but also gave me a sense of appreciation for the simplicity of villagers. To see things from their perspective has helped me understand that my views are not the only views, allowing me to be more open to others.

Another student determined that "understanding the perspective of the locals was easiest when by myself or with a small group. This helped me begin to reflect on the differences [between cultures] and shift my thinking." Increased empathy, through an expanded worldview, may aid in coping with stress and provide the student with more flexible thinking.

Establishing flexible thought patterns and developing perspective provides students with the ability to engage professors, other students, and future employers in meaningful ways. The capacity for one to communicate regarding a broader range of topics and experience, and the expanded ability to problem-solve, are benefits seen by students. An AAMRI student, on the verge of graduation and seeking employment, indicated that studying abroad made "having conversation with C-Level and Senior Executives easier and improved the way in which I view challenges." In a similar fashion, an AAMRI graduate student identified the underrepresentation of students of color traveling abroad and decided to concentrate his research efforts in filling this void. He stated:

Traveling abroad opened my eyes to the opportunities that exist beyond my environment. I want to understand the experiences of students of color traveling abroad, so that I can increase the number of students of color engaging in this experience. We will have to reach them through nontraditional ways.

An increased global worldview assists students in establishing an outlook that differs from the dominant narrative and work toward establishing a new normative. This same graduate student was able to realize his desire when he co-led a trip to Cape Town. He indicated that "leading over 20 Black students up Lions Head Mountain in Cape Town, South Africa was memorable for me. I had made the hike seven years prior and knew that I wanted to help other Black students accomplish the same."

Thematic Graduate Initiative

Given the overlap of students involved in AAMRI and in the partnerships as well as in the Thematic Graduate Initiative, it is not surprising that the findings on thematic graduate hires, both current and past, show complementary characteristics in the experiences of the Black male thematic graduates.

SUPPORT FOR RESEARCH

One of the greatest aspects of the Thematic Graduate Initiative is the opportunity for graduate students to build and expand their research agenda and portfolio, making them more competitive applicants after graduation. The research performed by AAMRI graduate students, faculty, and staff informs the programming and work done with students on campus. Thus, research is a cornerstone to AAMRI's agenda, as well as the work of the thematic graduate hires.

Within AAMRI's first cohort of thematic graduate hires, two have obtained tenure track positions at other institutes of higher education. One student, now a professor in the school of education at an East Coast university, stated, "Going into my tenure track position I feel I was ahead of the curve. Because I had been working on my own research projects since my first year, I was able to develop a steady pipeline of publications." The opportunity to work closely with various faculty members across departments offers increased support, a wider array of insight into research and publication, and added structure in regard to writing. It is through these relationships that AAMRI thematic graduate hires are able to engage in a range of research projects, while focusing on their personal research agenda. A current graduate reported that many of his publishing opportunities were established through faculty relationships that were cultivated through AAMRI. He indicated that he feels "connected to many faculty members that [he] may not have otherwise met had it not been for AAMRI. This has provided more accountability in terms of engaging in research, writing, and opportunities for publishing."

The emphasis on research through AAMRI encourages students to make research a priority. Although thematic graduate hires are responsible for programming and student advising, graduate students' responsibilities are refocused as they near their dissertation. One graduate student reported that he "felt supported by AAMRI, especially as I needed to concentrate more on my dissertation. They knew how much to utilize my assistance, while providing me the space to focus on my research."

MENTORSHIP

The mentorship aspect of AAMRI is designed to be a cascade mentorship model, where the thematic graduate hires are mentored by Black male faculty and staff and mentor undergraduate students in return. Graduate students find the holistic nature of the mentorship experience helpful in regard to academic, professional, and personal development. A fourth-year doctoral student indicated that "the mentorship really enhanced my ability to navigate a predominantly White space as an African American male. It also provided academic accountability and personal community." Graduate students meet with faculty and staff once a week, as a minimum, in order to program and discuss issues that have arisen with the graduate students. A fourth-year doctoral student described the mentorship in the following manner:

> They are always willing to help in any way possible. Whether serving as a resource or having the difficult conversations with us about life, academics, and personal development. The staff has also provided a lead by example mentality and challenged me to be better than I was when I started working with them. The staff's mentorship was most apparent during our trips away [study-abroad and recruiting trips].

Establishing an intentional and strategic support system for the graduate students enhances their ability to engage in self-care and to practice emotional well-being during difficult periods. Faculty and staff readily make themselves available to discuss personal challenges, as well as academic and professional issues. A graduate student who has been with AAMRI for three years reported that "during the time of my father's illness and eventual death, mentors and other graduate students were very supportive. This helped me remain focused and provided a platform for me to process my experience. I was not alone." Having this level of support was just as important for his academic and professional development since it permitted him to remain focused and connected to his professional pursuits.

Since AAMRI works in a cascade mentorship model, AAMRI thematic graduate hires found that their ability to mentor undergraduate students was improved through the mentor-mentee interaction they shared with AAMRI faculty. By modeling the role of a mentor and discussing various mentorship philosophies, AAMRI graduate students were able to tailor their mentorship style in keeping with the theories and practices demonstrated by faculty and staff. A fourth-year AAMRI graduate student stated that "given my experience with AAMRI I think that I am much better at mentoring students in holistic ways." The thematic graduate students mirrored staff and faculty's attention to intragroup diversity and the mentees' individual needs. By forming meaningful relationships with undergraduate Black males, they were better able to engage the students on a variety of levels (i.e., academic, personal, professional). A third-year graduate student was "shocked at the intensity and depth of problems that [were] faced by my mentee. I remember talking with him and reinforcing the resiliency that he had. It made me more determined to not allow obstacles to dishearten my progress."

Partnerships

DDCE partners with the Sigma Pi Phi Fraternity, also known as the Boulé, in order to provide extended mentorship and professional opportunities for the students. There is a significant amount of overlap from the partnerships between DDCE and the Boulé with the work of AAMRI. This also includes the partnership that DDCE has with the White House through the My Brother's Keeper initiative. Given that both are key initiatives within the Greater Austin Area My Brother's Keeper Initiative, which strongly promotes mentorship among young males of color, AAMRI and the Boulé have cultivated a multifaceted mentorship structure. This partnership manifests in three different actions: connect with the students through development workshops, partake in one-on-one career mentorship, and provide opportunities to the students to present research. The partnership impacts Black males on campus and challenges them to expand their personal narratives to include Black male success.

Through various student development programming, AAMRI invites Boulé professionals to network and speak with the students. Key events include a college-to-career program, the Collegiate Black Male Retreat, and Power Hour networking. During these events, Boulé members speak to AAMRI students about their path to their career, advice around college and graduate school, and opportunities available to them as students. AAMRI students are encouraged to ask questions and explore career avenues that are available. Through these interactions, one-on-one mentorship opportunities organically develop.

Boulé members provide one-on-one mentorship with AAMRI students in an effort to enhance and personalize the mentorship experience for students. As noted, the relationships develop organically through the programming or may be more intentional as faculty and staff introduce students to specific Boulé members depending on the student's needs and interests. AAMRI students are afforded the opportunity to shadow professional Black males within the career field in order to gain a comprehensive understanding of what is entailed with the profession, understand the benefits and challenges facing males of color within the field, and expand their narrative by witnessing a male of color in a position they may not have been exposed to previously.

Additionally, AAMRI students are invited to national and regional Boulé conferences to speak about their research, collegiate matriculation, and future goals. These opportunities allow AAMRI students to engage a larger body of Black male professionals within social and professional settings, which expand their network and support circles. A former AAMRI student reported that "the professional development opportunities such as speaking at the national and regional Sigma Pi Phi meetings helped me to network and develop supportive relationships where I currently live and work."

Implications

Research indicates collegiate academic success is significantly dictated by a sense of belonging-ness (Booker, 2007; Clark et al., 2012; Glass & Westmont, 2014). The Division of Diversity and Community Engagement has always believed this to be true, both empirically and anecdotally. But, on a campus which has hovered between 3 and 5 percent undergraduate Black enroll-ment, belongingness is, unfortunately, far from a given. In 2016, students on the UT campus continued to experience isolation, some going entire days without seeing those who look like them in class—whether it be their instructors or classmates. Dealing with these realities oc-curs while simultaneously combating the monolithic narrative specific to Black males—that they are not smart enough to compete.

Running parallel to feelings of isolationism is the history of the university itself. As previ-ously noted, it was just sixty years ago that UT admitted its first Black undergraduates. This decades-long lack of access that preceded integration created a legacy that still permeates the hearts and minds of many Black citizens across the state of Texas today, that UT was not and is not the place for them. After some momentum, that ideal was only further cemented in the aftermath of the *Hopwood* decision, which eliminated the university's opportunity to forcefully recruit and offer scholarships to Black students. In a history that spans some 135 years, the period in which the university has been dedicated to recruiting and retaining Black students spans less than two decades.

Although neither reality, be it student isolation or university history, is ideal, it also does not define UT or the experience of its Black male students. The university, and in particular the DDCE and AAMRI, made the decision to chart its own course. The summation of this choice is the division's commitment to intentionality—that wanting or hoping is not enough. Through the study-abroad program, thematic graduate student hires, and partnership with the Boulé, the DDCE and AAMRI have enhanced the sense of belongingness among Black male students and have combated decades of unfortunate history on UT's campus. This suc-cess has in turn disproved the monolithic, deficit-based, narrative surrounding young Black men. The evidence of these programs may be viewed in the graduation rates and GPAs of the Black male student body.

Although not easy, creating a positive and fulfilling experience for Black males is due more to hard work and insistence than to groundbreaking strategy. The foundation for increasing academic outcomes among Black male students exists in a strategic plan that is both organi-zationally and financially dedicated to holistic development programming, mentorship, and exposure to opportunity. Creating programs and cultivating relationships increases student capital, which increases participation of Black male students through programs and resources.

For example, as qualitatively expressed in the research, the thematic graduate hires in-dicated that mentorship, personal and professional development, and the Black professional network opportunity were significant contributors to their AAMRI experience. By gaining the intentional and purposeful mentorship of Black male faculty and staff, graduate students felt holistically supported across multiple facets of their lives. Discussing personal challenges and professional uncertainties and opportunities, and exposure to an increased number of Black male professionals, served to further feelings of belongingness.

Similarly, study-abroad programs have also been seen as a form of building a sense of belongingness within students of color (Lowe, Byron, & Mennicke, 2014). Although research indicates that there is an underrepresentation of students of color within study-abroad programs (Shih, 2009; Salisbury, Paulsen, & Pascarella, 2011), DDCE and AAMRI have found success through the implementation of programming that specifically targets the Black male student population. Programs have been developed that directly address specific concerns, and in turn participation has increased. This has led to greater interaction with a diversity of students among those students of color who partake in study abroad once they return to campus. Additionally, anecdotal evidence has shown that study-abroad students also encounter and interact with students of color they might not otherwise cross paths with on campus during their study-abroad experiences. One such student reported that what he experienced in South Africa was much more impactful because it occurred with other students who looked like him. This increased belongingness is in addition to previously noted benefits, including an expanded worldview, professional experiences, mentoring opportunities, and problem-solving for students who study abroad (Sutton & Rubin, 2004).

Given the holistic approach that AAMRI and the DDCE take, the mental health of these young men has to be considered given the impact that it has on academic and professional functioning. In regard to mental health, the stigma that exists within this community serves as a significant contributor to the underutilization of services among Black men. By providing relatable mentors and role models, young men are afforded organic relationships that cultivate an environment conducive to processing their emotions and experiences. Students and mentors have an opportunity to improve their emotional well-being through the processing of their lived experiences. Additionally, these mentors may serve as a trustworthy liaison between the students and available services on campus, thus increasing the likelihood that these young men seek help when appropriate.

Much of the literature speaks to the experiences of undergraduate Black males, with less research addressing the experience of graduate students. Although this chapter addresses the experience of both populations, it focuses primarily on the mentor experiences of graduate students and the study-abroad experiences of undergraduate students. Future research should further explore the experiences of graduate students, as well as the undergraduate experiences of current graduate students. By expanding the narrative around Black male graduate students' experience during their undergraduate studies, research may better inform the practices and programs that contribute to successful matriculation from undergraduate to graduate school.

Conclusion

While more needs to be done to ensure that Black men are not only entering higher education but also attaining a degree, the University of Texas at Austin through the Division of Diversity and Community Engagement is making substantial strides to ensure Black male success. All of the students who were interviewed for this study expressed their enjoyment of the processes as well as the tangible and intangible benefits of being part of the DDCE, through AAMRI, the thematic graduate, or the mentoring opportunities through its partnerships. Although these programs within this study are still developing, the administrators of the programs are confident in the work that is being done as well as what they have planned for the future.

■ References

Astin, A. W. (1984). Student involvement: A developmental theory for higher education. *Journal of College Student Personnel 25*(4), 297–308.

Battle, W. J. (2010). University of Texas at Austin. In *Handbook of Texas Online.* Texas State Historical Association. Https://tshaonline.org/handbook/online/articles/kcu09.

Booker, K. C. (2007). Perceptions of classroom belongingness among African American college students. *College Student Journal 41*(1), 178–86.

Bowen, W. G., & Bok, D. C. (1998). *The shape of the river: Long-term consequences of considering race in college and university admissions.* Princeton: Princeton University Press.

Brown, M. C., II, Davis, G. L., & McClendon, S. A. (1999). Mentoring graduate students of color: Myths, models, and modes. *Peabody Journal of Education 74*(2), 105–18.

Carly, I. (2013). Alend, George Louis. In *Handbook of Texas Online.* Texas State Historical Association. Https://tshaonline.org/handbook/online/articles/faldu.

Clark, C. R., Mercer, S. H., Zeigler-Hill, V., & Dufrene, B. A. (2012). Barriers to the success of ethnic minority students in school psychology graduate programs. *School Psychology Review 41*(2), 176–92.

Cocchiara, F. K. & Studdard, N. L. (2008). The effect of perceived value in the decision to participate in study abroad programs. *Journal of Teaching in International Business 4*, 346–61. doi:10.1080/08975930802427551.

Creswell, J. W. (2013). *Qualitative inquiry & research design: Choosing among five approaches.* Los Angeles: Sage.

Cuyjet, M. J. (1997). African American men on college campuses: Their needs and their perceptions. *New Directions for Student Services 1997*(80), 5–16. doi:10.1002/ss.8001

Dancy, T. E. (2012). *The brother code: Manhood and masculinity among African American males in college.* Charlotte, NC: Information Age.

Division of Diversity and Community Engagement. (2016a). About DDCE. Http://diversity.utexas.edu/about-ddce/.

Division of Diversity and Community Engagement. (2016b). Strategic plan. Http://diversity.utexas.edu/strategic-plan/.

Douglas, C., & Jones-Rikkers, C.G. (2001). Study abroad programs and American student worldmindedness: An empirical analysis. *Journal of Teaching in International Business 13*(1), 55–66.

Glass, C. R. & Westmont, C. M. (2014). Comparative effects of belongingness on the academic success and cross-cultural interactions of domestic and international students. *International Journal of Intercultural Relations 38*, 106–19.

Goldstone, D. (2006). *Integrating the 40 acres: The fifty-year struggle for racial equality at the University of Texas*. Athens: University of Georgia Press.

Greater Austin Area My Brother's Keeper. (n.d.) About us. Http://gaambk.org/about-us/.

Harper, S. R. (2007). Peer support for African American male college achievement: Beyond internalized racism and the burden of "acting White." *Journal of Men's Studies 14*(3), 337–58.

———. (2009). Niggers no more: A critical race counternarrative on Black male student achievement at predominantly White colleges and universities. *International Journal of Qualitative Studies in Education 22*(6), 697–712.

———. (2010). Peer support for African American male college achievement. In S. R. Harper and F. Harris III (eds.), *College men and masculinities: Theory, research, and implications for practice*, 434–56. San Francisco: Jossey-Bass.

———. (2012). *Black male student success in higher education: A report from the national Black male college achievement study*. Philadelphia: University of Pennsylvania, Center for the Study of Race and Equity in Education.

Harper, S. R., & Kuykendall, J. A. (2012). Institutional efforts to improve Black male student achievement: A standards-based approach. *Change 44*(2), 23–29.

Kuh, G. D. (2003). What we're learning about student engagement from NSSE: Benchmarks for effective educational practices. *Change 35*(2), 24–32.

Kuh, G. D., & Hu, S. (2001). The effects of student-faculty interaction in the 1990s. *Review of Higher Education 24*(3), 309–32.

LaVant, B. D., Anderson, J. L., & Tiggs, J. W. (1997). Retaining African American men through mentoring initiatives. *New Directions for Student Services 1997*(80), 43–53.

Lavergne, G. M. (2011). *Before Brown: Heman Marion Sweatt, Thurgood Marshall, and the long road to justice*. Austin: University of Texas Press.

Lowe, M. R., Byron, R. A., & Mennicke, S. (2014). The racialized impact of study abroad on U.S. students' subsequent interracial interactions. *Education Research*, 1–9. doi:10.1155/2014/232687.

National Association of Foreign Student Advisors. (2016). *Trends in U.S. study abroad*. Washington, DC: NAFSA: Association of International Educators.

Pascarella, E. T., & Terenzini, P. T. (1978). Student-faculty informal relationships and freshman year educational outcomes. *Journal of Educational Research 71*, 183–89.

———. (2005). *How college affects students: A third decade of research*. Vol. 2. San Francisco: Jossey-Bass.

Reddick, R. & Heilig, J. V. (2013). Considering African American population, crime, education and mentoring constellations. Public policy paper for Sigma Pi Phi Fraternity.

Salisbury, M. H., Paulsen, M. B., & Pascarella, E. T. (2011). Why do all study abroad students look alike? Applying an integrated student choice model to explore differences in the factors that influence White and minority students' intent to study abroad. *Research in Higher Education 52*(2), 123–50. doi:10.1007/s11162-010-9191-2.

Savicki, V. & Cooley, E. (2011). American identity in study abroad students: Contrast, changes, correlates. *Journal of College Student Development 52*(3), 339–49. doi:10.1353/csd.2011.0035.

Shih, K. (2009). Study abroad participation up, except among minority students. *Diverse Education*, November 16. Http://diverseeducation.com/article/13193.

Sigma Pi Phi. (2016) History of the Boulé. Https://www.sigmapiphi.org/home/history-of-the-boule.php?page=2.

Smith, W. A., Allen, W. R., & Danley, L. L. (2007). "Assume the position . . . you fit the description": Psychosocial experiences and racial battle fatigue among African American male college students. *American Behavioral Scientist 51*(4), 551–78.

Steele, C. M. (1997). A threat in the air: How stereotypes shape intellectual identity and performance. *American Psychologist 52*(6), 613.

Strayhorn, T. L. (2008a). Fittin' in: Do diverse interactions with peers affect sense of belonging for Black men at predominantly White institutions? *NASPA Journal 45*(4), 501–27.

———. (2008b). The role of supportive relationships in facilitating African American males' success in college. *NASPA Journal 45*(1), 26–48.

———. (2014). What role does grit play in the academic success of Black male collegians at predominantly White institutions? *Journal of African American Studies 18*(1), 1–10.

Sutton, R. C. & Rubin, D. L. (2004). The GLOSSARI Project: Initial findings from a system- wide research initiative on study abroad learning outcomes. *Frontiers 10*, 65–82.

Thomas, L. (2002). Student retention in higher education: The role of institutional habitus. *Journal of Education Policy 17*(4), 423–42.

Tinto, V. (1997). Classrooms as communities: Exploring the educational character of student persistence. *Journal of Higher Education 68*(6), 599–623.

———. (2006). Research and practice of student retention: What next? *Journal of College Student Retention 8*(1), 1–19.

University of Texas at Austin. (2016a). Facts & figures. Https://www.utexas.edu/about/facts-and-figures.

———. (2016b). Statistical handbook. Http://reports.utexas.edu/statistical-handbook.

———. (n.d.). Graduation rates 2014–2015. Https://sp.austin.utexas.edu/sites/ut/rpt/Documents/IMA_IPEDS_GraduationRates_2014_AY.pdf.

US Department of Education, National Center for Education Statistics. (2015). *The condition of education 2015* (NCES 2015-144), Educational attainment. Https://nces.ed.gov/fastfacts/display.asp?id=40.

US Department of Education, National Center for Education Statistics, Integrated Postsecondary Education Data System (IPEDS) (2014). Fall 2001 and spring 2007 through spring 2014, graduation rates component. Https://nces.ed.gov/programs/digest/d14/tables/dt14_326.10.asp.

Walton, G. M., & Cohen, G. L. (2007). A question of belonging: Race, social fit, and achievement. *Journal of Personality and Social Psychology 92*(1), 82.

Yin, R. K. (2009). *Case study research: Design and methods*. 4th ed. Thousand Oaks, CA: Sage.

 VIGNETTE

Given the climate of the university at which Ronnie worked, he started to develop research on how to better educate and prepare students from diverse and underrepresented populations. He met with students across campus who were struggling to find their way, and who were in need of additional assistance. He also encouraged them to participate in research and to help better understand things were the way they were. Ronnie was met with a great deal of opposition from academic leaders, as they felt their methods of instruction and content were timeless. Ronnie worked to show the academic team that additional approaches and updates to their current policies and procedures needed to take place. Today, Ronnie is still assisting with incorporating diversity initiatives in education approaches at his current institution.

Where Do We Go from Here?

We Need a Revolution

C. P. Gause

ince arriving in America in 1619, from the shores of Africa, members of the Black diaspora have experienced physical, psychological, spiritual, and cultural ramifications that continually plague our nation and people today. Throughout the five-hundred-year history of our presence in this country, African Americans, and specifically Black males, have borne the brunt of marginalization and disenfranchisement. The contested, infamous text of Willie Lynch's "The Making of a Slave" provided slave owners with a systematic method for breaking down and reordering the dynamics between Black males and Black females.

> The next step is to take a bullwhip and beat the remaining nigger male to the point of death, in front of the female and the infant. Don't kill him, but put the fear of God in him.... We reversed nature by burning and pulling a civilized nigger apart and bull whipping the other to the point of death, all in her presence. By her being left alone, unprotected, with the male image destroyed, the ordeal caused her to move from her psychological dependent state to a frozen independent state. In this frozen psychological state of independence, she will raise her male and female offspring in reversed roles. For fear of the young males life she will psychologically train him to be mentally weak and dependent, but physically strong. (1712)

This physical, psychological, and emotional exertion of power on African Americans continues to place its mark on the livelihood of Black people as a collective group, specifically with regard to Black males. This is evidenced by the significant number of Black males under the custody and control of the criminal justice system, the lack of adequate healthcare, and the lack of economic advantages provided through successful educational attainment. This has created

Black masculine anxiety (Harper, 1996). The notion of power executed via the slave master and continued by societal forces is best defined by Michel Foucault:

> [Power] is the moving substrate of force relations, which, by virtue of their inequality, constantly engender states of power, but the latter are always local and unstable. [It] is not an institution, and not a structure; neither is it a certain strength that we are endowed with; it is the name that one attributes to a complex strategical situation in a particular society. (1979, p. 93)

Through this process of exerting power, a system of oppression and hegemony has been constructed to reify a hierarchy and caste system. Oppression is the inequitable and unjust use of power and authority resulting in the privileging of the white-dominant culture over individuals, groups, and/or communities who are nonmembers—this creates a duality. According to Freire (1970) the oppressed experiences an inner conflict that results from not being free and internalizes the master's oppression. Once the oppressed are free, they themselves become the oppressors.

> The oppressed suffer from the duality, which has established itself in their innermost being. They discover that without freedom they cannot exist authentically. Yet, although they desire authentic existence, they fear it. They are at one and the same time themselves, and the oppressor whose consciousness they have internalized. The conflict lies in the choice between being wholly themselves or being divided; between ejecting the oppressor within or not ejecting him; between human solidarity or alienation; between following prescriptions or having choices; between being spectators or actors; between acting or having the illusion of acting through the action of the oppressors; between speaking out or being silent, castrated in their power to create and recreate, in their power to transform the world. This is the tragic dilemma of the oppressed, which their education must take into account. (32–33)

Reflection on men and masculinities research, and specifically the evolution of research on Black masculinity, must begin with the understanding of our duality—as gendered bodies, emotional beings, and spiritual entities. All of these forms are impacted by the spaces we occupy in the world, as well as by the Black public sphere.

(Re)Presentations of Black Masculinity

Scholars, researchers, and policymakers continue to inform our communities that children of color and children in poverty are being left behind, particularly the Black male. Many scholars and policymakers continue to limit the analyses of Black masculinity to detached statistical data and reports devoid of the authentic (re)presentations of the voice and performance of global masculinities across multiple landscapes. There exists a full range of gender expressions witnessed by all, globally; however, given the power of the media, the representation often presented of Black males is the duffle bag boy (drug runner and money carrier); the thug (an aggressive, no-holds-barred bad boy); or the convict (in and out of jail, or always in—a prison lifer). The underlying messages in these images are ones of heteronormativity, homophobia, and patriarchy. Negotiating the (un)contested terrain of transgressive Black masculinities, love, and intimacy continues to be wretched in most circles, yet applauded in others.

Constructions of transgressive Black masculinities are still prevalent because tolerance, and not affirmation, of the "other" continues to be the accepted norm in our society, and schools are microcosmic representations of our larger society. The affirmation of queering masculinities by society as a whole would expand white-dominated constructions of masculinity beyond the heteronormative. Queering masculine characteristics would move beyond typically viewed/accepted "male" behaviors and embrace behaviors of all members of the global community regardless of sexually identified, gender-perceived, and biologically confirmed positionalities.

The political disturbances and cultural representations of Black masculinity in popular culture require new and different readings and contextualization. Currently, Black masculinity is rooted in masculine hero worship in the case of rappers and as naturalized and commodified in the case of athletes. The combination of these two has yielded a new Public Enemy Number One, a sadistic and masochistic heterosexist Black masculine cyborg, devoid of emotion, thought, and remorse.

The current construction/representation of the Black male brings together the dominant institutions of (white) masculine power and identity—criminal justice system, the police, and the news media—to protect (white) Americans from harm. The heavily policed and illuminated image of the Black male is the object of adolescent intrigue, fascination, and commodification. By drawing on deeply felt moral pains presently regarding crime, violence, gangs, and drugs, numerous Black entertainers—namely athletes and rap artists—have rewritten the historic tropes of Black masculinity from provider and protector to pusher and pimp.

This corrosive nihilistic construction of maleness reifies notions of (hyper)sexuality, insensitivity, and criminality, which serve as the new tropes of fascination and fear for the dominant culture. It becomes a veil of Black masculinity, a veil in which, at times during my life, I was complicit. This is why I interrogate my own identity by queering Black masculinity. The status of Black men in America is a publicly discussed phenomenon that often limits its discourse to statics on high incarceration rates, low educational attainment, and family abandonment. As Neal explains in *The New Black Man*, the "Black Man in Crisis" is the theme of hundreds of conferences and newspaper, magazine, and journal articles over the last thirty years. According to Neal (2015), the influx of public messages about Black men has made it easy to "isolate the Tupac Shakurs, Allen Iversons, 'Pookies' and Nushawn Williamses of the world and make them the reason why the black man has failed" (p. 3). This causes me to question the ability of Black men to express acts of love while internalizing public attacks on their gender and racial identities. Hence we find currently the issues are still the same.

What Is Our Purpose?

Due to the sociopolitical, sociocultural, and similar issues surrounding our development as children and men, it is difficult to create the language or the tool with which to engage one another about our purpose. At birth, Black boys are socialized according to their gender in ways that differ from their white counterparts (Wallace, 2007). Studies examining the gender socialization of Black children show that

> Black children are taught that womanhood is something that one must grow into while man-hood is something that is both natural and automatic. Black boys are regarded as adult men from young ages and therefore are expected not to participate in behaviors associated with girls or childhood. (p. 15)

What is our purpose? Perhaps it is not within our destiny to make the assumptions that there needs to be a language to engage each other regarding our purpose. Maybe it is too much to ask that as Americans, as men, as Black men that we find a commonality to address the issues that will assist us in understanding the pathology of our existence. Our purpose is to build an inclusive society of brotherhood: "If we desire a society in which men are brothers, then we must act towards one another with brotherhood. If we can build such a society, then we would have achieved the ultimate goal of human freedom" (Rustin, 1943, p. 366). Dismissing racism, sexism, classism, and all other isms does not grant deniability. In order to transform our communities we must engage in antioppressive practices, create inclusive educational environments, and support a radical democracy that fosters collaborative activism and social movements for change. The foundation to all of this is the need for open, honest dialogue and education. This is our purpose being actualized and fulfilled in a radical democracy (Gause, Reitzug, & Villaverde, 2007).

A factual history of Black men and masculinity reveals the existence of multiple societies, tribes, nations, and cultures between and within groups. We have to acknowledge the issues that cause us to unite and to separate. As Blacks, our experiences and history of treatment in this country that united us are not necessarily over race. Sure, our race was certainly a means for treatment; however, we have never acknowledge that we are the same, so let's not portray our current challenges as rooted in our disagreements or lack of solidarity. For example, Martin Luther King, Malcom X, James Baldwin, Marcus Garvey, Booker T. Washington, and W. E. B. DuBois, are all vastly different in their perspectives on how to help the race and society, yet they are united in their quest to know one's way of being as a Black man.

Black Masculinity and Politics

Black males continue to be marginalized, stigmatized, and disenfranchised in America. Mass media allow us to see and witness events instantaneously—the shooting of unharmed Black men by white police officers; members of Black Lives Matter protesting across America; racial profiling and injustice on college campuses; the calling for the lynching of a Black congressmen because he believes President Donald J. Trump should be impeached; and the rise of crimes committed by white nationalists against communities of color. We need to continue to question how Black males are (re)presented in popular culture—American culture. The election of President Barack Obama created a false notion that we live in a postracial society; however, based upon the national political climate, it is indeed about race.

The election of Barack Hussein Obama as president of the United States in 2008 solidified the international face of America as African American and male. For the first time in the history of this country the image of a self-identified Black man took a place on the world stage, and it had nothing to do with rap music, hip-hop culture, or professional sports. Or did it? This president listens to rap music, was elected by a large margin of the hip-hop generation, and plays basketball; however, these stereotypical tropes of Black culture are not the only thing that defines him or his image. He is a graduate of Columbia University and Harvard Law School. He was born in Honolulu, Hawaii. His mother, Ann Dunham, was of English and German ancestry; in essence she was white. His father, Barack H. Obama Sr., was of Kenyan descent and therefore African. The election of former president Barack Obama was monumental and historic; however, it was not without controversy. Although his Black male image moved us away from the hypersexualized bestial aggressive Black male image often presented by the media, he was still considered by many to be a menace to society. The gridlock and partisan politics in Washington, DC, and the rise of white nationalism under President Donald J. Trump consistently serves as a reminder to the American people that the intersections of race, class, and gender, as well as white hegemony, continue to impact how decisions are made in this republic.

Black Masculinity and Popular Culture

Presently, in today's global community, we find ourselves bombarded on a twenty-four-hour, daily basis with mediated imagery and sounds that shape our values, belief systems, and moral structures. The constant bombardment of popular culture on our daily existence informs our global identities, as well as national identities. Throughout our global history, education has been viewed as the unkept promise of many societies and democracies. Under American apartheid the Black male image was nearly absent in popular culture. Except for the occasional butler, field hand, or driver, Black males were not characters in television or film. The past four decades have yielded an increase in Black male images in popular culture, although many of these roles are nihilistic, to say the least. With the explosion of hip-hop as a global music genre and the election of Barack Obama as president of the United States a shift occurred; however, the Black male continues to be viewed as a menace to society. The killing of Trayvon Martin, the killing of Michael Brown, the killing of Tamir Rice, the killing of Philando Castile, the stop-and-frisk policies of the New York City Police Department, the rollback of justice reforms by former attorney general Eric Holder by current attorney general Jeff Sessions of the Trump administration, and the ever-increasing school-to-prison pipeline for Black males cause the authors in the volume to pause and question how the (re)presentations of the Black male image are being constructed and (re)packaged for capitalistic consumption. There is still more work to be done. Where do we go from here?

We Need a Revolution

Black males across the global diaspora are one of the most powerful creations ever known to our humanity. As a testament to this belief, we must continue to bring together scholars, dancers, teachers, poets, educators, hip-hop artists, policymakers, spoken-word performers, politicians, and researchers to celebrate and affirm our Black masculinities. We must continue to create, actualize, and live out counternarratives to mediated hegemonic constructions of the bestial, hypersexualized, aggressive, co-opted, and commodified cyborg that is the Black male. We must seek, produce, and construct knowledge that represents multilingual, multiethnic, and nonconforming gender identities that are not rooted in Eurocentric constructs and paradigms. Several scholars are engaged in researching men and masculinities; however, the amount of critical and mediated discourse regarding Black males in our global society grows slowly. Finally, we need to explore and examine multiple-discourse and multiple-discipline analyses of issues and perspectives regarding Black masculinities. The heavily policed and illuminated image of the Black male is the object of intrigue, fascination, and commodification. Drawing on deeply felt moral pains and the notion of celebrity, numerous Black entertainers—namely rap artists and athletes—have rewritten the historic tropes of Black masculinity from pusher, pimp, and hype man to protector and provider. It is my hope that educators, policymakers, scholars, researchers, and media analysts continue to question and interrogate how Black male images and (re)presentations contribute to the marginalization and disenfranchisement of Black males in America. By doing so, we will make progress.

■ **References**

Foucault, M. (1979). *Discipline and punish: The Birth of the prison.* New York: Vintage Books.
Freire, P. (1970). *Pedagogy of the oppressed.* New York: Continuum.
Gause, C. P. (2008). *Integration matters: Navigating identity, culture, and resistance.* New York: Peter Lang.
Gause, C. P., Reitzug, U. R., & Villaverde, L. (2007). Beyond generic democracy: Holding our students accountable for democratic leadership and practice. In D. Carlson & C. P. Gause (eds.), *Keeping the promise: Essays on leadership, democracy and education,* pp. 217–31. New York: Peter Lang.
Harper, P. B. (1996). *Are we not men? Masculine anxiety and the problem of African-American identity.* New York: Oxford University Press.
Neal, M. A. (2015). *New Black man.* 2nd ed. New York: Routledge.

Rustin, B. (1943). Bayard Rustin in his own words: I must resist. In M. G. Long (ed.), *I must resist: Bayard Rustin's life in letters*, pp. 340–66. San Francisco: City Lights Books.

Wallace, D. (2007). It's a M-A-N thang: Black male gender role socialization and the performance of masculinity in love relationships. *Journal of Pan African Studies 1*(7), 11–22.

CONTRIBUTORS

KEVIN ALMASY serves as associate director for communications within the Division of Diversity and Community Engagement at the University of Texas at Austin. Previously he served as a communications coordinator within the Office of the President and as a policy adviser on public-private initiatives at the Federal Communications Commissions in Washington, DC. Born in Cleveland, Ohio, he holds a bachelor of arts from Denison University and a master of arts in journalism from the Newhouse School at Syracuse University.

J. MICHAEL ANDERSON is the associate director of disability services at Georgia State University. He has worked in the field of postsecondary disabilities for more than twenty years. He holds a bachelor of arts degree in sociology from Newberry College, a master of education degree from Clemson University, and doctor of philosophy degree from the University of Georgia.

ROBERT Q. BERRY III is a professor in the Curry School of Education with an appointment in curriculum instruction and special education. A former mathematics teacher, he teaches elementary and special education mathematics methods courses in the teacher education program at the University of Virginia. Additionally, he teaches graduate-level mathematics education course and courses for in-service teachers seeking a mathematics specialist endorsement. His research focuses on equity issues in mathematics education, pre- and in-service teachers' mathematical knowledge for teaching, and mathematics instructional quality. Berry has extensive experience in classroom observation and has collaborated with other researchers to develop an observation instrument, Mathematics Scan, to examine mathematics teaching quality.

RICHARD D. BESEL is an associate professor of communication studies at California Polytechnic State University, San Luis Obispo. His doctorate was awarded by the University of Illinois, Urbana-Champaign. He became interested in social justice concerns as an undergraduate student at North Central College. While at the University of Illinois, he explored connections between race, class, gender, science, and environmentalism. His background in rhetoric has allowed him to work with Bernard K. Duffy on several publications about African American orators.

JAMES BRIDGEFORTH serves as an adjunct professor in the College of Education and director of housing at the University of South Alabama. Dr. Bridgeforth holds a bachelor's degree in sociology from Catawba College, a master's degree in higher education administration from the University of Massachusetts, Amherst, and a PhD in higher education administration and institutional research from the University of Southern Mississippi. James is married to Valerie Bridgeforth and resides in Mobile, Alabama.

ROBERT G. BRYANT is the Assistant Director for The Multicultural Center at Georgia State University, and has an extensive background working in multicultural affairs. Bryant's research interests include diversity issues, organizational development, student development, and a host of other related topics. His more than fifteen years of experience in higher education include previous roles in multicultural programs, fund-raising operations, student orientation, and recruitment services.

JAMES H. CAMPBELL is an instructor in the Business College at Cincinnati Christian University. His doctoral degree was awarded by Miami University. He explores the narratives of black male athletics at predominantly white Division I institutions and their interactions with advocates, democracy, and social justice. As an athletic administrator at a Division I institution, he observed that the black male who participated in revenue-generating sports was denied the most common democratic liberties that are customarily afforded to other students and other student-athletes who do not participate in revenue-generating sports. It is his mission to make this phenomenon more salient and reveal that this systemic issue can be conquered.

JEFFREY K. COLEMAN is the director of the Multicultural Center and an adjunct faculty member in the departments of African American Studies and Sociology at Georgia State University. His doctoral degree was awarded by the University of North Carolina at Greensboro. He is passionate about challenging the system of education to find equitable approaches to college success for African American males. In his experience as an African American male attending a small, private, liberal arts, predominantly white institution, he had to overcome the race and gender culture shock of being one of a handful of African American students on campus and one of an even smaller number of African American males. He had to adjust to the socioeconomic barriers of being from a middle-class family, a graduate of a predominantly black public school system, a first-generation college student unprepared to manage academic and social life, and a recipient of financial aid in a campus environment where this was not the norm. It was these experiences that motivated him to build a career focusing on improving college adjustment for students coming from backgrounds similar to his own.

ARMONDO R. COLLINS is department head of the Digital Media Commons in the Jackson Library and an adjunct professor with the African-American and African Diaspora Studies program at the University of North Carolina at Greensboro. He is also a PhD candidate in rhetoric and composition at UNCG who holds a postbaccalaureate certificate in African American studies. His research interests include Black Nationalist literature, African American rhetorical culture, writing as activism, media constructions of black identity, and the influence of digital technology on composition. His forthcoming dissertation project explores the rhetoric of a "black God" as it is constructed by late twentieth-century African American writers.

STEVEN RANDOLPH CURETON earned a PhD in sociology from Washington State University in 1997. His areas of specialty are criminology and the family. He is currently an associate professor in the Department of Sociology at the University of North Carolina at Greensboro. His research interests remain focused on African Americans' life chances and life course outcomes relative to economics, justice processing, education, access to opportunities, gangs, street corner politics, norms and ethics governing lifestyle decisions, and the impact of family dynamics on behavioral outcomes.

TOMEKA DAVIS is an associate professor in the Department of Sociology, Georgia State University. Her research areas include the sociology of education, social stratification, and Inequality. Her interests in race and gender inequality in education were shaped by seeing the talent of young black students go unrecognized and unsupported.

KIMYA N. DENNIS is a sociologist and criminologist with a criminal justice background, and creator and coordinator of the Criminal Studies program at Salem College (the oldest continually operating women's college in the United States) in Winston Salem, North Carolina. She has a doctorate in sociology with concentrations in crime, deviance, and social control; and inequality in race, class, and gender. Her research and social activism are interdisciplinary, with particular emphasis on blacks and the African diaspora, particularly suicide and suicidal self-harm, mental health, childfree-by-choice, gender equality; and on challenging traditional beliefs and institutions of patriarchy and pronatalism.

BERNARD K. DUFFY is professor of rhetoric and chair of Communication Studies at California Polytechnic State University, San Luis Obispo. His PhD was awarded by the University of Pittsburgh. His interest in African American oratory was piqued when with Halford Ryan he published two encyclopedias on American orators in 1988. His experiences at Clemson University, where he taught for nine years, and in the South Carolina community where he lived taught him the importance of increasing awareness of the heroic struggles of African Americans. In 2013, with Richard Leeman, he published *The Will of a People: A Critical Anthology of Great African American speeches.*

CRYSTAL LEIGH ENDSLEY is assistant professor in Africana Studies at John Jay College of Criminal Justice, CUNY. Recognized by *Cosmopolitan Magazine* as a "Fun, Fearless Female," Crystal Leigh serves her community as an internationally acclaimed spoken word artist, activist, and actor. For the past decade, she has been leading global arts as activism workshops with a special focus on girls and women. Her work has taken her to Latin America, the Caribbean, East Africa, and across the United States. She was featured for TEDxHamiltonCollege's debut filming and the TEDxCUNYSalon. Her first book, *The Fifth Element: Spoken Word Poetry as Social Justice Pedagogy,* was published in 2017. Her second book, *Open Mic Night: Campus Programs that Champion College Student Voice and Engagement* (2017) is a co-authored text that features practical and theoretical implications of incorporating open mic programming for college student development.

DAVID A. FRANK is a professor of rhetoric in the Clark Honors College, University of Oregon. In his research he seeks to understand how rhetoric and argument might be used to foster the use of reason and promote good decision making and the humane treatment of others. Toward this end, he is in an ongoing interracial collaboration with Mark McPhail in which they study the rhetoric of racism, adaptive racism, and antiadaptive racism.

C. P. GAUSE is professor and chair of the Department of Educational Leadership and Counseling at Southeast Missouri State University. He is a former public school teacher, principal, and district administrator. His doctoral degree was awarded in educational leadership by Miami University. The current construction/representation of the black male brings together the dominant institutions of (white) masculine power and identity—criminal justice system, the police, and the news media—to protect (white) Americans from harm. The heavily policed and illuminated image of the black male is the object of adolescent intrigue, fascination, and commodification. By drawing on deeply felt moral pains presently regarding crime, violence, gangs, and drugs, numerous black entertainers—namely athletes and rap artists—have rewritten the historic tropes of black masculinity from provider and protector to pusher and pimp. Professor Gauss is inspired by his black male students and colleagues to provide a counternarrative, and it is through this work that he actualizes the tenets of social justice.

COREY D. GIVENS is an interim student conduct officer at Georgia State University. His juris doctor degree was awarded by Atlanta's John Marshall Law School. His research interest is the effects of legal practices and structures on communities of color. Initially, he pursued a career as a criminal defense attorney because of the lack of adequate representation for people of color in the criminal justice system. After taking several courses in higher education law, he became intrigued with how the law and education influence the overall achievement of communities of color.

THEODORE GREENE is an assistant professor of sociology at Bowdoin College. His research draws on gay neighborhoods to introduce and develop the notion of vicarious citizenship–cultural and political claims of ownership to community by actors lacking residential, network, and material ties.

ELIJAH K. HAMILTON-WRAY is a freelance artist who earned a bachelor of arts degree from Kalamazoo College. He uses art as both a therapeutic and a creative outlet. Though he usually works with oil paint and canvas, he enjoys branching out into other media, specifically charcoal on drawing paper for the project in this volume. The adinkra symbols are both structured and loose at the same time, which is what the artist attempted to channel through the use of charcoal with these hand-drawn adinkra symbols.

RYAN J. HENSON, M.Ed., currently serves as the Assistant Director for Student Affairs Maintenance at the University of Nevada, Las Vegas. With a Masters of Education from the University of Nevada Las Vegas, Ryan has worked to educate and support co-curricular efforts of students in various roles. During his time at Santa Fe University of Art and Design, he noticed a cultural divide among students, with students identifying as African American/Black students feeling ostracized from the community. He created the first African American Studies curriculum at the institution, continually being inspired by the students' passion and desire for continued growth and understanding. Ryan looks to continue working with diversity awareness initiatives, volunteering time to several community and university organizations that look to promote educational and cultural awareness worldwide.

ADRIEL A. HILTON is director of the Webster University Myrtle Beach Metropolitan Extended Campus. As the chief administrative officer, he is charged with implementing programs and policies to achieve Webster University's overall goals and objectives at the extended campus. Dr. Hilton's most recent positions include chief of staff and executive assistant to the president at Grambling State University and assistant professor and director of the Higher Education Student Affairs program at Western Carolina University.

DARRYL B. HOLLOMAN is associate vice president for student affairs and an affiliate faculty member in the Department of Sociology, Georgia State University, Atlanta. His PhD was awarded by Georgia State University. His research interest is the influence of societal factors such as family, work, and education on the advancement of marginalized communities within school settings, focusing on the effects of education on the development of disadvantaged communities. Early in his career working as an academic adviser, he was often struck by his interactions with black men specifically. In this role he was responsible for preparing graduation audits, and when he told a black male student that he was not going to graduate, more often than not he would just walk away. Those men, unlike other groups, would not argue or question why, but simply walk away from the office. That experience set Dr. Holloman on a charge to contribute to the discussion of black men in their relation to education, to primarily provide examples of men (and boys) who did not walk away.

AUSTIN JACKSON is a professor in the Residential College in the Arts and Humanities, Michigan State University. Dr. Jackson's scholarship examines how African American language and culture (especially Rap music and Hip Hop culture) can facilitate meaningful student engagement in social democracy. His original research has been published by National Council of Teachers of English Press/Routledge, *The International Journal of Africana Studies, Reading Research Quarterly, The Black Scholar, American Language Review,* and Stanford University's *Black Arts Quarterly.* In addition to his teaching and scholarship, Dr. Jackson has extensive experience as an administrator and facilitator of civic and community engagement programs. From 2009–2016, he directed the MSU My Brother's and Sister's Keeper's Program, a mentoring and service learning initiative for adolescent youth attending Detroit Public Schools. In 2016 he established the My Brother's Keeper Prison Outreach Program, a peer-mentoring program for inmates at the Richard A. Handlon Men's Correctional Facility, Ionia, Michigan.

JERLANDO F. L. JACKSON is the Vilas Distinguished Professor of Higher Education and the director and chief research scientist of Wisconsin's Equity and Inclusion Laboratory at the University of Wisconsin, Madison. As director of the WEI Lab, he is responsible for managing the Innovation Incubator, the National Study of Intercollegiate Athletics, and the International Colloquium on Black Males in Education. His central research interest is organizational science in higher education, with a special interest in hiring practices, career mobility, workforce diversity, and workplace discrimination. He also has a portfolio of research focused on interventions designed to broaden participation for underrepresented groups in the scientific workforce. He is credited with over one hundred publications that appear in high-impact journals and books.

TOBY S. JENKINS is an associate professor of higher education at the University of South Carolina. Her work focuses on the utility of culture (contemporary culture, folk culture, and pop culture) as a politic of social survival, a tool of social change, and a transformative space of nontraditional knowledge production. She is also interested in the ways in which culture influences one's leadership proxy and sense of citizenship/social commitment. She has authored a book focused on the evolving ideologies of culture, family, and education in contemporary society, *My Culture, My Color, My Self: Heritage, Resilience and Community in the Lives of Young Adults* (Temple University Press, 2013). It was named by the Association of American University Press to the list of "Top 100 Books for Understanding Race Relations in the US." *Family, Community, and Higher Education* (Routledge, 2012) is an edited volume that explores the critical role of family and community in the lives of first-generation college students.

ANDRE E. JOHNSON is an assistant professor in the Department of Communication, University of Memphis. His doctoral degree was awarded by the University of Memphis. In his roles as both academic and pastor, he has come to understand the need for black men to be examples of "living" role models for both boys and girls. His work on Turner and continued work in the community attempts to bridge those gaps. He is the editor of an award-winning book on Turner and the editor of a six-volume archive of Turner's works. A prolific author, Johnson also edited a book on hip-hop spirituality.

BRENT E. JOHNSON is a school counselor at Forest Park High School and an adjunct professor in the School of Education, Gordon State College. His doctoral degree was awarded by Miami University in Oxford, Ohio. His field of research is equity studies in school and society. As a middle-grades classroom teacher, he began to recognize the growing number of black and brown students not achieving in school. Conversations with students and parents, the deficit models being employed by teachers and administrators, and the increasingly inequitable conditions surrounding the school led him to employ more critical and humanist pedagogies and frameworks in his work as well as join others striving to end not only racism but all aspects of human oppression.

RAVEN JONES STANBROUGH is an assistant professor and the Detroit-area internship coordinator in the Department of Teacher Education at Michigan State University. Her teaching and research focus on literacy, culture, race, equity, and the educational and lived experiences of students of color in urban contexts. She creates and facilitates debate education programs to promote and expand the educative and creative engagement that debate offers and is committed to community and grassroots initiatives that create and sustain new ways of being, thinking, and doing. She is the co-founder of the Zuri Reads Initiative, an effort to provide and organize literacy-related events and resources for Detroit-area children, students, and families. Jones Stanbrough was a Fulbright-Hayes recipient in 2014 and received the King Chavez Parks Future Faculty Fellowship in 2015. In 2016 she received the Excellence in Diversity Award from Michigan State University for her outstanding efforts in promoting diversity and inclusion inside and outside of the classroom. She was also the 2016–17 awardee of the James and Grace Lee Boggs Center to Nurture Community Leadership Fellowship.

JESSICA M. KHALAF is Special Assistant to the President at Hobart and William Smith Colleges. She previously served as assistant director for policy and community engagement in the Division of Diversity and Community Engagement at the University of Texas at Austin, where she earned her doctoral degree. Dr. Khalaf has worked on research and policy that affects diversity issues both within the university and the community at large. Through her work in the division, Dr. Khalaf has recognized the importance of not only researching the effect of student support and mentoring for black males but also conveying the positive impacts of such programming through academic and general publications.

DAVID E. KIRKLAND is the executive director of the NYU Metropolitan Center for Research on Equity and the Transformation of Schools, and associate professor of English and urban education at NYU's Steinhardt School. He is also an activist and educator, cultural critic, and author. Dr.

Kirkland earned his PhD from Michigan State University and his JD from the University of Michigan. A Detroit native, his transdisciplinary scholarship explores intersections among race, gender, and education. With many groundbreaking publications to his credit, he has analyzed the cultures, languages, and texts of urban youth, using critical literary, ethnographic, and sociolinguistic research methods to answer complex questions at the center of equity and social justice in education and beyond.

CHELDA SMITH KONDO is an assistant professor in the Department of Teaching and Learning at Georgia Southern University and currently a Visiting Assistant Professor at the University of Notre Dame. Her research and teaching interests span the professional and educational experiences of people from traditionally marginalized backgrounds. From Somali youth refugees to university faculty of color, she explores how pedagogy, positionality, and institutional policies affect the socialization and learning experiences of underserved populations. The plight of black males is at the intersection of these research foci.

ANINDYA KUNDU is a Postdoctoral Research Associate at New York University. He is researching how to best create college and career pathways for South Bronx youth. Prior to arriving in New York, he worked with young Black and Brown men at the Cook County Juvenile Detention Center of Chicago, the largest juvenile center in America. His interaction with kids there shaped his continued sentiments toward disenfranchised youth of color, and he started to understand how sweeping inequities in mobility manifest through race and class. After a period working as an associate at the NYC Department of Education, he felt a strong desire to address the achievement and opportunity gap from an outside-in perspective, through research.

JAWANZA KUNJUFU is considered one of the foremost experts on black males and education and has been a guest speaker at most universities throughout the United States, as well as a consultant to most urban school districts. He has authored forty books, including national best sellers *Black Students: Middle Class Teachers*, *Keeping Black Boys Out of Special Education*, *An African Centered Response to Ruby Payne's Poverty Theory*, *Raising Black Boys*, *Understanding Black Male Learning Styles*, and *Changing School Culture for Black Males*.

RICHARD W. LEEMAN is professor of communication studies, University of North Carolina at Charlotte. His doctoral degree was awarded by the University of Maryland. He first became interested in African American oratory as a college junior, when his speech and debate coach suggested that he analyze Stokely Carmichael's "Black Power" speech for a rhetorical criticism event. It opened up to him a world about which he had been almost completely unaware. As a graduate student, he was fortunate enough to take a course titled The Rhetoric of Black America with Dr. Lyndrey Niles, then chair of the Department of Communication Studies at Howard University. Recognizing that African American oratory was then and still remains a field too little studied and known, Professor Leeman has devoted much of his scholarly work to the area. He is the editor of the encyclopedic *African American Orators: A Biocritical Sourcebook*, coeditor of *The Will of a People: A Critical Anthology of African American Orators*, and the author of *The Teleological Discourse of Barack Obama*.

GEORJ LEWIS is the vice president for student affairs at Georgia Southern University, a position to which he brings more than twenty years of higher education experience. His research interests include black males, administrative workings, organizational development, multicultural issues, and student affairs leadership. Lewis has a strong career in higher education that includes being a vice president and dean of students at four-year institutions.

JACK S. MONELL is an Associate professor of justice studies at Winston-Salem State University, North Carolina. He also serves on the faculty-in-residence, providing student-centered programming for undergraduate students residing on campus. Dr. Monell holds a PhD from Walden University and an MSW from Howard University, with postgraduate work in sociology at Appalachian State University. The author of *Delinquency, Pop Culture and Generation Why*, he conducts research in the areas of juvenile justice, popular culture, Afro-Latino urban youth and their families, and intervention programs for at-risk youths.

MAZI A. E. MUTAFA runs a large hip-hop nonprofit organization in Washington, DC. It sponsors multiple programs, including a hip-hop academy that runs after-school programs within several communities in DC. His organization has partnerships with several local schools and public libraries. Recently, the ambassadors of several countries have contacted his organization to help create similar programs abroad and to send his arts educators to other countries to facilitate workshops. He provides a very useful practice-based lens to understand the ways that hip-hop culture not only engages youth, but also provides a meaningful professional life experience for young adults.

LOUIS NAPOLEON was previously incarcerated as a juvenile in an adult prison. He is the publisher of the *Prison Life & Beyond* e-magazine. Napoleon was an inmate assistant to GED instructors in two prisons in 1970–1972. His specialized skills are beneficial to organizations working with the most difficult-to-place populations, particularly job seekers with low motivation and limited job search skills and work histories. He has developed and directed job-training programs, created survival skills' curricula, and written and published job development guides for ex-offenders.

SPENCER PLATT is an assistant professor of higher education administration at the University of South Carolina. He earned his doctoral degree from the University of Texas at Austin. His bachelor's degree is from the University of South Carolina, and he holds an MS from the University of Dayton. His research interests include black males in higher education, access to higher education, critical race theory, and the socialization of doctoral students of color at predominantly white universities.

DEVIN L. RANDOLPH currently serves as the assistant vice president for student development and services and the director of residential life at Claflin University. In this role, he is responsible for overseeing campus-wide student life programming, residential life, managing student clubs and organizations, Greek life, and the Office of Student Activities.

THEODORE S. RANSAW is a curriculum specialist for James Madison College, and a core faculty member in African and African American Studies, Michigan State University. His doctoral degree was awarded by the University of Nevada, Las Vegas. When Ransaw recognized that his black male undergraduate students did not have a "safe place" in which to explore their identity, he created one of the first black masculinity classes in the United States. That class established a mentorship program at three at-risk elementary schools for black and Latino boys with assessments as part of a class project. Ransaw's career was inspired by his black male students who wanted to know more about the journey of being black as well as male, and by their desire to work collectively to help other black males.

STUART RHODEN is an instructor in the Academic Success Program, College of Integrated Sciences & Arts, University College, Arizona State University. His doctoral degree was awarded by Temple University. A portion of his research focuses on the intersectionality of black males, college attainment, and positive academic achievement. He became interested in this particular research topic as a high school teacher who consistently graduated students who were "succeeding" despite being in a "toxic" public school and neighborhood environment. Rather than focusing on those who did not achieve, he wanted to focus on those who did and examine the factors that contributed to their social-emotional and academic growth.

TYREE ROBINSON is currently a Doctoral Candidate (who is researching and writing his dissertation entitled "The Perceptions and Lived Experiences of African-American Males in Higher Education Leadership in California Community Colleges") in the School of Education, Leadership Studies Department, Organization and Leadership program at the University of San Francisco. His own experiences as a young African American student who matriculated through the inner-city schools of San Francisco has encouraged him to research the issues in which he himself has personally experienced, with the hopes of changing America's public school systems to equitable institutions of learning for all.

LAWANDA M. SIMPKINS earned her doctorate from the University of North Carolina at Greensboro in cultural studies of education. She also has a certificate in women's and gender studies from UNCG. Simpkins's research focuses on dominant norms, more specifically, how these norms affect minority populations in the United States. Her interest in black masculinity originated from two very vivid experiences. First, much of what she has been taught in life about her femininity has been laden with traditional masculine ideals, and second, much of her collegiate experience working in various roles from advising to administration has been with male students. Her social justice background and the desire to learn more about the other has propelled her to do research on this population. Inspired by Freire, she researches fervently with the true belief that education can be used as a form of liberation to free people from their internalized oppressions. Currently Simpkins serves as the James Farmer Post-Doctoral Fellow in Civil Rights and Social Justice at the University of Mary Washington. In this role she is responsible for teaching and developing courses centered on her research. Concurrently, she works in the James Farmer Multicultural Center in an effort to provide social justice training for the university at large.

DARRON SMITH is an African American faculty member at the University of Memphis in the Department of Sociology. He is also an author and blogger. His research and writing focuses on injustices impacting African Americans and other marginalized groups. His work includes the study and impact of race on U.S. health care, the practice of white parents adopting black and biracial children, religion, sports, politics, and other pertinent subject matters of present time.

EDWARD J. SMITH is a PhD candidate, focusing on higher education, in the Graduate School of Education at the University of Pennsylvania. He earned a master's degree in education from Pennsylvania State University. Early in his career as a teacher and a mentor, he realized hip-hop culture could be deployed to understand, resist, and ultimately heal from structural oppression and various forms of trauma experienced by black boys and men.

RYAN M. SUTTON directs the African American Male Research Initiative (and serves as a fellow with the Hogg Foundation for Mental Health, all under the Division of Diversity and Community Engagement at the University of Texas at Austin. With a doctoral degree in counseling psychology from Howard University, Dr. Sutton focuses his research and practice on promoting positive mental and behavioral determinants of health for communities and students of color, specifically black males, in the educational and justice systems.

TAURA TAYLOR holds an MA in sociology from Georgia State University and anticipates completing her PhD in sociology at Georgia State University by 2018. Her research interests are varied, ranging from sociology of education to social movements to entrepreneurship, all of which converge in her interest in cognitive pluralism, intersectionality, and micro-level resistances. She is of the firm mind that sociologically relevant intraracial differences exist among black men and women but are rarely explored. It is her goal to explore the dimensions of racial consciousness among black men and women and to contribute to the theorizing of racial solidarity and resistance.

MICHELL L. TEMPLE currently serves as the Counselor and ADA Coordinator at Tusculum University. Formerly, and she served as the director of the Margaret A. Staton Office of Disability Services at Georgia State University. Dr. Temple conducts research and program evaluations to promote the access, equity, and inclusion of all people, with an emphasis on people with disabilities. She holds a doctorate in education in professional counseling and supervision from the University of West Georgia.

ROBERT E. TERRILL is professor of rhetoric in the Department of English at Indiana University. His doctoral degree was awarded at Northwestern University. He became interested in exploring the problematics of black masculinity as an undergraduate student, when he read the *Autobiography of Malcolm X* along with work by Stokely Carmichael (Kwame Ture), Eldridge Cleaver, Martin Luther King Jr., John Lewis, LeRoi Jones (Amiri Baraka), James Baldwin, Langston Hughes, and many others. These writers helped him, as a naive and sheltered young white man, to understand that his experiences were not universal. They also helped him to understand, through their varied voices, experiences, and insights, that no single perspective should be taken as representative of the experience of being a black male. The words of these black men helped to shape him. And throughout his career as an educator, first as a high school teacher and now as a college professor, he introduced students to these words and helped students to understand the ways that these words have shaped our world. He is the author of *Malcolm X: Inventing Radical Judgment* and *Double-Consciousness and the Rhetoric of Barack Obama: The Price and Promise of Citizenship* and the editor of the *Cambridge Companion to Malcolm X.*

KATERI THUNDER is a teacher and mathematics specialist at Burnley-Moran Elementary School in Charlottesville, Virginia. Previously, she was an assistant professor of middle, secondary, and mathematics education at James Madison University.

JULIAN VAN DYKE is the cover artist for the handbook, as well as an influential social activist in Lansing, Michigan. As he creates his works in oil paints on canvas, Van Dyke moves gracefully between a subdued richness of color and strong lines. Julian Van Dyke discovered his love of art at an early age through comic book illustration. Now working professionally as an artist, he is passionate about bringing artistic inspiration to children, self-publishing several books and working with young students in schools in his spare time.

GREGORY J. VINCENT is president of Hobart and William Smith Colleges in Geneva, New York. His doctoral degree was awarded by the University of Pennsylvania. Dr. Vincent previously served as vice president for diversity and community engagement at the University of Texas at Austin for eleven years, pioneering new organizational models so that the award-winning Division of Diversity and Community Engagement could become the most comprehensive and innovative program of its kind in higher education. Dr. Vincent has made it his life's work to support, enhance, and advocate for students of color through all of the positions that he has held in higher education for more than twenty years.

RANA WALKER is an Emmy Award–winning mental health therapist and wellness coach. She received her BS in psychology from Howard University and her master's in education in counseling psychology from Temple University. She has lectured and facilitated workshops domestically and abroad. Her overseas travel to Europe, the UK, Asia, South America, Africa, and the Caribbean and residence in Ghana, West Africa, has laid the groundwork for her far-reaching worldview. She has completed coursework in alternative medicine ranging from nutrition to shamanic healing. Ms. Walker was one of two life coaches on season 1 of NBC's groundbreaking program *Starting Over*, which aired daily and garnered Rana an Emmy for her role as life coach. Rana is a certified Yoga instructor and is dedicated to the development of the mind, body, and spirit. Her coaching system combines holistic life-changing guidance with innovative and intense mental, physical, and spiritual activities. She has translated her zest for life into her life's passion—helping others to see who they are in truth.

TERESITA WARREN is a native of Macon, Georgia, and currently resides in the Atlanta area. She received her bachelor's degree in psychology and human services from Clayton State University, a master's degree in rehabilitation counseling from the University of Kentucky, and a master's degree in industrial organizational psychology from Capella University. In 2008 she joined the family of Georgia State University, where she is currently the assistant director of the Margaret A. Staton Office of Disability Services.

RONALD W. WHITAKER II currently serves as assistant professor of education, director of district and school relations, and co-director of the Center for Urban Education, Equity, and Improvement at Cabrini University. Additionally, Dr. Whitaker is a current Schouver Fellow at Duquesne University. Dr. Whitaker specializes in culturally responsive pedagogy, urban education, educational programming for black males, and issues related to diversity, equity, and inclusion.

INDEX

ALSO IN THE

INTERNATIONAL RACE AND EDUCATION SERIES

Closing the Education Achievement Gaps for African American Males

edited by Theodore S. Ransaw, and Richard Majors
ISBN 978-1-61186-201-0 (paperback)

Internationalizing a School of Education: Integration and Infusion in Practice

by John Schwille
ISBN 978-1-61186-215-7 (paperback)

Emerging Issues and Trends in Education

edited by Theodore S. Ransaw, and Richard Majors
ISBN 978-1-61186-260-7 (paperback)

The Handbook of Research on Black Males: Quantitative, Qualitative, and Multidisciplinary

edited by Theodore S. Ransaw, C. P. Gause, and Richard Majors
ISBN 978-1-61186-297-3 (litho)